BUSINESS IMPERIALISM
1840–1930

AN INQUIRY BASED ON
BRITISH EXPERIENCE IN
LATIN AMERICA

BUSINESS IMPERIALISM
1840–1930

AN INQUIRY BASED ON
BRITISH EXPERIENCE IN
LATIN AMERICA

Edited by

D. C. M. PLATT

OXFORD
AT THE CLARENDON PRESS
1977

Oxford University Press, Walton Street, Oxford OX2 6DP

OXFORD LONDON GLASGOW
NEW YORK TORONTO MELBOURNE WELLINGTON
IBADAN NAIROBI DAR ES SALAAM LUSAKA CAPE TOWN
KUALA LUMPUR SINGAPORE JAKARTA HONG KONG TOKYO
DELHI BOMBAY CALCUTTA MADRAS KARACHI

British Library Cataloguing in Publication Data
Business imperialism, 1840–1930: an inquiry based on
  British experience in Latin America
  Index
  ISBN 0–19–828271–0
  1. Platt, Desmond Christopher St. Martin
  338.8'8   HD2810.5
  Corporations, British – Latin America – History

*Printed in Great Britain
at the University Press, Oxford
by Vivian Ridler
Printer to the University*

PREFACE AND ACKNOWLEDGEMENTS

THE inquiry which provided the material for this volume originated, some years ago, in my attempt to review a book in which words like 'hegemony', 'predominance', 'pre-eminence', 'informal imperialism', and 'control' were liberally employed without definition, explanation, or proof. The book had other merits, and I have since regretted the bad temper with which I completed that review. But one of its less uncomfortable consequences was a successful application to the Social Science Research Council (United Kingdom) for a three-year research grant to study the use of such terms in the context of the British connection with Latin America, and to come up with some conclusions. The grant was generous, and it enabled us to start work in the autumn of 1970 with Dr. Robert Greenhill and Dr. Charles Jones as the two full-time research fellows. Most of this book is theirs, and to them is due the major part of such credit as it may earn. Dr. W. M. Mathew (University of East Anglia), Dr. Colin Crossley (University of Leicester), Mr. Rory Miller (University of Liverpool), and Dr. Colin Lewis (Institute of Latin American Studies and the London School of Economics) have also been kind enough to supply chapters based on their independent but parallel research. My own contribution is limited to the initiation and supervision of the project, the editing of the papers, and the attempt to bring together a few of our principal ideas in the form of an introduction. The book is published with the help of a grant from the Latin American Publications Fund.

For so many separate inquiries in such a multitude of different places we have each accumulated more debts than we could possibly recognize. For my own part I am particularly glad to acknowledge the friendliness and co-operation of each of the contributors, which have made working together such a very pleasant experience, and I must also express my warm thanks to the Social Science Research Council for financing the project, to the Universities of Cambridge and Oxford for administering the grant, and to the Rockefeller Foundation and Dr. and Mrs. Olson for enabling me to complete my part of this book in the delightful but firmly labour-inducing surroundings of the Villa Serbelloni at Bellagio.

Dr. Jones would like especially to acknowledge the co-operation of the several business organizations on whose records he has relied. His thanks are due most of all to their archivists: Mr. T. L. Ingram of Baring Brothers & Co., Mr. W. E. H. Fuller of the Sun Insurance Group, and Mr. G. M. Hayward of the Phoenix Insurance Company. So many members of the staff of the former Bank of London and South America (now Lloyds Bank International) helped in one way or another—both here and in South America—that they cannot be named. However, as curator of the B.O.L.S.A. archive, Mrs. Janet Percival of University College Library was especially helpful. A special word of thanks is due to Mr. R. W. Haxell and his staff at Mandatos y Agencias del Río de la Plata, S.A., whose office became almost a second home to the Joneses while they were in Buenos Aires. Anonymity should in no way diminish the contribution made by the staffs of the Association of Foreign Insurance Companies in Argentina, the Biblioteca Nacional, and the library of the Banco Central in Argentina, nor of the Guildhall Library and the Chartered Insurance Institute in the United Kingdom.

Dr. Greenhill's thanks are due to the staffs of the Science Museum Library (in particular, Mr. Winser), the State Paper Room at the British Museum (Mrs. Eileen Davies), the Library of University College, London (Mrs. Janet Percival), the Guildhall Library, the Library of the National Maritime Museum (Mr. A. W. Pearsall and Miss Pipe), and the Library at Canning House. He wishes further to thank Balfour Williamson & Co., especially Mrs. Lee and Mrs. Taylor, for access to their papers; the Directors and Secretary of Naumann Gepp & Co. for the loan of their firm's early records; G. W. Penny of Furness–Withy & Co., who permitted him to see the Minutes of the Court of Directors of the Royal Mail Steam Packet Co.; and Mr. T. Forshaw of the Pacific Steam Navigation Co., who gave him office space when he examined the Company's papers. Dr. Greenhill also wishes to acknowledge the assistance of Dr. Harold Blakemore of the Institute of Latin American Studies, University of London, who read the section on nitrate, Dr. Roger Gravil of Portsmouth Polytechnic, who read the section on the refrigerated beef trade, and Mrs. Mavis Greenhill, who helped in so many ways.

Dr. Crossley is grateful for the financial assistance of the Astor Foundation, the Royal Geographical Society, and the University of Leicester. He also wishes to acknowledge the courtesy of Mr. K. R. M. Carlisle, former Chairman of Leibig's Extract of Meat Co., and his fellow directors, in giving him access to the Liebig company papers.

Dr. Mathew wishes to acknowledge generous financial assistance from the Nuffield Foundation, the Research Board of the University of Leicester, and the School of Social Studies of the University of East Anglia.

Mr. Miller would like to thank especially the Librarian of University College, London, for permission to use the Peruvian Corporation archive, Ing. Tito Gutiérrez and Sr. Silva Sansisteban for allowing access to the records of the Peruvian Corporation in Lima, and the archivist of Balfour Williamson & Co., London. In addition, Sr. Humberto Rodríguez of the Centro de Documentación Agrícola, Lima, and Sr. Ronald M. J. Gordon of Lima provided an opportunity to examine agrarian records, and the staff of the Biblioteca Nacional gave valuable assistance.

Mr. Lewis is particularly grateful to the Directors of Baring Brothers & Co., whose records provided the basic material for the early part of his chapter, and to the house archivist, Mr. T. L. Ingram. He would also like to acknowledge the kind assistance of the director and staff in charge of documents at the Ferrocarril Nacional General San Martín, the main repository in Argentina of material relating to the formerly British-owned railway companies.

Finally, may I say how continually grateful I am to my wife Sarah for her assistance and encouragement on this and so many other occasions; and to her, once again, I owe the index.

D. C. M. PLATT

St. Antony's College,
Oxford

CONTENTS

LIST OF TABLES

LIST OF MAPS

LIST OF ABBREVIATIONS

A.F.I.C.A.	Association of Foreign Insurance Companies in Argentina, San Martín 201, Buenos Aires.
Alexander Committee	*Report of the Committee on Merchant Marine and Fisheries on Steamship Agreements and Affiliations*, House of Representatives, 63rd Congress (Washington, 1914).
Anales	P. E. Dancuart and J. M. Rodriguez, eds., *Anales de la Hacienda Pública del Perú* (Lima, continuing series).
Balfour Williamson	Balfour Williamson & Co. Ltd., archive at Roman House, Wood Street, London, E.C. 2.
Baring, H. C. and L. B.	Baring Brothers & Co. Ltd., House Correspondence and Letter Books, 8 Bishopsgate, London, E.C. 2.
B.O.L.S.A.	Bank of London and South America, archive at University College, Gower Street, London, W.C. 1.
B.R.	*Brazilian Review* (Rio de Janeiro).
B.&R.P.M.	*Brazil and River Plate Mail* (London).
C.D.	*Chemist and Druggist* (U.K.).
Companies House	Companies Registration Office, Companies House, 55–71 City Road, London, E.C. 1.
D.G.F. *Estadísticas*	Dirección General de los Ferrocarriles, *Estadísticas de los ferrocarriles en explotación* (Buenos Aires, annual publication).
Diario de Diputados (Argentina)	Diario de Debates, Cámara de Diputados, Buenos Aires.
Diario de Diputados (Chile)	Diario de Debates, Cámara de Diputados, Santiago.
Diario de Diputados (Peru)	Diario de Debates, Cámara de Diputados, Lima.
Diario de Senadores (Chile)	Diario de Debates, Cámara de Senadores, Santiago.

D.O.T.	Department of Overseas Trade, trade reports published by H.M. Stationery Office, London.
E.R.	*Electrical Review* (U.K.).
E.T.	*Electrical Times* (U.K.).
F.M.	*Farmer's Magazine* (U.K.).
Gepp	Naumann Gepp & Co. Ltd., London & Santos coffee shippers, 45 Fenchurch Street, London, E.C. 3.
Gibbs	Antony Gibbs & Sons, Ltd., archive at Guildhall Library, London, E.C. 2.
Hac. Arch	Ministerio de Hacienda, Archivo Histórico, Lima, Peru.
House Docs.	Executive Documents, House of Representatives, United States.
Johnston	Edward Johnston & Co. Ltd., London and Santos coffee shippers, archive at University College, Gower Street, London, W.C. 1.
Liebigs	Liebig's Extract of Meat Company Ltd., archive at Thames House, Queen Street Place, London, E.C. 4, and at Paseo Colón 221, Buenos Aires.
Mandatos C.B.P.	Mandatos y Agencias del Río de la Plata, Chevalier Boutell's private letters, Avenida de Mayo 645, Buenos Aires.
Mandatos R.C.I.	Mandatos y Agencias del Río de la Plata, Rosario City Improvements Company papers, Avenida de Mayo 645, Buenos Aires.
Mandatos R.P.T.L.A.	Mandatos y Agencias del Río de la Plata, River Plate Trust, Loan & Agency Company papers, Avenida de Mayo 645, Buenos Aires.
Mandatos R.W.	Mandatos y Agencias del Río de la Plata, Rosario Waterworks Company papers, Avenida de Mayo 645, Buenos Aires.
PC/Lim	The Peruvian Corporation archive, Lima.
PC/UCL	The Peruvian Corporation archive, University College, Gower Street, London, W.C. 1.
Pearson	Weetman Pearson papers, Science Museum, London, S.W. 1.

Phoenix	Phoenix Assurance Company Ltd., papers at Phoenix House, King William St., London, E.C. 4.
Phoenix Valparaiso	Valparaiso Fire Insurance Agents' minutes, Phoenix House, King William St., London, E.C. 4.
P.P.	House of Commons (London) sessional papers (Parliamentary Papers).
P.R.O. B.T.	Public Record Office (London), Board of Trade papers.
P.R.O. C.O.	Public Record Office (London), Colonial Office papers.
P.R.O. F.O.	Public Record Office (London), Foreign Office papers.
P.S.N.	Pacific Steam Navigation Company Archive, Pacific Building, James Street, Liverpool, 2.
R.C.S.R.	Royal Commission on Shipping Rings, report and minutes of evidence, P.P. 1909, xlviii.
R.M.S.P.	Royal Mail Steam Packet Company, archives at the National Maritime Museum, Greenwich, and with the Furness–Withy Company, London.
R.R.P.	*Review of the River Plate* (Buenos Aires).
R.T.	*Railway Times* (U.K.).
S.A.J.	*South American Journal* (London).
Sun F.N.	Sun Insurance Office Ltd., foreign notebooks, 63 Threadneedle Street, London E.C. 2.
T.C.T.J.	*Tea and Coffee Trade Journal* (U.K.).
U.S.M.C.R.	United States' Monthly Consular Reports.
Weddels	W. Weddel and Company, *Review of the Frozen Meat Trade* (London, published annually).

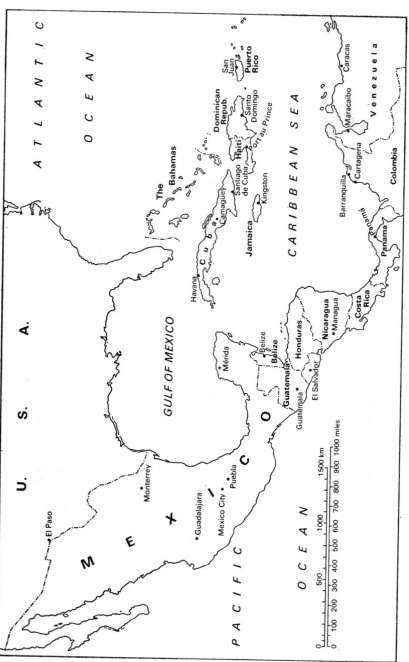

Map. I. Mexico, Central America, and the Caribbean.

INTRODUCTION

D. C. M. PLATT

I

WE have chosen to take Latin America as our exemplar, but it may not be unreasonable to expect that the studies which we now publish will have an interest and relevance beyond the place, period, and themes described. Financial and commercial practices were similar throughout the world before 1930, and our conclusions are likely to apply elsewhere. Many of the issues we raise may be relevant equally to the direction and control of modern business. Most of the chapters are themselves contributions to the economic history of the branches of trade, finance, public utilities, and communications which they discuss. But our central objective has been to furnish some part of the information, and perhaps of the balance and restraint, so needed in an argument for which these qualities are still in short supply. Business imperialism is an elusive concept in which emotion substitutes for reason, theories for facts, politics for history. Most businesses have their special problems and peculiarities, their expertise, which take time and trouble to master. But those who have traded with the notion of business imperialism have seldom examined the heart of the business itself —its records, its trade journals, its private correspondence. To take only one of many possible examples, Jonathan Levin's 'scissors', which as W. M. Mathew says have become a popular and important tool for the dissection of Peru's economic woes in the guano period, may have a certain elegance as economic theory. They are entirely implausible in the context of the long-term interests and strategy of the principal mercantile house in the trade, and Mathew's detailed investigation of the papers of Antony Gibbs and Sons (Chapter IX) makes this perfectly clear.

In this book we have started with the assumption that our first task is to understand how each business operated, for which the best source is clearly the archive of the business itself. So far as possible we have regarded the existence of a particular archive as the deciding factor in undertaking individual studies, and we have been able to draw further on the resources of an ample and generally expert trade press. However, we are well aware that the use of such material on its own can be misleading, and we have made abundant use of government archives, congressional records, printed documentary material, and the general press, Latin American and British, together with such secondary published work as already exists. The use of new material has brought us to the analysis of business imperialism from a different direction. We have not felt inclined to enter directly into the general debate on imperialism and dependency, which has now reached a level of abstraction difficult to associate with what may be understood to have happened in the past. But an inquiry of the character and scope of the one for which we now publish the results has never previously been undertaken, and there can be no doubt that the conclusions of each of its separate parts, though still far from definitive, can take us several stages further towards an understanding of both the mechanisms and the extent of business imperialism, informal imperialism, and control.

II

The quantity of foreign capital and expertise required to promote and maintain the momentum of Latin America's economic development after Independence will always be open to argument. Contemporary research suggests that the contribution of both has been exaggerated. But even if some of the first railways and public utilities were constructed with local capital, it would be difficult to deny that substantial quantities of foreign capital were needed for the extensive railway system which existed by 1930, as well as for ambitious plans for public works and utilities. Nor can it be said that foreign credit, connections, and expertise were entirely superfluous in the development of Latin America's commercial, financial, and manufacturing systems, although certainly replaceable at an earlier date than foreign capital. France in the mid nineteenth century may have needed foreign capital simply as a primer, to accustom local investors to the earning power of railways as an alternative to *rentes*. But few nations, even in Europe, had France's reserves of technical proficiency, capital, and natural resources, and certainly no equivalent existed for nineteenth-century Latin America.

Whatever the assets or liabilities of foreign interest in Latin American development during the nineteenth century, the fact that foreigners and their capital arrived in quantity is indisputable. In the circumstances, it is not easy to see how strain and conflict could have been avoided. Foreign merchants, with their superior contacts abroad, their cheaper credit, greater knowledge and experience in overseas markets, had obvious advantages over native Latin Americans in overseas trade. Furthermore, their interest in limiting costs and enlarging profits in the export trades made them progressively inclined to eliminate the native intermediary, which in turn brought them into direct contact, and often conflict, with the Latin American producer. In the case of the Argentine beef trade, where only 60 per cent of an animal provided saleable meat, a large margin was likely to exist between prices for live cattle and for beef, within which both producers and meat packers could feel aggrieved. Indeed, in the beef trade the conjunction of the notorious Chicago packing houses and of a general sensitivity towards the exploitation of Argentina's natural resources by foreign capitalists would have fomented suspicion and unpopularity even without the genuine bases for distrust which Colin Crossley and Robert Greenhill describe in Chapter VIII.

With some, but few, exceptions, friction of this kind was commonplace. It would probably have existed if both parties to the dispute had been Latin Americans, or if both were foreigners, but the introduction of a difference in nationality was clearly a further irritant. Nothing could have been more exposed in this respect than a large foreign public utility company. Squeezed between rising costs and regulated tariffs, the economic situation of the utility companies was always difficult. The Chilean Electric Tramway and Light Company, the misfortunes of which are analysed in Chapter III, could not have been more conspicuous. Its large payroll and the range of its customers and services made its every decision a matter of public interest, and no politician could have been expected to risk his career in its defence. Indeed, once one generation of politicians had made political capital out of an attack on the local utility company, it was not easy for their successors to reach agreement without being accused of a sell-out to the foreigner. The result, as the authors of Chapter III conclude, is a history of continued friction between the companies and the host countries, in which the final impression for the companies is one of painful vulnerability.

Basic conflicts of interest of this kind would have existed whatever the nationality, but others applied simply to foreigners in their relationship with Latin Americans, and others still more specifically to Britons. The unequal relationship between Latin American producers and foreign intermediaries is commented on in several of the trade and commodity chapters below, and inequality was as characteristic of the contact between German merchants at Bahía and the Brazilian cocoa planters, as it was of British and North American coffee export houses at Rio and Santos and the majority of their clients in the interior. But a classic misunderstanding, peculiarly British in origin, characterized the first decades of British banking in Latin America. British banking, long before it reached Latin America, had settled into a routine of short-term accommodation in which the tying-up of capital in long advances or loans was anathema. Charles Jones explains in Chapter I that although this was perfectly understood in British banking circles, it conflicted with the expectations of Latin Americans whose intention had been that the British banks should bring in substantial quantities of foreign capital, reduce the current interest rate on long-term credit, and accommodate politicians, landowners, and domestic entrepreneurs. Both parties had moved closer together by the end of the nineteenth century as the British, under pressure from increasing competition and falling interest rates, began to relax some of the rigidities of classical commercial banking, and as Latin Americans abandoned the cruder and less relevant forms of development banking. But the misunderstanding was there, and Jones points to its more damaging consequences.

III

It must be self-evident that, while all businessmen aim to make a profit, the majority enter and conduct their business in the expectation of a reasonable return on their capital and effort over a period of years, rather than a swift exit after a windfall gain. Similarly, a customer or creditor may normally be depended upon to settle his debts, since he expects to continue in business, to buy or to borrow, over many years. Exceptions are frequent enough, whether in the form of company promoters and fly-by-night financiers on the one part, or unsettled debts and insolvent governments on the other. But Baring Brothers in Argentina and

Rothschilds in Brazil, Antony Gibbs and Balfour Williamson on the West Coast, hoped and expected to remain in business permanently in their areas, and neither they nor the majority of respectable houses in the trade would have thought of sacrificing a safe and steady business for the chance of a once-off speculative gain. The same applied, with even greater force, to a railway company, a public utility, a land company, or a mine, with its capital locked immovably in the country in which it operated.

As for Latin American governments, so long as a need was felt for foreign capital, expertise, or management, indefinite default on loans or obligations was impracticable. The only long-term solution was to negotiate some form of composition with foreign creditors, or a working agreement with the companies already operating within national territory. Each of the governments in turn reached agreement with its creditors, more or less rapid and generous according to its need for money and its expectations for national credit. If foreign firms were supplying a useful service, for which no local substitute was as yet fully developed, they had to be left with just sufficient incentive to remain in business, more particularly if, as for the British insurance companies, the Latin American market proved to be only a marginal part of their business from which they might easily be persuaded to withdraw. A public utility company did not have this option, but somebody had to supply the services and politicians might well find it more convenient, and less politically invidious, to leave these services in foreign hands. Colin Lewis explains (Chapter XI) how the railway companies in Argentina, often in alliance with their own workers, could bring pressure to bear on the government by the threat to lay off men or reduce services unless government consent were given to a rise in tariffs designed to keep pace with costs. Lewis makes it clear that successful pressure of this kind presupposed both an unwillingness on the part of the government to take responsibility for the lines and the support of one or more of Argentina's more powerful sectional interests, so that without either the companies were in no position to resist. But in the normal course of events, Linda and Charles Jones's review of the sad history of the Rosario Waterworks and Drainage Companies (Chapter III) shows that the companies, after their early troubles, were permitted to make a small but steady profit. If British managers and directors, the Joneses explain, acquired some of the skills necessary in dealing with municipal authorities, so too did the municipality of Rosario learn to make political capital out of the presence of foreign-owned utility companies, to seem to persecute them, and yet always to allow them just enough air to breathe.

These were the basic constraints within the broad form of capitalism accepted at the time by businessmen, politicians, and officials alike. While these constraints could not prevent excesses and temporary distortions on either side, they reduced the possibility of any permanent imbalance of power. In each of the chapters which follow, the balance of power between British business and Latin America has been examined in some depth and an attempt has been made to identify the strengths and weaknesses on each side. Each case must be treated on its own merits, but it may not be unreasonable to say that the advantage lay with the party enjoying the better combination of flexibility, experience, local knowledge, market information, and access to credit, with political influence and government intervention as the jokers in the pack. Obviously, different equations bring very different results, with at one extreme the public utility company, a helpless giant tied down by its immovable capital at the mercy of the local politician, and at the other the powerful export house, its capital removable to better opportunities elsewhere, in control of several or all of the stages of production, purchasing, processing, shipment, and sale.

What emerges, however, from so many of our studies is that to speak in terms of control by one party over another, of antagonism between native and foreigner, is often to ignore the more fundamental elements in the equation. Indeed nationality is irrelevant in many or most of the cases described, since the business would have been conducted and controlled in the same way irrespective of nationality. Of more significance is the fact that each of the parties was subject to market forces over which it had no control, and where the flexibility it might command could amount only to a few per cent one way or the other on the transaction. This was clearly the case even for the powerful export house, when the commodities in which it traded faced competition in world produce markets. It was so for the monopolists, government or private, in Peruvian guano, Chilean nitrates, or Brazilian rubber, when monopoly prices encouraged substitution or the development of alternative products. Market forces were a major constraint for the influential meat packing houses in Argentina, whose ability to monopolize and control cattle prices was limited by the elements identified by Colin Crossley in his locational model for the industry, and where, as Greenhill observes, the final impression within Argentina's principal overseas market for frozen and chilled beef must be that constraints in the meat trade in Britain balanced the options open to the packer in Argentina (British, native, or North American).

In fact, it may not escape notice that what appear to be the most powerful of Latin America's commercial and financial alliances—in shipping, insurance, nitrate and iodine, and in the valorization scheme as applied to coffee—were in each case designed to postpone a long-term decline in rates and prices far more powerful than the combinations themselves. Charles Jones concludes from his study of the organizations uniting the foreign insurance companies in Latin America that they were essentially protective alliances gradually and unwillingly giving ground to outsiders. For shipping, Robert Greenhill points to the continuously downward trend in the freight rate from the 1870s, and decides that ordinary market forces within the shipping industry proved to be the most powerful and continuing restraint on the 'conference' system. In nitrates, the trend towards falling prices persisted, in spite of a series of nitrate combinations, until after 1900, and the combinations simply succeeded in 'decelerating the rise in output and the fall in prices'. For iodine the combination was more successful in maintaining the price, but the reason for its existence was 'a permanent change in the source of supply [i.e. the emergence of the Chilean nitrate industry as a producer of iodine], and a pronounced tendency towards overproduction which threatened competition and low prices' (Chapter VII).

The fact that combinations generally arose from *over*-production meant that instability was always marked. The entrance of a new competitor, the desire of one participant to increase his share, dissimilarities in costs or in aggressive spirit, could break a combination overnight, so that the pattern in combinations for all the industries we describe is of frequent suspension and re-formation. Governments could themselves become the most enthusiastic supporters of combinations, and for the same reason—to combat a strong and continuing trend towards falling prices in an important export product. The Chilean Government, after first opposing foreign-controlled combinations in the nitrate trade, became an enthusiastic convert to a system designed to secure high prices, limit production, and prolong the earning power of one of Chile's chief natural resources. The principle behind Brazilian official support for the valorization of coffee was no different: the restriction of sales to maintain prices in opposition to a strong secular trend towards falling prices in world coffee markets.

IV

Ultimately, it was the government which could do most to iron out inequalities. The valorization of Brazilian coffee is an example of the way that thinking developed, and of what could be done. Whatever its success, and opinions vary, valorization marked an important step in the acceptance of major responsibility for price control and maintenance by a producer government. It is unrealistic and unhistorical to expect a government in the nineteenth and early twentieth centuries to behave like a model socialist government today. But the studies which we now publish suggest that the extent of government regulation and control is commonly understated. Governments were sovereign; the citizen had no remedy against arbitrary power other than the overthrow of the government itself, and the foreigner, unless he were to join (at some disadvantage) in national politics, had no final sanction save diplomatic or forcible intervention by his own state. The rare appearance of the British Government in the course of this inquiry merely reflects the fact, for which evidence enough has been published elsewhere,[1] that tight limits were customarily set to the role of the government in the protection and promotion of Britain's trade and finance overseas. Certainly British businessmen and investors learnt not to depend on diplomatic support, and the assumption on which they operated, even at the highest level of international finance, was that in any operation with a national government, the government had the last word. Mathew's study of the Peruvian guano contracts (Chapter IX) spells this out. Antony Gibbs and Sons, over the twenty years for which they acted as government contractors, simply learnt to live with a

[1] D. C. M. Platt, *Finance, Trade and Politics in British Foreign Policy, 1815–1914* (Oxford, 1968), and W. M. Matthew, 'The Imperialism of Free Trade: Peru, 1820–70', *Economic History Review*, 2nd ser. xxi (1968), 562–79.

government chronically indebted, arbitrary in its acts, and politically unstable, and to accept its decisions as a necessary condition of doing business. The size of the guano contract, concentrated in the hands of a single commercial house, made it on commissions alone a good business while it lasted. But it was not easy to deal with such a government, and Gibbs, when dropped by the government in 1861, do not seem to have been particularly upset. Mathew detects an air of guano-weariness about their correspondence in the late 1850s and early 1860s; the business, said one of the partners, contained 'more *duras* than *maduras*, more kicks than halfpence'.

The question is not so much the sovereign political power of Latin American governments, which was seldom disputed, as the practical limits to the use which governments could make of it in their relations with foreign business. Peru needed the experience and expertise of Antony Gibbs in selling and promoting the use of guano in the principal market, the United Kingdom. On the whole the business seems to have been conducted fairly, and it passed, some time after the need for Gibbs's particular services were over, into the hands of Peruvians. The same was true of the use of foreign houses as sources of short-term credit and advances. Although local capital resources differed very much from one republic to another, it would have been difficult in most cases to find a local substitute for advances on the scale supplied by foreign houses to Latin American governments in the first decades of Independence. In the latter part of the nineteenth century, short-term government finance came to be handled by local banks, institutions, and capitalists, but whatever judgement one might now feel inclined to pass on the use made of advances in the early years of Independence, governments regarded them as essential so that they had little choice other than to negotiate terms with the foreigner.

With hindsight, one might wish that governments had taken a more positive role in the provision of services, in the protection of the producer and the conservation of natural resources, in the nationalization and municipalization of utilities, in the protection of crafts, in the promotion of local industry, in development banking and local insurance. Some action of this kind came with experience, but for the rest Latin America would have had to have been far in advance of the spirit of the times, even as shown in the most industrially advanced of contemporary societies. Latin

America, with its inequalities in the distribution of wealth and power and its unstable governments, could certainly not be numbered among these. The disposal of Peru's guano receipts, of which so unusually large a proportion passed through the hands of the Peruvian Government itself, was not a good omen for state ownership and exploitation of natural resources in the mid nineteenth century. And whatever the virtues of a well-organized state banking system, properly directed towards economic development in the home country, Charles Jones, whose sympathies clearly lie very much in that direction, is compelled to conclude from his investigation that it would have been of doubtful utility in the late nineteenth century to restrict private banks (national or foreign), which were performing their necessary if limited task efficiently, 'simply in order to protect State banks which were inherently unstable and patently corrupt, and whose commitment to the decentralization of credit was at best of times incomplete, composed more of rhetoric than action' (Chapter I).

In the circumstances, it is encouraging to learn of the progress which was actually made towards national legislative control. Jones feels that in banking the creation, after a series of financial crises, of a new generation of strong and more conservative official banks was more effective than legislation in resolving the deadlock between public and private banks in Latin America. In insurance, Jones argues, the common constraint of the market—its limited size and the development of competition—was far more instrumental in determining the course of events than aggression by foreigners or nationalist retaliation by local companies or Latin American governments. But for both banking and insurance a formidable body of regulatory legislation had developed by the turn of the century. Moreover, railways and public utilities in all countries have always been peculiarly subject to legislative control, for the enforcement of minimum standards and for safety requirements if nothing else, and Latin America was no exception. Colin Lewis remarks from his study of Argentine railways that an intention to place restraints upon individual companies was observable from the first, and that even before the general codification of railway legislation in 1891 (the Ley General de Ferrocarriles) the Argentine Government possessed extensive powers to regulate the affairs of private companies.

At a more general level it can be said that although no legislation is perfect and much of what passed through the legislatures fell far short of what was obviously desirable, there was no consistent reluctance to impose legislative controls on foreign business interests in Latin America. Both Rory Miller and Charles Jones have noticed that Congress was normally far more radical than the executive in proposals for legislative control over the foreigner, and that greater timidity was shown with the constraints of office. This accounts both for the strong language so often used of the foreigner and the relatively mild form taken by legislation. But where major legislative restraints were *not* imposed, the reason could well have been that the existing situation suited local interests rather better. Government intervention in the Argentine meat packing industry, so far as it related to foreign combinations in the trade, was postponed until after the First World War, since up to 1914 the competition of the Chicago meat packers with the established British firms on the River Plate was well directed to the interests of government and landowners. In Chile, while nitrate combinations continued to attract the close attention of legislators, the iodine combination was early recognized as a necessary element in preventing the lowering of prices under conditions of inelastic demand. Legislation was not felt to be necessary; restricted sales suited Chile's revenue, and the international iodine combination, classically monopolist in nearly every respect, itself caused little concern.

V

Given the limits to Latin America's capital resources in the nineteenth century, her need for at least some foreign expertise, and the genuine restraint which has to be accepted for government intervention over this period, is it possible to come to any conclusion on the nature of business imperialism, of informal imperialism and control, on the basis of British experience?

As the broadest of generalizations, it might fairly be said that although the returns derived from a political relationship between nations may be grossly unequal, any *economic* relationship, unless enforced politically, must offer at least some appearance of mutual benefit. Britain's political interest in Latin America was slight to non-existent, and she was unwilling to enforce economic interests, which were her sole genuine interests on the American continent, by military or diplomatic means. One may begin, then, with the assumption that British trade, enterprise, and investment in Latin America must have offered *some* benefit to at least *some* Latin Americans. The question than arises whether this benefit was very disproportionate, or just slightly unequal and in which direction, or not unequal at all. This is one of the main issues to which we have turned our minds in the chapters which follow. Where possible we have taken a look at profit levels, at the return to Latin Americans of each particular form of enterprise, at the advantages and disadvantages of the foreign connection. We have tried to establish in which businesses and in what countries the inequalities were most evident, whether for Latin Americans or for foreigners. We have tested some of the assumptions of general theories of imperialism and dependency against our own research at the level of particular industries and individual firms.

It would be unreasonable to attempt to anticipate the conclusions of each chapter, which are set out clearly enough as it is. If one accepts Latin America's need for foreign capital and expertise before 1930, the general level of return on productive investments in trade, railways, and public utilities was not extravagant. At 6 to 7 per cent it was 1 or 2 per cent higher than the yield to be obtained without risk or exertion on good Latin American government bonds or home industrial stock, which in turn was $1\frac{1}{2}$–2 per cent higher than the yield on British home and colonial government securities. Latin America would have found difficulty in obtaining the same services elsewhere on better terms. It seems unlikely that she could have supplied sufficient entrepreneurial talent or managerial and technical expertise, and she could hardly have accumulated the very large amounts of capital required within the same time-span from her own investors, even on the most optimistic of assumptions about reinvested profits.

In a competitive world—and the information we have gathered certainly suggests the reality of competition, even if only to force rival interests into defensive combinations—it would have been surprising if Britons had been able consistently to extract an unreasonably high price for their services. Others were ready enough to replace them if they did, and indeed the tendency of Englishmen over this period to drift out of Latin American enterprise into safer and more familiar openings in Britain herself, the Colonies, and the Dominions hardly implies an exceptional opportunity for profit in the Republics.[1] No more than conventional profit levels give a prima facie case for doubting the existence of any strong element of control in the business relationship of Britons to Latin Americans, and on the whole, with the exceptions we discuss, this is confirmed in our separate studies of industries and trades.

The case against British enterprise and capital in Latin America seems rather that it consistently outstayed its welcome, and came ultimately to serve as a barrier to, rather than the promoter of, Latin America's economic development. It reinforced tendencies which turned out to be not in Latin America's best interests, though few could have supposed this to be so at the time. W. M. Mathew, in the interesting conceptual categories which he develops for defining the term 'control' (Chapter IX), points to a form of control which derives simply from the circumstances that confront a government as a result of the presence of foreign merchants, their capital, and their willingness to enter into business. As residents in Lima, active in the guano business and backed by the capital resources of the City of London, Antony Gibbs 'held out to a weak, insecure, and inadequately financed governmental system in Lima irresistible temptations to sink ever more deeply into a costly and debilitating indebtedness'. Indirectly, then, Gibbs were contributing to the downfall of the Peruvian economy at the same time as they managed, efficiently and at no more than conventional cost, the sales of the Peruvian Government's guano overseas. In Gibbs's case too the welcome was overstayed; the twenty years of their guano contracts for the Peruvian Government well exceeded the period in which Gibbs's special qualities as a contractor might have earned the exclusion of Peruvian capitalists from so important a national enterprise. On the broader front of British banks, export houses, and railway systems later in the century and up to 1930, Britain's interest in Latin American export trades, and the belief which Englishmen shared with most Latin Americans at the time—and certainly with those in political authority—in the notion of comparative advantage, confirmed and reinforced all the tendencies towards the development of economies dangerously dependent on the export of a limited range of primary products, at the expense of a broader,

---

[1] Competitive pressures and the tendency among Britons to shift their interests to better opportunities outside Latin America are described in D. C. M. Platt, *Latin America and British Trade, 1806–1914* (London, 1972).

more balanced, and self-sufficient growth. Charles Jones, in the conclusion to his chapter on banks, goes further than this and makes the point, legitimately enough, that British banks lent a semblance of stability to inherently unstable national economies. By doing so they reinforced the position of those opposed to change, and they consistently abetted the concentration of credit in the administrative and commercial centres of the continent, tying the interior more and more to the apron-strings of the ports. All in all, Jones concludes, British banks 'proved a powerful agent in the maintenance of the political *status quo* during a period of turbulent economic change'.

It is on broad and general grounds such as these that the best case can be made against Britain's economic connection with Latin America before 1930. Leland Jenks once made the point, in the context of Argentine railway construction, management, and development, that Britons were not responsible for already existing anomalies in the social structure they encountered; 'their activity aided and abetted the tendencies that were already there, and in the case of Argentina, seemed for a time to have given them renewed strength'.[1] This is surely right. Whether genuine opportunities existed for a different pattern of development over the period we describe is still open to doubt. Poor communications, inadequate capital, restricted markets, shortages of labour, fuel, and raw material were formidable barriers to native development, which must have made the alternatives to a foreign connection as uninviting to Latin Americans at the time as they seem speculative to the historian today.

[1] Leland H. Jenks, 'Britain and America's Railway Development', *Journal of Economic History*, xi (1951), 388.

PART I

FINANCE

CHAPTER I

Commercial Banks and Mortgage Companies

CHARLES JONES

I

IN a discussion which centres on questions of control and economic power, several factors differentiate banking from most other activities. For whereas in many spheres of economic activity—in insurance, public utilities, or shipping, for example—there is at the very least a hint of combination or monopoly to be either substantiated or dismissed, the British banks in Latin America during our period were entirely free from this particular accusation. A railway line or a public utility company tends—of its nature—to be monopolistic. In insurance and shipping, on the other hand, it was in the nature of the business to be territorially dispersed, as it was for banking. Yet although the insurance agents of each major South American city formed themselves into a Local Board with the intention of maintaining rates, the bankers remained fiercely independent of each other. William Lough, reporting on South American banking to the United States Government in 1915, found this remarkable. He commented that only in Lima and Buenos Aires was there even so basic a facility as a clearing-house; that credit information was everywhere jealously guarded; and that there were no banking associations.[1]

Of course there are other charges which may be brought against any foreign company by its hosts and which were often applicable to the British banks. They were profitable—some would say excessively profitable—their dividends commonly ranging between double and four times the average yield upon British investments

---

[1] William H. Lough, *Banking Opportunities in South America* (U.S. Department of Commerce, Special Agents' Series, No. 106, Washington, 1915), pp. 101–2.

　　　　　　　　　B

in Latin America. They remitted home such of these profits as were to be divided amongst shareholders not resident in South America. That is to say, the greater part of the profits was remitted to England, although there was nothing to prevent Brazilians or Argentines from themselves taking shares and some did. When legislation was passed ordering them to be taxed, the banks reacted in a very natural way, setting their accountants to minimize the effects of the taxes. But over and above these minor sources of friction which are part of the matrix of relations between any foreign corporation and its host government, there are, in the case of banking, two questions which do not generally arise.

First, there is the source of the banks' funds. Whereas in the case of a railway company, a waterworks, or even a mortgage company, it was customary for the entire capital necessary to the enterprise to be raised in the home country, in colonial and foreign banking the rule was 'that where the money is lent there it should be mainly supplied'.[1] In other words, the banks relied mainly on deposits placed with their foreign branches as their means of business. They did not, as some Latin Americans had anticipated, introduce large amounts of British and European capital.

Second, and more important, is the question of the direction in which each bank lent its funds. A recent Indian commentator has claimed that 'in a country where there is acute scarcity of capital, the banking system has to bear the added onus of ensuring that the capital is used not only in a productive way, but in the most productive way'.[2] Clearly, differences of opinion may easily arise as to the most productive utilization of available capital in any given circumstances. There may also arise the rather more serious difference as to whether available capital should in fact be employed in what appears to be the most productive way possible, or whether it might be better employed in the most profitable way possible. And there would certainly have been some from the British nineteenth-century banking fraternity who would have argued that to employ capital in the most profitable way possible—though

[1] Nathaniel Cork, 'The Late Australian Banking Crisis', *Journal of the Institute of Bankers*, xv (Apr. 1894), pp. 182–3.
[2] T. A. Vaswani, *The Indian Banking System: A Critical Study of the Central and Commercial Banking Sectors* (Bombay, 1968), p. 3.

always in accord with the principle of safety—was itself the surest way of ensuring that such capital made its optimum contribution to production.

This might seem to be mere playing with words, but it is not. Indeed the central issue of this chapter, and of debates on banking in Latin America during our period, is between those who felt that the responsible pursuit of profit was not merely a principle of selfishness, but of utility—that, in short, the market would provide —and those who felt that the market must be *made* to provide by at least a minimal amount of government intervention and planning. And in this respect, foreign banks were early shown to be problematic. For if a government approved the plan of a foreign company to build a port or a railway, it could incorporate into the concession exact dimensions and distances. On the advice of its engineers, it could stipulate the quality of materials and know that, assuming honesty on the part of the contracting parties, it would get what it wanted. But in view of the imperfections—and occasionally even the absence—of commercial legislative systems and codes in nineteenth-century Latin America, governments were far less able to define and regulate the limits within which bank concessionaires would be permitted to work. Consequently they did not always receive what they had been hoping for, and on more than one occasion were bitterly disappointed by the lending policies of British banks to which they had hastily granted over-generous concessions—having had too much in mind, perhaps, the apparently immense contemporary achievements of French and German banks founded on principles quite out of line with those held by the majority of British bankers.

Having established our quarry in most general terms as an ideological disagreement about the ultimate purpose of banking and the way in which it should most effectively contribute to economic growth, we must now hunt with great circumspection. It is important to ascertain that the conflict was in fact, as well as in ideas, a genuine one; that each side in the debate was represented by active institutions; and that both profit-orientated and development-orientated banks really did exist and conflict in Latin America. It must also be established just who belonged on which side, and in doing this we shall have to distinguish between foreign and domestic banks, between British, French, and German banks, between private, semi-state-owned, and wholly state-owned banks, before arriving at a definition or division in terms of nationality, status of proprietors, or some other factor.

With these warnings in mind, however, it will be best to begin with the relatively straightforward history of the expansion of British overseas banking in Latin America, and to establish the geographical scope and the financial scale of this study.

II

Between 1862 and 1929 many companies were established in London to carry on banking business in Latin America. Some were no more than figments of the imagination of company promoters; they never opened branches in their declared fields of operation, and are best forgotten. But a few succeeded, and came to be numbered amongst the most successful of British investments in Latin America.[1]

The flotations followed a pattern dictated rather more by conditions in the British economy than by events in Latin America. The first wave, for example, came during the joint stock company boom which led up to the Overend Gurney crisis of 1866 and was made possible by the Companies Acts of 1858–62, which extended the privilege of incorporation with limited liability to banks.[2] In response to the new law a host of British banks was established to do business in almost every part of the world. Amongst them were the London and River Plate Bank, the English Bank of Rio de Janeiro, the London and Brazilian Bank, and the London Bank of Mexico and South America: all those banks, in short, which were eventually to come together in the Bank of London and South America with the exception of the Anglo-South American Bank, a later foundation.

---

[1] J. Fred Rippy, *British Investments in Latin America, 1822–1949; A Case Study in the Operations of Private Enterprise in Retarded Regions* (Minneapolis, 1959), p. 67, Table 18. Rippy gives the yield on British investments in Anglo-Latin American commercial banks in 1913 as 13·4 per cent. This was greatly in excess of the average return on British capital invested in railways, government bonds, and other economic enterprises in the principal Latin American countries. In Argentina, British capital at this time was earning 4·9 per cent per annum, in Brazil 4·8 per cent, and in Chile, where the yield was highest, no more than 5·9 per cent. Furthermore, bank shareholders were less often called upon to subscribe to fresh issues than were the holders of railway shares.

[2] B. C. Hunt, *The Development of the Business Corporation in England, 1800–67* (Harvard Economic Studies III, 1936), pp. 136–8; E. Nevin and E. W. Davis, *The London Clearing Banks* (London, 1970), pp. 70–3.

During the remainder of the century there were a number of attempts to found new Anglo-Latin American banks. The Mercantile Bank of the River Plate (1872) and the English Bank of the River Plate (1881) both came to grief within a few years, but the Anglo-Argentine Bank (1889) and the Bank of London and Tarapacá (1888) prospered. In 1900 they amalgamated to form the Bank of Tarapacá and Argentina, which became the Anglo-South American Bank in 1907 by change of name. From its base in the South, the Anglo Bank then moved northwards, absorbing the London Bank of Mexico and South America in 1912 and the Commercial Bank of Spanish America in 1914, so becoming by 1923 the largest, though not the most secure, of the British banks in Latin America (see Table I.1).

TABLE I.1

Total Assets of the Four Major Anglo-Latin American Banks,
1870–1923

(£000)

	1870	1880	1890	1900	1910	1923
London and River Plate Bank	3,742	4,482	12,031	21,612	26,204	46,854
London and Brazilian Bank	1,790	4,876	8,946	8,023	13,181	35,144
British Bank of South America	3,396	7,927	10,473	6,580	15,615	23,296
Anglo-South American Bank[a]	—	—	1,193	2,571	11,334	73,435
Total	8,928	17,285	32,643	38,786	66,334	178,729

SOURCE: Lough, *Banking Opportunities*, pp. 33, 35, 37, 40, 42.

[a] The assets for 1890 and 1900 are those of the banks which, in 1907, became the Anglo-South American Bank.

Two points must be added to complete this introductory outline of the expansion of British banking. The first concerns ownership. For whilst we have referred unquestioningly to those banks mentioned so far as British enterprises on the ground that they were registered in London, it was, of course, true that some shareholders of such companies were not themselves British and that, conversely, Britons held shares in some banks which were registered

abroad and were, to outward appearances, Latin American institutions. At one time, more than half the shares of the London
Bank of Central America were held in Nicaragua and El Salvador,
though nationality of the holders is unknown.[1] Throughout its
life, a part of the capital of the Mercantile Bank of the River Plate
was held by French, Belgian, and German capitalists.[2] 31·6 per
cent of the capital of the Anglo-Argentine Bank was held by persons living outside the British Isles, mostly Belgians.[3] And in 1865
as much as 42·4 per cent of the share capital of the English Bank
of Rio de Janeiro was held by Portuguese and Brazilians.[4] On the
other hand, by 1914 the Anglo-South American Bank, although it
operated conventionally through wholly owned branches in Chile
and the River Plate, made up the rest of its profit from substantial
minority holdings in Latin American banks such as the Banco de
la Provincia de Buenos Aires, the Banco del Perú y Londres, the
Banco de la Nación Boliviana, the Banca Agrícola y Comercial,
and the Banco de Londres y México.[5] In addition, the Anglo Bank
was providing funds on a profit-sharing basis to the Commercial
Bank of Spanish America which it was soon to control,[6] and in
1920 it took a controlling (60 per cent) interest in the largest
Chilean private domestic bank—the Banco de A. Edwards.[7]

[1] *S.A.J.*, 18 Apr. 1896, 442.

[2] P.R.O. B.T. 31 1736/6406.

[3] Companies House 27847/29 and 30. This was made up as follows:

	%
Belgians	19·5
Britons living abroad (mostly in the River Plate, where many were permanent settlers)	7·9
Argentines and Uruguayans	2·9
Germans and French	1·3
	31·6

[4] Companies House 548c, vol. i:

	%
Resident in U.K.	55·8
Portuguese names resident in Portugal	22·5
Portuguese names resident in Brazil	19·9
Britons resident abroad	1·8

[5] Lough, *Banking Opportunities*, pp. 39–40. The investments of the Anglo-
South American Bank amounted to about £1·3m. by 1913. It had held shares
in the Chilean Banco Mobiliario until that company failed in 1907.

[6] B.O.L.S.A., F8 Head Office to Roberto S. Fuerth (?), 11 Nov. 1912.

[7] 'We are on very intimate terms with that powerful institution [the Anglo-
South American Bank] which practically controls our share capital, and has
promised to help us in every possible way.' D. M. Joslin, *A Century of Banking
in Latin America* (London, 1963), p. 259.

Apart from institutional investments by British banks, there were some private British investors prepared to risk a part of their funds in Latin American banks in spite of their inability to exert effective influence on their management. The shares of the Argentine Banco de la Nación and the Banco Nacional de México were both dealt in on the London stock exchange, as too were those of the entirely privately owned (and therefore less prestigious) Banco Popular and the Banco Español del Río de la Plata—both of Buenos Aires. In short there was a considerable degree of internationalization of banking capital, significant in a few instances, but generally without effect on policy which, in so far as it had national leanings, was normally dictated by the nationality and consequent training of the directors and managers. Thus the Belgian directors of the Anglo-Argentine (and later the Anglo-South American) Bank may well have been responsible for the rather unorthodox style of that bank; and it was certainly Anglo-Argentine and continental influence in the board and management of the Mercantile Bank of the River Plate which brought about its downfall; by contrast, the Portuguese shareholders of the English Bank of Rio de Janeiro do not seem to have had any power over policy.

The second and concluding point concerns the growth of the British banks both in size and in geographical extent. We have already seen how the Bank of London and Tarapacá grew from modest beginnings in Chile in 1888 to comprehend operations of one sort or another in almost every part of the sub-continent as the Anglo-South American Bank. But the Anglo Bank was not the only British commercial bank to extend its operations during these years. It was unique only in the manner in which it expanded, for the three other major banks preferred to work mainly through branches, rather than wholly or partly controlled subsidiaries.

For the two Brazilian banks—the British Bank of South America and the London and Brazilian Bank—expansion consisted of the growth of their branch networks southwards into the River Plate area, and westwards into Chile. Conversely, the London and River Plate replied to the movements of its competitors by moving north and west into Brazil and Chile (see Table I.2). The London and Brazilian Bank had taken its first steps in this direction at a very early date. In 1864 they had planned a merger with Baron Mauá's Montevideo bank, the Banco Mauá y Cía, and the scheme might well have gone through had it not been for the opposition of the

Emperor of Brazil and the outbreak of the Overend Gurney crisis.[1]
As it was, no substantial expansion took place until the end of the
1880s.

TABLE I.2

Branch Offices of the Major Anglo-Latin American Banks, 1913

	Com- mercial	L. & B.B.	B.B.S.A.	Anglo	L.R.P.B.	Total
Argentina	—	2	2	7	13	24
Uruguay	—	1	1	1	4	7
Brazil	—	11	3	—	9	23
Chile	—	—	—	10	1	11
Central	5	—	—	—	—	5
Total	5	14	6	18	27	70

SOURCE: Lough, *Banking Opportunities*, p. 31.

Already, by 1913, the process of interpenetration had gone a
considerable way. The total number of branches (excluding those
of subsidiaries of British banks, and excluding agencies) of the five
major Anglo-Latin American banks numbered 70 (See Table I.2),
a figure which was not to be attained by United States banks in
Latin America until the 1960s.[2] No less impressive was the growth
of the principal banks as recorded in Table I.1. That the assets of
a group of young firms should have grown by 93·6 per cent during
the 1870s is perhaps unremarkable, but that this growth should
have been sustained and even surpassed between 1900 and 1923
surely is so (see Table I.3).

TABLE I.3

*Percentage Increase in the Assets of the Four Major Anglo-Latin
American Banks, 1870–1923*

1870–80	93·6
1880–90	89·0
1890–1900	18·8
1900–10	71·0
1910–14	10·1
1914–23	144·7[a]

[a] Distorted by the depreciation of sterling.
SOURCE: Lough, *Banking Opportunities*, pp. 33, 35, 37, 40, 42.

[1] Joslin, *A Century of Banking*, pp. 69–74.
[2] Harry Magdoff, *The Age of Imperialism: The Economics of U.S. Foreign
Policy* (New York, 1969), p. 75.

III

Viewed in isolation, this growth in British overseas banking suggests at least the possibility of an undue intrusion of foreign capital and influence into a vital area of Latin American economic life. However, as we have already explained, such control as the British did exercise was not the outcome of straightforward monopoly power in any major commercial centre. The British had to compete with domestic banks, both private and official, as well as with the German overseas banks, and a large number of nominally domestic banks with a substantial European element amongst their shareholders. It is not always even clear, owing to the scarcity and imperfections of the available statistical material, whether the British (or the foreign sector, or the private sector) were making ground against competition or not. Thus, in Mexico between 1901 and 1914, we know that the percentage of bank assets controlled by the Banco Nacional de México fell from 37·4 to 29·9 whilst that held by the Banco de Londres y México rose from 21·1 to 26·1.[1] Yet this cannot be taken as evidence of a trend towards greater British control over Mexican banking. For, whilst the Anglo-South American Bank held a substantial block of shares in the Banco de Londres y México, they did not have a controlling interest.[2] On the other hand, the Banco Nacional de México, in spite of its chauvinistic title, was about two-fifths British owned,[3] and was thought of by the *South American Journal* as an Anglo-Latin American rather than a Mexican institution.[4] It appears that in absolute terms, the value of the British shareholding in the Banco Nacional was actually larger than that of the British holding in the Banco de Londres,[5] which would imply a decline in the influence exercised by the British in Mexican banking over this period. However, in the present state of research, the deciding factor is missing; namely, what voice—if any—did the British have in the management of each of the two banks?

---

[1] Walter F. McCaleb, *Present and Past Banking in Mexico* (New York, 1920), pp. 136–7, 222–3.

[2] *Memoria de Hacienda*, Nos. 188–9, pp. xxxviii–xxxix, cited by McCaleb, *Banking in Mexico*, p. 66.

[3] Alfred P. Tischendorf, *Great Britain and Mexico in the Era of Porfirio Díaz* (Durham, N.C., 1961), p. 23 n. and Table 8 (p. 140).

[4] *S.A.J.*, Jan. 6 1912, cited in Hurley, *Banking and Credit*, p. 14.

[5] Tischendorf, *Great Britain and Mexico*, Table 8 (p. 140), gives the British investment (1900 and 1910) in British banking companies operating in Mexico as £350,000, and in Mexican banks, £590,000.

Peru presents similar problems. For the London Bank of Mexico and South America, which controlled about 30 per cent of Peruvian bank deposits in the early 1870s, was an entirely British institution,[1] whilst its successor, the Banco del Perú y Londres, which as government banker accounted for just over 50 per cent of Peruvian bank assets in 1913, had only a minority British shareholding. Again, in Argentina, where monthly figures for capital employed in banking were kept from 1909, the foreign share rose from 10 per cent to 19 per cent between 1909 and 1927.[2] This may be largely accounted for, however, by the number of domestic failures in the 1913–15 depression, and the entrance into the Buenos Aires market, for the first time, of North American banks.[3] So the share of bank deposits placed with the domestic banks, strengthened as a group by the loss of the more speculative of their number, actually rose slightly from 75 per cent to 80 per cent during the same period, whilst deposits with the diluted foreign sector fell by a corresponding amount.[4]

Yet if the study of longer-term trends in the relative size of the domestic and foreign-owned banking sectors is unrewarding and impracticable, the short-term fluctuations arising from the operation of the trade cycle are correspondingly rewarding. The pattern was simply this: that banks owned and directed by the British tended to weather crises far better than their competitors.

There are numerous instances of this phenomenon. In Brazil, in 1864 and again in 1875, there were a number of failures amongst the locally owned commercial banks which had emerged during the company boom of the late 1850s,[5] but the two British banks

[1] Carlos Camprubi Alcázar, *Historia de los bancos en Perú, 1860–79* (Lima, 1957), p. 217. Camprubi gives figures for the period Dec. 1872 to July 1875, during which the domestic banks suffered a severe fall in deposits owing to the Peruvian financial crisis of the mid seventies. At the start of this period the national banks controlled 81 per cent of deposits, but by the end they held only 55 per cent. I have taken an average of these two extremes as representing the 'true' position.

[2] Pedro J. Baiocco, ed., *Análisis estadístico y económico de algunas series bancarias y afines* (Buenos Aires, 1929), pp. 18–19.

[3] The Americans took advantage of the First World War to free their Latin American trade from dependence on British financial services. As Frank A. Vanderlip, President of the First National City Bank of New York, put it: 'If we find ourselves in a state of unpreparedness for war, we find ourselves at least in a state of preparedness for extending our banking facilities abroad' (*Chronicle*, 29 May 1915, 1794).   [4] Baiocco, *Análisis estadístico*, pp. 22–3.

[5] Alan K. Manchester, *British Preeminence in Brazil: Its Rise and Decline* (Chapel Hill, N.C., 1933), p. 318.

were under relatively little pressure, and were well placed to take their pick of the accounts of their less fortunate competitors in the aftermath of each crisis. During the 1875 crisis, Baron Mauá's bank failed, as did a recently established German bank. The board of the London and Brazilian Bank, in spite of the rather weak position which they had been in for some years past (indeed, ever since the failure of their attempt at amalgamation with Mauá) were at last able to look forward to better things. John Beaton, secretary of the London and Brazilian Bank, remarked upon the 'sudden and disgraceful collapse' of the German bank, and believed that 'the present crisis, bad as it is, and fraught with so much anxiety, must result in larger business for the two English banks; we hope to our bank particularly.'[1]

The same pattern may be observed in the Chilean banking crisis of 1897,[2] in the Argentine crises of 1876 and 1890/1, and in the Peruvian crisis of the early 1870s.[3] In each case, depositors withdrew their funds from the banks in general, but showed a markedly greater faith in the British banks than in their locally owned competitors. Throughout Latin America, at least until the 1890s, British banks were the place of deposit of last resort because it was believed that they would not fail, and that—even if they did—they would pay what they owed in good coin. An anecdote from the Argentine banking crisis of 1889 illustrates the high place given to the British. In spite of the fact that his own finance ministry was engaged in a private war with the English Bank of the River Plate, President Juárez Celman chose that bank, and not either of the official banks, in which to deposit his own large holdings of *cédulas* (land mortgage bonds).[4]

One consequence of short-term fluctuations of this kind was that in the aftermath of financial crises British banks frequently exerted a temporary and involuntary dominance in Latin American commercial centres. In Argentina the failure of the Banco de la Provincia de Buenos Aires and the Banco Nacional in 1891 left the London and River Plate Bank chief amongst the survivors, and strong enough to buy out its principal private rival, the Banco Carabassa, the same year, without reducing its customary dividend,

[1] B.O.L.S.A. G.1, J. Beaton to J. Gordon (Rio de Janeiro), 22 May 1875, p. 3.
[2] Ibid. C.1, 24 May 1897 and 21 June 1897.
[3] Camprubi, *Historia de los bancos*, p. 217, and see above, p. 26 n. 1.
[4] Mandatos R.P.T.L.A.: English Bank of the River Plate. Jones to Head Office, 5 June 1889, p. 2.

and in spite of the opposition of the Minister of Finance, Vicente Fidel López.[1]

It was particularly galling for the Argentines that this should have been the outcome of five years of government policy designed to strengthen the two official banks—especially the Banco Nacional —at the expense of the private banks. Conversely, it must have been a moment of some satisfaction for the British. They, whilst claiming that all their policies had been aimed at defence, and not at aggression against their competitors, had never made any secret of their attitude towards the style of business pursued by the official banks. As far as they were concerned, there were really two sorts of banks: banks like their own (the Banco Carabassa, for example, of which the balance sheet was—in view of the London and River Plate Bank—more or less like their own, though on a smaller scale[2]), and the political or speculative banks, of which no good could come, and to which no aid should be extended unless the stability of the entire market was threatened by their precarious condition. The London and River Plate Bank and other con- servative institutions were adamant. In the words of James Hackblock, a director of the London and River Plate Bank: 'Unless it became a question of necessity, for self-preservation, we con- sider it to be no part of our duty to prop up weak rival establish- ments in which we have no confidence, and the duration of which we consider to be only a question of time.'[3] So we find the London Bank refusing to hold the notes of the Banco Mauá in 1867,[4] the Banco Provincial de Santa Fé and the Argentine Banco Nacional between 1874 and 1876,[5] the Uruguayan National Bank from 1887 until its demise in 1890,[6] and the Banco de la República Oriental from its foundation in 1896 until at least ten years later.[7] And the attitude of the London Bank when such competitors failed was mirrored on the other side of the continent in the words with which the Santiago manager of the Bank of London and Tarapacá greeted the failure of the Banco de Santiago: 'We are inclined to

---

[1] B.O.L.S.A. D.75, 21 Jan. 1891 and 7 Mar. 1891.

[2] Ibid. D.75, 21 Jan. 1891.

[3] Ibid. D.94, Hackblock to Weldon, 8 Jan. 1868.

[4] Ibid. D.70, Holt to Jones, 8 Jan. 1867, and D.94, Holt to Weldon, 23 Mar. 1867.

[5] P.R.O. F.O. 6/345, St. John to Derby, 15 Aug. 1876, and B.O.L.S.A. D.35, Maschwitz to Head Office, p. 10.

[6] B.O.L.S.A. D.35, Anderson to Head Office, 14 Dec. 1887, p. 2.

[7] Ibid. D.35, Thurburn to Head Office, 24 Nov. 1905, p. 2.

look on the failure of the bank . . . as distinctly beneficial as it was
as an exclusively political bank doing . . . a large amount of bad
business for political purposes, and we have long felt that its
existence constituted a danger.'[1]

The British did not hide their dislike of such institutions and
openly worked to defend themselves in ways which could only
harm their competitors. Generally, they survived crises, whilst
the banks they most disliked failed. Yet they could not understand
why their action was unpopular. The British managers grumbled
at 'the jealousy shown towards the banks',[2] commented on the
'widespread desire to prejudice foreign interests',[3] and even recognized that these feelings arose from resentment against their own
dominance of bank deposits. What they could not grasp was that
their opponents could be motivated by anything more than self-
interest in their attempts to defend or strengthen the various
'political' banks.

The different rate of survival which we have described, when
coupled with the inability of so many orthodox commercial bankers
to sympathize with the liquidity problems of official or speculative
banks, was bound to result in unpleasantness between the orthodox
banks and the local political authorities. It is natural to attribute
the responsibility for disaster to those parties who benefit most by
it, and on these grounds the powerful British banks appeared in
the eyes of some Latin American governments to bear a large
part of the responsibility for the governments' own financial mis-
chances. However, as it stands, this argument is plainly as falla-
cious as it is attractive. The truth is more complicated, and if we
are to gain a closer insight into it than did the majority of contemporary British bankers, we shall have to go back a little and
try to understand the tenor of the domestic banking tradition in
Latin America as it existed prior to the influx of foreign capital,
and as it later developed in competition with the foreign banks.

IV

In many parts of Latin America experience of domestic ventures
in banking had jaundiced the views of both politicians and

---

[1] Ibid. C.1, Murray to Head Office, 21 June 1897, p. 3.
[2] Ibid. C.1, Murray to Head Office, 23 Dec. 1895, p. 3.
[3] Ibid. D.35, Maschwitz to Head Office, 14 May 1874, p. 8.

public by the middle of the nineteenth century. Too often in the past, so-called banks had been no more than a means by which governments were able to issue paper money, and had done nothing to further productive activity of any kind. In Rosas' Argentina the Casa de Moneda (1836), although it was founded as a bank and did a limited deposit and discount business for a year or so, neither received deposits nor made any discounts between March 1838 and its eventual demise in May 1851. But it did put into circulation $110 million to cover the budget deficits of an improvident government, making an increase of 733 per cent in the stock of paper money during a period of fifteen years.[1] These depreciated Argentine bank-notes circulated not only in Buenos Aires, but also in Montevideo, where there was no public bank at this time; and on both sides of the River Plate they brought about a great distrust of paper currency and of government participation in banking.[2] In Chile, also, there was a strong tradition of resistance to paper money, although there had been no experience of over-issue as there had been in the River Plate. In a memorandum submitted to the National Congress in 1824, the Chilean Minister of Finance made his government's attitude very plain when he described Chile as a country 'which has no paper currency and would admit it only at the point of a bayonet'.[3] And in Brazil, the first Bank of Brazil (1812–29) issued paper money, but apparently 'the fact that Dom João treated the bank as his private supplier of ready money did not tend to inspire confidence in the share-holders'.[4] As a result, an attempt to found a second bank in 1833 met with little public support.

But as well as serving the official role of government banker, many of the early banks provided whichever political leader controlled them with a means of paying his political debts and securing the continued adherence of his followers. Jobs in the official banks or loans from their coffers were and have continued to be a recognized part of the system of patronage throughout

---

[1] A. M. Quintero Ramas, *A History of Money and Banking in Argentina* (Puerto Rico, 1965), p. 35.

[2] Jose L. Buzzetti, *Historia económica y financiera del Uruguay* (Montevideo, 1969), p. 80.

[3] *Sesiones de los Cuerpos Legislativos*, ix. 68, quoted by G. Subercaseaux in *Monetary and Banking Policy of Chile* (Oxford, 1922), p. 62.

[4] Anyda Marchant, *Viscount Mauá and the Empire of Brazil* (Berkeley, 1965), p. 116.

Latin America into the present century. This meant that, in spite of the abject failure of so many banking ventures during the first half of the nineteenth century, both public and political obligations inclined all but the incorruptible Chileans to keep on founding new state banks, or to sacrifice the value of the currency in order to keep the existing ones going.

As for more genuine credit facilities, they were rare and limited in scope. In most commercial centres there were mercantile firms which carried on a trade in commercial paper as a part of their business.[1] There were also sporadic attempts to establish joint stock commercial banks independent of government. The Banco de Chile de Arcos y Cía (1849) was disbanded after only a few months, in 1850, when the government withdrew its right to issue notes.[2] The Banco y Casa de Moneda (1854-63) in Argentina, unlike its predecessor the Casa de Moneda, had all the characteristics of a commercial bank, albeit a government-controlled commercial bank.[3] And in Brazil, prior to 1850, authentic—though strictly illegal—banks were founded in Rio de Janeiro (the Banco

---

[1] According to Subercaseaux, *Banking Policy of Chile*, p. 57, in Chile 'it was a question of commercial establishments or individuals engaged in performing some of the functions of banks, such as that of issuing notes'. In Rosario de Santa Fé, Argentina, the choice of the premises of Don Esteban Rams y Rubert for the site of the Head Office of the Banco Nacional de la Confederación in 1854 may have been an indication that banking had previously formed a part of his business. Certainly, he did just about everything else. Naturally, such private firms are rather difficult to trace, but it is interesting that in some cases they formed the basis of branches of later joint-stock banks. When the London and River Plate Bank moved into Rosario in the 1860s, for example, they took over the banking business of Carlos Casado as the nucleus of their new branch, and the banking firm of Lumb, Wanklyn & Co. was later converted by its proprietors, with the assistance of European capital, into the Mercantile Bank of the River Plate. Camprubi (*Historia de los bancos en Perú*, p. 9) notes that before 1860 'las casas comerciales . . . venían efectuando ciertas operaciones del giro bancario confundidas con las mercantiles ordinarias', and (pp. 3-4) notes that a number of merchant firms in the guano trade issued notes payable at sight in the Peruvian pre-bank era: firms like Allsop, Gibbs, Templeman & Bergman, Pedro Denegri, etc. Camprubi also cites Ernesto Lobato López, *El Crédito en México* (Mexico City, 1945), who describes a similar situation in Mexico before 1864, and the same phenomenon in Colombia is mentioned by W. P. McGreevey, *An Economic History of Colombia, 1845-1930* (Cambridge, 1971), p. 163, who writes: 'Direct connection between exporting and importing was an obvious necessity given the primitive state of banking [before 1870]. Each commercial house had to handle for itself the acquisition and expenditure of foreign exchange.'

[2] Subercaseaux, *Banking Policy of Chile*, p. 61.

[3] Quintero Ramas, *Banking in Argentina*, pp. 39-40.

Comercial do Rio de Janeiro, 1838), in Bahía (1845), in Maranhão (1846), and in Pará (1847).[1] But in Uruguay, Peru, and most of the smaller republics, there was no effective joint stock commercial bank before 1850.

To sum up, until the middle of the century, merchants in the principal centres had to make do with the incomplete and insufficient services which they could provide amongst themselves. But it was the land-owners—the ruling group throughout Latin America at this time—who fared both best and worst. With no security except their land, they had no access to the credit offered by private bankers and were often thrown back on usurers who demanded upwards of 15 per cent per annum for mortgage loans.[2] So in Latin America, as in England a generation before, 'no one but a ruined man would attempt to raise money on the family estate',[3] unless, of course, he were a member of the ruling faction, in which case he might usually reckon to benefit financially either directly from government revenues, or indirectly through long-term advances from government-controlled banks.

Yet from these slender and unhealthy foundations there was to develop a tradition of experiment in policy and in institutional design that has received far less attention than it deserves from European banking historians. As early as 1877, Nicholas Bouwer, Baring Brothers' representative in Buenos Aires, was bound to admit, however grudgingly, that the Banco de la Provincia de Buenos Aires[4] had a quality which no British bank of the time possessed. Although he grumbled at the way in which so many Argentines regarded the bank as 'an institution specially created to supply them with funds without they being compelled to refund in due course', and fully recognized that 'if one were to dissect it according to the rules laid down in Europe the bank would be

---

[1] Marchant, *Viscount Mauá*, p. 117.

[2] The situation of landowners in Argentina before the creation of mortgage credit institutions is described in Santiago Alcorta, *Estudio sobre el Banco Hipotecario* (Buenos Aires, 1872). As late as 1895, William J. Buchanan, the United States Minister in Buenos Aires, claimed that borrowers on real estate in some provinces were paying rates of 15–18 per cent (U.S. Diplomatic Despatches, Argentina, Reel 26, Buchanan to State Department, No. 162, 21 Oct. 1895, Enclosure No. 1). By this time, the current mortgage rate in Buenos Aires was about 10 per cent.

[3] Anthony Trollope, *Can You Forgive Her?* (first published 1864–5, Oxford edition 1973), p. 36.

[4] Formed by a change of name in 1863 from the Banco y Casa de Moneda.

pronounced to be seriously compromised', he nevertheless affirmed that

> At the same time, the bank is perfectly sound both according to its friends and its detractors. It has always served the public without charging it commission; has always laid itself out, although injudiciously at times, to assist and foster enterprises of whatever nature; and the result is that the public at large looks on it as the mainstay of the nation ... Even merchants, though they confess that the establishment is not what it ought to be, are convinced that it can never break.[1]

The concept which found admittedly imperfect expression in the Banco de la Provincia was that of a bank lending cheaply and for long terms with a more or less conscious aim of furthering national development and the public good. This is certainly alien to the tradition of the first half of the nineteenth century, and requires some explanation.

Chronology and the absence of any other explanation would suggest that this new shift in banking policy was influenced by Henri de Saint-Simon whose ideas were transmitted via the brothers Péreire, although textual references supporting this view are admittedly rare. Saint-Simon had emphasized the role of the bank as the mobilizer of small savings in the service of industry, and also provided a theoretical justification for the participation of the state as systematizer and co-ordinator of the process of development. The Péreires, greatly influenced by Saint-Simon, established their *Crédit Mobilier* in 1852, and though not the first attempt to create a bank which would aid industry directly with long-term credits, it was certainly the most spectacular and influential of the century.[2] The *crédit mobilier* movement spread throughout continental Europe during the 1850s, and after a severe set-back in the crisis of 1857, continued into the sixties. It even touched Latin America briefly in 1856, at the height of the craze, when a Compañía Franco-Sud Americano de los bancos y créditos mobiliarios de la America del Sud was set up to create and operate a Uruguayan national bank with a capital of fifteen million *pesos*

---

[1] Baring H.C. 4. 1. 65, Part 1, 13 Jan. 1877, p. 4.

[2] The most convenient and readily available account of the influence of Saint-Simon on European banking and the *crédit mobilier* is to be found in Bertrand Gille, 'Banking and Industrialisation in Europe, 1730–1914', pp. 265–74, in Carlo M. Cipolla, ed., *The Fontana Economic History of Europe*, iii. 255–97. Barry Supple's chapter in the same volume on the state and the industrial revolution is also relevant.

fuertes. The scheme never came to anything, but its prospectus, modelled closely on those of the European *crédits mobiliers*, was circulated, and received attention in the national press.[1]

Less ephemeral, and closer at hand, was Baron Mauá: banker, financier, and industrialist. Mauá's biographer accepted that Mauá was a Saint-Simonian,[2] and this judgement is confirmed by his actions and thoughts. To Mauá, credit was the 'most powerful instrument of modern civilisation, in the creation of wealth everywhere in the length and breadth of our native land, in penetrating into the economic life of localities where the presence of sufficient means, already existing or to be created, would permit it to be employed with advantage'. Credit would 'bring to life the inert capital . . . abounding in all the corners of Brazil, converting it thus into an instrument of production, into resources otherwise dispersed and not used in the creation of individual and consequently national wealth'.[3]

Brazil was also the scene of a belated experiment with the pure *crédit mobilier* form. Come the end of the Empire, the first republican administration introduced legislation relaxing the regulations which controlled the chartering of corporations, and amongst the welter of new companies which followed were two government agencies—a new bank of issue, and a *crédit mobilier* set up 'on a scientific basis'.[4] The same government was responsible for the establishment of six regional banks, of which one, the Banco União do Estado de São Paulo, played a most active role in the financing of the textile and other industries over the next twenty years.[5]

At the very least, Saint-Simon and the Péreires were known about and discussed in the major cities of Latin America during the second half of the nineteenth century. They were abhorred and feared by some. Angel J. Costa, for example, an Argentine who adhered to the most conservative British principles of the time, attacked the creation of the Banco Nacional in 1872 and the

[1] The only copy of this prospectus of which I know is preserved in the Biblioteca Nacional, Buenos Aires (Ref. No. 113.760). It carries, rather inappropriately, an inferior engraving of Britannia, complete with Union Jack, on the front cover.

[2] Alberto de Faria, *Mauá* (São Paulo, 1933).

[3] Marchant, *Viscount Mauá*, p. 28.

[4] Stanley J. Stein, *The Brazilian Cotton Manufacture: Textile Enterprise in an Underdeveloped Area, 1850–1950* (Cambridge, Mass., 1957), p. 86.

[5] George Wythe, *Industry in Latin America* (New York, 1945), p. 165.

failure of both the National and the Buenos Aires Bank to adhere
to the Currency Principle, and denigrated the Péreire brothers
and the influence which they had exerted upon the lending policies
of the two official banks as an 'escuela retrograda'.[1]

Equally clear as the century progressed was the fact that the
industries of continental Europe, where the *crédits mobiliers* were
established, were advancing at a faster rate than those of Great
Britain, where they had not been. It was easy, therefore, for those
with no practical experience of banking to accept that the creation
of banks was both a necessary and a sufficient condition of the
development of a mature and prosperous economy; easy, too, for
those who were convinced of the automatic efficacy of banking
to believe that by making rather risky loans to a clique of progressive pastoralists, ambitious speculators, and company promoters which had the favour of government, the official banks
were following the trail blazed by the Péreires. Nor was there any
insincerity here, only a degree of self-deception which enabled
Rufino Varela, Vicente López, and their colleagues to ignore the
facts that both the Banco Nacional and the Banco de la Provincia
de Buenos Aires were constitutionally equipped, as deposit and
discount banks, to provide short-term and not long-term credit,
and that the Buenos Aires market was far narrower, riskier, and
more volatile than the markets of Europe.

Policies and attitudes very similar to those of López and the
Argentine economic nationalists flourished—with varying degrees
of success—elsewhere in Latin America. For the recently established and vulnerable Brazilian Republicans, the use of banks and
bank credit to establish a base of support in the growing industrial
sector was at least as important politically as were the Argentine
official banks. Thus, the action of the Banco da República under the
laws of September and December 1892 in supporting the textile
mills through the crisis of 1892–4 with *cédula* loans was not merely
a financial innovation, but a bid for political support.[2] In Chile,
also, faith in inconvertible paper, state banking directed towards
industrial and agricultural development, and economic nationalism
formed a matrix of beliefs and policies which received considerable
support. But here, even more than in Argentina, the economic

---

[1] Angel J. Costa, *El Banco de la Provincia decapitado por el Banco Nacional*
(Buenos Aires, 1873).
[2] Stein, *Brazilian Cotton Manufacture*, pp. 95–6.

nationalists or '*papeleros*' were ultimately unsuccessful. In 1887, Manuel A. Zañartu suggested the creation of a combined central bank and national development bank which would take the right of issue out of the hands of the private banks and direct credit to the nation's producers, but he failed to achieve acceptance for his project. As Finance Minister to President Balmaceda he tried again, but was thwarted by defeat in the Civil War.[1]

V

During the early 1860s, the first British banks to operate in South America stepped unwittingly into a world where the examples of the *crédit mobilier* and of Baron Mauá had already aroused expectations which it was not their intention to fulfil. The initial reaction amongst politicians and journalists seems to have been uniformly favourable. In Chile, for example, it was anticipated that foreign banks would serve as 'veritable channels for the conveyance of foreign capital into the country'.[2] And there is considerable evidence that landowners and politicians anticipated that some of this capital should be conveyed directly into their own hands. For, during their early years, the British banks met with a strong and overwhelming demand for advances from this class of client, as also from local governments and other banks, all of which were thirsty for credit.

At the start, Henry Bruce, the first chairman of the London and River Plate Bank, pursued a staffing policy which gave such would-be debtors a great opportunity. In Buenos Aires he appointed as manager John H. Green, formerly of the Buenos Aires and Rio de Janeiro merchant firm of Darbyshire & Green. To supervise Green, there were two local directors—John Fair, an Anglo-Argentine who had acted as Argentine Consul in London during the 1850s before returning to Buenos Aires to assist in the founding of the Argentine Great Southern Railway and the London Bank itself, and Norberto de la Riestra, an Argentine landowner and merchant who as National Minister of Finance had been instrumental in restoring Argentina's credit in Europe

---

[1] Peter J. Conoboy, 'The papeleros, or greenbackers, in Chile: 1891–1925' (unpublished Society for Latin American Studies Conference Paper, read at Leeds, Mar. 1973).

[2] Subercaseaux, *Banking Policy of Chile*, p. 131.

a few years before.[1] A similar course was adopted in Montevideo. After a brief, unsuccessful period during which the bank operated through a sole manager, a triumvirate was established on the Buenos Aires pattern. Thomas Hyne Jones was made manager, and once again two local directors were appointed to advise and watch over him. Vicente López we have already encountered in another role. The other was James Lowry, a local banker who, it was understood, would bring with him 'as many of his present customers as possible, and . . . as many of their current and deposit accounts as he can influence'.[2]

It was not long before the effects of this policy began to be felt. The Buenos Aires committee, used to the ways of the local market, blithely extended credit to clients who would never have passed muster with the ultra-orthodox board in London. By April 1863, Bruce was already aware that a large proportion of the bills which Green was discounting were accommodation bills—not backed by any genuine trading transaction, but simply fictitious as a means of raising capital. He urged Green 'to adopt a much more stringent system', explaining to him 'that the great monied interest of London watch such operations with the greatest jealousy, and when times of pressure arrive . . . the acceptances of parties in the habit of making "accommodation paper" are rejected by the Bank of England and can only be discounted at extreme rates by money dealers'.[3] Yet in spite of a succession of appeals, commands, and threats from the London board, the managers in Buenos Aires, Rosario, and Montevideo continued to bend the rules, tempted, no doubt, by the high profits offered by risky business.

[1] B.O.L.S.A. D.91, 29 Sept. 1862 and 6 Nov. 1862. See also Joslin, *A Century of Banking*, pp. 31–2.

[2] B.O.L.S.A. D.91, 8 Aug. 1864. The lengths to which Bruce was prepared to go in order to secure Lowry's services may be taken as evidence of the importance which he attached to local experience. Lowry at first proposed that in addition to his salary he should receive 10 per cent of the branch profits and 7 per cent on its capital plus a *carte blanche* to invest his own capital in whatever way he might choose without interference from the board. Bruce was quick to point out that a profit-sharing arrangement could easily damage the harmony which should exist between the branches, and that in no circumstances could an official of the bank be permitted to become a partner in any business venture on his own account. Lowry finally settled for a salary of £2,000 per annum (twice that of de la Riestra), free accommodation, 5 per cent of the profits of the two River Plate branches (when these exceeded 7 per cent per annum), and freedom to invest his money in the purchase of land and in other ways which would not interfere with his duties as a local director of the bank, excluding land speculation and sheep-farming.

[3] Ibid. D.91, Bruce to Green, 8 Apr. 1863.

Three kinds of client particularly offended Head Office. First there were the more speculative businessmen and financiers—people like Anacarsis Lanús and Ambrosio P. Lezica, who between them controlled a number of enterprises in Argentina and Uruguay during the 1860s and 1870s, including the Banco Argentino, with branches in Buenos Aires and Rosario. By 1870, Lanús and Lezica had succeeded in securing considerable advances from the Buenos Aires branch of the London Bank despite the serious doubts of Head Office as to the wisdom of aiding their competitors.[1] Also, as we have already remarked, the London Bank kept well clear of those banks which they considered to be political or speculative.

Next in line for attack from Head Office was the practice of lending on mortgage to clients who, unlike Lanús and his kind, had not the opportunity to kite bills on the pretence of genuine merchant business, and had only their property to offer as security. James Hackblock, of the London board, made the attitude of Head Office crystal clear. He wrote to Francis Weldon, the Rosario manager:

> If you unfortunately should see reason to doubt the safety of any account, then it becomes your duty to seek some security, and to obtain the best in your power—whether mortgage or any other collateral security. But under no other circumstances do we consider mortgages justifiable as a security in a well-conducted bank.
>
> You will invariably bear in mind that *safety* is the *first* consideration.[2]

And Hackblock was all the more convinced of the wisdom of his policy when it became known, in 1868, that the London and Brazilian Bank—which a short time before had been threatening to join forces with Baron Mauá and move south into the River Plate Bank's territory—had fallen into the mortgage trap, locking up large amounts of capital to the detriment of its business and profits.[3]

---

[1] B.O.L.S.A. D.70, extract from Head Office to Buenos Aires, confidential, 8 Oct. 1870, also D.35, Green to Head Office, 15 Nov. 1870.

[2] Ibid. D.94, Hackblock to Weldon, 6 Sept. 1867 (the emphasis is Hackblock's).

[3] Hackblock made quite sure that his managers in the River Plate should be made aware of the misfortunes of the London and Brazilian Bank and their cause. In ibid. D.94, 8 Jan. 1868 to Weldon, and D.70, 8 Jan. 1868 to Jones, he referred to the plight of his bank's competitor, citing it as an example of 'the evil effects of locking up capital in mortgages and overdrawn accounts and advances'. Unfortunately, the principal London–Rio series of the London and Brazilian Bank has survived only from 1868, so there is no direct evidence

If financiers and landowners were unwelcome to the London and River Plate Bank as clients, so too were governments and those in government, at least during these early years. In Rosario, the Bank was particularly hard hit by the failure of Mariano Cabal, an ex-Governor of the Province of Santa Fé and chairman of the Banco de Comercio. Weldon, in Rosario, had advanced considerable sums to Cabal, and both he and his superiors in London were bound to admit that conciliation would achieve more 'than can be achieved by pressing legally our rights, more especially out of consideration of the position occupied by Cabal in the Province'.[1] Clearly, the advice offered by Bruce five years before that 'it is generally considered very dangerous policy to lend money to parties who are beyond the reach of the law' had been neglected, if not forgotten.[2] There was a difference, of course, between dealing with individual members of any past or present government, and dealing 'out in the open', as it were, with a government in its official and collective capacity. From an early date, the London Bank engaged in operations on account of the Uruguayan Government. Even here they were cautious, however, and G. A. H. Holt, writing on behalf of the board to Jones in Montevideo, warned that 'the fewer transactions you have with the Government the better we shall be pleased, the intention of this bank having always been to confine its transactions to purely commercial affairs'.[3] Moreover, there were governments and governments, and the board determined to keep well clear of the Argentine national administration so long as they continued to consort with such financial reprobates as Lezica, Lanús, Edward Lumb, and Frederic Wanklyn.[4]

During the first decade of their operations, then, both the London and River Plate Bank and the London and Brazilian Bank

to corroborate Hackblock's account of just how the London and Brazilian got into difficulties.

[1] Ibid. D.94, Hackblock to Weldon, 23 Nov. 1868. See also D.94, 8 Aug. 1868, 7 Nov. 1868, 8 Dec. 1868, 23 Dec. 1868, and 8 Jan. 1869. The Cabal disaster sparked off an internal inquiry from which Weldon was fortunate to survive. In spite of Head Office orders he had made considerable advances on mortgage, and was eventually obliged to admit to having accepted a *steamship* as sole security for a loan to one Leopoldo Arteaga.

[2] Ibid. D.91, Bruce to Green, 23 Apr. 1863.

[3] Ibid. D.70, Holt to Jones, 21 Oct. 1865.

[4] Ibid. D.70, copy of Drabble to Smithers (Buenos Aires manager), 19 July 1870, p. 2. See also D.1, Smithers to Green, No. 126, 8 Jan. 1866, and No. 144, 8 Jan. 1866, p. 7.

found themselves with large lock-ups. This was a consequence of their early preference for merchants as branch managers, combined with a very considerable pressure from local governments, landowners, and businessmen of the more speculative sort. The London and Brazilian Bank suffered badly as a result. Between 1865 and 1874 the shareholders received no dividend, and it was found necessary, from 1868, to set about reconstructing the company.[1] The London and River Plate Bank was more fortunate. In George Wilkinson Drabble, who joined the board in 1867 and was elected chairman in 1869, the bank found a leader who had both banking and River Plate experience. Moreover, soon after becoming chairman, Drabble reorganized the management of the branches. He appointed two Germans with financial experience—George Maschwitz and Ludwig Behn—to officiate in Buenos Aires and Rosario, and moved Weldon to Montevideo. Maschwitz and Behn excelled in their caution, and were able to restore the liquidity of their respective branches in preparation for the difficult times of the mid-seventies. But in the process they inevitably made many enemies both for themselves and for the bank.

To set up banks in Latin America in the middle of the nineteenth century, then to refuse to do more than a bare minimum of business with the most important and influential groups there —the politicians, the landowners, and the domestic entrepreneurs —may seem rather an odd thing to have done. Yet to the directors of the Anglo-South American banks it was the most natural thing in the world. They were *commercial* bankers, and they conceived their business to be the provision of short-term credit to facilitate the conduct and extension of Latin American external trade. There was no secret about this, and yet it was at first not understood, and later resented, by groups of some importance in the host countries.

VI

It is clear that during the second half of the nineteenth century there was a profound difference both in ideology and in policy between certain of the British overseas banks and economic nationalist factions, and that disagreement between the two centred mainly on the question of the correct lending policy to be pursued in Latin American conditions. In distinguishing between

[1] Joslin, *A Century of Banking*, pp. 75–9.

what may be called 'orthodox commercial banks' and 'development-orientated banks', it will be as well to bear in mind earlier qualifications and caveats. Thus, whilst the British were foremost amongst the orthodox, they found hardly less purist allies amongst their local competitors—the Banco Carabassa in Argentina and the Banco Edwards in Chile, for example. Equally, although state or semi-state banks customarily carried the developmentalist standard, then as now there were some private companies, and even one British bank, which belonged more with this latter group than with the orthodox banks.

The Mercantile Bank of the River Plate not only serves as a warning against generalizations based on nationality, but also helps to show that whatever part the infamous corruptibility of Latin American officials may have played in the failure of the official banks, the root causes of failure of nineteenth-century development-orientated banks in Latin America were the structural inadequacy of local markets and the limitations of available institutional forms. For, although clearly equipped to carry on the same kind of commercial business as the London and River Plate Bank, the Mercantile Bank was used instead in an attempt to play a profitable *and* modernizing role in the growth of industry in Argentina and Uruguay. Bearing in mind the character of the major participants,[1] it seems more than probable that this was a deliberate policy. But it was also misconceived, since it meant that the bank's management had to act as though their resources were long- and not short-term. After only three years of operation, the bank had more than £500,000 of its £1·5 million assets locked up in the Montevideo Waterworks, the Pando Railway, the Central Tramway (Montevideo), and a handful of lesser projects—all undertakings owned by Argentine, Uruguayan, or immigrant capitalists.[2] Even in the opinion of the hostile Montevideo manager of the London and River Plate Bank, these investments were fundamentally sound.[3] The Waterworks, it was thought, could pay a dividend of about 5 per cent; the Pando Railway, when completed, would also be profitable; and the Central was a paying line, hindered only by persistent lawsuits challenging its concession.

---

[1] C. A. Jones, 'British Financial Institutions in Argentina, 1860–1914' (unpublished Ph.D. thesis, University of Cambridge, 1973), pp. 40–3.
[2] *Bankers' Magazine*, May 1877, 490–1.
[3] B.O.L.S.A. D.68, 27 Mar. 1876.

The point here is that the term structure of the bank was quite impractical. With the usual short- and medium-term deposits of a commercial bank of the period, it was very foolhardy to advance venture capital to assist in projects which could not be expected to mature within less than three years; the more so when it is realized that in the small stock markets of Montevideo and Buenos Aires such shares and bonds as were given as security would immediately become unsaleable at the least hint of trouble. Deposits of a term to match such enterprises were not available to the banks of the late nineteenth century, and methods of resolving the resultant liquidity problem were still in the experimental stage, even in Europe.

Virgil M. Bett has described a similar situation in Mexico during our period. He draws attention to a market in which 'there was a very limited demand for strictly commercial credit, and yet most of the banks were organized to grant only commercial credit',[1] and one cannot but be reminded of Green's assertion to the board of the London Bank in 1870 that 'the amount of real trade bills, in the full acceptation of the term, offering for discount [is] by no means adequate to the capital seeking employment'.[2] In such a situation it was perhaps inevitable that

a great subterfuge developed to cover long-term loans so that they should appear to be of short-term . . . In this fashion many long-term loans were granted to ranch-owners and small industrialists, with the result that the portfolios of the banks were in fact highly illiquid, though they were composed of six-months paper. This situation constituted a serious threat to the banks, to the borrowers, and to the general public who held bank notes. The borrowers were in constant danger of having great pressure put on them by the banks when their six-month notes were due, even though their borrowed funds were sunk in long-term investments. The banks were in constant danger owing to the illiquidity of their portfolios.[3]

Stated baldly, the dilemma was this: in markets as small and immature as those of nineteenth-century Latin America the supply of venture capital was bound to be a risky business. Only a reliable and constant fund of deposits could lower the risk, but depositors,

---

[1] Virgil M. Bett, *Central Banking in Mexico: Monetary Policies and Financial Crises, 1864–1940* (Michigan Business Studies, XIII, No. 1, Michigan, 1957), pp. 11–12.

[2] B.O.L.S.A. D.95, Green to Smithers, 15 Nov. 1870.

[3] Bett, *Central Banking in Mexico*, pp. 11–12.

well aware of the style of business pursued by each bank in the market, reacted to the first flecks of financial drizzle by moving their deposits out of development-orientated or political banks, and into the coffers of the British banks. At the same time, holders of the notes of the already weakened development-orientated banks, fearing that they might soon become depreciated, hurried to convert them into more solid assets, with the result that they came pouring back to their point of origin, often via the British banks, creating bad feeling, the suspicion of conspiracy, and further liquidity problems for their issuers.

The problem was therefore how to break this deadlock between banks which meant well but could not perform adequately, and banks which were immensely capable and professional but relatively unconcerned with wider issues of development. No final answer was ever found, but four main paths towards a solution were discovered and explored during the years after 1895.

The first of these paths was legislation, which, during our period, had three broad objectives. The first was to give a clear legal definition of what should constitute a bank. The second was to protect the shareholders and depositors of banks by insisting on minimum capital requirements, the deposit of guarantees, the disclosure of accounts and publication of balance sheets, the restriction of loans by banks to governments or to their own directors, and the maintenance of safe ratios of cash and capital to deposits and notes. The third was to offset the disadvantages experienced by public service or development-orientated banks in relation to their profit-motivated competitors. Here a distinction was made, either between public and private or, more usually, between domestic and foreign banks. A differential was then secured by taxes on deposits, profits, or capital; by demanding greater guarantees from one class than from the other; by varying the privileges (e.g. of note issue) open to each class; or by insisting that foreign banks should operate through locally registered subsidiaries, making uniform regulations possible.[1] No single country used all these measures, and the degree of bias against foreign banks, as also the date at which legislation gathered pace, varied from one part of the continent to another, influenced by the extent

---

[1] The *S.A.J.* and both British and American Consular Reports for the period contain copious details of the many individual laws from which this list has been abstracted.

and nature of foreign penetration and by the degree to which it differed from domestic practice.

Probably it was because foreign banks were established in the River Plate region from an early date, and because their success was so markedly greater than that of the official banks, that the River Plate countries passed the most aggressive anti-foreign legislation before 1914. The Uruguayan Banco de la República (1896), although founded before the accession to power of President Batlle, became incorporated into his broad programme of state intervention and monopoly, a policy which was in large measure a reaction against the extensive penetration of the economy by foreigners.[1] In Argentina, also, experience of the incompatibility of official and private banks during the 1870s and 1880s gave rise to aggressive banking legislation between 1887 and 1891. The Guaranteed Bank Law of 1887 and subsequent fiscal measures were intended by the architects of the policy—Wenceslao Pacheco, Rufino Varela, and Vicente López—to strengthen the Banco Nacional at the expense of the private banks and to bring the latter under the effective control of the state. But in 1891, overwhelmed by the Baring crisis, the official banks failed, robbing the policy of even the logical possibility of success. None the less, discriminatory taxation directed against private institutions remained, and the new Banco de la Nación (1891), although in some ways a far more orthodox institution than its predecessor, the Banco Nacional, was conceived of—even by its relatively conservative founders, José Terry and Carlos Pellegrini—as continuing the public service traditions of earlier official banks.

This brings us to the second of the four paths towards a solution of the deadlock between public and private banks, and the one which was ultimately most fruitful. Financial crises brought the failure of official banks and necessitated the creation of new ones, providing opportunities for improvement and fresh thought. In the train of the Baring crisis, the insecure Argentine Banco Nacional was replaced by the secure (and extant) Banco de la Nación, and the privately owned Uruguayan National Bank gave way to the state-controlled Banco de la República. Later, the shock of the 1913-15 crisis and of the First World War itself brought about new developments in the 1920s. In Chile, the Caja

[1] S. G. Hanson, *Utopia in Uruguay: Chapters in the Economic History of Uruguay* (New York, 1938), pp. 70–8.

de Crédito Minero, the Caja de Colonización Agrícola, and the Caja de Crédito Hipotecario were established; in Mexico a central bank—the Banco de México (1925)—was formed. Again, during the 1930s, in the aftermath of the crash of 1929, there was a further wave of institutional innovation, born of necessity, during which the Argentine Banco Central (1934), the Mexican Nacional Financiera (1934), and the Banco Industrial del Perú (1937) were founded.

The later foundations were purpose-built, but the Banco de la República Oriental de Uruguay and the Banco de la Nación Argentina worked on a different principle, employing many of those safeguards which were the best features of the British banks in order to acquire such overwhelming size in proportion to the markets in which they operated. This was done on the assumption that size would bring confidence, confidence deposits, and deposits the possibility of pursuing an independent and constructive lending policy.

The Banco de la República, for example, was established to cope with a situation in which banking facilities outside the cities of Montevideo, Salta, and Paysandú were non-existent, in which the idea of state banking had been discredited by the experience of the 1890 crisis, and in which the bulk of banking business rested in the hands of the British. The new bank sought to gain the confidence and deposits of the public at large by laying stress on small savings and a broad branch network, neither of which was likely to prove conducive to any rapid growth in profits. By 1909, branches in the interior numbered 24; by 1931, 50. And despite the fact that between 1921 and 1932 three branches lost money every single year, and another six in at least five years, the Uruguayans were able to show that it was indeed possible for a Latin American state bank to overcome the heritage of public mistrust and the tradition of bureaucratic defalcation, and to regain the kind of widespread affection and esteem which had been granted to the Banco de la Provincia de Buenos Aires in its early days. For the bank was soon able to dominate the market; to enforce agreements on interest rates paid on deposits; and to support a welfare system for the benefit of its employees and their dependents. In 1919, with already 52 per cent of the country's banking capital, the Banco de la República controlled 41 per cent of all bank deposits and 53 per cent of loans. By 1934—in spite of the world economic crisis and Uruguay's own internal political problems—the bank controlled 46 per cent of deposits and 60 per cent of loans, with only 48 per cent of total bank capital.[1]

The Argentine Banco de la Nación was similarly concerned to establish a nation-wide branch system and facilities for small savers, and, like its Uruguayan contemporary, was able within a very few years to achieve a remarkable growth, and to dominate the market. On this basis, the bank was able to pursue in safety a lending policy which went a good way towards satisfying Argentina's needs.[2] It did not achieve all that it might have done. The establishment of a banker's clearing-house was left to the London and River Plate Bank, and no move was made to establish rediscount facilities until the war forced a makeshift attempt. None the less, the Banco de la Nación, like its Uruguayan contemporary, survived, prospered, and achieved some of its aims. Most of all, both banks were big enough not to have to worry overmuch about the opinions held by the British banks with regard to their lending policies.

But if some of the requirements of the Latin American market were met by the adaptation of the European commercial bank, it should not be forgotten that others were satisfied by the importation of the *crédit foncier*, or mortgage bank. The Caja de Crédito Hipotecario of Chile (1855), the Peruvian Banco de Crédito Hipotecario (1866), the Crédito Hipotecario de Bolivia (1870), the Banco Hipotecario de la Provincia de Buenos Aires (1872), the Caja de Crédito Territorial del Uruguay (1872), and the Mexican Banco Internacional e Hipotecario (1882), by no means exhaust a long list of nineteenth-century foundations all of which offered long-term credit to local landowners and emitted mortgage-bonds or *cédulas* for sale in local and European markets.

Small savings and mortgage operations were also taken up by some private domestic institutions such as the Argentine Banco Popular (1887). This experimental co-operative bank featured shares of small denominations which could be purchased by a series of small monthly payments, and insisted on a ceiling of 100 shares (worth about £292) per shareholder, with one vote only for each member regardless of the size of his or her holding.

---

[1] Hanson, *Utopia in Uruguay*, p. 75.

[2] For the Statement of Intent of national Minister of Finance José Terry as to the policies to be pursued by the bank (and for the scepticism with which this was greeted by British journalists), see the *S.A.J.*, 7 Apr. 1894, p. 375.

During the latter part of our period, then, Latin American banks made both concessions and innovations in order to regain public confidence. Increasingly their constitutions and policies reflected the need for lending to government and government participation in management (as opposed to ownership) to be limited, and for the more doctrinaire fantasies derived from Saint-Simon to be dropped or at the very least substantially modified to take account of local needs and circumstances. Equally, in response partly to legislative assaults upon them, but far more to changes in the conditions of the Latin American markets, the British overseas banks modified their initially severe lending criteria to take into account the susceptibilities of their host governments and the opportunities for profit which Latin America offered them. Mainly, it was increased size, and especially the growth in their deposits, which enabled the British banks after 1895 to move into mortgage business, industrial enterprises, and new crops (Tucumán sugar, for example), which they would previously have shied away from. Size *enabled* them to do this, but what caused them to make use of their new potential to the limited extent which they did was the increasing growth of French, German, and domestic competitors, the need to conciliate hostile factions in government or in the legislatures, the degree of maturity which had already been attained without their help by their new clients, and, most of all, the persistently low rates on money which prevailed during the years between the Baring crisis and the outbreak of war. This modification of the early rigidities of the British overseas banks, grudging though it was, formed the third path towards conciliation between the British and domestic traditions in Latin American banking.

The last of the four paths lay strictly outside banking, and its relevance was confined to the River Plate area. British mortgage companies established on the model which had been pioneered in Australasia and North America moved into Argentina and Uruguay from 1881. The River Plate Mortgage Company, the Mortgage Company of the River Plate, and the Trust and Agency Company of Australasia all operated on the same basic principle. They loaned money at what were, by the standards of the time, moderate rates, raising capital cheaply in London by the issue of debentures secured on their uncalled capital. In this way they overcame the problem of term structure which so troubled the

commercial banks. Hard on the heels of the mortgage companies
came the insurance companies, notably the Law, Union and Rock
and the Standard Life Insurance Company, so that by 1901 it
appeared to F. H. Chevallier Boutell of the River Plate Trust,
Loan and Agency Company that 'there is not an English firm of
any importance that is not engaged directly or indirectly in mortgage business'.[1]

A criticism often levelled at the early Latin American official
mortgage banks—companies like the Banco Hipotecario de la
Provincia de Buenos Aires—was that they did little to help agriculture, concentrating their resources too much on pastoral activity.
But the European mortgage lenders were even more selective.
They restricted their lending to the very best pastoral areas of the
provinces of Buenos Aires, Santa Fé and Entre Rios, and of
Uruguay.[2] Furthermore, the terms on which they loaned money
were such as to exclude most agriculturists. Unlike the official
mortgage banks which permitted repayment over twenty years or
more, the foreign firms customarily advanced funds for a period of
four years, sometimes on the understanding that a part of the loan
might afterwards be renewed. As H. A. C. Cox, the first manager
of the River Plate Trust, Loan and Agency Company, put it:
'A poor man who has nothing but his camp [estate] cannot afford
to come to us, for he knows that he will not be able to pay us back
the capital in the four or five years stipulated . . . This class of
borrowers, who only require small sums, as their property is small,
naturally prefer the Mortgage Bank.'[3]

So although they partly met the criticism made of the British
banks by the more conservative elements in the local population,
and helped to satisfy that need for credit which had previously
been experienced as an illegitimate demand for their funds by the
commercial banks, the mortgage companies made little positive
contribution to diversification—even to so basic a diversification
as that from pastoralism to agriculture. However, they were well
in tune with the governments of the time, which were drawn largely
from that class which benefited most from the sort of credit which
they had to offer. And it must surely tell something about the real
nature of the credit facilities desired by the Argentine ruling classes

[1] Mandatos R.P.T.L.A., C.B.P., 18 Oct. 1901.
[2] Ibid., Anderson to Bramwell, 21 Dec. 1904.
[3] Ibid., Cox to Head Office, 5 July 1884, pp. 2–3.

that the River Plate Trust, Loan and Agency Company not only made profits almost as great as the London and River Plate Bank, but was never pestered by hostile legislation as was the London Bank.

VII

Almost without exception, the British banks in Latin America conformed to a pattern. As commercial banks ultimately responsible to their shareholders, they placed a high value on survival and growth, the safety of their capital always taking precedence over increase in profits. They had no mission to develop the economies of the countries where they operated along this or that path. In a quite objective fashion they loaned money to those clients who could provide satisfactory security and refused it to those who could not. This policy, which was simply that of any commercial bank, had two important consequences. It created considerable public trust in the foreign banks and led to a rapid growth in bank deposits. But it also meant that these deposits were directed disproportionately into the finance of external trade, benefiting a commercial sector itself dominated by foreigners. Landowners, artisans, and manufacturers found that Britons looked askance at mortgages, which were not considered to be adequate security for advances.

Many Latin American bankers behaved similarly to the British. Carabassa in Buenos Aires and the Edwards family in Chile ran their businesses in accordance with the British tradition. This, indeed, was what made them such attractive subjects for take-over by the British, whose strong international connections and broad geographical spread put them at a considerable advantage. Takeovers by the British of the business of failed or failing domestic commercial banks commonly took place in the wake of financial crises. They aroused concern, but in terms of lending policy they mattered very little.

Some Latin American banks, however, pursued a different style of business. These included the Banco Mauá, the (British) Mercantile Bank of the River Plate, the Banco de Santiago, and the great majority of the official banks—either wholly or partly state-owned. Their style was closer to that of the European *crédits mobiliers* of the 1850s and 1860s than that of the commercial banks. They tended to lend to clients who had no security sufficient to satisfy the criteria of a commercial bank: to landowners, governments, and even industrialists. Their advances, though nominally short-term, were often renewable and sometimes perpetual. It was a crude and clumsy instance of the public sector being operated at a loss so as to awaken and encourage private enterprise. Commonly, it led to illiquidity and eventual failure.

British bank managers were infuriated by such institutions, considering them anachronistic survivals from the mercantilist past rather than heralds of modernization. The British rarely, if ever, took deliberate steps to eliminate official banks, for that would have been political suicide. Instead, they allowed structural contradictions to do the job for them. Funds borrowed by Latin American governments were invested in infrastructure projects of long maturation. During the construction phase imports outpaced exports whilst the official banks advanced money wildly and issued fresh supplies of paper currency, discounting the economic miracle which surely lay just around the corner. When the flow of funds from Europe was interrupted, the balance of payments deficit assumed giant proportions, currency-notes flowed into the banks for conversion, but bank advances—tied up in long-term projects—could not be recovered in time to prevent failure. The British banks played their part in the process in several ways. During the boom years the generous lending policies of the official banks kept unwelcome clients away from their doors. Always the first to smell trouble ahead, the British often appeared to precipitate crises by calling in their own advances and instituting the daily conversion of the notes of banks whose business they considered unsafe. When the crisis did come, they were generally seen to benefit. Their deposits held up better than those of the official banks and, in the aftermath of bank failures, they were able to pick up good accounts from their erstwhile competitors.

This incompatibility led to legislation aimed at strengthening the official banks and bringing private banks—especially the British—to heel. Such measures were fiercely resisted. When and if they became law they were evaded, and in the long term they seem to have had only a marginal effect on the growth and profitability of the British banks.

To have placed more than minimal constraints on the operations of the British banks would have raised insuperable problems, many of which are indicated by the events surrounding the failure of the

Argentine banking law of 1887. Liberal clauses in national constitutions and international commercial treaties, backed up by considerable liberal sentiment at home, made it difficult for some Latin American governments to pass laws directed specifically at *foreign* banks. Yet to act against all private banks inevitably meant hitting domestic as well as British institutions, and the former were less able to resist. Besides, it was of doubtful utility to hit private banks which were performing their chosen and necessary task efficiently simply in order to protect state banks which were inherently unstable and patently corrupt, and whose commitment to the decentralization of credit was at the best of times incomplete —composed more of rhetoric than action. Throughout Latin America the majority of politicians were suspicious of state participation in banking, and the experiments of Rui Barbosa in Brazil or Wenceslao Pacheco in Argentina did little to quell those suspicions. So, whilst financial crises were commonly accompanied or followed by attempts to tackle the banking question, prolonged periods of prosperity tended to reduce the influence of the reform lobbies and strengthen the case for letting well alone.

The consequence was that during the years of prosperity—as, for example, in Argentina and Uruguay between about 1895 and 1912, conservative thinking prevailed in banking as elsewhere, and nothing was done to utilize the balance of payments surplus imaginatively. The Banco de la Nación and the Banco de la República followed the example of the British by placing emphasis on long-term growth and the creation of a strong deposit position, and appear to have all but abandoned the provision of venture capital to nascent industries. Pleas that the balance of payments surplus should be used as the basis for a rediscount bank were successfully resisted by politicians who had seen previous expansions of credit end in apparent disaster.

At the same time that Latin American state banks were veering away from their early Saint-Simonian ideals, increasing competition and falling interest rates went some way towards altering the style of the British banks. In the more advanced economies the British embraced a new class of borrowers in the last decade or so before the First World War—Argentine wine and sugar and Brazilian textiles benefited from this relaxation. The landowners of the River Plate region also found the British more amenable as a surge of money seeking investment in mortgage came into

Argentina and Uruguay, displaced by the Australian recession and
by falling rates on traditional British institutional investments.

By 1912 much of Latin America had achieved the banking
system it deserved: a system mainly devoted to the production of
exports and the financing of external trade. The great majority of
those in power benefited from this system, and prosperity had
largely eroded the support of the proto-bourgeois elements in the
political élite who had earlier tried to modify the system to their
own advantage. The British banks had played an important part in
bringing about this state of affairs. They had lent a semblance of
stability to inherently unstable national economies. They had consistently assisted the concentration of credit in the administrative
and commercial centres of the sub-continent, making the interior
increasingly dependent on the ports. They had inadvertently (but
not unwillingly) brought strong sanctions to bear on banks which
differed radically from themselves, and in doing so had impressed
upon the post-1890 generation of official bankers the utility of a
'safe' business. They had made minimal concessions in the face of
hostile legislation and adverse market conditions, but in doing so
had neither sacrificed profits nor induced any significant structural
changes in their environment. All in all, they had proved a powerful agent in the maintenance of the political *status quo* during a
period of turbulent economic change.

CHAPTER II

Insurance Companies

CHARLES JONES

I

AFTER 1860 the major British insurance companies extended their business beyond the British Isles, setting up a far-ranging system of agencies and branches throughout America, South Africa, Australasia, and the East. The continuing expansion of world trade offered great opportunities in every class of insurance. Marine business grew with the development of new shipping services, though owing to the predominance of the British merchant fleet the greater part of this could be done in London. Fire insurance also benefited from the growth of trade, since trade found concrete expression in railways, warehouses, and processing plants, many of which were owned by British companies or merchants, and all of which required insurance. Unlike marine business, this could not safely be handled in London; the risks involved in insuring buildings in comparatively new cities where wooden structures were still common and the elements an incalculable factor greatly exceeded those of home business, as many found to their cost after the San Francisco earthquake and conflagration of 1906. Consequently, it was found necessary to employ agents or representatives on the spot, not only to win new business, but also to supervise the inspection of risks.

Because of the dangers involved, not all British companies were equally forward in exploiting new areas, and of those that did, some lost heavily. The Albert Life Assurance Company, one of the foremost of the progressive companies of the 1860s, failed in 1869 along with its twenty-six subsidiary companies.[1] On the other hand, the Commercial Union—another pioneer of foreign business—was earning rather more than two-thirds of its fire premiums outside the United Kingdom by 1885. Clearly there was

[1] B. Supple, *The Royal Exchange Assurance* (Cambridge, 1970), p. 142.

business to be had, and many of the less forward companies soon revised their initial decisions and followed the example set by their more adventurous competitors. The Royal Exchange Assurance, considered a rather stuffy and old-fashioned enterprise in the sixties, raised the proportion of its fire premiums earned abroad from 2 per cent in 1885 to 64 per cent in 1910.[1]

In building up its foreign business, each company was at pains to spread its risks as widely as possible; this, after all, was an essential principle of insurance. The required spread of risks was achieved not only through reinsurance arrangements with other companies, but also by taking in a wide geographical range. Thus, although existing patterns of trade and cultural bonds led most companies to prefer the opportunities offered by the British Dominions and the United States of America, almost all established bridgeheads in the major Latin American centres. By 1866 the Royal, the Imperial, the London Assurance, the Queen, the Commercial, the Albert, the Northern, and the Sun were all established in Valparaíso.[2] A year later they had been joined by the London, Liverpool and Globe, the Lancashire, and the North British and Mercantile.[3] By 1872, the Albert Life Assurance had failed, but four of the companies already mentioned had set up agencies in Brazil.[4] Two years later the Northern opened in Bogotá.[5] By 1875 eight British companies were operating in Buenos Aires.[6] By 1883 thirteen were represented in Lima.[7] And so it went on. The pioneers were joined from 1880 onwards by a second generation of expansionist companies—amongst them the Guardian, the Royal Exchange, the Phoenix, and the Norwich Union—so that even allowing for amalgamations the number of British agencies in some major cities reached twenty or more by 1914. In 1904 there were twenty-eight foreign agencies—mostly British—in Valparaíso; by 1921 there were twenty-three in Buenos Aires.[8] Valparaíso, Lima, and Buenos Aires continued to support the highest concentrations of British offices, but Mexico City, with eight in 1897, could not complain of neglect, and even

[1] Supple, *Royal Exchange*, pp. 241–2.
[2] Phoenix Valparaíso, 5 Sept. 1866. [3] Ibid., 28 Feb. 1867.
[4] Phoenix, 'Preliminary Notes . . . on Insurance in Brazil' (1964), by G. Warner, of the Federacão de Seguradores Terrestres, Rio de Janeiro.
[5] Sun F.N. Colombia. [6] A.F.I.C.A., *Argentine Association*, p. 7.
[7] Sun F.N. Peru, ii. 34.
[8] Ibid., Chile, v. 119; A.F.I.C.A., *Argentine Association*, pp. 2–3.

San Salvador was covered by an agent of the Sun from as early as 1873.[1]

It was usual for companies to operate—initially at least—through British merchants, paying them commission on the business which they found. In this way the large expenses involved in setting up a branch, buying or leasing premises, and sending out an employee from the home office could be avoided, or at least deferred until the market had proved itself. In North America, branches or subsidiary companies were soon established, and for some British firms the United States alone came to account for a third or more of premium income by the end of the century.[2] In South America growth was less spectacular, and agencies remained the predominant form of organization until the eve of the First World War. South America, in short, remained a marginal market for British companies; they had to compete with each other, with numerous European companies, and with local firms for what were all too often very limited opportunities. Latin American insurance legislation—whilst not radically different from patterns pursued in other parts of the world—made matters worse. It was one thing to be made to hold deposits in the securities of European or North American governments, but quite another to be obliged to take the more speculative internal bonds of Peru or Argentina. Just how limited the opportunities were may be seen from the premiums collected in a selection of South American cities: during 1883, twenty-three companies in Valparaíso, of which twenty were British, collected only £75,000 in premiums;[3] the same year, in Lima, the ten British companies in operation collected just under £10,000;[4] in 1899, twenty-one companies—British, colonial, and German—collected £41,000 in Santiago.[5] These figures represent average gross premium incomes per company of £3,261, £1,000, and £1,949 respectively, and appear insignificant when compared with the total of £20,270,000 in fire premiums collected in 1901 by fifty-two British insurance companies—an average of £389,808 per company.[6] For example, the 1899 Santiago premiums collected by the five largest British insurance companies expressed as a percentage of those companies' total

---

[1] P. G. M. Dickson, *The Sun Insurance Office* (London, 1960), p. 219.
[2] Supple, *Royal Exchange*, p. 214. [3] Sun F.N. Chile, iv. 223.
[4] Ibid., Peru, ii. 34. [5] Phoenix Valparaíso, 20 May 1899.
[6] Supple, *Royal Exchange*, p. 213 (Table 10.1).

premiums for 1901 indicate that Santiago may have accounted for about 0·45 per cent of business done by British offices at the turn of the century.[1] It seems unlikely that the entire Latin American market can have yielded more than ten times the business done in Santiago, and this would confirm the isolated figures which suggest that Latin America at best never provided much more than a small percentage of the total business done by British companies. It is true that as late as 1938 the Phoenix group were still dependent on South America for about 8 per cent of their business, Central America and the Caribbean accounting for a further 8 per cent. However, the total of 16 per cent is probably misleading as an indication of the importance of the area to other British firms. The Phoenix had two particular interests in Latin America—a large share in Cuban workers' compensation, and a subsidiary company, El Fénix Peruano, in Peru—which tend to distort the picture.[2] The Commercial Union, on the other hand, had been amongst the first to move into Latin America in the 1860s, and was the leading British insurance company in Chile during the 1890s. Yet Latin America and the Caribbean accounted for only 4·4 per cent of the Commercial Union's *foreign* business in 1889—a mere £35,000 in premium income.[3]

Profit statistics, like those of turnover, are elusive; and where companies claimed to be making a loss, one must of course beware of ulterior motives. In Colombia, for example, following a charge in the local press that the five foreign insurance companies in Bogotá had spirited away a million pesos profit from the country during 1914, the British retorted with figures which showed a loss. The Northern, which was the longest-established office in the country and had the lion's share of the business, declared that it had remitted about £2,500 in premiums to London during 1914, but had paid out £10,000 locally in claims.[4] Unpublished statistics from the Phoenix Insurance Company carry more weight; they show a net profit on Chilean business between 1890

[1] Phoenix Valparaíso, 20 May 1899; and Supple, *Royal Exchange*, p. 214. A calculation for the same five companies for Buenos Aires in 1900 yields 0·925 per cent.

[2] Phoenix, Report of the Victory Committee (1942) on Post-War Development Overseas (hereafter *Victory Committee*), pp. 9–10.

[3] E. Liveing, *A Century of Insurance: the Commercial Union Assurance Group, 1861–1961* (London, 1961), p. 45.

[4] Sun F.N. Colombia, p. 191.

and 1904 of a mere £2,156 (£144 per annum), and a loss in
Argentine business over the same period of £15,954.[1] Of course,
the Phoenix was a comparative late-comer. Companies which had
been established since the 1860s were almost certainly profiting
from Latin America by the 1890s; if not, it is hard to see why they
should have remained. The list of premiums collected by companies operating in Santiago in 1899 (compiled in order to calculate the contribution which each company should make to the
local fire service) shows that the older-established firms certainly
had much larger turnovers than newcomers like the Phoenix.
Eight companies which had been in Chile since the 1860s averaged
£2,256; eight companies which had come to Chile since 1870
averaged about £1,640 each.[2] Again, in Valparaíso, during 1883,
the average premiums of seven established companies were almost
double those of ten newer entrants.[3] Turnover is no guarantee of
profit; indeed, both the Commercial Union and the Royal made
substantial losses in Chile during the 1890s.[4] But it seems likely
that, in general, those companies which were first on the scene
took not only the bulk of the business, but the best of it.

It is also clear from the Valparaíso list of 1883, which includes
British, German, and local companies, that the British dominated
the market. Twenty British companies collected 76 per cent of premiums, two local companies held 21 per cent, and the sole German
company a mere 3 per cent. These proportions may well have
been typical for most South American cities prior to 1885, before
the recently formed local companies had had time to develop, and
before the continental firms had moved in in any strength. As
late as 1911, two-thirds of Uruguayan fire insurance was still
handled by foreign firms, though this implies a British share of
less than 66 per cent, since there were by this time several continental companies in Montevideo. Again, in Chile, local companies
already controlled 40 per cent of the market by 1910, and the
British had been reduced to 53 per cent.[5]

Poor though it is, the quantitative evidence presents a picture
which is confirmed by other sources. From the point of view of
the present inquiry the salient features of this picture are three.
First, Latin America, unlike North America, was never an

---

[1] Phoenix, Annual Results of Foreign Agencies, Drawer C. 9, vol. 3.
[2] Phoenix Valparaíso, 20 May 1899.   [3] Sun F.N. Chile, iv. 223.
[4] Ibid., v. 119.   [5] Ibid.

overwhelmingly important market for British insurance companies. Therefore, if any sector of the Latin American market became unduly unprofitable or difficult to work in, whether through excessive competition or hostile legislation, London head offices could take the decision to withdraw without too much heart-searching. Second, there is nothing to suggest that British insurance companies generally made more than a marginal profit from Latin American fire insurance: it was worth being in Latin America, but not worth expanding this area of business beyond a certain point. Third, British offices dominated the fire insurance business in most Latin American cities until about 1885. Thereafter they generally gave ground to European (mostly German) and local companies.

However, a word of qualification is necessary. If the stakes were low for the British head offices, the same was not equally true for their local agents. To Anglo-South American merchants and businessmen, the agency of a British insurance company was a source of relatively risk-free and trouble-free profit, and it could be made to dovetail nicely with other business interests—mortgage lending, for example. After 1900, when legislation increased the amount of paperwork involved, the business became less attractive; but in the earlier period it was the men on the spot rather than the directors in London who had the motive to achieve and maintain British hegemony. This was an entirely different situation from that encountered by a railway or public utility company, where the attention of directors and managers alike was focused on the economic and political environment in which their fixed assets were imprisoned.

II

In view of the picture of the Latin American market and of the constitution of the British insurance companies given in the first section of this chapter, it should come as no surprise that competition was frequently severe, and that the initiative in controlling it was taken by the local agents of British companies. As soon as a handful of British agencies was established in any Latin American city, they banded together to form a local board of agents, modelled on and affiliated with the London Fire Offices Committee.

Co-operation between fire insurance companies in England had begun in the late eighteenth century. Initially it was restricted to a few of the larger companies which joined together to finance local fire services, a step which was clearly in the interest of all, clients included. Agreements over rates came later. High losses in Liverpool between 1816 and 1825 resulted in a joint tariff being agreed by the four companies most closely concerned—the Sun, the Royal Exchange, the Phoenix, and the Imperial. The Liverpool tariff led to other similar attempts to maintain rates in cities throughout the United Kingdom, not all of which were equally successful. The system was not formalized until 1868, when the London Fire Offices Committee established a written constitution and regulations, though even before 1868 the Committee acted as a supervisory body, approving or disapproving the regulations and rates set up by the many local tariff committees throughout the world.[1] In Latin America, local agents' boards were established in Valparaíso (1866), Buenos Aires (1875), Montevideo (1897), Mexico City (1897), and elsewhere.[2] In Lima, and possibly in Mexico City, the local agents had met informally for many years prior to the setting up of a local board, but the tariff to which they adhered had been fixed in London by the Fire Offices Committee. Similarly, the Montevideo tariff prior to 1897 was fixed by the Buenos Aires local board.

Whilst the rates maintained by each local tariff committee, the regulations which it operated, and the success with which it carried out its self-appointed task of controlling competition naturally varied from city to city according to local circumstances, it is possible to isolate common features.

One of the advantages of the agency system was that it saved on overheads. The local boards facilitated further savings; members pooled their resources to employ inspectors of buildings and electrical installations, and to promote and sustain local fire services. Furthermore, when the British agents were threatened by hostile legislation they could afford to employ the best legal advice available by sharing the fees. The essential purpose of the boards was, however, to agree upon a tariff, regarded as a confidential document for circulation amongst the member agents and such non-members as it was hoped might abide by it, and to maintain this tariff against all comers.[3]

---

[1] Supple, *Royal Exchange*, p. 282.
[2] Phoenix Valparaíso, 5 Sept. 1866; Montevideo, 11 Aug. 1897; Mexico City, 22 Feb. 1897; A.F.I.C.A., *Argentine Association*, p. 7.
[3] Phoenix Valparaíso, 20 June 1899; Sun F.N. Chile, v. 7.

Yet, once rates had been fixed, competition began to break out in new ways. By appointing his larger clients as sub-agents and paying them a commission on the business they gave him, an insurance agent could effectively reduce the rate he charged, whilst nominally keeping to the tariff rates. Increasingly, local boards found it necessary to make regulations limiting the number and nature of sub-agents to be appointed by each agent. Another way in which competition could seep out was through the brokers who, in many cities, took on the task of distributing large risks amongst the various offices. Agents paid a commission to any broker bringing them business, but the brokers often returned a part of their commission to their clients, so that—once again—the tariff was only nominally maintained. There was also disagreement over the size of the commission which should be paid by agents to brokers, local and continental companies tending to pay higher rates to attract business away from their British competitors. Local boards attempted to regulate these matters, and occasionally, as in Buenos Aires during the early 1890s, blacklisted brokers who did not conform.[1] This, though, was only safe policy when the tariff companies controlled so large a proportion of the market that the ostracized brokers could not easily dispose of their business elsewhere.

The issue of long-term policies provided yet another means of circumventing the tariff. The customary term of fire insurance policies during the mid-nineteenth century was one year. In many instances the original regulations of local boards did not specifically outlaw the granting of discounts to clients who were prepared to pay three or five years' premiums in advance. When companies on the fringe of, or outside, the tariff organizations began to offer large discounts on long-term policies, the local boards responded with regulations governing the maximum permissible discounts for each class of business.

Finally, reinsurance by a tariff company with non-tariff companies made it possible for the former effectively to undercut its fellows. It was customary for insurance companies to minimize their risks by sharing out large businesses. An agent who controlled the insurance of a local railway company would probably take no more than 20 or 25 per cent for his own company, sharing the remainder between three or four other companies. Such arrangements were usually reciprocal, and one of the greatest difficulties

---

[1] A.F.I.C.A. Minutes, 10 May and 2 Aug. 1892.

facing any new entrant to a market was the establishment of satisfactory reinsurance arrangements which would enable him to take on large clients. So long as the tariff companies dominated the market in any particular city and reinsured only amongst themselves, it was very difficult for any intruder—local or European—to gain a firm place in the market. But if a tariff company agent arranged to reinsure a risk with a group of non-tariff companies which worked on rates below the tariff, he could offer his client an over-all rate which was below the tariff rate, though he himself would not be breaking the tariff since the policy issued for his company's share of the risk would be at the tariff rate. Because they were a breach of the spirit of the tariff, and because they presented a chance for local and foreign non-tariff companies to develop their business at the expense of the tariff companies, such arrangements were generally frowned upon, and regulations forbidding reinsurance with non-tariff companies were passed at different times by most of the local boards and by the London Fire Offices Committee.

The tariff system savoured very much of monopoly, and aroused criticism not only in Latin America, but also in Britain, where *The Economist* complained that the tariff offices had 'banded themselves together into what is virtually a great trades union, having for its object the restraining of competition and the upholding of rates'.[1] However, the undoubtedly monopolist intent of the tariff system was somewhat mitigated in Latin America—as elsewhere—by its failure. In each city, the local board appears as a defensive alliance, gradually and unwillingly giving ground to outside companies; never as an aggressive force forcing rates upwards. Two examples may help to illustrate the general pattern.

As early as 1871, the local board at Valparaíso found that their members were losing business to two new Chilean companies, and were obliged to cut their rate for customs sheds by 25 per cent. The next few years saw the rates charged by local companies rise fractionally, but in 1876 the tariff offices were once again forced to sanction a cut in rates to defend themselves against continental companies which were trying to break their way into the Chilean market.[2]

---

[1] *The Economist*, 30 Apr. 1881, 532 (quoted by Supple, *The Royal Exchange*, p. 282).
[2] Sun F.N. Chile, iii. 307 (Valparaíso Local Minutes, 10 Jan. 1876).

The 1876 cut was successful, in that it persuaded the new continental companies—the Hamburg Magdeburg, La Confiance, and the Prussian National—to join the local board, and abide by its rates and regulations for the time being.[1] The outcome was that by 1881 the remaining non-tariff companies did not appear to be doing much business.[2] But by 1885 competition from national companies was as bad as ever, and the local board felt it necessary to take strong action, refusing to reinsure even at tariff rates with non-tariff companies.[3] The policy of the local board was a curious mixture of concessions, intended to bring in as many companies as possible, and aggressive measures designed to discomfit those companies which remained outside. Until the mid-1880s it seemed to be working, but by 1887 it was clear that ostracism had not had its desired effect of limiting the growth of outside competition. Nineteen non-tariff offices were operating in the city: eight German, eight Chilean, and one each from New Zealand, Sweden, and France.[4] Of these, some voluntarily kept to the tariff, but others were aggressive in their competition. It was plainly impossible to be rid of them, and local board policy from this date tended to concentrate on making just such minimal concessions as would protect members' business against outsiders. In 1896, the tariff for the North Chilean ports was cut when it was found that business was being lost to continental and Chilean offices, and customs house rates were also reduced.[5] In 1898 the local board attempted to bring non-members into a less aggressive frame of mind by threatening to suspend the tariff altogether.[6] The local board was no longer strong enough to be able to control non-members by refusal to coinsure with them, and admitted as much in February of the following year, when they dropped the prohibition against reinsurance with non-tariff companies.[7] Instead they had to resort to their only remaining sanction—the threat of all-out rate war. This did produce results. In August 1899 the Asociación Chilena de Aseguradores was formed—a tariff union embracing the majority of British, continental, and Chilean companies—but it was a union which was achieved only at the

[1] Sun F.N. Chile, iv. 103–25.
[2] Ibid., iv. 138, memorandum, 4 May 1881.
[3] Ibid., pp. 240 and 245.   [4] Ibid., v. 7.
[5] Phoenix Valparaíso, 3 Jan. 1896.
[6] Ibid., 18 Mar. 1898, and circular to non-tariff offices, 22 Mar. 1898.
[7] Ibid., 22 Feb. 1899.

expense of considerable concessions over commission and rebate regulations by the British companies.[1]

The history of the local board in Buenos Aires bears marked similarities to that of Valparaíso both in chronology and in its ultimate result. Board members began to feel severe competition from continental and local companies from the late 1880s. In 1888 they applied to the Fire Offices Committee for permission to reduce their rates should this be necessary in order to meet the assault of the non-tariff companies.[2] In 1889, as a possible gambit towards the formation of a broader union, they agreed to limit the tariff to the contents of buildings, leaving the rates on the buildings themselves to be decided by each company individually.[3] However, these concessions proved to be insufficient, and during the 1890s the board was obliged to make further compromises over brokerage, the return of commission to the insured, long-term policies, and rates.[4] In 1901 the regulation forbidding reinsurance with non-tariff companies was dropped; the strength of the non-tariff companies had made it an anachronism.[5] The same year, the local board and the Comité de Aseguradores Argentinos (the trade organization of the Argentine insurance companies) set up a joint tariff committee, and agreed to synchronize their rates and regulations.[6]

The arrangements made with non-tariff companies in Valparaíso (1899) and Buenos Aires (1901) were by no means final, and did not bring competition to an end in either city. However, they amounted to an admission by the British that they were no longer sufficiently strong to manage these markets to their own advantage without the co-operation of German and local firms. Although the volume of business done by British companies in Latin America continued to increase after 1900, their share of the business and their power over the market were already in decline by the 1890s.

III

Besides the control of competition, the local boards of agents were concerned to protect their members against hostile legislation. To

---

[1] Phoenix Valparaíso, 11 Aug. 1899, 27 Aug. 1900 and circular no. 32.
[2] A.F.I.C.A. Minutes, 10 Sept. 1888.   [3] Ibid., 2 July 1889.
[4] Ibid., 12 Feb. 1891, 10 May and 2 Aug. 1892, 7 Nov. 1893, 7 Sept. 1894, 5 Feb., 7 May, 4 June and 2 July 1895, 4 Feb., 4 Aug. and 1 Sept. 1896.
[5] Ibid., 3 Dec. 1901.   [6] Ibid., 2 Sept. 1901.

some extent, these two objectives were incompatible, since the hostile attitude initially adopted by the British towards their Latin American competitors led the latter to use their influence to secure legislation specifically designed to break the hold of foreigners over the market. One great advantage which local companies had over foreign offices was that their boards of directors were composed of local men, often of considerable political influence.[1] This not only helped in the development of business, but gave the local companies privileged access to the legislatures. However, the insurance legislation which was passed in South America during the twenty-five years or so before the First World War was not solely the outcome of pressure from immediately interested parties. On the broader political front, insurance legislation was just one of the many spheres of conflict between liberal and nationalist elements—the former favouring equality of treatment for foreigner and national, the latter attempting to secure protection by discriminatory legislation for local businessmen against foreign products and services.

There were four principal objections shared by economic nationalist elements in all Latin American states against the foreign insurance companies. First, it was recognized that foreign insurance companies—like any other form of foreign enterprise—exported the profits which they earned locally for payment to British or European shareholders. Second, the strength of foreign —and especially British—insurance companies prevented local enterprises from achieving as fast a rate of growth as they might otherwise have done. The foreigners were all the more resented since they kept a firm hold on the more valuable commercial business of the principal cities, leaving local companies with the thankless task of developing provincial and 'public service' business (e.g. agricultural insurance and workmen's compensation). Third, it was felt that foreign companies did not invest in Latin America an amount of their funds proportionate to the premiums which they earned there. Thus, Latin American govern-

---

[1] Take, for example, the Argentine national insurance companies. In 1875 the board of the Estrella company included two of the most prominent Buenos Aires merchants, Thomas Armstrong and George Temperley. Armstrong was also chairman of the Fire and Marine Insurance Company, which included amongst its directors the then powerful Argentine banker Ambrosio P. Lezica. Another member of the Lezica family, Juan, was a director of the Bienhechora company, as was the Irish journalist and businessman, Edward T. Mulhall.

ment and industry as borrowers did not benefit from the investment role of insurance companies to the same extent as did Great Britain. The fourth objection was that insurance—and other financial services—were businesses which came well within the technical competence of local businessmen, even if it might be necessary to raise capital abroad. With railways and public utilities, where technical expertise in engineering was an evident need, the most ardent nationalists agreed that foreign management was necessary for the time being; but they saw no reason why insurance could not be handled entirely by South American nationals.

It was these objections which influenced the general outline of most of the insurance laws passed by Latin American legislatures between 1890 and 1914. Naturally, each law had its own individual characteristics, and some nations, notably Uruguay, followed a quite different pattern from the majority. But the greater number of insurance laws of the period may be reduced, in essence, to the following standard form, ultimately derived from mid-century New York State legislation:[1]

1. All insurance companies, whether national or foreign, were obliged to register with an appropriate government department, to publish some form of balance sheet, and to submit to inspection by a government inspector of insurance companies, or similar official.

2. All companies were obliged to deposit with the Treasury a substantial sum in guarantee of good faith. Usually, there was a scale of deposits which differentiated between companies on grounds of nationality and size, and according to the nature of their business. Fire and Life offices paid more than agricultural insurance departments (which were usually allowed to operate free of most taxes); and larger organizations paid more than their smaller competitors.

3. Furthermore, the form in which the deposits were to be made was stipulated by law. Bonds of the legislating authority, or of provinces or municipalities within its territories, shares of local companies, mortgage bonds of the local state mortgage bank, titles to real estate within the territory, or cash—any or all of these might be acceptable; but foreign (especially British) bonds or shares were not.

4. All companies had to pay a percentage tax, generally levied on their gross premiums. As with the deposit, distinctions were commonly made between foreign and national companies so as to favour the latter.

[1] Liveing, *A Century of Insurance*, pp. 30–1.

The agents of British insurance companies found this sort of legislation obnoxious, and made every effort to suppress or delay it whenever it appeared. In Chile the first proposals for a deposit-style insurance law came as early as 1888.[1] Further attempts to legislate followed, and were opposed with considerable success by a defence committee established by the local representatives of the foreign companies.[2] It was not until 1904 that a revised version of an 1896 Bill eventually became law.[3] The fate of the 1898 version of this project illustrates the power of the foreign agents. Whilst the project was in its committee stage, under the consideration of the Comisión de Hacienda, the local board of agents managed to reduce the scale of deposits from $1·5 million (pesos) to $300,000 for life insurance departments, and from $250,000 to $150,000 for fire departments. The board also succeeded in extracting an assurance that the deposits would be payable in internal bonds or national mortgage bonds to be purchased at an agreed market rate, instead of at a mandatory 80 per cent of nominal value.[4] Even when the project finally became law six years later, these modifications still stood.[5]

A fairly modest project put forward in Colombia in 1912 was also opposed by the foreign agents. They clubbed together to buy space in the leading newspapers, though the opposition of President Zapata probably did more to delay the passing of the law until the 1915 session.[6] In 1922 the foreign agents once again combined to fight a more radical proposal. Securing the reluctant support of two local companies by threatening to withdraw re-insurance facilities, the foreigners put their own more moderate project before Congress.[7] The crux of the original 1922 project had been a clause stating that at least half of the deposits made by insurance companies should be in the form of Colombian real estate. Although a modified proposal was eventually passed, the pressure of the foreign representatives ensured that it lost this cutting edge.[8]

The Peruvians had better luck. In spite of the resistance of

[1] Sun F.N. Chile, iv. 256, memorandum, 11 Mar. 1886.

[2] Phoenix Valparaíso, 10 June 1898.

[3] *S.A.J.*, 27 June 1896, 711, 716, and Dickson, *The Sun*, p. 215.

[4] Phoenix Valparaíso, 10 June 1898.

[5] U.S. M.C.R. No. 263 (Valparaíso, Aug. 1902), p. 591, and No. 294 (Santiago, Mar. 1905), pp. 148–9.   [6] Sun F.N. Colombia, pp. 199–203.

[7] Ibid., p. 201.   [8] Ibid.

foreign companies, their deposit law passed first time, in 1895. But the local agents' board agreed unanimously that they would not comply with the provisions of the law, and that they would refuse to reinsure with the local Compañía Internacional, or with any other company working under the law.[1] However, by December 1896 all had given way except for the Sun, which withdrew from Peru.[2]

As elsewhere, the first serious legislative attack on the foreign companies in Argentina came during the 1890s—a time when British investment in Latin America was at a standstill. In 1890 Congress levied a tax of 7 per cent on the profits of all foreign companies, and introduced deposit requirements for insurance agencies.[3] As a result of these measures, three recently established North American life offices withdrew from the country, and new Argentine companies, favoured by the law, sprang up in their place—and with the aid of their staff.[4] In 1892 and 1896 attempts to increase the controls and taxation exercised over the foreigners failed.[5] Then in 1897 a new comprehensive insurance law was proposed which insisted, amongst other things, that the deposits made by foreign insurance companies should be in specially issued national five per cent internal bonds, to be purchased at 80 per cent of their nominal value.[6] A special issue such as this amounted to a forced loan in the opinion of the foreign insurance offices, since the bonds would not be marketable in the same way or at the same price as publicly issued national loans. It was this clause more than any other which accounted for the special efforts made against the 1898 law by the foreign companies.

The local board first approached Wenceslao Escalante—the Minister of Finance—asking that they might be allowed to make their deposits in publicly issued bonds rather than in the special issue authorized under the new law.[7] The Minister claimed that he could do nothing, and advised the board to petition Congress;[8] but the petition had no effect. However, at the last moment, the forced loan deposit scheme was abandoned due to the combined

[1] Sun F.N. Peru, vol. ii (Valparaíso Minutes, 31 Jan. 1896).
[2] Ibid., p. 148 (Valparaíso Minutes, 4 Dec. 1896).
[3] A.F.I.C.A. Minutes, 20 Mar., 23 and 29 Dec. 1890; *S.A.J.*, 5 Mar. 1898 (editorial gives a résumé of insurance legislation 1890–8).
[4] *S.A.J.*, 19 Sept. 1896, 307.   [5] Ibid., 5 Mar. 1898, 256.
[6] A.F.I.C.A. Minutes, 19 Jan. 1897.
[7] Ibid., 15 Jan. 1898.   [8] Ibid., 12 Mar. 1898.

pressure of the local agents and of the British Foreign Office
(traditionally opposed to forced loans). Instead of the special
bonds, foreign companies were allowed to make their deposits in
easily negotiable treasury bills.[1] The local agents also understood
from their negotiations with government that they had been
promised equal tax status with local companies; but in this they
were deceived.

Before the furore aroused by the 1897/8 law had entirely
subsided, voices were once again raised in reaction to a further
insurance law brought before the new session of Congress towards
the end of 1898.[2] Attention moved from the terms of deposit
payments to the premium tax differential between foreign and
local companies which, promise or no promise, still stood at 10
per cent for foreign agencies and 2 per cent for local companies.
The finance committee of Congress recommended a reduction of
these rates to 7 and 1 per cent respectively.[3] But this seeming
reduction represented an increase in the differential from 5:1 to
7:1. In November the foreign agents made a proposal; they were
prepared to accept the bonds which they had refused earlier in the
year if Congress would now put an end to the discriminatory tax.[4]
But Congress—more radical than the national executive—stood
firm, and the increase became law; the rates were eventually fixed
for 1899 at 10 per cent for foreign companies and 1·4 per cent for
Argentine companies, thus establishing the 7:1 ratio.[5] The *Buenos
Aires Standard*, organ of the local British community, remarked
that 'if this dead-set at foreign capital is to be allowed a foothold,
we may prepare a coffin for interment of our credit abroad'.[6] *El
Diario*, a leading Argentine daily newspaper, referred to 'this
protectionism [which] has degenerated in the hands of congress-
men into a morbid, incongruous, little-minded policy',[7] and
commended those Argentine politicians—especially Finance
Minister Escalante—who had opposed the tax.

In Uruguay events took a different course.[8] It was not until
1908 that a deposit law was passed obliging foreign agencies to

---

[1] *S.A.J.*, 26 Mar. 1898, 340; 23 Apr. 1898, 453; 29 Oct. 1898, 494; 5 Nov.
1898, 510.

[2] Ibid., 19 Nov. 1898, 566.　　　　　　[3] Ibid., 29 Oct. 1898, 494.

[4] Ibid., 19 Nov. 1898, 566.　　　　　　[5] Ibid., 26 Nov. 1898, 594.

[6] Ibid., 24 Dec. 1898, 712.　　　　　　[7] Ibid., 7 Jan. 1899, 9.

[8] This account relies principally on S. G. Hanson, *Utopia in Uruguay* (New
York, 1938), pp. 26–39.

place 150,000 pesos in government securities as a guarantee of good faith. Three years later the government of President Batlle put forward a far more radical, and—in Latin America—an unprecedented plan. All foreign operators were to be expropriated without compensation, and a state insurance monopoly was to be established. The project was opposed not only by the board of local agents, but by influential elements in the political establishment. Those who opposed the law claimed that it was unconstitutional, and pointed out that the Standard Life Office had actually incurred losses in the process of instilling the habit of life insurance amongst the Uruguayan public, and that despite their tariff system, the foreign companies had reduced fire insurance rates by 50 per cent over the past twenty-five years. It was also feared that politics might intrude into the administration of a state company, and that the profits to be gained from it might not compensate for the loss of revenue (about 40,000 pesos per annum) previously gained from foreign agencies. By the time the project became law, in December 1911, it had suffered some modification as a result of pressure from its Uruguayan and foreign opponents, but the essential feature—the state insurance bank—remained. By 1915, 41·67 per cent of total insurance premiums in Uruguay were already being paid to the state bank, and private companies, largely excluded from fire, life, and workmen's insurance, soon went into decline. The fortune of this experiment in state control lies beyond the scope of the present study; none the less, it is worthy of note that between 1928 and 1932 the state insurance bank distributed 271,400 pesos of its profits amongst its employees—a gesture to equitable distribution of income which would hardly have been forthcoming from private companies of that era, whatever their nationality.

Most of the tactics employed by foreign insurance companies in their efforts to fight Latin American legislation prejudicial to their interests were open to all other interested parties. Newspaper space, access to congressional committees and individual politicians, were used as much, or more, by local companies as by the local boards of agents. British diplomatic support could rarely be relied upon to achieve results, and by the 1890s local companies in most countries were well enough able to withstand any market pressures which the foreigners might bring to bear.

The British were well aware of both the strengths and the

weaknesses of their position. They lost, ultimately, in every case; but the often substantial delays and concessions which they achieved secured profits which would otherwise have gone elsewhere.

IV

The tariff system and legislation have so far been considered separately. Of course, the two were interconnected, since although the Latin American insurance companies established themselves largely without government assistance during the 1880s and early 1890s, they were greatly assisted in consolidating their position from the later 1890s by legislation favouring them at the expense of foreign companies. Differential taxation must certainly have affected the growth of fire insurance business done by foreign companies, especially those which had only recently moved in. But almost all felt that what was left to them was worth the price which they had now to pay in order to do business, even though the deposits—a forced investment—represented a considerable expense. The following figures for the Phoenix Insurance Company, even though they refer to a rather later period, illustrate the nature of the problem. The Phoenix, with a world-wide business, was obliged to make deposits in many territories. By 1938, deposits made by the company in British Dominions and possessions at a cost of £293,184 had risen in value to £299,561. On the other hand, Central and South American deposits originally costing £266,049 had depreciated by £87,993. The records of the Phoenix do not disclose over what period the depreciation took place. However, they do state that the average profit on Latin American business during the period 1929–38 was £36,823 per annum—enough to extinguish the total loss arising from the forced investments in less than three years.[1] When one considers the adverse course of the world's money markets during the 1930s, this loss does not appear intolerable.

The deposit clauses represented efforts on the part of Latin American governments to benefit from the role of insurance companies as institutional investors. Clearly, they achieved their object in some measure, but that they did so was due as much to market trends as to their own efforts. Just as the market was moving naturally in favour of local companies even before

[1] Phoenix, Victory Committee, p. 18.

governments established tax differentials in their favour, so there was a growing tendency for British insurance companies to invest abroad which may even have been curtailed—rather than promoted—by the forcible extraction of deposits. Towards the end of the nineteenth century the yield from many of the traditional investments of insurance companies was falling. Consols were earning only 2½ per cent by 1896–8, and colonial government stocks were not a great deal better.[1] The objection of the insurance companies to deposit legislation at this time was not based on any fundamental aversion to foreign investment, but rather on the way that they were obliged to buy internal bonds—often specially issued for the purpose—and were not allowed to buy external bonds of the legislating country on the open market in satisfaction of their obligations. This very often meant that the risk of depreciation outweighed the attraction of a relatively high yield. However, they did not withdraw in the face of deposit laws; on balance, the risk was obviously considered acceptable.

By 1913, the proportion of the funds of the Royal Exchange which were invested in foreign government and municipal securities was 12 per cent; in 1890 it had been 0·8 per cent.[2] A great deal, if not all, of this investment may have been specifically occasioned by deposit legislation. It was tolerable because the danger of depreciation was balanced by a high nominal yield, and because only by paying these deposits could a company hope to maintain and increase its world-wide business. At a time when the bi-national, and even the multi-national, company was becoming increasingly important, insurance companies with wide geographical cover and influence stood to win extensive business at the expense of more limited competitors.

As the yields of home and colonial government stocks fell during the late nineteenth century, therefore, foreign government stocks presented a natural refuge for some part of the funds of the major companies—even though it was only after considerable prompting and with deep misgivings that they condescended to take up the bonds of Latin American states. However, in two other ways insurance companies more willingly directed their funds towards Latin America. First, they moved a large portion of their funds into debentures and shares. Together these had accounted for 13 per cent of the total investments of the U.K. Life offices in

---

[1] Supple, *Royal Exchange*, p. 331.   [2] Ibid., p. 334 (Table 13.6).

1870, but by 1913 this figure had risen to 31·1 per cent.[1] Most of this investment was certainly in British companies doing business in Britain, but some Anglo-Argentine companies made their appearance in the portfolios of the insurance firms from the end of the nineteenth century. As early as 1903, the Refuge Assurance Company had acquired a small block of shares in the River Plate Electricity Company.[2] The 1888 list of shareholders of the Mortgage Company of the River Plate includes no insurance companies. By 1913, however, six companies held 2,548 preference shares, about 5 per cent of the total paid-up capital.[3]

Of course, it is arguable whether such investments were to the long-term advantage of Latin America (or of the insurance companies), and they can have accounted for only a very small fraction of the portfolio of any one company, or of the total British investment in Latin America. Of more significance was the move pioneered by the Scottish life insurance offices into foreign mortgages. The Scottish Widows' Fund led the way, placing large amounts in Australian mortgages during the pastoral boom of the 1880s.[4] When Australia turned sour in the mid-1890s, the Fund followed the example set by a number of the Australasian mortgage companies, transferring much of this money to the River Plate.[5] A mortgage rate of 10 per cent (1895) could hardly fail to attract funds, and by the turn of the century every English firm of any importance was engaged in some way or another in mortgage business, not only for ordinary clients but on behalf of the large insurance companies.[6] Even when the rate dropped to 7 per cent in 1905 in response to the vast inflow of funds, Argentine mortgages were still a worthwhile investment for the British offices, whose average portfolio yield was by this time not much in excess of 3·5 per cent.[7]

It is impossible to give precise figures for aggregate investment by British insurance companies in Latin America, since the available statistics group investments by type, and not by country. What is clear is that before 1895 such investment was minimal, and that it was only with reluctance, and under the pressure of

[1] Supple, *Royal Exchange*, p. 333 (Table 13.4).
[2] P.R.O. B.T.31/15640/48662.
[3] Companies House, 26562.   [4] Supple, *Royal Exchange*, p. 344.
[5] Trust and Agency Company of Australasia, Ltd., *Centenary, 1860–1960* (privately printed for the company, London, 1960), p. 3.
[6] Mandatos C.B.P., 18 Oct. 1901.   [7] Supple, *Royal Exchange*, p. 331.

falling yields from traditional investments, of Latin American legislation, and of depression in Australia, that the British invested anything at all. Furthermore, however much one may sympathize with the moral claims put forward by Latin American politicians for an investment proportionate to the premiums earned in their territories by foreign companies, it must be admitted that subsequent events fully justified the initial reluctance of the British to put their funds at risk. Latin American stocks did not justify the optimistic forecasts of the 1880s and 1900s; on the contrary, they gave a poor long-term return to the investor.

V

British insurance in Latin America bore many of the features commonly associated with economic imperialism and control. British companies worked in concert, on a more or less national basis, to fix prices and limit the growth of local competitors. They also fought tooth and nail against legislation which threatened their profits, employing every legitimate means open to pressure groups, and some which were not legitimate. Furthermore, the investment policies of the London head offices markedly favoured British and colonial investments even in the face of falling yields, though more through conservatism than any overt spirit of nationalism. But what is striking about the British experience in Latin America is neither the aggressive intent of the British, nor the nationalistic role of Latin American companies and governments; rather it is the way in which both sides were constrained by the market. The British local boards were continually obliged to give way to non-tariff companies and insurance brokers over rates and regulations, even before the legislative assault upon them gave their local competitors an artificial advantage. The local agents fought valiantly against the terms of deposit laws in spite of the fact that foreign investment was fast becoming as necessary to the insurance companies as it was desirable to Latin Americans. In each case, extra-market activities tended to harmonize with market trends rather than cut across them, and both parties were conscious of this. Thus, the Queen Insurance Company noted in 1899:

Experience had proved that the non-tariff companies, and especially the local companies, were much too strong to be crushed by any boycotting policy that could be adopted . . . [and that] almost the whole strength of the movement in favour of harassing legislation came from the fact that the boycotting policy was considered an act of hostility to Chilean companies in their own country.[1]

On the government side, too, Latin Americans seem to have been aware of the marginal character of the Latin American market in the eyes of the British, and on many occasions tempered the enthusiasm of more enthusiastic and less informed lower Chambers by responding to the pleas and petitions of the foreigners, aiming always to leave them with just sufficient incentive to remain in business. Each side made some losses and gains against the trend of the market; the insurance companies managed to retard the inclination towards lower rates and sometimes delayed or prevented the passage of legislation; the Latin Americans occasionally forced the companies to invest before they were ready to do so, and on terms which they did not much care for. Yet each side acted within market limitations which were ultimately beyond their control. Business imperialism and economic nationalism both contributed to the process as recognizable and even considerable forces, but the protagonists of neither creed had yet developed the ideology, the power, or the techniques to subvert the prevailing condition of capitalism to any serious extent.

[1] Phoenix Valparaíso, 22 Feb. 1899.

PART II

PUBLIC UTILITIES
AND TRANSPORT

CHAPTER III

Public Utility Companies

LINDA AND CHARLES JONES
AND ROBERT GREENHILL*

I

DURING the second half of the nineteenth century the increasing production for export in Latin America was accompanied by a rapid process of urbanization, particularly in the major ports of shipment. Travellers exclaimed at the pace of building in Buenos Aires,[1] Montevideo, São Paulo,[2] and other commercial centres, marvelling at the fortunes made and lost by speculation in urban construction. Such developments were generally seen as vigorous indications of the pervasive spirit of progress. But observers could hardly fail to notice that the congested cities were still reliant on public services appropriate to villages a fraction of their size. Thus Scobie describes Buenos Aires: 'Enough sewage also found its way into the streets and into the ground to contribute to the cholera and yellow fever plagues that decimated the *porteño* populace and emptied the city during several summers in the late 1860s and early 1870s.'[3] Similarly, a British clerk, Robert Thurburn, recently arrived in the River Plate, reported the disastrous effects of the yellow fever epidemic in Buenos Aires during 1871. The port was closed to ships, which left the telegraph as the only communication with the outside world, business houses remained shut and the government was forced to declare a public holiday. 'The only way to prevent the city being visited again', he declared, 'would be to burn it down.'[4]

Clearly, on both social and economic grounds improved public

---

* Dr. and Mrs. Jones are responsible for the Rosario case study and Dr. Greenhill for the Chilean.
[1] For a description of the conditions in and the growth of Buenos Aires see J. R. Scobie, *Buenos Aires, Plaza to Suburb, 1870–1910* (New York, 1974).
[2] For example, Richard Morse, 'São Paulo in the Nineteenth Century: Economic Roots of the Metropolis', *Inter-American Economic Affairs*, v (1951).
[3] J. R. Scobie, *Argentina: A City and a Nation* (New York, 1964), p. 163.
[4] B.O.L.S.A. D.111, R. A. Thurburn to J. Thurburn, 15 Apr. 1871.

services could confer substantial advantages. Unless conditions improved, trade normally handled by Buenos Aires would pass instead to Montevideo which would threaten the standing of the smaller merchants in the Argentine capital.[1] Efficient water supply, in particular, had further significance for the businessman and for the local inhabitants in fire-fighting. William Wheelwright, when constructing the Valparaíso waterworks, responded to the request of local British merchants that he should build into his system an efficient fire-fighting capacity, on the completion of which one London insurance company offered to halve its Valparaíso fire premiums.[2] Similarly, street-lighting, whether by gas or electricity, meant a higher level of security against criminal attack on person and property and would, perhaps, reduce the alarming rise in accidents. Tramways would improve the state of urban transport to the benefit of employer and shopkeeper alike. In the Latin American city a case existed for a marriage between philanthropy and enlightened self-interest, which so often characterized nineteenth-century commercial liberalism.

Local participation in the provision of improved public utility services was not, however, always forthcoming. Some domestic Latin American interests would undoubtedly benefit from such enterprise. Local bureaucrats, government officials, lawyers, other professional groups, and native businessmen large and small stood to gain substantially from capital invested in urban real estate which would appreciate considerably with an improved infrastructure. But the political masters of Latin America, resident on estates well outside the congested urban areas, were less immediately interested. As producers of export commodities they could avoid the unpleasant consequences of epidemics in the ports of shipment by consigning to merchants elsewhere and, unlike urban interests, did not benefit to any great extent from the cost reductions which improved services might bring. A landowner investing, say, in a waterworks might with luck receive a six or seven per cent dividend, but a local merchant investing in the same project would obtain his dividend, plus a rebate on his insurance premiums and the business which he normally lost when periodic epidemics brought trade to a halt.

[1] B.O.L.S.A. D. 111, R. A. Thurburn to J. Thurburn, 1 May 1871.
[2] Jay Kinsbruner, 'Water for Valparaíso: A Case of Entrepreneurial Frustration', *Journal of Inter-American Studies*, x, part 4 (Oct. 1968), 654.

It is also doubtful whether those local enthusiasts in favour of promoting public utilities could have alone raised sufficient funds for such undertakings. In many cases native capitalists, who preferred more immediate returns, were unable or unwilling to shoulder the burdens of developing projects which were necessarily capital-intensive enterprises of long gestation. On the other hand, funds were readily available in North America and Europe. If foreigners, sometimes expatriate businessmen in Latin America who stood to gain considerably from public services, could mobilize outside *rentier* capital for concessions to build the waterworks, lay the drains, and pave the streets, was it not perfectly rational for Latin Americans to let them go ahead? Again, even when native interests did pioneer public utility enterprises why should they refuse an attractive offer from overseas investors? Promoters and capitalists abroad willingly purchased locally based concerns which had overcome their teething troubles but which required further improvement and expansion, or unworked concessions in towns which held a promising future. A new company incorporating the concession or native firm would be floated abroad at a higher capitalization both to develop the enterprise and to satisfy the promoters.

But it was not, of course, merely the foreigner's access to funds and his willingness to lend that accounted for the increasing overseas participation in Latin America's utilities. Urban improvement in both North America and Europe, largely preceding similar Latin American developments, had accustomed investors to public utility companies and, despite inevitable vicissitudes, demonstrated that such undertakings could be profitable. Moreover, utilities largely exploited technical innovations pioneered in Europe and North America where a generation of engineers and technical experts now more fully understood the problems of designing and constructing public services, and enjoyed easier access to patents.

Furthermore, the construction of public utilities in Latin America was closely associated with the work of foreign contractors and concessionaires like William Wheelwright in Argentina[1] and on the West Coast, and Francisco Cisneros in Colombia,[2]

[1] Colin M. Lewis, 'The Problems of Railway Development in Argentina, 1857–1890', *Inter-American Economic Affairs*, xxii (1968), part 2, pp. 55–75.
[2] Hernán Horna, 'Railroads and the Development of Nineteenth Century Colombia: the Role of Francisco J. Cisneros', a paper read to the American Historical Association in 1972.

who built major railways and port works from the mid-nineteenth century when the accelerating pace of development provided lucrative opportunities. While the price of failure was high, since the work of concessionaires has an almost unique public prominence and enjoys considerable attention from officials and the press, one contract, gained competitively and completed successfully, generally led to others. Thus in Mexico the close relationship of S. Pearson & Sons with the Díaz Government and the company's considerable prestige,[1] both of which stemmed from the successful draining of the Valley of Mexico and the reconstruction of the Tehuantepec Railroad,[2] brought further contracts, while from the accumulation of work emerged economies of scale which anyway permitted Pearsons to undercut rival tenders. Many of Pearsons' subsequent contracts involved electrical installations, at the terminal harbours of the Tehuantepec Railroad (Coatzacoalcos and Salina Cruz) and at Orizaba where Pearsons built a power station for a local jute mill.[3] Thus, by the 1920s Pearsons supplied electricity to four major Mexican cities, Puebla, Vera Cruz, Orizaba, Córdoba, and their surrounding districts from a power station at Tuxpango, and to Tampico where three local concerns were amalgamated. Although the scale of these enterprises remained local and small[4] they provided an essential background to the firm's decision to undertake electricity supply and tramway services in Chile, the subject of the second case study in this chapter.

In principle, then, there was nothing, not even in the last resort lack of capital, to stop Latin Americans from developing their own public utility concerns. After all, some local initiative showed what might be achieved, capital could always be acquired at a price, and the technical obstacles were not insurmountable. But in practice, native interests preferred to allow the foreigner to develop the public services. Private interests in Latin America had more

[1] See J. A. Spender, *Weetman Pearson: First Viscount Cowdray 1856–1927* (1930), and R. K. Middlemass, *The Master Builders* (1963).

[2] Edward B. Glick, 'The Tehuantepec Railroad: Mexico's White Elephant', *Pacific Historical Review*, xxii (1953), 373–82.

[3] *E.R.*, 9 Feb. 1906, 214, and 2 Oct. 1925, 531; *The Times* (Engineering Supplement), Sept. 1921, 268.

[4] For details of these enterprises see Pearson, B1–4; *Manual of Electrical Undertakings*, xxiv (1920–1), 789; *E.T.*, 27 Dec. 1917, p. 462. By 1922 Pearsons' Mexican holdings represented just 166 miles of tramway, and the electricity supply reached only 40,000 consumers.

immediately rewarding investments, especially in real estate. Municipal authorities did not yet seem enthusiastic to follow the lead set, for example, by Birmingham which municipalized its gas supplies in 1873. Local government had no well-developed revenue system able to cope with the considerable initial costs and running expenses, nor a sufficiently responsible bureaucracy.

Foreign investment in Latin America's public utilities, whether provided through expatriate businessmen based in the republics, *rentiers* from Europe and North America, glib-tongued promoters, or concessionaires and constructors whose chief interests were in much larger projects, thus proceeded apace from the mid nineteenth century. Britain's involvement was considerable from the first even in the electricity supply companies, as well as in the gas and water concerns where she was traditionally strong. Restrictive legislation and Britain's sources of cheap power—coal supplied both steam and gas—limited her role in the world's electrical industry before the First World War. By 1913 Britain's output of electrical goods was little more than a third of Germany's and her firms could not compete with such giants as the Siemens group, A.E.G., or Westinghouse,[1] which encouraged the development of electricity supplied abroad to widen their markets. Much of Britain's industry was developed by foreigners; it was mainly American capital, for example, that electrified London's underground system in 1905.[2] Nevertheless, according to Professor Rippy's tentative figures British investment had, by 1900, established fifty public utility enterprises of which fourteen were electricity companies. By 1913, he continues, British capital was interested in eighty electrical concerns, and by 1926, the peak year, over a hundred.[3]

Irving Stone's figures for British investment in public utilities (Table III.1) confirm the impression of a far from negligible British interest in electrical utilities. During the period before

[1] *Report of the Departmental Committee on the Position of the Electrical Trades after the War*, P.P. 1918, xiii, 355–68; I. C. R. Byatt, 'Electrical Products' in D. H. Aldcroft (ed.), *The Development of British Industry and Foreign Competition 1875–1914* (London, 1968).

[2] John K. Dunning, 'The Growth of U.S. Investment in U.K. Manufacturing Industry 1856–1940', *Manchester School of Economic and Social Studies*, xxiv (1956), 249.

[3] J. Fred Rippy, 'British Investments in Latin American Electrical Utilities', *Hispanic–American Historical Review*, xxxiv (1954), 251–5; id., *British Investment in Latin America, 1822–1949* (Minneapolis, 1959), pp. 33–45 and 242–5.

1895, utilities as a whole never accounted for more than 5 per cent of the total British investment in Latin America. By 1913 a substantial growth in electricity supply and in tramways (mostly powered by electricity) had raised the share of utilities to 11·8 per cent of the British portfolio.

TABLE III.1

British Investment in Latin American Public Utilities, 1865–1913[a]

(£000)

	1865	1875	1885	1895	1905	1913
Canals and docks		116	201	457	1,760	15,036
Electrical					1,207	24,915
Gas	848	1,919	2,443	2,250	5,003	7,166
Telegraph and telephone		5,380	5,614	7,699	7,199	9,953
Tramways and omnibuses		991	1,539	5,383	23,243	79,185
Waterworks			703	2,012	1,823	2,837
(a) Total public utilities	848	8,406	10,500	17,801	40,235	139,092
(b) Total British investment in Latin America	80,869	174,611	246,620	552,505	688,268	1,177,462
(c) (a) as percentage of (b)	1·05	4·8	4·3	3·2	5·8	11·8

[a] These figures are formed by adding paid-up share capital to outstanding loan capital and are therefore rather more reliable than the figures based on nominal capital given by J. Fred Rippy, *British Investments in Latin America, 1822–1949* (1959), pp. 33–45. One slight drawback is the omission of drainage companies, generally classified in *Burdett's Official Intelligence* under the heading 'Commercial and Industrial'.

SOURCE: Irving Stone, 'British Long-Term Investment in Latin America, 1865–1913', *Business History Review*, xlii (1968), 323.

As early as 1844 the first gas company was established in Havana and by the 1860s gas was in common use in limited areas of the major cities—Rio de Janeiro, São Paulo, Buenos Aires, Santiago, and Caracas.[1] William Wheelwright's Valparaíso water supply scheme was under way by 1851. From the 1880s telephones and electricity brought a new surge in the establishment of utilities although, again, their immediate impact was not wide. The River Plate Telephone and Electric Light Company was formed in 1882; the rival Argentine company set up by the English-born Cassels brothers became, in 1889, the British-registered River Plate Electricity Company. By 1890 fifteen telephone companies were operating in Latin America.[2] Traditional enterprise in water

[1] J. Fred Rippy, 'Notes on Early British Gas Companies in Latin America', *Hispanic–American Historical Review*, xxx (1950), 111–14.

[2] Id., 'Notes on Early Telephone Companies of Latin America', ibid. xxvi (1946), 116–18.

supply and drainage also continued. The 1870s saw the construction of a technically daunting system of water supply for Montevideo by local and Argentine capitalists supported by the (British)
Mercantile Bank of the River Plate, although the whole enterprise
soon passed into the hands of a British company, the Montevideo
Waterworks Co. Ltd.

The two case studies of British utility companies in Latin
America in this chapter cannot, of course, do justice to the wide
variety of experience within the republics' very different economic,
political, social, and institutional environments. But these two
examples do demonstrate clearly many of the severe limitations—
financial and legal—on the day-to-day operation of foreign-owned
utilities. Capital invested in plant and buildings and subject to
a long period of gestation could not be easily withdrawn, and was
often at the mercy of notoriously fickle municipal authorities and
a leisurely legal process. While Latin America apparently offered
excellent prospects for foreign-owned public utility companies,
the two cases examined here seemed to have turned out rather
less fortunately. But these studies may not indicate the extent
to which some businessmen, often the original promoters who
enjoyed a wide range of interlocking commercial and financial
interests in Latin America, benefited from the existence of improved services at the expense, perhaps, of both local consumers and
British investors.

The advantages derived by individuals from public utility
services constitute a factor not lightly dismissed, but this chapter
examines other important issues, namely the operating methods
of British companies and the consequences for the host countries.
Were local resources unduly monopolized by foreign capitalists?
Were consumers in Latin America exploited? What were the
points of friction in the relationship between expatriate utility
companies and local interests? What was the extent and the limit
of the powers which foreign companies exercised in supplying
public services?

II

John Morris's Rosario Public Utilities, 1882–1914

The business empire which John Morris built for himself in the
River Plate between 1880 and 1895 was modest by post-1914
standards. At the centre, the River Plate Trust, Loan and

Agency Company—usually known simply as the Trust Company
—co-ordinated the activities of the member companies both in
London and South America. Control, which was never absolute, was
exercised by several means. Morris and his colleagues on the Board
of the Trust Company also sat on the boards of other companies
in the group, so that by 1895 the seven directors of the Trust
Company between them held a total of forty-nine River Plate
directorships in twenty-seven companies.[1] Ashurst, Morris,
Crisp, the firm of company solicitors in which Morris was senior
partner, acted for most of these companies.[2] The River Plate and
General Investment Trust (1888), the Mortgage Company of the
River Plate (1888), and the Trust Company itself held blocks of
shares (sometimes quite small) in many of the companies, as did
members of the Trust Company board.[3] From time to time, new
issues of shares and debentures for group members were handled
by the Trust Company. And in Argentina and Uruguay the local
manager of the Trust Company, Francis H. Chevallier Boutell,
was available to act as agent in dealings with the local authorities
and as management consultant, advising the London boards of
the strengths and weaknesses of their staff and organization in the
field.

At the heart of this group of companies were a number of public
utilities.[4] All but the smallest railway companies had sufficient
resources to manage their own affairs more or less unassisted; the
geographical isolation of land and *estancia* companies necessitated
self-reliance; but public utility companies, less highly capitalized
than the railways and situated in the major urban centres, were
well placed to take advantage of the services of Chevallier Boutell
and his colleagues.

Loose and immature though it was, the structure of the Morris
group might have been expected to place the public utility com-

---

[1] *Directory of Directors* (London, 1895).

[2] *Burdett's Official Intelligence* (London, 1895).

[3] For example, in December 1889 Morris and his family (including the
Puleston family—connected to Morris by marriage) between them held 2,083
1st Preference and 4,166 Ordinary shares in the Rosario Waterworks (New) Co.
Ltd. The Trust Company held 1,000 1st Preference: P.R.O. B.T., 29508/4516.

[4] In 1895, of the seven directors of the Trust Company, four sat on the board
of the Buenos Aires and Belgrano Tramway Company, one on the board of the
Rosario City Improvements Company, three on the board of the Rosario
Waterworks, and four on the board of the Montevideo Water Works Company:
Directory of Directors (1895).

panies within it at an advantage compared with similar companies elsewhere in South America. In an era when it was still considered possible for an Anglo-Latin American utility company supplying a single service to a single city to operate successfully without even the minimal economies of scale achieved by the Morris organization, why should not his utilities have done as well as any, and better than most? Some, of course, did prosper, but the Rosario enterprises failed signally, at least for the first twenty years of their existence. The Rosario Waterworks Company (1883) and the Rosario Drainage Company (1887) went through a series of enforced reconstructions during the 1890s, emerging as the Consolidated Waterworks of Rosario and the Rosario City Improvements Company, and during these years they failed to pay any dividends to their ordinary shareholders and were sometimes unable even to service their debentures.

The reason for this failure in Rosario is easily stated. Constant municipal obstruction made efficient operation at best difficult and often impossible. But to understand the rationale of this policy of obstruction it is necessary to go back almost thirty years before the establishment of the British utility companies to the time when Argentina was divided into two independent and hostile states— the Province of Buenos Aires and the Argentine Confederation. During the 1850s Rosario had enjoyed a period of considerable prosperity. As the chief port and commercial centre of the Confederation, it had been the site of the Banco Nacional de la Confederación.[1] Foreign shipping, deterred from sailing up-river to Rosario before 1852 by the Buenos Aires authorities, was encouraged to do so between 1856 and 1859 by the differential import duties sanctioned by the National Congress. Even more important, however, was the growth of Rosario as an outlet for the produce of the confederate provinces, which had previously been shipped from Buenos Aires.[2]

Expansion continued during the 1860s in spite of the reunification of Argentina and the renewal of the differential duties. Spanish-born capitalist Aaron Castellanos raised funds locally to dredge a deep-water channel in the Paraná river and make a dock at Rosario; the great Brazilian financier Baron Mauá opened a

---

[1] Julio Martinez, *Origen de los bancos en Rosario: el Banco Mauá y cía— contribución al estudio de su historia* (Rosario, 1942).
[2] T. J. Hutchinson, *Buenos Aires and Argentine Gleanings* (1865), p. 71.

branch of his bank and introduced gas lighting; a stock exchange was established under the presidency of Francis Weldon, manager of the local branch of the London and River Plate Bank;[1] and several local land owners set up colonization schemes to develop the agricultural production of the hinterland.[2]

In short, Rosario in the 1850s and 1860s was a rapidly growing centre of production and distribution with a cosmopolitan outlook. British, French, and Brazilian capital supplemented, but did not yet overwhelm, local and immigrant enterprise. It was a city of great expectations—both economic and political. For Rosario, flushed by its experience under the Confederation, aspired to replace Buenos Aires as the capital of the Republic. The provincial legislature went so far as to offer Rosario to the nation. The offer was refused, but the campaign in its support spawned a newspaper, *La Capital*, which continued for many years to print a strong line in localism—a sort of Santa Fé nationalism.[3]

Nationalism is not too strong a word, for the municipal pride of the people of Rosario was accompanied by one of the classic accoutrements of nationalism—a fierce xenophobia directed not only against Europeans, but also against the political control exerted by the magnates of Buenos Aires province. Always latent, this xenophobia was exacerbated by the economic setbacks of the mid 1870s and the early 1890s. These crises, which were felt throughout the Republic, were especially severe in Rosario. That of the 1870s followed immediately upon the cessation of the war against Paraguay, during which Rosario had profited from the supply of provisions to the armies of the Triple Alliance. Both this and the later crisis must be seen, in Rosario, against a background of relative decline in comparison with Buenos Aires. The secular tendency of the Rosario economy remained—to 1914 and beyond— one of rapid growth, but its relative importance as a port was

---

[1] B.O.L.S.A., London and River Plate Bank, D.94, Head Office to Weldon, 23 Apr. 1869.
[2] Camilo Aldao, who stood for election as Governor of Santa Fé in 1868, founded six colonies. His victorious rival, Mariano Cabal, was responsible for two.
[3] D. A. de Santillán, *Gran Enciclopedia Argentina* (Buenos Aires, 1956–63), articles on *La Capital* and its editor, Ovidio Lagos. Later, after the failure of the campaign to make Rosario the national capital, local politicians continued to press for the diminished honour of replacing Santa Fé City as the provincial capital. See Mandatos R.W., Martin's Annual Reports for 1904 and 1908, 22 Feb. 1905 and 15 Feb. 1909.

undermined by the development of improved facilities at Buenos Aires which led many importing firms to withdraw from Rosario altogether in favour of the capital.[1]

This, then, was the lion's den into which Morris and his colleagues stepped during the 1880s. It is probable that no foreign company, however blameless, could have avoided becoming embroiled in the elaborate political game which followed, since the reasons given for obstruction were generally no more than pretexts, and the real aim of the succession of local politicians who opposed the foreigner was to tap the xenophobia of those sections of the population which were in the process of incorporation into the effective body politic: the urban middle classes, the sons of immigrants, and, not least, the companies' own employees. All the same, the Morris companies laid themselves open to persecution from the very beginning by the manner of their entry into Rosario.

When the drainage concession was put on offer in 1887, Morris and his colleagues were already interested in the Rosario Waterworks Company. The advantages of running both water and drainage services were obvious, but it was also evident that—in accord with local custom—bribery would have to be employed to gain the concession. So, on signing the contract for the construction of the works, sweeteners were distributed to the municipal council by prior arrangement at a cost to the new company of just over $200,000.[2] Had they not turned out their pockets, it is more than likely that the Morris faction would have seen the business pass elsewhere. But by doing so they provided a pretext for criticism, and this was not long in coming.

In 1890 Rosario was plunged into economic crisis and power changed hands. The relatively anglophile faction of the late 1880s was replaced by more nationalist politicians. By these men, who were to remain a powerful force in local politics, the drainage works and other foreign-owned public utilities were presented as a visible expression of the foreign capital which, in their view,

---

[1] Ezequiel Gallo, 'El gobierno de Santa Fé vs. el Banco de Londres y Río de la Plata, 1876', *Instituto Torcuato di Tella, Centro de Investigaciones Sociales*, working paper (Buenos Aires, 1972). Gallo points out that during the 1860s and 1870s many of the leading politicians of Santa Fé—men like Mariano Cabal and Camilo Aldao—were import–export merchants as well as large land-owners. This was generally not the case in Buenos Aires, where the merchants were mostly foreigners, and helps to account for the immediacy with which economic depression in Santa Fé was translated into political action.

[2] Mandatos C.B.P., Boutell to Morris, 7 Jan. 1888, pp. 21–2.

had been largely responsible for the downfall of the local economy. Equally, the atmosphere of corruption surrounding the granting of the drainage concession provided a symbol of the alleged moral corruption of the outgoing administration.

In October 1890, *La Capital* moved into attack against the Water Company. The management themselves admitted that the quality of their product could have borne improvement, but they were quite taken aback by *La Capital's* claim that 'on repeated occasions the water supplied to consumers had been bad, unhealthy, and unhygienic . . . [containing] bodies of human beings and animals in the most complete state of putrefaction'.[1] To make matters worse, the last section of the drainage works, just completed, was refused approval by the new municipal authorities on the grounds that it had been constructed with inferior materials in breach of the contract of 1887.[2]

To any company finding itself in this situation there were three courses open. Appeal could be made to the British Foreign Office, which recognized its obligation to protect the interests of British subjects and companies abroad. Alternatively, help might be sought from higher authorities within the host country—pitting the national government against a provincial government or municipality. Last, the company could try to fight the local authorities on their own ground and with their own weapons.

As for the first option, the Rosario affair of 1876 had shown the limitations of forceful British Government action.[3] Santa Fé had shrugged off the attentions of the British navy. Moreover, financial pressure was effectively ruled out during the 1890s. The city and the province were in default on their debts, and any threat to withhold further credit would have been empty. Support from national authorities had also been found wanting in the 1876 incident, and there was no reason to believe that the *Santafecinos* would be any more likely to respond to pressure from above in the 1890s than they had been in the 1870s. Nor, indeed, was there any obvious advantage to be gained at this time by Argentine national politicians in openly supporting the British; rather the reverse. It was, therefore, up to the Water and Drainage Companies to

---

[1] *La Capital*, 25 Oct. 1890.
[2] Mandatos R.C.I., Hamilton to Boutell, 20 Dec. 1890.
[3] There are several accounts of the Rosario incident of 1876. The most recent and comprehensive is Ezequiel Gallo, op. cit.

defend themselves against their adversaries within the local arena by adopting local customs and conventions.

J. Farquhar MacDonald, the manager of the Drainage Company, being on the spot in Rosario and in constant touch with the undercurrents of opinion there, understood the real nature of the problem better than his superiors in London could hope to do. In his report for 1890 he blamed the failure of the company to secure acceptance of the last section of the works on

the insensate personalism of the Press, and of a small but powerful minority of political enthusiasts, who carry their hatred of the deposed municipality to such unjustifiable limits by making war on concessions granted in their regnum . . . Rightly or wrongly, a feeling inimical to the residence in Europe of the head offices of these companies whose capital is invested here, is making ground, [and] the means of acquiring concessions usually employed here have given ground for this, also the persistent want of consideration for the very customers by whom [the] said companies make their often very large profits.[1]

MacDonald's advice to his board of directors was that steps be taken to earn the esteem of the townsfolk, especially by admitting the inequitable nature of the rating system set up under the original water concession, and that this course of action should be adopted even if it entailed the surrender of some of the companies' strict rights.[2] MacDonald argued that water consumers had been overrated by the Company throughout the mid 1880s. 'In prosperous times this made little matter', he remarked, 'but all the same a feeling of ill-will was growing, and for three years past it has found vent in the newspapers, and in resistance to the Water and Drainage Companies.'[3]

MacDonald's political instinct was accurate. The character of local politics was beginning to change, personally based alliances between oligarchic factions giving way to a system in which politicians were to depend increasingly for office on their support among a limited but growing section of the public. Hence the central importance of the rates charged for public services—rates which bore on just that section of urban property owners whose support was now being seriously courted for the first time. He

---

[1] Mandatos R.C.I., MacDonald's Report for the six months ending 31 Dec. 1890.   [2] Ibid.

[3] Mandatos R.P.T.L.A., Letters to José Toso, vol. i, MacDonald to Toso, 24 Dec. 1892, p. 2.

recognized that the dispute over the standards of workmanship on the last section of the drainage works was a trumped-up affair and not one to be settled by engineers' inspections and reports. It would last just so long as public opinion remained opposed to the British companies, and could be resolved only by winning back public favour. MacDonald pointed out that

> Former intendants did all they could to get as much benefit for themselves individually as was possible out of the foreign companies established here, while the present one tries to get as much for the public as he can, irrespective of the justice of his demands or requirements so long as he himself becomes popular. In either case, the companies pay.[1]

There was a further argument in favour of making concessions. Once the Water and Drainage Companies had been publicly identified as 'enemies of the people', it became extremely difficult, even on those occasions when municipal power fell into the hands of elements sympathetic to the British, for any municipal council to come to an agreement with the companies without seeming to sell out to the foreigners. If they were not to place their opponents at a distinct advantage *vis-à-vis* the electorate, such men had to seem to have wrung substantial concessions out of the companies in exchange for any points on which they themselves yielded.[2]

However, realism at management level was generally met with obduracy at board level: an obduracy which seemed reasonable enough, and indeed necessary, to the directors in view of the serious financial predicament of the companies—a factor which MacDonald may not have fully appreciated. By 1891, the Drainage Company had already had to default on the service of its debentures and was in the hands of a receiver—albeit a friendly one in the person of James Anderson, Morris's principal *aide* in London. Furthermore, the Baring crisis of 1890 had quite destroyed the confidence of British investors in River Plate ventures. All in all, London could not see their way to making any concessions whatsoever in exchange for what they considered to be their existing rights. 'Head office seem satisfied that when it is in the concession, or when it is our indisputable right, all is well', MacDonald complained; 'the purely ethical ground taken by

---

[1] Mandatos R.C.I., MacDonald to Boutell, 6 July 1891, pp. 1–3.
[2] Ibid., Hamilton to Boutell, 17 Jan. 1891, p. 3.

Mr. Morris is undeniably just, but this fact does not weigh one iota with the Municipality and the Rosario public.'[1]

By 1891, political constraints on the Rosario politicians and financial constraints on the Morris companies had brought about a stand-off in which no agreement could be reached which did not threaten the base of support of one or other of the interested parties. Only a sustained burst of prosperity or a radical change in political circumstances could break the stalemate, and in the presence of neither, the struggle went on.

For Morris and his associates, the 1890s were a period of adaptation to the changing political environment of Rosario. They soon realized that they could survive only by the diligent exercise of tact and diplomacy. Even if, as seems likely, Chevallier Boutell and his friends were not guilty of attempting to secure the defeat of the Radical Party candidates in the 1891 municipal elections, the attacks made upon them at that time in *La Unión Cívica*, the Radical Party journal, must be considered justified,[2] since the Trust Company had bribed municipal officials on at least five occasions over the previous four years.[3] It may be said that Boutell was slow to learn that the old understanding, whereby bribery was more or less accepted, was coming to an end, and that it had never really been intended to extend to foreigners anyway. Nevertheless, he did eventually learn his lesson, and in future much greater care was taken to cover the tracks of money paid by the Trust Company on behalf of its clients.[4]

Boutell concentrated on the elimination of friction. Weak and inefficient early managers were weeded out. Fairlie Bruce, for example, had been in the habit of calling on the *intendente* on official business dressed in an old coat and gum-boots and accompanied by a large and boisterous dog. The *intendente* was a stickler

[1] Ibid., MacDonald to Boutell, 6 July 1891.

[2] *La Unión Cívica*, 27 May 1891.

[3] Mandatos C.B.P., 7 Jan. 1888, pp. 21–2; 8 Dec. 1889, p. 3; Mandatos R.P.T.L.A., Letters to José Toso, vol. i, Anderson to Toso, 2 Oct. 1891 and 28 Oct. 1891; Nield to Boutell, 12 Sept. 1888; and Morris to Boutell, 17 Apr. 1889 and 19 Apr. 1889, all bear on the Trust Company's policy towards bribery.

[4] Already, in his letter of 17 Apr. 1889 to Boutell, Morris had stressed the need for the Trust Company to avoid association 'with any transaction which might involve any possible irregularities'. But this often meant little more than that Boutell and Toso would leave the room whilst the payments were being made, as happened with the drainage concession. Later, such payments were usually made through an Argentine intermediary having no permanent or public association with the Morris group.

for good manners, so Bruce was dismissed. A team of able managers and advisers was formed. W. J. Martin was brought from the Paraná Water Works (another Morris company) to manage both the Drainage and Water Companies on the spot in Rosario; Boutell watched over the affairs of these and other companies from Buenos Aires; José Toso, a former Buenos Aires provincial Minister of Finance valued for his contacts amongst the ruling élite, acted as a general trouble-shooter; and the team was completed by expert lawyers like Pedro Arias, a schoolfriend and close associate of ex-President Julio Roca.

Tact was equally necessary in London, where the Trust Company with its staff of lawyers and accountants was able to engineer the dismal capital reconstructions and debenture issues made necessary by the continued hostility of the municipality with the least possible disturbance. Morris himself, a master at handling annual general meetings, was able—most of the time—to retain the support of the shareholders and debenture-holders in spite of the failure of dividends, and to bolster up their faith in the ultimate success of the Rosario enterprises.

The achievement of the Water and Drainage Companies during the 1890s was a minimal one: they survived. But after 1900 came indications of improved prospects. There were signs that the troubles with the municipality might be coming to an end. The stabilization of the Argentine peso against sterling in 1899 simplified the rates question, eliminating some of the bitterness of former years and making it easier for the companies to forecast their revenue and to plan expenditure. At the end of the same year the drainage works were at last accepted by the council on the understanding that certain modifications and improvements detailed in the so-called Huergo contract should be carried out.[1] In his report for the year ending 30 June 1904, Martin was able to inform the board that the general prosperity of the community seemed to have reduced tension between the municipality and the local utility companies.[2] The municipality even showed signs of a willingness to compromise on the long-standing issue of the validity of the Water Company's concession.[3]

It was a false spring. The lawsuit over the Water Company's

---

[1] Mandatos R.C.I., Martin to Proctor, 16 July 1909.
[2] Mandatos R.W., pp. 8–9.
[3] Ibid., Martin to Anderson, 26 Dec. 1904.

concession dragged on, and in April 1905 it was rumoured that the municipality, should they lose the case, planned to permit a local syndicate to set up in competition against the British.[1] In the meantime, the municipal lawyer had been preparing a case against the Drainage Company claiming that its concession was invalidated through non-fulfilment of the Huergo contract of 1899.[2] Rumours of expropriation were rife, and in May 1907, Luis Lamas—formerly *intendente* in Rosario and now a national deputy—brought in a bill to the National Congress for the expropriation of the drainage works.[3] This came to nothing, but was soon followed by an attack from Lisandro de la Torre's *Liga del Sur*—a local political group dedicated to ending the system whereby the taxes of prosperous Rosario passed into the hands of a small clique of landowner politicians from the smaller and less wealthy provincial capital of Santa Fé. They also included in their programme the nationalization of the Rosario public utilities.[4] On top of all this, although the suit against the Water Company for nullity of contract was finally settled in favour of the Company in 1905,[5] the municipality refused to accept this verdict, and their appeal dragged on for another decade.[6]

The water and drainage works of Rosario remained in British hands until the Second World War. The bickering continued in much the same vein as it had done up to 1914.[7] All the same, the later period—say from 1900 onwards—was distinguished from the earlier years by one vital factor. Both companies started to make profits—small at first, but later quite steady. Indeed, had they not, the companies could scarcely have continued to exist. If the British managers and directors acquired certain skills necessary in dealing with the municipal authorities, so too the municipality learned how to make political capital from the presence of foreign-owned utility companies, seem to persecute them, and yet always

[1] Ibid., 13 Apr. 1905.
[2] Mandatos R.C.I., Martin to Proctor, 2 Mar. 1906, p. 2.
[3] Ibid., 22 June 1907.
[4] Ibid., 3 Feb. 1909, 9 June 1909, and 23 June 1909.
[5] Mandatos R.W., Martin to Proctor, 12 Oct. 1905.
[6] Ibid., 31 July 1913.
[7] P.R.O. F.O. 371/45131, AS 1234/184/46, F. S. Gibbs (Rosario Consulate) to Storey (Buenos Aires), 13 Jan. 1945, shows how little things had changed. One of the first acts of the incoming *comisionado municipal* was to attack the Water Company on the ground that its service was inadequate, threatening expropriation if improvements were not made.

allow them just enough air to breathe. The struggle between the companies and the municipality in Rosario was exceptional in its severity, its duration, and the early stage in the history of the utilities at which it occurred. None the less, it was a pattern which was soon to become a familiar feature of the Anglo-Latin American business world.

III

S. Pearson & Sons: Electricity Supply in Chile, 1919–28

The interest of S. Pearson & Sons in electric light, power, and tramway companies in Chile after the First World War was, as indicated in the first section of this chapter, part of the firm's established pattern of investment in Latin America from the turn of the century. The company's original and major business enterprise lay in contracting for the construction of public works schemes, which later drew it into the actual operation of utility services. The particular reasons for Pearsons' subsequent interest in electrical undertakings in Chile are not clear, though successful development in Mexico must have provided some impetus. Growing interest in contracting work on the West Coast—especially at Valparaíso—also gave the firm an opportunity to study Chile's needs and potential.[1] The development of electrical utilities in Chile was well established since major concessions around Santiago had been granted in 1897.[2] Cheap hydro-electric power was available in rivers flowing from the Andes, and the bulk of Chile's population and industry was concentrated into the relatively small area of the central valleys. Short transmission lines distributed electricity from the foot of the mountains to the cities. Alexander Worswick, Pearsons' chief engineer, was convinced that 'there are exceptionally good opportunities for a powerful public utility company in Chile'.[3] An official survey showed that Chile's hydro-electric capacity was five million horsepower, of which only 100,000 was being used.[4] By 1918 the German-owned

[1] Pearson, files 6, 15, 26, 37–8, and 43.

[2] Diario de Diputados (Chile), 22 Jan. 1897, p. 567, and 27 July 1897, pp. 596 and 605; Consular Reports (Valparaíso), P.P. 1899, xcviii, 466, and (Chile), 1900, xcii, 510–11.

[3] Pearson, B5 LCO 10/125, Worswick to Clive Pearson (Lord Cowdray's second son), 26 June 1920; see also ibid., 7/113, MacDonald to Cowdray, 23 Sept. 1919.

[4] *The Times* (Trade Supplement), 13 Nov. 1920, 204d.

Deutsche Uberseeische Elektrizitäts Gesellschaft (D.U.E.G.), Chile's most important electrical concern, operated a large, well-equipped power station, La Florida. La Florida supplied the Chilean Electric Tramway and Light Company (C.E.T.L.), which was also owned by D.U.E.G. and which worked the light, power, and traction concessions in Santiago.[1]

The occasion of Pearsons' entry into Chile's electrical supply industry was, however, fortuitous. The Chilean Electric Tramway and Light Company (C.E.T.L.), though German-owned, was registered in Britain (under the original concessions awarded to a British partnership), and throughout the First World War was administered from London. During the post-war seizure of German assets, Whitehall decided to sell the concern through the Public Trustee's office. The anxious British diplomatic representative in Santiago, Vaughan, had telegraphed 'that position of company should be regularized as soon as possible as British private property'.[2] He recognized its value to the Chilean economy, and felt that British owners would probably order British goods where German equipment had previously been used.[3] Moreover, a long-running dispute between C.E.T.L.'s German managers and the local authorities raised the very real fear of expropriation. The Central Mining and Investment Corporation introduced the business to Pearsons, and the two firms' joint bid of £1 million (Pearsons staking 60 per cent) was accepted.[4]

The British Government was thus involved in Pearsons' undertakings in Chile. A Foreign Office official minuted that C.E.T.L. was 'deserving of diplomatic support in view not only of its present importance but of the greater importance it will obtain from the point of view of British export trade', an opinion no doubt fostered by the ambitious Vaughan.[5] Moreover, Pearsons, noting Vaughan's view that losing C.E.T.L. would cause 'incalculable harm' to Britain's commercial interests and prestige in Chile, declined to sell their new property to the Compañía

[1] *Consular Reports* (*Chile*), P.P. 1902, cv, 624, and 1905, lxxxvii, 563–4; Philip S. Smith, *Electrical Goods in Bolivia and Chile* (Special Agents Series 167, Washington, 1918), pp. 38–9.
[2] P.R.O. F.O. 371 3679/110436, Vaughan to F.O., 30 July 1919.
[3] P.R.O. F.O. 371 3679/130942, Vaughan to F.O., 17 Sept. 1919.
[4] P.R.O. F.O. 371/3679 A137/36/9, B.O.T. to F.O., 4 Nov. 1919; Pearson, B5 LCO 10/122, Sir Leonard Phillips to Cowdray, 14 July 1920. Phillips was a director of the Central Mining and Investment Corporation.
[5] P.R.O. F.O. 371/4451 A436/366/9.

Hispano-Americana de Electricidad (C.H.A.D.E.), a Spanish consortium busily acquiring the remnants of D.U.E.G.'s assets in South America. Lord Cowdray told the Department of Overseas Trade:

In following the above course my company loses a very handsome immediate profit on its original investment. The future development of the undertaking will involve the expenditure of large sums . . . and in the difficulties which undoubtedly will arise from time to time, my Company trusts that it may rely on the goodwill of H.M. Government and its assistance, should this be necessary, in any dealings with the Chilean authorities.[1]

The Department of Overseas Trade agreed to this course.[2] Later Clive Pearson told Worswick that 'we received . . . strong representations from the Foreign Office [which] urged us very definitely to forego a sale'.[3] And throughout the negotiations Vaughan had taken an aggressive line. If agitation for expropriation occurred, he explained, 'we should of course stoutly resist'.[4] The Foreign Office became alarmed. 'It seems to me', an official noted, 'rather a dangerous practice . . . to commit H.M. Government to the support of a company by persuading it not to accept an advantageous offer of purchase from a foreign group.' 'We are', another minuted, 'pledged to support something we do not quite understand.'[5]

Although C.E.T.L. owned considerable property in Santiago— eighty-four miles of tramway track, more than 400 cars, and a steam turbine plant[6]—it did not yet enjoy a monopoly. It provided lighting for only a third of the city's users, possessed no hydroelectric resources (renting power from La Florida for £75,000 per annum), and did not supply Valparaíso, the republic's chief port less than 100 miles away. But although C.E.T.L.'s concessions expressly forbade a monopoly, in practice some degree of unity existed between the light and power tariffs of rival firms which Vaughan certainly recognized. 'If some combination could be effected with the new hydro-electric syndicate and Valparaíso

---

[1] P.R.O. F.O. 371/4451 A5926/366/9, Whitehall Securities to D.O.T., 12 Aug. 1920.　　[2] Ibid. D.O.T. to Cowdray, 24 Aug. 1920.
[3] Pearson, B5 LCO 10/122, Clive Pearson to Worswick, 11 Aug. 1920.
[4] P.R.O. F.O. 371 3679/130942, Vaughan to F.O., 17 Sept. 1919.
[5] P.R.O. F.O. 371/4451 A5926 and A7011/366/9; P.R.O. F.O. 371/4451 A6613/366/9, D.O.T. to F.O., 17 Sept. 1920.
[6] Pearson, B8 LCO 10/385, memo, 23 Feb. 1923.

tramway could be secured', he telegraphed, 'possibility of development and control over electric imports would be enormous.'[1] It
was important, therefore, for C.E.T.L. to preserve its source of
electrical power. When C.E.T.L. was sold to Pearsons, D.U.E.G.,
its former owners, began legal proceedings in Chile to recover
their La Florida station. D.U.E.G. alleged non-payment of rent
from 1914[2] since, of course, a firm registered in Britain could not
deal with a German concern during the war. Once again, Vaughan,
eager to press C.E.T.L.'s case in Santiago, intervened. 'It looks',
he telegraphed, 'as if object of Germans was to obtain verdict on
technicality when they could demand preposterous prices or
refuse to sell thus obliging the company either to shut down or
sell.'[3] The Chilean Government, Vaughan continued, 'must devise
means for putting an end to German action'.[4] C.E.T.L. preferred
to continue the lease, the terms of which conferred practical
ownership, and thus released capital for development elsewhere.

C.E.T.L. sought to neutralize rivals. As Deputy Vergara, a
severe critic of C.E.T.L., later explained: 'faced with the danger
of competition the foreign company [C.E.T.L.] began negotiations
during which it bought concessions and established works,
paying for them generously'.[5] The Compañía Nacional de Fuerza
Eléctrica (C.N.F.E.), a local concern formed to develop hydro-
electricity at Maitenes on the Rio Colorado for Santiago and Ran-
cagua, was the closest rival, and union between C.E.T.L.'s domestic
light and power business and C.N.F.E.'s industrial capacity
appeared crucial.[6] Hydro-electric concessions gave C.N.F.E. a
strong bargaining position, since C.E.T.L. would eventually
have to buy their power. 'Instead of they depending on us',
explained Worswick, 'we are much more dependent on them, and
apparently they have the key enterprise of this whole Santiago–
Valparaíso situation.'[7] Nevertheless, C.N.F.E.'s weakness, access
to capital to develop Maitenes, was C.E.T.L.'s longest suit

[1] P.R.O. F.O. 371/3679 130942, Vaughan to F.O., 17 Sept. 1919.
[2] P.R.O. F.O. 371/4451 A436/366/9, Vaughan to F.O., 28 Oct. 1919; P.R.O.
F.O. 371/4451 A1368 and A1418/366/9, C.E.T.L. to F.O., 15 and 17 Mar. 1920.
[3] P.R.O. F.O. 371/4451 A1728/366/9, Vaughan to F.O., 26 Mar. 1920.
[4] P.R.O. F.O. 371/4451 A1864/366/9, Vaughan to F.O., 30 Mar. 1920. An
official minuted: 'Mr. Vaughan seems to have put it fairly strongly.'
[5] Diario de Diputados (Chile), 9 Aug. 1927, pp. 1783–9.
[6] Pearson, B5 LCO 10/123, Worswick to Pearson, 12 Jan. 1920. *E.R.*, 9 Jan.
1920, p. 47.
[7] Pearson, B5 LCO 10/123, Worswick to Pearson, 19 Apr. 1920.

because of Pearsons' high reputation and close links with the London market. In 1920, therefore, C.E.T.L. and C.N.F.E. merged their assets into the Compañía Chilena de Electricidad.[1] The union included a good deal of watering.[2] Stock was allotted on a 3:1 basis in C.E.T.L.'s favour. C.N.F.E. raised its capital from £650,000 to £1·5 million for which it received £1·5 million ordinary shares in the new company plus £750,000 preference and £750,000 debenture stock. C.E.T.L. in addition to placing a value of £3 million on its assets (for which it had recently paid Whitehall £1 million), provided £1·5 million working capital, receiving, therefore, a £9 million stake. The injection of capital would now complete the Maitenes power-station, cover the laying of transmission lines, and raise the capacity available for Santiago. *The Times* reported local enthusiasm for the Compañía Chilena since it lowered industrial fuel costs, provided hydro-electric capacity second only to Brazil's, and demonstrated British financial confidence in Chile.[3] Pearsons, too, were jubilant. 'We have made', Worswick explained, 'the first important step towards laying the foundation of a great enterprise . . . We are safe now so far as our power requirements are concerned.'[4] And at this point Pearsons took over the stake in C.E.T.L. of Central Mining, their partners in the original purchase, who had earlier preferred the immediate profitable sale to C.H.A.D.E. and now opposed union with C.N.F.E.; Central Mining had also objected to Pearsons acting without consultation.[5]

The Compañía General de Electricidad Industrial (C.G.E.I.), formed in 1905 with local and German capital, was a further competitive obstacle. It operated at first in Nuñoa and San Bernardo, suburbs of Santiago, and then at Curicó south of the capital. By 1919 it owned several power stations and was authorized to lay underground supply cables. 'This company', Vaughan

[1] Pearson, B5 LCO 10/123, Pearson to Worswick, 18 Aug. 1920 and Worswick to C.N.F.E., 14 Aug. 1920; *E.R.*, 25 Nov. 1921, p. 712, and 9 Dec. 1921, p. 793; D.O.T., *Chile* (Dec. 1921), p. 51.

[2] Vergara later spoke of 'the very great inflation of this elastic capital', Diario de Diputados (Chile), 9 Aug. 1927, pp. 1783–9.

[3] *The Times* (*Trade Supplement*), 26 Nov. 1921, 206b. See also D.O.T., *Chile* (Apr. 1923), pp. 41 and (Sept. 1924) 51; F. M. Halsey and G. B. Sherwell, *Investments in Latin America III: Chile* (Trade Information Bulletin 426, Washington, 1926), p. 51.

[4] Pearson, B5 LCO 10/125, Worswick to Pearson, 31 Aug. 1920.

[5] Ibid. 10/122, Phillips to Cowdray, 14 July 1920.

told the Foreign Office, 'will of course do all in its power to become a formidable rival . . . It is impossible for the two companies to cooperate.'[1] Worswick warned that the consequences of competition would be 'far-reaching and costly'.[2] C.G.E.I., disputing the value put on its assets, preferred territorial agreement with Compañía Chilena to outright purchase. By 1921, however, terms were agreed, C.G.E.I. transferring its plant to a new concern, Compañía Hidro-Eléctrica (C.H.E.), a subsidiary of Chilena, for cash and a stake in Chilena.[3]

Valparaíso also appeared an attractive prospect. The port, relatively close to the capital, was Chile's major international trading outlet and well known to London financial circles from whom help might be needed. The light and power business in Valparaíso was worked by the Spanish consortium, C.H.A.D.E., which had replaced the previous German owners, D.U.E.G., here and at La Florida after the war. Relations with the Municipality were steadily deteriorating. Equipment which had not been repaired or up-dated since 1914 caused inefficient service. Rioting mobs damaged property.[4] The city authorities welcomed competition in Valparaíso where no company, apart from the Viña del Mar sugar refinery, produced electricity. A memorandum from the British consulate summarized the position: 'The present occasion is most favourable for the capture of this enemy position with its valuable contingent trade. The company is down and once a scheme were evolved to carry on in their place either by buying them out or by setting up in competition they could be forced to loose their hold.'[5] The Valparaíso company's coal supply, the consulate continued, could be interrupted to bring it to terms. It possessed no hydro-electric resources and its steam plant was poorly equipped. Further, good reasons existed for C.H.A.D.E. to sell the property to the Compañía Chilena. C.H.A.D.E., badly needing cash, could not increase its business in Valparaíso without

[1] P.R.O. F.O. 368/2079/136593, Vaughan to F.O., 7 Aug. 1919; see also *E.R.*, 26 Dec. 1919, p. 816.

[2] Pearson, B5 LCO 10/124, Worswick to Hyde, 9 Oct. 1920.

[3] Ibid., Hyde to Worswick, 10 Dec. 1920, Worswick to Pearson, 21 Dec. 1920, and Pearson to Hyde, 6 Jan. 1921.

[4] P.R.O. F.O. 371/4451 A2399/366/9, Cottenham-Smith to F.O., 11 Mar. 1920 and includes *El Mercurio* and *South Pacific Mail*, 28 Sept. 1918; *E.R.*, 19 Mar. 1920, 366.

[5] P.R.O. F.O. 371/4451 A447/366/9; see also Pearson, B10 10/126, memo, Feb. 1920, and *E.R.*, 2 June 1922, 772.

buying power from Chilena, and the city was remote from
C.H.A.D.E.'s other South American holdings. The Chilena company, however, possessed ample capacity and was conveniently
situated.[1] Pearsons had earlier expressed interest in Valparaíso, but
the asking price had been high. In 1921 territorial limitations and
power sales were discussed—although Compañía Chilena preferred
not to co-operate. Worswick explained:

> We are not at all inclined to supply them with bulk power and are
> seriously considering entering the field ourselves if we cannot make a
> reasonable deal for the purchase of [the] property . . . I am quite con-
> vinced that we must have Valparaíso and it would be a calamity if we
> made a contract to sell them power which would put them on their
> feet . . .[2]

Under any power contract, Worswick continued, 'the conditions
should be made so difficult that they will revert to the idea of
sale'.[3] In early 1923 C.H.A.D.E. sold out for £1·3 million.

The deal included not only plant in Valparaíso but La Florida
which Chilena had continued to rent. Separate subsidiary companies were formed to effect purchase. The Compañía de Electricidad de Valparaíso (C.E.V.) operated in the port and C.H.E.
(originally established to run C.G.E.I.'s assets) received La
Florida.[4] Pearsons provided £3 million to satisfy old shareholders
and for working capital. These arrangements avoided the appearance of the Compañía Chilena monopolizing the electrical supply
industry and eased negotiations with municipalities. Each concern
had to pay, and separate accounts could now be presented to local
authorities when tariffs required revision. If the Chilena company
were profitable *in toto*, it was difficult to convince officials that
certain parts were unremunerative.[5] C.E.V. now contracted with
Compañía Chilena for power and settled its territorial limits.

The Chilena company developed further business at San

[1] P.R.O., F.O. 371/4451 A366/9, Vaughan to F.O., 23 Jan. 1920; P.R.O.
F.O. 371/4451 A447/366/9, Pearsons to F.O., 4 Feb. 1920; Pearson, B10 LCO
10/126, D.O.T. to C.E.T.L., 29 April 1920, and memos, 11, 13, and 14 Apr.
1920.
[2] Pearson, B10 LCO 10/126, Worswick to Grant, 15 Apr. 1921.   [3] Ibid.
[4] Pearson, B5 File 10/352 and B8 LCO 10/385, memo, 15 Aug. 1922; *The
Times*, 20 Aug. 1923, 16b; *E.R.*, 24 Aug. 1923, 295.
[5] Pearson, B5 10/352, Whitehall Securities Corporation to Pearson, 3 Jan.
1924; D.O.T. *Chile* (Sept. 1924), 71, and (Sept. 1925), 46; Halsey and Sherwell,
op. cit., p. 51.

Bernardo where the electric railway, linking the capital to this popular summer resort, also provided light and power. The concern, covering a wide area with limited resources, was already partly supplied by Chilena. Its rates were not subject to control from Santiago and its profits were good. The only competitor was the state railway, eight trains of which stopped daily *en route* for the capital. Although the concern required outlay for improvements, it offered easy amalgamation with Chilena's existing business. A high asking price prolonged negotiations until the levers of Chilena's powerful competitive position, the fact that it supplied electricity to San Bernardo and the local concern's shortage of capital, were applied.[1] In 1926 Compañía Chilena bought a 56 per cent share in the Empresa Eléctrica de San Antonio, which served a small port south of Valparaíso, and C.H.E. developed concessions at Queltepues for business in the Central Valley.[2]

By the mid 1920s the Compañía Chilena de Electricidad dominated electrical supply in the rich, populous, and industrial regions around Santiago and Valparaíso, satisfying 80 per cent of Chile's needs. Mergers, purchases, territorial agreements, exclusive municipal concessions, and threats of tariff wars or power reductions had eliminated competition, imposed uniformity, and strengthened the original investment. Small local concerns had been expelled. Even the geography of Chile reinforced Pearsons' monopoly. Although there were in the republic 140 electric light and power concerns—since all major towns of 15,000 or more enjoyed electricity[3]—and eight companies, the division of the country into deep valleys running west to east effectively prevented companies at a distance from invading the territory operated by the Compañía Chilena. Moreover, the distribution of power over a wide area was centralized at large stations. The Chilena company was the only major developer of hydro-electricity in the important Central Valley.[4] By 1923 the firm's local and national influence was enormous. It owned all the trams in Santiago and Valparaíso, and most of the light and power. It supplied all the state railways' power needs and was already negotiating further contracts so that 'the whole of the railroad communications

[1] Pearson, B10 LCO 10/129, Pearson to Worswick (?), 15 June 1922, and memo, 3 Feb. 1921.
[2] Pearson, B9 LCO 7/135.
[3] D.O.T., *Chile* (Nov. 1927), 34; Halsey and Sherwell, op. cit., pp. 51–2.
[4] Pearson, B8 LCO 10/385, memo, 23 Feb. 1923.

around Santiago would be . . . at the command of Messrs. Pearson'.[1] The value of Chilena's assets exceeded those of any native concern. Juan Tonkin, a director, emphasized that although Pearsons wished to treat Chile fairly and remove the stigma of German mismanagement, the republic had to recognize that the company would 'form a lever of great weight to be used when the Chilean Government became obstructive'.

The organization of the firm's electrical companies reinforces the view of Pearsons as monopoly capitalists. Their holding company, Whitehall Securities, had purchased the Mexican concerns before acquiring C.E.T.L. in 1919. Then, in 1920 it provided fresh capital to finance the union with C.N.F.E. from which the Compañía Chilena emerged. In 1922 a separate company, Whitehall Electric Investments, was formed to consolidate Pearsons' electrical interests and provide funds (especially for Santiago). Public subscription for preference and debenture stock was invited in an attempt to extract working capital from British investors for foreign utilities, by now normally regarded with suspicion, under cover of a British-based holding company. Whitehall Securities took the ordinary shares, thus retaining voting control, and a proportion of the receipts from the preferred and debenture stock to repay its original purchase of, and outlay on, the business which Whitehall Electric now owned.[2] Therefore, while the Compañía Chilena had a preponderantly Chilean directorate, the chief decisions were taken in London. Clive Pearson recognized the dangers: 'It may be that for the Whitehall Trust to be the trustees [for Chilena's debentures] would give an appearance of affairs being altogether in the hands of Pearsons. Hence it is likely that we should prefer some completely independent company to act as trustees.'[3]

Critics in Chile had no doubt that Pearsons enjoyed wide, uncontrolled powers. Vergara told the Chamber of Deputies in 1926 that 'the Compañía Chilena de Electricidad had established a practical monopoly, a monopoly which I desire—as my fellow citizens must desire—to end some day'.[4] Others considered that

---

[1] P.R.O. F.O. 371/8443 A5729/2722/9, Grant Duff to F.O., 24 Aug. 1923.

[2] *The Times*, 30 Mar. 1922, 19b, 31 Mar. 1922, 19b, and 3 Apr. 1922, 21a; *The Economist*, 24 June 1922, 1315.

[3] Pearson, B5 LCO 10/125, memo, 7 May 1921.

[4] *Diario de Diputados* (Chile), 29 Dec. 1926, 2230–2. See also ibid. 12 July 1926, 1332–9.

this monopoly encouraged poor service and harsh conditions. The company's tariffs, particularly the standing meter charges, were said to be unreasonable in view of Chile's wealth of natural hydro-electric resources.[1] While modern lights, underground cables, and steel posts had been installed in the centre of Santiago, the outer suburbs of the poor still contained old fittings, wooden poles, and dangerous aerial lines. The hydro-electric stations were allegedly liable to floods and droughts which interrupted power supplies. Vergara summarized the position: 'The provision of electrical power in our country is too dear, given the natural resources which we possess to generate it and it is agreed, moreover, that this industry is in the hands of enterprises so restricted . . . that they constitute a real monopoly.'[2]

Nevertheless, Pearsons were realistic enough not to press their luck. 'It may be convenient', Worswick argued, 'to take in the gas companies of Santiago and Valparaíso [and] the telephone properties might also be absorbed.'[3] Both sectors, needing working capital which Pearsons could provide, would be easily and profitably assimilated. Clive Pearson firmly rejected these proposals, however attractive. Financial resources had to be conserved for the vital light and power sectors, and not dispersed into subsidiary ventures. He wished to avoid monopolizing Chile's public utilities. 'The greater the ground we cover', Pearson explained, 'the more open we are to complaint and attack.'[4]

In addition important private suppliers of electricity existed. The Chilean Exploration Company, which worked copper mines at Chuquicamata, was said to own the largest hydro-electric plant in South America, and the Braden Copper Company and some nitrate works had also electrified their mining operations. At Valdivia the Compañía Eléctrica Siderúrgica e Industrial was harnessing the falls at Huilo-Huilo.[5] The rapid growth in Chile's electrical goods trade further indicates a widening use of electricity, and suggests that the influence of the Compañía Chilena, the largest power supplier, was developing rather than retarding

---

[1] *Diario de Diputados* (Chile), 4 Aug. 1922, 1295, 4 Jan. 1927, 2486–8, and 9 Aug. 1927, 1783–9.

[2] Ibid., 26 Dec. 1927, 878–9.

[3] Pearson, B5 LCO 10/125, Worswick to Pearson, 26 June 1920.

[4] Pearson, B10 LCO 10/150, Pearson to Worswick, 21 Sept. 1920.

[5] *E.R.*, 30 Jan. 1920, 144, 2 July 1920, 13, 20 Mar. 1925, 455, and 27 Mar. 1925, 511; D.O.T., *Chile* (Sept. 1924), 51, and (Nov. 1927), 35.

the economy. In 1926 Chile was said to be the United States' fourth-best customer for electrical goods, after Canada, Japan, and Australia.[1] And the wide use of electric signs in Santiago suggested that tariffs were reasonable. Moreover, in 1927 two native companies began manufacturing electrical apparatus and wire.[2]

Again the major users of electricity were not domestic consumers. Many of the rich enjoyed electric light, but the several domestic tasks which electricity eased—washing, cleaning, and cooking—could still be cheaply performed by servants. Rather, users were large industrial concerns, mines and manufacturing, where savings could prove decisive. The majority of Chile's imported electrical goods comprised equipment—motors, dynamos, machines, and transmission cables, not consumer products. The small number of large consumers, rather than a greater number of insignificant users, acted as a restraint against high charges or poor service. The most important users of electricity were the railways, under pressure from rising coal costs and operating losses. Between 1921 and 1923 the Chilean Government placed contracts with Westinghouse to electrify two sections of the state lines, from Valparaíso to Santiago, and the shorter branch to Los Andes. The Compañía Chilena de Electricidad provided the power for £90,000 per annum. Further schemes electrified the lines between San Antonio and the capital and between Talca, Talcahuano, and Temuco.[3] By 1925 a third of Chilena's bulk power was sold to the railways. It is difficult to imagine Chilean state railways arranging long-term, disadvantageous contracts with Pearsons.

Official interest in state railways formed only a part of the much wider question of government regulation of the electrical supply industry. It is quite unrealistic to expect any utility company, foreign or native, to operate unchecked. A framework of safety legislation and land concessions must exist. Officials naturally prefer more costly underground cables to dangerous overhead

[1] *The Electrical Equipment Market in Chile* (Trade Information Bulletin 515, Washington, 1927); D.O.T., *Chile* (Nov. 1929), 43–7.

[2] *E.R.*, 1 Apr. 1927, 514, and 3 June 1927, 884; *Electrical Equipment Market in Chile*, op. cit., pp. 10–12.

[3] *Diario de Diputados* (Chile), 10 July 1923, 615; *E.R.*, 14 Oct. 1921, 502, 21 Oct. 1921, 534, 2 Nov. 1923, 672–3, and 18 Apr. 1924, 610; D.O.T., *Chile*, (Sept. 1924), 51–3, and (Apr. 1923), 34; *The Electrical Equipment Market in Chile*, op. cit., p. 19.

wires. Domestic and industrial wiring must be standardized. In 1925 Chile formulated new regulations concerning installation, and the Compañía Chilena introduced safer fittings. Señor Navarette called attention in the Chamber of Deputies to the need to protect electrical workers from industrial accidents.[1] The increasing national importance of electricity provided the greatest incentive for government intervention. According to the Departmental Committee on the Electrical Trades, Britain's wartime experience, particularly in the manufacture of munitions, 'proved the electrical industry to be a *key industry*'.[2] Cheap, efficient power was essential for industrial and public well-being. In the Chamber, Vergara agreed 'that electricity today is a service which can be considered indispensable'.[3] He bitterly regretted the Chilean Government's failure to purchase C.E.T.L. when it was offered for sale in 1919, and persistently pressed ministers for action. But from the 1920s a formidable body of legislation was enacted in Chile. There were official inquiries into hydro-electric resources. In 1922 regulations covering the rights of way of transmission lines over private property were announced;[4] in 1923 a bill authorized the government to take over the industry in a national emergency;[5] in 1925 regular inspection was established under the Dirección de Servicios Eléctricos;[6] and in 1930 the policy of rationalizing vital industries was extended to electricity. The Sociedad Nacional de Electricidad amalgamated diverse electrical interests under one body comprising local capitalists and government representatives, 'the first step', the President announced, 'in the effective nationalization of the electrical industry'.[7]

The Pearson group resented increasing official control—possibly a testimony to its effectiveness. The Compañía Chilena de Electricidad criticized what it termed the hasty, unpractical legislation of

---

[1] *E.R.*, 12 June 1925, 934; *Diario de Diputados* (Chile), 12 July 1926, 1332–9, and 16 Nov. 1927, 130.

[2] *Electrical Trades after the War*, P.P. 1918, xiii, 355–68.

[3] *Diario de Diputados* (Chile), 29 Dec. 1926, 2230–2; see also 9 Aug. 1927, 1783–9, 26 Dec. 1927, 878–9, and 4 July 1928, 715.

[4] P.R.O. F.O. 371/7207 A4851/4851/9, Bateman to F.O., 17 June 1922.

[5] P.R.O. F.O. 371/8443 A3232/2722/9, D.O.T. to F.O., 30 May 1923; P.R.O. F.O. 371/10613 A6127/6127/9, Hoblen to F.O., 29 Oct. 1925; *Diario de Diputados* (Chile), 14 Mar. 1923, 1915–32, and 20 Mar. 1923, 1959–65.

[6] D.O.T., *Chile* (Nov. 1929), 13; *The Times*, 18 June 1926, 22e.

[7] *Diario de Diputados* (Chile), 24 Jan. 1930, 2693–4; see also D.O.T., *Chile* (Nov. 1930), 13.

successive governments, administered by inexperienced personnel and aimed directly at the firm: 'We do not think that it is too much to say that if there had not existed an entity of the importance of the Compañía Chilena, the Law of Electrical Services would not have been dictated until 20 years later.'[1] But official intervention was not always one-way. The Dirección de Servicios Eléctricos fixed Chilena's tariff at Chillán at $1 per kWh, 20 per cent above the figure the municipality had already negotiated with the company.[2]

Nor was national intervention the only level of government participation. Public utility services were important issues for local authorities. Electrical consumers and tram passengers were voters. A municipality which could not ensure cheap, efficient services from the concessions it granted lost electoral support.[3] And the failings of utility companies were immediately apparent. Public lighting was a particularly sensitive issue. Consumers complained both if service were poor and if modernization required increased rates. There were continual pressures to lower tariffs, though public lighting was in fact often unremunerative. Contracts, arranged for a number of years, rarely recognized rising costs. And given seasonal fluctuations, demand was inelastic. Once a certain level of street lighting was achieved, demand would not alter greatly from year to year. Far more profitable were industrial and private users whose consumption continued to rise as business and domestic appliances expanded, and with whom long-term contracts were less common. And to raise public lighting tariffs if wages or depreciation were inflating costs, was fraught with difficulty.

The labour question also aroused municipal interest in the public utility companies which, although capital- rather than labour-intensive, were still among a town's chief employers. Utility concerns throughout Chile had a labour force in the 1920s of some 30,000 of which Valparaíso alone accounted for 1,000.[4] And the well-being of a community partly depended on adequately paid workers who, again, were potential voters. Clashes were frequent. In light and tramway companies the large percentage

[1] Pearson, B8 LCO 10/520.
[2] *Diario de Diputados* (Chile), 6 Aug. 1928, 1256–7.
[3] This point is well made by E. J. Hobsbawn, 'British Gas Workers 1873–1914', in his *Labouring Men: Studies in the History of Labour* (London, 1964), pp. 169–71.   [4] Halsey and Sherwell, op. cit., pp. 51–3.

of skilled and semi-skilled workers—electricians, drivers, and conductors—were both vocal and unionized. In Santiago the tram employees formed a strong section of the *Federación Obrera*. Local authorities, anxious for mass support against their political rivals, could not therefore side with the operating companies, particularly if foreign-owned, in any labour dispute. The labour question was linked to tariffs. A successful wage claim generally led to demands to raise rates, which caused further debate with the authorities.

Tramway rates aroused heated disputes. While electricity was fitted in relatively few houses, most people regularly used the trams. One report in 1927 stated that Santiago had 120 million fares on its trams and Valparaíso 40 million, compared with only 30,000 domestic consumers of electricity throughout the whole of the Santiago–Aconcagua valleys.[1] Fare revisions or poor service received blanket condemnation. At the same time tramways were attacked on the question of street accidents,[2] road repairs, and the hazards of embedded rails and overhead wires. It was generally impossible to secure the operating margin necessary to service the enormous capital—for rolling stock, track, and running equipment—which tramways required. Electrical supply could be installed far more cheaply. Nor were trams immune from competition. By the 1920s motor-bus competition, aided by road-building programmes, was severe. Chile was said to have the largest bus fleet in South America—totalling 1,000 units by the late twenties when Santiago and Valparaíso enjoyed thirty-five regular bus routes in addition to a host of irregular operations. The buses milked the trams' best routes at peak times and were well adapted for the many narrow streets which trams could not penetrate. They worked beyond town boundaries, attracting passengers from rural areas who normally walked to the outlying tram termini or used other means of transport. The Compañía de Autobús de Santiago ran a freight service in the capital. Operated by owner-drivers or small private concerns, which aroused public sympathy against the large, foreign-owned trams, motor-buses were low-cost competitors. Local authorities were slow to

---

[1] *Manual of Electrical Undertakings*, xxxi (1927–8), 1260–1; see also *Consular Reports (Chile)*, P.P. 1905, lxxxvii, 563–4, and *E.R.*, 7 Aug. 1925, 220.

[2] *Diario de Diputados* (Chile), 18 Oct. 1926, 428–40, and 23 Oct. 1928, 2972–8.

levy their contributions for road repairs and to impose safety regulations.[1]

In general, therefore, light and power undertakings were more remunerative than tramways. In Santiago the operating ratio (expenses divided by receipts) of the trams remained at about 90 per cent in the 1920s, compared with 30 per cent in the light and power businesses. To some extent it is unrealistic to distinguish between sectors. Tramway receipts were in depreciating paper, where those of light and power, especially under contracts, were in gold. Most companies in fact operated light, power, and trams as one enterprise, in which the trams contributed materially to the receipts and profits of the power sector, and, hence, to over-all profits. Nevertheless, as Lord Cowdray explained to his son Clive, trams 'where they represent the primary value of a public utility company's undertakings, are clearly a troublesome and unprofitable business'.[2]

The history of negotiations between the Santiago municipality and the Compañía Chilena epitomized the problems facing expatriate tramway companies. Relations were strained from the start. Pearsons inherited a legacy of bad labour relations and contractual disputes from C.E.T.L.'s German managers. Between 1897 and 1905 alone there were twenty-five lawsuits. Vaughan distrusted the local authorities, concessions to whom would 'only lead to further trouble as Municipality are corrupt and unscrupulous'.[3] Nevertheless, in 1919 the new board asked to negotiate a fresh concession which raised wages and financed costly development if tram tariffs were increased to compensate for persistently low earnings in that sector. The municipality was offered a share in net receipts to give it an interest in lowering costs. Relations worsened in July 1921 when blacklegs broke a tram strike. Protracted negotiations finally forced the company to apply the 'tourniquet', reducing services to the minimum level authorized under the 1905 concession. Tram shortages and overcrowding coincided with a typhoid outbreak which increased confusion.[4] 'You will appreciate',

[1] H. C. Schuette, *Motor-Bus Transportation*, Part II: *Canada and Latin America* (Trade Information Bulletin 404, Washington, 1926), pp. 1–2 and 23; *The Tramway and Railway World*, 16 July 1925, 45.

[2] Pearson, B10 LCO 10/126, Cowdray to Pearson, 27 Jan. 1921.

[3] P.R.O. F.O. 371/4451 A366/366/9, Vaughan to F.O., 23 Jan. 1920; see also ibid., A436/366/9, Vaughan to F.O., 28 Oct. 1919.

[4] *E.R.*, 17 Sept. 1920, 372; *Diario de Diputados* (Chile), 21 July 1921, 1289–93, 9 Dec. 1921, 811–12, and 10 May 1922, 494–7.

Pearson told Agustín Edwards, the banker, 'our desire to give the public a full and efficient service and that we deplore the necessity of having to reduce our services, but . . . we cannot go sinking money down a non-paying business.'[1]

The company's tougher policy seemed effective. In September 1922 the municipality seized the opportunity of the absence abroad of the Mayor, the main obstacle to agreement, to arrange terms, which included tram tariffs and no restrictions on light and power rates if full services were restored, £1 million spent on new lines, and the city's debt to the company of £20,000 erased.[2] To confirm the agreement's validity—although it already possessed legal force—the company insisted on Congressional approval. This cautious approach backfired. The Senate delayed its decision. Radical deputies encouraged agitation against terms which benefited foreign shareholders at their customers' expense. Deputy Pradenes accused the company of flagrantly violating the Republic's laws.[3] There were hostile demonstrations and calls for expropriation. The ministry of the day was tottering and the municipality now rejected the terms. The Compañía Chilena stubbornly resumed its coercive measures. The municipality retaliated by fining the company for the resulting overcrowding on the trams. And when the firm strictly enforced passenger regulations, thereby heightening confusion, the government suspended services. Agustín Edwards then arranged a conference of interested parties, from which an interim agreement to double tariffs outside peak periods emerged.[4]

The Compañía Chilena, apart from reducing its services, exerted other pressures on the municipality. The need for inspired press articles to arouse public sympathy was recognized. *La Unión* and *El Mercurio*, which had been anti-German, were to be exploited. One deputy spoke of Chilena's 'seditious propaganda'.[5] London explained its policy in a memorandum:

publicity should be energetically followed up to accustom the people

---

[1] Pearson, Bɪo LCO 10/504, Pearson to Edwards, 2 Jan. 1922.

[2] P.R.O. F.O. 371/7207 A6053 and A7325/6053/9, Bateman to F.O., 30 Sept. and 31 Oct. 1922; *E.R.*, 23 Nov. 1923, p. 783.

[3] *Diario de Diputados* (Chile), 6 Dec. 1922, 789; 7 Dec. 1922, 822–9; 8 Mar. 1923, 1861, and 14 Mar. 1923, 1915–32.

[4] P.R.O. F.O. 371/8443 A2722/2722/9, Bateman to F.O., 21 Mar. 1923; P.R.O. F.O. 371/9534 A239/239/9, Grant Duff to F.O., 7 Dec. 1923.

[5] *Diario de Diputados* (Chile), 10 May 1922, 494–7.

to the coming alteration in the tramway tariff . . . and it might be worth while to pay a certain fee . . . to keep up the press agitation in favour of the company for some time . . . it never does any harm to have the press and local propaganda to boost the company's operations and show how exceedingly well it has served the community.[1]

The Compañía Chilena also employed local agents and representatives in Santiago. Most of the board was Chilean-based, including Ismael Tocornal, a highly respected former Minister, and Samuel Claro, a company lawyer. More important, however, was Juan Tonkin, formerly with C.N.F.E., who represented the company with the authorities, handled labour questions and propaganda, advised the general manager (Worswick), and was a link between the board and departmental heads. Nevertheless, their impact was probably small. Clive Pearson considered the company's business with officials 'could be more happily handled along strictly commercial lines, that is by the management, rather than by a representative with a political position'.[2] Pearson particularly feared entanglement in local politics. Despite rumours, no evidence of association was discovered during an internal investigation, although the personal politics of the company's directors must have been recognized and reflected in the firm.[3]

The dispute between the Compañía Chilena de Electricidad and the Santiago authorities was rekindled in 1924 when the municipality repudiated the terms of March 1923.[4] From negotiations concluded in May 1925, under pressure from outer suburbs seriously compromised by lack of transport, two new dimensions emerged. The company offered the municipality $2\frac{1}{2}$ per cent of gross receipts, and formed a separate operating company for the capital's light, power, and trams, the Compañía Tracción e Alumbrado de Santiago, entirely owned by the Chilena from whom the new concern 'bought' its plant. The separation of assets had several advantages. The municipality could more closely supervise operations. The Compañía Chilena's business in Santiago could not now be confused with earnings outside, which facilitated either the justification of higher tariffs or liquidation.

    [1] Pearson, B5 LCO 10/119, memo (undated), and Pearson to Worswick, 4 May 1920.
    [2] Ibid., Pearson to Worswick, 14 June 1920.
    [3] Ibid., Worswick to Pearson, 29 Apr. 1920.
    [4] *Diario de Diputados* (Chile), 1 Aug. 1924, 1605; 7 May 1924, 338 and 363; 12 May 1924, 421; 22 May 1924, 528, and 25 June 1924, 823.

Chilena was freed from the burdensome tramways, and avoided the possibility of delay over the renewal of other concessions to force it to terms over the trams.[1]

The new contract (14 May 1925) worked no better than before. The municipality refused to pay its lighting bills or regulate buses. The press and Congress remained hostile. The contract, explained Señor Retamales, 'neither represents nor consults the interests of the city of Santiago'.[2] Deputies Ayala and Navarette accused the Compañía Tracción of failing to fulfil its obligations by running old stock and withdrawing services. At the same time Tocornal and Claro were bitterly attacked. Although both denied any collusion between their political posts and their new company positions, Claro was eventually exiled as *persona non grata*.[3] In 1927 the matter went to a commission which merely confirmed prejudices against the firm. It rejected the 1925 contract and demanded both lower tariffs and improved service.[4] The Compañía Chilena was rapidly losing patience, and in 1928 it approached the President for settlement.

At the end of 1928 Whitehall Electrical Investments sold its holdings in utility companies to the American and Foreign Power Company.[5] During the 1920s the United States, which had emerged after the First World War with enormous productive and capital surpluses, rapidly increased its foreign investments. This was particularly so for South American utilities which appeared to offer sound prospects both for investors and for U.S. manufacturers.[6] The price which Whitehall Electrical received was attractive. *The Economist* estimated the profit at £2·7 million, less £650,000 to pay a five-shilling bonus on the 2·5 million × £1 preference shares, and £729,000 to meet the outstanding discount on the debenture issue.[7]

[1] Pearson, B10 LCO 10/131, Memos, 10 Sept. and 8 Dec. 1925.

[2] *Diario de Diputados* (Chile), 3 Aug. 1927, 1629–30; see also 16 June 1926, 747–50, 20 July 1927, 1256–60, 9 Aug. 1927, 1782, and 17 July 1928, 927–32.

[3] Pearson, B5 LCO 10/169, Pearson to Antonio Huneeus (Chilean Minister in London), 24 Aug. 1927.

[4] *Diario de Diputados* (Chile), 21 June 1927, 665; Pearson, B8, 7th Directors' Report, Compañía Chilena de Electricidad, 1927–8.

[5] *The Times*, 10 Oct. 1928, 22e and 12 June 1929, 21b; *Diario de Diputados* (Chile), 21 Oct. 1929, 24–5; Pearson, B7.

[6] Henry W. Balgooyen, 'Experience of United States Private Business in Latin America', *American Economic Review*, xli (1951), Part 2, 330–42; D.O.T., *Chile*, Nov. 1927, 43. In 1927 the International Telephone and Telegraph Company (ITT) had bought the Chile Telephone Company.

[7] *The Economist*, 15 June 1929, 1374, and 22 June 1929, 1416.

The favourable price was not the only reason for the sale. Negotiations with Santiago and the government—'our unfortunate experience'—had inevitably soured business relations in Chile, the main area of interest. Worswick's view was that the company had genuinely sought co-operation with the authorities to develop a permanent investment, but had 'experienced constant opposition amounting at times to persecution';[1] Clive Pearson had refused an extremely attractive offer in 1921 but, he continued, 'I doubt whether we could see our way to repeat such action.'[2] When negotiations with the municipality failed in 1927, the Compañía Chilena feared expropriation. The sale caused few regrets.

The eagerness with which Whitehall Electric sold its utility companies does not suggest that they were particularly profitable; there would have been little reason to accept an offer if they had been. The published results of Whitehall Electric which, as chief shareholder, received the bulk of their net revenue, support this view. Whitehall Electric's gross profits rose from £537,000 in 1922, the first year of operation, to £722,000 by 1927, although the bulk was absorbed by heavy fixed interest charges on the debentures (6 per cent) and the preference stock ($7\frac{1}{2}$ per cent) and by the fund to wipe out the debenture discount. In the period 1922–7, dividends on ordinary stock, which Pearsons' holding company (Whitehall Securities) almost totally owned, averaged only $2\frac{1}{4}$ per cent. Even after an 18 per cent bonus in 1928 from accumulated reserves after selling the electric company shares, the average dividend was only $4\frac{1}{4}$ per cent. Such figures did not impress the City. *The Times* noted in 1922, when Whitehall Electric was first placed before the public, that investors were suspicious, which was unusual in a period when electricity shares normally found a ready market. Similarly, *The Economist* warned that 'these offers will not appeal to conservative investors'.[3] Underwriters were left with 75 per cent of the debentures and 92 per cent of the preference stock. *The Economist* still warned against the stock in 1924 when fresh issues were made to finance the Valparaíso purchases, but now the debentures were over-subscribed.[4] No doubt the fixed

[1] Pearson, B10, LCO 10/103, Worswick to Tonkin, 25 Oct. 1928.
[2] Pearson, B5 LCO 10/169, Pearson to Sir Edward Crowe (D.O.T.), 22 June 1927.
[3] *The Economist*, 8 Apr. 1922, 682, and 24 June 1922, 1315; *The Times*, 7 Apr. 1922, 19a.
[4] *The Economist*, 28 June 1924, 1308–9 and 1336; *The Times*, 25 June 1924, 19b.

interest shares represented a comfortable, if not spectacular, investment, but taken with the ordinary stock an over-all return of about 6 per cent emerges which is hardly unreasonable considering the risk.

It is possible, of course, to disguise profits—although how far Whitehall Electric sinned in this respect is uncertain. Juan Tonkin strenuously denied, in a memorial to Congress, that this firm used a double accounting system whereby one set for the public authorities showed a less rosy picture than the real accounts. The true balances had been verified at the highest level and inspected at the Chilean Legation in London.[1] Similarly, there is no evidence that the Pearson firms, despite their close relations, employed an interlocking equipment company from which to buy plant at grossly inflated prices, thus smuggling out embarrassingly high profits without publicity. This device had been employed by C.E.T.L.'s German management through its links with the parent company, A.E.G., but it was specifically repudiated by Pearsons in 1920.[2]

On the other hand, the creation of the Compañía Chilena and its holding company, Whitehall Electric Investments, almost certainly involved some watered capital—although exactly how much is not known. After all, the original purchase price of C.E.T.L. paid to the Public Trustee in 1919 by Pearsons and Central Mining, whose share Pearsons later acquired, was £1 million. Yet, by 1928 the total book capital of Compañía Chilena de Electricidad exceeded £12 million. Of course extra capital was required to develop current assets and to finance mergers, but it may be asked whether valuations of existing and projected assets were accurate or inflated and whether total book capital was unduly inflated beyond the value of the assets and not paid up. It was perfectly possible for Pearsons to pay what appeared to be a moderate dividend on diluted fixed capital and ordinary stock which in reality was a much larger return on the original investment. Certainly, Pearsons employed blatant tactics at Tampico in Mexico, where it was proposed to conceal the substantial gains from the unexpectedly rapid growth of the oil industry after the First World War in a new operating company, the capital of which was much inflated. The company thus hoped to disguise its windfall

---

[1] *Diario de Diputados* (Chile), 26 July 1921, 1361.
[2] P.R.O. F.O. 371/4451 A436/366/9, B.O.T. to Vaughan, 6 Feb. 1920

profits, retain the existing assets without investigation, and avoid publishing the original balance sheet.[1] An internal memorandum concisely stated Pearsons' problem:

> The earnings of Tampico are going to be most difficult to handle. When the true position is realised by the State Government the company will be subject to many attacks which may take the form of a demand for decreased charges etc. The simply phenomenal earnings of the current year cannot, in any way, be effectively wrapped up in the next balance sheet.[2]

Yet the fact that Pearsons could rarely interest local investors in their electrical undertakings further suggests that profits were not startlingly high. Clive Pearson fully realized the advantages of including a large sector of native capitalists, which would protect the company from charges of exploitation for expatriate shareholders and forge a closer bond with consumers and officials. Pearsons wanted to encourage not merely the large institutional investors and the Chilean banks but also the small saver so as to assure the Pearson group of widespead support.[3] Nevertheless, local financial interest was slight. In the Compañía Chilena, Chilean holdings totalled less than £50,000. Local investors also ignored the stock issues of the Chile Telephone Company. According to the *Financial Times* the native capitalist 'much prefers to leave the financing of public utility companies to outsiders'.[4] Perhaps Chileans found more lucrative investments elsewhere, perhaps their savings were inadequate, or perhaps they resented the fact that ordinary stock with voting control and opportunities for capital gains (in the event unrealized) was seldom offered. Certainly the yield on debentures and preference stock was locally uncompetitive.

IV

The history of foreign public utilities in Latin America is predominantly one of friction between the companies and the host countries. Officials, the press, and the public all suspected and resented foreign control over the valuable natural resources necessary for the successful operation of utilities. Electricity

---

[1] Pearson, B2 64–71. [2] Ibid., B2 64, memo, 25 Aug. 1921.
[3] Ibid., B7 LCO 10/151, memo, 17 Feb. 1921; ibid., B5 LCO 10/352, Pearson to Worswick, 27 Apr. 1923; ibid., LCO 10/169, Pearson to Crowe, 22 June 1927. [4] *Financial Times*, 2 July 1925.

generation, for example, required ownership of fuel and water supplies and access to land for transmission. Utility companies *ipso facto* raised fears of monopoly. Vertical and horizontal integration, the elimination of competition, and rationalization conferred considerable economies of scale on capital intensive enterprises but reduced the choice open to consumers—although optimum operational size varied. Waterworks and drainage concerns worked efficiently in a compact city area, while companies supplying electricity from one power station preferred a wider locale. Exclusive, long-period concessions protected operators against rivals, but also prevented consumers from improving terms. Once a utility company had established plant and fittings, it enjoyed a natural monopoly. Under a new operator, consumers ran the costly risk of altering or replacing equipment to conform to a different distribution network. The nationality of utility companies, particularly in the case of light and power, strongly influenced standards, operating practice, and the purchase of hardware. Moreover, demand for utility services, once established, is relatively inelastic. Consumers needed water, drainage, heat, light, and transport whether wages or business were increasing or on the decline. The close contact between utilities and their consumers heightened distrust. Any rise in tariffs or decline in service was immediately and widely felt. Public utility companies, which were substantial local employers, and their shareholders abroad, appeared to benefit at the community's expense. And, most important, utilities were now a basic factor in modern urban life. Public health and well-being depended on water supply, drainage, heat, and light. Cheap fuel, particularly in South America where coal was dear, was vital for industry. Increasingly, therefore, local interests resented what appeared to be undiluted foreign control over issues of national and strategic importance.

The conflict between British utility companies and Latin American municipalities was damaging to most of the parties. British shareholders received a meagre return, politicians gleaned votes from issues which never failed to arouse attention, but the public lost on all counts. Interminable lawsuits and frequent disputes over the quality and quantity of services cost money which both sides ultimately recouped from the townsfolk. The utility companies were not always able to renew machinery or expand services to keep pace with growing urban requirements. Even when they had capital available, they remained cautious under constant threat of expropriation. Further, there was always the temptation to delay improvements as a bargaining-counter against the municipality; a promise to renew plant might ensure agreement to higher rates or legal concessions. Without these disputes with local authorities, or in less contentious hands, extension and renovation would undoubtedly have taken place sooner and more willingly. Yet what alternatives were there to large, foreign-owned utility companies? If Chilean electrical development had remained the responsibility of small, independent concerns the problems of undercapitalization would have been even more intractable. The Chilena company, generating 80 per cent of the republic's electricity, probably contributed materially to the development of a national outlook towards utilities. And without the security of lengthy concessions, both consumers and operators would have suffered from an unstable, hand-to-mouth policy even more discouraging to long-term development.

The methods used by British utility companies in Latin America were, as it turned out, quite unsuited to the running of a public service. But the tenacity of investors unwilling to admit their mistakes and realize at a loss kept such enterprises as the Rosario utilities in British hands for sixty years. The capital could have been better employed elsewhere, and the export orders which Britain won were probably outweighed by the damage done to British prestige and hence to the more general interests of her trade. Nationalization or municipalization was the logical solution, a view with which the Foreign Office was becoming increasingly sympathetic. Not only did the British Government lack the means, but it was also rapidly losing the will, to protect British utility enterprise in Latin America. Vincent Perowne summarized this attitude in 1942. It was natural for Latin Americans, he wrote, 'to wish to own their public utilities and to resent the foreign tribute which the companies continue to exact . . . British prestige suffers, both because the company is not being run to local satisfaction (albeit probably through no fault of its own) and because His Majesty's Government are publicly shown to be unable to protect their nationals from being bullied and exploited.'[1]

---

[1] P.R.O. F.O. 371/33929 A3479/3479/51, Perowne to Waley, 21 Dec. 1942; see also P.R.O. F.O. 371/8430 A7511/818/6, C.R.T. 6500/23, B.O.T. to F.O., 21 Dec. 1923.

Yet little local enthusiasm in fact existed for investment in public utility companies. As Deputy Vergara, the Compañía Chilena's most persistent critic, pointed out, although Chile possessed good natural resources she lacked experienced personnel, know-how, and above all capital to exploit them.[1] Indeed, as long as the British utility companies maintained a minimum service, which could usefully be turned to political ends, there was no incentive for either local or national authorities to offer more than minimally acceptable terms. Municipalities did not really want the bother of running public services themselves, or the embarrassment of collecting tariffs. Opportunities for patronage which expropriation provided might well be outweighed by the unpopularity which accrued to the authorities as managers and entrepreneurs. On balance, it seemed better at the time to let the foreigner earn a modest profit and take the blame for shortcomings and deficiencies. The pretence, if not the reality, of persecution was kept up to please the electorate. As Martin had remarked in 1905 about the Rosario enterprises:

I have had good opportunity of observing this Municipality . . . and all through in all its business it has always taken a tortuous course and found it paid. In fact I do not see, from their point of view, why the Municipality of Rosario should ever be honest, because it is obviously profitable to be the reverse.[2]

The final impression is of the vulnerability of British utility firms, which supports the warnings of City financial columns. What effective redress had the companies against labour troubles, the non-payment of municipal debts, the imposition of harsh operating terms by politically powerful users, press hostility, and the expulsion of legal representatives? Once utilities had invested huge sums they could not suddenly depart if local conditions deteriorated. Their capital was tied up in long-term investments. Even if competition were eliminated, operating concerns still had to modernize and improve services. Legislation had to protect the consumer against exploitation from a natural monopoly. In reality the power available to utility companies was limited, and the dependence of Latin America on the foreigner was not absolute. The options open to officials for the control of utilities were wide,

[1] *Diario de Diputados* (Chile), 1 June 1927, 175–6.
[2] Mandatos R.C.I., Martin to Anderson, 9 Mar. 1905.

and the restraints on operating companies increased as time went
by. One writer has considered government regulation of United
States public utilities in South America particularly hostile.
Immediately after the Second World War their earnings, 3 per cent
over all, were amongst the lowest in the United States' investment
portfolio.[1] A letter from the Foreign Office to the Department of
Overseas Trade as far back as 1923 best summarized the situation:

Both the legislative and administrative bodies [in Latin America]
have developed what is practically a system of deliberate obstruction
vis-à-vis the important British companies which hold concessions to
operate services of public utility. This obstructiveness appears to be
marked by disregard of promises given, unreasonable refusals, and by
extreme dilatoriness, so that the Companies are often forced to work
in an atmosphere of uncertainty, prejudice, and frequently at a dead
loss due to the refusal of the relevant authority to permit, for example,
any increase in the tariffs proportionate to increased costs.[2]

[1] Benjamin A. Rogge, 'Economic Development in Latin America: the Preb-
isch Thesis', *Inter-American Economic Affairs*, ix (1956), 24–49.
[2] P.R.O. F.O. 371/8430 A6208/818/6, Foreign Office to Department of
Overseas Trade, 19 Oct. 1923.

CHAPTER IV

Shipping 1850–1914

ROBERT GREENHILL

I

BRITAIN's shipping dominated the ocean trades before 1914. Early industrialization, which ensured the rapid application of iron and steam in her shipyards, enabled British ship owners to meet the new demands. The country's rising population required imported foodstuffs and supplied an expanding labour force for industry which, in turn, provided two-way cargo; raw materials inwards and manufactures and coal outwards. Imperial possessions, which provided a major source of imports and an export market, demanded an efficient communications network; emigration was proceeding apace; and Britain's substantial entrepôt trade, founded on an early maritime lead and commercial links abroad, helped to confirm an already strong position in shipping. Even by 1890, when newly industrialized nations were developing fleets, Britain's 25 million tons still represented 50 per cent of the world's ocean tonnage.[1]

Britain's shipping industry was broadly based. Although steel steamships predominated by 1900, specialized trades still retained wooden sailing vessels. Tramp steamers, loading where and when cargo was offered, comprised the bulk (nearly 60 per cent) of British tonnage. They were usually small, even single-ship enterprises which seldom attracted public notice. Better known were liner companies, normally large, highly capitalized public concerns working regular time-tables.[2] And British shipping embraced every major trade route. Although the bulk of tonnage had one home terminal, many ships, particularly tramps, operated between foreign ports.

It was customary to assume that ocean shipping forged a vital

---

[1] S. G. Sturmey, *British Shipping and World Competition* (1962), pp. 4–14.
[2] Peter Mathias and A. W. Pearsell in their *Shipping: A Survey of Historical Records* (Newton Abbot, 1971) list available records of liner companies.

link in international economic interdependence, integrating advanced countries with the less developed, and overcoming the inefficiences of internal transport which prevented contact overland. Steam-engines and regular routes constituted a revolution in communications, removing the obstacles imposed by distance, reducing costs, and widening markets.[1] The impact of innovations in transportation has since been questioned.[2] Was steam-shipping an essential prerequisite of economic development? The influence of one element, improved transportation, on growth can be exaggerated, and the initial impact of steam-shipping on Latin America was certainly unimpressive. Expensive early steamships were better suited to short-haul trades; the institutional environment of the republics, commercial backwardness, political instability, inadequate harbours and navigational aids impeded the use of steam-power; and without steam-power the use of sail would have continued. Nevertheless, by the end of the century it is clear that whatever hypothetical alternatives may have existed, modern steamship links were now in practice essential to Latin America. They formed part of the infrastructure crucial to development, since the republics depended on the export overseas of a narrowly based range of primary commodities.

The fact that Latin America did not operate ocean-going tonnage made her reliant on the great industrial powers, her trading partners. In the circumstances, Britain's shipping could hardly fail to exercise a strong and sustained influence over Latin America's economic and political development. By 1913 British companies accounted for 50–60 per cent of oceanic tonnage at Buenos Aires and at Brazilian ports. Such a degree of dependence can of course create a perceived community of interest, but more usually

[1] Douglas North, 'Ocean Freight Rates and Economic Development 1750–1913', *Journal of Economic History*, xviii (1958), 537–55; Charlotte Leubuscher, *The West African Shipping Trade 1909–1959* (Leyden, 1963), pp. 9–12.

[2] Kent T. Healy, 'Transportation as a Factor in Economic Growth', *Journal of Economic History*, vii (1947), Supplement, 72–88. This controversy largely surrounds the economic impact of railways and the concept of 'social saving'. See particularly R. W. Fogel, *Railroads and American Economic Growth: Essays in Econometric History* (Baltimore, 1964). Social saving measures the importance of a particular innovation from observed facts and postulations. It may be defined as the difference in the costs of economic output under two states, the actual which includes the innovation, and the 'hypothetical alternative' which excludes it. This technique has been applied to measuring the impact of steamships; see Gerald Gunderson, 'The Nature of Social Saving', *Economic History Review*, xxiii (1970), 209, n. 3.

it arouses the hostility associated with fears of overcharging and complaints of poor service. Volume of tonnage alone is not evidence of control or exploitation. British ship owners, perhaps more efficient than their rivals, may still have acted harmoniously with local interests, and only a more careful examination can establish the facts of the relationship, one way or the other. Where, then, were the points of friction between British ship owners and Latin Americans? What were the options available to the republics? In short, what were the limits to, and extent of, the influence of British ship owners in the control and manipulation of commerce and development in Latin America?

II

Exclusive contracts and concessions, which prevent fair competition and protect privileged monopolies, constitute one area of friction. The earliest British liner companies in Latin America, the Royal Mail Steam Packet Company (R.M.S.P.) which began a Caribbean service in 1842, and the Pacific Steam Navigation Company (P.S.N.) which from 1840 loaded along the West Coast between Valparaíso and Panama,[1] were mail contractors for H.M. Government. Their mail subventions, not merely for services rendered but as subsidies for working, cost far more than postal value.[2] The companies also negotiated smaller subventions in Latin America. Under the guise of mail contracts, islands in the West Indies and the Brazilian port of Maceio (Alagôas) paid Royal Mail to call. West Coast republics supported the Pacific Steam Navigation Company.[3] Competitors like Alfred Holt and Company found existing contracts with H.M. Government, at first

[1] Robert G. Greenhill, 'British Shipping and Latin America 1840–1930: The Royal Mail Steam Packet Company' (unpublished Ph.D. thesis, University of Exeter, 1971), pp. 13–15. House histories of both R.M.S.P. and P.S.N. exist, see T. A. Bushell, *'Royal Mail': A Centenary History of the Royal Mail Line, 1839–1939* (London, 1939), and A. C. Wardle, *Steam Conquers the Pacific* (1940).

[2] *Report of the Select Committee into Packet and Telegraph Contracts*, P.P. 1860, xiv, 452. The postage on items carried by Royal Mail averaged less than a third of the company's contractual income which, in turn, comprised 30–40 per cent of the firm's total revenue.

[3] P.S.N., *Reports of General Meetings* (henceforth P.S.N., *Meetings*), 25 Sept. 1856 and 22 Aug. 1857.

arranged privately and not by public tender, a great obstacle.[1] And the West India and Pacific Line declared in 1873 that 'the large subsidy enables the Royal Mail Company ... to carry goods at lower rates than will pay'.[2] P.S.N. negotiated a contract with Whitehall in 1850 'to lessen the chances of competition', and West Coast arrangements fortified the company against 'wanton competition'.[3]

Critics deprecated the wider effects of these contracts. In Britain, where the mid nineteenth century marked the apogee of *laissez-faire*, the use of public money for shipping, an industry noted for individual enterprise and well able to stand unaided, was unpopular. Gladstone certainly believed, like *The Economist*, that postal subsidies had been 'carried too far and ... required to be confronted and exposed'.[4] Robert McCalmont, an independent shipowner, condemned 'intolerable commercial monopolies which are being reared up by this monstrous parasytical system of ocean contracts', the effect of which was to deter competition and prevent better services.[5] Observers in Latin America adopted a similar line. William Hadfield, a frequent traveller to Brazil, believed that Royal Mail's subsidies gave it a monopoly which was 'exercised injuriously for the interests of the countries they were trading to'.[6] In the Cámara de Senadores in Santiago, Senator MacIver condemned contracts with P.S.N. and with a local concern, which 'have given bad results for our commercial interests'.[7]

Like men-of-war, the earliest mail carriers (R.M.S.P. and P.S.N.) enjoyed a range of privileges and concessions at ports in Latin America which reduced harbour dues and expenses and permitted preferential handling. The directors of P.S.N. considered that 'the preservation of the privileges granted by the South American governments is an object of paramount importance to the best interests of the company'.[8] In 1851 William Wheelwright succeeded in obtaining for the company an extension of the exclu-

[1] F. E. Hyde, *Blue Funnel: A History of Alfred Holt and Company of Liverpool from 1865 to 1914* (1957), pp. 17–18.

[2] West India and Pacific Company to Post Office, 30 July 1879, Post Office Archives, St. Martins-le-Grand, London, 29 fo. 193/400Z/1874.

[3] P.S.N., *Meetings*, 25 Sept. 1850 and 22 Aug. 1857.

[4] Quoted in Greenhill, op. cit. (1971), p. 38.

[5] R. McCalmont, *Some Remarks on the Contract Packet System* (1851), pp. 3–13.

[6] W. Hadfield, *Brazil and the River Plate in 1868* (1869), p. 11.

[7] *Diario de Senadores* (Chile), 22 Oct. 1894, 64–5.

[8] P.S.N., *Minutes of the Court of Directors* (henceforth P.S.N., *Minutes*), 4 May 1839.

sive privileges, and in 1857 the Peruvian Government waived local dues amounting to £2,400.[1] British shipping in Latin America also owned dockside services, and thereby reinforced its position. Royal Mail and Pacific Steam received land off Rio and Panama for bunkering and anchorages, and Pacific Steam formed the Callao Dock Company in 1863, which enjoyed local exemptions in return for preferential treatment of government vessels.[2] The Booth Steamship Company worked lighter and tug services at its Amazon ports.[3]

The disabling and contentious effects on competition of contracts and concessions should not be exaggerated. P.S.N. considered local and West Coast agreements a public relations exercise, 'to draw close the connection with local governments'.[4] The fact that West Indian islands and small mainland ports had to find subventions for steamships strongly suggests that their everyday business was insufficient to attract ordinary commercial services, rather than that the unfair advantages of subsidized lines excluded competition. The major ports handling the bulk of Latin America's trade experienced little shortage of tonnage. Shipowners always responded to commercial pressures. The quickening pace of Latin America's economic development at the end of the nineteenth century was a stimulus to independent services far stronger and more influential than the deterrent effect of exclusive privileges. Without contracts, the level of shipping services which governments wished to maintain for undeveloped areas could not have survived. Early steamships in the long-haul trades, which burned too much coal and carried little cargo, were unprofitable.[5] While the subsidies on Britain's steamships were initially for imperial and military reasons, they may, in fact, 'be considered as examples of infant industry subsidies which . . . succeeded . . . precisely because they were working with, not against, the economic tide'.[6] Britain's shipping supremacy was

---

[1] P.S.N., *Meetings*, 24 July 1851 and 22 Aug. 1857; see also Claudio Véliz, *Historia de la Marina Mercante de Chile* (Santiago, 1961), pp. 70–3, 116.

[2] P.S.N., *Meetings*, 28 July 1863; P.R.O. F.O. 177/174, Callao Dock Co. to Consul St. John, 8 Dec. 1882.

[3] A. H. John, *A Liverpool Merchant House: Being the History of Alfred Booth & Company, 1863–1958* (London, 1959), pp. 99–100.

[4] P.S.N., *Meetings*, 22 Aug. 1857, 10 Aug. 1859, and 28 July 1863.

[5] G. S. Graham, 'The Ascendancy of the Sailing Ship 1850–1885', *Economic History Review*, ix (1956), 74–88.

[6] Sturmey, op. cit., p. 30. See also S. Pollard, 'The Economic History of

already based on international market forces, an industrial lead, a substantial overseas trade, and an expanding empire.

Moreover, if the initial advantages of the Latin American mail contracts were necessarily substantial, their impact by the end of the century was limited. Royal Mail's West Indian subvention fell from £240,000 to around £80,000 per annum by 1880, which barely covered costs.[1] Although imperial sentiment encouraged the British Government to continue assistance to the West Indian service, which no firm would work unaided, the subvention of £30,000 for Brazil was discontinued when commercial possibilities attracted carriers. By the end of the century, too, West Coast contracts were small; Chile paid P.S.N. £5,600 a year in the 1890s to serve her southern ports.[2] And, in general terms, the ability of subsidies to create permanent advantages is questionable. Germany, the least state-aided of European shipowners, proved Britain's most formidable rival in the ocean trades. In Italy and France, where subsidies ran 'counter to economic considerations they produced little worthwhile result'.[3]

Similarly, the effect of operating concessions can be overrated. Tonnage and light dues became payable once mail ships carried cargo. P.S.N. lost its Chilean privileges in the 1850s under pressure from *laissez-faire* and Free Trade lobbies.[4] Where operating concessions remained, the savings were small. Again, preferential handling was only sensible for an efficient mail service. No ports in Latin America, as opposed to berths, were the exclusive possession of one steamship company. Freedom of the seas permitted any ship to dock. Therefore, British shipping in Latin America did not enjoy the same sort of monopoly as railways with an exclusive right to operate between given termini.

III

The strategic importance of maritime transportation and communication in the nineteenth century gave shipping a political role in Latin America, and created another possible area of friction. In

British Shipbuilding 1870–1914' (unpublished Ph.D. thesis, University of London, 1950), pp. 21 and 228.

[1] *Report of the Select Committee on Steamship Subsidies*, P.P. 1902, ix, 300.
[2] *Diario de Senadores* (Chile), 29 Oct. 1894, 110–12.
[3] Sturmey, op. cit., p. 33; *Report on Steamship Subsidies*, P.P. 1902, ix, *passim*.
[4] Véliz, op. cit., pp. 117–18.

general, British companies anxiously avoided political entangle-
ments. They preferred peace and the *status quo* which permitted
normal business. Yet, by the very nature of their business, most
companies were likely to be compromised by the unsettled political
situation in Latin America. P.S.N.'s experience during the Chilean
revolution in 1891 affords a striking example of the political traps
which awaited neutral commercial enterprises.[1] The conflicting
demands of the legitimate government and of the insurgents were
impossible to resolve, each side accusing the P.S.N.'s directors of
running arms and importing war materials. The British Naval
Commander in the Pacific rebuked the Company for loading
government cargo: 'to carry military stores or munitions of war
for either side', he explained to Kennedy, the British Minister, 'is
contrary to the strict neutrality which British vessels should
observe'.[2] During the Brazilian naval revolt of 1893 newspapers in
Rio charged British firms with intrigue.[3] Royal Mail was accused
of signalling to rebel ships in the bay, which the Company's agent
emphatically denied in a letter to the British diplomatic representative at Rio. On the other hand, Royal Mail permitted Brazilian
naval personnel to travel aboard the *Thames* to Montevideo to join
a loyal government warship,[4] and a demand for government
services of this kind, even in contravention of neutrality regulations, was difficult to reject.

The instructions which the British steamship companies gave
to their officers were clear enough. 'It is to be distinctly understood', P.S.N.'s directors minuted, 'that officers are not to interfere except in cases of urgent or immediate necessity . . . Any Act
which seriously affects the neutrality of the Company's vessels . . .
is directly at variance with the orders of the Court.'[5] Similarly,
Royal Mail was careful to abstain from alignment when the Canada
–West Indies contract became part of the political tug-of-war between supporters of private enterprise and the Canadian Government's mercantile marine. The directors refused to contribute
to the Conservative Party's funds, although its policies fitted the

---

[1] *Correspondence on the Chilean Revolution*, P.P. 1892, xlv, 151–431. See also
P.R.O. F.O. 132/29.
[2] P.R.O. F.O. 132/29, Admiral Hotham to Kennedy, 10 Apr. 1891.
[3] P.R.O. F.O. 128/211, Royal Mail to Wyndham, 4 Jan. 1894. See also
P.R.O. F.O. 13/706, Wyndham to Rosebery, 17 Oct. 1893.
[4] P.R.O. F.O. 13/707, Wyndham to Rosebery, 22 Dec. 1893.
[5] P.S.N., *Minutes*, 23 June 1841, 6 Apr. and 11 May 1842, and 11 Oct. 1843.

company's contractual interests. They thought it inadvisable to depart from their traditional policy of abstaining from partisanship in matters of public interest.[1]

Yet when business was threatened it would be unrealistic to expect companies to remain detached. The opinion of G. C. Anderson, Royal Mail's agent at Rio during the naval revolt, that armed intervention 'should take place to force the insurgents to cease from worrying commerce and to free the customs house from molestation', was doubtless shared by many.[2] The sheer distance between head office and South American ports gave considerable authority to local agents, which might be abused. Head office expected to continue business whatever the local difficulties. And faced with rapid decisions in a fluctuating situation, agents made mistakes. Captain Jones, master of the Lamport & Holt steamer *Vandyck*, certainly used his position to aid Brazilian rebels in 1893, but was quickly dismissed for 'not having confined himself strictly to the performance of his duties in accordance with his orders'.[3]

Nevertheless, there were resources more subtle than open intervention by which steamship companies might exercise influence. Representation in Latin America was one. Locally based managers and agents protected their company's interests in negotiations with officials when disputes arose. And despite competitive considerations, agents in important ports formed their own representative association, the Centro de Navegación. Ostensibly theirs were legitimate commercial interests which helped solve long-standing institutional problems. But an interest in harbour administration, taxation, subsidies, and the collection of dues could be construed as unnecessary interference in local affairs.[4] Good relations with local officials, which obviated problems for British companies abroad, could also be misinterpreted. In 1910 Royal Mail granted free passages to delegates who supported the company's postal contracts at a conference in Barbados.[5] Similarly, the directors authorized a free trip for F. E. Bawden, a Canadian official, during

---

[1] R.M.S.P. Correspondence, Canada–West Indies Contract.
[2] P.R.O. F.O. 13/707, Wyndham to Rosebery, 20 Dec. 1893.
[3] P.R.O. F.O. 13/726, Wyndham to Kimberley, 18 June 1894.
[4] *Diario de Diputados* (Argentina), 27 Nov. 1905, 564, and 10 Aug. 1910, 938. See also *Consular Reports* (Brazil), P.P. 1907, lxxxviii, 243 and 1909, xcii, 684.
[5] R.M.S.P., E. C. Skinner (Trinidad agent) to London, 26 Oct. 1926, West India Correspondence.

the delicate negotiations on the mail contract between Nova Scotia and the Caribbean, because he was well informed and anxious to assist. Publicity and 'inspired' articles were a device which British shipowners, like most expatriate concerns in Latin America, regularly employed. Royal Mail 'informed' local English language newspapers and those native newspapers which supported the British standpoint, so that they might publicize a view or correct inaccurate information. The Prince Line published complaints in the local newspapers against the prefect of the port of Buenos Aires.[1]

IV

The greatest causes of dispute between Latin America and British shipowners were the fixing of rates and the limiting of competition. Issues of mutual interest (taxation and the law) had for long forged links between shipping companies. Royal Mail and Pacific Steam, despite intervals of independent working, co-operated closely on the overland route from Panama, where P.S.N. loaded for south Pacific ports, to Colon, R.M.S.P.'s West Indian terminal.[2] Rate control, apart from the apportionment of revenue from through bills, developed later once shipowners began to invade each others' territory. In 1862, when the Compagnie Générale Transatlantique (C.G.T.) started trading, Royal Mail negotiated a tariff agreement to blunt its competitive edge.[3] In 1868, when P.S.N. began a service to the West Coast through the Straits of Magellan, thus tapping business in the River Plate, Royal Mail proposed a meeting for 'the discussion of mutual interests'.[4]

At first British shipowners, alone or under sectional agreements, easily handled competitors. P.S.N. 'still ruled west coast trade' into the eighties—though its position was not unchallenged—simply because it was more efficient and because it could lower rates temporarily to expel competitors invariably less well equipped to

[1] P.R.O. F.O. 118/245, James Knott (Prince Line) to Barrington, 23 Feb. 1899. For a case study of the methods which R.M.S.P. used to preserve its West Indian mail contract, see Robert G. Greenhill, 'The State under Pressure: The West Indian Mail Contract 1905', *Business History*, ix (1969), 120–7.

[2] P.S.N., *Minutes*, 8 Nov. 1855, 20 Apr. 1858, and 11 Jan. 1859; P.S.N., *Meetings*, 22 July 1862; *The Times*, 5 Sept. 1846, 6a, and 9 Feb. 1847, 6b; J. Kemble, *The Panama Route 1848–1869* (Los Angeles, 1943), pp. 3–5.

[3] M. Barbance, *Histoire de la compagnie générale transatlantique: un siècle d'exploration maritime* (Paris, 1955), p. 87.

[4] P.S.N., *Minutes*, 9 June 1868.

withstand a protracted fight.[1] But changing conditions at the end
of the nineteenth century broke informal, bilateral understandings.
From 1870 available cargo space rapidly outstripped the rise in the
volume of trade.[2] Enormous building programmes for steamships
in Britain and continental Europe were stimulated by private and
state investment. Technical advances—compound and triple
expansion engines, steel hulls and powerful boilers—cheapened
fuel and running costs, increased speeds, and raised efficiency.
Shifting patterns in world trade, as Britain lost her old entrepôt
status and the Suez Canal was opened, developed new steamship
routes and regular schedules.[3] Competition thus intensified on the
west coast of South America where, in addition to invasions by
casual outsiders seeking berths, the German Kosmos company
from 1874 and the Compagnie Maritime du Pacifique (C.M.P.) in
1881 started rate wars with P.S.N.[4]

When supply exceeds demand for a commodity or service in a
free market, the price for that commodity or service, *ceteris
paribus*, will decline. Thus the trend for the price of shipping
services, the freight rate, was continuously downward from the
1870s and the high ratio of cargo to capacity, which ship owners
had once enjoyed, was threatened. A characteristic of liner ownership and operation is that fixed costs form a high proportion of total
costs. As the size of a liner increases so the percentage of fixed
costs rises, while that of variable costs (handling, storage) falls.
Since liners must have a high utilization of capacity—rising output
of services causes a rapid fall in average costs—the conditions
which prevailed at the end of the nineteenth century (i.e. a decline
in freights and cargoes) sharply interrupted the profits of the liner
companies.[5] 'Rates were so ruinous', explained one shipowner,
'that working agreements and combinations became a sheer
necessity.'[6] *Fairplay*, the weekly shipping journal, agreed that

---

[1] David M. Pletcher, 'Inter-American Shipping in the 1880s: A Loosening
Tie', *Inter-American Economic Affairs*, x (1956), 27; Véliz, op. cit., *passim*.
[2] B. M. Deakin, *Shipping Conferences: A Study of their Origins, Development
and Economic Practices* (Cambridge, 1973), p. 21, estimates that between 1873
and 1897 the volume of British overseas trade rose at 2·62 per cent per annum
while the effective capacity of British ships rose at 5·33 per cent per annum,
after allowances are made for increased speeds.
[3] *Royal Commission on the Depression in Trade and Industry*, P.P. 1886,
xxiii, QQ. 10068–72, 10087, 10270 *et seq.*, and 10778–934.
[4] P.S.N., *Minutes*, 7 Dec. 1874, 2 Dec. 1878, 20 May 1881, 9 Jan. 1882, and
16 Apr. 1883.   [5] Deakin, op. cit.   [6] R.C.S.R., P.P. 1909, xlviii, Q. 19092.

'the concerted action of well-established shipowners who know the Plate' was needed.[1] In 1896 British and European lines formed the international River Plate conference, and agreement among the Caribbean carriers quickly followed.[2] Conferences of shipowners to regulate competition particularly suited the liner companies, whose highly capitalized industry and inelastic operations (fixed and regular timetables) were vulnerable to casual poaching by tramps at peak shipping seasons. Brazil's coffee harvest from July to November attracted tonnage which creamed off valuable trade, but which did not return for the slack period after December. British shipping in Latin America was relatively slow to adopt conference procedure, first introduced to the Calcutta trade in 1875.[3] Commercial and economic backwardness before 1880 and continued use of sail for the few, low-value cargoes, delayed regular steamship services and, hence, working arrangements. And where agreement was desirable, it was frustrated by persistent rivalry. On the West Coast protracted negotiations between P.S.N., the Gulf Line, Lamport & Holt, Kosmos, Kirsten, and C.M.P. failed to achieve an acceptable formula.[4]

Conferences among shipowners thus arose from a fusion of several factors: established business links, the depression in rates, and the particular needs of liner companies. Originally, conferences were limited to informal discussion, but they quickly became private sessions arranged geographically under permanent secretariats. Member lines contributed towards the costs and provided office space and personnel. Arthur Cook (Lamport & Holt) was chairman of the Brazil and River Plate Conference, the largest in

[1] *Fairplay*, 3 Sept. 1896, 396.

[2] *S.A.J.*, 28 Sept. 1895, 314, and 17 Oct. 1896, 406; *Fairplay*, 18 June 1896, 1086–7; P.S.N., *Minutes*, 4 Sept. 1896, 23 March, 31 May, 20 Sept., and 12 Oct. 1897.

[3] Literature on the conference system is vast. The best starting-point, from which the following paragraphs are taken, is R.C.S.R., P.P. 1909, xlvii and xlviii, *Report of the Committee on Trusts*, P.P. 1918, xiii, 789–833, and Alexander Committee. Among general works used are A. E. Sanderson, *Control of Ocean Freight Rates in Foreign Trade* (Washington, 1938); D. Marx, *International Shipping Cartels: A Study in Industrial Self-Regulation by Shipping Conferences* (Princeton, 1953); F. E. Hyde, *Shipping Enterprise and Management 1830–1939: Harrisons of Liverpool* (Liverpool, 1967); and S. Marriner and F. E. Hyde, *The Senior. John Samuel Swire: 1825–98: Management in the Far Eastern Shipping Trades* (Liverpool, 1967); Deakin, op. cit., adopts a more theoretical approach.

[4] P.S.N., *Minutes*, 22 and 28 Dec. 1892; 5 Apr. 1893; 23 Apr. and 11 June 1894, and 21 June 1895.

the Latin American trades and the model for the Caribbean and
West Coast conferences. By 1913 most of the established carriers
were associated with one or more organizations. Royal Mail,
operating in the West Indies and on the East Coast, and Lamport
& Holt, loading for Brazil and the Pacific, were members of two.
Interlocking membership facilitated inter-conference agreements
to respect spheres of influence. Nortons, who shipped to the River
Plate,[1] and the United Fruit Company in the Caribbean were not
formal members, but they tacitly accepted conference rulings.
Occasionally one line, like P.S.N. on the West Coast, dominated,
but generally the Latin American conferences were broadly based.
Continental European lines were founder members, unlike the
South African Conference in which they were given subordinate
status.[2] Breaches of regulations were subject to arbitration and
fines.[3]

Conferences devised a range of broadly similar tactics to control
prices and regulate traffic. Their actions were normally secret,
which has hampered investigation and on which most observers
have placed the worst interpretation. Undertakings were oral as
well as written, although none the less formal. Such caution prevented unwanted publicity and circumvented trust regulations.
Tariffs, too, were kept confidential except from brokers and large
shippers, to avoid assisting competitors and because rates were
liable to change. Confidential bilateral arrangements—P.S.N. and
R.M.S.P. undertook in 1902 to regulate sailings to the East Coast[4]
—reinforced conference agreements. And conferences raised
institutional barriers to new members, who were admitted only
after a formal vote.

Shipping conferences were price makers on a large scale. To
raise freight levels in Latin America, a fixed tariff common to all
members was normally introduced. But the Red D and Dutch
West Indian lines merely imposed minimum rates on their
Caribbean routes, while the West Coast companies included a
differential which permitted Kosmos, whose service was inferior,
to undercut P.S.N. Conferences designed a comprehensive classifi-

[1] Alexander Committee, evid., p. 416.
[2] R.C.S.R., P.P. 1909, xlvii, 20.
[3] R.M.S.P., *Minutes of the Court of Directors* (henceforth R.M.S.P., *Minutes*),
7 Sept. 1904.
[4] Ibid., 19 and 26 Feb. 1902; P.S.N. *Minutes*, 28 May and 4 July
1902.

cation of goods, although its scope in the homeward trades from underdeveloped countries was limited by the small number of different products shipped. Charges were levied according to weight or value (whichever was the higher), with additions for special services rendered on dangerous or refrigerated cargoes. Shippers, officials, and public representatives naturally considered conference rates, which increased Latin America's import bill and lowered export earnings, excessive.[1] In the Cámara de Diputados in Santiago, members frequently complained at P.S.N.'s charges.[2] The Alexander Committee reported that coffee freights from Brazil to New York were 'fixed at the highest possible level'.[3] And although equality of tariffs from British and continental ports was a condition of the South American conferences, greater opposition to Conference tariffs at continental ports consistently depressed rates so that British merchants were penalized and complained bitterly at what they considered unfairly exacting terms.[4]

It is of course difficult to compare rates or assess their fairness. Their level in any trade depends on many economic variables— distance, density of traffic, return cargo, port charges, produce values, supervision, and competition.[5] Nevertheless, grounds for concern existed. Rates fixed in conference must be profitable for the weakest member, so that shippers were denied the economies to be derived from more efficient operation. Accusations of over charging may be upheld, as they can for any combination of this kind, since what is profitable to the least efficient is excessively profitable to the efficient. Shipowners exploited the fragmented and uneducated market for shipping services. Buyers rarely compared notes about charges for different commodities over the same routes, and remained uninterested in rates on goods not manufactured by themselves or by their competitors. Rate increases were imposed either across the board, which normally reflected cost-based pressures, or on selected items, which reflected demand factors. If elasticity of demand for transport was high—at the bottom end of the market where tramps and sail were able to compete for

[1] *Consular Reports* (Brazil), P.P. 1914–16, lxxi, 179, suggested that freights rose from 15 to 18 per cent of Brazil's import bill, 1905–12.

[2] *Diario de Diputados* (Chile), 21 Nov. 1893, 249; 2 Nov. 1901, 179–80, and 7 Nov. 1901, 228.   [3] Alexander Committee, report, p. 156.

[4] *Worthington Reports*, P.P. 1899, xcvi, 462, 512, 553.

[5] E. S. Gregg, *Rate Procedure of Steamship Companies* (Trade Information Bulletin 221, Washington, 1923), pp. 1–3.

commodities on which freights formed a high proportion of final cost and speed was not essential—the discretion of conferences over rates was limited. But if elasticity of demand for transport was low —where goods enjoyed a high unit value in the market or required rapid shipment—conferences had considerable power.[1]

It was not enough simply to control rates. Improved levels merely encouraged additional tonnage. To retain more continuous control of their trades, conferences limited output and apportioned business under spheres of influence and spatial monopolies. Companies were generally granted a free hand at their home port but were excluded from those of fellow members. Routes and time-tables were allocated to regulate the total volume of available tonnage and avoid direct clashes on berths. Firms operated exclusively to north or south Brazilian ports, Royal Mail and Chargeurs Réunis obtained special privileges to load Brazilian coffee for Le Havre, and Royal Mail was unopposed at Trinidad to give Hamburg-Amerika a free hand at Haiti. Each member-line loading at New York for Brazil was granted a quota of sailings.[2] Sometimes all or part of the earnings of members over specified routes and business were pooled and divided *pro rata*, to ensure an even distribution of revenue among lines of varying efficiency. The agreed shares were normally the percentage of business that each interested line had earned in the last, unregulated year's working. Further, a pool might pay to eliminate a rival. Caribbean lines bribed Norddeutscherlloyd not to contest the Cuba–Mexico trade for three years.[3] Again, large contracts won by conference lines were shared amongst members, and identical quotations prevented shippers from obtaining different terms unless they went to outside lines.[4] Control of business and output thus restricted the shipper's choice and promoted inefficiency. The least effective lines could retain a portion of the business which free competition would otherwise have denied them.

Tying arrangements, which limited the merchant's choice, further controlled the shipping trades. Long-term contracts and discounts, negotiated privately with large shippers of bulk goods (coal, cement, iron, grain and nitrate), were unpopular since they

[1] Deakin, op. cit., *passim*, but especially pp. 72 and 143.

[2] Alexander Committee, report, pp. 212–18 and evid., pp. 157–66.

[3] R.M.S.P., *Minutes*, 12 Aug. 1908 and 13 Jan. 1909.

[4] Ibid., 12 and 19 Apr. 1899. In 1899 the conference lines agreed to divide the emigrant business conducted with the Brazilian Government.

discriminated against the small man whom conferences purported to protect. F. H. Colley told the Royal Commission on Shipping Rings that large shippers of machines to the River Plate were granted special terms to keep their loyalty.[1] Regular Brazilian lines placed textile manufacturers under contract to prevent them from using the cheaper tonnage of Manchester Liners which attacked the conference in 1904–6.[2] Central American coffee was also shipped under contract to outflank competitors.[3]

A more common engagement, which created a great deal of friction, was the deferred rebate. After a six- or twelve-month period of uninterrupted loyalty to the conference lines, shippers were repaid a portion, 5 or 10 per cent, of earlier freights. The coffee trade negotiated a sliding scale of 5 per cent rebates on shipments of up to 100,000 bags, rising to $12\frac{1}{2}$ per cent for 400,000 bags or more.[4] 'This system', the Royal Commission on Shipping Rings reported, 'imposes a continual obligation on the shipper to send his goods by the conference lines.' The deferred rebate was not new; it had been first applied on a regular basis to the Manchester cotton goods trade to the East, and was intermittently employed in Latin America until permanently installed in the Brazilian trade in 1895 and on the West Coast in 1904. 'The regular lines', the British consul at Santos explained in 1910, 'by means of the rebate system have striven for a number of years to keep the bulk of the coffee trade exclusively in their hands.'[5] Rebates gave considerable scope for abuse. Robert MacLaren, a Scottish steel manufacturer, told the Shipping Rings Commission that rebates were 'in restraint of trade and thereby injurious to it and the interests of the country'.[6] Rebates were withheld from disloyal shippers who might be penalized further by higher rates in any future business. Arthur Cook denied the use of such discrimination in the Latin American trades, although provision for it existed under the rebate circular of the Brazilian conference.[7] British exporters

[1] R.C.S.R., P.P., 1909, xlvii, QQ. 9360–5.
[2] Ibid., xlviii, QQ. 19136–52; *S.A.J.*, 10 Feb. 1906, 162; *U.S.M.C.R.*, Feb. 1906, 305, p. 69.
[3] P.S.N., *Minutes*, 19 Aug. 1901.
[4] Gepp, London to Santos, 17 June 1896.
[5] *Consular Reports* (Santos), P.P. 1910, xcvi, 503.
[6] R.C.S.R., P.P., 1909, xlvii, Q. 9586 (statement of evidence).
[7] Ibid., xlviii, QQ. 19126–7; Arbuckle Brothers, important coffee shippers from Brazil, claimed that conference members deliberately excluded their cargoes because they used cheap outsiders: *Spice Mill*, Feb. 1912, 116–18.

might thus see their continental rivals enjoying cheap, non-conference rates from European ports, but would have lost accumulated rebates if they too had shipped to Antwerp or Rotterdam for transit to Latin America. And rebates were substantial. Naumann Gepp calculated that its rebates in the 12 months to June 1906 with Royal Mail and Chargeurs Réunis totalled £6,000.[1] The deferred rebate was in fact at its most effective in the Brazilian coffee trade, where one conference operated to New York and to Europe. Merchants could not load outside tonnage on either route with impunity. And the fact that merchants would not jeopardize rebates for occasional cheap loads obstructed any competition for business from outside tonnage. Rebates, the Alexander Committee concluded, were 'an almost insuperable obstacle to the successful entrance . . . of any independent line which does not possess the most powerful financial backing'.[2]

Railway connections in Latin America further extended the power of British shipowners. Railroads linking the Pacific to the Atlantic formulated exclusive through-agreements, which tied merchants, who depended on railways to reach an export outlet, to particular steamship companies without the right to negotiate rates. Royal Mail collaborated with the Costa Rica Railway[3] and the Buenos Aires and Pacific Railway. The strategy was most blatantly used at Panama where P.S.N. and the Compañía Sud Americana de Vapores (C.S.A.V.) were the only South Pacific lines to call, thus controlling shipments via the Panama railroad to Europe and the eastern seaboard of the United States.[4] The situation did not seriously handicap Chile or the southern ports of Peru since 80 per cent of shipments from Arica and Antofagasta passed through the Straits of Magellan. Further north at Callao the decision was difficult: the Panama route was dearer but much shorter—although the Straits were always a potential competitor. For Ecuador the situation constituted a particular hardship. Cocoa, a relatively high-value, perishable commodity comprised the bulk of Guayaquil's exports and was perforce shipped at the isthmus.

[1] Gepp, *Board Minutes*, 27 Dec. 1906.

[2] Alexander Committee, report, p. 164, and evid., pp. 4–36.

[3] R.M.S.P., *Minutes*, 16 June 1897.

[4] Lincoln Hutchinson, *Report on Trade Conditions in Central America and on the West Coast of South America* (Special Agents Series 9, Washington, 1906); C. M. Pepper, *Report on Trade Conditions on the West Coast of South America* (ibid. 21, Washington, 1908).

Shipping conferences had a further range of weapons available. While normally glad to broaden and strengthern membership, conferences opposed occasional poachers who jeopardized profitable working. Members berthed 'fighting' ships against rate-cutting outsiders, which offered still lower rates and then shared operating losses—an openly aggressive tactic to protect business by ruining a rival. Gepp advised his partner: 'reflect that if you sever our connection with Lamports you break with a firm which may break the opposition . . .'[1] Deputy Mena told the Chilean Congress that 'foreign shipping companies which serve our coasts . . . will operate under agreement to preserve their freight monopoly by adopting temporarily low rates to make all competition impossibly ruinous'.[2]

Shipping companies, too, traded on their own account (particularly in bulk products) at nominal rates to force merchants to heel or to outflank rival shipowners. Booths' unique position as merchant-shipowners preserved their role on the Amazon. Again, establishment advantages, goodwill, agents, and dockside service for goods which needed careful handling, deterred rivals. Hyde explains that South American routes, like those elsewhere, had 'emerged from an initial period of unregulated growth and now became subject (in the relation of shipping space to cargo) to systematic control'.[3]

Beyond these conference loyalties, shipowners conducted their everyday business (building-contracts, brokers, and agents) independently. Concentration of financial and administrative control by amalgamation and absorption, as distinct from conference organization, was an additional means by which competition was restricted and terms imposed. It permitted permanent co-operation, where conferences were essentially short-term arrangements. Fluctuations in earnings also encouraged owners to spread their risks by buying established fleets, often a cheaper way of entering a conference than operating loss-making steamers until admitted. And the personal influence of ambitious individuals was an important impetus to amalgamation.

From 1900 a well-defined process existed whereby a small and

---

[1] Gepp, Gepp to Broad, 1 Apr. 1896.

[2] *Diario de Diputados* (Chile), 7 June 1913, 89–94; see *Fairplay*, Oct. and Nov. 1891, for an account of the 'fighting' ships used by the Kosmos and Kirsten lines against Lamport & Holt on the West Coast.

[3] Hyde, *Shipping Enterprise and Management*, p. 59.

declining number of companies absorbed their rivals and acquired an increasing volume of British tonnage. In particular the bulk of twelve-knot ships of 4,000 tons or more was operated by seven large liner groups, of which Royal Mail and Furness-Withy constituted two, controlling nearly 50 per cent of Britain's shipping after 1920 and enjoying increased authority in fixing ocean freight rates.[1] In addition to acquiring interests in Africa, the Far East, and the Mediterranean, Royal Mail purchased three of its main rivals in the South American trades before the First World War: P.S.N. (1910), Lamport & Holt (1911), and H. &. W. Nelson (1913). Similarly, the Furness-Withy group worked Manchester Liners, Houlder Brothers, the Prince Line, the Quebec Steamship Company, and the British and Argentine Line. Easy access to the capital market reinforced the large groups. Royal Mail raised £7 million before 1914 to finance its deals. The motives for merging aroused suspicion. P.S.N. was acquired when it advertised a direct line to the River Plate against Royal Mail. Nelsons were a non-conference line loading at Liverpool, which from 1910 threatened Royal Mail's meat and passenger businesses at London. The merger policies of British steamship companies in Latin America thus weakened competition and seemed to place the republics at the mercy of an oligopoly of large corporations.

V

Nevertheless, clear limitations on the powers of shipping conferences existed. The attitude of merchants was crucial to the shipowner. 'The strength of a monopolist', explains Robinson, 'lies in his power to raise prices without frightening away all his customers.'[2] The fact that many shippers in continental Europe and Latin America continued to support the regular lines challenges the view that the tactics of British shipowners were wholly damaging. Of course, some shippers supported a particular line through habit and convention (the brand name effect), often on national grounds. The largest shippers had substantial incentives, including preferential terms on bulk contracts[3] and conciliation

---

[1] E. T. Chamberlain, *Liner Predominance in Transoceanic Shipping* (Trade Information Bulletin 448, Washington, 1928), *passim.*

[2] E. A. G. Robinson, *Monopoly* (London, 1945), p. 5.

[3] Naumann Gepp tied Royal Mail and two German lines to a carriage contract n 1898: R.M.S.P., *Minutes*, 19 Oct. 1898; Gepp, *Board Minutes*, 19 Oct. 1898.

machinery for disputes, to encourage them in the use of conference lines. In addition, large shippers like E. Johnston & Sons,[1] who held steamship agencies and signed conference circulars, had direct access to shipping managers and exerted considerable influence. In the Singapore trade the deferred rebate was successfully imposed, after years of intermittent use, only in 1896 when it was accepted by the three largest shippers.[2] In turn, the lines preferred bulk loads which cut handling costs and reduced delays in ports. Yet to suggest that conference members deliberately allied themselves to an oligopoly of large, normally expatriate merchants in Latin America at the expense of smaller shippers would be wrong. A relationship of some kind was inevitable, since exports were usually handled in bulk by a few large foreign merchants. But it was in the long-term interest of shipping conferences to ensure the survival of the small man against the dominance of more substantial merchants.

Moreover, conferences offered merchants real advantages, namely frequent, efficient, regular, stable, and dependable services by first-class tonnage whether full cargoes were available or not, which permitted the confident forward planning that tramp shipping could not supply. Shippers often expressed strong preference, even under higher rates (which only formed a fraction of final cost), for quality shipping. More than anything else merchants feared damage *en route* and irregular delivery, and they willingly paid more to any service which guaranteed them against both. Arthur Cook told the Royal Commission on Shipping Rings that two shipping firms gave widely differing quotations on piping for Latin America. The dearer liner, a conference member, arrived with only 0·5 per cent breakages, while the cheaper tramp had losses of 42 per cent.[3] Similarly, coffee, a valuable cargo needing regular shipment, had to be carefully handled and stowed. Thus, Hard Rand, coffee shippers at Santos, told the Alexander Committee that they did not oppose the deferred rebate, and actually preferred conference tonnage to the cheaper outside competitors who could not guarantee reliable shipment.[4] These considerations also applied to those whom the merchants served,

---

[1] Johnston, Rio to London, 28 July 1902, Letter Book II.
[2] Chian Hai Ding, 'The Early Shipping Conference System of Singapore 1897–1911', *Journal of South East Asian History*, x (1969), 56.
[3] R.C.S.R., P.P. 1909, xlviii, QQ. 19155–66.
[4] Alexander Committee, evid., pp. 60–85. See also report, pp. 162–3.

whether producers or consumers of foodstuffs and manufactured goods. Naumann Gepp feared that loading coffee in tramp tonnage would alienate buyers in New York.[1]

Similarly, combination among shipowners realized benefits for the consumer—although these were not necessarily the prime motive. Services were rationalized. Royal Mail and Nelsons developed the River Plate trade from Britain, P.S.N. loaded only for the West Coast, and Lamport & Holt shipped only to New York. The shipper received at least some of the benefits of economies of scale, combined representation and advertising, improved terms for bulk stevedoring and shipbuilding contracts, and the cheaper credit available to a large group which permitted faster investment in improved technologies. Nor were shipowners normally a direct threat to merchants. Merger movements before 1914 were horizontal rather than vertical. Shipowners did not take over merchant firms or enter buying and retailing.

If shipowners' tactics became unacceptable, merchants could undertake effective bargaining both to represent their views and, if necessary, in reprisal. The Shipping Rings Commission concluded that merchant associations were 'our main recommendation' to restrain shipowners.[2] Critics considered such co-operation 'absolutely impossible';[3] merchants were relatively small-scale, disorganized, and scattered at various ports or in the hinterland; there were mutual jealousies and conflicts of interest; meat shippers had little in common with nitrate exporters who required totally different services. The Minority Report of the Royal Commission on Shipping Rings also considered the limitations imposed by merchants to be illusory. Nevertheless, a measure of association was possible between firms to lobby officials and shipowners and to organize opposition. H. H. Clarke, who attacked the South African lines, formed the British Mercantile League, a commercial pressure group.[4] A deputation of Members of Parliament and commercial interests to Lloyd George at the Board of

---

[1] Gepp, London to Santos, 17 June 1896.

[2] R.C.S.R., P.P. 1909, xlvii, 85; P.R.O. B.T. MT9 869 M1569 (1910), memo on the report of the R.C.S.R.

[3] R.C.S.R., P.P. 1909, xlvii, Q. 837.

[4] H. H. Clarke, *The Shipping Ring and the South African Trade* (London, 1898); *B.R.*, 11 July 1899, 457, and 25 July 1899, 478; *The Times*, 9 June 1899, 13e; *Fairplay*, 15 June 1899, 1035 and 1059; P.R.O. B.T. MT9 734 M11869 and M12390 (1902).

Trade in 1906 encouraged the formation of the Royal Commission on Shipping Rings. The Manchester cotton trade, the Federation of British Industry, Chambers of Commerce, and the British Iron and Steel Federation were also active.[1] Similarly, semi-official organizations in South America united shippers.[2] Arthur Cook insisted that the Brazilian conference should listen to merchants' views, and Owen Philipps, Royal Mail's chairman, visited textile manufacturers in Manchester in 1904 to discuss the onset of cheap competition at that port.[3]

Large shippers, too, proved tough opponents. E. Johnston & Sons, who played one line against another, gave their Le Havre coffee to the Royal Mail steamers, abandoning the accumulated rebate on their Chargeurs Réunis shipments. Subsequently Johnston threatened to abandon Royal Mail, 'to bring home to the directors that it was necessary to show some attention to their large customers'.[4] Merchants in the bulk trades could charter or load outsiders if conference terms were unreasonable, a tactic less suitable for small merchants whose business consisted of small parcels at a number of calls. The United States Steel Corporation employed Wessel Duval, a non-conference firm, or chartered its own tonnage.[5] In 1912 Balfour Williamson chartered shipping, declaring 'war to the knife' against P.S.N.[6] Edward Greene, Johnston's manager in Brazil, explained that the availability of outsiders and the current unpopularity of Lamport & Holt made shippers 'determined not to ship by the combination . . . Knocking down freights has become the popular amusement of the hour'.[7] Conferences could not ignore shippers with impunity. When Lamport & Holt tried to squeeze Naumann Gepp who, annoyed at conference tactics, had loaded outsiders, the resulting battle forced Lamports to sue for peace.[8]

As a last resort merchants operated their own shipping. Considerable difficulties—such operations required expertise and

---

[1] P.R.O. B.T. MT9 926 M20232 (1913), Manchester Association of Importers and Exporters to Board of Trade, 3 July 1913; see also MT9 792 M9628 (1906); J. R. Galloway, *Shipping Rings and the Manchester Cotton Trade* (London, 1898).   [2] Sanderson, op. cit., pp. 118–33.

[3] R.M.S.P., *Minutes*, 16 Mar. 1904.

[4] Johnston, Rio to London, 3 Nov. 1902 and 26 May 1903.

[5] Alexander Committee, evid., pp. 490–9.

[6] Gibbs, 11470/20, Valparaíso to London, 1 Aug. 1912.

[7] Johnston, Greene to New York, 4 May 1896.

[8] Gepp, Naumann Gepp to F. & S. Hampshire, 23 Jan. 1898.

capital, and ships might sail half-full—made many attempts short-lived. Nevertheless, W. R. Grace & Co., New York merchants whose rough cargoes comprised about 75 per cent of their total freights, loaded tonnage for South America.[1] And if the merchant shipowner handled bulk cargoes, business was assured. The Nitrate Producers Steamship Company, formed by John Thomas North to serve his several *oficinas* in Chile, became a powerful West Coast line.[2] After the First World War the Vestey meat-packing company operated its own Blue Star line of refrigerated ships, in response to unacceptable terms imposed by Royal Mail and Furness-Withy.

VI

Official intervention also restrained British shipowners. Latin American governments interfered not so much to help all shippers —since the largest were foreign and probably well able to look after themselves—but to prevent abuses and protect the smaller local houses and the producer, whose net income was threatened by rising rates. Intervention at the local level constituted one constraint. Petty officials harassed steamship companies in the ports.[3] Costly and delaying quarantine and sanitary rules, important since epidemics along Latin America's coasts were frequent, could also be applied coercively. 'There can be no doubt', one angry shipowner claimed, 'that hanging would be too good for the heads of the sanitary department in Rio.'[4] Particular officials made life difficult. The inspector of the Rio custom house was, Royal Mail explained to the British Minister in 1897, 'only occupied in raising obstacles and imposing unjust fines'.[5]

Local governments withheld essential berthing privileges (*patentes*) from liners, unless companies complied with certain regulations. In 1876 Argentina threatened delays unless British ships carried six emigrants free. Such harassment succeeded

[1] Alexander Committee, evid., pp. 464–79 and report, p. 184; P.S.N. *Minutes*, 4 Aug. 1896 and 13 July 1909.

[2] *Fairplay*, 1 Feb. 1895, 258, and 22 Mar. 1895, 656.

[3] P.R.O. F.O. 128/196, Wilson Coaling Co. to Grenville, 14 June 1893, and P.R.O. F.O. 118/245, Wilson Coaling Co. to Barrington, 6 Apr. 1899; P.R.O. F.O. 13/729, F.O. to Grenville, 21 Sept. 1894.

[4] P.R.O. F.O. 128/222, Raeburn & Vesel to Samson, 1 Apr. 1895.

[5] P.R.O. F.O. 128/233, Royal Mail to Phipps, 5 Jan. 1897; cf. P.R.O. F.O. 118/245, Knott to Barrington, 23 Feb. 1899.

because shipowners could not 'offer any effectual resistance and through fear of seeing their vessels excluded from the port of Buenos Aires'.[1] Companies lost their *patentes* if they refused to carry mails free, or if they omitted calls to avoid postal obligations. 'It is an absurdity', Royal Mail's representative in Rio informed London, 'that the Brazilian government . . . should arrogate the right to keep a mail line to a particular itinerary when it does not pay that line a penny.'[2] Harassment, not necessarily part of an organized policy, reminded British companies of the powers which could be employed against them if their tactics became unacceptable.

Local competition gave Latin American officials a further weapon against foreign shipowners. The fact that privately owned tonnage in Latin America was on a small scale until the end of the century created difficulties. Chilean shipping practically disappeared from the West Coast during the 1860s–1870s.[3] The expansion of the late 1840s, under the attraction of trading with California and an end to restrictive legislation, was short-lived. Local investors preferred mines and agriculture to shipping, and Chilean registries were transferred to neutrals when Chile declared war on Spain in 1865. Lack of local shipbuilding was also a handicap. Thus, the emergence of a national mercantile marine depended on government initiative. But subsidies and preferences to local companies were not necessarily the answer (see above, pp. 123–4). And the era of fleets totally government-owned and government-operated was not to come until after the First World War.

Nevertheless, government assistance to shipping in Latin America took three forms. Coastal services, the first form of opposition to the established lines, were from the late nineteenth century increasingly nationalized. Native concerns, trans-shipping small parcels at a succession of tiny harbours to ocean-going tonnage at the major ports, provided a buffer between local producers and the foreign shipowners, and formed the nucleus for wider operations. Coastal shipping was a training ground for men, managers, and ships. Thus before the First World War, Brazil, Argentina and Chile, with their long coastlines and natural

---

[1] P.R.O. F.O. 6/361, Egerton to Granville, 25 May 1880; see also correspondence in P.R.O. F.O. 6/352.

[2] R.M.S.P. Brazil and River Plate Correspondence, Greenwich, Rio to London, 13 Mar. 1903.

[3] Véliz, op. cit., pp. 88–174.

interests in local shipping, restricted coasting to national lines. The impact on British companies was small. Their coastal interests in Latin America were confined to south Brazil, which they abandoned, and the West Coast. In Brazil, where in 1888 eight native coastal shipping concerns existed,[1] and in Argentina, where Nicholas Mihanovitch constructed a wide network of services, local firms in any case already predominated. The Germans, the main foreign interest in Latin American coasting, merely re-registered their ships while retaining full control. Subsidies, particularly to southern ports which Argentina hoped to develop, reinforced her coasting policy. Nevertheless, it continued to be said that exclusively native concerns provided a poor service, charged high rates, and could not meet demand.

A second point at which governments intervened was to offer subsidies to foreign competitors against the existing lines. This was a policy favoured by Argentina, who alone of the larger republics failed to establish an ocean-going fleet. But it was not a success. The onerous terms offered—flying the national flag, free passages for officials and military personnel, and abstention from rate wars—were unattractive. Argentina formulated proposals in 1887, the 1890s, and 1905, when a bill presented by Pedro Luro, deputy for Buenos Aires and President of the Asociación de la Marina Mercante Nacional, offered £5,000 per round trip, Europe to the River Plate, for fast steamers.[2] Chile, too, offered subsidies to Italian lines to improve links with Brazil and encourage emigration.[3]

The promotion of local ocean-going tonnage was the third form of state intervention. The Chilean Compañía Sud-Americana de Vapores (C.S.A.V.), an amalgam of two coastal concerns assisted by generous subsidies and preferential government cargo contracts, challenged P.S.N. from 1872.[4] The resultant rate-cutting, P.S.N.'s directors reported, seriously affected revenue. By 1873 P.S.N. wanted an arrangement which would raise fares and

---

[1] U.S.M.C.R., Aug. 1888, xxvii, 96, pp. 260–1.

[2] Ibid., Nov. 1905, 302, pp. 56–8, and Dec. 1905, 303, p. 223; *Diario de Diputados* (Argentina), 7 Aug. 1905, 121–7, 23 Aug. 1905, 501, 11 Sept. 1905, 841–54, 27 Sept. 1905, 161; R.M.S.P., *Minutes*, 23 Aug., 13 Sept., 8 Nov., and 6 Dec. 1905.

[3] *Diario de Diputados* (Chile), 25 Jan. 1911, 1784–5.

[4] Véliz, op. cit., pp. 177–9 and 207–22; P.R.O. F.O. 61/318, St. John to Salisbury, 16 Apr. 1879.

freights to an equitable level.[1] The directors considered outright purchase of their rival but preferred a sailing scheme 2:1 in their favour. P.S.N. allowed C.S.A.V. to load south of Valparaíso, but not at the lucrative ports north of Callao. The Chileans accepted a five-year agreement on these lines rather than continue ruinous competition. After the War of the Pacific, when the two companies came to co-operate closely, operating joint services north of Panama and pooling revenue, C.S.A.V. achieved parity with P.S.N. and prevented a British monopoly of West Coast services.[2] Indeed, the futility of competing with C.S.A.V. taught P.S.N. a valuable lesson. In 1907, when the Compañía Peruana de Vapores bought tonnage in Europe to load on the West Coast, P.S.N. was not prepared to fight a costly battle which would have encouraged retaliation by the Peruvian Government.[3]

Lloyd–Brasileiro, a merger of four coasting lines which monopolized Brazil's ocean-going tonnage, experienced a turbulent financial history.[4] It was, Dering told Lansdowne, 'a badly managed and corrupt Shipping Society'.[5] Under massive public support— the Brazilian Government owned 66 per cent—it struggled to maintain the services until the outbreak of war in 1914. It loaded for New York from 1906, proposed a service to Europe in 1910, and attacked Booths at Pará in 1912. Its only consistent northbound shipper was Arbuckle Brothers who loaded coffee.[6] Cargoes were more readily available southbound where no rebate existed since many coffee carriers returned to Brazil via Europe. Lloyd–Brasileiro thus blamed conference tactics for the dearth of cargo for New York. But, as Hard Rand made clear, the cheaper

[1] P.S.N., *Minutes*, 8 Dec. 1873, 2 Mar. 1874, 8 and 12 Mar. and 13 Sept. 1875; P.S.N., *Meetings*, 11 Aug. 1874, 14 July 1875, and 7 June 1876.

[2] P.S.N., *Meetings*, 3 May 1882 and 9 May 1883; P.S.N., *Minutes*, 14 Sept. 1881, 8 May 1882, 3 May 1887, 19 Aug. 1889, 27 Mar. 1891, 29 Oct. 1894, and 4 Feb. 1895; *Diario de Diputados* (Chile), 8 June 1893, 33, 30 July 1896, 252–5; U.S.M.C.R., Feb. 1901, lxv, 245, p. 263.

[3] P.S.N., *Minutes*, 30 Jan. 1906, 12 Apr. and 13 Sept. 1911; see also U.S.M.C.R., Oct. 1906, 313, pp. 60–1; P.R.O. F.O. 368/484/853, Jerome to Grey, 1 Nov. 1909.

[4] *B.R.*, 18 July 1899, 474, and 14 Nov. 1899, 746–7; R. Graham, *Britain and the Onset of Modernisation in Brazil, 1860–1914* (Cambridge, 1968), p. 198; U.S.M.C.R., Feb. 1902, lxviii, 257, pp. 253–5, and Nov. 1909, 350, pp. 53–4.

[5] P.R.O. F.O. 13/236, Dering to Lansdowne, 28 Dec. 1903.

[6] G. Jones, *Government Aid to Merchant Shipping* (Special Agents Series 119, Washington, 1916), pp. 229–32; *Fairplay*, 5 May 1904, 715; U.S.M.C.R., Nov. 1906, 314, pp. 134–5, and Apr. 1909, 343, p. 59; Alexander Committee, evid., pp. 144–5.

rates of Lloyd-Brasileiro were simply unattractive so long as its service was poor. Its influence, therefore, on the East Coast was less than C.S.A.V.'s on the Pacific.

Legal restraint formed a further weapon to control foreign shipowners. The growth of conferences soon attracted attention as examples of cartelization and oligopoly. The years before 1914 marked a wide variety of official policies. In Britain the majority report of the Royal Commission on Shipping Rings recommended no legislative action. The view was that most shipowners of conference lines were 'public spirited men fully alive to the desirability of increasing trade'.[1] Officials, adopting a traditionally *laissez-faire* attitude, would not intercede between two sets of businessmen (merchants and shipowners) who were the best judges of their needs, nor would they legislate against or handicap an industry crucial to national well-being. The Royal Commission recognized the good service which conferences gave and the real restraints which existed. British courts, too, tended to ignore the coercive tactics of conferences.[2] And officials were not prepared to establish a costly supervisory body when rate control in an international industry presented such enormous difficulties. Who could prevent foreign lines from cutting or increasing tariffs, changes which British shipowners could not ignore under whatever legal restraints? The problems were rather different for railway control which had a long tradition in Britain, since the scope of operations was confined and the danger of monopoly more apparent.[3]

The United States, which depended on foreign ocean tonnage, adopted a firmer line. She considered that European companies, among which the British predominated, unfairly discriminated against American merchants by providing older tonnage at New York and overcharging on Latin American routes by comparison with services from Europe.[4] She particularly resented the fact that

---

[1] R.C.S.R., P.P. 1909, xlvii, 85; see also P.R.O. B.T. MT9 869 M1569 (1910), memo on the Report of the R.C.S.R., and Sanderson, op. cit., pp. 47–90.

[2] P. H. Guenault and J. M. Jackson, *The Control of Monopoly in the United Kingdom* (London, 1960), pp. 12–13; G. C. Allen, *Monopoly and Restrictive Practices* (London, 1969), pp. 59–62. The famous Mogul case, when an outsider indicted the Far East conference, was lost.

[3] P. J. Cain, 'Railway Combination and Government, 1900–1914', *Economic History Review*, 2nd ser. xxv (1972), 623–41.

[4] U.S.M.C.R., Dec. 1905, 303, p. 229, Mar. 1906, 306, pp. 30–57, Nov. 1909, 350, pp. 47–53; J. Bristow, *Report on the Panama Canal*, Senate Document 429, 59th Congress, first session (1905), p. 47; Pletcher, loc. cit., pp. 20–30.

services between Latin America and the United States seemed totally dependent on conference decisions made in Europe. At the same time trust scandals in America's domestic industry, which were requiring legislation (the Sherman Act of 1905 and the Clayton Act of 1914), had alarmed the country. Conferences and mergers among foreign shipowners thus assumed sinister proportions. 'In issues relating to monopoly', Guenault and Jackson have explained, 'the reactions of government and people are based more on fears and suspicions than upon firm facts.'[1] The Alexander Committee thus recommended closer supervision of such abuses as secret tariffs and preferences, and an end to the deferred rebate. In 1914 legal proceedings were taken against the Prince Line and the Brazilian conference, alleging unlawful conspiracy and restraint of trade. The outbreak of war rendered the case academic, but Judge Lacombe in fact found for the lines.[2]

British Dominions and Colonies, themselves dependent on overseas tonnage, were also suspicious. South Africa, pressing for the Royal Commission on Shipping Rings in 1906, continued to threaten restraining legislation.[3] Australia, too, had been active. At Singapore, where since 1901 a succession of inquiries had investigated the effect of the shipping conference and pressed Whitehall for action, successful legal restraint was ultimately imposed. In 1910 the colony introduced the Freight and Steamship Bill outlawing rebates and imposing penalties. The shipping companies then agreed to abandon rebates if the bill were withdrawn.[4]

Latin America's position was close to that of the United States and the British Empire. Brazil framed legislation aimed at foreign shipowners, although before 1914 it was not extensively applied. The Alexander Committee was told that Brazil began, but did not press, a case against the conference lines in 1908. The deferred rebate was not outlawed until 1933, when the São Paulo Chamber of Commerce still wanted its retention.[5] In 1912 the foreign firms

---

[1] Guenault and Jackson, op. cit., p. 3.
[2] P.R.O. B.T. MT9 973 M9002 (1915).
[3] P.R.O. B.T. MT9 784 M23600 (1905), Colonial Office to Board of Trade, 23 Dec. 1905.
[4] Chian Hai Ding, loc. cit., pp. 50–66; see also P.R.O. C.O., 273 247, Minute 12302, and 256, Minute 14113.
[5] Sanderson, op. cit., pp. 118–23; Marx, op. cit., pp. 98–9; Alexander Committee, evid., p. 36.

at Rio protested against double taxes in the Brazilian budget
(which discriminated against those who applied rebates), and
were said to be marshalling impressive support against the imposition of rate control.[1] And Antony Gibbs & Sons, whose
employment of outsiders the conference lines resisted, certainly
recognized that, while rebates and other tactics were not illegal in
Britain, 'Chilean and Peruvian law would be much more likely to
be of service . . . These countries might with more justice consider
themselves prejudiced by being unable to avail themselves of the
cheapest outlets available for their products.'[2]

In the years before 1914 Latin American interference, whether
at a local level, in the development of competition, or in the courts,
did not seriously impede British liner companies. Local and legal
intervention was a threat rather than a reality, though none the
less important. Native competition was not normally decisive. At
the same time, Latin American policy appeared contradictory.
Argentina tried to subsidize foreign lines to develop shipping
links. Chile supported P.S.N. as well as its national rival, C.S.A.V.,
which in turn became one of the West Coast conference lines.
Senator MacIver certainly saw the irony here. 'We have', he
explained, 'a twin colossus of navigation on our coasts . . . two
companies but only one interest.'[3] Similarly, Brazil acted against
the conference, but also 'persuaded' the lines to accept Lloyd–
Brasileiro in conference decisions and benefits.[4] Chile complained
of high rates, but resented the long freight war with Kosmos
which depleted C.S.A.V.'s finances. While coasting theoretically
excluded foreign tonnage, rates rose since local concerns could not
cope. Legal resources were not much more helpful. Thoroughgoing merger, long-term contracts, or verbal arrangements often
circumvented attacks on rebates and conferences.

Nevertheless, the success of United States and Singapore
legislation showed what might be achieved. And despite the
limited short-term effects of Latin America's shipping policy, a
new determination was apparent immediately before the First
World War. The expansion of C.S.A.V. and Lloyd-Brasileiro, the
onset of the Compañía Peruana, and Pedro Luro's Bill, all occurred

[1] R.M.S.P. *Minutes*, 13 Nov. 1912; *Consular Reports* (Brazil), P.P. 1914–16,
lxxi, 212.
[2] Gibbs 11471/77, London to Valparaíso, 14 Sept. 1905.
[3] *Diario de Senadores* (Chile), 22 Oct. 1894, 64–5.
[4] Alexander Committee, report, p. 158, and evid., pp. 7 and 123–4.

in the years 1905–7. Afterwards Brazil initiated her legal attacks on foreign shipping, and Chile debated the formation of a national mercantile marine.[1] The view, therefore, that British and foreign shipowners could operate without local constraint in Latin America is unacceptable.

VII

Ordinary market forces within the shipping industry proved the most powerful and continuing restraint on the conference lines. Despite the substantial barrier created by the large amount of capital necessary for ocean-going shipping services, outside tonnage (tramps, chartered ships, or new lines) always existed. Immediately before 1914 the Scandinavians, the Japanese, and the Dutch became formidable competitors.[2] Shipping was a wholly international trade in which units were easily transferable. Rising rates and profits in a particular trade attracted outside tonnage, which soon restored equilibrium. Freedom of the seas did not exclude shipowners from any ports, and the conference lines had little control over shipbuilding. Because the expenses of steamship operation were largely unaffected by the volume of cargo shipped, it paid owners to load at low rates if ballast were the only alternative. Moreover shipping was traditionally a stronghold of small-scale but vigorously independent operators, in which the fittest survived. Despite the obstacles which conferences erected— rebates, specialized services, long-term contracts, and fighting ships—no monopoly was safe for long.

Moreover, conferences had little influence in the bulk, low-value seasonal traffic which formed a substantial proportion of Latin America's cargoes, and for which tramps were able to compete. Nitrate from Chile and grain from Argentina, among homeward trades, as well as coal outwards, were exclusive to tramps and sail. They required no specialized tonnage or handling and demanded the cheapest freights. Time was no object in shipment. They were loaded at one or two ports, nitrate at Iquique and Antofagasta and grain at Rosario or Buenos Aires, which particularly suited non-conference tonnage. Indeed, the West Coast was for years the

---

[1] *Diario de Diputados* (Chile), 7 June 1913, 89–94; P.S.N., *Minutes*, 22 Mar. 1910, 29 Jan. 1913, and 18 Mar. 1914.

[2] The Norwegian Johnson Line loaded for Buenos Aires from 1905, see U.S.M.C.R., Apr. 1905, 295, pp. 82–3.

preserve of sailing ships. When Colonel North launched one of the Nitrate Producers' vessels in 1895, he recognized that the 'nitrate trade seems to be the only trade of any magnitude that has not received any development from the use of steam'.[1]

Internal instability also prevented conferences from exercising permanent control on the shipping trades. Like all associations to maintain prices and restrict output, they suffered strains and stresses. Unscrupulous members offered special discounts, illegal rebates, and unauthorized underquotations to outflank their conference partners, and blamed their agents or 'invented' competition to justify these tactics. The Booth Committee reported in 1918 that German companies 'did not scruple to increase [their] advantages by the employment of unfair methods'. Cases of evasion of conference commitments and subterfuge in South and Central America were 'too numerous to be regarded as accidental'.[2] Market sharing and pooling were unlikely to endure, since no two firms had an identical cost structure. Strong, aggressive companies seized additional business where possible; weaker lines were defensive, anxious only to retain what they had. Under new management from 1903, Royal Mail became consistently aggressive, attacking its old ally P.S.N., seeking berths at Antwerp, and challenging Hamburg–Amerika in the Caribbean.[3] Cartelization and oligopoly need not, therefore, imply a static situation. Partition of business was intermittent, not permanent. At the same time powerful outsiders had to be accommodated. The Brazil and River Plate conference admitted the French companies, Messageries Maritimes and Chargeurs Réunis, in 1897, the Italians in 1899, Houlder Brothers in 1906, and the Dutch in 1908.[4] And to prevent twenty or more international shipping companies from squabbling in an increasingly difficult market was impossible. In 1907, Hamburg-Amerika's attempt to raise its representation at New York began a twelve-month rate-war to Brazilian ports.[5] Booths,

[1] *Fairplay*, 1 Feb. 1895, 258.

[2] *Report on the Shipping and Shipbuilding Industries After the War*, P.P. 1918, xiii, 575–7.

[3] R.M.S.P., *Minutes*, 27 Apr. and 2 Nov. 1904, 13 Feb. and 31 July 1907; P.S.N., *Minutes*, 13 Mar. 1906 and 10 Feb. 1907; *Fairplay*, 21 Jan. 1904, 78.

[4] P.S.N., *Minutes*, 23 Mar. 1897, 18 Dec. 1899, 18 Sept. 1906, and 7 July 1908.

[5] U.S.M.C.R., Jan. 1903, lxxi, 268, p. 150; John, op. cit., pp. 101–3; *B.R.*, 16 Apr. 1901, 283, and 16 Sept. 1902, 455; R.C.S.R., P.P. 1909, xlviii, QQ. 19244 *et seq.*

whose control of ports in northern Brazil had hitherto been unchallenged, could not prevent the inroads of the Germans from 1901.[1]

Nor did fixed rates and berthing-control end competition. They diverted attention to non-price competition, facilities, and quality of tonnage. The race to build fast, modern liners between Royal Mail and Hamburg-Sud Amerika, both conference partners, was a marked feature of pre-war development in the Latin American trades. Services before and after shipment (warehousing, dock charges, and brokerage) became a competitive area within which the customer gained. Firms which could not satisfy demand in these respects lost business. Pooling may certainly delay the impact of non-price competition. Although traffic is naturally attracted to the best ships (given that rates are equal), pooling ensures a more even distribution of earnings among companies whose ships vary in age and efficiency. But this situation will not last long. Companies which improve tonnage will inevitably demand and take a greater share of business. 'Monopoly', explains G. C. Allen, 'is . . . always more or less vulnerable to innovations in demand and technique.'[2] And the competitive search for traffic is increased at the ports, where agents try to boost their earnings. Non-price competition continues to test a firm's enemies without commitment to a full-scale encounter.

Freight levels do not suggest that the power of the organized shipowners was excessive, or that ordinary commercial forces did not apply in the industry. Of course conference rates were inevitably higher than those ruling in the rough, bulk trades which required the cheapest services. At all levels the service of the regular lines was superior, at a cost, and this attracted rather than lost business. But over-all freight rates fell consistently from the 1870s as available tonnage outstripped cargo,[3] a trend against which shipowners were powerless.

It is true that tramp rates, which form the major part of available indices, may prove misleading. Specialized liner trades, requiring better facilities, were relatively isolated from general trends. But

---

[1] Alexander Committee, evid., pp. 153–237; *S.A.J.*, 28 Sept. 1907, 327.

[2] Allen, op. cit., p. 13.

[3] A. K. Cairncross, *Home and Foreign Investment 1870–1913* (Cambridge, 1953), pp. 132 and 176; E. A. V. Angier, *Fifty Years Freights 1869–1919* (London, 1920); E. S. Gregg, 'Vicissitudes in the Shipping Trades, 1870–1920', *Quarterly Journal of Economics*, xxxv (1921), 603–17.

the few categories of bulk cargo which represented 60 per cent of Britain's shipping business ultimately determined rates. A fall in the earning power of the tramp's traditional traffic inevitably forced it into competition with liners (as in the case of the Brazilian coffee trade), and widely influenced rates. The persistent availability of outsiders and tramps limited the rates which conferences could charge. Nor were major increases attributable to shipping conferences. Improving rates from 1896 to 1901 were influenced by the Spanish–American and Boer Wars when tonnage was scarce. Coffee shippers in Brazil complained that they could not secure tonnage at 50 cents a bag in 1900. Within months the level had fallen below 35 cents.[1] 'Despite some noticeable exceptions,' explained Professor North, 'the ocean freight market was competitive . . . and the long-term secular decline in the nineteenth century reflected the operations of an impersonal market.'[2]

Likewise, shipowners' profits did not suggest that rates were unduly high. Liners and tramps suffered together. Of course, operating charges had decreased as a result of greater port efficiency and declining coal costs. Nevertheless, the gap between outgoings and revenue had persistently narrowed. According to Derek Aldcroft: 'Few industries have been subject to such violent fluctuations as the shipping industries . . . on balance the bad years outnumbered the good. In the 45 years before 1914 the number of poor years exceeded the prosperous ones by two to one.'[3]

Between 1901 and 1911 the state of British shipping was particularly depressed and unprofitable. The worst year, 1908, was marked by 'unexampled depression in all freights'. These facts strongly suggest that the ability of shipowners to influence rates was limited, and that the cost of their services to Latin America was falling.

VIII

In the years before 1914 British shipowners in Latin America exercised a prima facie control over a crucial economic sector. Expatriate shipping companies, which the British still dominated,

---

[1] U.S.M.C.R., Mar. 1900, lxxii, 234, p. 362; *B.R.*, 30 Apr. 1901, 310.
[2] North, loc. cit., p. 539.
[3] Derek H. Aldcroft, 'The Depression in British Shipping, 1901–1911', *Journal of Transport History*, vii (1965), 14; see also, Gregg, loc. cit., pp. 614–15.

had almost totally captured the republics' ocean-carrying trades. Firms loading at and developing small ports enjoyed enormous influence, apparently reinforcing Britain's international commercial monopoly.[1] Similarly, Richard Graham writes that 'Great Britain's control of the world's largest shipping trade gave it one more stake in Brazil's export-import economy'.[2] Merchants, officials, and the public resented what they took to be dependence on foreign shipowners. Deputy Subercasseaux expressed his fears of 'the complete absorption of the Chilean flag by foreigners, the purchase of our companies by foreigners; once this is realized, the companies which dominate the Pacific could impose rates at the maximum that trade and passengers could bear'.[3] And the American Consul at Pará agreed that the British shipping firms in Pará 'have not used their monopoly in such a way as to win popularity'.[4] Strategic and national issues were also at stake. The republics with long seaboards wanted effective merchant fleets, but they were undersold by foreigners. In one sense shipping constituted an absolute monopoly. No alternative existed to shipment by sea. Much of Latin America's external trade was with Europe and the United States; it was not intercontinental, when railways might have been used. Railways tended to link the hinterland to the ports, thus complementing, not competing with, shipping. The capital required to start an ocean-going service also restricted entry.

Beyond these general considerations, particular areas of friction developed. In the mid-nineteenth century contracts and concessions seemed to protect companies against competition. Interference in local affairs, and the power to influence opinion through agents and the press, aroused animosity. Most important, conferences of shipowners represented a collective, continuing monopoly which set prices for consumers, fixed output, shared business, and excluded outsiders over specified routes. Latin Americans naturally resented the apparent power of large, rich, expatriate corporations—in sharp contrast to small, local shipping concerns—over Latin American producers, merchants, consumers, and commodity prices. The concentration of control and ownership appeared to

---

[1] Gibbs to Evarts, 6 Aug. 1877, *Foreign Relations of the United States* (Peru), 1877, p. 449, includes a description of P.S.N. as 'a powerful link in a commercial chain'. [2] Graham, op. cit., p. 88.

[3] *Diario de Diputados* (Chile), 15 Dec. 1909, 909.

[4] U.S.M.C.R., Feb. 1901, lxv, 245, pp. 216–17.

restrain commerce, 'tying' merchants and preventing them from employing cheaper tonnage or redirecting trade. At their worst, conferences, which diverted income from native producers, threatened Latin America's economic and social stability. They were also extravagant, since they reduced or destroyed competition in prices. Why should merchants pay for luxury ships at regular intervals, when their own needs fluctuated? Conferences, too, had an international impact, giving rise to fears of a plot by the developed nations against the underdeveloped. Conferences were against the public interest because they induced inefficiency, wasted resources, and prevented the spread of benefits from improved technologies. Robinson, while acknowledging some advantages in mitigation, considered that conferences 'have in many instances used their monopoly powers, not to give the best or most desired service at a reasonable cost but to make unreasonable charges'.[1] And if the larger republics, Argentina, Chile, and Brazil, could take care of themselves, the smaller ones like Ecuador seemed to have few options.

However, fears that British shipowners would control Latin America's economic and political development were exaggerated. The fact that sea-lanes and ports were open to all militated against a permanent monopoly. 'In ocean shipping', explained MacRosty, 'we have complete freedom of competition. The ship is neither tied to port nor trade but can go where-ever cargo and profit call.'[2] A railway company, on the other hand, often operated exclusively; where lines did compete, creating a radius of competition around each terminal, intermediate stations did not benefit. Units were easily transferred between the ocean trades. Tramps, representing 50 per cent of British shipping before the First World War, rarely attempted to combine or to regulate working. Liner owners could not, therefore, permanently control rates, subject to world economic conditions. Shipping was an international industry and was not made up of several exclusive, unrelated routes. The effects of overtonnage or rising rates were quickly transmitted along international sea-lanes. If rates rose or fell in Latin America, her competitors in world markets were already experiencing or would soon experience a similar phenomenon.

---

[1] Robinson, op. cit., p. 71.
[2] H. W. MacRosty, *The Trust Movement in British Industry* (London, 1907), p. 285; see also Kurt Wiedenfeld, *Cartels and Combines* (Geneva, 1927), p. 10.

The degree of concentration among Britain's shipowners may be overestimated. Certainly before 1900, shipping was still a strong-hold of the independent entrepreneur whose innovative and competitive aggression limited the power of the liner companies. In Germany, where two groups owned 80 per cent of tonnage, and in Holland, the merger process had progressed much further. British owners were often reluctant to abandon their independence.[1] If the corporate image became a threat—Royal Mail opened the Edificio Británico in Buenos Aires in 1917—liner companies did not have the physical presence of railways, always targets of economic nationalists. The fixed assets of shipowners were fewer. They did not directly employ local labour.

Specific charges against British shipowners are not easily maintained. The short-term advantages of the early contracts and concessions did not prevent the emergence of rivals. Entanglement in domestic political affairs was unavoidable but unwanted. Nor were conferences an unmitigated evil. They removed some of the disadvantages of persistent cut-throat competition—fluctuations, sharp practice, and inefficient duplication of plant and services. Co-operation and combination permitted rationalization and economies of scale. Conferences did provide a good service, which many merchants recognized. If conferences were at times guilty of a want of tact and moderation, the charges of a handful of malcontent shippers must be treated with caution. To permit continued warfare would eventually deprive shippers of many lines, leaving their trades at the mercy of the few strong companies which survived. And real restraints existed—merchant organizations, local initiatives, legal devices, and outside tonnage. Conferences failed to eliminate competition or to impose the deferred rebate throughout the carrying trades. Alternative means of ocean shipment were available and were frequently employed. Although British shipping companies gained from conferences, they did not enjoy undiluted control. Rather, conferences were a mixture of rivalry and co-operation. Operating within a monopolistic framework, the business of shipping comprised more competitive features than are at first apparent. Conferences were not static, inflexible organizations, but adaptable and pragmatic.

[1] Admiral Chatfield, chairman of Royal Mail, told P.S.N. in 1894 that he 'declined to participate in arrangements with competing lines', P.S.N. *Minutes*, 2 and 23 Apr. 1894.

Moreover British shipping, like any foreign enterprise abroad, was vulnerable to external stresses. Shipowners wished to avoid any scandal and prejudice overseas which the use of questionable tactics might encourage. They looked for good relations with local-governments. 'A conciliatory and good feeling', the P.S.N. directors minuted, 'must be shown towards the interests of the governments referred to.'[1] Otherwise, what effective redress had British companies against harassment and discrimination? What were Britain's long-term chances against the increasing competition of the Germans, Japanese, and Scandinavians? How would Britain fare when national fleets became a priority after the war? Britain had no ultimate sanction. Boycotting Latin America's ports would merely transfer business to her rivals. And the rising corporate image of British liner companies merely made departure from Latin America, if conditions deteriorated, that much harder. Britain's superiority rested on a thin basis, her ability to provide better services. Moreover, British shipowners relied on Latin America's ability to export and on her purchasing power. Although freights were rarely more than a fraction of total commodity cost, no shipowner would so raise rates as to threaten trade. He had no control over supplies, and he could not risk the production of cheaper substitutes elsewhere. Again, shipowners were vulnerable to new routes. American control at Panama, the plan for and ultimately the construction of a canal, and the development of the Tehuantepec railway, destroyed the old monopoly which the Panama railroad and the favoured shipping lines had enjoyed.

In fact, relations between British shipowners and Latin America were reasonably calm before 1914. Each side permitted the other a few indiscretions rather than risk a full-scale engagement. 'I venture to think', Consul Egerton explained, 'that collective action would only be desirable in the case that the steamship companies . . . should have *serious* cause for complaint.'[2] The fact that Argentina formulated no consistent maritime policy, that C.S.A.V. co-operated with P.S.N., and that Brazil's legislation was essentially mild suggests that foreign shipping was not coercive. The situation made sound economic sense. Latin Americans lacked sufficient resources to develop their own ocean fleets, at least in competition with the rate of return on capital in other

[1] P.S.N. *Minutes*, 11 Oct. 1843.
[2] P.R.O. F.O. 6/367, Egerton to Granville, 29 Aug. 1880.

occupations. The play of market forces was the republics' greatest protection against exploitation. Profit was not evidence of exploitation; it was necessary for renewals and improvements, and as a fair reward for managers and investors. And while all shippers naturally consider freights too high, every index shows that the cost of shipping services had fallen sharply from the late nineteenth century, although a rise did occur from the low point of 1905–8. The Latin American experience suggests that before 1914 expatriate shipping operations were less harmful to the economies of developing countries, and provoked less complaint, than most foreign-owned sectors.

PART III

TRADE

CHAPTER V

Merchants and the Latin American Trades: an Introduction

ROBERT GREENHILL

I

THE development of international trade in the nineteenth century depended increasingly on a chain of intermediaries to transfer ownership of goods from producer to consumer. In primitive societies, exchange of produce involved merely buyer and seller, normally in a barter transaction. But the rise of money economies and the problems which distance imposed required middlemen to perform specialized functions. Large concerns and government organizations sought direct transactions and established independent import/export agencies. Similarly, producers whose goods needed after-sales service developed their own marketing structure. Nevertheless, most businessmen preferred to leave shipment and selling to experts who performed these tasks more efficiently. When a producer lacked capital and an effective sales organization, or handled unbranded bulk goods where personal goodwill was relatively unimportant, he employed intermediaries. Britain, which dominated international commerce in the nineteenth century, employed a long chain of middlemen in her import/export trades. Crucial were the merchant houses abroad, who were experienced in foreign markets and who enjoyed valuable connections with consumers and suppliers.

British houses participated in Latin American trade before Independence on an informal basis. Goods flowed indirectly through metropolitan Spain and Portugal to their colonies in the New World. Economic development in Brazil had long determined the level of British trade with Lisbon. Britain's Caribbean colonies also provided a commercial base for an important contraband trade, and the *asiento* permitted a limited number of British ships to enter Spanish ports. However, the Napoleonic Wars, which obstructed the operations of British houses in Europe, and the independence movement in Latin America, which publicized potential markets and helped remove colonial restrictions, stimulated direct British commercial interest in the New World. Local officials in Spanish America favoured an increase in overseas trade,[1] while the removal of the Portuguese court to Rio under British naval protection exposed Brazil to foreign commercial penetration. Moreover, consumers in the New World, frustrated by blockade in Europe where a war economy ended the export surplus, welcomed new trading opportunities.[2]

There were soon few large cities in Latin America where British houses were unrepresented. The British commercial community became, despite continued local discrimination, a valuable source of scarce imports. Multiple small commission houses, contracted to merchants and manufacturers at home, dominated Britain's pattern of trading in Latin America. The wide range and type of imports, not sold in bulk nor individually of great value, permitted the participation of many businesses in specialized lines. Working for commissions rather than owning the goods they handled, each merchant firm required little capital and minimized its risks. Manufacturers at home preferred commissions. Before the onset of rapid and reliable communications, sellers ran risks from changing supply and demand in any market between the time that they transmitted news of its needs to the point that their goods arrived. Intermediaries who required a large margin to cover risk could buy only well below the intended selling price. Manufacturers preferred to consign on commission, retaining ownership and reaping the trade and risk profit. Thus Antony Gibbs & Sons, whose earliest commercial links were forged in Spain, established commission businesses for textiles and hardware on the Pacific coast.[3] And two families of Yorkshire woollen dealer/manufacturers,

[1] For the role of Viscount Liniers in Buenos Aires see H. S. Ferns, *Britain and Argentina in the Nineteenth Century* (Oxford, 1960), p. 67.

[2] Ibid., p. 80. In 1806–7 British firms sold goods worth £1 million in the River Plate and its hinterland; in 1808–9 forty-one British ships arrived with goods worth £2·7 million; by 1822, the first year when complete customs house figures are available, Britain supplied 60 per cent of Buenos Aires's imports valued at $11·3 million.

[3] J. A. Gibbs, *The History of Antony and Dorothea Gibbs and of their Contemporary Relatives* (London, 1922), pp. 164–8; C. W. Maude, *Antony Gibbs & Sons Limited: Merchants and Bankers 1808–1958* (London, 1958), pp. 11–23.

Luptons[1] and Rhodes,[2] excluded from Europe, sent agents to Rio, who, while chiefly handling their principals' goods, also represented outside firms on a commission basis.

The presence of expatriate merchants was not always welcomed in Latin America. Francisco Encina recognized that after 1850 Chile's overseas trade was increasingly dominated by foreigners. 'In less than 50 years', he wrote, 'the foreign merchant suppressed our expanding commercial enterprise abroad; and in our own backyard eliminated us from international traffic largely replacing us in every respect.'[3] Similarly, Luis Aldunate explained that in Chile 'all the intermediate agents between producers and consumers are foreign', and also that 'into their hands fell all commercial and industrial profits'.[4] British officials in Latin America noted similar developments at the local level. Sir Reginald Tower, British minister in Argentina, explained that the republic's grain trade was in the hands of foreign firms.[5] Milne-Cheetham reported expatriate merchants operating a chain in the Amazon valley. They bought rubber during seasonal gluts which they hoarded until shortages occurred abroad. If prices fell overseas, merchants would not buy from local producers except at unrealistically low levels. 'The mutual sweating which makes life impossible', Milne-Cheetham explained, '. . . is initiated by the foreign exporting merchants.' He had no doubt of 'the control of the industry by the foreign firms who act as intermediaries between the Brazilian producer and the main markets'.[6] And it was Milne-Cheetham who noted similar developments in the cocoa trade where the multiplicity of small farmers hindered united action to resist injustice. 'A group of foreign merchants', he reported, 'having taken advantage of the want of cohesion among the Brazilian growers, have them entirely in their power.'[7] More recently, Harry Magdoff has drawn attention to the tendency of large houses and

[1] Herbert Heaton, 'A Merchant Adventurer in Brazil 1808–1818', *Journal of Economic History*, vi (1946), 1–23.

[2] R. G. Wilson, 'The Fortunes of a Leeds Merchant House 1780–1820', *Business History*, ix (1967), 70–86.

[3] Francisco A. Encina, *Nuestra Inferioridad Económica: Sus Causas, Sus Consecuencias* (Santiago de Chile, 1955), p. 5.

[4] L. Aldunate, *Estudios de Actualidad*, quoted in Aníbal Pinto Santa Cruz, *Chile, Un Caso de Desarrollo Frustrado* (Santiago de Chile, 1959), p. 56.

[5] P.R.O. F.O. 368/786/40153, Tower to Grey, 30 July 1913.

[6] P.R.O. F.O. 368/172/32464, Milne-Cheetham to Grey, 30 Aug. 1908.

[7] P.R.O. F.O. 368/173/31056, Milne-Cheetham to Grey, 19 Aug. 1908.

corporations to control sources of raw materials and markets abroad in order to protect their dominant position and their investments, making use both of economic and political influence.[1]

This chapter examines the nature and extent of the control British merchants exercised over the economy of Latin America. Magnitude of commercial interest does not necessarily imply manipulation. How was influence really exercised? Where does the separation of damaging elements from normal business procedure occur? Where were the areas of friction between British merchants and Latin America's political and economic interests? What resources were available to the producer, the merchant, and the consumer—the three main market forces? Within what boundaries did each sector operate?

II

Latin America at the beginning of the nineteenth century was not in fact a merchant's paradise; it offered simply a temporary solution to the short-term problem of restricted European markets. Obvious limits existed to the volume of specie which Latin America could afford to release for imports, and the further resource of foreign loans soon dried up after the financial crisis of 1825–6. John Owens, a Manchester merchant who retained interests in Brazil and the River Plate until his death in 1846, knew that South America rarely supplied more than a moderate portion of sales.[2] Again, Antony Gibbs did not immediately regard South America as a permanent alternative to Spain. In 1826 the house still had eighty-six clients in Spain, twenty-six elsewhere in Europe, and only thirty-one in the Americas.[3] The market in Latin America was still disappointingly narrow. The small, scattered population, whose purchasing power was low and whose economic growth was limited, lived at subsistence level, and supplied its own needs. Independence did not accelerate population increase, redistribute income, or raise demand. Only the wealthy sophisticated few in

[1] H. Magdoff, *The Age of Imperialism: The Economics of U.S. Foreign Policy* (New York, 1969), pp. 9, 19.

[2] B. W. Clapp, *John Owens: Manchester Merchant* (Manchester, 1964), pp. 120–1.

[3] W. M. Mathew, 'Anglo-Peruvian Commercial and Financial Relations, 1820–1865, with Special Reference to Antony Gibbs and Sons and the Guano Trade' (unpublished Ph.D. thesis, University of London, 1964), pp. 351–4, 375.

the major cities wanted and could afford imported luxuries. One or two mixed cargoes of textiles and hardware, ordered when supplies were scarce or pressed on to agents, soon overstocked markets and sharply depressed prices. Once peace returned to Europe and Latin America's immediate needs were satisfied, trade resettled at not much above its old level. Foreign communities, new tastes, and demand *had* increased trade, but not dramatically. British merchants were responsible not so much for a great enlargement of trade as for its redirection.

The failure of *imports* to provide adequate business, and the release of resources and energy which this implied, inevitably encouraged British merchants to seek opportunities in Latin American exports. British merchants increasingly diversified into handling and marketing local produce abroad, a role emphasized subsequently by Latin America's entry into international trade as communications improved and demand rose. At first, of course, Spanish America had little except hides or specie to offer exporters, though Brazil, as an exporter of cotton, coffee, tobacco, and sugar to continental Europe and North America, was better placed. A crude triangular trade also existed in jerked beef from the River Plate to Brazil and Cuba, where commodities were loaded for Europe. Nevertheless Balfour Williamson, trading on the West Coast from 1851, abandoned their original plan to import dry goods on commission, and began to use funds in South America to finance produce deals.[1] During the 1870s Antony Gibbs & Sons, who had already abandoned Guayaquil, recognized that their wholesale business on the West Coast had long been unremunerative. The house, anticipating new options and opportunities in trade, broke with suppliers in England and closed its store at Valparaíso. 'Our business here', a report stated, 'will soon be almost a produce one and we shall have to try and conduct it with more keenness and special study than hitherto. . . .'[2] Of course, the pace at which British importers rationalized their businesses must not be exaggerated. At the turn of the century British coffee houses in Brazil continued to handle imported foodstuffs and textiles.[3] Gibbs and Balfour Williamson remained principal importers

---

[1] Wallis Hunt, *Heirs of Great Adventure: The History of Balfour Williamson & Company Limited* (London, 1951 and 1961), i. 21–34.
[2] Gibbs, Valparaíso to London, 16 Feb. 1877. For details of Gibbs's wholesale business see Gibbs, 11033, 11120, and 11124.
[3] *Consular Reports* (*Rio de Janeiro*), P.P. 1899, xcviii, 313.

into Chile and Peru before 1914. Nevertheless, the significance of the business was diminishing. Edward Greene, manager of the coffee shippers E. Johnston & Co. (Santos) who also imported flour, fish, and timber, summarized the position: 'There is no doubt . . . that working on our present lines we are in the position of middlemen whose intervention in the business is daily becoming less necessary to the better class of wholesale buyers in São Paulo.'[1]

Intervention in exporting raised wider issues than the mere transfer of ownership of commodities from producing to consuming areas. What was the relationship between local growers and expatriate merchants? How far did British houses control commercial links or coerce farmers? The agricultural commodities which British merchants handled in Latin America represented a high proportion of the total volume of these goods entering international trade. More important, these primary exports played a crucial national role. While only a small fraction of total output was consumed locally—exceptionally meat, wool, and wheat enjoyed local demand—the remainder was exported to the richer industrialized communities of Europe and North America, and thus provided a substantial portion of overseas income and of government revenue based on export duties. These goods directly redressed the balance between poor countries (the producers) and rich (the consumers). They paid for manufactured imports, public works, and loan servicing. Successful production stimulated employment, population growth, agricultural and industrial development, and urbanization. The wealth and well-being of communities throughout Latin America were irrevocably linked to primary production for export, to overseas markets, and to the expatriate merchants who handled the goods. Caio Prado Júnior has noted this dangerous reliance on the foreigner. 'All the real rubber business', he explained, 'from the financing and trading to the processing and the consumption of the product, was abroad.'[2]

A prima facie case can be formulated that the local producer of agricultural commodities in Latin America was weak and thus easily exploitable. No individual or even group could decisively influence total output, or, therefore, prices. Despite the traditions of latifundia, despite the advantages derived from economies of

---

[1] Johnston, Greene to E. Johnston & Co., 18 May 1903, Letter Book III.
[2] C. Prado Júnior, *História Econômica do Brasil* (São Paulo, 1967), p. 240.

scale, and despite the existence of a minority of large landowners, the great majority of Latin American agricultural producers were small-scale and isolated. Land was contracted to small-holders, tenants, squatters, and sharecroppers, so that in practice control was fragmented. Favourable natural conditions encouraged newly arrived immigrants or *colonos* of modest means to farm on land bought during a fragmentation of estates. Such farms were normally worked by their family and not by hired labour. Further, farmers valued their independence, co-operatives were rare, and capital to merge farms was usually unavailable. In the up-country cocoa regions of Brazil and Ecuador, the isolation of farmers was extreme. Only rivers, near which farms were sited, linked them to towns. Absentee landownership, which the harsh climate in the cocoa- and rubber-planting areas encouraged, further contributed to disunity. In Ecuador, foreign managers and agents, foremen and estate administrators, were not empowered to make far-reaching agreements. One British representative wanted men of initiative and energy to organize planters in Brazil, but apparently such leaders were 'not to be found amongst the class of small planters here'.[1] The argument can be exaggerated. Neighbouring farmers were often related, interlocking directorships existed amongst estate companies, and local identities might be strong

Again, the pattern of production was often precarious, to which small-scale and absentee ownership often contributed. Farmers were dangerously dependent on one crop, their farms representing total capital. They were vulnerable to harvest fluctuations, and yields which were over-reliant on natural fertility and weather varied alarmingly; these were problems which the relative concentration of many of Latin America's commodities increased. Inefficient cultivation on virgin soil, extensive rather than intensive farming, and lack of costly science-based inputs added to the difficulties. In the longer-term, inelastic supply also proved disruptive. Although more intensive picking, adulteration, and the sacrifice of quality for quantity raised output marginally if prices rose, supply lagged behind demand until new crops were harvested, some five years later in the case of cocoa and rubber. Labour and seasonal factors also delayed response to upward prices. And since demand might fall again between planting and harvest, overproduction was always a threat which in turn restricted fresh output

[1] P.R.O. F.O. 368/275/8064, O'Sullivan-Beare to Grey, 25 Jan. 1909.

until undersupply recurred. But farmers could not afford to sell up at a discount and invest elsewhere. While annual crops like cereals permitted a more flexible approach, many producers hung on grimly for some return. Where plant lifespan was long, a slump was likely to be prolonged. Falling prices did not immediately arrest the flow of supplies.

The middlemen, who in theory performed a necessary and valuable service, formed a second element in the commodity trades. Produce was not shipped direct by farmers but passed through a hierarchy of native itinerant buyers and up-country agents who collected small lots, harvested by each of their principals, to transmit to larger intermediaries and consignees in the cities and ports. These factors formed the first links in the marketing chain between producer and consumer. Nevertheless, cultivation and handling were not always so distinct. Considerable overlapping occurred, because farmers and native middlemen might be relatives, friends, or partners, and because firms undertook several tasks. A large producer often acted as intermediary to his tenants and *colonos*.

The local middleman's role was not confined to receiving his principal's produce. In addition to settling business in the city he provided supplies and equipment and became, as a local capitalist, the farmer's banker and creditor. Sources of agricultural credit in Latin America were limited, a permanent and serious handicap to rural development. 'Want of organisation and particularly of agricultural credit', Milne-Cheetham reported, 'has been shown to exist in the cocoa areas and is a blemish on Brazilian production in general'.[1] Commercial banks disliked risky advances to farmers, which tied up capital, and they operated few up-country branches. Although Latin American producers required less capital than, say, plantation owners elsewhere, they still became heavily dependent upon outside finance. The long lag between sowing and harvesting and the need to meet current expenses, especially during harvest, caused financial strain. Farmers required cash to pay labour, cover supplies, or settle outstandings. Sharecroppers and tenants hired equipment from their landlords. Their security was their crops; the harvest profits repaid debts.

Credit, on which most businessmen depend, was not at first sight damaging, especially when harvests were full and prices rising. It

[1] P.R.O. F.O. 368/172/32464, Milne-Cheetham to Grey, 30 Aug. 1908.

provided an opportunity for outside capital to finance abnormal expenditure in local economies which would otherwise have had to go without. Sometimes the net sum of rural income could be unaffected since creditors were neighbours, relatives, or close friends of the borrower. But the system operated unfavourably during short crops or falling prices, particularly if it financed marginal cultivation or extravagance. Repayment periods were short, necessitating a succession of loans, and interest rates were often usurious since few financial sources existed and risks were high. The farmer's debt became continuous since his surplus, after rent and labour, was often barely sufficient to service, let alone reduce, the principal. He lost control of his operations to the creditor to whom he mortgaged his crop, a monopsony which removed discretion over price and market. Creditor-middlemen were thus ideally placed to harass planters, deliberately lowering prices for crops which had been pledged but raising their terms for essential supplies purchased with the contracted loans. This squeeze might represent the creditor's legitimate interest, but in too many cases it was an arbitrary form of profiteering and control. Credit which tied the producer to the native middleman thus formed a major area of friction in the commodity trades. Only the few largest farmers escaped. Milne-Cheetham reported that 'it appears that the cocoa growers, like the coffee planters and rubber producers, are in the hands of money lenders'.[1]

Abuses aggravated the position. Buying agents, having advanced cash on a farmer's standing crop, rejected bag after bag on inspection on grounds of inferior quality, threatening to sue for breach of contract until the hard-pressed farmer settled for well below his crop's true value.[2] Intermediaries imposed on ignorant producers arbitrary gradings and classifications, severe penalties for defective produce, and generous allowances for weight losses in transit; they even falsified accounts. Frequently, their control of road- and river-transport compelled farmers to accept unrealistically low prices. The farmer's reliance on the goodwill and credit of intermediaries, and on narrow marketing channels which gained control of crops, further weakened his position. A large

[1] P.R.O. F.O. 368/173/31056, Milne-Cheetham to Grey, 19 Aug. 1908.
[2] For examples, see *R.R.P.*, 29 Sept. 1911, 861; James R. Scobie, *Revolution on the Pampas: A Social History of Argentine Wheat 1860–1910* (Austin, Texas, 1965), p. 100.

number of middlemen-buyers ought to erase the advantages gained from abuses of this kind. 'Competition among traders', explained Professor Bauer, 'safeguards the interests of producers even if traders resort to sharp practices.'[1] The buyer's need to offer higher prices offsets the sharp practices he may employ. But where competition among buyers is absent, unfair tactics can flourish and the farmer is helpless. And in the remoter areas of production in Latin America, these latter conditions probably prevailed. The few marketing channels could impose their own terms.

The larger native middleman in turn acted for foreign merchants seeking export shipments at the ports. Financing and shipping an increasing surplus brought a new dimension which strained local relations and forced producers to face an international rather than a domestic market. The typical exporter was an expatriate merchant of large capital, with important contacts in world trade. The vastly greater credit and marketing requirements of the export trade rapidly exhausted the local resources of producer and intermediary. Only very exceptionally did the large farmers or plantation companies export directly (Ecuador's cocoa was one example), while the same was true of the first users of the product, the manufacturers. Export houses replaced the older domestic channels, and redirected the flow of trade. The exporter accumulated produce from farmers and native intermediaries which he cleaned, graded, and rebagged for the needs of importers and first users abroad. He could spread the harvest over the year by meeting interest and storage charges in the country of origin or in warehouses overseas, which neither the producer nor the consumer were inclined or could afford to undertake. The foreign merchant borrowed more cheaply, and his growing expertise promoted confidence. British houses began to finance native intermediaries, both on commission and joint account. They advanced a proportion of a crop's estimated value and remitted the remainder after sale, deducting interest on the advance and their commission. The credit nexus, particularly if outlets were limited, now restrained the options open to local middlemen. The local *aviador* (up-river middleman) was indentured to foreign rubber exporters at Pará and Manaos, whose financial connections and resources gave them a crucial role

[1] P. T. Bauer and B. S. Yamey, *Markets, Market Control and Marketing Reform* (London, 1968), p. 50.

in distributing supplies and shipping produce.[1] Native firms had to order return imports through the exporter and his partners abroad through whom rubber was sold.

In practice the relationship between the grower and the intermediary (who was accused of exploiting the grower's weaknesses) was unhappy. The expatriate merchant was particularly liable to criticism. Farmers sometimes claimed there were too many middlemen between grower and manufacturer, each deriving interest and commission and thus lowering the producer's income. Such complaints should be taken cautiously. It is important to differentiate between the rightful claims of producers, and the inevitable but misplaced resentment against intermediaries who produced nothing concrete and therefore seemingly contributed nothing, but who in fact performed vital functions in the transfer of ownership. Completely redundant middlemen are in time bypassed, either on the producers' or the first users' initiative. And a large number of intermediaries offer certain advantages. They will provoke such competition between themselves that higher prices are offered to farmers, their margins will be small, and they will widen the area of growth and distribution. Then, the pattern of Latin American production, in small, scattered, and isolated farms, inevitably created a long chain of intermediaries. The low level of capital formation and development forced each buyer to sell quickly to a slightly more important buyer, which process, repeated many times, eventually brought produce to the ports.[2]

Although the penetration by export houses of up-country areas at first widened the producer's options, it alarmed native intermediaries. Their fear was that expatriate shippers, enjoying substantial resources and economies of scale, would overbid and eventually expel local buyers. Foreign houses now employed factors, formerly independent, as their agents. Their financial facilities, increased by the willingness of banks to support them, again threatened to replace the traditional credit relationship between farmer and local intermediary. Producers, continuing to receive advances from their agents who now used funds provided by exporters, were bound, in Ortíz's words, by '*los consorcios*

[1] P.R.O. F.O. 368/172/32464 and 42640, Milne-Cheetham to Grey, 30 Aug. and 14 Nov. 1908. See, e.g., the role of the house of Suárez: J. Valerie Fifer, 'The Empire Builders: A History of the Bolivian Rubber Boom and the Rise of the House of Suárez', *Journal of Latin American Studies*, ii (1970), 113–46.

[2] Bauer and Yamey, op. cit., pp. 32–42 and 139–40.

vinculados al comercio exterior'.[1] Chilean deputies were told that lack of rural capital forced farmers, through extravagance or carelessness, to become 'slaves of foreign capitalism . . . Chileans' own money and banking organs serving as blind instruments of the hegemony which foreign capital has established over national production'.[2] Not all exporters continually financed producers. Chronic overdrawing by native intermediaries might put a house at risk. Gibbs and Balfour Williamson sometimes preferred to reduce advances, retaining only their better clients, and to buy from dealers rather than lock up capital. An ungathered crop was not a first-class security. Nevertheless, the equation of power persistently favoured overseas shippers at the expense of local intermediaries.

Further, the relative concentration of merchants *vis-à-vis* the multiplicity of scattered producers caused alarm. Many Latin American commodities were channelled through only a few outlets where the export houses gathered. The absence of serviceable deep-water ports and the fact that regions like the Peruvian valleys were isolated from the rest of the country tended to funnel shipments. Even where an economy appeared diversified, the same concentration occurred. Before 1914 Brazil exported increasing quantities of coffee, cocoa, and rubber, which gave her some protection if world conditions in one product deteriorated. But the Brazilian economy remained localized. Each regional economy was tied to one product and to the one or two ports which served the immediate hinterland. Bahía shipped all the cocoa, Rio and Santos the coffee, and Pará and Manaos the rubber. Consequently a handful of export houses specialized in isolation, competition between them appeared to be limited, and the fear was that they would agree prices and spheres of influence to the producer's detriment.

A fairly high degree of oligopolistic concentration in the export trade of an underdeveloped country was usual and, as Professor Bauer has shown, not hard evidence of collusion. The far greater range in price and type in the same country's import business permitted the participation of numerous small import houses, some local and others foreign. But only a few substantial merchants could successfully handle the one or two low-value and standardized exports. 'The more standardized the commodity', Bauer explained,

---

[1] Ricardo M. Ortíz, *História Económica de la Argentina 1850–1939* (Buenos Aires, 1955), ii. 121.   [2] *Diario de Diputados* (Chile), 29 Dec. 1912, 1120.

'the more probable is a high degree of concentration.'[1] And such exporters were normally foreign. The great risks of trade in tropical goods required capital and reserves on a scale few local firms could afford to purchase the ancillary services (transport and storage) which were poorly developed in the areas of production, and to permit economies of scale, bulk transactions and handling. Thus, given world supply and demand, merchants whose costs and experience were similar were likely to offer equal prices independently of each other. And it was normal business practice for smaller firms to follow the prices of their larger rivals.

But the danger was real enough that an oligopoly of foreign shippers, controlling a substantial share of the local market, would combine, offer artificially low prices to producers, and squeeze consumers. And the gradual elimination of rivals through severe competition increased that danger, since the largest could sustain short-term losses for longer-term gains. The grain trade is an instructive example. 'There is no doubt', Gibbs's Valparaíso branch informed London, 'that it is very absurd that practically the only three wheat buyers [in southern Chile], Gibbs, Duncan Fox and Balfour Williamson, should not have an understanding.'[2] The Big Four grain exporters, who handled 75 per cent of Argentina's grain trade, maintained the appearance but not the substance of competition. Each of the four Buenos Aires houses led the bidding in turns, the others agreeing to stay below a set price; a sudden raising of price levels soon eliminated any unexpected outsider.[3] And at Arequipa, where in the 1870s four houses, Gibbs, Fletchers, Staffords, and Woodgate, dominated wool shipments, a secret agreement fixed prices and quotas and ended competition.[4] Again, *The Economist* reported that most Brazilian rubber was 'dealt with by so few people that they are able to exercise some control over the selling price'.[5]

---

[1] P. T. Bauer, *West African Trade: A Study of Competition, Oligopoly and Monopoly in a Changing Economy* (London, 1963), p. 226 *et seq.*; see also Bauer and Yamey, op. cit., pp. 201–7.

[2] Gibbs 11470/20, Valparaíso to London, 17 Apr. 1912; see also ibid. 11116 and 11471/78, London to Valparaíso, 8 Mar. 1912. Archibald Williamson expressed similar views: Balfour Williamson, A. Williamson to Harry Williamson, 27 Mar. 1912.

[3] Scobie, op. cit., *passim*. See also p. 190, n. 1 below.

[4] Gibbs 11124, Arequipa to Lima, 12 Aug. 1873, 17 Mar. and 21 Apr. 1874; ibid., Hayne to Harrison, 17 Mar. 1875, 19 Jan. 1876, and 3 Jan. 1877.

[5] *The Economist*, 19 July 1913, 110.

The foreign exporter did not confine his operations to the collection and shipment of produce. Increasingly he interfered at every stage of the marketing chain. Such extended business, often taken originally for quite independent motives, tended to exploit the farmer's already weak position, to reinforce the direct tactics of intermediaries, and to contribute further to the removal of commodity control from local to foreign hands. British merchants invested in land, a common and convenient outlet both for avoiding loss-making remittances when local currency was depreciating, and for its own sake. Later, estates and plantations were bought as going concerns, cocoa in Ecuador and rubber in the Amazon. Antony Gibbs & Sons undertook cattle-rearing and wine-growing in the Wellington Islands, and Balfour Williamson developed farms on Easter Island. Output from merchant-owned estates was, however, never more than a small fraction of total production. And gullible shareholders, especially in the Brazilian rubber companies, appear to have suffered most.

This analysis of the intermediary's function, particularly that of the foreign exporter *vis-à-vis* the producer, has shown that the number of middlemen, their nationality and concentration, their provision of credit, all of which concerned farmers directly, were major issues in the struggle for market dominance. What is clear, however, is that there was no single control exerted by expatriate middlemen over local producers. Coercion could occur at all points in the marketing chain. Nor were the different intermediary functions confined to foreigners. The local middleman might predominate because he was a creditor, because he had few rivals, or because he practised deception. The foreign firm might exercise control because it was one of a few large houses concentrated at the ports of shipment and dealing with many clients. Time and place, as much as size and nationality, determined market control.

III

It is necessary to examine the world marketing organization to understand fully Latin America's agricultural trades and the position of British merchant houses. Most Latin American cash crops—essential staples which enjoyed regular harvests or collection, did not deteriorate in storage, and were open to accurate grading—adapted easily to formal market organization. From the mid nineteenth century international markets opened, especially in the consuming countries. The telegraph, the steamship, and the general expansion of world commerce now united isolated and hitherto restricted local markets. Trading rules, information services—closely linked to the shipping and insurance markets and to news sources—and a basic world price from continuous trading over thousands of transactions, were established. Grain markets emerged at Chicago in 1846, New York in 1850, and Liverpool in 1853. A committee and paid secretariat controlled membership, devised uniform contracts between buyers and sellers, standard units of delivery, gradings, storage charges, and an arbitration procedure. A clearing-house registered all deals and required both sides in any contract to place margins, altered as the daily price rose or fell, as a pledge of completion.[1] Dealers offset contracts, settling in margins. Some exchanges established independent prices—although, after allowing for local circumstances and freight differences, levels would be similar since the same information was discounted—while others followed one leader market, like Hamburg in the cocoa trade.

Users of exchanges, merchants and jobbers both buying and selling, first users, and large manufacturers obtained certain advantages. Exchanges permitted not only distribution through space (the 'spot' market) but also in time (the forward or 'futures' market),[2] enabling merchants to order ahead rather than hold stock (which tied up capital, and incurred interest and storage charges). Futures also permitted speculation, which, in theory at least, eliminated price fluctuation. While some dealers continued to undertake physical marketing (i.e. transferred goods), the additional burden and complexity of appraising international factors (crop reports, weather, political events, and demand) created a

---

[1] Many books describe the working of commodity exchanges. Among the best, from which much of the following is taken, is J. W. F. Rowe, *Primary Commodities in International Trade* (Cambridge, 1965), pp. 46–8. See also Julius B. Baer and G. P. Woodruff, *Commodity Exchanges* (New York, 1929), H. C. Emery, *Speculation on the Stock and Produce Exchanges of the United States* (New York, 1896), and A. A. Hooker, *The International Grain Trade* (London, 1939) and *Grain Futures* (London, 1955).

[2] The futures price normally exceeds the spot to allow for storage and interest charges. Nevertheless, even if futures prices were lower (inverse carrying charges) users might prefer to store rather than order ahead either to avoid the nuisance of frequent delivery necessitated by production schedules and seasonal factors or to safeguard themselves against wildly fluctuating prices.

band of specialists who 'corrected' prices by astute trading to the level conditions warranted. At best theirs were valuable services which helped to equalize supply throughout the world and secure uniform prices, thus protecting producer and consumer. Unequal prices in two markets were quickly levelled by buying in the cheaper and shipping to the dearer market for resale. If prices appeared too high, speculators 'sold short' (that is, in the future without owning stocks), anticipating that they could buy cheaply when prices actually fell and thus be enabled to cover their contract. If prices unaccountably rose, speculators switched to a more distant position to cover the original deal and sold further forward. The high return on the second deal, if successful, more than recouped the loss on the first. If prices were too low the speculator went 'long', buying for a rise. The speculator benefited from accurate guesswork and knowledge. His economic role is controversial, but his actions permitted all to see the eventual trend in prices and gave merchants advance warning to adjust and prevent more violent, unexpected fluctuations when the foreseen conditions became effective—an important commercial gain. The more speculative the transaction, discounting the news of the day, the more likely it was that the right level of prices would be achieved.

A developed futures market and speculation facilitated another advantage to merchants in commodity exchanges—hedging. Hedging involved an equal but opposite deal in futures, which would not be physically exercised, for every genuine spot transaction. A buyer in spot, fearing a price fall, would sell futures; when he sold his commodity (for example, after transport or processing) he would buy futures, not taking delivery but offsetting his earlier sale in futures. If the price did fall, his loss in spot was balanced by a gain in futures since he bought in cheaply, covering his forward sale. If prices in fact rose, an increased trade profit would offset a loss in futures. The perfect hedge was unlikely since spot and futures rarely coincided exactly, but divergences were small and equalized over several deals. Hedges gave merchants an important insurance and credit facility since banks more readily lent on produce which had been hedged.

The fact that British shippers in Latin America possessed offices, agencies, and contacts in the international produce exchanges gave them considerable influence in determining trading rules and prices. They also enjoyed the advantages which futures dealings, speculation, and hedging conferred. Moreover, Britain, the most powerful commercial nation in the nineteenth century, sited between Europe and the United States and a major importer of primary goods, was the busiest centre for intermediaries and middlemen, giving British firms advantages in their international dealings based on Latin America.

Latin America did not adopt formal commodity organization until immediately before 1914. Producers and native factors, whose lack of overseas contacts barred them from exchanges abroad, were thus denied commercial facilities locally. The quantities which they handled were normally too small to hedge, and they preferred immediate sales. Lack of local commodity markets further reinforced the position of expatriate merchant houses. First, exporters remained consistently better informed through their many overseas contacts. Although the low level of local market information in Latin America impeded all sectors of trade, the foreign merchant was better placed to exploit confusion, and sophisticated enough to ignore bias and misleading reports. And without formal standards and price differentials, most careful businessmen, even if honest, imposed their own rough, rule-of-thumb gradings which lowered prices. The less scrupulous offered still lower prices which producers could not refuse. Local merchants, explains Rowe, are 'apt to give the small producer less than a fair price because the producer's information about prices . . . is out of date'.[1] Low levels of information in Latin America resulted from inaccurate or uncollected statistics of production. Latin America was thinly populated and poorly served by up-country communications. Farmers, isolated in the interior and rarely journeying to the city, ignored opportunities to anticipate needs and protect themselves under production plans. Either the long-run average price or the local spot price influenced farmers, *not* future, foreseeable needs; they produced regardless of returns and adjusted only slowly. Inexperienced officials collected statistics haphazardly and provided widely different estimates of output. 'The tendency to exaggerate any storm of wind or hail', reported the *Review of the River Plate*, 'is only too apparent.'[2] Boundary disputes and a lag between planting and exporting further confused matters.

Second, Latin America's lack of storage space forced producers

[1] Rowe, *Primary Commodities in International Trade*, p. 36.
[2] *R.R.P.*, 7 Feb. 1908, 355.

to sell soon after harvest, thus depressing prices and preventing them from holding for a rise. Despite important gains for producers and consumers and despite derived improvements in quality, the handling, distribution, and marketing processes were generally neglected.[1] In practice, each farmer rushed to market to secure the highest prices made by the first shipments, but as crops flooded the ports so prices crashed. Storage remained a specialized function, normally provided by the foreign merchant who had access to the capital necessary to cover the cost of stockholding, weatherproofed buildings, and staff. No developed elevator system existed in Argentina before the First World War, in contrast to North America, and much of what there was was owned by Bunge y Born, one of the Big Four cereal exporters.

Thus, low prices *per se* did not mean unfair trading. Imperfect marketing arrangements, the possibility that world prices might fall in the long lag between buying up-country and export, and the lack of information created huge risks for merchants whose function was to gather produce, pay farmers, and store for sale abroad. While some merchants unfairly exploited the system, the risks were real enough.[2] Accordingly merchants charged a high-risk premium so that the prices they gave farmers seemed to bear little relation to those ruling in consuming markets.

An effective warrant system also depended on storage and gradings. When delivering produce to a recognized warehouse, a depositor was handed certificates or warrants which guaranteed ownership and were generally negotiable for sale or credit. Holders of warrants had a general claim on a fixed quantity and quality of produce, though not on their original deposit. Because public warehouses were reliable, banks normally lent more readily on a warrant's security than on crops held up-country, where verification was difficult. Warrants eased credit and helped producers to obtain fairer prices. They enabled sale by description rather than by personal inspection, and by curtailing physical transfers promoted speed and efficiency. In Latin America these advantages could rarely be enjoyed by producers except on terms dictated by the foreign merchants who controlled storage.

[1] C. D. Vincent, 'Marketing and Economic Development', in T. K. Warley, ed., *Agricultural Producers and Their Markets* (London, 1967), pp. 75–81.

[2] *United States Monthly Consular Reports*, Mar. 1902 (lxviii), No. 258, pp. 438–9; *S.A.J.*, 7 June 1902, 650–1 (the example of the failure of two important German houses in Guayaquil).

Of course, commodity exchanges contained abuses which prompted international investigation and legislation. The German Government, under pressure from agrarian interests, prohibited futures on the Berlin bourse to prevent manipulation.[1] The danger existed that a speculator or group might out of self-interest influence prices and disrupt trade. Leiter in 1897 and Patten in 1909 accumulated millions of tons of wheat at Chicago hoping that short sellers, finding themselves compelled to liquidate forward contracts, would buy at their monopoly price.[2] Such operations were worked by moneyed outsiders who poached for a casual profit, and by established merchants. The successful corner required considerable nerve and resources, the exploitation of a number of devices, inadequate information in the market generally, and trading irregularities. A further weakness was that speculators exploited an uninformed public, buying in a market for a rise which conditions did not in fact warrant. Public participation in exchanges was rare in Britain but strongly affected American markets. Certainly Milne-Cheetham believed that 'the speculating middleman injures the producer today and the manufacturer tomorrow and prevents legitimate trade . . .'.[3] And the British rubber market was said to be weak and coercible.[4]

Latin America's farmers thus suffered from a locally undeveloped marketing structure. Even the long-established coffee industry, Brazil's most important source of wealth, was slow to organize itself. For her cocoa business, a relative newcomer to international commodity trading, and for her cocoa-planter, almost certainly less wealthy or informed than the São Paulo planter, matters were considerably worse. Cocoa was grown in some of the most backward regions of Latin America under very primitive conditions of cultivation, collection, and sale. Farmers had little idea of their cost structure, did not seek to match production to foreseeable requirements, and could not forecast prices. They failed to establish any of the usual conventions of international commodity trading, information services, grading, regulated exchanges, warehouses, and warrants. Haphazard harvesting and

---

[1] H. C. Emery, 'Legislation against Futures', *Political Science Quarterly*, x (1895), 62–86, and 'The German Exchange Act 1896', ibid. xiii (1898), 286–320.

[2] *The Economist*, 10 Apr. 1909, 776–7.

[3] P.R.O. F.O. 368/172/39917, Milne-Cheetham to Grey, 27 Oct. 1908.

[4] *The Economist*, 19 July 1913, 110; *The Times*, 30 Sept. 1913, 17f, and 1 Nov. 1913, 20c.

unskilled preparation paid little attention to quality. Produce deteriorated while awaiting shipment at up-river moorings or at the
quayside.

The growers' weaknesses—small-scale production, isolation,
lack of storage and of information—constituted one dimension of
control in the commodity trades. Professor Bauer's studies of West
African trade, which was in several respects similar to the Latin
American pattern, have suggested that these weaknesses need not
be crucial. The structure of world demand and price levels may not
justify raising costs to achieve higher quality. Delimiting exchanges
and storage may in fact *reduce* the options open to producers and
prevent them from exercising their traditional methods of sale.
Market conditions, not the wealth or number of producers, determine their ability to extract a higher price from buyers. Nevertheless, the facts of the case suggest that the Latin American producer
was vulnerable. His living standards depended on commodity prices
over which he exercised very little control.

IV

British merchants were industrialists. Their deep interest in agricultural marketing and the importance of primary production in
Latin America inevitably led them into the processing of commodities—although they were not excluded from secondary manufacturing. Local industrial enterprise constituted useful diversification
and an attractive outlet for surplus funds, particularly if transfer
to London would seriously deplete the value of these surpluses
or if profits needed to be disguised. The processing of local raw
materials complemented the merchant's productive and handling
functions. The addition of value by the industrial refinement
and processing of commodities in the countries of production,
which would otherwise have taken place abroad, raised prices and
profits in international markets. It also lowered the impact of
freight rates. At the same time commodities like flour had a large
local demand. British merchants saw industry as serving both
Latin American and overseas markets, particularly when countries
like Chile protected local flour and sugar against foreign competition. Moreover, expatriate merchants, if not the original owners,
were likely to finance and eventually take over industrial processing
which had been started by local entrepreneurs. The large British

export house, with easier access to cheap capital, would lend and then assume control (as leading creditor) if the enterprise faced bankruptcy. If, however, the business expanded, a limited company might be formed in which the merchant was a principal shareholder.

Balfour Williamson became a leading miller on the West Coast. In 1869 a bad debt brought them the Molina de la Fé which soon paid its way before being sold in 1875. In 1871 the firm bought a linseed mill in Valparaíso. Then, in 1892–3 Balfour Williamson built a mill at Concepción using Cooper & Co., their agents at the Molina de la Fé, as managers, and buying their wheat locally, from Argentina and from Australia. Since most existing mills in Chile were small, Balfour Williamson appreciated the possibilities of producing a cheap, good quality flour for a wide market, and in 1895 enlarged the property, forming a new operating company, the Sociedad Molinera de Concepción.[1] At the same time the house had an interest in a mill at Callao (Peru), which proved exceptionally profitable. The two mills were combined under the Santa Rosa Milling Company in 1913 to conceal the Peruvian plant's success, which might tempt the Lima Government to lift protective tariffs.[2] By the outbreak of war the two mills were the largest in their respective countries. Such developments were not exceptional. Gibbs & Sons operated mills in southern Chile, Graham Rowe managed the very profitable Compañía de Azucar de Viña del Mar,[3] and, of course, several British firms packed meat in Argentina.

Processing Latin America's commodity trades also raised the danger of an oligopoly of foreign enterprises which operated the largest, most efficient concerns and controlled both domestic and overseas markets. They might come together to divide output and fix prices. The Rio Flour Mills, started in 1886 by the established British import/export house of Knowles & Foster, enjoyed agreements with rivals covering quotas and discounts in São Paulo.[4]

[1] Hunt, op. cit. i. 76–7 and 181–3.

[2] A. Williamson to Milne, 17 May 1904 and 24 Aug. 1912; to Harry Williamson, 29 Aug. 1912; and to Anstruther Williamson, 24 July 1913: Balfour Williamson, Letter Book I, pp. 16–19; II, pp. 244–6; and V, pp. 49–56 and 458–65. Hunt, op. cit. ii. 17, 69, and 88.

[3] Gibbs 11470/17, Valparaíso to London, 16 Oct. 1899.

[4] R. Graham, 'A British Industry in Brazil: Rio Flour Mills, 1886–1920', *Business History*, viii (1966), 34.

A millers' combination on the West Coast was discussed by Gibbs and Balfour Williamson.[1]

Mining interests expanded in much the same way. Easier access to capital and readiness to assume risks contributed again to the initial penetration of British merchant houses like Gibbs into this sector of the Latin American economy. A remunerative consignment business in minerals could not be developed without persuading a merchant to take an active financial interest in the product shipped. Quite apart from Gibbs's long-standing interest in nitrate (both in Peru and Chile), its West Coast mining business included gold, silver, copper, tin, cobalt, coal, and salt, although in small quantities. Such a spread of interests acted as a hedge if one sector failed, since machinery and personnel could easily be transferred. Gibbs's original function as consignees—handling ore for producers on an advance and commission basis for shipment to Europe, much like the agricultural trades—was soon extended. Gibbs financed operations, acted as agents (thus supplying imported inputs) and managers, acquired ownership through bad debts, and promoted mining companies. The house independently sought mines or bought out existing owners.

Mining, like the commodity trades and processing, was also subject to cartelization and price-fixing. Nitrate, iodine (a by-product of nitrate), and copper, the main props of the Chilean economy in the nineteenth century, were all subject to private control of output to prevent competition and raise prices, and in such control the house of Gibbs was deeply involved. British merchants, therefore, progressively broadened and deepened their role in the Latin American economy.

V

Merchants, handling export commodities as well as importing capital and consumer goods, required a range of business services such as shipping, insurance, banking, exchange, and credit. These had normally to be developed independently, since few facilities existed locally. At the same time firms in London who handled business services wanted to place agencies among British merchants already based in commercial centres and at the ports, since

[1] Balfour Williamson, Letter Book V, pp. 49–56, A. Williamson to H. Williamson, 29 Aug. 1912.

insufficient business existed for independent branch offices. British merchants, on the other hand, could conveniently combine a number of agencies under one or two clerks, using their business expertise and their range of contacts more effectively than managers sent out cold from England. Insurers and shipowners wanted to exploit the commercial reputation of British merchants, who, in turn, would themselves be the largest customers for business services and would desire the maximum rebates which an agency would confer. Agency work was easy and supplied a steady income; it was linked with the merchant's main business interests; and it required little outlay.

Thus, Gibbs were agents for the American Barber Line and lobbied for the Pacific Steam Navigation Company's agency held by Balfour Williamson. Threats by shipowners to close agencies were treated with alarm. 'My only fear', wrote Greene to Head Office when he considered leaving Hamburg–Sud Amerika for the Royal Mail Steam Packet Company, 'is that our coffee business might suffer by the loss of the agency.'[1] Gibbs & Co. also worked for several insurance companies: Phoenix, London Assurance, Ocean Marine. Both Henry Gibbs and Stephen Williamson, heads of their respective houses, were directors of leading City insurers.[2] Taking several agencies at any port did not necessarily imply conflict of interest. Most of the major insurance companies operated under agreed tariffs and divided business *pro rata*. The fire insurance side of their business was usually good, and life insurance could be developed by propaganda in the villages. The value of an agency 'can only be measured by the time and energy displayed by the agents'.[3] Agency work was not confined to shipping and insurance—although these were the main areas. Johnstons were agents for the London and Brazilian Bank, and Gibbs for the Anglo-Peruvian Bank in the 1870s and later for the Trust, Loan and Agency Company of Australia.[4]

From the merchant's functions as shipping agent and shipper, it was an easy step to ownership. Links between commerce and

---

[1] Johnston, Letter Book II, Rio to London, 3 Nov. 1902.
[2] See, for example, Maude, op. cit., pp. 69–73.
[3] Gibbs 11116 and 11471/80, London to Valparaíso, 24 Mar. 1911; see also ibid. 11470/11 and 14, Valparaíso to London, 9 Nov. 1888, 6 July 1892, and 27 July 1893.
[4] Gibbs 11120, Hayne to Henry, 10 Oct. 1874; ibid. 11115, Gibbs to Trust, Loan and Agency Co., 29 Jan. 1899.

shipowning were traditionally close. Shipowners traded on their own account, while merchants chartered tonnage, using ships as cheap warehouses in emergencies. Merchant houses bought and operated ships to prevent delays, to serve ports ignored by the regular lines, to compete against unreasonable tariffs, or to bring produce from outlying communities for transhipment by the regular lines. British merchants with offices in London were well placed to charter ships on terms denied to natives. Shipowning might also arise out of a debt settlement. Of course, problems existed. Merchants were inexperienced and sometimes unsuccessful shipowners. Money was better invested in commerce or kept in cash than tied up in costly, depreciating fixed capital like ships, especially when freights were falling as they did during the last quarter of the nineteenth century. Merchants could not always fill their ships both ways, essential if the enterprise were to pay, especially if regular shipowners resented their intrusion. Nevertheless, as Claudio Véliz has noted, British merchants were among the largest shipowners on the West Coast.[1] 'Like most merchants in the nineteenth century', writes Wallis Hunt, 'Stephen Williamson & Company were shipowners as well as shippers.'[2] Archibald Balfour preferred liquidity, but Williamson persistently enlarged his commitment to shipowning and by 1876 operated twenty vessels valued at £90,000. Such investment represented still further penetration into local economies. Booths were accused of monopolizing transport along the Amazon and of raising charges.[3] Chilean deputies criticized West Coast merchants for their control of shipping space at harvest, by which they forced local producers to sell cheaply or incur high freights.[4]

British merchants also followed the familiar development from commerce into banking. They provided the capital which the public would not subscribe for high-risk ventures, floated the enterprise on the capital market once established, and released their resources for fresh enterprises. British merchants used their reputation to mobilize support, and probably retained a management and agency function as well as a large block of shares. Gibbs

[1] Claudio Véliz, *Historia de la Marina Mercante de Chile* (Santiago, 1961), pp. 110–12.

[2] Hunt, op. cit., i. 24.

[3] A. H. John, *A Liverpool Merchant House: being the history of Alfred Booth & Company, 1863–1958* (London, 1959), pp. 99–100.

[4] *Diario de Diputados* (Chile), 19 Dec. 1912, 1071–4.

provided a range of banking services. In 1878 when the Associated Peruvian Bank was unable to meet its liabilities, Gibbs provided short-term accommodation. The house also invested widely in locally owned and British firms in South America as useful outlets for idle funds. Such investments had to yield at least ten per cent since, unless they did so, partners preferred a safer seven per cent in London; they led to representation on local boards.[1] Gibbs's banking business also included private facilities for friends, family, and selected clients, for whom securities were traded and deposit terms arranged. The house undertook exchange deals, remitting homewards when local exchanges were rising against the pound, speculating in local bills of exchange, and playing off one West Coast currency against another. Such activities were not always successful. 'We notice with regret', London wrote, '. . . that the liquidation of the exchange speculation carried forward from 1893 left a considerable loss. We note with satisfaction that . . . you have altogether abandoned speculation in exchange and that it has entirely ceased to be a part of your business.'[2]

Although banking facilities, short-term loans to outsiders, and exchange deals were often temporary phenomena—they tied up capital which any house could more usefully employ in its regular business—investment and credit interests soon brought Gibbs their own bond-issuing and agency business. It was small, especially in Chile where the government agents were the Rothschilds whom Gibbs could not afford to offend. But loans were floated for the Greek and Mexican governments and for a number of South American railways, and approaches were made by Bolivian officials.[3] Indeed, links with Argentina seemed likely to implicate the house in the Baring crisis when it was feared that Gibbs too might be unsound, a suggestion which Herbert Gibbs quickly denied. Gibbs's outstandings, he said, had been much exaggerated; their liability in the Argentine North Eastern Railway was only 25 per cent, of which much had been sold, and their business, while similar to Barings, was on a 'small and prudent scale'.[4]

---

[1] Gibbs 11039 and 11040, London to Valparaíso, 16 Jan. 1914; Hunt, op. cit., i. 37.

[2] Gibbs 11471/51, London to Valparaíso, 7 Nov. 1895.

[3] Gibbs 11116 and 11471/77, London to Valparaíso, 28 Jan. and 25 Feb. 1910; Maude, op. cit., pp. 32–4.

[4] Gibbs 11042, Herbert Gibbs to Mareo (?), 27 Jan. 1891.

VI

The prominent position of British houses in Latin America's financial and commercial framework, the range of business services they offered, and their connections with Europe and the United States inevitably fashioned links with local officials, professional classes, and politicians. Movement of commodities, contracts, monopoly trading rights, the purchasing of stores, and local financial needs were central to establishing a relationship between officials and merchants. At the same time British merchants sought and found local lawyers to defend their interests and supervise contracts, politicians sympathetic to their cause in Congress, business contacts, and ministerial friends. Evidence for these contacts rarely survives, conducted as it was in clubs, board rooms, and cabinet offices. Yet the range of Gibbs's interests on the West Coast indicated the level of influence which a foreign merchant might attain. The house became agents for Chile's state railways, and later sold two of her warships after the settlement of a boundary dispute with Argentina.[1]

Gibbs's interest in Peru's guano shipments, and subsequently in Peru's nitrate trade, provides some of the better-researched material for the relations between merchants and officials in Latin America (see Chapter IX). Gibbs liked working with governments, despite its risks, since competitors were automatically eliminated. From the first Peru claimed the guano deposits on her coasts and islands,[2] and in 1875 expropriated the nitrate industry, originally financed by foreign and domestic private capital.[3] In both cases the temptation of receiving large cash sums in advances from foreign merchants—as a solution to the Peruvian Government's short-term budgetary difficulties, to supply capital and to service existing loans—encouraged Peru to approach British houses. The trading monopolies which resulted gave the appearance of enormous power to British merchants. Gibbs, who held successive

[1] Maude, op. cit., pp. 30–5.

[2] W. M. Mathew, 'Peruvian Contractors and the Peruvian Government at the Outset of the Guano Trade', *Hispanic–American Historical Review*, lii (1972), 598; see also id., 'Peru and the British Guano Market, 1840–1870', *Economic History Review*, 2nd ser. xxiii (1970), 112–28; and Chapter IX, below.

[3] Robert G. Greenhill and Rory M. Miller, 'The Peruvian Government and the Nitrate Trade, 1873–1879', *Journal of Latin American Studies*, v (1973), 107–31.

guano contracts from 1842 to 1861, and who were the nitrate consignees for 1875–8, apparently controlled Peru's major export earners in the second and third quarters of the nineteenth century, from which the house derived substantial profits. Ostensibly Gibbs, deeply entrenched in the industry and economy of an underdeveloped country which was struggling for financial credibility and dependent on a narrow export front, remained omnipotent. Its tentacles penetrated every level of business; it managed government shipments to Europe, where the house enjoyed valuable retail connections, and it extracted commissions on its sales, and interest on its advances.

VII

Businessmen, T. S. Ashton wrote in 1958, have suffered from a poor press. No one has provided the eulogies which Samuel Smiles gave to the engineers. Businessmen are said to be ostentatiously rich or mean, taciturn, secretive, caring only for money, and saying little in their own defence.[1] The expatriate British merchant certainly won little love or respect in Latin America. He was a 'parasite', producing and contributing nothing. The accusation of *monopolistas* was an old cry of the Chilean press against Gibbs.[2] In the Santiago Chamber of Deputies, Arteaga explained that export houses, whom he likened to bandits, 'extend their range of influence over all the visible and invisible organs of political groups, over constitutional powers and public opinion. They conspire to facilitate the triumph of the foreign exporter over the national producer.'[3] Inevitably, as middleman between producer and consumer, the merchant was blamed by both. He squeezed the producer whom he underpaid, and the consumer whom he overcharged.

The question of British merchants' profits in Latin America is difficult to resolve. Since merchant houses were rarely public companies, no balance sheets were published nor were dividends paid (however misleading these may often be as profit indicators). Most firms were partnerships or private concerns—although they sometimes floated public companies and took a large stake in them,

---

[1] T. S. Ashton, 'Business History', *Business History*, i (1958–9), 1–2.
[2] Gibbs 11115, Cokayne to Gibbs, 4 April 1913.
[3] *Diario de Diputados* (Chile), 21 Dec. 1912, 1122.

for which records do remain. Nevertheless, what evidence exists suggests that for those who survived, mercantile profits were attractive, whether divided among partners or reinvested. Gibbs's guano trade provided remunerative contracts, and losses in Peru were recorded only in 1834 and 1865 (the year of the Spanish blockade). Again, the nitrate trade in Peru and Chile was mainly responsible for Gibbs's net profit of some £581,000 over the period 1875–85, during which losses were sustained in only three years, 1882–4, as a result of the War of the Pacific. Brokerage and commissions, the principal sources of revenue, came from a variety of interests: selling, buying, forwarding, insuring, acceptances, and freights.[1] B. W. Clapp, in his excellent history of John Owens based on Owens's correspondence, set out the problem of trading profits:

> Valuable as the letters are [Clapp writes], no merchant willingly admits that he is doing well: he is much more likely to grumble about goods badly sold than offer praise when they go off well. In the Owens correspondence praise is sparingly distributed indeed; and a writer using the letters would be puzzled to explain how the partners acquired a substantial fortune.[2]

Yet acquire a substantial fortune they did. John Owens owned several houses and carriages and property worth £100,000. An income of £5,000 per annum in days of low income tax and fewer declarations enabled him to live well. Silence, then, is the record of success in business.

But profits were not the only object of criticism. Rather, British merchants appeared to have achieved an unassailable economic, social, and even political position. They were firmly entrenched in the emergent economies of Latin America. They entered commerce at every level. They monopolized the commodity trades, vital to the republics; they were important industrialists; they dominated the range of business services as bankers, investors, speculators, insurers, and shippers. Integrated operations were soon developed. H. S. Ferns cites the Robertsons at Buenos Aires, who from the 1820s advanced cash for produce, enjoyed wide up-country contacts, bought and sold hides, hired carters, chartered tonnage, and financed all stages of the trade from purchasing live-

---

[1] Mathew, 'Commercial and Financial Relations', pp. 270 and 359–61; Gibbs 11042, London to Valparaíso, 28 July 1886.
[2] Clapp, op. cit., p. 7.

stock to shipping the finished product.[1] Business services, if small compared with the merchant's role in the commodity trades, were nevertheless a valuable complement to other commercial interests. Advantages lay persistently with British houses, whose London contacts permitted agencies and business on terms denied to local firms.

The fact that the relationship between British merchants and native Latin Americans appeared unequal inevitably caused tension. The merchant depressed prices for the produce which he held until levels in consuming markets rose. He supplied certain needs, but on harsh terms. He exploited the lack of rural capital, inferior productive methods, isolation, and ignorance. An unsophisticated marketing pattern and lack of local storage gave him further bargaining power. Local prices, perhaps, bore little relationship to world supply and demand. Producers complained that too many intermediaries, of which British merchants formed one or more levels, appropriated farmers' surpluses and reduced their net income; whereas too few specialized exporters, reinforced by mutual agreements concerning prices and spheres of influence, raised a real fear of monopsony. The need for substantial credit and overseas contacts, and the foreign merchants' ability to cut margins temporarily, expelled native traders. Any refusal by British merchants to purchase, perhaps in an effort to squeeze producers, paralysed whole areas. At best, therefore, prima facie evidence existed that British merchants did well, while local interests were not so fortunate. At worst, Latin America's primary economy depended on selfish coercive houses, powerful links in the chain of international marketing, who deceived and exploited farmers and native intermediaries.

These conclusions are, however, only one side of the equation of control which determines the power of British merchants in Latin America. Did the British seek to control the Latin American economy? What restraints limited their influence? What resources were open to the local producer? In short, who controlled whom?

VIII

The opening of business archives, the publication of house histories, and a study of trade journals now make it possible to get

[1] Ferns, op. cit., p. 81.

a clearer impression of the functions and methods of businessmen. Despite well-publicized disputes and criticisms, old-established and respectable British merchants in fact worked reasonably well with the emergent governments of Latin America. Antony Gibbs & Sons had an instinct for co-operation which depended much on their moderation, their conformity to a strict code of business morality, and their rejection of capitalism's more free-wheeling ethics. The house established rules of conduct, explained Maude, which would 'always avoid doing anything on the propriety of which rested the least doubt'.[1] The London office drew Valparaíso's attention to the danger of inducing investors to support an enterprise for which the house was unable to vouch. Good reasons must exist before a partner's name could be attached to a public company.[2] And Lord Aldenham, formerly Henry Gibbs, explained his business philosophy to a partner in 1906:

I had considerable misgivings about assigning such a large percentage to partners with little or no capital; my feeling was that to partners who have very little capital to lose there is much greater inducement to try what are called 'short cuts to fortune' instead of laboriously building up steady business which during the process of building will only yield them a modest income.[3]

These were honest, intelligent, liberal, and patient men, working long hours, whose wives saw little of them, and whose record of philanthropy was creditable.[4] Their success, not always easily explained, excited jealousy. But if luck played a part, if the economic conditions were right, still the quality and the character of the men themselves were crucial.

Nor were British merchants in Latin America casual poachers. Their business success depended upon the accelerating pace of Latin America's economic development. They did not condemn the republics to primary production. Like most politicians and economists of their day, they recognized that under comparative advantage Latin America could best produce foodstuffs and raw materials in exchange for capital and consumer goods. Merchants like Gibbs, permanent residents on the West Coast, rejected the maximization of short-term gains. Under their commitment to

[1] Maude, op. cit., p. 20.
[2] Gibbs 11471/76, London to Valparaíso, 13 Apr. 1905.
[3] Gibbs 11115, Aldenham to Daubeny, 1 Feb. 1906.
[4] Hunt, op. cit., i. 59–66.

Latin America, they could not afford to antagonize local political or commercial feeling. When they became engaged in fixed capital projects, like processing or mining, where the risks were high and the necessary resources considerable, their flexibility was much reduced. If conditions deteriorated they could not suddenly depart without heavy loss.

Real restraints existed on British merchants in Latin America. Fierce competition between adventurous and independent men had characterized foreign commerce in the republics during and immediately after their independence, and had persuaded many houses to leave. The growth of direct producer–customer relations, particularly in Latin America's imports, bypassed the merchant house, thus saving commissions and promoting more personal links. This development, which ended the highly specialized division of labour in international trade from which Britain had benefited, went far on the East Coast but was less important along the Pacific. Inevitably, manufacturers of branded goods preferred to market their products themselves.[1]

Later in the nineteenth century agreements concerning prices and output collapsed. Some merchants demanded a larger share, were refused, and initiated open competition. Negotiations at Arequipa between Gibbs and three other wool shippers broke down when the largest firm, Staffords, became dissatisfied.[2] Moreover, if commercial requirements largely excluded local exporters, important European and American houses directly competed with the British and could destroy their entrepôt trade. Immigrant communities established their own houses to meet their particular needs. The telegraph, the steamship, and overseas banks all made it possible for British merchant houses to be replaced, reducing overheads and risks. To expect merchant houses of different nationality to co-operate permanently was unrealistic. Even in the Brazilian rubber trade, where produce was pledged to established intermediaries, pirate middlemen would successfully trade up-river offering marginally better prices. Again, the British consul at Bahía reported in 1905 that keen competition between exporters had lowered commissions.[3] Indeed, in some commodity

[1] D. C. M. Platt, *Latin America and British Trade, 1806–1914* (London, 1972), pp. 140–50.

[2] See correspondence in Gibbs 11068, 11124, and 11132.

[3] *Consular Reports* (*Bahía*), P.P. 1905, lxxxvii, 405.

trades the British role was small. While Britain was a large importer of Argentine grain, British houses handled only a fraction of the trade.[1] The cocoa and tobacco trades of Bahía were financed by German houses.[2] None of the cocoa exports from Bahía and from Guayaquil in Ecuador, explained a British merchant inelegantly, 'are financed in the same way by British houses like Central and South American coffee is'.[3] In world commodity markets, speculators were opposed by equally determined rivals. Rising prices encouraged shipments in such quantities to those markets where corners were being worked that the speculators' resources became exhausted. Again, producers and their governments could play off one merchant against another. The Peruvian Government forced Gibbs to accept less favourable terms on its guano and nitrate businesses under the threat of handing contracts to rival houses, and in both cases the house was replaced after years of service. In 1861 Thomson, Bonar and Co. became guano consignees, and in 1878 Sawers, and later Graham Rowe, assumed responsibility for nitrate shipments.[4]

The rise of alternative suppliers acted also as a constraint. The versatility of many crops ensured production elsewhere, particularly if prices were attractive. British merchants in Latin America could not permanently squeeze both producers and consumers. An attempt to limit shipments and raise prices in the final market would inevitably promote competition elsewhere from new growers, substitutes, or synthetic products. The high prices which the Peruvian government, through her merchant contractors, demanded for guano and nitrate encouraged the search for alternative supplies of natural and artificial fertilizer. Cocoa, which had begun to be produced in Africa, was no longer dominated by Latin America. Newly opened copper mines in Spain and the United States ended Chile's favourable supply position, lowered prices, and limited the success of the copper syndicate. The most remark-

[1] P.R.O. F.O. 368/928/71594, Consul Dickson (Rosario) to Tower, 14 Oct. 1914, and Tower to Grey, 16 Oct. 1914; P.R.O. F.O. 368/1207/185729, memo. of Consul General Mackie. The Big Four shippers were Dreyfus & Co., Bunge y Born, Huni y Wormser, and Weil Bros.
[2] *Consular Reports (Bahía)*, P.P. 1905, lxxxvii, 403; 'Cocoa Trade and Production' (Special Consular Report 50, Washington, 1912), p. 15; *The Economist*, 23 Apr. 1910, 888.
[3] P.R.O. C.O. 96/586/4427, Ganzoni to Colonial Office, 15 Jan. 1917.
[4] Mathew, 'Peruvian Contractors and the Peruvian Government', loc. cit.; Greenhill and Miller, loc. cit., 127.

able switching of supplies occurred in rubber, world output of which was practically monopolized by the Amazon region before 1910; exorbitant prices and shortages directly contributed towards substitution by plantation rubber, and the development of reclaimed and synthetic materials. Plantation-produced rubber from the Far East soon outstripped Brazilian shipments and lowered prices to a fraction of their former level, ruining Brazilian producers and merchants alike. While the depression in rubber had previously been attributed 'to the manipulations of speculators', even Brazilians now pointed to 'the extraordinary development of rubber planting'.[1]

Further, British merchants had little influence over demand. Some primary products were staples, the demand for which was inelastic. Thus, in years of dearth merchants were rewarded with high prices, but when gluts occurred and prices slumped demand would not increase. Some switching did in fact occur. If wheat were scarce, taste might favour other cereals (rye, maize, or barley) or substitutes like rice and tapioca, particularly in poor countries. Again, demand for rubber in America and Britain, the chief markets, depended not on price but on the general level of business expectations, especially when the automobile industry was the most telling market factor. Cars could only sell when real incomes were rising and employment prospects good. The slump in the United States in 1907, which severely damaged business confidence, therefore proved disastrous for Brazilian rubber. Latin American grain merchants could never eliminate imports of Empire or European grain into Britain, whatever the level of prices, since the British market preferred bread produced from a mixture of grains. Moreover, the fact that most of Latin America's commodities were not sold locally made resident merchants highly dependent on overseas demand. They could not afford to antagonize consumers.

British merchants in Latin America did not always enjoy a ready market in Britain where they might have expected to have exerted greater influence. Before 1914 Britain increasingly tapped the Empire for supplies of foodstuffs and raw materials. The United States was the big consumer of Latin American coffee and rubber before 1914, and Germany was the acknowledged centre for cocoa and nitrates. Moreover, in Britain a strongly entrenched network

---

[1] *The Economist*, 20 Jan. 1912, 118; see also *The Times*, 25 Feb. 1910, 15d–e.

of first users (importers, jobbers, brokers, and manufacturers)[1] limited the options open to exporters from Latin America. Like the shipper at the Latin American end, importers in Britain gathered at selected reception centres, and manufacturing was steadily concentrated into fewer hands. In Britain the number of independent millers fell from 10,000 in the 1880s to less than 1,000 by 1914, when such large concerns as Ranks and Spillers had effected amalgamations and rationalizations. If merchants became too coercive, first-users could establish direct links with producers, or even purchase their own sources of supply.

Recourse to government action in Latin America by producers and by local commercial interests also restrained foreign merchants. Strong links between officials and powerful producers ensured intervention at several levels. A general economic policy which facilitated immigration and the development of railways and banks lowered costs and improved marketing. Specific measures which promoted production, raised tariff barriers, established marketing boards, and fixed prices constituted more direct intervention. Latin America's use of export taxes also provided a dimension of control. Brazil readily intervened on behalf of her coffee, cocoa, and rubber producers when low prices, caused it was alleged by foreign speculators, threatened stability. In each case the Brazilian government raised funds from taxes or loans to satisfy producers, while reducing output until conditions improved. 'The history of the rubber market', writes Knorr, 'is replete with efforts of the producers to protect and advance their interests by interfering in the free market.'[2] Of course, intervention did not always occur. Argentine cereal farmers, who lacked political influence, failed to attract attention among governments composed of ranchers, and this became even more marked when producers were isolated and their output constituted a small proportion of total product. And *laissez-faire*, the theoretical justification for official non-intervention, was still popular among some Latin American politicians.

Although the success of valorization schemes varied—Brazil's *Defesa do Borracha* in 1912 failed to prevent falling rubber prices —the radical implication that government should and could

[1] Peter F. Payne, *British Commercial Institutions* (London, 1969), pp. 14–15 and 68–87.
[2] K. E. Knorr, *World Rubber and its Regulation* (Stanford, 1945), p. 88.

intervene to protect producers against abuses was an important advance, with repercussions for those British merchants who previously enjoyed substantial economic power. But given that Latin America's economy depended on exporting primary products, such intervention was inevitable if exports were threatened. Peru took the policy of extending control over her natural resources a stage further. Her dependence on foreign capital seemed well defined. To alleviate a financial crisis, budget deficits, and problems in the servicing of the internal and foreign debts, she needed the help of skilled foreign capitalists. Her crucial weaknesses—contacts, sales, and marketing overseas—were the strength of expatriate merchant houses. But Peru's bold policy towards guano and nitrate effectively extended control despite the opposition of foreign capitalists and consumers. She could and did dispense with the services of overseas intermediaries when she wished.

Moreover, it was undeniable that British merchants provided basic and valuable services which were of assistance to Latin America's long-term development. They were not redundant middlemen who contributed nothing. They moved primary goods from producers to manufacturers and consumers. They accumulated small lots from farmers and native factors, and performed the specialized functions of cleaning, grading, and packing, according to the customer's needs. They bore the risks of buying and storing produce over periods during which prices could be volatile. Their links with overseas markets, their efficiency and expertise, were crucial when a large portion of output was exported. Enjoying access to cheap money in Britain (which gave them distinct advantages over other houses in Latin America), British merchants supplied credit to producers and buyers. The reputation of British merchants was such, and debt collection in Latin America so hazardous, that small firms and buyers could not get credit unless a well-known British house undertook the business or endorsed their bills.[1] And where trade was still small or a manufacturer reluctant to employ his own agent, the merchant's knowledge of local needs, regulations, and tariffs was invaluable. British merchants also supplied storage. While these services naturally added to the role and power of the foreign house, it is difficult to see what alternative existed when local initiatives were insufficient to meet the need themselves.

[1] Platt, op. cit., pp. 145–9.

Nor was the merchant's business persistently profitable. Like all businessmen he suffered unavoidable losses and made the wrong decisions. Enormous risks had to be faced in Latin America, as the early merchants discovered. Time and distance created misunderstandings and the wrong goods or quantities were sent. In the 1820s the return of the post was delayed for six months or longer so that partners were isolated from their branch offices and had to place a great deal of faith in their local representatives. A careless or dishonest agent who invented persistent excuses for lapses caused untold damage before his principals discovered the truth. Agents, experts only in one or two products, sold a range of goods about which they knew little.[1] Overcrowded ports in Latin America forced vessels to discharge into lighters, cargo was stored unattended and unprotected, duties were imposed arbitrarily, and official procedures were slow. Freights and insurance were high to cover demurrage and risks heavy enough to erase a man's capital. John Owens placed small loads in several ships to minimize risks and regulate arrivals.[2] Continuing political instability made matters worse. The greatest problem was in returning receipts from sales to England. Quick turnover and short-term credit constituted the safest course, but remittances normally lagged far behind sales, giving merchants an anxious wait for their money. Local currencies were liable to depreciation, and merchants who waited for a rise lost money, while further falls erased any paper profit. Successful merchants had to forecast fluctuations in exchanges as well as prices.[3] Remitting in bullion or precious stones entailed high insurance and freight costs. Some merchants disliked investing locally (to earn interest or to await an appreciation in value) since it loosened their personal hold over their fortune. Merchants were also vulnerable to liquidity crises and to sharp breaks in prices if they retained produce too long and had capital tied up in unsaleable stock.

British merchants, far from exercising political control, were vulnerable to local political pressure. Gibbs, once replaced, were unable to retrieve their consignment contracts in the guano and nitrate trades. British merchants were commercial, not political animals, at a disadvantage in any contest with an experienced professional politician. A recent article concludes that even in the

---

[1] Gibbs, op. cit., pp. 410–14; Maude, op. cit., p. 79. Gibbs dismissed their agent, Moens, in Lima.   [2] Clapp, op. cit., pp. 26–7.   [3] Ibid., p. 125.

precarious days of Chilean independence, when the British influence was strong, when a British fleet cruised in the Pacific, and when the new Republic needed recognition, the actual political discretion of British merchants was limited against 'the resolute independence of mind demonstrated by the Chilean Government'.[1]

British merchants did not deliberately aim at controlling local economies, and many aspects of 'control' were simply the normal pattern of business. To hire shipping space in advance was not to deprive local trades but to ensure shipment after the harvest. To establish backward or forward linkages in production and processing, in marketing and financial services, was only prudent when there were few local alternatives. Oligopoly among exporters was virtually inevitable in Latin America's commercial pattern, rather than part of a plot to exploit the republics. Merchants were unlikely to have deliberately held down prices for consumers of their own nationality when their livelihood depended on the gap between producer and consumer prices. They could hardly refuse to buy when local prices were low (which would merely further depress levels), or fail to take advantage of high prices abroad. Nor were the powers of British merchants unique. The pattern of primary production in Latin America—small, scattered, and isolated farms—inevitably created a long chain of intermediaries.

By 1900 British merchants did not in fact exist in any great numbers in Latin America. After the first inflow of speculators, agents without capital, and manufacturers dumping what was unsaleable elsewhere, British trade was confined to a few houses.[2] This trend, visible immediately after the 1825–6 crash, continued from the 1860s—despite a greatly increased volume of trade—until the First World War. Houses became extinct because their partners were extravagant or incompetent, because they were bankrupt, because of the climate, or because they looked for more comfortable conditions and safer profits in North America, Europe, or the Empire where Britons predominated. Illiquidity, debts, and the need to protect their reputation in the West Riding, forced the Rhodes family to recall their agent from Brazil in 1816. John Luccock, representing the Luptons, returned in 1818 through ill

[1] Jay Kinsbruner, 'The Political Influence of the British Merchants resident in Chile during the O'Higgins Administration, 1817–1823', *The Americas*, xxvii (1970–1), 26.

[2] Platt, op. cit., pp. 136–50, from which most of this paragraph is taken.

health: unable to sell cloth and ironmongery, he had tried retailing, auctions, bartering, and reshipment to Buenos Aires with equal lack of success. While British houses remained in diminished numbers at the principal commercial centres, which were entrepôts for other coastal and up-country communities, they withdrew rapidly from the smaller markets. In Mexico, Britain was completely eclipsed by the Germans, and in Central America her representation was scattered. Even the strong British houses which remained in Latin America developed important links elsewhere. Gibbs operated in Australia and New York, and Balfour Williamson's interests on the north Pacific coast soon exceeded those in Chile and Peru. Moreover, while the nature of Latin American trade favoured large merchant houses, particularly when bulk unbranded goods or high value products were handled, houses like Gibbs and Balfour Williamson were not necessarily typical of those that survived. The depth of their penetration into finance, manufacturing, and marketing were the exception rather than the rule.

This introduction, then, illustrates both sides of the equation of power between British merchants and Latin America's economic and political interests. Certainly the republics were initially very reliant on British houses, which could offer solid advantages such as credit facilities, contacts abroad, knowledge, and expertise. Sheer size gave cause for alarm. Some tactics sharpened resentment. At the intersection of the three market forces—producer, native intermediary, and exporter—conflict was inevitable. The exporter preferred low prices which were not in the farmer's interests; and where farmers were small, ignorant, and unable to influence either marketing or officials, abuses could become practically institutionalized. The latent power of British merchants in Latin America was enormous.

Nevertheless, some fears now appear unreasonable. Real restraints on exporters existed in the shape of market forces and government intervention. Nor was it a simple case of foreigners exploiting native interests. The injection of outside capital was beneficial at a point when economies lacked resources. And foreign intermediaries provoked competition with local factors which raised prices for the producer, lowered margins, widened the area

of production and distribution, and erased the advantages conferred by fraud.[1] The case studies which follow in Chapters VI–
VIII re-examine and develop further the issues raised here. The
conclusions which emerge may together suggest the limits and
extent of British mercantile power in Latin America.

[1] Bauer and Yamey, op. cit., pp. 32–50.

CHAPTER VI

The Brazilian Coffee Trade

ROBERT GREENHILL

I

FROM the mid nineteenth century Brazil became the major force in the world's coffee trade. Her share rose rapidly from 30 per cent in 1850 to over 70 per cent immediately before 1914, while in absolute terms shipments increased from two to fifteen million bags (Table VI.1). Coffee cultivation, first introduced on a commercial basis in the Paraíba Valley behind Rio de Janeiro, spread west and south-west from the 1860s into São Paulo (which soon produced three-quarters of Brazil's output), Minas Gerais, and Espírito Santo. Between 1890 and 1910 the number of trees in São Paulo more than trebled to 700 million, covering three million acres.[1] Coffee dominated the Brazilian economy. It earned more than three-fifths of Brazil's foreign exchange for the purchase of manufactured imports and technical skills, and it provided a similar proportion, through an export tax, of government revenue by which overseas loans were serviced and public works financed. Successful cultivation stimulated immigration, urbanization, and industrial development. Railways and roads to transport the crops opened up the hinterland.[2] Moreover, coffee was a substantial employer. Its potentially high returns were crucial not only to the large landowner or *fazendeiro* who hired labour, but also to the smallholder and sharecropper.[3]

[1] M. L. Bynum, 'International Trade in Coffee' (*Trade Promotion Series* 37, Washington, 1926), pp. 2–16; W. G. McCreery and M. L. Bynum, 'The Coffee Industry in Brazil' (ibid. 92, Washington, 1930), pp. 55–8; C. Prado Júnior, *História Econômica do Brasil* (São Paulo, 1967), pp. 226–7.

[2] Warren Dean, 'The Planter as Entrepreneur: The Case of São Paulo', *Hispanic–American Historical Review*, xlvi (1966), 138–52; id., *The Industrialisation of São Paulo 1880–1945* (1969), p. 85; G. Wythe, 'Brazil: Trends in Industrial Development' in S. Kuznets, Wilbert E. Moore, and Joseph Spengler, *Economic Growth in Brazil, India and Japan* (Durham, N.C., 1955), p. 31.

[3] United Nations Food and Agriculture Organization (F.A.O.), 'The World

TABLE VI.1

Quantities of Coffee at Brazilian Ports, 1880–1908

(000 bags of 60 kilos)

	Rio	Santos	Vitória	Bahía	Other	Total	World
1880–1	4,521	1,126		136		5,783	9,975
1881–2	3,841	1,723		126		5,690	9,803
1882–3	4,736	1,968		147		6,851	11,796
1883–4	3,186	1,872	none	109		5,167	9,145
1884–5	4,276	2,095		121		6,492	10,641
1885–6	3,797	1,669		208		5,674	9,222
1886–7	3,499	2,583		150		6,232	10,428
1887–8	1,911	1,121		106		3,138	7,203
1888–9	4,189	2,635	27	164		7,015	10,834
1889–0	2,428	1,872	14	170		4,484	8,697
1890–1	2,421	2,952	62	156	none	5,591	10,382
1891–2	3,719	3,386	94	306		7,505	11,941
1892–3	3,112	3,206	150	192		6,660	11,235
1893–4	3,856	1,685	358	370		6,269	10,580
1894–5	2,693	4,007	252	290		7,242	11,499
1895–6	2,399	3,093	303	211		6,006	10,553
1896–7	3,579	5,104	292	323		9,298	13,949
1897–8	4,305	6,153	454	302		11,214	16,070
1898–9	3,320	5,570	289	268		9,447	13,851
1899–0	3,395	5,712	282	175		9,564	13,943
1900–1	3,015	7,973	204	181		11,373	15,158
1901–2	5,372	10,171	468	242	30	16,283	19,928
1902–3	4,002	8,357	414	198	21	12,992	16,746
1903–4	4,056	6,402	435	274	25	11,642	15,821
1904–5	2,592	7,423	389	179	14	10,597	14,417
1905–6	3,406	6,982	397	229	40	11,054	14,535
1906–7	4,440	15,392	409	150	17	20,408	24,135
1907–8	3,409	7,302	483	230	24	11,448	14,831
1908–9	2,927	9,533	396	176	8	13,040	16,664

SOURCES: *Brazilian Yearbook* (1909), p. 632; W. G. McCreery and M. L. Bynum, 'The Coffee Industry in Brazil' (*Trade Promotion Series* 92, Washington, 1930).

The enormous rise in coffee production needed a complementary marketing organization to collect and distribute produce overseas. If not the main agrarian staple—the values of world production of rice, wheat, and sugar were larger—the proportion of coffee

Coffee Economy' (*Commodity Bulletin Series* 33, Rome, 1961), pp. 1–3; C. R. Krug and R. A. de Poerck, *World Coffee Survey* (Rome, 1968), p. 438.

entering international trade was, and still is,[1] the highest of all agricultural goods. Coffee was exported to temperate regions, where customers enjoyed higher standards of living, from less developed areas which consumed relatively little, thus directly redressing the balance between rich and poor countries if not necessarily dividing the return value fairly.[2] Probably 95 per cent of Brazil's coffee was exported before 1914, giving the mainly foreign export firms in Rio de Janeiro and Santos, her chief international ports, an undeniable influence in the national economy in general and on producers' incomes in particular.

The interest of British capitalists in Brazilian coffee was long established. Edward Johnston, for example, who had reached Brazil in 1820, became an important shipper by the mid century and the second largest exporter in the 1870s.[3] Another British firm, Naumann Gepp, formed in the 1860s and incorporated in 1897, led shipments from Santos.[4] Around 1900 other British houses included Quayle Davidson, Nicholsons, Moore & Co., Norton Megaw, and Edward Ashworth.[5]

Many contemporary observers agreed that the power which the coffee trade's structure conferred on foreign capitalists was abused. Producers and their agents considered that export houses deliberately depressed local prices and exploited the consumer abroad. Dr. Neiva told the Brazilian Congress in 1901 that the difficulty facing the coffee industry was 'exporters who in combination with the big roasting houses monopolize the markets and persistently and systematically "bear" coffee'.[6] In 1902 the Governor of Rio reported that the coffee business had been 'handed over to the triumphant spectre of capitalism'.[7] Again, Dr. Antonio Candido Rodrigues, Secretary for Agriculture in São Paulo, explained: 'The present organization of the coffee trade places us entirely at the mercy of speculators who, availing themselves of the wide

[1] Coffee is currently second only to oil in value among primary commodities traded internationally.

[2] V. D. Wickizer, *Coffee, Tea and Cocoa: An Economic and Political Analysis* (Stanford, 1951), p. 4; *Financial Times*, 27 Feb. 1970, 13–15.

[3] Anon., *One Hundred Years of Coffee* (London, 1942); R. Graham, *Britain and the Onset of Modernisation in Brazil, 1850–1914* (Cambridge, 1968), p. 73.

[4] Gepp, Board Minutes 1897.

[5] *Consular Reports (Rio de Janeiro)*, P.P. 1899, xcviii, 313.

[6] *B.R.*, 28 May 1901, 379.

[7] Stanley J. Stein, *Vassouras: A Brazilian Coffee County 1850–1900* (Cambridge, Mass., 1957), p. 283.

margins of profit in their transactions are able, with perfect security, to maintain their control over prices.'[1] Similarly, later writers have assumed that foreign capitalists, particularly the British whose commercial power and representation were substantial, exercised a disruptive influence. Richard Graham, for example, takes the whole question of Britain's control over Brazil's external trade for granted. Her merchants, he explained, were 'probing the export economy in search of the weaker spots to be controlled'.[2] J. R. Normano described the commercial battles of coffee houses, where adversaries 'became allies and collaborators unceasingly striving towards control of the market'.[3]

The present chapter will examine these issues. What was the precise nature of the limitations imposed by intermediaries on Brazilian planters? What resources were available to the planters? Who controlled whom? How were prices determined? The chapter also discusses the identity of these middlemen and the extent of Britain's role in the coffee trade. Were British merchants responsible for alleged mistreatment? Did the demands of British consumers encourage unfair practices?

II

The first stage in studying the problem of control in the Brazilian coffee trade is to evaluate the planter's position. Production followed a familiar pattern in Latin America. For all but the smallest planters the fixed capital employed in planting, labour accommodation, welfare, and equipment was heavy.[4] But working costs over a large cultivable area were relatively low, particularly when paid in depreciating paper currency against receipts in gold. Probably 70–80 per cent of total costs were fixed, while the remainder varied according to output; the more bags harvested, the lower was the

[1] *B.R.*, 1 July 1902, 321.
[2] Graham, op. cit., pp. 73–8, and his 'Sepoys and Imperialists: Techniques of British Power in Nineteenth Century Brazil', *Inter-American Economic Affairs*, xxiii (1969), 23–37.
[3] J. R. Normano, *Brazil: A Study of Economic Types* (Chapel Hill, 1935), p. 43.
[4] F.A.O., *Coffee in Latin America: Productivity Problems and Future Prospects*, Part 2 (1): *São Paulo* (New York, 1960), pp. 9–17; *T.C.T.J.*, Nov. 1928, 555–7; Richard Morse, 'São Paulo in the Nineteenth Century: Economic Roots of the Metropolis', *Inter-American Economic Affairs*, v (1951), 14–16.

cost per bag. The coffee *fazenda* thus adapted well to economies of scale, giving every incentive to increased production. And to maximize such economies (or to raise earnings during periods of high return) farmers discouraged interplanting of all but a few subsistence foodstuffs. The fact that their entire income now depended on the coffee harvest made them particularly vulnerable.

Producers tended to extend rather than intensify cultivation. Scientific planting, fertilization, irrigation, pruning, pest control, and mechanization were applied sparingly and irregularly. To exhaust land and plant virgin soil on a large scale was cheaper—although continual movement from old producing areas required a complementary infrastructure of roads, railways, and ports.[1] Before 1914 yields fell sharply outside the main productive centres and on exhausted farms around Rio, and poor quality produce realized only low prices. São Paulo alone improved yields and encouraged better practices. An agricultural institute, established at Campinas in 1887, was soon taken over by the state government, but although some valuable research was published, improvements were generally left to a minority of enterprising *fazendeiros*.[2] Unscientific cultivation increased *fazendeiros'* vulnerability, since it failed to reduce the effects of fluctuations in the harvest. Several short crops were likely to follow a heavy yield which had exhausted soil and trees. Weather conditions, disease, and pests continued to exercise a strong but unpredictable influence. If coffee's adaptability were 'probably unequalled by any other important perennial tropical crop'[3]—in Brazil it grew in fourteen states and to an altitude of 3,000 feet—the great concentration within the hot, moist climate of São Paulo created problems. Although the geography of Brazilian cultivation was wide enough to ensure some ecological differences, and even within states conditions sometimes varied

[1] McCreery and Bynum, op. cit., pp. 55–61; Krug and de Poerck, op. cit., pp. 280–4. There was a similar story in Brazilian cocoa production, see *Cocoa Trade and Production*, Special Consular Report 50 (Washington, 1912), p. 15.

[2] Krug and de Poerck, op. cit., pp. 294, 360, and 439–42; V. D. Wickizer, *The World Coffee Economy with Special Reference to Control Schemes* (Stanford, 1943), p. 21; Stanley J. Stein, 'The Passing of a Coffee Plantation in the Paraíba Valley', *Hispanic–American Historical Review*, xxxiii (1953), 331–64; House Docs., No. 401, 50th Congress, 1st Session (1887), pp. 5–6; U.S.M.C.R., Nov. 1908, 338, pp. 96–7, and June 1909, 345, p. 96.

[3] Krug and de Poerck, op. cit., p. 436. In contrast to coffee, cocoa required special climatic conditions which severely limited cultivation. In both Brazil and Ecuador the bulk of cocoa was grown in one province, Bahía and Los Rios respectively.

sharply, a broader scattering would certainly have helped to average out damage by climate or pests.

In the long run, however, coffee experienced a recurring cyclical pattern of rising production. The good prices which resulted from short crops encouraged renewed planting, but for five years, by which time favourable conditions might have ended, seedlings bore no fruit and the impact of high prices on supply was postponed. Overproduction and falling prices then restricted planting until under-supply recurred. But the fact that estates with large fixed assets were long-term investments, while working costs were relatively low, discouraged *fazendeiros* from uprooting trees in unfavourable years. To grow less conferred marginal savings when overheads were high. To adopt an alternative main crop was impracticable. Farmers awaited better returns, even intensifying production to compensate for falling receipts since coffee trees enjoyed a productive life of about thirty years (although output declined over the last decade). Falling prices did not, therefore, immediately reduce supplies. A long period of overproduction and depression normally ensued before a new balance was struck between supply and demand. Prices then rose until a fresh cycle of planting and production occurred.[1]

The pattern of late nineteenth-century production illustrates these fluctuations. Relatively good prices prevailed until 1879; then new planting in São Paulo became effective and Rio enjoyed bumper harvests, so that markets were depressed, particularly for the lowest grades.[2] After 1884 equilibrium was slowly re-established with smaller crops in Brazil and Java (Brazil's chief competitor), and coffee in the nineties, almost alone amongst primary commodities, enjoyed price levels ruling twenty years earlier. Inevitably, massive planting brought oversupply and low prices by the end of the decade. During 1897 alone, when Brazil's crop totalled 8·7 million bags compared with an average of 5·5 million in the preceding three years, prices fell 40 per cent with 'hardly any prospect of improvement'.[3]

---

[1] F.A.O., *Commodity Bulletin Series 33*, p. 5; Wickizer, *Coffee, Tea and Cocoa*, p. 21; Federal Trade Commission, *Economic Report of the Investigation of Coffee Prices* (Washington, 1954), pp. 2 and 21–3.

[2] Gepp, Gibbes to Naumann, 9 Feb. 1879, Guard Book.

[3] Gepp, Naumann to Gibbes, 18 May 1897, Naumann Letters; cf. *Statist*, 2 June 1894, 718–19, and 20 Nov. 1897, 802; and P.P. 1898, xciv, 264; 1899, xcviii, 275, and 1900, xcii, 364.

The variability of coffee harvests caused acute distress to producers in times of dearth. Extensive rather than intensive cultivation depressed quality. As a result of the expansion of estates, climatic factors, and the farmers' response to temporary high prices, coffee also experienced occasional bumper crops and oversupply which permanently threatened prosperity. And to these variations was added the short-term inelasticity of supply. 'This delayed adjustment of supply to demand', a report concluded, 'is the prime cause of the periodic crises which afflict the world's coffee industry.'[1] Disunity among *fazendeiros* made things worse. Despite the presence of a minority of large landowners, the majority of farmers were small-scale, producing relatively insignificant crops. At the turn of the century over 11,000 estates in São Paulo, more than two-thirds of the total, contained less than 50,000 trees. Only 1,650 had over 100,000 trees.[2] No single or even several growers could decisively influence shipments.

Direct reliance of coffee growers on native middlemen in the shipping centres gave further cause for alarm. Farmers consigned produce to *comissários*—Brazilian brokers or general merchants who performed a multitude of agency services such as forwarding supplies, settling rail charges, checking weights, and storing output for isolated clients.[3] Export shipments were laboriously compiled from numerous consignments by intermediaries in Rio and Santos, the chief railheads for the up-country stations to which farmers hauled their crop. Generally, *comissários* did not buy coffee but merely handled it for their principals. Once buyers were found, *comissários* deducted commission and expenses, and forwarded the balance of the sale price to the growers. If supplies were limited, *comissários* dispatched representatives up-country to buy on the *fazendas* or at local stations. At Rio, a further middleman, the *ensacador*, intervened. He was a broker preparing transactions on commission between *comissário* and exporter for whom consignments were assembled according to needs. The origin of the system is obscure, but later developments which permitted a more stream-

---

[1] Commonwealth Secretariat, *Plantation Crops* (1970), p. 29; cf. Prado, op. cit., pp. 228–9.

[2] *S.A.J.*, 25 Aug. 1900, 213; *B.R.*, 18 July 1899, 472; Normano, op. cit., p. 41; J. W. F. Rowe, *Primary Commodities in International Trade* (Cambridge, 1965), pp. 40–2; P. Yates, *Commodity Control: A Study of Primary Products* (London, 1943), p. 68.

[3] Stein, op. cit., pp. 81–2; Normano, op. cit., p. 42.

lined commercial structure probably account for its absence at Santos. The *ensacador*, normally a merchant of greater resources than the *comissário* with storage and handling machinery, usually bought produce outright. The Comercio e Lavoura Cia., for example, owned four warehouses with a capacity of 125,000 bags, and Messrs. Camara y Gomes handled 100,000 bags a month.[1] The intervention of successive middlemen delayed the transfer of produce, increased costs, and diminished the grower's share of the current export price. Thus, some *comissários* tried to bypass the *ensacador*, though this was still only at its early stages before 1914.[2] Weight of tradition and the complex network of understandings between intermediaries were difficult to overcome. The *ensacador* represented a useful buffer to the exporter. Moreover, a decree in 1882, which limited brokers in Rio to 70, conferred profitable intermediary functions on a privileged few who would not surrender them.

The *fazendeiro*'s need for cash further constrained him. Before the last quarter of the nineteenth century the majority of growers could plant and harvest without permanent resort to credit. But cultivation of marginal land which required dearer inputs, some sudden breaks in price (in 1875 and 1897), and extravagance forced farmers to seek outside capital. In the 1880s, admittedly an unfavourable decade, Laërne calculated that only 20 per cent of farmers were solvent, another 30 per cent could repay loans if pressed, but the rest, in need of fresh capital yet unable to service current debts, were beyond retrieval. In 1899 the *Brazilian Review* calculated that debts exceeded £14 million.[3] Before 1914 few long-term sources of specialized agricultural credit existed. Although banks lent before 1880, increasing agricultural indebtedness and opportunities for more remunerative investments elsewhere steadily raised interest rates to prohibitive levels. The hard-pressed *fazendeiro* thus applied to his *comissário* for funds to meet expenses, especially at harvest, sending him bills for settlement. The *comissário*, unable to refuse since his business depended on viable *fazendas*, covered himself by charging up to 24 per cent interest on advances and seldom advanced more than 60 per cent of a crop's

---

[1] C. F. van Delden Laërne, *Brazil and Java: Report on Coffee-Culture in America, Asia and Africa* (The Hague, 1885), p. 231; *B.R.*, 10 July 1900, 436.
[2] *S.A.J.*, 20 July 1901, 71; *B.R.*, 23 July 1901, 530, and 13 Mar. 1909, 289.
[3] Laërne, op. cit., p. 224; *B.R.*, 18 July 1899, 472; Stein, op. cit., p. 352.

value. He raised the necessary cash from banks in Rio or Santos which were more ready to lend to him than to a *fazendeiro* because his assets were easily realizable and his credit better known. Thus the farmer, in debt and paying heavy interest charges, rarely regained solvency. He lost control of his crop to the *comissário*, could not seek competitive terms elsewhere, and forfeited a portion of the final price.[1] The system worked smoothly while credit and coffee revenues were forthcoming. However, deteriorating prices and restricted credit, which forced the farmer to accept what he could obtain and indirectly harmed the *comissários*, threatened collapse.[2]

One dimension, then, of control in the Brazilian coffee trade was, on the one hand, the grower's weaknesses (a pattern of production tending to oversupply, disunity, and the credit nexus) and, on the other, the dominance of the native intermediary. Of course this relationship was not inevitably damaging. No clear demarcation of business existed where planter and *comissário* were relatives or partners, and where one firm undertook farming and brokerage.[3] Nevertheless, apart from the minority of large *fazendeiros*, able to function unaided, most farmers depended on native intermediaries to finance and manage their crops. The first stage in marketing Brazilian coffee favoured the local middleman.

III

The resources open to foreign capital formed a second factor in the equation of power in Brazil's coffee trade. The elimination of the native middleman directly removed control from local to foreign hands. Exporters established up-country agencies to tap centres like Ribeirâo Prêto to which *fazendeiros* hauled their crops. Such rough and ready markets, without adequate classifications, supplied cheap coffee once good personal relations with planters had been established. To secure loyalty and bypass *comissários*, the expatriate shipper offered small premiums and credit facilities.[4] Johnstons soon adopted this policy, constantly widening their interior contacts and preferring their own buyers to independent

---

[1] *B.R.*, 14 Oct. 1902, 502, and 18 Nov. 1902, 568; Stein, op. cit., pp. 353–63.
[2] House Docs., No. 401, pp. 69–79; McCreery and Bynum, op. cit., pp. 37–52; W. K. Ukers, *All About Coffee* (New York, 1935), pp. 323–32.
[3] Johnston, Greene to Norty, 9 Sept. 1903, Letter Book II; Laërne, op. cit., p. 213; Stein, op. cit., pp. 84 and 238.
[4] *B.R.*, 16 July 1901, 506.

brokers.[1] Similarly, Arbuckles, an American house, established up-country buying offices.[2] The battle for consignment of up-country coffee from 1895 resulted in the 'rout' of the *comissários* by exporters, who thenceforward squeezed the planters.[3] Shippers, whose knowledge of the coffee trade was extensive and whose financial resources were greater, threatened to usurp the *comissários'* functions of grading and pricing produce and advancing capital. Middlemen came together in 1901 to reverse these trends, which diverted business, pared down their commissions,[4] and made them into mere clients of the foreign exporter.

Ownership of coffee-processing facilities reinforced the exporters' powers. Although coffee was normally roasted in consuming markets, British merchants could undertake stages in the processing of coffee denied to native coffee interests who could rarely afford the necessary outlay. Both Naumann Gepp and Johnstons invested in cleaning and hulling mills, paying their owners a retainer for preferential treatment, or encouraging *fazendeiros* to use mills which the exporting houses owned outright. Johnstons successfully centralized milling in plant erected around 1900. Large crops and falling prices were strong inducements to minimize handling costs, introduce labour-saving machinery, and improve quality.[5]

The fact that Brazilian coffee shipments were concentrated in relatively few hands at two main ports, Rio and Santos—Vitória and Bahía accounted for less than 5 per cent of exports (Table VI.1)—also aroused concern. Although the total of interested houses was high since some forty firms exported coffee, an oligopoly of large shippers, especially at Santos, handled the bulk of the trade. Between 1895 and 1910, as Table VI.2 shows, six or seven firms exported up to 60 per cent of the Brazilian crop.[6] Firms

---

[1] Johnston, Greene to Johnston, 11 Nov. 1899; Santos to London, 10 Aug. and 23 Nov. 1903; *S.A.J.*, 6 Jan. 1900, 4.

[2] *Spice Mill*, June 1908, 354, and Feb. 1912, 116–18; U.S.M.C.R., June 1908, 332, pp. 121–4.

[3] Stein, op. cit., p. 283.

[4] *B.R.*, 15 Jan. 1901, 48, and 25 June 1901, 457.

[5] Johnston, Greene to Johnston, 6 Apr. and 3 Nov. 1896; 21 July and 11 Nov. 1899; 21 Mar. and 10 Dec. 1900, and 25 Aug. 1904. Gepp, Naumann to Michaelson, 9 June 1897, Naumann Letters; 26 Jan. 1898, Naumann Board Minutes.

[6] H. W. Spielman, 'Brazilian Coffee Goes to Market', *Agriculture in the Americas*, v (1945), 95; Wickizer, *Coffee, Tea and Cocoa*, p. 56; *S.A.J.*, 28 Sept. 1907, 331.

which, like Naumann Gepp, shipped entirely from one port further concentrated exports. The fear was that these few large shippers would combine and offer artificially low prices to consumers, a possibility which the gradual elimination of important houses—J. W. Doane & Co. closed their doors in 1905—increased. Following on from the process which eliminated native dealers,

TABLE VI.2

Leading Coffee Exporters from Rio de Janeiro and Santos, 1895–1911: Quantities Exported

(ooo bags of 60 kilos)

	1895[a]	1898/9	1899/ 1900	1900/1	1901/2	1902[b]	1907	1895/6– 1910/11
Wille	177	780	870	1,498	2,560	1,165	6,340	21,032
Naumann Gepp[c]	n/a	973	1,068	1,507	1,632	584	n/a	16,246
Johnstons	190	757	676	964	1,208	561	n/a	9,068
Doane	135	616	857	951	816	474	n/a	n/a
P. Chaves	n/a	n/a	n/a	n/a	n/a	n/a	n/a	7,550
Hard Rand	155	536	559	632	867	183	1,261	6,410
Arbuckles	409	869	908	1,045	1,193	365	n/a	6,325
Zerreiner, Bulow	n/a	147	303	246	n/a	n/a	n/a	3,569
Krische	n/a	180	225	220	n/a	n/a	n/a	3,200
Holsworthy, Ellis	n/a	95	72	39	n/a	n/a	n/a	2,841
Nossack	n/a	112	128	153	n/a	n/a	n/a	2,635
McLaughlin	130	259	289	264	272	68	n/a	1,410
All Shipments[d]	2,764	9,547	9,703	11,148	15,632	6,421	17,125	124,007

[a] Rio shipments only. [c] Naumann Gepp shipped only from Santos.
[b] July to November only. [d] Including smaller shippers.

SOURCES: *Spice Mill*, Jan. 1912, 29; *Brazilian Review*; *South American Journal*.

Brazil's coffee trade 'concentrates itself', an American consul reported, 'more and more in the hands of relatively few houses in the United States and in Europe commanding large capital'.[1] At the turn of the century coffee, explained Morse, was 'delivered in Santos to a half-dozen exporters who set their own price'.[2]

Foreign capitalists directly exploited the weak position of the producers. Their ownership of plantations became a persistent element in the coffee trade. The high returns of the early 1890s attracted outside investment, and after 1897 *fazendas*, often heavily mortgaged and unable to resist the sharp downturn in prices, increasingly passed to creditors, agents, and brokers who in turn resold. Alternatively, planters auctioned property. The fact that

[1] U.S.M.C.R., May 1905, 296, p. 149. [2] Morse, op. cit., pp. 31–2.

estates sold at a discount—though an exceptional fall often indicated bad siting or an unsettled mortgage—attracted foreign interest. 'Before long', the *Brazilian Review* commented, 'we shall hear of plantations being given away.'[1] By 1902 Naumann Gepp calculated that nearly 'a third of coffee plantations have passed into the hands of banks, financial institutions and other firms that had originally no intention of owning and working them'.[2] Edward Greene, Johnstons' manager in Santos, urged his principals in London to consider investment in holdings, scattered to ensure good soil and protection against localized climatic conditions. 'If London capitalists felt half the confidence I feel', he explained, 'they would jump at such a chance.'[3] The Dumont Coffee Company and the São Paulo Coffee Estates, both formed early in 1896 at the peak of prices to amalgamate *fazendas* around Ribeirão Prêto, were prominent examples of British ownership. They introduced model estate management methods, constructed light railways to the main Mogyana line, and brought in modern machinery to lower costs and raise output and quality.[4] United States consuls viewed such developments with alarm. Ownership of 'a vast share of the productive area' would give Britain 'a controlling influence over the coffee trade between Brazil and the United States'.[5]

The access enjoyed by exporters to the world's coffee exchanges gave them some familiar advantages. Coffee, a regularly harvested staple which did not deteriorate under storage and was open to accurate grading, adapted readily to an organized commodity market. The New York Exchange, formed in 1882 after a succession of disastrous commercial failures, was the first modern international coffee market, followed by Le Havre and Hamburg (1887) and London (1890). Handling 50 per cent of world output and 60 per cent of Brazil's production before 1914, New York dominated the trade. It classified Brazilian coffee into nine grades based on the size, colour, and uniformity of beans, grade seven

---

[1] *B.R.*, 18 July 1899, 472; cf. ibid., 15 Aug. 1899, 541, 12 Sept. 1899, 608.
[2] *S.A.J.*, 11 Oct. 1902, 416.
[3] Johnston, Greene to Johnston, 21 Dec. 1903; cf. ibid., letters, 15 and 28 Dec. 1903.
[4] *Consular Reports (Rio de Janeiro)*, P.P. 1898, xciv, 267; 1899, xcviii, 278; 1900, xcii, 371; and 1902, cv, 427; U.S.M.C.R., Sept. 1909, 348, p. 151; *S.A.J.*, 5 Jan. 1903, 11, 9 July 1904, 37, and 15 July 1905, 58.
[5] U.S.M.C.R., Nov. 1898, 218, pp. 334–40.

being the standard against which premiums or discounts were paid; the unit of delivery was 250 pounds.[1] Through their contacts in the exchanges abroad, foreign coffee exporters could help determine and control world market prices, a role normally denied to native Brazilian interests. The successful merchant, employing large resources, daring, foresight and understanding—qualities in short supply—operated the specialized market functions of futures, speculation, and hedging.[2] These facilities, it was alleged, encouraged a sinister speculative element which depressed prices to the producer, but raised them for the consumer. International houses profited from links between exchanges and from manipulation.[3] New York was certainly not free from imperfections. Henry Sielcken, a partner in a coffee business, worked several corners there. Guzmán Blanco, an ex-dictator of Venezuela, apparently manipulated coffee stocks at Le Havre in 1895.[4] Similarly, New York suffered from exploitation of an uninformed public by insiders who bought for a rise which conditions did not warrant. Around 1900, although visible supply was in fact rising, the heavily backed Lewisohn copper syndicate bought coffee, a trend which the speculators and merchants encouraged and which upset markets and prices.[5]

Brazil unsurprisingly developed the most advanced marketing arrangements among coffee producers. Nevertheless, in practice the machinery was inadequate for the complexity and volume of business, and techniques in Brazil were crude and archaic compared with the refinements introduced at New York. Brazil, suspicious of dealings and gradings, formed the first official exchange at Santos only in 1914 after much debate, and at Rio not until after the First World War.[6]

Exporters were able to remain consistently better informed than producers since an important function of exchanges was to furnish data on estimated supply, stock, and demand, continuously modi-

[1] G. G. Hubner, 'The Coffee Market', *Annals of the American Academy of Political and Social Science*, xxxviii (1911), 292–302; Federal Trade Commission, op. cit., pp. 282–318; U.S.M.C.R., June 1907, 321, pp. 148–9; *B.R.*, 30 Jan. 1900, 76; *Spice Mill*, Jan. 1907, 23–7.

[2] For an analysis of these activities see above, pp. 172–5.

[3] *S.A.J.*, 31 Aug. 1901, 226.

[4] *Statist*, 2 Feb. 1895, 157; Ukers, *All About Coffee*, pp. 448–50.

[5] *B.R.*, 26 Mar. 1901, 224; 21 May 1901, 373; 18 Mar. 1902, 141; and 2 Sept. 1902, 437; *S.A.J.*, 11 Apr. 1903, 350 and 361.

[6] McCreery and Bynum, op. cit., pp. 48–53; Ukers, *All About Coffee*, p. 323; Wickizer, *Coffee, Tea and Cocoa*, p. 36.

fied by weather conditions, crops, political decisions, and daily transactions. Limited access to the information which circulated in commodity markets, compiled from unpublished reports and private correspondence between agents and their principals, enhanced the power of the privileged few in the struggle for local control. In Brazil, however, the level of information remained low, particularly amongst *fazendeiros*. Apart from the largest, they remained in the interior and rarely visited the cities,[1] hence isolating themselves from commercial contact and relying on the goodwill of successive intermediaries. A working, if imperfect, knowledge at least helped farmers to formulate long- or short-term production plans and realize fairer prices. But despite the institution of a coffee census by the São Paulo government, wide margins of error survived. 'The want of organization in the compilation of the daily coffee statistics of Rio de Janeiro', complained *The Times*, 'is a scandal.'[2] Estimates for the 1908–9 crop varied between 10 and 15·5 million bags.[3] Unsystematic collection of information, remote family farms unsure of their output, fear of tax assessments, exaggeration of crop damage, inefficient officials, and misleading press opinion inevitably coloured estimates. As late as 1956 one investigation concluded that 'coffee perhaps more than any other important world crop is without an adequate and reliable system of crop estimates and production reports by the leading producer countries'.[4] If misinformation sometimes outwitted exporters, who paid dearly in the unfounded expectation of short crops,[5] sophisticated shippers were better equipped to discount bias and hence to exploit confusion.

Brazil also lacked storage capacity in the interior, at main railway termini and at ports of shipment, which further weakened the producer. Few *fazendeiros* could store even a fraction of their crops, a serious disadvantage during a bumper crop or when rising prices were expected after a short harvest. Instead, coffee lay exposed and deteriorating at up-country stations, or was briefly warehoused at ports before shipment.[6] Deliberate attempts to retain crops, a

---

[1] Normano, op. cit., p. 42.
[2] *The Times*, 17 Apr. 1908, 5b; cf. 19 Aug. 1907, 5f.
[3] *S.A.J.*, 11 July 1908, 32; 11 Sept. 1909, 284; and 25 Sept. 1909, 341; cf. *The Times* (*Financial and Commercial Supplement*), 15 Jan. 1906, 32c.
[4] Federal Trade Commission, op. cit., xvi–xxiv.
[5] *B.R.*, 25 Dec. 1900, 858; 11 Mar. 1902, 127–8; and 30 Sept. 1902, 485.
[6] *Consular Reports* (*Rio de Janeiro*), P.P. 1900, xcii, 370, and 1902, cv, 326.

crude method to exert pressure on prices, thus rarely succeeded;[1] each producer, in debt and requiring cash, rushed to market hoping for the high returns obtained by the first sales but naturally only enfeebling prices.[2] Adequate storage was also important for an efficient warehouse and warrant system which would have promoted speed and efficiency, improved handling, prevented deterioration of stocks, and expanded credit. If the considerable original working costs of warehousing deterred local initiative, foreign capital was less reluctant, and its intervention in this area both constrained native middlemen and provided a new level of interest in Brazilian coffee. Edward Greene mobilized British and native funds to form the Cia. Paulista de Armazéms Gerais (bonded warehouses), which handled produce under warrants, and the Cia. Registradora de Santos, which operated a clearing-house for dealers. In 1909 both companies were amalgamated, together with property owned by E. Johnston & Co., into the Brazilian Warrant Company, capitalized at £600,000.[3] This firm's tactics— direct purchase under commissions from up-country planters, low interest advances, and better prices—steadily increased its business from 1·5 to 2 million bags between 1911 and 1913, and enabled it to pay dividends of $7\frac{1}{2}$ per cent. But they angered *comissários*, although the inspired press attacks and a threatened boycott of those using its facilities merely advertised the company and ensured further patronage.[4]

The elimination of native middlemen, the concentration of shippers, ownership of processing plant, *fazendas* and warehouses, and links with the international commodity exchanges gave British houses like Naumann Gepp and E. Johnston & Co. an increasingly direct interest in every stage of the Brazilian coffee trade. They operated a chain of marketing and financial support from up-country centres through the ports of shipment to consuming markets, where influence over prices, information, and sophisticated trading techniques offered decisive advantages. They could exert pressure on supplies and prices at all levels, which conferred on them substantial power in the battle for

[1] *Consular Reports (Brazil)*, P.P. 1893–4, xcii, 532; House Docs., No. 401, p. 9.

[2] *B.R.*, 14 Oct. 1902, 508; Prado, op. cit., p. 230.

[3] *The Economist*, 1 Jan. 1910, 16; 26 Apr. 1913, 1002; and 18 Apr. 1914, 931–2; *S.A.J.*, 13 Apr. 1907, 409, and 27 Feb. 1909, 229 and 241; *The Times*, 8 Apr. 1907, 127c, and 5 Aug. 1909, 3f; McCreery and Bynum, op. cit., pp. 35–6.

[4] *S.A.J.*, 7 Aug. 1909, 149.

market control. The exporter benefited from the producer's weaknesses, and threatened to relegate the native middleman to a similar, subordinate role. And complaints that merchants— like most businessmen, conservative, cautious, and pessimistic— tended to depress farm prices could be justified. They expected the worst, a glut, and offered low prices to protect margins, a particularly tempting policy when producers' knowledge of standards and world conditions was restricted. Dealers learned to discount exaggerated reports of crop failures. But merchants would release stocks stored after a glut during the following lean harvest, preventing the planter from realizing the higher prices which the current shortfall would lead him to expect. Although merchants, who distributed and processed produce and bore risks of price change, performed an essential service, the commercial structure favoured them against native interests. During a coffee shortage producer and merchant benefited from rising prices, but when a glut occurred—a persistent tendency from the late 1890s—the dealer insured himself against loss in ways denied to the farmer, so that he might even increase his profit.

IV

The weakness of the producer's position and the resources available to foreign houses, one side of the equation of control in the Brazilian coffee trade, were balanced by restraints on merchants. British coffee exporters did not operate in a competitive vacuum. Indeed, the trade's potential profits attracted a growing number of native commission businesses. Around 1900 Greene noted that at Santos some 150 local brokers handled coffee, which strengthened their hold on trade.[1] No evidence exists of formal, market-sharing agreements between foreign exporters. Given certain conditions in world supply and demand, shippers, whose costs and experience were alike, would independently offer similar prices. And the prices of the larger firms were regarded as a useful standard by the small firms, a normal business practice. Moreover, the fact that only two British firms, Naumann Gepp and Johnstons, featured among the seven leading shippers does not suggest that Britain, handling only 20 per cent of Brazilian coffee, could through informal understandings exert undue influence. American and German houses

[1] Johnston, Greene to Johnston, 31 Aug. 1903; see *B.R.*, 20 Mar. 1900, 187.

were tough opponents. Indeed, an impression of fierce competition
emerges. In Santos, where Naumann Gepp and Johnston clashed
frequently,[1] trade was so vigorously contested that 'only those
shippers with a reputation sell at all'. Its cut-throat rivalry,
particularly in a depression, caused 'the collapse of many firms
and the difficulties of others'.[2]

Similarly, British ownership of *fazendas*, if on the increase, was
still uncommon. Dutch, Belgian, and German syndicates, the last
supported by improved shipping links, competed strongly for purchases. The largest São Paulo planters, owning forty-one *fazendas*,
were German, and *The Economist* noted that they 'clearly take the
lead in this great trade'.[3] Despite Greene's exhortations, Johnstons
failed to promote British estate companies. In fact, the whole
question of the elimination of native ownership has been exaggerated. In 1911 *The Economist* recorded only 8,000 foreign
fazendas out of 57,000 in São Paulo. A census in 1925 indicated
that of 990 million trees, 716 million were locally owned, and of
the remainder resident Italian *colonos* owned half.[4] Plantation
profits remained in Brazil. Moreover, investment in backward and
forward linkages, like plantations and processing, was not intended
to exercise any sinister form of control; it was normal business
prudence to reduce risks. The assimilative policies of British
exporters had the effect of raising their commitment to Brazil.
Investment in plant and property prevented rapid departure or
transfer of resources if conditions deteriorated. The British houses'
stake in the republic forced them to recognize local sensitivity and
to seek rather than avoid co-operation. Greene refused to raise
capital in mortgages: 'if the property is left unencumbered', he
explained, 'Brazilians see that they are dealing with people who
have a greater share in the country than an office table and a
chair'.[5]

Demand factors also restrained the exporter. The very magni-

[1] Gepp, Naumann to Broad, 24 June 1898, Naumann Letters; Johnston,
Greene to Schneider, 7 Sept. 1898.

[2] Johnston, Greene to Johnston, 30 Dec. 1899 and 31 Aug. 1903; cf. ibid.,
Greene to Schneider, 27 Mar. 1899, Greene to Johnston, 21 July 1899.

[3] *The Economist*, 16 Jan. 1909, 107–8; cf. *S.A.J.*, 10 Apr. 1897, 408, and 8
Jan. 1898, 32; *B.R.*, 20 Feb. 1900, 119; *Spice Mill*, Aug. 1910, 571; Normano,
op. cit., p. 76.

[4] *The Economist*, 25 Mar. 1911, 620; McCreery and Bynum, op. cit., p. 30.

[5] Johnston, Greene to Johnston, 15 Mar. 1904; cf. ibid., letters, 14 Jan.
1900, 5 May and 21 Nov. 1903.

tude of the American market, the chief consumer of Brazilian coffee, precluded any attempt at overseas, particularly British, control. That the United States would permit foreigners to direct the trade in coffee, her third largest import, was inconceivable. The complex distributive structure in America through importers, jobbers, roasters, and wholesalers, excluded British houses. Despite the presence of numerous small firms, a handful of domestic importers dominated shipments at New York and New Orleans (Table VI.3), from which coffee was distributed throughout America.[1] Crossman Sielcken and Arbuckles alone ordered nearly 50 per cent of the coffee landed at New York around 1900, an oligopoly which small outside shipments to Charleston and Baltimore hardly endangered.[2] Moreover, the largest roasters, Arbuckles, Woolston Spice Company (Crossman Sielcken), McLaughlin, Chase & Sanborn, and Levering imported 80 per cent of their green coffee needs through their own agencies, or through direct links with exporters who bought and graded coffee exclusively for their principals.[3] Arbuckle and Hard Rand purchased their own coffee in Brazil, where they featured amongst the largest shippers. And American traders formed influential bodies, like the United States Coffee Roasters' Association, to protect their interests.[4]

The independent influence of American importers and roasters, particularly over prices, was considerable. The buying policies of manufacturers differed from those of the exporters. A short harvest would raise the level of market demand in Brazil where a given number of exporters competed for less coffee—although consumption abroad might remain stable. Indeed, as market demand increased, final demand might fall as higher prices forced roasters to live on stocks. Similarly, bumper crops which lowered market demand might raise final demand as roasters seized the opportunity to stockpile cheaply. Moreover, American roasters altered prices of processed coffee as soon as that of green beans changed, responding to replacement rather than contracted costs, even if ordered more cheaply. On the other hand, competition amongst

[1] *Spice Mill*, Sept. 1908, 572, and July 1910, 496.
[2] Ibid., June 1908, 355.
[3] *B.R.*, 3 July 1900, 431; *Spice Mill*, Apr. 1910, 264; U.S.M.C.R., June 1908, 333, pp. 121–3.
[4] Federal Trade Commission, op. cit., pp. 228–38; *S.A.J.*, 27 Sept. 1902, 354.

TABLE VI.3

Leading Importers of Brazilian Coffee at New York, 1899–1913: Quantities Imported

(000 bags of 60 kilos)

	1899	1900	1901	1906	1907	1908	1909	1910	1911	1912	1913
Crossman S.	872	839	1,786	498	961	426	624	163	397	616	115
Arbuckle	1,382	910	1,466	892	750	316	398	466	77	410	306
Hard Rand	355	303	230	337	374	543	615	249	219	224	287
Phipps Bros.	115	70	77	111	80	154	142	49	52	141	163
McLaughlin	304	211	278	172	156	151	151	114	75	88	110
Hills Bros.	36	77	167	─n/a─							
Bayne	79	50	113	90			98	53	68	36	102
Crenshaw	15	47	97	─n/a─							
Chase and Sanborn	40	22	90	48	74	128	143	115	75	96	105
Doane	89	120	70	─n/a─							
Leon Israel				58	101	100	166	119	144	116	158
Wessels, Kuhlenkampf Steinwender, Stoffregen	n/a			185	113	323	312	191	299	205	233
Aron				99	186	255	170	120	78	103	136
								50	266	205	206
All Shipments[a]	4,690	3,749	5,602	3,303	3,839	?	4,474	2,735	2,780	3,324	2,814

Leading Importers of Brazilian Coffee at New Orleans, 1906–1911/12: Quantities Imported

(000 bags of 60 kilos)

	1906	1907	1908	1909	1910	1911	1911/12
Hard Rand	208	176	188	197	133	120	139
Leon Israel	153	156	188	212	104	90	87
Aron	138	192	233	281	203	199	192
Crossman	103	38	41	8	20	8	5
Steinwender, Stoffregen	52	70	45	67	48	35	43
Thomson & Taylor Spice Co.	74	71	84	103	97	60	99
All shipments[a]	1,593	1,697	1,946	2,515	?	1,821	1,994

[a] Including smaller importers.

SOURCES: *Spice Mill*; *Brazilian Review*.

roasters lowered prices. In 1887, for example, Arbuckles and Woolston began a long price war, raising payments to producers and decreasing prices for customers.[1] Wholesalers and retailers,

[1] *S.A.J.*, 23 Jan. 1897, 105, and 18 Aug. 1900, 181; *B.R.*, 1 Jan. 1900, 6 and 8; 12 Feb. 1901, 127; 7 May 1901, 331; and 25 Feb. 1902, 99; *Spice Mill*, Apr. 1912, 294–6; *T.C.T.J.*, Sept. 1926, 315; Ukers, *All About Coffee*, pp. 450–2.

neither of whom were normally specialist coffee dealers and whose margins for coffee were kept deliberately low to attract customers to other lines, had a less direct influence on prices. Only long-term price movements were reflected in the retail trade, when alterations in prices were likely to be sharp.

The pattern of consumption was also an important constraint. Demand was relatively inelastic, benefiting merchants during short crops but creating marketing problems for bumper harvests. Once coffee-drinking was established in the chief consuming countries, increasing population more than other factors influenced the long-term rise in buying. Though strictly a non-essential, coffee occupies a place in western living and diet equal to that of a basic food. It is indispensable to social and psychological, rather than physical and nutritional, well-being.[1] But although demand is more flexible than, say, for wheat, a saturation point is soon reached. Between 1890 and 1913 Dutch and Danish consumption remained constant at 23 and 15 pounds *per capita* respectively, and Belgian demand rose annually by only 1 per cent.[2] Rising incomes were not spent on basic foodstuffs, and a marked rise in demand could be achieved only at the expense of other beverages—difficult since beverages are habit forming. On the other hand, if a sustained upward movement occurred, consumers bought or wasted less, used substitutes (tea or cocoa), and synthetics (chicory and ersatz). Exporters, like other levels in the coffee trade, could not permanently squeeze consumers.

The pattern of demand created particular disabilities for British merchants. Britain was a tea-drinking nation and no substantial home market existed on which British firms could base their sales.[3] Britain's coffee consumption fell from one pound per head in the 1850s to 0·7 pounds by 1914, and total imports ran at 10,000 tons per annum compared with America's 400,000. Moreover, the coffee drunk in Britain was not Brazilian. Britain's chief consumers, the middle class, preferred and could afford mild coffee either from imperial suppliers such as Jamaica, India,

[1] Wickizer, *Coffee, Tea and Cocoa*, pp. 3–7; Bynum, op. cit., p. 1.
[2] Wickizer, *World Coffee Economy*, pp. 64–6; Bynum, op. cit., p. 11; *The Grocer*, 13 Jan. 1900, 87.
[3] *Statist*, 27 Nov. 1897, 848; *The Economist*, 25 June 1910, 1408; Wickizer, *World Coffee Economy*, pp. 74–7; Imperial Economic Committee, 19th Report, *Coffee* (1931), pp. 48–9.

Ceylon, and East Africa,[1] where cultivation was encouraged, or from Central America which supplied 50 per cent of British purchases.[2] Nor did Britain consume all her purchases; a considerable re-export trade existed, in spite of which London's role in the world's coffee trade remained small and she handled less than 10 per cent of total output.

V

The options open to planters form a further dimension in Brazil's coffee trade. During the 1880s and early 1890s, when returns were good, *fazendeiros* could ignore debts and increase their reliance on intermediaries. Subsequent depression forced them to think seriously about getting together,[3] but an unwillingness to compromise personal freedoms eventually compelled the government to intervene. A good case for assistance existed for coffee, critically important as it was for Brazilian economic development. Wickizer calculated that planters, encouraged by a sharply depreciating currency and an unfounded optimism for the future, had trebled the number of trees, so that production more than doubled between 1890 and 1900 (when newly planted estates approached full output).[4] Given relatively inelastic demand, overplanting sharply reduced prices and threatened the planters' and Brazil's prosperity. Few estates were now unencumbered, as farmers borrowed heavily when margins narrowed. The desperate need for cash strained financial and transport resources when crops were marketed. And the now appreciating milreis further narrowed the gap between expenses and receipts. The planter was easily persuaded that low prices benefited foreign middlemen who 'waxed fat upon his ruin'.[5]

---

[1] 'The Development of Coffee Production in the Empire', *Bulletin of the Imperial Institute*, lxxx (1933), 507–35; Clive Y. Thomas, 'Coffee Production in Jamaica', *Social and Economic Studies*, xiii (1964), 188–217; *T.C.T.J.*, Sept. 1926, 314, and July 1928, 72; *Statist*, 6 May 1899, 720.

[2] Sandford Mosk, 'The Coffee Economy of Guatemala, 1850–1914: Development and Signs of Instability', *Inter-American Economic Affairs*, ix (1955), 6–20; Imperial Economic Committee, op. cit., pp. 9 *et seq.*; *The Economist*, 15 Oct. 1892, 11 (Monthly Trade Supplement).   [3] *S.A.J.*, 17 Aug. 1901, 173.

[4] Wickizer, *World Coffee Economy*, p. 137; cf. Celso Furtado, *The Economic Growth of Brazil: A Survey from Colonial to Modern Times* (Los Angeles, 1963), pp. 193–5.

[5] J. W. F. Rowe, *Studies in the Artificial Control of Raw Material Supplies*, No. 3: *Brazilian Coffee* (1932), pp. 6–7.

Moreover, a strong identity existed in Brazil between plantation and political élites. Land represented political influence. A relatively small body of rich planter-oligarchs filled local official roles and controlled the machinery of politics and government, which they used consistently in their own interests.[1] 'The entire period of the First Republic (1889–1930) is dominated', Normano explained, 'by the interrelation between coffee and politics.'[2] Paulista and Mineiro politicians, who represented the chief coffee growing states, held many of the highest offices of the Republic.[3] And the decentralization of power within the Republic enhanced the *fazendeiros'* influence at state level. In São Paulo, the wealth of which was vital to Brazil, planters were supreme in the political and administrative machinery of the state.[4]

Coffee, the 'spoilt child' of successive Ministers of Finance, thus dominated legislation. The subsidizing of immigration to expand labour supplies, and railway and harbour legislation designed to cheapen transport, gave some indirect assistance. Other essentially compromise measures, variously tried from 1900 as the crisis deepened, provided no long-term answers. Lower duties, while cheapening exports, merely decreased the major source of government revenue, and persistent devaluation, while raising export receipts, made imports and loan servicing dearer. Discriminatory duties on low-grade coffee were resisted by the large sector whose primitive methods were the cause of the poor quality.[5] Permanently lower production levels, envisaged by the law of 1902 which restricted planting, were unpopular with planters facing high overheads. In any case, trees could not be prevented from flowering, and relatively low labour costs still made harvesting worth while. Evasion of the restrictive law and the five-year lag before flowering meant that output continued to expand until 1907.[6] And given inelastic demand, attempts to raise consumption achieved little.

[1] R. Graham, ed., *A Century of Brazilian History since 1865* (New York, 1969), pp. 106–11; L. F. Hill, ed., *Brazil* (1947), p. 629; Furtado, op. cit., p. 137; Stein, op. cit., pp. 16–17 and 119–22.

[2] Normano, op. cit., p. 42.

[3] P. Monbeig, *Pionneurs et Planteurs de São Paulo* (Paris, 1952), pp. 122–3.

[4] P.R.O. F.O. 368/8/36463, O'Sullivan Beare to Grey, 2 Oct. 1906.

[5] *Consular Reports (Rio de Janeiro)*, P.P. 1899, xcvii, 278; 1900, xcii, 359; 1902, cv, 427; U.S.M.C.R., July 1903, 274, pp. 343–5; *Statist*, 24 Jan. 1903, 202; *S.A.J.*, 7 Mar. 1903, 230.

[6] U.S.M.C.R., Nov. 1907, 326, pp. 158–60; *The Economist*, 20 June 1903, 1087; *S.A.J.*, 24 Jan. 1903, 89; Normano, op. cit., p. 44.

Propaganda and advertising, which all sectors of the trade welcomed, were financed both privately and officially. Sustained British preference for tea and insufficient capital wrecked three attempts to increase demand in London, in 1899 when a resident Brazilian merchant agreed to popularize consumption,[1] in 1903 when the Anglo-Brazilian Coffee Company distributed samples on which steamship companies had waived freights,[2] and in 1908 when the São Paulo Government subsidized a company formed by Johnstons and by Joseph Travers & Co., a London house.[3] At the same time officials tried to prevent adulteration, to raise quality, and to lower import duties abroad. Shortage of capital prevented sustained native investment in warehouses, for which São Paulo offered guaranteed returns under a law in 1903, although in addition to the Brazilian Warrant Company two local enterprises were formed, the Central de Armazéms and the Internacional de Armazéms.[4]

By 1906, when a bumper crop reduced prices to less than half those ruling a decade before, matters reached a head. Far-reaching state intervention had been advocated in the Brazilian press, in Congress, and even abroad since the turn of the century. In 1902 the coffee states discussed but did not implement a minimum price plan.[5] Then, in February 1906 representatives of São Paulo, Minas Gerais, and Rio met at Taubaté to formulate what became known as valorization, a scheme to raise or valorize planters' incomes over a period of years by regularizing shipments and thus equalizing crop fluctuations. During bumper harvests prices were inevitably low (although unit costs were also low); in successive short crops, when unit costs were higher, prices rarely rose in sympathy since merchants released stocks on the market. Valorization sought to replace the merchant's stock-holding capacity and

---

[1] *B.R.*, 10 Oct. 1899, 665, and 27 Aug. 1901, 605; *The Grocer*, 7 July 1900, 46.

[2] *S.A.J.*, 6 Jan. 1900, 3; 17 Mar. 1900, 284; 7 Dec. 1901, 620; and 20 June 1903, 602.

[3] P.R.O. F.O. 368/173/23254 and 23915, Milne-Cheetham to Grey, 14 and 24 June 1908; F.O. 368/173/27315, B.O.T. to F.O., 5 Aug. 1908; U.S.M.C.R., July 1908, 334, pp. 72–4; *Hansard* (Commons), 4th ser. cxc, 1275 (22 June 1908); *S.A.J.*, 28 Mar. 1908, 347; *Brazilian Year Book* (1909), p. 805; *The Times*, 25 Jan. 1909, 15d.

[4] *S.A.J.*, 3 Sept. 1898, 256; 12 Nov. 1904, 510; *B.R.*, 26 Mar. 1901, 218; *Brazilian Year Book* (1909), pp. 658–701; U.S.M.C.R., Mar. 1902, lxviii, 258, p. 429, and Feb. 1907, 317, p. 47.

[5] Pierre Denis, *Brazil* (London, 1911), pp. 244–7.

to reserve that profit for the farmer. Officials would buy coffee from farmers at minimum prices, say 55–65 francs per bag, and store it in the main consuming centres until undersupply again occurred, anticipating that the withdrawal of crops would soon influence prices.[1] Valorization was not designed to raise prices *per se* nor permanently to reduce output. The intention was to prevent fluctuations in price and supply, an important advantage both to consumer and producer; and in this respect it differed from crude restrictive schemes. The release of stocks during shortages would prevent undue price rises.

To the classical economist, hardened to the traditions of *laissez-faire*, such direct government interference with supply and demand was heresy. Valorization, Consul-General Chapman explained, was 'so impracticable and immature that it is not likely to be adopted'.[2] The Board of Trade considered it 'a wonderfully mis-guided scheme'.[3] And, an official warned, serious repercussions occurred when a government 'allows itself to be drawn into wild-cat schemes for bolstering up industries'.[4] Merchants were alarmed. McLaughlins in New York labelled the huge risks Brazil was undertaking as 'decidedly wrong and unprincipled',[5] and Rothschilds feared that valorization might compromise their financial agency to the government. Press reaction in Rio, London, and New York was unenthusiastic.[6] 'When', *The Economist* asked, 'will governments learn to let trade alone?'[7]

Of course, serious problems existed. Brazilian producers, advocating different needs and solutions, remained divided. Minas Gerais and Rio opposed the destruction of low-grade coffee, the bulk of their crops. Resentment in Pernambuco and Bahía at the apparent favouritism shown towards coffee, and demands that their own crops, sugar and cocoa, should also be protected, made any federal action more difficult.[8] Nor was there international

---

[1] Rowe, *Primary Commodities*, p. 122, and *Markets and Men: A Study of Artificial Control Schemes in some Primary Countries* (Cambridge, 1936), pp. 179 and 219–22; U.S. Diplomatic Despatches (Brazil), lxxii. 135, Richardson (Chargé d'Affaires) to Root (U.S. Secretary of State), 3 Jan. 1906.

[2] P.R.O. F.O. 368/8/10944, Chapman to Grey, 12 Mar. 1906.

[3] P.R.O. F.O. 368/8/minute 29822.

[4] Ibid., minute 31390.   [5] *Spice Mill*, Aug. 1908, 482.

[6] *S.A.J.*, 6 Oct. 1906, 368; 6 June 1908, 639; 13 June 1908, 667; and 25 July 1908, 104; Furtado, op. cit., p. 196; Denis, op. cit., pp. 236–7; Prado, op. cit., pp. 230–1.   [7] *The Economist*, 18 July 1908, 108–9.

[8] P.R.O. F.O. 368/91/24268, Haggard to Grey, 28 June 1907.

harmony.[1] As it turned out the Taubaté proposals were not ratified. Rio demanded monetary reform, which São Paulo rejected since depreciation raised paper earnings, and by the end of 1906 Rio's attitude to intervention was lukewarm.[2] While the Taubaté proposals passed through Congress and Senate, President Rodriguez Alves, though a Paulista, refused to commit Federal resources; he preferred such well-tried solutions to the crisis as raising consumption and expanding credit.[3] Nevertheless, São Paulo, confident that her enormous share of Brazilian and world production would prove decisive, remained 'grimly determined to put this risky scheme through'.[4]

Even more serious were the financial difficulties. Valorization required capital to pay planters for surplus bags and to cover storage and administrative costs, so that São Paulo was forced to borrow. These funds, some £4 million from Europe and New York issued at 91 per cent of nominal value, raised £3·64 million.[5] Repayments to the Bank of Brazil and Theodor Wille & Co., São Paulo's valorization agents, halved the £3 million credit which Rothschilds had furnished through the federal government. At the same time, the terms offered were probably less generous than those applied to regular merchants whose credit and commercial standing were established. The planters' assets, their estates, were illiquid and unsuitable as collateral. The absence of direct federal intervention also raised uncertainties. São Paulo was additionally burdened by heavy interest charges of up to 9 per cent, to cover which the state government levied a three franc (12½ p) surcharge per bag on planters, anticipating that long-term price rises would later cover the surtax, interest, and principal.[6] But the withdrawal

[1] *S.A.J.*, 25 Oct. 1902, 465–7; Wickizer, *World Coffee Economy*, p. 137.

[2] U.S. Diplomatic Despatches (Brazil), lxxii. 139–58, Richardson to Root, 12 and 23 Jan. and 12 and 20 Mar. 1906.

[3] *The Times*, 3 May 1906, 9f, and 28 May 1906, 9a.

[4] P.R.O. F.O. 368/173/30193, Milne-Cheetham to Grey, 11 Aug. 1908.

[5] *The Times*, 29 Sept. 1906, 4b, and 29 Oct. 1906, 370c; U.S. Diplomatic Despatches (Brazil), lxxiii (telegram), Richardson to Root, 28 Jan. 1907; U.S.M.C.R., May 1907, 320, p. 200. São Paulo borrowed £1 million in Germany, £2 million in London, and £1 million in New York. The state additionally raised £1 million in Treasury Bills.

[6] P.R.O. F.O. 368/8/36384, 36463 and 368/91/13800, Barclay to Grey, 3 Oct. 1906, O'Sullivan-Beare to Grey, 2 Oct. 1906, and Chapman to Grey, 9 April 1907; *Consular Reports (Brazil)*, P.P. 1908, cix, 646; U.S.M.C.R., Sept. 1908, 336, pp. 192–3 and Nov. 1908, 338, pp. 96–7; *S.A.J.*, 4 Aug. 1906, 117, and 3 Nov. 1906, 493 and 499; *The Times*, 9 Apr. 1906, 134b.

of eight million bags[1] failed to influence prices, since bumper crops in 1906–7 (when twenty million rather than the usual twelve million bags were harvested) and cautious buying continued to depress trade. Continental houses, now anxious for their advances, threatened to sell stocks for what they would fetch. The Bank of France, recognizing that visible stocks were dangerously high, refused further credit except under impossibly stringent conditions.[2] São Paulo, now the owner of eight million bags which could not realize their purchase price, faced bankruptcy.

Henry Sielcken, one of the original New York consignees, persuaded reluctant bankers to float a consolidating loan of £15 million at 85 to repay consignee and storage charges under the collateral of the outstanding bags, thus ensuring that valorization continued. Strict conditions were imposed: an end to São Paulo's buying until stocks were exhausted, a governing committee of seven (one of whom São Paulo nominated), regular disposal of bags at a minimum price, a five franc export tax (thus raising costs) in return for a federal guarantee, and an additional 20 per cent *ad valorem* duty (later replaced by 10 per cent tax in kind) to restrict shipments.[3] These draconian measures provided such security that São Paulo 'could probably have dispensed with the Federal guarantee'.[4] The succession to the Presidency of Alfonso Peña, a Paulista, and to the Vice-Presidency of Precanta, a signatory at Taubaté, ensured a new level of federal government participation. São Paulo's direct participation in valorization was now reduced, though a British official recognized that the loan was 'specially intended to enable the State Government to go on with the Trust'.[5] But continued reliance on external financing, 'negotiated at a great disadvantage, discount and loss to the State',[6] was crippling. To raise planters' incomes immediately, São Paulo probably over-borrowed, creating

[1] Consignees, who included Arbuckles, Kleinwort & Schroeder, Nathan & Co., C. S. Latham, T. Wille, and Ferdinand Souguet, also advanced money.

[2] *S.A.J.*, 16 Mar. 1907, 306; 23 Mar. 1907, 335; 25 May 1907, 589; 11 Apr. 1908, 408; 23 May 1908, 577; and 30 May 1908, 607; Prado, op. cit., p. 232.

[3] *The Economist*, 29 Aug. 1908, 397; 5 Sept. 1908, 446; and 14 Nov. 1908, 929; *Consular Reports (Santos)*, P.P. 1909, xcii, 556–8 and *(São Paulo)* P.P. 1911, xc, 442–3; U.S.M.C.R., Dec. 1908, 339, pp. 140–9; Sept. 1909, 348, pp. 151–2; and Mar. 1910, 354, pp. 58–9.

[4] P.R.O. F.O. 368/173/30193 and 368/274/3226, Milne-Cheetham to Grey, 11 Aug. and 28 Dec. 1908.

[5] P.R.O. F.O. 368/274/5150, Milne-Cheetham to Grey, 18 Jan. 1909.

[6] W. Chantland, *Valorisation of Coffee*, Sen. Doc. 36, 63rd Congress (1913), 1st session.

payment and servicing problems.[1] Certainly, European and American houses seem to have done well by it. Devised in Brazil's interest, valorization earned huge profits for 'the eminent international firms and their coffee trade friends',[2] and Milne-Cheetham anticipated that the banks would make 'enormous profits on recent transactions'.[3] Yet the risk involved entitled supporting bankers, without whose co-operation São Paulo's position would have been untenable, to safeguards and a reasonable return.

A third problem was that valorization, which benefited from inelastic demand, antagonized consumers on to 'whose shoulders the final cost of raising farmers' incomes was shifted'.[4] In theory valorization was not designed to exploit consumers, since long-term prices should not have been markedly higher. Lower prices in a shortfall, when surpluses were released, offset higher than normal prices in a bumper crop when coffee was stored. Nevertheless, the largest importer of Brazilian coffee, the United States, which was unrepresented in the valorization committee and which contemporaneously was applying measures to limit domestic trusts, threatened to impound coffee stored in Brooklyn; tempers rose in Brazil and diplomatic relations were imperilled.[5]

A fourth problem was that valorization encouraged the very conditions it was designed to solve, a classic weakness of restrictive schemes of this kind. To raise incomes and fix prices merely promoted production as short-sighted *fazendeiros* farmed more intensively, reinvested their extra income in their farms, and replanted. Overplanting and the call for further valorization became recurrent themes after 1906. And higher prices encouraged rival producers inside and outside Brazil, who benefited without paying the surtaxes.[6] Unlike the free market, valorization preserved high-cost farmers, thus sustaining output and limiting efficiency. In the long term valorization could only stimulate production and prepare the way for the next crisis.

The costs and complexity of storage and administration created

[1] Rowe, *Markets and Men*, pp. 249–52.   [2] Chantland, op. cit., p. 8.

[3] P.R.O. F.O. 368/274/3226, Milne-Cheetham to Grey, 28 Dec. 1908.

[4] B. B. Wallace and L. R. Edminster, *International Control of Raw Materials* (Washington, 1930), pp. 274–84; Rowe, *Markets and Men*, pp. 199–201.

[5] L. F. Sensabaugh, 'The Coffee Trust Question in United States–Brazilian Relations: 1912–13', *Hispanic–American Historical Review*, xxvi (1946), 480–96.

[6] U.S. Diplomatic Despatches (Brazil), lxxii, 145, Richardson to Root, 27 January 1908; Imperial Economic Committee, op. cit., pp. 12–16; Normano, op. cit., pp. 44–5.

further difficulties. In Brazil, where smuggling was rife and friends outflanked rivals by ensuring shipments without tax or favoured treatment in warehouses, corruption was of 'tremendous importance in nearly all artificial control schemes'.[1] A report in *The Times* recognized the attractive possibility 'of fat sinecures and . . . large sums of money' under valorization.[2] Inexperienced administrators undertook the functions of skilled middlemen. Then, valorization sapped confidence abroad. The fear that São Paulo must soon liquidate its huge stocks at low prices put an end to speculation and encouraged first users to buy only as the need arose. The large coffee roasters and merchants, on whose services trade normally depended, although they obviously preferred stable prices, considered that Brazil was going too far. Valorization, the *South American Journal* reported, 'has paralysed the regular coffee trade'.[3]

Before 1914 these issues were resolved. A federal policy for the defence of coffee reduced regional objections. Necessary financial support was obtained. A serious consumer revolt was avoided when stocks in New York were discreetly sold. Administrative problems were eased by improvements in the bureaucracy and by the planning and construction of an internal network of warehouses.[4] And the advantage conferred by valorization in the lag before fresh planting matured seemed valuable. From 1908, when crop returns showed welcome reductions, prices moved upwards, and more intensive farming earned higher returns from better qualities. Demand increased rapidly as dealers struggled to complete orders in anticipation of a rise in American tariffs and a dock strike at Santos. The bankers' committee, once confidence was restored with the regular disposal of stocks, realized good margins.[5] In 1912 prices were at their highest since 1897, and twice those ruling when valorization began.[6] By the outbreak of war the loans were repaid and the coffee stocks profitably liquidated. Moreover, valorization achieved one of Brazil's main objectives, market control. By 1907 *The Economist* had reversed its view that valorization would be

---

[1] Rowe, *Brazilian Coffee*, p. 10.
[2] *The Times* (Financial and Commercial Supplement), 19 Feb. 1906, 74c.
[3] *S.A.J.*, 6 July 1907, 19; cf. *The Economist* (Annual Commercial Review), Feb. 1909, 11. [4] Rowe, *Markets and Men*, pp. 247–9.
[5] *The Times*, 22 May 1908, 16e; 1 June 1908, 16d; 17 July 1908, 16d; 30 Oct. 1908, 16d; 7 Jan. 1910, 15e; and 8 Feb. 1910, 13c; *The Economist*, 19 Sept. 1908, 529, and 28 Nov. 1908, 1027.
[6] *The Times*, 14 Oct. 1911, 15f; 4 Sept. 1912, 11e; *The Economist*, 12 Aug. 1911, 338.

ignored, and reported that the coffee business had been 'rendered largely nominal by the manipulation of the Brazilian Government'.[1] The very fact that speculation diminished—the volume of business on the New York Exchange was halved between 1905 and 1907— gave some indication of Brazil's influence.

Whatever its faults, most observers agreed that valorization provided short-term benefits; it stabilized prices and supplies, particularly after 1909 when crops were short, and boosted farmers' incomes. By encouraging the construction of warehouses and teaching useful lessons for the future, valorization, the *South American Journal* explained, was the only measure to save growers 'from a very serious crisis'.[2] The São Paulo Estate Company attributed its higher receipts to the scheme.[3] In the longer term, valorization, by preventing the elimination of weak, high-cost planters and by strengthening the basic imbalance between supply and demand, may have been mistaken. But in 1906, when a *laissez-faire* solution was impracticable and the government could hardly permit economic and social collapse, what alternative was there? Certainly, a private co-operative solution had foundered because planters were conservative and disunited; it needed the state to bring them together.

Theoretically there was little to choose between valorization and *laissez-faire*. Under the latter, merchants financed storage of a bumper crop by paying producers less per bag—although since unit costs were lower a larger return was earned, which the wise planter would then save to compensate for lower earnings from a short crop. But in practice the producer did not save. Valorization compelled a producer to save, since it guaranteed a minimum income during bumper crops but deferred full payment until surplus bags were sold during the anticipated short harvest. Producers' taxes to cover interest and administration were recoverable from a higher average income; and the participation of the national government, with its ability to attract capital and finance operations more easily than merchants, lowered the storage and credit costs normally charged to the producer.[4]

[1] *The Economist* (Annual Commercial Review), Feb. 1908, 12; cf. ibid., Feb. 1907, 11. The *South American Journal* also shared this revised view, e.g. *S.A.J.*, 16 Mar. 1907, 306; 18 Jan. 1908, 65; and 15 Feb. 1908, 185.

[2] *S.A.J.*, 13 July 1907, 43; cf. ibid., 15 Feb. 1908, 185; Furtado, op. cit., pp. 197–9.

[3] *S.A.J.*, 20 June 1908, 695.   [4] Rowe, *Markets and Men*, pp. 242–7.

Critics suggested that it was external factors—soil exhaustion, bad weather, and prohibitions on new planting—which reduced coffee crops, rather than valorization. Nevertheless, valorization anticipated that shortfalls *would succeed* bumper harvests. Moreover, the fact that between 1907 and 1912, when prices doubled, supply only fell short of demand by 5 per cent, indicates that official manipulation was important.[1] João Muñiz, Brazil's Acting Consul-General in New York, defended valorization as an 'emergency measure' which the crisis 'entirely justified'.[2] It was intended as a temporary support for the state of São Paulo and its coffee planters. But Brazilians fully attributed their good fortune to the *defesa*, which raised incomes, regulated supplies, and excluded middlemen. Thenceforward, coffee was subject to artificial control of a more thorough, prolonged, and deliberate character, in 1917–18, in 1922 (when regular warehousing was introduced), and in 1928.[3] Brazilian farmers, confident that valorization solved short-term fluctuations in supply, devised similar schemes for sugar, cocoa, and rubber. As Rowe admitted, whatever the real value of official market control, 'what matters is that both the Government and the planters were quite certain there was a great benefit'.[4] Valorization came to be adopted as a permanent resort by planters and officials, and as such it became the most significant element in the fixing of prices and the regulation of supply in the international coffee trade.

VI

The coffee exporter in Brazil gathered small lots from producers and agents which he then distributed abroad. He spread the produce of a few months' harvesting over the whole year, paid storage and interest charges, and offset bumper crops against shortages from his warehouses. He borrowed cheaply, his expertise promoted confidence, he provided the marketing machinery which producers lacked, and he co-operated with producers to improve quality and consumption.[5] For these services the merchant derived a legitimate

---

[1] Ukers, *All about Coffee*, p. 460.
[2] *T.C.T.J.*, Sept. 1926, 318; cf. Wickizer, *World Coffee Economy*, pp. 136–7.
[3] Rowe, *Brazilian Coffee*, p. 5; Yates, op. cit., pp. 74–5.
[4] Rowe, *Markets and Men*, p. 33.
[5] Both producers and shippers criticized bulk shipments which damaged beans, *S.A.J.*, 16 Dec. 1905, 644.

profit. Around 1900, British exporters expanded their interest in the Brazilian coffee trade, buying up-country, bypassing local middlemen, investing in processing and plantations—new functions which streamlined handling and lowered costs, but which increased market control. Moreover, successive bumper harvests, which glutted markets and diminished prices, increased the planters' reliance on foreign merchants, and were not offset by high returns during shortfalls since existing stocks maintained the flow of supplies to the market. But the merchant did not reduce prices *pari passu* to consumers, so that his profit margins increased.[1] The scope of the world's coffee business, and the facilities supplied by Exchanges in the major consuming centres, which were largely denied to planters and native intermediaries, further favoured the international house.

There were, of course, restraints on the discretion of foreign houses like Johnstons and Naumann Gepp. Competition among exporters, the existence of powerful importing interests in the principal overseas markets, and the pattern of international demand (particularly hostile to British merchants), did not permit unrestricted enterprise. Rising prices to the consumer were not always attributable to greedy merchants; they could come from higher credit costs and taxes over which merchants had no control. Nor was there in the coffee trade a straight conflict between two well-defined forces, but rather a series of contests on various levels of power. Some planters owed allegiance to the larger *fazendeiros*, who dominated the trade during the mid nineteenth century when demand and prices were persistently high. Native intermediaries in the marketing chain were said to have coerced exporters in the 1880s,[2] and they formed a strong, if not impregnable, position *vis-à-vis* producers. And the removal of *comissários* was not a process initiated solely by selfish foreign exporters. The pressure of prices encouraged *fazendeiros*, impressed by the example of the major tea distributors who controlled output from plantation to consumer, to attack the bewildering number of interests directly or indirectly dealing in coffee.[3] *The Brazilian Review* explained that the country's coffee trade 'must be simplified by the elimination of the

---

[1] *The Economist* (Annual Commercial Review), Feb. 1899, 8–9.

[2] Stein, op. cit., p. 283.

[3] *Consular Reports (Brazil)*, P.P. 1898, xciv, 265; 1900, xcii, 368–70; and 1902, cv, 426; Ukers, *All About Coffee*, p. 333; *S.A.J.*, 25 Jan. 1902, 95, and 28 Feb. 1903, 216–17.

useless intermediaries who at present absorb so considerable a share of the planters' profits'.[1]

Nevertheless, the coffee trade's structure increasingly favoured the foreign merchant, who forced lower prices on the producer in a depression while protecting himself by his employment of the world's marketing machinery. Producers, unable to reduce wages and overheads, naturally resented 'the fat profits which the merchant seemed to be making'.[2] The very fact that disorganized *fazendeiros* depended on a few powerful houses, financed abroad and working in close proximity, inevitably aroused suspicion. The results of two British houses, the São Paulo Estate Company, which recorded uneven results between 1897 and 1914 and amassed huge arrears on preference dividends, and Naumann Gepp, which consistently paid 15 per cent, illustrate the different experience of farmer and shipper.[3]

But government valorization, the Brazilian solution, maintained producers' margins against world market forces by exploiting inelastic demand and Brazil's quasi-monopoly of world coffee supplies. Valorization controlled the flow of supplies, bolstered prices, supplanted mercantile functions, and prevented market fluctuations. Despite market, press, and diplomatic hostility, finance, the main limiting factor, was always available at a price. Though there is little to choose between governments and merchants as a means of directing trade, official interference, offering substantial short-term advantages to producers, became a permanent instrument of Brazilian policy. Valorization did not solve every difficulty, principally the need to raise consumption and establish international control, but at least it gave planters some respite. Coffee was a commodity 'ill adapted to the regime of *laissez-faire*'.[4] The significance of the Brazilian example should not be lost. In the following years government control schemes became important and distinctive features of organized commodity trades. Government intervention, 'the key with which primary countries hoped to open the door to prosperity', now played an increasing role in international economic policy.[5] The novelty lay in official

[1] *B.R.*, 20 Mar. 1900, 187, and 18 Sept. 1900, 617.
[2] Rowe, *Markets and Men*, pp. 31-2.
[3] *S.A.J.*, 30 June 1900, 727, and 22 June 1907, 101; Gepp, Board Minutes, 1897 and subsequently.
[4] Yates, op. cit., p. 74.
[5] Wallace, op. cit., pp. 3-20; Rowe, *Primary Commodities*, p. 120.

adoption of the same business techniques to control foodstuffs, which had long characterized private manufacturing and mining. Brazil helped primary producers to redress the balance against industrialized consumers, Britain amongst others, whose merchants dominated marketing. In the last resort (and within the limits determined by market forces) it was not private interests but the government, representing politically influential producers, which could control the trade.

CHAPTER VII

The Nitrate and Iodine Trades 1880–1914

ROBERT GREENHILL

I

FOR some decades before the First World War politicians, officials, and the informed public in Britain, despite an apparently free trade and *laissez-faire* business ideology, had become increasingly concerned about the formation of monopolies and cartels. 'Any observer of trade of late', a correspondent to *The Economist* declared in 1890, 'must have been struck by the very much greater disposition which exists among producers and capitalists to combine rather than try to exterminate each other.'[1] Although business organizations had reached a more refined stage in Germany and the United States,[2] the Committee on Trusts reported in 1918 that 'there is at the present time in every branch of industry in the United Kingdom an increasing tendency to the formation of Trade Associations and Combinations having for their purpose the restriction of competition and control of price'.[3] If wartime conditions accelerated this process, a marked inclination towards commercial compromise had existed from the end of the nineteenth century. The chemical industry was a prominent example. From the 1880s complicated industrial diplomacy among alkali and explosive producers adjusted international markets and prevented unprofitable competition. In 1883 twelve British firms joined the Bleaching Powder Manufacturers' Association, a forerunner of the more elaborate and comprehensive United Alkali

[1] *The Economist*, 11 Jan. 1890, 48.
[2] The literature on monopolies is vast. See T. MacRosty, *The Trust Movement in British Industry* (London, 1907), H. Levy, *Monopolies, Cartels and Trusts in British Industry* (London, 1927), P. Fitzgerald, *Industrial Combination in England* (London, 1927), E. A. G. Robinson, *Monopoly* (London, 1945), P. H. Guenault and J. M. Jackson, *The Control of Monopoly in the United Kingdom* (London, 1960), and G. C. Allen, *Monopoly and Restrictive Practices* (London, 1969).
[3] *Report of the Committee on Trusts*, P.P. 1918, xiii, 789–833.

Company formed in 1891. In 1886 and 1889 British and European firms working Nobel's discoveries in dynamite and detonators negotiated agreements.[1] Lever Brothers were an important factor in cartels among soap manufacturers during the eighties,[2] and a Sulphate of Ammonia Federation was also formed.

This chapter examines the combinations governing the mining and manufacture of Chilean nitrate (sodium nitrate) and of its by-product, iodine. Why were they formed and how were they organized? What were their relations with the Chilean Government? What were the limits and the extent of their powers on the West Coast and in markets abroad? A clear picture emerges of the detailed working of a combination, its internal strains and external stresses in a period characterized by increasing cartelization. Further, the chapter discusses the role of those British merchants on the West Coast who were closely linked to the success of the nitrate and iodine business, and thereby extends the debate on the power of foreign business enterprise and its control over natural resources in an underdeveloped area.

II

The Nitrate Trade

The international importance of Chilean nitrate, a mineral fertilizer, grew steadily in the second half of the nineteenth century. Worked from the 1830s, Chile's original nitrate resources were small-scale, costly, and far from ports. But victory in the War of the Pacific and the annexation of territory from her neighbours, Peru and Bolivia, gave Chile full control of deposits on the West Coast in a coastal strip some 400 miles long by up to ninety miles wide.[3] The major nitrate ports, rapidly developing from the first boom in 1868, extended southwards from Pisagua in Tarapacá, where substantial fields were exploited from an early date, through the Atacama desert to Taltal. Iquique in the north, the most important outlet, was the main terminus of the Nitrate Railways

---

[1] Fitzgerald, op. cit., pp. 79–90; Levy, op. cit., pp. 261–4; W. J. Reader, *Imperial Chemical Industries: A History* (Oxford, 1970), pp. 59–125; L. F. Haber, *The Chemical Industry in the Nineteenth Century* (Oxford, 1958).

[2] Charles Wilson, *The History of Unilever: A Study in Economic Growth and Social Change* (London, 1970), i. 59–71.

[3] G. W. Stocking and M. W. Watkins, *Cartels in Action: Case Studies in International Business Diplomacy* (New York, 1947), p. 119; *The Times* (South American Supplement), 31 Jan. 1911, 10c.

serving up-country *oficinas* (nitrate works) and the entrepôt for local ports like Caleta Buena, Junín, and Punta de los Lobos which also enjoyed rail links to the *oficinas*.[1] Tarapacá's paramountcy in nitrate production—the province contained forty-eight of Chile's fifty-three nitrate works in 1892—was not permanent. Immediately before the First World War the relatively untapped southern fields of Antofagasta (embracing Tocopilla, Caleta Coloso, Mejillones, and Taltal), now linked by the Longitudinal Railway, overhauled production at the older northern deposits. In 1904 Tarapacá accounted for three-quarters of Chilean production, in 1905 two-thirds, and in 1908 half. By 1913 eighty-two *oficinas* in Tarapacá produced 1·1 million tons, but in the south fifty-five works shipped 1·6 million tons.[2] Productive capacity rose sharply as its base broadened.

The importance of nitrate to the Chilean economy also rose steadily after the War of the Pacific, coincidentally with a decline in the price of copper, hitherto Chile's principal export commodity. One estimate suggested that Chile mined thirty-six million tons of nitrate from 1830 to 1907, earning £222 million, of which the last decade accounted for 40 per cent.[3] In 1880 a nitrate export tax provided 5·2 per cent of the republic's revenue. By the late eighties it earned an average £1·5 million (43 per cent), and in 1894 £2·5 million (68 per cent). The windfall wealth of nitrate exports furnished 60 per cent or more of Chile's overseas earnings, which paid for essential imports, financed public works, and serviced the foreign debt. The prosperity of Pisagua, Iquique, and Taltal, where fitting shops and foundries served up-country *oficinas*, depended exclusively on nitrate. The position of Antofagasta, which was an outlet for copper and borax and also a port for Bolivia, was exceptional. On the other hand, nitrate was rarely used locally since it was expensive and commanded a better price abroad.[4] Its significance was financial and as an employer.

---

[1] George M. MacBride, *Economical and Social Progress of the Republic of Chile* (Santiago, 1906), pp. 36–8 and 194–8; H. Foster Bain and H. S. Mulliken, 'Nitrogen Survey: Part I. The Cost of Chilean Nitrate', *Trade Information Bulletin*, 170 (Washington, 1924), pp. 5–7.

[2] B. L. Miller and J. T. Singewald, *The Mineral Deposits of South America* (New York, 1919), p. 284; *Consular Reports* (*Antofagasta*), P.P. 1914, xc, 53. Compare the remarks of Consul Rennie who visited Antofagasta in 1907: P.R.O. F.O. 369/127/2941, Rennie to Grey, 7 Dec. 1907.

[3] *The Economist*, 7 Mar. 1908, 482.

[4] *Consular Reports* (*Chile*), P.P. 1900, xcii, 490–1.

Despite its importance to Chile, the nitrate industry was largely foreign-owned before 1900. During the 1870s European capital had expelled or bought out Chilean entrepreneurs in Peru and Bolivia,[1] a process continued after the War of the Pacific. Like most major mining enterprises, nitrate required capital accumulation on a scale beyond the scope of the resources which native businessmen were prepared to allocate to it at the time. The industry profited from economies of scale and erected high-cost plant, light railways, and living quarters. The harsh and difficult conditions of the Atacama desert forced managers to import expensive factors of production—labour, foodstuffs, water to dissolve the *caliche* (nitrate-bearing ore), fuel, carts, mules and their feed.[2] Coal accounted for 20 per cent of Iquique's imports of £2·3 million in 1909.[3] The fact that practically all Chilean nitrate output was exported gave a preponderant place to large foreign firms who handled nitrate in bulk and held marketing contracts abroad.

Britain's participation in the nitrate industry was substantial. During the 1870s British firms had shipped Peruvian nitrate homewards for British farmers, who were increasingly critical of Peruvian guano. Although early nitrate miners were small-scale local prospectors, British capitalists in Lima and Valparaíso willingly provided increased financial backing, and British manufacturers supplied machinery. Further, Britain shipped coal to power the *oficinas* in British vessels which then loaded nitrate homewards, a two-way traffic that employed sail long after its disappearance elsewhere and which was maintained until immediately before 1914. Although the Continent received the bulk of nitrate from the eighties, British tonnage continued to load 60 per cent of cargoes.

Among British firms on the West Coast, Antony Gibbs & Sons enjoyed an important role in every branch of the nitrate business, continuously influencing production and marketing. The House owned *oficinas* managed locally but supervised from Valparaíso. It undertook agency work for other *salitreros* (owners of nitrate works), drew commissions on shipments to Europe and on imported supplies, financed enterprises, and bought nitrate for

[1] Robert G. Greenhill and Rory M. Miller, 'The Peruvian Government and the Nitrate Trade, 1873–1879', *Journal of Latin American Studies*, v (1973), 107–31.

[2] Bain and Mulliken, loc. cit.; Gibbs 11131, *Oficina* Reports.

[3] *Consular Reports (Iquique)*, P.P. 1910, xcvi, 635.

sale abroad. The House also chartered tonnage and insured shipments on its own account and for clients. Head Office in London dictated long-term policy, studied market openings, and rented storage. From 1876 to 1878 Gibbs acted as consignees when the Peruvian Government nationalized the nitrate industry; Peru paid *salitreros* for their mines in short-term bonds, permitting them to work and manage their former properties under contract.[1]

Indeed, nitrate was crucial to the House's future on the West Coast where its other interests were diminishing. Guano, once an important business for Gibbs, offered few openings,[2] wool at Arequipa had become highly speculative, copper was in decline, and monetary crises and over-competition threatened the wholesale trade. Commitment to nitrate was high. At the outbreak of the War of the Pacific in 1879, the House held nitrate for sale in Europe, production contracts, and nitrate certificates.[3] Expensive property had been acquired and plant erected, which prevented the firm from departing quickly or transferring resources from the West Coast if conditions deteriorated. Nor could Gibbs sever valuable connections with nitrate dealers in Europe. At the end of 1880, therefore, under the twin prospects of a Chilean military advance and forced Peruvian loans, the firm decided to abandon its business at Lima and Arequipa in order to hold on to the nitrate at Iquique now in Chilean hands.[4] The accumulation of certificates, the purchasing of mines and nitrate, and the renting of other *oficinas* were the means by which Gibbs consolidated its position in the Chilean nitrate trade immediately after the Pacific War.[5] Although the House was anxious not to be overcommitted, it recognized that 'our business as nitrate manufacturers is likely to be our preponderant interest for many years to come'.[6] 'The firm's major preoccupation', agreed Wilfred Maude, its historian, 'was nitrate business.'[7]

[1] Greenhill and Miller, loc. cit.

[2] W. M. Mathew, 'Peru and the British Guano Market, 1840–1870', *Economic History Review*, second ser. xxiii (1970), 112–28, and see Chapter IX below.

[3] Gibbs 11470/4–5, Valparaíso to London, 10 Feb. and 8 Mar. 1881, and 11 Feb. 1882.

[4] Gibbs 11471/9–10, London to Valparaíso, 31 Dec. 1879, 16 Jan., 1 and 30 Dec. 1880.

[5] Gibbs 11471/13–18, London to Valparaíso, 20 Oct. and 29 Dec. 1881, 21 Jan., 23 Mar., and 18 Apr. 1882, 5 Jan. 1883, and 15 Feb. 1884.

[6] Gibbs 11470/9, Valparaíso to London, 24 July 1886.

[7] C. W. Maude, *Antony Gibbs & Sons Limited: Merchants and Bankers 1808–1958* (1958), pp. 29–49.

If the depth of Gibbs's penetration into the nitrate industry was exceptional, most of the British houses on the West Coast took an interest in nitrates. James Sawers & Sons and Graham Rowe had succeeded Gibbs as the Peruvian Government's consignees in 1878. Balfour Williamson exploited nitrate from the 1870s, purchasing *oficinas* during the War of the Pacific and opening an office at Iquique to import bags, fuel, and hardware.[1] In the mid 1880s Balfour Williamson was on the look-out for consignments from *salitreros*, and added to its business by arranging ships' charters.

The 1880s marked a boom in Britain's participation in Chile's nitrate industry through 'the exertions of a small but powerful group of company promoters'[2] led by John Thomas North.[3] During the War of the Pacific, North, who had left England for the West Coast as an engineer, met Robert Harvey, who became Chilean Inspector-General of Nitrate, and John Dawson, manager of the Iquique branch of the Bank of Valparaíso (which had financed mines in the 1870s). Using Dawson's access to local funds —it is not proven whether North also had advance warning from Harvey that Chile would recognize Peru's expropriation terms— North accumulated certificates from *salitreros* anxious to sell in the uncertain economic climate of the day. The coincidence of commercial depression on the West Coast, 1879–82, which interrupted nitrate working and shipment, with the requirements of continental sugar-beet farmers, maintained an apparently high level of demand for nitrate. Returning to England in 1882, North enlisted two merchant firms, W. & J. Lockett & Co. and Inglis & Co., and devised simple but effective methods of extending the nitrate boom. Using the British investors' traditional regard for Chilean stock, 'puffing' businesses, and exploiting speculative market enthusiasm for mining shares, North floated a succession of public companies which paid heavily for the *oficinas* that he himself had acquired so cheaply. A gullible public accepted

---

[1] Balfour Williamson, Stephen Williamson to Duncan, 16 Apr. 1862, and to McCulloch, 16 May, 16 June, and 24 Aug. 1876: S. Williamson Letters II, pp. 290–6, and III, pp. 76–86. These three men were partners in the House. See also Wallis Hunt, *Heirs of Great Adventure: The History of Balfour Williamson & Co. Ltd.*, 2 vols. (London, 1951 and 1961).

[2] *The Economist*, 7 July 1888, 858.

[3] Harold Blakemore, *British Nitrates and Chilean Politics, 1886–1896: Balmaceda and North* (London, 1974), pp. 22 *et seq.* See also Osgood Hardy, 'British Nitrates and the Balmaceda Revolution', *Pacific Historical Review*, xvii (1948), 170–5.

prospectuses at face value without examining claims. In 1883 the Liverpool Nitrate Company bought the Pampa Ramírez *oficina*, for which North had paid £5,000, for £110,000. The company's very lucrative early dividends placed its shares at 300 per cent premium when a Stock Exchange quotation was arranged, at which point the promoters began to sell their holdings.[1] The *Financial News* reported the example of the San Sebastian Company: its concessions, sold in 1882 for £1,268 and added to those at Sacramento for £1,000, were enlarged and re-equipped at a cost of £25,000 before sale to the public in 1886 at £135,000.[2] Additionally, North organized and financed related enterprises, the Nitrate Railways Company, the Iquique Gas Works, the Tarapacá Water Company, the Nitrate Provision Supply Company, the Bank of Tarapacá, and later the Nitrate Producers' Steamship Company. Before the Bank's prospectus appeared, shares were quoted unofficially at a £10 premium on £50 called, and days before issue the company's offices were besieged by eager applicants.[3]

The financial implications of the nitrate boom on the stock market during the 1880s may easily be exaggerated. According to Professor Rippy, although Britain's Chilean portfolio rose from £8·4 million in 1880 to £64 million by 1913, investment in nitrate came third after government stock and railways—though nitrate may well have stimulated interest in other Chilean stock. Nevertheless, as others imitated North, some thirty British nitrate companies, besides many privately owned *oficinas*, were floated in the period 1882–96, raising a capital of £13 million.[4] At the height of the boom, 1887–9, fourteen companies were formed, more than half of them North's.

Inevitably the nitrate boom, based as much on expected as actual

---

[1] Gibbs 11471/15, London to Valparaíso, 6 Oct. 1882. *The Economist*, 7 July 1888, 858, however, questioned the speed with which North disposed of his holdings in nitrate company promotions.

[2] *Financial News*, 6 May 1890; Blakemore, op. cit., pp. 36–7. North and his associates also formed the Colorado (1885), Primitiva (1886), and London (1887) nitrate companies, all of which paid generous early dividends on shares quoted at high premiums. See J. Fred Rippy, *British Investments in Latin America 1822–1949* (1959), p. 139.

[3] *The Economist*, 22 and 29 Dec. 1888, 1606 and 1635. For details of these concerns see Blakemore, op. cit., pp. 56–64.

[4] *Report on the Nitrate Industry of Chile*, P.P. 1889, lxxvii, 451–5; Rippy, op. cit., pp. 56–8 and 133–9; id., 'Economic Enterprises of the Nitrate King and his Associates in Chile', *Pacific Historical Review*, xvii (1948), 457–65.

profit, was short-lived, given the normal lag between investment and mining under full capacity. The formation of so many joint stock companies saturated the market. The fact that the best *caliche* was worked first in a period of exceptional demand ensured that most companies earned their largest returns early. Rising transport costs to cover cartage and roads as mining became more remote, and the rapid exhaustion of some grounds which required more labour and explosives, inevitably reduced later returns. The capacity of *oficinas*, like Lautaro and Santa Luisa, which contained only 33,000 tons to cover a capital of £550,000, failed to reach expectations.[1] The high rate of depreciation on equipment raised repair charges and permitted no resale when grounds were worked out. The London Nitrate Company, which averaged 89 per cent from 1888 to 1897 on nominal capital, distributed only 14 per cent per annum, 1898–1907. The Primitiva Company, paying 20 per cent in 1888 and 40 per cent in 1889, was liquidated by the mid nineties when its £5 shares, once quoted at £39, changed hands at five shillings.[2] The shares of other weak companies, like San Pablo and Julia, were soon at a discount, reflecting their true value. The dilemma was that although not all *oficinas* could consistently work at full capacity without exceeding demand, their high costs and the need to service watered capital required maximum operation. Nitrate stocks in Europe rose alarmingly. The enormous dividends of concerns like the Liverpool Company, judged against nominal capital, were never earned by the investing public who had paid a high premium for the stock. Yet precisely because mining ventures, subject as they were to diminishing returns and considerable risks, were often relatively short-term, high dividends were needed to replace and service capital over, say, fifteen years.

Colonel North was not solely responsible for the doubtful promotions. Gibbs criticized the German, Gildemeister, 'who should have been satisfied with the profit he made out of the poor Rosario shareholders and . . . left them whatever profit was going now, instead of again competing with the poor victims'.[3] Gibbs themselves, imitating the success of their rivals, were not blameless. Their Tamarugal Company, floated in 1889 to amalgamate the

[1] *The Economist*, 22 Mar. 1890, 371; *Oficina* Reports, Gibbs 11131.
[2] *Financial Times*, 29 Nov. 1895; *The Economist*, 23 June 1894, 763, and 1 Aug. 1896, 998–9.
[3] Gibbs 11471/41, London to Valparaíso, 3 Nov. 1892.

practically exhausted *oficinas* at La Patria and La Palma, quickly lost popularity when its machinery incurred large repair bills, the *caliche* deteriorated, and the gap between anticipated and actual profits widened.[1] Gibbs remained as agents to both the Rosario and the Tamarugal companies.

The problem, then, for nitrate promoters, particularly North and his associates, was to ensure sufficient profits to service the watered capital of current flotations during temporary recession, and to maintain confidence in nitrate so as to continue their policy of company formation. At the same time a profitable nitrate business was essential for those like North who retained large interests in concerns which serviced the industry. The fortunes of merchants like Locketts and Gibbs also depended on nitrate since, apart from their holdings in incorporated companies, they retained important interests as agents and bankers, earning commissions on sales, supply, and financial services.

The answer was combination among *salitreros* to monopolize and restrict output, and raise prices. Indeed, such was the excitability of the mining stock market that news of negotiation and approaching agreement was enough to lift share prices.[2] A nitrate combination, which would achieve privately what the Peruvian Government had unsuccessfully tried to do in 1876, was discussed as early as 1881 when Gibbs's branch in Valparaíso, much influenced by the benefits of Pardo's scheme, explained that 'a few years of adversity will teach nitrate producers that their only safety is to be found in combination. In our opinion the saving of the nitrate business lies in a limitation of production.'[3] The first nitrate combination, formed in March 1884 when overproduction threatened closures and falling prices,[4] lasted until 1887 when stronger demand in Europe anticipated the boom of 1888. At regular intervals thereafter, 1891-4, 1896-7, 1901-6, and 1906-9, the *salitreros* again resorted to combination.[5] Beginning as a

[1] Ibid. 11042, London to Valparaíso, 3 Nov. 1888; ibid. 11471/33-5, London to Valparaíso, 17 Apr. and 15 Nov. 1889 and 19 Feb. 1890; *Financial News*, 12 June 1889.   [2] Gibbs 11470/12, Valparaíso to London, 22 Nov. 1889.

[3] Ibid. 11470/4, Valparaíso to London, 8 Mar. and 24 May 1881; see also ibid. 11471/17 and 19, London to Valparaíso, 26 Apr. 1883 and 31 July 1884.

[4] Ibid. 11471/19, London to Valparaíso, 20 June 1884; U.S.M.C.R., Sept. 1886, 68, p. 603.

[5] J. R. Brown, 'Nitrate Crises, Combinations and the Chilean Government in the Nitrate Age', *Hispanic–American Historical Review*, xliii (1963), 230-46; Stocking and Watkins, op. cit., p. 121.

temporary expedient to solve a particular problem, combination became a recurring feature of the nitrate trade.

Few industries lent themselves to combination as easily as nitrate. Cartelization within the chemical industry as a whole provided encouraging examples, while the accumulation of considerable fixed capital and the advantages of economies of scale within the nitrate trade concentrated working. Nitrate was a homogeneous product without a natural competitor, highly localized in Chile, and under predominantly British control. The purchase of depreciated nitrate certificates raised British ownership of nitrate *oficinas* from 13 per cent in 1878 to 70 per cent by 1890. Communication problems were not serious, and output, independent as it was of harvest variations, was relatively easy to forecast.

Each combination comprised the same broad principles. Informal discussions during a crisis in prices and profits preceded the creation of a permanent organization and secretariat, to which the member *oficinas* contributed funds, office space, and personnel. In 1884 Schmidt, later president of the combination, and Sloman, two German *salitreros*, met in Gibbs's Iquique office to circularize firms. An executive council of managers supervised exports and accounts, and representative commissions arranged production stoppages in their areas to determine the volume of visible nitrate throughout the *bodegas* and stores of Tarapacá and Antofagasta. A permanent committee in London and a local nitrate producers' association in Iquique (which moved to Valparaíso in 1914) were created.[1] Some *salitreros*, like Folsch & Martin, tacitly adhered to agreed terms but remained outside the formal nitrate combination.

Like any trade association, the nitrate combinations devised a range of tactics. They increased the consumers' burdens by imposing a fixed or minimum level of prices above that ruling immediately before the combination. It is difficult to assess the fairness of prices which depended on economic variables beyond the *salitreros'* control (the cost of inputs, freight rates, and storage charges), but some cause for concern exists. Prices imposed by combination must be profitable for the weakest member, preventing the efficient from charging less and the consumer from deriving economies from their efficiency. By implication, prices for the least efficient are excessively profitable to the most efficient.

[1] Gibbs 11470/8, Valparaíso to London, 21 July 1884; Fitzgerald, op. cit., pp. 87–8; U.S.M.C.R., Sept. 1886, xix, 68, pp. 609–13.

Merely to govern prices was insufficient, since improved levels encouraged further production and eventually increased competitive pressures. To retain more continuous control, combinations limited and apportioned output, but the withholding of nitrate when prices fell for release when they rose (again encouraging overproduction) proved an unsuccessful stabilizer. More drastic and refined action was required to place voluntary or formal restrictions on production and prevent the accumulation of unmanageable stocks. Temporary closures of *oficinas*, with free working at other times, was suggested, but it was a drastic measure suited to high-cost *oficinas* which operated best under full capacity. A second method was to fix maximum output for a given period at the previous year's or current demand, reckoned as a percentage of total capacity.[1] Each member *oficina* was then given a quota, normally the same percentage of its own capacity. Basic quotas varied between 40 per cent in 1884 to more than 50 per cent of capacity in 1901, sharply curtailing output but permitting continuous if partial production.[2] The first combination drastically lowered output between 1884 and 1886, as Table VII.1 shows. Any shortfall in production by companies which did not meet their quotas was reallocated, while those which overproduced were fined. Pensioned *oficinas* were paid not to work, and owners of several mines could allocate output as they pleased. Gibbs's quota in 1884 of 1·4 million quintals was concentrated at one *oficina*.[3] The Valparaíso house considered these terms very satisfactory but warned that 'we must . . . maintain a very firm attitude in defence of the position we have acquired'.[4] To avoid jealousy, combination officials obtained individual agreements without revealing what rivals received. Rising demand and the rapid increase in the number of participating *oficinas*—the combinations preferred to be inclusive not exclusive—considerably expanded capacity but reduced quotas to each *oficina*. The 'make', fixed at ten million quintals in 1884 and at twenty million in 1897,[5] exceeded thirty million by

---

[1] *The Economist*, 20 Oct. 1900, 1466, and 27 Oct. 1900, 1497; *Consular Reports* (*Chile*), P.P. 1906, cxxiii, 190.

[2] W. H. Russell, *A Visit to Chile and the Nitrate Fields* (London, 1890), p. 331.

[3] Gibbs 11471/20, London to Valparaíso, 7 Nov. and 31 Dec. 1884.

[4] Ibid. 11470/8, Valparaíso to London, 27 Dec. 1884.

[5] *The Economist*, 26 Oct. 1895, 1410, and 25 Apr. and 8 Aug. 1896, 530 and 1040.

TABLE VII.I

Nitrate Oficinas, Work Force, Exports, and Prices, 1878–1913

Year	Number of oficinas	Work force 000	Export 000 tons	Prices per quintal c.i.f. (shillings and pence)
1878			1	
1879			59	
1880			224	
1881			356	13/3 to 15/6
1882			492	12/3 to 15/-
1883			590	10/6 to 12/9
1884			589	8/9 to 10/9
1885			435	8/6 to 10/3
1886			451	8/9 to 11/3
1887			713	8/9 to 12/-
1888			767	8/9 to 10/9
1889			953	8/1 to 11/6
1890			1,063	7/10 to 8/6
1891			789	7/6 to 9/6
1892	40		804	7/9 to 9/7
1893	48		948	9/6 average
1894	51		1,098	9/- ,,
1895	53	22	1,238	8/- ,,
1896	53	19	1,107	7/10 ,,
1897	42	17	1,078	7/4 ,,
1898	46	16	1,294	8/6 ,,
1899	58	20	1,398	7/4 ,,
1900	51	20	1,454	7/5 ,,
1901	66	20	1,260	n/a
1902	80	25	1,384	n/a
1903	72	24	1,458	n/a
1904	76	n/a	1,500	n/a
1905	90	n/a	1,650	n/a
1906	96	n/a	1,727	n/a
1907	110	40	1,656	7/10 to 9/1
1908	113	41	2,050	7/6 average
1909	103	38	2,135	6/10 ,,
1910	102	44	2,335	6/4 to 7/3
1911	107	44	2,450	7/4 average
1912	118	47	2,493	7/6 ,,
1913	127	53	2,738	7/11 ,,

Source: Ministerio de Minería, *Servicio de Minas del Estado, Departamento de Salitre* (unpublished statistical information in Markos Marmalakis, 'Historical Statistics of Chile', A-481).

1906, while the largest quota, 14 per cent (which Gibbs enjoyed in 1884), fell to 7 per cent by 1890 (for the Primitiva).

From the 1880s Gibbs, North, and the German companies favoured a single consignment scheme or cartel, whereby one selling agency handled total output. Such a cartel would prevent local underselling, derive substantial economies in freight, insurance, and handling, control quality, shipment, and price, and curtail the charges of middlemen and dealers, thus stabilizing and complementing the powers of the combinations. Any firm which undertook the cartel needed strong links on the West Coast and in Europe, a sound knowledge of the trade, considerable financial resources to pay producers, and vast storage during the off-season—though sales afloat would be encouraged to reduce warehouse charges and shrinkage. The choice was limited, in effect, to a handful of powerful houses who could hardly lobby for themselves. The entire transference to one consignee of all commercial relations between producers and buyers would unduly benefit the successful firm, and reduce the competitiveness of rivals now deprived of their business. 'The time has not yet come', Gibbs's Valparaíso house explained, 'for going into any scheme.'[1] Gibbs considered dividing continental markets between two consignees, and a partial consignment scheme by which a few firms pooled shipments successfully operated in 1907–8.[2] But despite the persistent exhortations of company chairmen like Herbert Gibbs (Alianza), H. W. Sillem (Salar del Carmen), and Rau (Lagunas), no comprehensive cartel emerged before the First World War.[3]

The fact that *salitreros* controlled several, apparently independent *oficinas* reinforced the power of the nitrate combinations. North and his associates, by stock holdings and interlocking directorships, controlled a dozen or so companies in the 1890s and 'a very large quantity of nitrate', perhaps 25 per cent.[4] Later, Gibbs formed the Salar del Carmen, Pan de Azúcar, and Alianza companies. Take-overs further consolidated ownership. The Salar del Carmen purchased control of the Fortuna Nitrate Company, *The Times* reported the amalgamation of the Britannia and Tricolor

[1] Gibbs 11470/17, Valparaíso to London, 18 Feb. 1898.
[2] Maude, op. cit., pp. 35–6.
[3] *The Times*, 16 Apr. 1909, 3f, 22 May 1914, 20d and 23b; *The Economist*, 16 Jan. and 15 June 1909, 115 and 1196.
[4] Gibbs 11470/11, Valparaíso to London, 14 Sept. 1888; see also ibid., Valparaíso to London, 4 Jan. 1889.

oficinas, and the *Financial Times* that of the Santa Rita and San Patricio companies.[1] North's exceptional position in the trade led him to advocate further refinements, 'a gigantic scheme for turning the whole nitrate business into a share capital of £5 million';[2] that is, buying existing companies, paying them with shares in the new concern, and thus monopolizing nitrate under a single management. Such concentrated control would rationalize mining, and reserve the southern fields until those in the north were exhausted. Some doubted North's sincerity and considered his plan merely a stock-jobbing move to raise share prices,[3] and others opposed a syndicate which profited at their expense. Nevertheless, Gibbs's Valparaíso office certainly liked 'the idea of a buffer company to buy all the nitrate at a certain price'.[4] North considered using the Nitrate Railways as a lever to coerce producers, and encouraged foreclosures on *salitreros* which would allow him to purchase their works cheaply.[5] However, inability to raise money in London in 1890 (the year of the Baring crisis and of a collapse in South American stocks) and hostility in Chile against an apparent foreign monopoly killed the scheme.

The nitrate combinations and their refinements replaced rivalry with compromise. The smaller, high-cost, and near-exhausted mines (such as Santa Luisa, and Rosario in Taltal) were not eliminated, as was likely under free competition. Limitations on production and minimum prices discouraged modern economies, efficiency, and innovation. The Shanks process, introduced in the 1870s and not replaced until the adoption of the Guggenheim recovery method after the First World War, preserved wasteful, obsolete, and costly working, thereby damaging consumption and preventing the exploitation of lower-quality *caliche*.[6] Of course, complete technological standstill was impossible. Lighter German machinery replaced British plant, larger works in the south introduced economies of scale (although the output per *oficina* in fact

[1] *The Times*, 14 Dec. 1908, 18c; *Financial Times*, 20 Jan. 1909.

[2] Gibbs 11470/10, Valparaíso to London, 24 June 1887; see also ibid. 11471/35, London to Valparaíso, 5 Mar. 1890; Blakemore, op. cit., pp. 51–2.

[3] Gibbs 11470/12, Miller (partner on West Coast) to London, 6 May 1890. This view, which Miller reported, was in fact held by President Balmaceda and his minister Gandarillas.

[4] Ibid., Valparaíso to London, 23 June 1890.

[5] Ibid. 11471/26, London to Valparaíso, 6 May, 2 July, and 26 Aug. 1887; ibid. 11470/10, Valparaíso to London, 19 Aug. and 14 Oct. 1887.

[6] Stocking and Watkins, op. cit., pp. 134–5.

fell from 1900 to 1914), and cheaper oil power superseded coal immediately before 1914. However, this one major innovation raised freight costs since oil tankers could not load a return cargo of nitrate, and nitrate ships lost their outward cargo of coal.[1] *The Times* commented in 1914 that 'it is not a little remarkable that in this scientific age Nitrate of Soda is the only thing produced ... in virtually the same way as it was 60 years ago'.[2]

Congress, the press, and public opinion in Chile were critical of British nitrate concerns, and indeed of all foreigners who appeared to exploit local resources for their own profit.[3] Largely sited in Tarapacá, the richest province because of its nitrate fields but in other respects infertile and sparsely populated, the mines were economically and physically isolated from the rest of the republic. The foreign *salitreros* seemed to have created an 'enclave' economy. Their exports from Iquique affected only a limited sector, leaving the bulk of the country untouched since agriculture remained the chief employer. 'The English', explained Ramírez, 'dominated Tarapacá's vital centre exercising an unchallenged influence in this province ... The nitrate region was converted into a British factory.'[4] The industry had little direct effect on native entrepreneurs, or on labour mobility. Large British firms like Gibbs & Sons handled consignments and sales, extracting fat commissions, providing capital, and importing equipment. Net income went overseas as foreign managers transferred their earnings abroad and expatriate shareholders demanded dividends. Low-wage local labour barely stimulated demand for goods already exorbitantly priced.[5] No reason existed why the nitrate industry should not contribute to the hard-pressed national exchequer, nor why Chile should not profit from, and exercise stricter control over, the development of her physical resources, particularly since a unique, natural monopoly apparently existed. Chileans also

[1] *Consular Reports (Antofagasta)*, P.P. 1912–13, xciv, 523, and 1913, lxix, 334; Gibbs 11471/68 and 69, London to Valparaíso, 22 Feb. 1901 and 17 May 1901.   [2] *The Times*, 17 June 1914, 21a.

[3] Gibbs 11470/14, Valparaíso to London, 27–8 July and 10–11 Aug. 1893; *Consular Reports (Valparaíso)*, P.P. 1895, xcvi, 567–604; Blakemore, op. cit., *passim*.

[4] Hernán Ramírez Necochea, *Historia del Imperialismo en Chile* (Santiago, 1960), pp. 117–18.

[5] *Financial News*, 6 May 1890, explained that *salitreros* 'put the price of ... first necessities of life to an exorbitant figure to correspond with their swollen capitals'.

resented the fact that the superior organization and wealth of foreign capitalists seemed to have outwitted those native concerns which had enjoyed an early foothold in the nitrate trade, and seized the fruits of victory from the War of the Pacific.[1]

The particular tactics of the nitrate combinations, which lowered production, weakened competition, fixed prices without reference to cost, and preserved inefficiency were resented. They forced reductions in consumption, in employment, and in Chile's export duties (crucial to her economy), yet raised profits for foreigners.[2] 'The English companies', an American Consul reported, 'are making strenuous efforts to secure a monopoly of the nitrate trade', at Chile's expense.[3] Short-term foreign exploitation paid no attention to Chile's long-term needs. *La Libertad Electoral* claimed that *salitreros* could 'modify nitrate prices in Europe at their whim defrauding the Chilean Government of sums anticipated from collecting duties'.[4] *La Patria* compared Britain's exploitation of nitrate to Spain's rape of her South American colonies.[5] Later Chilean writers have also emphasized British power over their country's financial and commercial affairs through the nitrate trade. 'Control of the nitrate industry', explained Ramírez, 'was taken by foreign capitalists who . . . began to exercise a decisive influence over the whole economy.'[6] Similarly Aníbal Pinto considered that 'Chile had within its territory a kind of factory, an industrial colony for the exploitation by and profit of foreigners'.[7]

III

Combination, price-fixing, manufacturing restrictions, and cartelization, the weapons which *salitreros* used to preserve their profits but which also influenced wider issues concerning Chile's society and economy, formed the points of friction between the republic and British nitrate interests. Nevertheless, they are only one side

[1] Francisco Encina, *Nuestra Inferioridad Económica: Sus Causas y Consecuencias* (Santiago, 1911), p. 5; Aníbal Pinto Santa Cruz, *Chile: Un Caso de Desarrollo Frustrado* (Santiago, 1959), pp. 52–3.

[2] Hernán Ramírez Necochea, *Balmaceda y la Contrarevolución de 1891* (Santiago, 1st ed., 1955), p. 67.

[3] U.S.M.C.R., Mar. 1890, 114, p. 407.

[4] Quoted in *El Heraldo*, 7 and 9 Aug. 1893, and *La Patria*, 3 Aug. 1893.

[5] *La Patria*, 3 Aug. 1893.

[6] Ramírez, *Historia del Imperialismo*, p. 102, and compare p. 118.

[7] Pinto, op. cit., p. 56.

of the equation of power. What were the limitations on British nitrate companies? How far did market forces prove a continuing restraint? What retaliatory measures were available to Chilean officials and politicians?

British *salitreros* had no control over the demand for nitrate which, though chemical uses included explosives and dyes, relied to a very large extent on agricultural fertilizer. Nitrate did not, in fact, justify every extravagant claim for its properties, since certain soils and crops responded poorly. Agricultural demand, in turn, was heavily dependent on such variables as the weather (obviously difficult to forecast), world economic conditions, and the size of farmers' incomes. Late frosts or a wet spring (the period of maximum manuring), or abundant farmyard manure from a heavy straw crop, sharply reduced consumption. Nor was demand perfectly elastic. Farmers were highly sensitive to rising prices, but reacted slowly when prices fell and stocks accumulated. If general conditions were particularly adverse farmers would not buy nitrate at any price, while increased manuring did not always substantially improve results.[1] Moreover, Britain, as Table VII.2 shows, was a minor market for nitrate. The agricultural depression after 1878 forced economies on British farmers who, as Professor Voelcker (the Royal Agricultural Society's analyst) told the Richmond Commission, immediately reduced expenditure on fertilizer;[2] and the depression encouraged a permanent shift in Britain from arable to pastoral farming.

The major nitrate users were sugar-beet growers in Europe, particularly Germany which imported 35 per cent of Chilean production, and France. German *salitreros*, shipping to their houses in Hamburg, the market centre and a clearing-house for information and dealings, sold ahead more easily and avoided intermediate commissions, benefits which were lost to British merchants without the same home market.[3] Gibbs felt 'at a great disadvantage with the Hamburg houses who appear to have means of obtaining orders for such cargoes which are not within our reach'.[4] The creation of a syndicate of German agriculturists, which bought *oficinas* in Taltal to ensure nitrate supplies, further narrowed the

---

[1] Gibbs 11471/8, London to Valparaíso, 18 Jan. 1884.
[2] *Royal Commission on Agriculture*, P.P. 1881, xvii, 56, 953–7, and 985; *C.D.*, 15 Jan. 1887, 81.
[3] Gibbs 11470/6, Valparaíso to London, 13 Mar. 1883; *C.D.*, 2 Sept. 1899, 430.   [4] Gibbs 11471/25, London to Valparaíso, 5/6 Nov. 1886.

TABLE VII.2

Principal Nitrate Importers, Nation and Quantity, 1880–1913

(000 tons)

Year	Britain	Germany	France	Belgium	Holland	United States	For orders in Europe (mainly France and Germany)
1880	└──────────181──────────┘					12	
1881		276				33	
1882	96	333	182	99	44	86	
1883	103	304	134	88	52	104	
1884	106					58	
1885	95					45	
1886	106	390				60	
1887		275					
1888		└──────680──────┘				79	
1889		└──────570──────┘					
1890							
1891							
1892	114	└──────646──────┘					
1893	104	└──────643──────┘					
1894	114	└──────734──────┘					
1895	110	└──────800──────┘					
1896	118	└──────841──────┘					
1897	13	277	100	50	45	108	380
1898	50	382	180	74	60	130	290
1899	65	377	200	98	50	145	317
1900	61	372	170	70	83	190	345
1901	50	345	155	50	60	180	290
1902	55	317	130	55	60	240	345
1903	65	370	204	80	85	255	240
1904	60	377	213	83	104	255	230
1905	50	372	150	50	65	335	413
1906	60	370	120	50	104	322	526
1907	50	350	100	25	80	326	540
1908	55	460	130	60	80	323	700
1909							
1910	44	465	78	52	90	535	774
1911	82	530	78	78	78	487	852
1912	56	531	108	90	87	460	878
1913	44	600	113	95	113	600	900

SOURCE: Antony Gibbs & Sons, Ltd., archive at Guildhall Library, London.

largest European market for British *salitreros*.[1] Moreover, sugar-beet growers were dangerously dependent on government bounties (limited under the Brussels Convention of 1903) to outflank cane producers and buy essential manure, and on the state of the world sugar market. And to extend the use of a relatively expensive fertilizer beyond the richer European farmers was difficult. Only the United States and South Africa (as agriculture recovered after the Boer War) imported substantial supplies.

[1] Gibbs 11471/72–3, London to Valparaíso, 30 May, 24 July, and 11 Dec. 1902.

On the other hand, the gap between output and demand was rather the result of overproduction, since world consumption of nitrate rose consistently from the late nineteenth century. Further, the general improvement in world agricultural conditions and prices in the decade before the First World War helped double exports to a peak of 2·7 million tons (Table VII.1). The smaller explosives market for nitrate was not only dependent on military outlets but also on mining, quarrying, road and rail construction, and land clearance, activities which enjoyed an upsurge before 1914.

TABLE VII.3

Sources of Chemically Combined Nitrogen

(per cent)

	1900	1913	1934
Chilean nitrate	66·6	55·4	6·9
Coal (ammonia)	34·4	37·3	18·6
Air (nitrogen)	—	7·3	74·5

SOURCE: United States Tariff Commission, Report No. 114, *Chemical Nitrogen* (Washington, 1937).

Nor did nitrate enjoy the monopoly in world markets which is commonly assumed. Guano, an alternative natural fertilizer still shipped from the West Coast during the 1880s under a succession of consignees, despite its poor quality continued to attract some buyers who might otherwise have bought nitrate.[1] The Chilean Government only stopped guano shipments to encourage local use during the 1890s, when in any case nitrate's falling price undersold guano.[2] At the same time reports of nitrate fields outside Chile further alarmed *salitreros*.

Artificial manures and synthetic ammonia (a chemical combination of nitrogen and hydrogen) also threatened Chilean nitrate before the First World War, as Table VII.3 shows. Any rise in the price of nitrate which combination or world conditions imposed inevitably accelerated the search for mineral and chemically

[1] Maude, op. cit., p. 30; *Statist*, 9 June 1888.
[2] *Diario de Diputados* (Chile), 11 Feb. 1896, 203; *Diario de Senadores* (Chile), 15 June and 6 July 1897, 111–12 and 262.

produced substitutes. Moreover, nitrate's commercial and industrial importance to agriculture and munitions raised political and strategic issues which encouraged governments, particularly Germany's, to seek domestic substitutes and ensure their independence of imports. From 1900 the Haber–Bosch method successfully extracted nitrogen from the air, combining it with hydrogen to manufacture ammonia; it was convertible into explosives and fertilizers, and could thus replace mined nitrate.[1] For some years officials of the nitrate combination ignored this development, confident that 'nothing . . . should cause uneasiness on the part of those interested in nitrate of soda'.[2] Again, sulphate of ammonia, a low-cost by-product of coke-burning for, say, the production of town gas, was increasingly used from the 1880s. Artificial fertilizer—'that sinister cloud . . . on [Chile's] financial horizon'[3]—as a result of Liebig's experiments with sulphates from the 1840s and of the discovery of superphosphates, first in decomposed bones by Lawes at Rothamsted in 1843 and later naturally in East Anglia and North Africa, also threatened Chilean nitrate.

The crucial self-defeating weakness of combination, the inability to eradicate competition, further reduced the control exercised by British *salitreros*. A cyclical pattern emerged, causing the rise and fall of successive combinations, whereby high prices expanded output from existing and new works until overproduction occurred when lower price levels ensued. Weaker mines were then temporarily suppressed until price levels rose again. Nevertheless, a general tendency towards rising output, which threatened long-term prosperity, is noticeable. To eliminate weaker mines permanently was difficult. Highly capitalized firms continued to produce (provided that working costs were covered), since permanent stoppages permitted no inroads on overheads and the sale or dismantling of *oficinas* was impracticable. Then, new outside production, the result of reckless promotion and management particularly when prices were rising, was endemic. *Caliche* was readily accessible, production was easy, no secret patents or rapidly changing innovations presented technological barriers, and capital

[1] G. T. Morgan and D. D. Pratt, *British Chemical Industry: Its Rise and Development* (London, 1938), pp. 89–90; *The Times*, 2 June 1913, 17c–d, and 29 Oct. 1913, 19d–f.

[2] Gibbs 11471/74, London to Valparaíso, 25 Sept. 1903.

[3] *Diario de Diputados* (Chile), 13 and 15 June 1908, 101 and 106.

was usually available. Rising nitrate prices under the first combination merely attracted investors, causing 'a recurrence of the abnormal and unwise expansion of production'.[1] Moreover, economies of scale encouraged working at full capacity, inevitably increasing output. Finally, the very increase in the number of operational *oficinas*, from seventy-eight in 1901 to over 150 by 1911, not only raised production, but made agreements more difficult to arrange and enforce.

Rivalries in the industry were never easily settled. No two mines had perfectly similar costs so that fixed market shares could not be maintained for long. Aggressive firms wanted more business and larger quotas at the expense of defensive or weaker mines. The existence of large, low-cost producers, difficult to entice into a combination since they easily undersold its terms and profited by unrestricted working, unsettled agreements. Combination was not renewed after 1909, 'owing, it is said, to the unjust demands . . . by the majority of producers, especially of the British and German companies'.[2] *Oficinas* could establish little goodwill among buyers, who readily abandoned their suppliers for cheaper competitors since nitrate was a uniform product and contact after sales negligible. Small, ignorant *salitreros* on the coast, normally locally derived and hard to convince of the virtues of any co-operation which removed their direct control over sales, tried to squeeze the larger British firms handicapped in turn by their watered capital. Gibbs's Valparaíso house explained that the many small *oficinas* would not co-operate 'till their profits had been hit hard with lower prices'.[3] Groups of *salitreros* which assumed disproportionate influence were also resented. The Rosario company rejected the committee at Iquique, 'which is chiefly composed of Mr. North's friends'.[4]

Further, the trust and goodwill on which a combination's success ultimately depended were selfishly abused. If a joint consignment scheme evolved, it was not easy to prevent outsiders or an unscrupulous member of the combination from independently selling forward cheaply, or demanding extravagant advances which would endanger consignees if prices should break. Gibbs,

[1] Gibbs 11470/8, Valparaíso to London, 24 Jan. 1885.
[2] P.R.O. F.O. 368/280/19511, Consul Hudson to Grey, 20 Apr. 1909.
[3] Gibbs 11470/12, Valparaíso to London, 23 June 1890.
[4] Ibid. 11471/34, London to Valparaíso, 17 Jan. 1890.

fearing a break in 1888, made cheap forward contracts, and Don Juan y Castro sold 1·5 million quintals forward in 1892 before the second combination began.[1] Dealers in the United States shipped stocks to Europe, underselling direct loads from the West Coast. High-cost producers, who needed full working, exaggerated capacity or overshipped (especially from accumulated stocks) immediately before restrictions came into force so as to raise their quotas. Yet Gibbs & Sons recognized that 'the introduction of a little distrust and malice will not do us any harm' since it would discourage powerful outside interests, like Barings, from handling nitrate.[2]

Rivalry between Gibbs and Colonel North was a permanent feature of the nitrate trade. Despite early co-operation between them—Gibbs partly financed North's first dealings on the West Coast and managed property for him—Gibbs remained suspicious of North on personal grounds and because he had so obviously out-smarted them in the industry.[3] Nor had Gibbs any illusions about North's free-wheeling business ethics. While the House preferred a safe and steady return, North's policy maximized short-term gains.[4] North was, Herbert Gibbs explained, 'quite free from scruples . . . a very dangerous antagonist in any South American state'.[5] During the 1880s minor areas of conflict included North's interference in negotiations over two *oficinas*, La Patria and La Palma, his anger at Gibbs's refusal to lower their quotas under the first combination, and the opening of the Primitiva mine in 1887.[6] The Nitrate Railway sharpened rivalries.[7] North, who owned the railway, levied exorbitant rates on *salitreros* like Gibbs who lobbied the Santiago Government and sought concessions of their own.

[1] Gibbs 11042 and 11471/40, London to Valparaíso, 3 Nov. 1888 and 23 May 1892.

[2] Ibid. 11471/34, London to Valparaíso, 17 Jan. 1890.

[3] Ibid. 11042, Herbert Gibbs to John Smail, 28 Nov. 1888; Blakemore, op. cit., p. 36.

[4] Gibbs 11471/27, London to Valparaíso, 26 Aug. 1887.

[5] Ibid. 11042, Herbert Gibbs to Bruce Miller, 2 Dec. 1887; ibid. 11471/27, 12 Jan. 1888.

[6] Ibid. 11471/18–25, London to Valparaíso, 6 Dec. 1883, 2 June and 14 July 1886, and 25 Aug. 1888; ibid. 11470/7, Valparaíso to London, 18 Jan. 1884.

[7] This involved issue is well explained by J. R. Brown, 'The Chilean Nitrate Railway Controversy', *Hispanic–American Historical Review*, xxxviii (1958), 465–81, and by Blakemore, op. cit. See also correspondence in P.R.O. F.O. 16/266–8 and 298.

IV

Official intervention in the nitrate trade constituted a further restraint on British *salitreros*. Two arguments have been formulated which appear to weaken the impact of government control. First, it is said, Chilean officials, staunch supporters of *laissez-faire*, were unwilling to act on philosophical grounds. A commission set up in 1880 to examine the conduct of the nitrate trade, now that Chilean troops controlled Tarapacá, believed firmly in free enterprise and private ownership. It rejected the Peruvian state monopoly, a decision confirmed by a second commission of inquiry in 1881.[1] At the same time officials wished to preserve Chile's international credit and her attraction to overseas investors, which government intervention in a predominantly foreign-owned enterprise would endanger. Nevertheless, once Chile had seized *de facto* and then *de jure* control of Tarapacá and Antofagasta she could not abdicate her responsibilities. Santiago, recognizing the claims of Peruvian bondholders, ended the expropriation scheme and returned *oficinas*, under a succession of decrees, to those who presented 75 per cent of their value in nitrate certificates and 25 per cent in cash.[2] Keen to end the question of outstanding certificates, Chile agreed in 1885 to redeem them at £105 per 1,000 soles, for which it negotiated a loan with Rothschilds—although the matter remained unsettled until the 1890s.[3] Thus, the Chilean Government, involved from the first in the administration of the nitrate trade, now actually owned *oficinas* since their former proprietors either could not be traced or preferred to accept cash for their certificates. These developments gave Santiago, notwithstanding any reluctance which may have been felt at the time, a platform for further, more decisive intervention.

Second, a view has emerged that British *salitreros* successfully intervened in Chilean politics to frustrate local control over nitrate. John North and his associates certainly enlisted the Foreign Office's help against official attempts to curb the Nitrate Railway's monopoly.[4] Their wide use of influential local lawyers and

---

[1] Blakemore, op. cit., p. 20.

[2] *Diario de Diputados* (Chile), 30 Nov. 1889, 291. Chilean decrees were dated 11 June and 6 Sept. 1881, 28 Mar., 28 May, and 31 July 1882.

[3] *Diario de Senadores* (Chile), 16 June 1897, 133–4. Chilean decrees were dated 18 Apr. and 23 June 1887.

[4] Brown, loc. cit., and Blakemore, op. cit., pp. 129 *et seq.*; for Foreign Office correspondence, see P.R.O. F.O. 16/266–8 and 298.

advisers to canvass support, seek favours, and 'fix' solutions has also been criticized.[1] In particular, British *salitreros* were accused of supporting and actually encouraging opposition to President Balmaceda, whose policy was to restrain foreign participation in the nitrate industry and the nitrate combinations. Despite North's denial of complicity with the Congressionalists who replaced Balmaceda in 1891 (and similar denials by all British *salitreros*),[2] many observers stressed North's role in the revolution which accelerated in Tarapacá. Patrick Egan, the United States Minister in Santiago, told Washington of the sympathy and active support of Britons for the revolution, of *oficina* managers who encouraged their labourers against Balmaceda, and of North's contributions to the revolutionary campaign fund.[3] 'The accession to power of the Congress Party', Kennedy (the British Minister at Santiago) explained, 'will relieve the fears of many persons whose interests were threatened by the Government of President Balmaceda.'[4] Ernest Spencer, Member of Parliament and a leading *salitrero*, stated that 'British interest in Chile . . . in all probability stands or falls with the fortunes of the Congress Party'.[5] Indeed, wild statements circulated that the revolution and the blockade of Iquique were merely devices by Colonel North to raise sagging nitrate prices by creating shortages.[6]

No doubt, many British *salitreros* favoured the new government in 1891. If their interests had been threatened by Balmaceda, such a view was inevitable. Yet the fact that Antony Gibbs & Co. had formed a good working relationship with Balmaceda and were negotiating with him over the Nitrate Railway question until late 1890, does weaken the case for unanimity among Britons against the President. Herbert Gibbs, Chairman of the House, congratulated Bruce Miller, a West Coast partner, on 'your cultivating good relations with the President'.[7] The view is also becoming more

---

[1] Blakemore, op. cit., pp. 125–9, fully examines this question. For a hostile view of this practice, see Ramírez, *Balmaceda*, p. 72.

[2] Gibbs 11470/13, Valparaíso to London, 13 Sept. 1891. *The Times*'s view that Balmaceda was 'hostile to all foreign interests and was especially directed against the English' supplied the motive, see *The Times*, 21 Jan. 1891, 5b.

[3] Egan to Blaine, 14 Mar. 1891, *Foreign Relations of the United States* (Chile), 1891, p. 107.   [4] P.R.O. F.O. 16/266, Kennedy to F.O., 24 Sept. 1891.

[5] P.R.O. F.O. 16/272, Spencer to Salisbury, 15 Mar. 1891.

[6] *Financial News*, 6 Mar. 1891.

[7] Gibbs 11471/27, Herbert Gibbs to Miller, 12 Jan. 1888. See correspondence, ibid. 11470/12, and Blakemore, op. cit., pp. 143–8.

widely held that Balmaceda's real enemies were not British *salitreros* but the *ancien régime* in Chile, who resented loss of power to the Presidency and feared government manipulation of the elections of 1891.[1] The Chilean revolution was an expression of internal party struggle rather than a function of the wider questions of economic nationalism. Moreover, the year 1891 was not a watershed in Chile's economic (or political) life, particularly in the nitrate trade where government interference continued unchecked. The Congressionalists adopted no new order at the behest of British *salitreros*. Gibbs's Valparaíso house explained in 1894 that 'the present government held exactly the same views as Balmaceda . . . and was determined not to deliver the Province of Tarapacá bound hand and foot to the foreigner'.[2]

Thus Chilean governments, not deterred from intervention in the nitrate trade, constituted a real force. Government ownership of mines permitted influence over production, since *oficinas* could be released to outsiders (preferably Chileans) whenever the combinations raised prices or restricted output. Furthermore, supervision of the unworked *oficinas* and *caliche* against bogus claims and thieving required an army of officials under the Delegación Fiscal de Salitre, set up to administer mining laws, settle boundary disputes, and inspect and value property. The mines themselves were meanwhile losing value as machinery deteriorated and nitrate prices fell. From the 1880s, therefore, Santiago arranged successive auctions of *oficinas*, setting an official valuation and a reserve price. Successful bidders paid an immediate deposit in sterling and interest on the outstanding sum, terms which favoured foreign buyers who borrowed more cheaply abroad at 2 or 3 per cent against the 12 per cent ruling in Chile. Expatriate houses, like Gibbs who bought Alianza at an official auction, participated strongly to gain control over good *caliche*, pre-empt rivals, or consolidate holdings. To favour native buyers unduly would have aroused jealousies from other sectors of the economy, lowered Chile's intake of sterling (vital to repay and service debts), and permitted unscrupulous local capitalists to resell immediately to foreigners at a profit.[3]

---

[1] McBride, op. cit., pp. 204–5; Blakemore, op. cit., *passim*; H. Bernstein, *Modern and Contemporary Latin America* (Chicago, 1952), pp. 511–24.

[2] Gibbs 11470/15, Valparaíso to London, 23 Aug. 1894.

[3] *Diario de Diputados* (Chile), 24 Dec. 1896, 309, 4 Feb. 1897, 796 and 801, and 28 Jan. 1899, 1113–14; *Financial News*, 7 Apr. 1897; *Diario de Senadores* (Chile), 15 Sept. 1898, 900.

Nevertheless, privileged terms with respect to repayment and lower deposits encouraged local ownership. Auctions, the *Financial News* explained, now enabled the government 'to control the market by opening up at a key time the virgin grounds which it still holds'.[1]

The nitrate export duty, levied by the Santiago Government, in addition to the import duties on machinery and bags, also served crudely to regulate the industry. Payable in gold, despite *salitreros'* protests, to insure against the depreciating peso, the duty formed the largest element of the f.o.b. price on the West Coast, rising from £1·5 million per annum, 1884–8, to £5·5 million by 1911.[2] Inevitably, official responsibility for so large a part of the cost of nitrate strongly influenced the industry. It discouraged cost-cutting innovation since the greatest element in the f.o.b. price would remain unaltered, and a lower duty might possibly have increased consumption among those poorer farmers who were unable to afford nitrate. Moreover, coercive threats to raise duty if prices and profits were rising soon ensured reform. Gibbs actually suggested a sliding scale of duties according to price to replace the flat rate, giving officials a continuous but flexible influence. Nevertheless, constraints existed on the levels which Santiago might impose. Overtaxation devalued the government's own *oficinas* since no one would bid for them. Rising costs would depress sales, perhaps lowering total revenue, and thus damage Chile's financial stability.

Labour problems within the nitrate industry also ensured a degree of government participation—though official attitudes were equivocal. The size of the nitrate work force and its crude political consciousness forced the government to pay some heed to its demands. But strikes, which prevented the exports on which the country depended, encouraged officials to ensure a rapid return to work rather than a prolonged confrontation, and thus made them inclined to favour the mine-owners. By 1913 there were 53,000 nitrate workers, of whom 23,000 were in Tarapacá (see Table VII.1), in addition to the many thousands in Iquique and other nitrate towns whose livelihood depended indirectly on the industry.[3] Although *oficinas* staggered closures under the nitrate

[1] *Financial News*, 10 Feb. 1890.
[2] Bain and Mulliken, op. cit.; Russell, op. cit., p. 335; *C.D.*, 22 Mar. 1912, 454.
[3] Miller and Singewald, op. cit., p. 284; Markos J. Marmalakis, 'Historical Statistics of Chile', unpublished work, part 4, A-481. Employment more than doubled between 1895 and 1913. See also McBride, op. cit., pp. 121–5.

combinations, serious unemployment still occurred (and was aggravated when the copper industry was slack, since a degree of mobility existed among miners). One report to Congress in 1896 estimated that closing forty-four of the seventy-seven *oficinas* under the third combination made 30,000 idle, who were now drifting south to seek work and disrupting social life.[1] Again, friction developed from the *salitreros'* use of truck and *fichas* (credit notes in lieu of pay, which were redeemable only at *pulperías* or company shops where exploitative prices were charged, wages exhausted, and savings made impossible), and it was brought to a head when 2,250 nitrate workers petitioned Congress.[2] Charges that families were split, that wages were unpaid, and that cheap agricultural labour was deliberately imported to depress wages, were also current.[3] But strikes and disorder in the nitrate fields in 1890 and in 1907, when 5,000 workers were said to have been killed or injured, required federal troops to restore order.[4] Agitators, like the leader of La Fraternal (the nitrate workers' union) in Iquique, where strikes paralysed the industry, were imprisoned with the result that local *intendentes* were accused of favouring the *salitreros*.

While government auctions, export duties, and labour policy constrained *salitreros*, constructive links were also forged between industry and government based on propaganda to encourage consumption. Senator Montt (Minister of the Interior) recognized their importance. He thought 'the State must co-operate to develop the use of nitrate. The interests of the Exchequer and the industry are the same.'[5] In the early 1880s *salitreros* formed a fighting fund to promote new uses and markets by means of advertisements, deputations to New York and European capitals, circulars, experiments, and prizes for research.[6] The Chilean Government contributed an annual £15,000 by 1890, £20,000 by

---

[1] *Diario de Senadores* (Chile), 13 July 1896, 147. Stronge telegraphed to Grey in 1913 that fifty-seven *oficinas* were closed, making 15,000 idle: P.R.O. F.O. 368/945/41821, Stronge to Grey, 21 Aug. 1913.

[2] *Diario de Diputados* (Chile), 13 Aug. and 5 Sept. 1901, 495, 506, and 869.

[3] Ibid., 26 and 27 Oct. 1903, 132 and 143, and 4 Jan. 1912, 1705.

[4] Gibbs 11471/78, Gibbs to F.O., 19 Dec. 1907, and London to Valparaíso, 3 Jan. 1908; P.R.O. F.O. 369/127/2491, Rennie to Grey, 7 Dec. 1907; *Consular Reports* (Chile), P.P. 1908, cx, 63; *The Times*, 23 Dec. 1907, 3c.

[5] *Diario de Senadores* (Chile), 31 July 1893, 356, and *La Unión*, 2 June 1893.

[6] *The Economist*, 3 Jan. 1891, 16; *El Heraldo*, 7 Aug. 1893; *C.D.*, 15 Apr. 1885, 188.

1897, and £40,000 by 1913. When a subsidy was proposed in 1889, Congress was told that propaganda was 'indispensable not only to give new impetus to production and to obtain in this way an increase in the fiscal revenues but to ease the difficulties which the industry has encountered . . .'.[1] The Chilean Government also instructed its legations abroad to advertise nitrate, created experimental farms and *oficinas*, and shipped output to Japan.[2] Although results from such propaganda were not immediate and bureaucratic handling of the campaign was criticized, the Chilean Government offered the Asociación Salitrera de Propaganda—the promotional committee of nitrate owners—the permanent assistance of two officials.[3]

The Chilean Government supported *salitreros* when crisis and depression affected the industry. Chilean buyers at government auctions, who like the Compañía Internacional de Salitre de Tarapacá found their grounds overvalued or were unable to redeem the purchase price, were regarded sympathetically in the sudden downturn after the relatively prosperous years of 1896–7. In 1907 the government established the Caja de Crédito Salitrera (a loan agency for *oficina* owners) when La Granja & Co. failed, after over-speculation, and other closures were threatened.[4] Officials could not allow crisis in the industry to go unchecked.

Government policy had also achieved a considerable degree of Chileanization in the nitrate industry from the nineties, when foreign-dominated combinations had seemed to be in control. Nitrate's economic significance ensured official sympathy for the demands for protective legislation against expatriate ownership expressed in Congress and before investigating commissions. In 1902 Deputy Darío Sánchez believed that 'to redeem past errors we have not, I believe, any other way . . . than to nationalize the nitrate industry'.[5] In 1912, when the formation of a national nitrate company was suggested, Deputy Ibañez claimed that 'nothing will be more satisfactory than that all the nitrate . . . should be

---

[1] *Diario de Diputados* (Chile), 21 Dec. 1889, 537–9.

[2] Ibid., 15 June 1908, 126, 28 Aug. 1912, 1653–5, and 1 and 5 July 1913, 423 and 514; *Consular Reports (Antofagasta)*, P.P. 1911, xc, 570.

[3] *The Times*, 5 May 1911, 22e.

[4] *The Economist*, 7 Mar. 1908, 482; *Consular Reports (Chile)*, P.P. 1908, cx, 63; *The Times*, 27 Aug. 1907, 3c.

[5] *Diario de Diputados* (Chile), 24 Oct. 1902, 48–50.

exploited by and belong to Chileans'.[1] Adherence to *laissez-faire* and the difficulties arising from Peru's experience made most officials and politicians reluctant to commit Chile to any thoroughgoing nationalization by the expropriation of existing foreign owners.[2] But all governments paraded their hopes for increased local owner-ship. In 1894, forty-six out of fifty-two *oficinas* producing 92 per cent of output were foreign-owned, thirteen large British com-panies mining over 60 per cent. At the turn of the century British firms accounted for 55 per cent of production, while Chileans shipped 15 per cent. Just before 1914, Chilean capital in the industry totalled $55 million (representing half the *oficinas*), Britain held $50 million (40 per cent of *oficinas*), Germany $20 million, and others $25 million. Of sixteen new mines about to open in 1911, two were British and the rest Chilean.[3] To some ex-tent the naturalization of foreign-born businessmen, the holdings of resident expatriates, and transfers of company registration to avoid taxation at home, accounted for the change, but the rapidly increasing participation of native capital, officially encouraged from the late nineties, was the prime element. The new situation, according to Señor Alessandri (Minister of Finance), 'makes the error of believing the nitrate industry to be absolutely and totally controlled by foreigners disappear'.[4] Far from being the small, undercapitalized, poor relation of their European-owned rivals, Chileans now owned four out of the five largest nitrate concerns.

Co-operation between *salitreros* and officials reached its peak, surprisingly, in negotiations concerning the combinations. At first the declared policy of Congress was to denounce their formation, since combinations restricted output and employment, threatened Chile's finances, and increased profits which then went abroad.[5] Gibbs's branch in Valparaíso believed that 'the Chilean Govern-

[1] Ibid., 18 Oct. 1912, 44–54; see also Gibbs 11471/82, London to Valparaíso, 24 Dec. 1912.

[2] See, for example, Senator MacIver's remark as Minister of the Interior that nationalization seemed patriotic but was unobtainable, *Diario de Senadores* (Chile), 1 Aug. 1894, 410, and *El Mercurio*, 7 Aug. 1893.

[3] *Financial News*, 24 Apr. 1890; *Diario de Senadores* (Chile), 23 Nov. 1894, 257; F. M. Halsey and G. B. Sherwell, 'Investments in Latin America III: Chile' (*Trade Information Bulletin* 426, Washington, 1926), pp. 59–60; *Consular Reports* (Iquique), P.P. 1910, xcvi, 631.

[4] *Diario de Diputados* (Chile), 5 July 1913, 506–13. This statement certainly made nonsense of Consul Rennie's claim that nitrate would 'gradually fall more into English hands', P.R.O. F.O. 369/127/2941, Rennie to Grey, 7 Dec. 1907.

[5] *Chilean Times*, 29 Dec. 1888.

ment will never [accept?] any monopoly scheme brought forward
principally in the foreign interest'.[1] A commission in 1893
examined the abuses of the combinations, 'which seize from the
nation and the industry millions of pesos which legitimately
belong to it'.[2] Nevertheless, persuasive arguments existed for
official approval of the combinations. Eduardo Matte, a Deputy
for Santiago, realized the need for recovery from depression and
for a fair return on capital.[3] While official reports remained confident of Chile's nitrate resources the mines were not inexhaustible,
and the restricted output which a combination achieved might well
be desirable. A Senate Committee reported in 1894 that 'the system
of raising production to sell the article at a low price . . . appears to
us uneconomic and unpatriotic'.[4] The higher prices which a combination might obtain would simplify the collection of duties.
Moreover, the increasing Chileanization of ownership, and the
political influence of some *salitreros*, caused officials to rethink
their policy towards the combinations. Any downturn in activity
now affected local investors whom the government had encouraged. The new depth of official involvement surprised even
Antony Gibbs & Co., who had long supported closer government
rapport with the combinations. Chileans 'have so much got the ear
of the Government', the firm's Valparaíso House explained, 'that
for the first time . . . we find the Chilean Government proposes
to take active steps to force the producers to make a combination'.[5]
Indeed, the government eventually supported cartelized sales in
London, linked with debt servicing, thereby encouraging privately
what Peru had forced publicly on the industry in the 1870s. In
1901 officials delayed auctions of mines which 'would produce an
immediate breach in the nitrate combination whose advantages
to the Treasury and to the nitrate industry are evident'.[6] By 1906
a complete volte-face had occurred since the government now
lobbied reluctant, low-cost *oficinas* to join the combination when
the *oficinas* themselves would have preferred to undersell com-

[1] Gibbs 11470/10, Valparaíso to London, 24 June 1887.
[2] *Diario de Senadores* (Chile), 31 July and 11 Aug. 1893, 354 and 409, and
28 Dec. 1894, 666; *La Unión*, 6 Aug. 1893.
[3] *Diario de Diputados* (Chile), 9 July 1892, 155–60.
[4] *Diario de Senadores* (Chile), 5 Nov. 1894, 158–62; see also *Financial News*,
17 Sept. 1898.
[5] Gibbs 11470/18, Valparaíso to London, 17 Aug. and 7 Nov. 1899.
[6] *Diario de Diputados* (Chile), 5 Sept. 1901, 840; see also ibid., 29 Aug. 1901,
693.

petitors on the free market. Realizing that Chile must maintain high nitrate prices to improve her financial position, and regulate shipments to preserve natural resources, Deputy Carlos Avalos explained the new attitude to combinations:

Fortunately there is no one today who does not recognize the importance of the nitrate combination. It regulates nitrate production to the needs of consumption and increases the article's value in a convenient way, and protects the interests not only of industrialist owners of nitrate but also of intermediaries in the operation of this industry and those of its own workers. It is evident, then, that the public interest is linked to the existence of the nitrate combination.[1]

V

British investment in the Chilean nitrate industry created many points of friction with the host country. Although Britain supplied badly needed capital at a point when local financiers could find more remunerative outlets, although Britain provided know-how and technical leadership, and although British firms created employment, Chilean officials, the press, and the public resented foreign control over natural resources crucial to the country's economy. By the 1880s nearly half the nitrate mines were British-owned, including most of the largest, as well as much of the nitrate service industries, the banks, the public utilities, and the railways in Tarapacá. Additionally, a high proportion of these concerns were managed by an oligopoly of British capitalists, particularly by powerful merchant houses like Antony Gibbs & Sons and by Colonel North and his associates 'who had been creating there, little by little, and with tendencies which were daily more marked, an almost total monopoly'.[2] Although export duties constituted the greater proportion of nitrate's f.o.b. price, one semi-official estimate considered that in the late eighties practically two-thirds of the final price still went abroad as profit, freight, insurance, managerial expenses, and fuel costs, so that the local economy benefited far less than it might have done from its natural wealth. Chile struggled 'against the economic superiority of foreigners from whom neither sufficient compensation nor proper reciprocity

[1] Ibid., 30 July 1904, 900.
[2] Ministerio de Hacienda, *Fomento de la Industria Salitrera* (Santiago, 1888), p. 143.

were obtained'.[1] The formation of nitrate combinations reinforced fears that a handful of foreign capitalists would direct Chile's economic and social life, regulating employment, revenue, and investment.

The profitability of the British nitrate firms aroused particular animosity. Although *The Times* warned that the successful record of the Liverpool Nitrate Company, which paid dividends of 100 per cent or more six times between 1905 and 1913, 'must be regarded as unique' in the history of Chilean nitrate,[2] the handful of outstanding *oficinas* inevitably attracted more attention in Chile than the majority of merely or barely profitable concerns. The weaknesses of *oficinas* like those at Lagunas, San Donato, Santiago, Fortuna, and San Patricio—their bad siting, overcapitalization, depleted reserves, and burdening debentures—were well known. Yet what attracted greater scrutiny were the extremely profitable years, 1912–13, when nearly twenty British *oficinas* paid more than 10 per cent and five paid over 20 per cent.[3] Both the Salar del Carmen and the Alianza works, incorporated by Gibbs & Sons in the nitrate boom, paid handsomely from the late nineties, the former returning over 20 per cent per annum from 1897 to 1914 and wiping off its debentures.[4]

Yet it is misleading to exaggerate the unanimity between British *salitreros*. Antony Gibbs & Sons always differentiated sharply between North's policy of short-term gains and their own, linked, as they saw it, to Chile's permanent prosperity. Nor did North win undiluted acclaim at home. *The Economist* and the *Financial News* remained hostile to his schemes which 'puffed' values and misled investors; both papers were severely critical in their editorial comment, and published 'inspired' letters which warned of over-production, rising costs, and exhausted *caliche*. Long before North's death in 1896, Gibbs knew that his position on the West Coast was weak. 'Any prestige', the Valparaíso House explained, 'which Mr. North may have had in the times of his greatest popularity and success appears to us to have disappeared completely.'[5] Nor should the weakness of expatriate mining companies be under-

---

[1] Min. de Hac., *Fomento de la Industria Salitrera*, pp. 140–2.
[2] *The Times*, 29 Oct. 1913, 18b.   [3] Rippy, op. cit., pp. 64 and 138.
[4] *The Economist*, 28 May and 4 June 1910, 1209 and 1265; 17 June 1911, 1318; and 10 and 24 May 1913, 1110 and 1308.
[5] Gibbs 11470/15, Valparaíso to London, 9 Aug. 1894; cf. Blakemore, op. cit., pp. 35–7 and 65.

estimated. Once a concern had invested huge sums in a concentrated, capital-intensive business, it could not suddenly depart if conditions deteriorated. No effective redress existed against rising duties or delay in the granting of concessions. *Oficinas* were also vulnerable to the notoriously high risks of exhaustion and rapidly diminishing returns.

Moreover, despite the advantages which co-operation conferred on *salitreros*—economies of scale, common research and propaganda campaigns, and bulk deals (which omitted middlemen and reduced the cost of credit and insurance)—the nitrate combinations were surprisingly ineffective in restricting output and raising prices. Production rose steadily from the 1880s, as Table VII.1 shows, and prices continued to fall until after 1900, narrowing profit margins. The combinations were powerless to prevent competition from other *salitreros*, the growth of substitutes, or changing patterns of demand. The greatest boom in prices and profits occurred outside the combinations, in 1888 when Gibbs & Sons were 'astounded at the leap in prices',[1] and after 1909, 'striking testimony', *The Economist* remarked 'to the recuperative powers of any trade which has been demoralized by the breaking up of a price-raising combination'.[2] The *Financial News* explained that 'the lesson taught by the nitrate combination of 1885 and 1886 was that however cleverly managed . . . control over output could not be other than partial and ephemeral'.[3] W. H. Russell also noted the difficulties facing combination:

> It is much to be regretted that the unanimity and cohesion which characterized the action of the nitrate makers assembling to maintain a fair average price to the consumer, moderate profits for the producer and an equable revenue to the government, was not preserved.[4]

The success of combination depended on lasting goodwill and selflessness, rare commodities among entrepreneurs in an industry seeking immediate rather than long-term results. The nitrate combinations were defensive rather than offensive, decelerating the rise in output and the fall in prices. The fact that agreements were not secret or oral but well-publicized, adds weight to the view that their purpose was not sinister exploitation. The collapse of successive combinations indicates how temporary, intermittent,

---

[1] Gibbs 11470/11, Valparaíso to London, 23 Nov. 1888.
[2] *The Economist*, 16 Dec. 1911, 1255.
[3] *Financial News*, 20 Mar. 1890.   [4] Russell, op. cit., p. 334.

and impermanent their control was. 'Even among firms which seem to dominate the market', G. C. Allen has remarked, 'monopoly is never for long unqualified.'[1]

Indeed, the fact that nitrate extraction involved no secret processes, that it evolved little technical innovation, and that reserves of *caliche* remained large even by 1914, permitted no single firm or group to dominate the industry for long. While estimates of Chile's nitrate resources varied, and allowing for official exaggeration (since to inflate the size of Chile's chief asset helped to maintain the confidence of investors), it is clear that nitrate resources were far from exhausted. Official estimates of reserves rose from 140 million tons in 1892 to 220 million by 1909.[2] In the case of the nitrate industry the reaction of Chileans to the monopoly issue was based more on fear and suspicion that on firm facts. And in the absence of any marked enthusiasm among Chileans for nitrate properties during the 1880s, what alternative was there to foreign ownership?

Nevertheless, nitrate combinations inevitably caused conflict between British *salitreros* and all Chilean governments, both before and after 1891. And if officials anticipated real evils from foreign mines, then government intervention was a proper and practical solution. The once temporary expedient of state interference became permanent, although the failure of Peru's expropriation policy, entrenched *laissez-faire* views, and the fear that investors would panic, made total nationalization out of the question. Balmaceda's policy was not directed at foreign capital *per se*, as his negotiations with Gibbs indicated,[3] but at monopoly and restricted sales. Gibbs themselves usually preferred to work with, rather than against, local governments in Latin America to ensure protection for their commercial interests; they developed an instinct for amicable relationships with small, emergent countries and for satisfying those countries' political and economic requirements. The government pursued effective measures to obstruct the action of the nitrate monopoly, namely levying export duties to reduce profits, selling unworked grounds to increase competition, and promoting Chileanization. If the ideal, which Cocq Port proposed in his pamphlet, of 'one manufacturer, one shipper and one seller

[1] Allen, op. cit., p. 13.
[2] *C.D.*, 6 Feb. 1909, 242; *Financial Times*, 1 Nov. 1913; *Diario de Diputados* (Chile), 9 Jan. 1914, 1548.   [3] Blakemore, op. cit., pp. 145–58.

of nitrate'—the state—was unobtainable at this stage, government action increasingly regulated the industry.[1] And by 1914 officials recognized the importance of the nitrate combination's aims. Competition between *oficinas* unnecessarily duplicated energies and resources. An article like nitrate, where goodwill and brand-name were unimportant, benefited from bulk sales centrally directed. Moreover, since supplies were finite (although exhaustion seemed distant) and demand unresponsive when prices fell, to maximize revenue at a higher price was sensible enough. By the outbreak of the First World War, therefore, government participation in the industry was effective and the co-operation of *salitreros* genuine, particularly in areas like propaganda and research, in anticipation of more thoroughgoing official intervention after 1919.

VI

The Iodine Trade

After twenty years of uninterrupted growth, the introduction of new techniques, fresh sources of supply, and the replacement of existing materials caused a sharp crisis in Britain's chemical industry in the 1870s.[2] The production of iodine, an element comparable to bromine and chlorine in its properties and found naturally in minute quantities, reflected these fundamental changes. Discovered in 1811, iodine was first extracted from kelp or seaweed on the coasts of Ireland, Scotland, and Brittany. Seaweed was dried and burned locally and the ash shipped to chemical manufacturers, a method which yielded some fifteen pounds of iodine per ton of kelp.[3] Serious drawbacks existed: work was seasonal and depended upon drift seaweed; rain during collection or incineration washed out valuable salts; other less precarious industries—fishing, agriculture, or rural crafts—attracted labour; farmers demanded seaweed as a fertilizer, particularly in the west of Ireland where soil was poor.

[1] Ministerio de Hacienda, *Fomento de la Industria Salitrera* (Santiago, 1888), p. 147.

[2] Reader, op. cit., pp. 3–15; Morgan and Pratt, op. cit., pp. 339–40; H. W. Richardson, 'Chemicals' in D. H. Aldcroft, ed., *The Development of British Industry and Foreign Competition 1870–1914* (London, 1968), pp. 278–305.

[3] F. S. Taylor, *A History of Industrial Chemistry* (London, 1957), p. 192; H.M.S.O., *The Mineral Trade of the British Empire and Foreign Countries: Iodine* (1928), p. 5; 'The Trade in Iodine' (*Trade Information Bulletin* No. 561, Washington, 1928), pp. 11–15; *C.D.*, 15 Apr. 1874, 148, and 14 Apr. 1877, 149.

In the 1840s an American chemist, A. A. Hayes, and a Frenchman, Lembert, observed iodine as a by-product in nitrate manufacture. Iodine production in *oficinas*, although yielding barely one pound per ton of untreated ore, was considerably cheaper and easier than extraction from seaweed.[1] Relatively little effort or outlay gave South American producers highly satisfactory results. The surge in West Coast production—iodine output rose 600 per cent between 1869 and 1880—threatened the established commercial framework. More efficient shipping links at rates which scarcely influenced the high market value of iodine ensured transportation to Europe. The competitive advantages of nitrate producers terminated the monopoly which kelp manufacturers had hitherto enjoyed.[2] The traditional marketing of iodine through the firm of Leisler Boch in Glasgow, close to major suppliers and customers, was imperilled.

During the 1870s Gibbs developed links in the iodine trade which complemented their nitrate interests. The established reputation of the House attracted West Coast manufacturers like Gamboni who retained no regular European agency. Gibbs's London office was 'in the habit of supplying all the continent and had agents who must know all about the trade'.[3] Its policy was to advance a modest proportion of the anticipated market price upon a producer's shipments to cover his working costs, then to ship and sell in Europe and remit the difference between final price and advance (less commission and carriage charges). The importance of shipping through one house was considerable. European buyers, confident of production exceeding consumption, would not order ahead but merely covered immediate needs. A single consignee, however, limited buyers' options, stabilized business, and guaranteed prices, and therefore negotiated more effectively.

But at first, firms who resented the House's increasing power would not consign to Gibbs. In 1873 Read, one of Gibbs's managers, wanted to show Hainsworth, an important West Coast producer, 'the folly of endeavouring to take the sale of iodine out

---

[1] M. B. Donald, 'History of the Chilean Nitrate Industry', *Annals of Science*, i (1936), pp. 41–4; Francis C. Kelly, 'Iodine in Medicine and Pharmacy since its discovery: 1811–1961', *Proceedings of the Royal Society of Medicine*, liv (1961), 831–6.

[2] Haber, op. cit., p. 58.

[3] Gibbs 11120, Miller to Hayne, 24/25 Jan. 1879; see also ibid. 11123, Read to Henry, 15 June 1873.

of Antony Gibbs & Co.'s hands'. Although Hainsworth might save a half penny per ounce commission by avoiding Gibbs, he risked 'losing 2*d*. or 3*d*. per ounce on the price of the article', as competing distributors weakened the market.[1] Folsch & Martin, a German house, which appeared 'most apprehensively jealous' of Gibbs, would not co-operate, and repeatedly shipped to their Hamburg principals.[2] Read fully understood London's delay in reaching agreement with the Hamburg office, 'knowing the slippery elements that have to be dealt with on this side'.[3]

Gibbs's ambitions, however, went beyond the centralization of West Coast consignments to the possibility of regulating the trade internationally. There were two principal issues. First, annual production exceeded the level of consumption. Stocks accumulated at a rate for which no outlet existed, and posed a continuing threat to prices and stability. Then, price scarcely influenced demand since the pharmaceutical industry, the major user, had no satisfactory substitute. Competition between producers would merely lower prices and raise freight charges, without markedly increasing consumption. If, however, the two sources of iodine, Europe and South America, could be jointly controlled, the restriction of manufacture (and therefore of competition) and the maintenance of artificially high prices could become practicable. Gibbs did not consider that the elimination of European makers was in the long-term interests of West Coast firms. Conflict would prove costly in terms of price and stability. Before long South American producers would squabble. Moreover when prices rose again, European producers would reopen. Then, Leisler Boch, the European selling agency, had built-up market confidence and enjoyed valuable commercial contacts which there was no reason to disturb. The head of this firm had 'by the labour of his whole career in drugs and chemicals created for himself a position of influence in this particular branch with which nobody can compete . . .'; he controlled the iodine market with a skill and precision on which Gibbs could confidently base their more far-reaching international understandings.[4]

The first task, however, was to teach European producers the

[1] Ibid. 11123, Read to Henry, 15 June 1873.
[2] Ibid. 11472, London to Read, 11 Aug. 1878.
[3] Ibid. 11132, Read to Valparaíso, 2 Nov. 1876, Read to London, 28 Jan., 21 Feb. and 8 Mar. 1877.
[4] Gibbs 11471/4, Gibbs to Folsch & Martin, 15 June 1877.

need for compromise. The shock of South American iodine was felt from 1873 when there was 'a sensational downward leap in prices' from two shillings an ounce to ten pence. Gibbs would sell 'at a loss to beat any rival out of the field'. Iodine was no longer 'a safe product to prophesy about'.[1] Then, in 1874 Gibbs considered the question of limiting competition internationally. The fact that only six West Coast firms made iodine, and that the Europeans faced higher working costs, would facilitate negotiations. But discussions were premature. Lower prices, which were still giving good returns, did not encourage the South Americans to compromise. 'The majority of the producers', wrote Read, 'oppose the idea of combination with the Scottish manufacturers.'[2] Campbells, who owned works in Tarapacá, preferred selling until the Scottish and French makers were driven to the wall. And European firms retaliated. It seemed to Read that 'the Scottish producers are trying to prevent direct contact with the consumer by creating distrust as to the final course of the market . . .'.[3]

The first effective West Coast combination, restricting annual output and assigning manufacturers a quota, made its appearance early in 1877 when prices had fallen to $5\frac{3}{4}d$. New price levels alone were not enough. Without a limit on production and quotas, members would merely increase output and in the long run aggravate the situation. After Gibbs had smoothed over local objections and negotiated consignment contracts, only Campbells remained aloof. The House bought the Hamburg iodine stocks of Folsch & Martin, which eliminated one major problem. Henceforth Gibbs would receive all West Coast output for sale through Leisler Boch, who in turn, since they managed European production, would ultimately control supply and price. 'We may consider', Read informed his principals, 'the combination completed as far as Peru is concerned.'[4] Leisler Boch charged a 5 per cent handling commission, but returned 2 per cent to Gibbs. The House thus assumed a position between South American producers and the European marketing organization. By November the price of iodine had settled at $9d$.[5]

The combination soon dissolved. By December Folsch appeared

---

[1] *C.D.*, 15 Jan. 1873, 1 and 34; 15 Feb. 1873, 72; 15 June 1874, 215; 15 Oct. 1874, 390.　　　　[2] Gibbs 11122, Read to Lima, 9 Oct. 1875.
[3] Ibid., Read to Lima, 15 Oct. 1875.
[4] Ibid. 11138, Read to London, 20 Jan. and 3 Apr. 1877.
[5] *C.D.*, 15 Nov. 1877, 457.

'so perverse as to break the monopoly', refusing to consign through Gibbs.[1] 'We are very sorry', Folsch explained, 'that the contract is very advantageous to Mr. Leisler and so very little so to us.'[2] Moreover, the rising number of outside iodine producers on the West Coast in response to higher prices weakened Gibbs's influence. Although the Peruvian Government had expropriated *oficinas*, iodine production remained in private hands as an attractive sideline for *salitreros* who resented official interference in the nitrate trade. Read warned that 'this business will get beyond our control if we are not very careful'.[3] The Antofagasta Company, which consigned to Paris, was opposed to any combination with the Scottish producers. Disagreements inside Messrs. Leon induced one partner unilaterally to abrogate the agreement with Gibbs, and Messrs. Ugarte consigned to Folsch who had helped construct their iodine house. Producers also claimed outrageous advances upon their shipments.[4] During the next two years Gibbs struggled to influence the growing number of South American manufacturers and thus reassert authority. 'I have no doubt', a West Coast partner explained, 'that the Peruvian iodine producers will only be too glad to accede to Messrs. Antony Gibbs & Sons' consignments.'[5]

From April 1878 Gibbs established the first international combination. Folsch & Martin, after independent negotiations through their Hamburg principals, tacitly adhered to its decisions (without joining formally) and shipped direct to Leisler Boch. Terms were highly satisfactory: French manufacturers received 25 per cent of estimated sales, the Scottish producers 29 per cent, and the South Americans 46 per cent—equivalent to 100 tons—divided *pro rata*. Prices rose to 14*d*. in July 1879, where they remained for nearly eighteen months.[6] In January 1880 the international combination was renegotiated. The War of the Pacific created a new situation. Quotas had to recognize a rapid expansion in the output of West Coast *oficinas*, without antagonizing European producers

[1] Gibbs 11121, Bohl to Comber, 12 Dec. 1877.

[2] Ibid. 11471/4, Folsch to Gibbs, 8 May 1877.

[3] Ibid. 11472, Read to Miller, 26 Aug. 1878.

[4] Ibid. 11472, Smail to Bohl, 20 June 1878; Smail to Read, 28 Jan. and 13 Aug. 1879.

[5] Ibid. 11132, Smail to Read, 28 Sept. 1879; see also ibid. 11121, Valparaíso to Lima, 15 Oct. 1879, and ibid. 11126, Smail to Bohl, 25 June 1878.

[6] Ibid. 11472, London to Read, 11 Apr. 1878, and Smail to London, 6 June 1878; *C.D.*, 15 Feb. 1879, 85, and 15 Apr. 1879, 175.

now increasingly sensitive to their diminished importance.[1] And from July, international co-operation ceased as Fairlie, a leading Scottish manufacturer, demanded revised quotas and lowered prices to 6*d*.[2]

But Gibbs, who enjoyed more settled relations with West Coast producers, now led a strong South American lobby. The House made attractive overtures to Gildemeister and Folsch, the leading Chilean iodine producers. By 1884, Folsch & Martin had largely abandoned the practice of independent shipments, which had undermined earlier negotiations. Gibbs were able to rationalize and consolidate their iodine business. The House stockpiled on the West Coast, and reduced its shipments to the level of European demand rather than consign the whole of South American output. This policy diminished risks and prevented consumers from speculating on available supplies. It required firmer supervision of producers to ensure that they did not exceed quotas or ship independently. Thus Gibbs encouraged the formation of a Directory at Iquique comprising elected representatives of recognized iodine manufacturers. Gibbs's branch in Valparaíso maintained the link with London, where the House appointed a manager permanently responsible for iodine matters.[3] The Iquique Directory levied contributions, regularly inspected plant and stocks, admitted new members, imposed fines for unauthorized sales of iodine or iodoferous property, and fixed quotas.[4] Periodic negotiations revised quotas. The West Coast committee, a forum for disputes and difficulties, relieved Gibbs of considerable labour by reducing friction in South America. The House also ended its advances, believing that the excellent selling arrangements alone would attract consignors. These changes did not please everyone. German firms, envying the power that Gibbs wielded, complained that the Valparaíso and London offices settled matters internally without adequately consulting the Iquique Directory.[5] The decision to end advances antagonized smaller producers whose resources were slender.

---

[1] Gibbs 11471/9, Gibbs to Leisler Boch, 12 Nov. 1879 and 20 Jan. 1880, and London to Valparaíso, 16 Mar. 1880; H.M.S.O., op. cit., p. 10.

[2] *C.D.*, 15 Jan. 1880, 41; 15 July 1880, 304 and 321; 15 Nov. 1880, 501.

[3] Gibbs 11471/22–3, London to Valparaíso, 10 Apr. and 9 Sept. 1885; Anon. 'Trade in Iodine', pp. 7–9; *C.D.*, 22 Dec. 1894, 877–8.

[4] Gibbs 11471/26, Iquique to London, 1 Apr. 1887. In 1887, for example, Gibbs received a 10·692 quota, Folsch 11·245, and Gildemeister 10·771.

[5] Gibbs 11118, 41–4.

In January 1885, after four years of low prices, Gibbs and Leisler Boch negotiated a second international combination, which
came to be renewed triennially (though not without periodic
crises) until 1914. Scottish producers proved obstinate, but the
French, whose kelp crops were deteriorating, preferred a rapid
settlement. Thus before 1900 iodine's market value was usually
9*d.* and only once fell below 7*d.*[1] But the increasing power of the
South Americans, as a result of their developed local organization and steadily expanding output, demanded recognition. Their
share of sales increased from 46 per cent in 1880 to 75 per cent in
1914. European output had decreased from 117 to 60 tons between
1880 and 1883 in response to low prices, while West Coast output
had doubled. The fact that Leisler Boch pledged their loyalty
to the South Americans rather than to their traditional allies, the
Europeans, indicated the change in relative strength. Furthermore, Gibbs now extracted a larger return commission of $2\frac{1}{2}$ per
cent, since the House's co-operation was essential to Leisler
Boch.[2]

VII

The smooth operation of successive international iodine combinations was more apparent than real. Notwithstanding the Iquique
Directory, little machinery in practice existed to enforce contracts
or coerce recalcitrant firms. The difficult task for both Gibbs and
Leisler Boch was to control their respective producers and adjust
supplies to market needs. 'The international agreements', wrote
London in 1885, 'are waste paper if anyone wanted to break
them.'[3] Indeed, the organization of the iodine combination was
remarkable for the absence of binding contracts, since some
producers accepted the combination's decisions only informally.
Even Gibbs and Leisler Boch discontinued their formal alliance
after 1884, tacitly acknowledging the established quotas, prices,
and conditions. Such a fluid situation inevitably forced Gibbs to
balance conflicting claims of South American producers and wider
international issues.

[1] Ibid. 11471/18–21, London to Valparaíso, 14 Feb. and 7 Aug. 1884,
Rottenburg to Sillem, 9 Sept. and 10 Oct. 1884, Valparaíso to London, 24 Nov.
1884; *C.D.*, 15 Jan. 1885, 15, and 15 July 1885, 399.
[2] Gibbs 11471/9 and 21, Leisler Boch to Sillem, 24 Nov. 1879 and 27 Jan.
1880; ibid. 11118, 253, Gibbs to Watjen Toel, 4 Dec. 1884.
[3] Ibid. 11118, 6 and 82.

The state of the nitrate trade, the main source of income for *oficina* operators, constituted a disruptive factor to which iodine negotiations were subordinated. When *salitreros* failed to compromise over nitrate, distrust was unavoidable in the iodine trade. The need to offset losses incurred in nitrate production encouraged *salitreros* to make iodine, which in turn weakened the combination, reduced the quotas of older manufacturers, and exaggerated grievances. By 1903 more than twenty *oficinas* out of eighty made iodine.[1] The rivalry between Gibbs and North illustrated the links between nitrate and iodine. Despite their protestations of loyalty, the North group of *oficinas* remained at the edge of the iodine combination, ready to sell stocks for what they would fetch. 'As we have opposed his railway', Herbert Gibbs explained, 'it is war to the knife.'[2] Again, consigning iodine from his Buena Ventura works to outsiders was merely 'part of the policy . . . pursued by Colonel North with the object of coercing the two Nitrate Companies which are blocking the proposed Nitrate Combination'.[3]

Outside shippers also disturbed West Coast business. In 1885 Retzlaff, whose head office was in Danzig, shipped iodine to a Scottish pharmaceutical maker through Liverpool. He was, explained Rottenburg (a partner in Leisler Boch), 'worse than an eel and always slips out of your hands when you think you have him'.[4] In 1888 Daniel Oliva decided to remain aloof from the combination. 'We very much fear', explained Valparaíso, 'that it will cost . . . a good deal of work and money to bring him to his bearings.'[5] Then between 1890 and 1896 Eduardo Charme consigned his iodine through a Berlin house at one penny below the combination price. General policy was to secure the allegiance of outsiders if they could not be defeated. Unfortunately, the onset of new producers materially reduced existing quotas, while outsiders, suspicious of the virtues of compromise, continued a competition which was costly to themselves and to existing

---

[1] *C.D.*, 22 Dec. 1894, 877–8; 24 Oct. 1896, 267; and 31 Oct. 1903, 743.

[2] Gibbs 11040, Herbert Gibbs to Vicary Gibbs, 29 Jan. 1894; see also *C.D.*, 7 Sept. 1889, 333; 19 and 26 Oct. 1889, 570 and 607–8; and 8 Feb. 1890, 189.

[3] Gibbs 11471/49, London to Valparaíso, 21 May 1895; see also ibid. 11471/44, London to Valparaíso, 2 Feb. 1894, and ibid. 11470, Valparaíso to London, 9 March 1894.

[4] Ibid. 11471/42, Rottenburg to Sillem, 12 Dec. 1892.

[5] Ibid. 11470/10, Valparaíso to London, 27 Apr. 1888.

members. In 1889 Gibbs feared that outside manufacturers might even enter into a combination against the regular makers.[1]

Unauthorized shipments to the United States, where no direct representation or marketing organization existed, proved particularly embarrassing. Not only did they avoid intermediate commissions to Leisler Boch and Gibbs, but they were reshipped to Europe where they undersold combination iodine. Before 1884 Leisler Boch had supplied American needs, but now West Coast producers shipped direct, threatening to exclude those who had first developed the trade. The dispute was soon settled. Outside South American shippers were allotted 75 per cent of the market, and their agent, Watjen Toel, was officially recognized by Gibbs and Leisler Boch who charged a 2 per cent return commission on all American sales.[2] Subsequently Grace Brothers, New York merchants with extensive South American interests, tempted West Coast producers to ship cheap iodine direct, upsetting regular buyers who paid the combination price. In 1898, when Frederico Varela consigned to Grace Brothers, the Iquique Directory imposed reductions and a boycott.[3]

Similarly, outsiders threatened the established commercial framework in Europe, where the burden of defending the combination's interests fell on Scottish producers (Table VII.4). In 1897 the Scottish Acid and Alkali Company reduced prices and demanded an increased quota. The combination seized kelp supplies, but the company tapped fresh deposits in Ireland and further reduced prices before compromise was reached, in 1904.[4] Other Scottish firms attempted similar tactics, but their small output was not a serious threat. Norwegian kelp produced in Stavanger and sold in Hamburg was a continuing menace from 1880.[5] The demands of Scottish firms for Norwegian kelp to outflank the

[1] Ibid. 11471/33, London to Valparaíso, 21 Aug. 1889; ibid. 11135, John Gibbs to Smail, 27 Nov. 1896.

[2] Ibid. 11471/20–5, London to Valparaíso, 6 Nov. 1884, Leisler Boch to Watjen Toel, 15 Dec. 1884, Rottenburg to Sillem, 5 Sept. 1886.

[3] C.D., 22 and 29 Jan. 1898, 157 and 216, and 5 and 26 Mar. 1898, 404 and 518; Gibbs 11118, pp. 42–3.

[4] Gibbs 11471/26 and 33, Rottenburg to Sillem, 24 Mar. 1887 and 13 June 1889; ibid. 11118, pp. 80–1; C.D., 15 May 1897, 775, and 22 Apr. 1899, 626.

[5] 'Trade in Iodine', op. cit., p. 17; C.D., 15 Mar. 1880, 131, 29 Aug. 1891, 346, 18 June 1898, 1001, 3 Aug. 1912, 231, and 14 Dec. 1912, 899; Gibbs 11471/ 49, Rottenburg to Sillem, 3 June 1895; and ibid. 11471/72, Leisler Boch to Gibbs, 12 and 14 Feb. 1902.

combination had also encouraged local makers to challenge the market. Norwegian production was on a significant scale from 1902, but successive working agreements in 1905 and 1907 achieved stability. In France, the major outside force was the Co-operative Society of Chemists for the Manufacture of Iodine, an attempt by retail chemists in 1895 to exploit resources in Finisterre

TABLE VII.4

Distribution of World Iodine Production and Prices, 1840–1914

(tons)

	Seaweed/kelp					Nitrate	Waters	Price per ounce (old pence)	
	Britain	France	Norway	Japan	Total	Chile	Java	Lowest	Highest
1840–9					31ᵃ			3¾	26
1850–9					65	nil			
1860–9					90ᵃ	2ᵇ	nil		
1870–9			n/a		92ᵃ	26ᵃ		5¾	30
1880–9					72ᵃ	164ᵃ		4	9
1890–9					100ᵃ	345ᵃ	2ᵃ	7½	9
1900–2					158ᵃ	303ᵃ	nil	6	7½
1903	95	28	11	34	168	382	nil		6
1904	91	34	10	36	171	370	nil	6	9
1905	66	43	11	45	165	270	nil	6	10½
1906	87	63	14	54	218	460	1		6
1907	80	60	12	64	216	380	nil		6
1908	80	60	12	64	216	370	nil		6
1909	94	58	12	68	232	400	12		6
1910	92	49	14	73	228	420	nil		6
1911	70	42	16	73	201	420	nil		6
1912	61	48	12	89	210	490	12	6	7¼
1913	71	39	11	91	212	480	30	7½	9
1914	86	41	7	101	235	570	nil	9	

ᵃ Annual average.   ᵇ 1868 only.

SOURCES: *Chemist and Druggist*; Parliamentary Papers; Gibbs; Donald, op. cit., 214–15; Kelly, op. cit., viii; Annual Iodine Reports, Nitrate Corporation of Chile, London.

and free themselves from the bondage of the combination. Its limited success required no retaliation. 'It would be tantamount', explained Leisler Boch, 'to shooting with heavy artillery at sparrows.'[1]

The most important new producer was Japan, whose extensive coastline provided abundant seaweed and whose rapid economic development conferred strong competitive advantages. Substantial

[1] Gibbs 11471/49, Rottenburg to Sillem, 6 Apr. 1895; see also *C.D.*, 5 Jan. 1895, 17; 19 Jan. 1895, 88; and 7 Aug. 1897, 244.

iodine manufacture after 1892 was a small part of the general development of import substitution in Japan's chemical industry.[1] The raw iodine worked by subsistence communities around Hokkaido was of good quality. Instead of collecting drift seaweed, kelpers dived for high iodine-bearing specimens which were carefully prepared before delivery to processors.[2] By 1894 production above domestic needs at $4\frac{1}{2}d$. an ounce alarmed Leisler Boch. They appointed agents to prevent exports, who were instructed to offer an iodine monopoly to Japan's leading wholesale druggists at below domestic costs in the hope of ousting local makers and then raising prices. Provided the druggists bought chemicals exclusively from the combination and did not re-export, the combination would in return boycott their smaller rivals.[3]

Attempts at permanent market control failed. Japanese iodine production rose 250 per cent between 1898 and 1902. In 1897 an American export house won over four leading native firms, and Japanese iodine found buyers abroad like Unilevers and Parke-Davis. Imports which undermined Japanese home sales merely promoted cheap native exports, often under pirated brand-names. Seasonal production forced the combination to face a heavy influx within relatively short periods. To buy up local kelp, thus preventing manufacture, was an expensive solution which encouraged local divers. Although any opposition to the combination was costly, in the short run strong Japanese chemists were able to withstand low prices. Indeed, native firms retaliated, and demanded protection against cheap foreign imports.[4] Gibbs approached the Imperial Government, whose influence was central to Japan's economic development, offering the Far East market and a small European quota. John Gibbs admitted in October 1904 that negotiations 'are not going very well . . .'.[5] In 1907 the possibility of

---

[1] *C.D.*, 7 Apr. 1900, 578, 13 Dec. 1902, 977, and 2 May 1914, 700; G. C. Allen, *A Short Economic History of Japan* (London, 1962), pp. 33–4 and 87; W. W. Lockwood, *The Economic Development of Japan: Growth and Structural Change, 1868–1938* (Princeton, 1954), pp. 3–33.

[2] 'Trade in Iodine', pp. 17–18; H.M.S.O., op. cit., p. 19; *C.D.*, 27 Mar. 1897, 516, and 14 July 1900, 71.

[3] Gibbs 11471/46–50, Rottenburg to Sillem, 20 June and 29 Aug. 1894, 5 Mar. and 24 July 1895.

[4] *C.D.*, 19 June 1897, 979, 24 Oct. 1897, 609, 28 Nov. 1897, 799, and 22 Oct. 1899, 684; Gibbs 11118, pp. 160–2.

[5] Gibbs 11040, John Gibbs to Alban Gibbs, 6 Oct. 1904; see also *C.D.*, 16 Mar. 1907, 427, and 11 Jan. 1908, 66; Allen, op. cit., pp. 31–5.

government subsidies encouraged Japanese manufacturers to combine under the Japanese Chemical Industry Company, the cost-cutting innovations of which promised to quadruple output within a year.

Although the combination negotiated no formal agreement before 1914, the threat posed by Japan probably receded somewhat after 1905. Local producers became disenchanted with heavy losses in regular or prolonged competition. The onset of the Russo-Japanese War, an increased domestic demand for iodine, and the reallocation of manpower, put a temporary end to Japan's exports. Indeed, an iodine shortage raised prices to 10½d. A succession of poor kelp harvests from 1908, aggravated by prolonged rainfall, seriously damaged production.[1] Moreover, the threat of Japanese competition may have strengthened links between South American and European producers, and thereby the authority of the combination. Certainly, examples of recalcitrant outsiders in the two older producing areas diminished markedly after 1900.

Minor manufacturing centres developed also in Russia, Java, Korea, and Jersey (Channel Islands), this last closely linked to the Boots chain of chemist shops. In Russia, iodine was associated with petroleum discoveries around Baku where an experimental plant was erected. Kelp supplies were also treated near Vladivostock. In Java, iodine was found in mineral springs but it was not exported in quantity before 1914.[2]

Competition was not the only influence on the international combination. Pharmaceutical makers and wholesale chemists were a powerful market force. Leisler Boch recognized the work of buyers in encouraging consumption. 'It would be a most shortsighted policy', Gibbs were informed, 'were the combination to cut out said middlemen and only do business direct with the consumer for the sake of saving 1 or 2 per cent.'[3] In 1888 the largest European pharmaceutical firms organized a complementary association to negotiate with producers and prevent internal friction.

---

[1] *C.D.*, 5 Mar. 1904, 387, 17 Feb. 1906, 263, 21 Aug. 1909, 352, and 4 Dec. 1909, 872; 'Trade in Iodine', op. cit., p. 18; H.M.S.O., op. cit., p. 19.

[2] *C.D.*, 24 Mar. 1900, 496, 16 May 1908, 736, 12 Mar. 1910, 116, 7 Jan. 1911, 5, 16 Sept. 1911, 453, 6 July 1912, 30, and 26 Sept. 1914, 460; H. A. N. Bluett, *Reports on the Economic Situation of the Netherlands East Indies* (D.O.T.), June 1923, p. 78, and July 1924, p. 37; Gibbs 11118, pp. 210–12.

[3] Gibbs 11471/30, Leisler Boch to Gibbs, 12 June 1888.

Operating a tacit understanding rather than a formal contract, the Preparations Combination agreed to confine purchases to Leisler Boch, who in turn would not sell to outsiders. This compact, if not in the interests of the retailer or the public, 'proved most beneficial' to both associations, protecting the pharmaceutical makers and the producers.[1] The restriction of outlets was no hardship, because sales of iodine preparations were relatively stationary. The iodine sold to outside pharmaceutical firms merely diminished trade with the older companies. In the United States, where no buyers' combination existed, and in France, where the chemists' co-operative was formed, dealings were less easily controlled.

Public and private pressure also restricted the iodine combination. Iodine's links with nitrate were enough to incur scrutiny. Gibbs reported 'the denunciation of the iodine combination as almost an equally nefarious robber of the Chilean Government with the nitrate combination'.[2] Artificial restrictions on output curtailed employment opportunities, discouraged industrial use of iodine, and damaged national revenue, since iodine export duties exceeded £50,000 per annum.[3] The *Chemist and Druggist* claimed in 1887 that Chile could make annually six times the world's needs.[4] Already two years' consumption lay in stock. Then local consumers, the National Chemical Society of Santiago and Weidmayer in Valparaíso, resented buying iodine on the combination's terms. Indeed, the combination actively discouraged direct Chilean demand which might imperil control over supplies and initiate low-price competition with established European markets, its best customers.[5] The situation also alarmed the United States which imported 97 per cent of its iodine from Chile. In 1914 supplies became so scarce that Austria reduced tinctures to half strength, Holland imported from Java, and Mr. Boland, Member for Kerry, asked in the House of Commons whether Irish kelp could be treated.[6]

---

[1] Ibid. 11471/44 and 56, Leisler Boch to Gibbs, 24 Jan. 1894, Watjen Toel to Leisler Boch, 2 Dec. 1896; *C.D.*, 23 Jan. 1909, 126; 'Trade in Iodine', op. cit., p. 10.

[2] Gibbs 11471/42, London to Valparaíso, 27 Oct. 1893.

[3] *C.D.*, 21 May 1887, 632, and 10 Aug. 1889, 216; H.M.S.O., op. cit., p. 11; 'Trade in Iodine', pp. 9–10.   [4] *C.D.*, 18 June 1887, 749–50.

[5] Gibbs 11471/56–7, Leisler Boch to Gibbs, 27 Jan. and 25 Feb. 1897, Iquique to London, 2 May 1897.

[6] *C.D.*, 3 Oct. 1914, 471, and 4 Nov. 1914, 644; *Hansard* (Commons), 5th ser., lxvi. 782 (14 Sept. 1914).

The iodine combination adopted a wide variety of tactics to offset competition and enforce control. The encouragement of consumption in wider markets was an obvious answer to over-production. Yet before 1914 the use of iodine beyond its pharmaceutical properties, for which it was difficult to stimulate demand, remained marginal. At first iodine was used in photography and enjoyed brief popularity as a dye, particularly in France until tastes changed and improved fast colours were discovered. Iodine producers advertised, exhibited preparations, offered prizes for new uses, sponsored research, and reduced prices for manufacturers outside the pharmaceutical trade. Gibbs preferred to sell at the highest possible prices, but recognized that a temporary sacrifice could prove advantageous. Subsequently iodine found limited use for refining metals and processing rubber.[1] Consumption did increase, from 6,400 cwt to 9,400 cwt per annum between 1887 and 1908, but evidence suggests that the increase was due to population growth and to the number of chemist shops, rather than to successful promotion. Vigorous salesmanship and advertising alone would not influence sales, and propaganda to create demand was, therefore, rather half-hearted. Manufacturers bought little iodine even at the lowest rates. Doctors rarely took account of prices before prescribing. In 1886 and 1887 pharmaceutical uses accounted for 80 per cent of sales. 'The consumption of iodine', Rottenburg explained, 'for any other purpose than drugs is mere moonshine.'[2] Moreover, increased demand merely encouraged further production without, therefore, permanently improving prices.

The combination also employed an extensive intelligence network to locate and discourage outsiders. The threat of unauthorized shipments to London required 'a reliable detective on that beat'. Gibbs's Liverpool House promised to search customs entries and watch landings for suspected iodine. Again in 1897 the Iquique Directory, fearing that outsiders were 'pulling the strings', made a check on the local collection of iodine duty. Such watchfulness made evasion increasingly difficult. Five kegs of iodine were smuggled to Hamburg in blankets; unmarked

---

[1] Gibbs 11471/18–29 and 57, Rottenburg to Sillem, 14 Jan. 1884, 1 Feb. and 9 Sept. 1885, Leisler Boch to Gibbs, 16 Mar. 1897; *C.D.*, 9 June 1888, 758; 'Trade in Iodine', p. 2.
[2] Gibbs 11471/28, Rottenburg to Sillem, 17 Dec. 1887.

consignments mysteriously arrived in London or Paris; sales were anonymously advertised in German newspapers. 'If outsiders have to resort to such means of selling their iodine', Rottenburg explained, 'it is hoped they will soon get tired and join.'[1] But Gibbs had no wish to broadcast the fact that other supplies of iodine were on sale in Europe. Such news would upset buyers and encourage further unauthorized shipments. 'We wish we could prevent that publicity', Gibbs informed the Preparations Association confidentially, when outsiders shipped to Hamburg, 'and thereby allow your business to continue unmolested.'[2] An *ex gratia* payment to a Scottish producer compensated him for his fight against the Acid and Alkali Company in 1897. Again, in 1898 South American producers paid £2,100 to terminate Grace Brothers' contracts on the West Coast.

An arbitrary pricing policy further strengthened the combination. Although changes in prices were relatively infrequent—eight occurred between 1900 and 1913—secret negotiations and sudden price movements deterred speculators and upset merchants. Buyers, anticipating low prices and covering only current needs, were outmanœuvered when without warning a restructured combination raised charges. Conversely, sudden decisions to reduce rates surprised those who had forecasted high prices. Attractive prices to selected industrial firms, leaked by the *Chemist and Druggist*, upset some pharmaceutical companies.[3] But discrimination in favour of the Preparations Combination retained its loyalty and damaged outsiders. Large customers received a 2½ per cent discount for every 250 barrels, since bulk orders saved administrative and carriage costs. Again, contracts with loyal merchants included reduction clauses. If market prices fell below an agreed figure within a fixed period, the lower rate would apply. *In extremis*, producers imposed an interregnum, selling iodine at prices negotiable later when the competition had retired. This measure, used against Grace Brothers in the 1890s and against the Japanese, created uncertainty and gave outsiders no basis on which to work.[4]

[1] Ibid. 11471/29–56, Rottenburg to Sillem, 5 Feb. 1888 and 25 Apr. 1890, Leisler Boch to Gibbs, 14 Jan. 1889 and 29 Jan. 1897, Liverpool to London, 28 Sept. 1894.   [2] Ibid. 11471/52, circular, 10 Dec. 1895.
[3] Ibid. 11471/29, Rottenburg to Sillem, 24 Jan. 1888.
[4] Ibid. 11471/25–52, Rottenburg to Sillem, 22 July 1886 and 19 Feb. 1890, Leisler Boch to Gibbs, 21 Dec. 1895; *C.D.*, 14 Dec. 1895, 865, and 30 Mar. 1912, 63.

Gibbs could be ruthless. In 1880 Smail, a West Coast partner, considered that because of Gildemeisters' independent stand

the price at home should be brought down to a point at which they cannot afford to sell, thus obliging them and the refractory Scotchmen to come to terms . . . the day any iodine is shipped outside the combination the price should be reduced to 1*d*. per ounce, or even lower, and kept at that price until every producer both here and at home agrees to join the combination. Afterwards prices might be raised to a point which would recuperate us and others for the sacrifice made in crushing the competition . . . Half measures will not do . . . the producers must first be taught that competition in the iodine trade means loss and that profit can only be found in the combination.[1]

VIII

Though unimportant in world trade, iodine was an essential item in the international supply of medicine. The combination which controlled production and sales arose from two main causes: a permanent change in the source of supply, and a pronounced tendency towards overproduction which threatened unrestricted competition and low prices. From the 1870s *oficinas* in Tarapacá, aided by relatively cheap transport costs, broke the old European monopoly based on kelp production. Between 1879 and 1913 Chile exported 11,000 tons of iodine valued at £11 million, nearly 70 per cent of world output.[2]

Organization of the iodine trade raised important issues. First, it indicated the range of powers available to a British merchant house in an underdeveloped area during a period ostensibly loyal to Free Trade. Gibbs & Sons developed a commercial framework typical of their interest in local produce trades. The House endeavoured to 'keep the iodine trade in our hands and control it', establishing a strong international bargaining position.[3] Within the major area of iodine production the House collected, shipped, and insured; it negotiated terms in Europe and centralized sales; it fought outsiders and disciplined recalcitrant consignors; it arranged quotas and developed a permanent secretariat in South America and London maintaining a link, at times strained, between

---

[1] Gibbs 11472, Smail to Bohl, 9 Dec. 1880.
[2] Miller and Singewald, op. cit., p. 301.
[3] Gibbs 11472, Read to Miller, 26 Aug. 1873.

separately organized but mutually interested producers. Of course, Gibbs's control depended upon their ability to serve West Coast manufacturers and European customers, delicately balancing production against consumption and improving prices and profits. Although prepared to fight, the House generally preferred compromise. It resisted the temptation to eliminate competitors. It opposed conditions which might attract adverse comment or attention. It preferred to work through, rather than to overthrow, the traditional marketing organization. Gibbs favoured the elimination of risk, not the short-term maximization of profit. In formulating the iodine combination, the House perfected the businessman's art of subtlety and discretion.

Of course, Gibbs drew substantial double profits from iodine as producers and consignees. Although it is difficult to measure the cost of production in Chile—iodine works were not separately charged, the nitrate industry preserved secrecy about its cost structure, and the experience of individual *oficinas* varied markedly—estimates agree on a production cost of 1*d.* an ounce, just under £150 per ton. The Chilean Government levied export duties of £95 per ton and carriage charges averaged some £70, so that the gross cost was about £300 or 2*d.* per ounce.[1] From 1884 the market price moved between 5*d.* (£750 per ton) and 10*d.* (£1,500). In 1885 Gibbs informed their West Coast office that 'a total gain in iodine of $177,000 is very handsome indeed'. In 1888 Valparaíso revalued stocks from 2*d.* to 4½*d.* per ounce, since 'the course of the iodine business during the current year has fully justified the alteration'. Similarly, the Rosario Company earned £25,000 net from iodine in 1889, a year when for three months the lowest prices prevailed.[2] Gibbs also enjoyed a steady growth in commissions, both absolutely as the volume and direction of trade expanded and relatively as West Coast quotas increased. The consigning business, which needed little outlay, was 'a nice thing whilst it lasts'.[3]

The organization of the iodine trade was also a striking example of combination before 1914. First established in 1878, it became a permanent feature of the pharmaceutical trade from 1884 and

[1] Ibid. 11472, Smail to Read, 29 June 1879; Donald, op. cit., pp. 208–9; 'Trade in Iodine', p. 6; H.M.S.O., op. cit., p. 9.

[2] Gibbs 11042, London to Valparaíso, 30 Dec. 1885 and 3 Nov. 1888; *The Times*, 28 Oct. 1890, 11d.

[3] Gibbs 11040, Herbert Gibbs to Vicary Gibbs, 29 Jan. 1894.

remained under British control despite the rise of the German and American chemical industries. The controlling association did not operate unchecked. Emergencies required swift action to preserve a delicate organizational framework. The combination faced dissatisfied members, outside competition, new sources of supply, seasonal variations, buyers' associations, and government hostility. A long period of disturbed conditions and wildly fluctuating prices from the onset of South American exports yielded to a more settled state only after the second international combination in 1884.

The iodine combination found its defenders. Experience taught, they claimed, that however low the prices, consumption was not materially raised. Only the potential, not the commercial, use of iodine had been demonstrated.[1] The combination created stable prices, uniform contracts, and regular negotiating machinery between producers and buyers. It averted the evils of undiluted self-interest and vicious competition. Sensitive to possible scandal and to its commercial future, the combination did not reject conciliation. Bonds between members were at times informal within a loosely organized structure. The very fact that producing iodine from kelp required little skill, capital, or equipment prevented the introduction of totally unrealistic terms. Moreover, the combination and its central marketing agency could prevent unnecessary duplication of plant and activity, and therefore promote efficiency. They could negotiate with buyers, distribute output equitably, study markets, and centralize research. Bulk shipments and joint advertising saved transportation and administrative costs. If sales were not increased, they were achieved more cheaply.

The lasting impression of the combination, however, is that subtly and discreetly it committed most of the business sins elsewhere denounced as against the public interest. The *Chemist and Druggist* deplored a combination 'based on principles so essentially vicious from an economical point of view'.[2] It was dictatorial, oppressive, and arbitrary in search of international control. It moved prices without warning, established fighting funds and tying arrangements, and undersold small outsiders at ruinously

[1] C. A. McQueen, 'The Cost of Chilean Iodine Production', *Weekly Commercial Reports* (Washington), Apr. 1922, p. 112.
[2] *C.D.*, 18 June 1887, 749–50.

low prices which it later raised to recoup losses. It discriminated in favour of bulk orders, and resisted the claims of emerging South American chemists. Close links with buyers ensured permanent control. The *Chemist and Druggist* claimed that in 1891 only 1 per cent of shipments to London were unauthorized.[1] To acquit the combination of charges that, far from well-intentioned, it deliberately limited output and raised prices to a level bearing little relation to costs, is not easy. Profit for weaker members represented an enormous margin for the strong.

The iodine combination was a remarkable example of organization and consistency. It employed a central selling agency on the German kartel pattern—a sophisticated development still unusual in Britain before 1914. Its continuity owed much to the fact that it aroused few fears. In Chile the nitrate combinations always attracted closer attention. The importance of the iodine combination, however, lies in demonstrating the power of businessmen and in describing their tactics. The remarks of the Committee on Trusts in 1918 are particularly to the point. Although business consolidations were slower to develop in Britain than elsewhere, and less formidable in structure than their American and German counterparts

it should not be readily assumed that British industries lagged far behind those of other countries in effectiveness of internal organization . . . British trade organizations made little parade of their existence or achievements, but there are few corners of British industry in which some kind of trade association is not to be found and some of them can show a thoroughness not easily surpassed.[2]

[1] *C.D.*, 5 Nov. 1892, 679.
[2] *Committee on Trusts*, P.P., 1918, xviii, 807.

CHAPTER VIII

The River Plate Beef Trade

J. COLIN CROSSLEY AND ROBERT GREENHILL*

I

BY 1930 Britain, the principal beef-importing nation, was supplied by many parts of the world with the various forms of beef in demand: fresh, chilled, frozen, and corned beef, and beef extract. The spatial pattern of production of these respective forms of beef accords very closely, both at world level and within Argentina and adjacent nations, with what might be predicted from a location model of beef-product manufacturing based on the assumption of perfect competition. The general course of events leading to that pattern was also predictable. Yet in detail there is abundant evidence, especially in the refrigerated beef sector, that firms individually or collectively sought to manipulate the trade to their own advantage, that others voiced fears of the possible consequences, and that degrees of monopoly control were at times achieved. Governments, too, maintained a watching brief and intervened to protect national interests. In this chapter the theoretical interpretation is presented first and is followed by empirical examination of the forces operating both in the refrigerated beef trade in general, and in particular in the corned beef and extract trades in so far as they influenced the leading producer, Liebig's Extract of Meat Company.

II

In a world of perfect competition and rational economic man, the beef-product manufacturer (including the fresh-beef slaughterer) is faced by competition of several kinds: competition between beef-cattle farming and other types of agriculture for the use of the land, competition between manufacturers of the same and other

* The first author, a geographer, is responsible for most of Sections I and II and for Section IV; the second author is responsible for most of Section III.

Map II. Beef production and processing zones in the River Plate area

beef products for the available cattle, and competition between producers of all forms of meat for the meat market. The location of competing types of agriculture has long been the subject of theoretical exploration;[1] the location of competing types of beef-product manufacture has hitherto been neglected by theorists of economic location.[2]

The price which the cattle purchaser can afford is restricted by the initial weight and grade of the animal offered, by the costs of transferring it to the slaughter-house, of processing it and of transferring the end-products to the market, and by the price which those products command at the market. The range of beef products includes, besides those mentioned, *tasajo* or jerked beef.[3] It is assumed initially that all beef products are destined for a single market. A peculiar feature of the meat trade is that the fresh beef derived from a single head of cattle, and constituting the raw material from which the other products are prepared, commands the highest price, whilst the chilled, frozen, corned beef, *tasajo*, or extract command successively lower prices at the market. In the cases of chilled and frozen beef, this arises because refrigerated beef carcasses are considered inferior to fresh beef carcasses; in the remaining cases the products have undergone a process of concentration and, whilst commanding quite high unit prices, in fact yield lower returns per animal (Table VIII.1). Hence no other beef-product manufacturers can outbid the fresh-beef slaughter-house for cattle unless constraints on the latter outlet exist. Similarly, manufacturers of less rewarding beef products cannot secure cattle in the face of competition from manufacturers of more rewarding beef products without corresponding constraints on the latter. The constraints lie in the relative perishability and relative transport costs incurred. Thus fresh beef, with the short-

---

[1] P. Hall, ed., *Von Thünen's Isolated State* (Oxford, 1966); E. S. Dunn, *The Location of Agricultural Production* (Gainesville, 1954), and 'Equilibrium of Land Use Patterns', *Southern Economic Journal* (1955).

[2] The following paragraphs summarize the first chapter of J. Colin Crossley, 'The Location and Development of the Agricultural and Industrial Enterprises of Liebig's Extract of Meat Company in the River Plate Countries 1865–1932' (unpublished Ph.D. thesis, Leicester University, 1974), and the article, 'The Location of Beef Processing', *Annals*, Association of American Geographers (1976).

[3] *Tasajo* consists of strips of salted and dried beef. Jerked beef is an inaccurate translation, being derived from *charque*, which was unsalted. Unlike the other beef products, *tasajo* found its principal markets in Brazil and Cuba rather than Britain.

est life, cannot undergo a journey to market of more than a few days. With increasing distance from the market, slaughter for fresh beef, therefore, gives place to the preparation of chilled beef.[1] The latter, deteriorating more slowly and having a life of about forty days, in turn cannot with safety be prepared at locations more than three-and-a-half weeks' journey from the market

TABLE VIII.1

Yields of Beef Products

End product	Wholesale price of end product		End products yielded per ton of cattle:		
	per lb	per ton	Weight	Wholesale price	Transport cost per 100 miles
	shillings and pence	£ p.	% of 1 ton	£ p.	£ p.
English fresh beef sides	10d.	93 33	61·00	56 93	0 61
Argentine chilled quarters	5½d.	51 33	61·00	31 31	0 61
Argentine frozen quarters	4½d.	42 00	61·00	25 62	0 61
Corned beef	9d.	84 00	25·33	21 15	0 32½
Beef extract	4s. 0d.	448 00	1·52	6 81	0 01½
	(1)	(2)	(3)	(4)	(5)

SOURCES: Col. 1. Fresh, chilled and frozen beef: approximate values at Smithfield, Jan.–June 1924, quoted in *Meat Trades Journal*, 1924. Corned beef and extract: Liebig records.
    Col. 2. Calculated from Col. 1.
    Col. 3. See pp. 287–8.
    Col. 4. Calculated from Cols. 2 and 3.
    Col. 5. Arbitrarily assumed freight rate of £1 per ton per 100 miles.
    NOTE: No comparable figures are available for *tasajo*.

and gives place to frozen beef which is effectively imperishable. Frozen beef is transported in carcass form[2] (as are chilled and fresh beef), which represents about 61 per cent of the live weight of the animal. By contrast, the weight (including the can) of corned beef derived from an animal is only 32½ per cent of the live weight. Additionally, refrigerated beef requires specialized transport which is three times more costly per ton than the transport needed by corned beef, *tasajo*, and extract. Therefore, it costs almost six times as much to transport the beef from an animal in frozen form as in cans. A point will, therefore, occur beyond which

[1] The recent development of air-freighting fresh beef may ultimately lead to the destruction of all other kinds of beef-product manufacturing.
[2] In the last decade, with the exclusion of refrigerated beef on the bone from the British market, boneless cuts that are more economical to transport have been substituted.

it is more profitable to prepare corned beef than frozen beef. In
turn, for a similar reason, *tasajo*, which is unburdened by the
weight of a can and represents only 25 per cent of the live weight,
will replace corned beef with increasing distance from the market.
Finally extract, weighing only $1\frac{1}{2}$ per cent of the live animal, will
replace *tasajo*.

Thus a series of concentric zones about the market may be
theorized, each characterized by the preparation of a distinct beef
product as the primary outlet for the cattle.[1] The manufacturer
of a given beef product who locates in the zone of a superior beef
product will normally be outbid for cattle by zonal firms. His
survival will, therefore, depend upon either the failure of zonal
rivals to enter the area or their agreement to combine with him to
restrict cattle prices to his level. In either case the situation will be
precarious and inviting to a more aggressive zonal firm. In contrast, the prospects for a manufacturer of a given beef product
locating in a remoter zone will be naturally limited by perishability
or high transport costs.

At this point the initial assumption of a single market may
temporarily be relaxed in order to allow consideration of the
impact of a second market, located, let us suppose, within the
chilled beef zone of the first market. In that zone the chilled beef
manufacturer can afford for cattle a price which is determined by
the price realized by chilled beef in the first market, less costs of
production and transfer. The fresh-beef slaughterer catering for the
second market need, therefore, only marginally outbid the chilled
beef manufacturer in order to secure as many cattle as local demand
warrants. Survival of the chilled beef industry, therefore, depends
entirely on cattle supply continuing to exceed local demand.

The second stage of the theoretical analysis concerns the location of individual firms within any beef-product zone. Factors
already discussed determine the zonal price which may be offered
for cattle at the factory gate; farm-gate prices will be reduced to
take account of the cost of transferring cattle to the factory. The
principal component of this cost is not, as might be supposed, the
charge for droving or hauling the cattle, but the value of the meat
and fat lost through shrinkage in transit. Shrinkage costs increase
with the quality of the animal and the duration and rigours of the

---

[1] For several reasons, in each zone inferior beef products will additionally be
prepared as by-products of the primary product.

journey. Low total transfer rates will extend the factory's out-reach, high rates will restrict it. Thus if the factories within a zone are evenly dispersed, high rates will allow each to exercise monopoly control over nearby supplies of cattle and hence to offer low prices, whilst low rates will stimulate competition through the overlapping of supply areas and hence lead to higher prices. The replacement of overgrazed and hence costly drove roads by rapid-haul rail networks will have predictable consequences. If, in contrast, factories are clustered together, high rates will induce keen competition and low rates reduce it. Whatever the cause, high farm-gate prices will encourage and low prices discourage improvements to land and cattle.

The relative costs of transferring live cattle and the beef products derived from them will also affect the location of factories within a zone. Where the latter cost is—or is perceived to be—the higher, factories will locate along the market edge of the zone; where the former cost is the higher, dispersal throughout the zone will be preferred.

The final stage of the theoretical analysis introduces a dynamic element. Beef extract and *tasajo* require only the poorest *criollo* (native) cattle, whilst chilled beef requires steers of predominantly European breed. How therefore can an area initially stocked with *criollos* become a producer of chilled beef? The answer lies in the requirements of other beef products and in the purchasing policies of the different beef-product industries. Corned beef requires cattle of roughly 25 per cent improved blood and frozen beef 50 per cent. The manufacturers of each beef product, whilst requiring cattle of only a given grade, will find it more profitable to pay somewhat higher prices for somewhat better cattle, thus stimulating farmers to improve their herds. In time, sufficient cattle of a higher grade will exist to permit the entry of the manufacturer of the next superior beef product. If other locational factors favour the entry of that industry, it will outbid the existing manufacturers for those cattle and displace the inferior beef product to a remoter location—that is, existing factories will be obliged to convert to the new beef product or to relocate. In time this process will lead to the concentric zonation of beef-product manufacturing already hypothesized.

It remains to be seen how far this location model of beef-product manufacturing (based upon the assumption of perfect competition) accords with actual historical developments. During the colonial period, River Plate *criollo* cattle were reared almost solely for their hides and tallow. At the start of the nineteenth century, *saladeros* (beef-salting works) were established on both sides of the Plate Estuary to prepare *tasajo* for export to Brazil and Cuba,[1] but the meat of remoter herds continued to be wasted. Further *saladeros* were erected along the lower reaches of the River Uruguay, navigable by ocean-going vessels. By 1862 the herds and *tasajo* industry of Uruguay had been overexpanded and *tasajo* and cattle prices fell.[2] Increased slaughters in Argentina and Rio Grande do Sul[3] doubtless contributed to this excess of supply.

Conditions now favoured G. C. Giebert's attempts to prepare beef extract according to the formula of Baron Justus von Liebig, and the Fray Bentos *saladero* was converted to an extract factory. Proving commercially successful, Giebert's enterprise was rapidly expanded through the flotation in London in 1865 of Liebig's Extract of Meat Company which provided the capital required. Extract production and the company's dividends advanced steadily until 1891 when they attained 1·5 million pounds and $23\frac{1}{3}$ per cent respectively.[4] Fray Bentos benefited from the stagnation of the *tasajo* trade[5] and also from its locational advantage with respect to local supplies of cattle.[6]

1893 saw a sharp rise in *tasajo* demand and in 1893–5 total River Plate and Rio Grande *saladero* slaughters exceeded 1·7 million head,[7] probably for the only time in history. Most of the

[1] Alfredo J. Montoya, *História de los Saladeros Argentinos* (Buenos Aires, 1956), parts I–III.

[2] Uruguayan *saladero* slaughter rose from 168,000 head in 1858 to 505,000 in 1862; meanwhile *tasajo* prices fell from U.G. $7 to U.G. $2¼ (Uruguayan gold pesos) per quintal and cattle prices from U.G. $20 to U.G. $10: E. Acevedo, *História Económica y Financiera de la República Oriental del Uruguay* (Montevideo, 1903), ii. 20; A. Barrios Pintos, *De las Vaquerías al Alambrado* (Montevideo, 1967), p. 140.

[3] By 104,000 and 172,000 head respectively: Acevedo, op. cit., p. 20.

[4] Liebig's Extract of Meat Co. Ltd.: *Board Minutes* and *Annual Reports to Shareholders*, various dates. Many of the *estancia* and factory reports cited below are still in Argentina, either at the head office, Paseo Colón 221, Buenos Aires, or out at the Colón factory.

[5] The Uruguayan *saladero* slaughter was 495,000 in 1890: A. Ruano Fournier, *Estudio Económico de la Producción de las Carnes del Río de la Plata* (Montevideo, 1936), p. 364, and Liebig's *Slaughter Statistics*.

[6] The nearest *saladeros* to the north and south lay 100 and 300 km away, at Paysandú and Montevideo respectively.

[7] Ruano Fournier, op. cit., p. 364.

increase of 132,000 in 1893 over 1892 was concentrated in western Uruguay, whose *saladeros* now enjoyed (unlike Fray Bentos) access by railways built in 1890–1. Under conditions of perfect competition, where 'the price of *tasajo* practically rules the cattle market',[1] Fray Bentos's locational disadvantage was recognized, production of extract was reduced, and in 1894 Liebigs secured a ten-year lease on the Kemmerich Company's extract factory which lay at Santa Elena in north-western Entre Rios, more than 200 kilometres beyond the nearest *saladero*.[2]

Meanwhile, in the mid-nineteenth century, experimentation with other forms of meat preservation had proceeded. Meat-canning was developed in the 1840s to 1860s in Australia, the United States, and elsewhere, but commercial success was first achieved with the American product in the 1880s.[3] The River Plate, despite endeavours by Liebigs and other companies, had still not succeeded in producing a marketable canned beef even by 1900.[4] Through Eastman's efforts, the United States was also the first country to ship chilled beef with commercial success to Britain, in 1875. Thanks to the relatively short journey the trade developed rapidly.[5] The feasibility of shipping chilled and frozen meat from the more distant Plate was demonstrated in 1876 and 1877 respectively,[6] but a successful trade in refrigerated beef took more than twenty years to develop. Meanwhile, Australasia had developed exports to Britain of frozen beef, the spatially logical complement to United States chilled beef (Table VIII.2).

Argentina's first four *frigoríficos* began production in 1883–6, at San Nicolás, Campana, and Zárate on the Buenos Aires shore of the Lower Paraná, and at Barrancas, just outside the capital. From the start all concentrated on frozen mutton, and the attempt by cattlemen in 1884 to establish a beef-freezing plant failed.[7] In the absence of United States shipments of mutton, Argentine *frigoríficos* had only to compete with New Zealand packers. In

[1] Liebigs, *Board Minutes*, 11 Oct. 1893.
[2] Ibid., 31 Oct. and 15 Nov. 1894.
[3] S. G. Hanson, *Argentine Meat and the British Market* (Stanford, 1937), pp. 20–1, 34–5.
[4] Uruguayan production of canned meat fell from an annual average of 3,400 tons in 1881–5 to 140 tons in 1896–1900: Acevedo, op. cit. (1903), ii. 23.
[5] Hanson, op. cit. (1937), p. 42.
[6] H. C. E. Giberti, *História Económica de la Ganadería Argentina* (Buenos Aires, 2nd ed., 1961), p. 169.
[7] Hanson, op. cit. (1937), pp. 53–5.

TABLE VIII.2

British Imports of Refrigerated Beef, 1881–1925

(Quinquennial totals, ooo cwts rounded to nearest ooo)

	United States	Argentina	Uruguay	Brazil	Australia	New Zealand	Total[8]
1881–5	2,844	2[2]			13[6]	9[7]	3,050
1886–90	5,158	29			57	222	5,541
1891–5	8,614	86			1,098	203	10,104
1896–1900	12,242	805			2,611	640	16,702
1901–5	12,792	c 1,230 / f 5,873	40[3]		486	945	21,764
1906–10	7,668	7,260 / 10,906	506		1,560	1,966	29,900
1911–15 (f)	1,270	11,775	f 1,306	18[4]	5,735	1,973	f 21,496
1911–15 (c)		19,192		c 481			c 20,486
1916–20 (f)	6,430	15,113	1,368	372	3,831	3,279	31,592
1916–20 (c)		3,557		306			4,667
1921–5 (f)	378[1]	13,641	2,550	448[5]	5,822	3,267	26,779
1921–5 (c)		29,628		1,048			33,232

f Frozen beef shipments only.   c Chilled beef shipments only.

[1] 1921 and 1922 only.   [2] 1884 and 1885 only.   [3] 1905 only.   [4] 1915 only.   [5] 1920 only.   [6] 1883–5 only.   [7] 1885 only.   [8] From all sources.

SOURCES: *Annual Statements of the Trade of the United Kingdom with Foreign Countries and British Possessions* (Parliamentary Papers); W. Weddel & Co., (Annual) *Review of the Frozen Meat Trade*.

contrast, by virtue of inferior breeding, poor fattening, and deterioration on the long journey, Argentine beef could not compete with the United States product. In consequence the River Plate refrigerated beef trade had to await the results of herd improvement which was stimulated by other forces.

By 1895 half of Buenos Aires cattle and 10 per cent of Entre Rios cattle were of *mestizo* (half *criollo*/half European) breed or better; the better animals were especially to be found beside the Plate and Lower Uruguay, the areas of concentration of the *saladero* industry. Such a distribution bore out the truth of Gibson's observation in 1908 that for thirty years the Argentine *saladeros* had 'strongly supported cattle breeding by paying a good price for bullocks'.[1] But there was a limit to the price which *saladeros* could afford, and after 1892 Buenos Aires' *saladero* slaughter declined with the growth of fresh beef markets.[2] The domestic metropolitan market, though not a discerning one, was growing rapidly.[3] Of greater significance was the export of live cattle, especially to Britain, which in 1898 received almost 100,000 head.[4] Compared with the *saladeros'* £2·50–3, cattle exporters paid £7–8 per head and preferred heavy, tame beasts. 'The great difference is therefore a powerful incentive to the breeder', wrote Gibson in 1896.[5]

In 1900 British ports were closed to live animals to prevent the importation of foot and mouth disease. The now improved cattle of Buenos Aires province were deflected to the *frigoríficos*, which rapidly seized the opportunity for preparing an acceptable frozen beef. Exports rose from 28,000 carcasses in 1899 to 303,000 in 1904.[6] More distant Australia was eclipsed as a supplier of frozen beef (see Table VIII.2). By 1907 frozen beef represented 51 per cent of all Argentina's meat exports, compared with 1 per cent in

---

[1] H. Gibson, in *Argentina: Censo Agropecuario, 1908* (Buenos Aires), iii. 91. Uruguayan *saladeros* behaved similarly: V. Sampognard, *L'Uruguay* (Paris, 1910), p. 221. More recent writers have wrongly regarded the *saladeros* as a retarding influence on cattle improvement: Ruano Fournier, op. cit., pp. 150–1 and S. G. Hanson, *Utopia in Uruguay* (New York, 1938), p. 216.

[2] From 443,000 in 1892 to nil in 1904: Ruano Fournier, op. cit., p. 364.

[3] In 1907 it consumed 670,000 cattle: R. Pillado, in *Argentina: Censo Agropecuario 1908*, iii. 382.

[4] Montoya, op. cit., p. 97. A history of the Argentine livestock trade is fully documented in P.R.O. F.O. 6/473 and 495.

[5] *S.A.J.*, 1896, i. 44.

[6] Ruano Fournier, op. cit., pp. 374–5. See also Tables VIII.2 and VIII.3.

1897, as Table VIII.3 shows. This speedy response was facilitated in Argentina by the availability of huge areas of natural pasture suitable for fattening freezing-grade cattle and accessible by the dense network of railway lines which radiated westwards from Buenos Aires and the ports along the Lower Paraná.[1] It was also stimulated by the decline in United States chilled beef exports to

TABLE VIII.3

Relative Values of the Different Argentine Livestock Exports, 1887, 1897, and 1907

	1887 %	1897 %	1907 %
Tasajo	48	22	4
Live cattle	28	43	7
Live sheep	1	13	1
Meat extract	2	2	7
Meat flour	<1	<1	6
Frozen mutton	19	17	20
Frozen beef	<1	1	51
Preserved and other meats	1	2	3
Total value (Million gold pesos)	5	12	27

SOURCES: Crossley, 'The River Plate Countries' in Blakemore and Smith, *Latin America: Geographical Perspectives*, p. 427; data derived from Pillado, op. cit., p. 361.

Britain as the domestic market absorbed an increasing proportion of available cattle (see Table VIII.2).

The same decline led American chilled beef exporting firms to seek new sources of supply in Argentina in 1907. Significantly they chose to buy out the *frigoríficos* with a tidewater location at La Plata and Buenos Aires (and later, in 1911, at Montevideo), eschewing those plants along the Lower Paraná and the shallow Riachuelo at Buenos Aires whence journeys to Europe took several days longer. Spatial as well as entrepreneurial factors may, therefore, be seen as explaining the relative importance of chilled and

[1] For a general description of these developments, see J. C. Crossley, 'The River Plate Countries', in H. Blakemore and C. T. Smith, eds., *Latin America: Geographical Perspectives* (London, 1971), pp. 409–30.

frozen beef in the shipments from different *frigoríficos* (see Table VIII.4). With the arrival of the American firms, chilled beef exports increased and by 1910 had surpassed frozen beef. Their expansion was paralleled by the development of the cultivated

TABLE VIII.4

Argentine Mutton and Beef Shipments per Leading Frigoríficos
1885–1913

1. Mutton (Quinquennial totals, 000 carcasses rounded to nearest 000)

	1885–9	1890–4	1895–9	1900–4	1905–9	1910–13*
Sansinena	794	2,158	4,263	5,495	4,444	2,841
R.P.F.M.	1,392	2,086	3,460	4,713	2,549	1,378
Terrason	929	503	16[1]			
Nelsons		1,354	3,255	4,697	3,316	1,220
La Blanca (later Morris)				637[2]	731	1,167
La Plata (later Swifts)				129[3]	2,530	3,576
Smithfield & Argentine					115	139
Frigorífico Argentina					1,268	704
Total shipments[4]	3,115	6,040	11,198	15,670	14,946	12,433

2. Beef (Quinquennial totals, 000 quarters rounded to nearest 000)

	1885–9	1890–4	1895–9	1900–4	1905–9	1910–13*	
						f	c
Sansinena	15	41	158	1,094	1,727	1,080	597
R.P.F.M.	4	8	57	1,287	2,017	1,272	954
Nelsons		29	83	1,093	1,652	985	670
La Blanca (later Morris)				221[2]	1,498	351	1,842
La Plata (later Swifts)				140[3]	2,155	904	3,876
Smithfield & Argentine					810	591	616
Frigorífico Argentina					720	621	489
Total shipments[4]	19	78	298	3,836	10,575	15,529	

* Because of the outbreak of the First World War this last period covers only four years.
f Frozen beef.   c Chilled beef.
[1] Terrason works closed. [2] La Blanca opened 1903. [3] La Plata opened 1904. [4] From all sources.
SOURCES: P.R.O. F.O. 368/785/20837, taken from *La Argentina Agrícola 1912–1913* (Buenos Aires, 1914), pp. 179–80; *Review of the River Plate*.

pastures, mainly of alfalfa, that were necessary for the year-round fattening which the chilled beef trade required. From these superior grazings, located in north-western Buenos Aires and adjacent parts of Córdoba and Santa Fé, cattle could be speedily delivered to the tidewater plants. The Lower Paraná *frigoríficos* in contrast had to a greater extent to depend on the freezing-grade cattle fattened seasonally on the natural pastures of Entre Rios.[1] Access to these was greatly facilitated in 1908 with the opening of the Zárate–Ibicuy rail ferry and associated lines on the further shore.

Meanwhile, in 1903 Liebigs had acquired a second factory for extract at Colón on the Entre Rios bank of the Uruguay. Like Fray Bentos it was flanked by *saladeros* that still remained extremely active. Liebigs' chairman would appear to have envisaged only a temporary gain from this expansion. But late 1908 and 1909 saw a dramatic upturn in the Company's fortunes when the trapezoidal can was introduced in Colón's struggling corned beef department.[2] At the same time, urban beef consumption in the United States had converted that country from an exporter of corned beef into an importer.[3] As a result production of 'Fray Bentos' corned beef quadrupled from 6 million lb in 1908 to 25·9 million lb in 1911.[4] Cattle in eastern Entre Rios were now deflected from the *saladeros* to Colón.[5] Cattle prices rose accordingly and extract now also became unprofitable as a primary product.[6] Besides Fray Bentos and Colón, corned beef also began to be produced at Santa Elena which Bovril Ltd. acquired in 1908.

With *tasajo* ousted from Buenos Aires province in the 1890s, and in retreat in Entre Rios and western Uruguay by 1910, the cattle of remoter regions began to be utilized for *tasajo*. In the first decade of the twentieth century, *saladeros* were opened along the River Paraguay in northern Paraguay[7] and the Mato Grosso, though their scale was limited by a shortage of cattle. Liebigs gave serious consideration to the same areas as possible sites for an extract factory, and only misfortune prevented the construction of a plant on land south of Asunción in 1908.[8] Instead, in view of the absence of plentiful but cheap cattle supplies in remote areas,

[1] For an early appreciation of these spatial patterns, see *S.A.J.*, 1909, ii. 291–2.

[2] Evidenced in a series of cables exchanged between Liebigs' Head Office and River Plate manager, Nov. 1908–May 1909.

[3] *S.A.J.*, 1908, i. 66.

[4] Liebigs, Fray Bentos and Colón Factory Managers' Annual Reports, 1908 and 1911.

[5] *Saladero* slaughter declined from 226,000 in 1908 to 142,000 in 1911, whilst Colón's slaughter increased from 114,000 to 188,000: *S.A.J.*, 1909, ii. 201; E. Acevedo, *Anales Históricos del Uruguay* (Montevideo, 1934), v. 594; Liebig's Slaughter Statistics.

[6] Liebigs, Fray Bentos Factory Department, *Annual Report*, 1912.

[7] Consular Reports (Paraguay), P.P., 1901, lxxiv, 8–9; *S.A.J.*, 1902, ii. 226.

[8] Liebigs, Fray Bentos, Cattle and Estancia Department, *Annual Report*, 1908.

long-term programmes for developing their own herds were embarked upon in Paraguay, German South West Africa, and Rhodesia.

The impact on beef-product manufacturing of the First World War, though abnormal in character, gave rise to wholly predictable spatial consequences. Frozen beef, less vulnerable to shipping delays and more economical in shipping space than chilled, replaced the latter: Argentine chilled beef exports fell from 748,000 carcasses in 1913 to 5,000 in 1918 whereas frozen beef rose from 276,000 to 1,554,000 carcasses.[1] But corned beef was even more preferable than frozen, and Argentine exports of canned meats rose from 13,000 to 191,000 tons.[2] This massive increase came primarily from *frigoríficos'* expanded canning departments and secondly from existing canning factories.[3] Over 70 per cent of Uruguayan *frigoríficos'* output was also of canned meat.[4] Further supplies of corned beef came from converted *saladeros* or newly established factories in Rio Grande do Sul and Paraguay.

In the cattle market, competition focused on inferior *mestizos*, suitable for freezing and canning, and on *criollos* which were adequate for a poorer grade of corned beef. Cattle prices responded accordingly and producers of inferior animals profited handsomely.[5] Unable to compete, the *saladeros* closed down and the domestic fresh-beef consumer had to be content with mutton.

Cessation of hostilities in 1918 left the allies with huge stocks of frozen and corned beef. By 1922 Argentine corned beef exports had fallen to 19 per cent of their 1918 level and frozen beef exports to 27 per cent.[6] In contrast domestic demand recovered rapidly, as did chilled beef exports surpassing their 1913 peak by

---

[1] Hanson, op. cit. (1937), p. 184; *R.R.P.*, 1920, i. 596.

[2] *R.R.P.*, 1918, i. 645; 1920, ii. 899. The higher tonnage probably represented the product of 1·5 to 1·7 million cattle.

[3] Whilst Colón's output quadrupled, its share of Argentine production fell from one-third to one-tenth.

[4] In 1918 only 165,000 of the 611,000 cattle slaughtered were destined for freezing, whereas all the 141,000 carcasses handled in 1913 had been frozen; Ruano Fournier, op. cit., p. 357; Acevedo, op. cit. (1934), v. 596; *R.R.P.*, 1920, i. 596.

[5] The average price realized at Buenos Aires cattle market by fat *criollo* steers rose from $104 (paper) in 1913 to $126 in 1918: Ruano Fournier, op. cit., p. 346.

[6] *R.R.P.*, 1920, i. 596 and ii. 899; *R.R.P.*, 1925, i. 313 and 27 Mar. (volume pagination ceased).

1922.[1] Prices of the lowest grades of cattle plummeted[2] and Paraguayan factories ceased operations. Old *saladeros* reopened and new ones, financed by *estancieros*, were erected on both sides of the Uruguay. In circumstances analogous to those of 1862, Liebigs in 1922 acquired Swifts' Paraguayan factory for extract,[3] and for several years provided almost the sole outlet for cattle.

By the mid-twenties demand for good quality corned beef had recovered and a new trade in frozen beef with continental countries had developed. With this market preferring a leaner beef than the British market, demand focused on the same inferior *mestizo* cattle as required by the canning factories and domestic market. Demand was intense and corned beef production at Colón was hardly profitable.[4] Even when, in 1927, European countries imposed restrictions on frozen imports,[5] *frigorífico* demand remained high as the animals were now prepared for the growing domestic market.[6] Argentine *saladeros* collapsed for ever. In its search for a profitable supply of corned beef, Liebigs began production in 1930 at its Paraguayan plant and, albeit unsuccessfully, sought sources of cheap cattle for extract in remote eastern Bolivia and western Mato Grosso. Able to offer somewhat higher prices for Paraguayan cattle destined for corned beef than it could afford for extract cattle, Liebigs hoped to stimulate the herd improvement necessary for better-quality corned beef.[7]

Thus, by 1930 a spatial pattern of beef-product manufacturing had evolved that clearly reflected the relative abilities to compete of the different beef products. In Argentina the domestic fresh-beef market absorbed 4·26 million of the 6·40 million cattle slaughtered; whilst home demand had traditionally focused on cow beef, the percentage of steers that were killed for export had fallen from 70 per cent in 1924 to 58 per cent in 1930.[8] Among the exported products, chilled beef prepared especially at tidewater locations

---

[1] Junta Nacional de Carnes, *Reseña 1957* (Buenos Aires); Hanson, op. cit. (1937), p. 184; *R.R.P.*, 1923, i. 286.

[2] Fat *criollo* steers fetched $60 in 1922 at Buenos Aires: Ruano Fournier, op. cit., p. 346.

[3] Liebigs, Buenos Aires to London, 29 Oct. 1921; London to Buenos Aires, 27 Oct. 1922.

[4] Liebigs, 'Memo on the Argentine Meat Trade', 5 Apr. 1926.

[5] Hanson, op. cit. (1937), pp. 253–4.

[6] Junta Nacional de Carnes, *Reseña 1957* (Buenos Aires).

[7] Liebigs, K. M. Carlisle to C. D. Noble, 15 Aug. 1929.

[8] Junta Nacional de Carnes, *Reseña 1957* (Buenos Aires).

from the finest animals fattened on the western Pampas continued to dominate. Frozen beef was prepared either from inferior parts of good animals received at tidewater locations or from inferior *mestizo* animals received at riverside *frigoríficos*, such as Swifts' Rosario plant, opened in 1925 for the purpose of handling the cattle of Mesopotamia and northern Santa Fé. The corned beef factories at Santa Elena and Colón, decreasingly able to compete for *mestizo* animals, had to seek the less improved cattle which were steadily retreating to the most northerly provinces of the Chɛ ɔo and Corrientes.[1] The *tasajo* trade had collapsed, partly through the *saladeros'* inability to obtain cheap cattle and partly through former consumers' ability to purchase more attractive beef products. The best *criollo* cattle of Paraguay were now destined for corned beef or the local fresh-beef market, and the worst for extract.

If allowance is made for the distorting effects of climate[2] and of higher transport costs over land than sea,[3] and for the dating of the relevant technological innovations, the actual pattern of evolution of beef-product manufacturing accords well with the theory outlined earlier. The Argentine experience as a whole thus emphasizes the key role which competition played in the long term, since the location model theory, to which the historical pattern of development in practice conformed, is based upon the assumption of perfect competition. Nevertheless, some questions remain unanswered, and it is to these that we shall now turn our attention. How far could individual firms within these industries, separately or collectively, establish monopoly control either of cattle markets in the River Plate area or of meat markets abroad, and for how long? What were the opportunities which such firms were able to exploit, and what weapons did they use? What restraints placed limits on their freedom of action? What was the impact of govern-

---

[1] Had Liebigs relocated their corned beef factory in western Corrientes, calculations by the author reveal that Colón's marginal profit of 1 per cent in 1926 on manufacturing could have been converted into a handsome 10 per cent through savings on cattle transfer costs: Crossley, op. cit. (1974), pp. 475–7.

[2] For example, in Argentina, Patagonia is too cold and dry for cattle farming (but not for sheep), Cuyo is too arid, and the north too hot for purebred animals of European breeds.

[3] In the River Plate area, freight rates even by river were twenty times higher than those by sea. Thus, of two locations, one inland and one coastal, equidistant from the market by great circle routes, the former is always in cost terms remoter.

ment intervention? How important were backward and forward linkages into ranching and marketing? What were the internal and external pressures which influenced the behaviour of individual beef product firms? In the long run, competition rather than monopoly characterized the River Plate beef trade, but what of the short run?

III

The Argentine Refrigerated Beef Trade

Argentina's meat packing was exceptional among Latin America's export trades, since processing, with attendant by-product manufacturing, occurred in the country of production. The *frigoríficos* performed useful, integrated functions, slaughtering, cleaning, and converting raw material into a transportable product for distribution abroad. Nevertheless, their reputation was low. First, the fact that the industry was largely foreign-owned created fears that control over Argentina's vital resources would be exercised abroad.[1] In 1885, James Nelson & Sons, a British concern, erected a factory at Zárate supplementing the British-owned River Plate Fresh Meat Company's Campana works and two native-owned plants. Other British firms followed, and in 1907 American packers took over two existing works. Second, combinations between the foreign-owned *frigoríficos* not only threatened *estancieros'* prices but also squeezed consumers.[2] The president of a committee of Argentine deputies investigating the meat trade in 1917 reported that the packers 'suppress real competition, maintaining it only in appearance, and they determine by common agreement the prices which are to be paid to producers, reserving the right to sell at the highest price possible to obtain enormous profits which do not remain in the country . . .'.[3] Later writers like Jaime Fuchs, who remarked that expatriate packers 'established a total monopoly in the meat trade which constituted an enormous plunder of the nation's patrimony', echoed this

[1] For a general view see Rodolfo and Julio Irazusta, *La Argentina y el Imperialismo Británico* (Buenos Aires, 1934), and Julio Irazusta, *Influencia Económica Británica en el Río de la Plata* (Buenos Aires, 1963).

[2] *Diario de Diputados* (Argentina), 27 July 1910, 640, and 13 May 1913, 57 et seq.

[3] Quoted in Federal Trade Commission, *Report on the Meat Packing Industry* (Washington, 1919), ii. 106–7.

theme.[1] In Britain, too, the prospect was viewed with some alarm. In 1909, when a departmental committee of the Board of Trade investigated combinations in the meat trade, Consul-General Bennett told the Foreign Office that 'there is no reasonable doubt that the Beef Trust is seriously considering whether it would not pay to seek complete control of the Argentine beef trade and that . . . the same tactics which have been employed in the States to crush or absorb competing concerns will be adopted'.[2]

The pattern of meat packing in Argentina strongly influenced the formation of combinations, in marked contrast to Australian and New Zealand experience. In 1902, when in Argentina the three pioneer firms, the River Plate Fresh Meat Co., Nelsons, and Sansinenas, were taking 'the first tentative steps to monopolize the meat trade',[3] New Zealand had twenty-five independent plants and Australia sixteen.[4] Even when the American companies and Vestey entered the River Plate before and during the First World War, the number of *frigoríficos*—excluding the few small mutton works in Patagonia—did not exceed a dozen. Similarly, Argentina's chief factories were clustered at the tidewater ports of Buenos Aires and La Plata or along the banks of the River Paraná (like Campana and Zárate), at the centre of the republic's railway network and ideal for direct maritime links abroad, while New Zealand had twelve exit ports. Such concentration—in numbers and locality—of Argentine *frigoríficos* inevitably facilitated negotiation and agreement. Managers knew each other well, met regularly, and could easily keep an eye on output and prices. And, unlike Australasian farmers, Argentine *estancieros* did not enjoy personal access to *frigoríficos*. No farmers' manufacturing companies existed once the Americans had entered the River Plate, and factories operated only on their own account (that is, cattle were bought outright and not processed on behalf of *estancieros*).

The *frigoríficos* further eliminated competition amongst themselves. The Terrason works, seized by creditors in 1894, was leased

[1] Jaime Fuchs, *La Penetración de los Trusts Yanquis en la Argentina* (Buenos Aires, 1958), pp. 196–7.

[2] P.R.O. F.O. 368/266/20436, Bennett to Grey, 24 May 1909.

[3] José V. Liceaga, *Las Carnes en la Economía Argentina* (Buenos Aires, 1952), p. 20.

[4] Weddels, 1899, p. 6, 1908, p. 8, and 1913, p. 12; *R.R.P.*, 26 May 1900, 29; *Report of the Royal Commission on Food Prices*, P.P., 1924–5, xiii, vol. 3 (appendix xxx lists forty meat works in New Zealand).

by its rivals in 1898, who closed it. Thenceforward, remarks Hanson, 'the paucity of competitors facilitated the making of gentlemen's agreements'.[1] The arrival of American packers, whose reputation for integrated working and dubious competitive tactics was well established in the United States,[2] brought a new dimension to the Argentine meat trade, and marked the opening of a 'struggle without mercy' with the existing Anglo-Argentine companies.[3] In 1908 Swifts purchased their La Plata works, and within a year Armour & Morris, under the guise of the National Packing Company, bought the La Blanca plant.[4] In the period immediately before 1914 the Americans modified and expanded their acquisitions, Swifts gained control of frozen mutton factories, and Sulzberger & Sons purchased the Frigorífico Argentina which found itself unable to meet the strains of dearer cattle at the farm gate and cheaper meat in the consuming markets—two major tactical weapons in the American competitive armoury.[5] Such pressures and the need for economies of scale forced other companies to rationalize. In 1914 the River Plate Fresh Meat Company and Nelsons merged under the style of the British and Argentine Meat Company (later acquired by Vesteys) and concentrated its operations at Campana.[6] Armours relinquished interests at La Blanca and opened a large modern factory outside La Plata. The closure of *frigoríficos* as a result of aggressive competition was normally permanent and, therefore, potentially serious. Low overheads in the more flexible *saladeros* permitted them to shut down under competition and reopen when prices improved.

[1] Hanson, op. cit. (1937), p. 62.
[2] *Report of the Select Committee on the Transportation and Sale of Meat Products* (1890), Senate Documents, 51st Congress, 1st Session, No. 829; *Report of the Commissioner of Corporations on the Beef Trust* (1905), House of Representatives Documents, 58th Congress, 3rd Session, No. 382; *Consular Reports (United States)*, P.P., 1902, ciii, 341–408; Alfred D. Chandler, 'The Beginnings of "Big Business" in American Industry', *Business History Review*, xxxiii (1959), 1–31.
[3] Nemesio de Olariaga, *El Ruralismo Argentino: Economía Ganadera* (Buenos Aires, 1943), p. 102.
[4] *Report of the Departmental Committee on Combinations in the Meat Trade*, P.P., 1909, xv, 15; *The Economist*, 12 June 1909, 1237; *The Times*, 17 June 1913, 17c–d; *Consular Reports (Argentina)*, P.P., 1912–13, xciv, 119–28.
[5] *R.R.P.*, 25 Sept. 1908, 783; 17 Sept. 1909, 725; 26 Sept. 1913, 791; and 3 Apr. 1914, 845.
[6] Weddels, 1914, p. 16; *The Times*, 24 Jan. 1914, 8c, 26 Jan. 1914, 15e, 30 Mar. 1914, 21a and f; *The Economist*, 4 Apr. 1914, 819; *R.R.P.*, 30 Jan. 1914, 273.

The most important outside competitor eliminated before 1914 was the livestock cattle trade which, under the impetus of the Boer War and South African demand,[1] dominated Argentina's meat exports until 1900 when British ports were closed. Though not responsible for this measure, the *frigoríficos* were able to take full advantage of it. They not only captured the British market but were able to buy cattle cheaper from *estancieros* who now faced a monopoly. While the British farmer gained directly by reduced competition from imported livestock, many interests—*estancieros*, shipowners, slaughterers (at Deptford and Birkenhead), butchers, and consumers—were alarmed, lobbying Whitehall to remove the ban, particularly when reports from Argentina suggested that the incidence of foot-and-mouth disease was confined.[2] Harford warned the Foreign Office that 'the frozen meat companies are naturally interested in maintaining the *status quo* and statements emanating from that quarter as to the alleged existence of foot and mouth disease . . . should be looked on with distrust'.[3] But only in 1903 were British ports briefly reopened, and the triumph of refrigerated beef over live cattle shipments (always subject to criticism on humanitarian grounds) was assured.[4]

The packers used a further range of tactics to control Argentina's meat trade. The three pioneer *frigoríficos*, having eliminated the Terrason works, became accustomed to informal meetings to reduce competition. They discussed local prices, markets, and returns, though the size of the British market and the high profits possible at the time made formal combination as yet unnecessary. Published accounts show that the River Plate Fresh Meat Company paid 10 per cent, 1899–1902, when the directors also placed £150,000 to reserves, and when Nelsons returned a spectacular 50 per cent dividend and put £210,000 aside.[5] 'The present

[1] *Diplomatic Despatches of the United States* (*Argentina*), xxxix, 75, William Lord to Hay, 3 Nov. 1900; *R.R.P.*, 25 May 1901, 28, 1 June 1901, 19, 21 Dec. 1901, 105, and 1 Mar. 1902, 549.

[2] *Diplomatic Despatches of the United States* (*Argentina*), xli, 202, Lord to Hay, 6 Sept. 1902; P.R.O. F.O. 6/495, Ross to F.O., 1 Mar. 1902.

[3] P.R.O. F.O. 6/495, Harford to F.O., 20 Jan. 1903.

[4] *R.R.P.*, 19 Jan. 1901, 27; 4 May 1901, 27; and 14 May 1904, 949. The value of frozen meat exports rose from $4m. in 1900 to $14·7 m. in 1903, while cattle exports fell from $9·5m. (1898) to $2m. (1902). The launching of two refrigerated steamers by the Houston Company for the River Plate in 1901 indicated the relative importance of the two trades.

[5] See reports of annual meetings in *The Times*, e.g. 19 June 1903, 14b, and 1 May 1903, 13a.

comparatively low price of livestock suitable for export or freezing', complained *El Diario*, 'is undoubtedly due to . . . the freezing companies . . . not competing freely against one another.'[1] The American *frigoríficos* developed more refined and permanent market sharing in 1911, when they seized 43 per cent of the chilled shipments to Britain under quotas based on average exports from 1909[2] (Table VIII.4), in 1914 when they secured 59 per cent, and in the 1920s.[3] At the same time formal agreements with the shipping companies through the packers' Freight Committee, which contracted all refrigerated space, tended to obstruct the entry of outsiders.[4]

Nevertheless, *frigoríficos* were vulnerable to competition. Refrigerated meat did not require unobtainable patents or secret processes, nor did it need unlimited capital or rare expertise. The relatively slow rate of technical change protected competitors from innovations which might have upset the balance of production. Cheap and rapid transport in Argentina gave some locational flexibility within the zone around Buenos Aires. Although refrigerated meat manufacture required dearer plant than *saladeros* and benefited from economies of scale, the early *frigoríficos* had cost only £500,000 apiece, enabling native interests to participate. Indeed, the locally owned Sansinena works, which like the British firms sought to expand output, was said to be the world's largest factory.[5] Moreover, profitability inevitably attracted competition. Four new works, the Smithfield & Argentine (a British concern),[6] La Blanca and Frigorífico Argentina (two local companies),[7] and La Plata (formed with British and South African capital)[8] started operations from 1903. By expanding Argentina's annual slaughtering capacity, the outsiders freed producers 'from the supposed

---

[1] Quoted in *R.R.P.*, 2 Nov. 1901, 689, although this British-owned paper consistently denied that a combination existed, e.g. ibid., 1 June 1901, 10, and 14 Sept. 1901, 405.

[2] P.R.O. F.O. 368/785/31012, Tower to Grey, 11 June 1913; Federal Trade Commission, op. cit., i. 165; Weddels, 1913, p. 9.

[3] See, for example, Hanson, op. cit. (1937), pp. 210–70 *passim*; Weddels, 1921, p. 19.

[4] *Report of the Royal Commission on Food Prices*, QQ. 6222–6 and appendices lxvi–lxvii.

[5] *R.R.P.*, 18 Mar. 1899, 31; 31 Mar. 1900, 21; 19 May 1900, 19; 20 July 1901, 99; and 11 Oct. 1902, 622.

[6] Ibid., 28 Mar. 1903, 539, and 11 Apr. 1903, 641.

[7] Ibid., 2 Nov. 1901, 697; 25 Jan. 1902, 329; 7 June 1902, 1158 and 1165; and 2 May 1903, 765.   [8] Ibid., 22 Nov. 1902, 897.

ring of the freezing companies . . . who are said to be keeping down prices'.[1] The chairman of Nelsons explained to shareholders in 1904 that competition had wrecked agreements, and in 1907 the River Plate Fresh Meat Company's chairman, announcing a fall in profits, considered renewed arrangements between *frigoríficos* the best solution.[2] Indeed, unremunerative competition between *frigoríficos* partly accounted for the sale of native-owned works to the Americans whose invasion of Argentina's meat trade then further expanded competition, a development repeated after 1914 when the British Vestey group established the Anglo-South American Meat Company at Zárate.[3] While factories became larger, more costly and sophisticated, they could not permanently prevent the inroad into their business and profits of outsiders, who pushed cattle prices upwards and meat prices downwards.

Internal disagreements also restricted the duration of combinations. Dissatisfaction with their share, agreed in 1911, induced Morris & Co. to claim a 50 per cent rise in quotas, after which combination gave way to sharp conflict before agreement was renewed in 1914.[4] Similarly, meat wars (1925–7) resulted from firms seizing business at their rivals' expense. The Smithfield & Argentine Company, hitherto an inefficient plant taking 5 per cent of the market in 1922, modernized and expanded capacity before beginning a competitive struggle in 1925. Vesteys also constructed new plant and ended pooling agreements.[5]

If the impression that the packers' combinations were essentially temporary and fluctuating institutions is justified, tactics abroad and limited periods of control may still have coerced consumers. Fears existed about Britain's dependence on Argentine beef—an alarm sharpened by the arrival of the Americans and reflected in a series of official British reports. Bennett informed Grey in 1909 that 'a grave position appears to be developing as to the feeding of the British public',[6] and Pellegrini told the Chamber of Deputies

---

[1] Ibid., 17 May 1902, 1025, and 11 Oct. 1902, 622.

[2] Weddels, 1904, *passim*; *R.R.P.*, 7 May 1904, 885, and 28 May 1904, 1041; *The Times*, 31 May 1904, 13e, and 5 Apr. 1907, 9c; *The Economist*, 20 Apr. 1907, 683.

[3] Weddels, 1916, p. 15; Hanson, op. cit. (1937), pp. 206–7; *Diario de Diputados* (Argentina), 25 June 1913, 313–19.

[4] P.R.O. F.O. 368/785/26229, Gaisford to Grey, 15 May 1913; P.R.O. F.O. 368/1203/135523, Memorandum to Tower; Hanson, op. cit. (1937), pp. 163–73.

[5] Weddels, 1925, *passim*; Hanson, op. cit. (1937), pp. 243–7.

[6] P.R.O. F.O. 368/266/20436, Bennett to Grey, 24 May 1909.

that packers were fixing prices in Britain.[1] Technical obstacles to shipments of chilled beef from Australasia[2] restricted the Empire to supplying merely 15 per cent of all British beef imports (6 per cent of total needs), while America's domestic market reduced her shipments to Britain after 1901 (Table VIII.2). In 1913 the United States became a beef importer. By contrast, Argentina, relatively close to the final market and apparently enjoying expanding production under favourable natural conditions, supplied 30 per cent of Britain's beef needs (75 per cent of imports).[3] From 1911 to 1924 shipments of Argentine beef rose to over 80 per cent of Britain's imports, exaggerating the imbalance between foreign and imperial supplies and enhancing the opportunities for River Plate packers to coerce and disrupt British meat markets.

The structure of Britain's wholesale markets apparently increased the power of Argentina's packers. While individual experience differed—Newcastle, Dundee, and Norwich, for example, sold mainly domestic meat—Liverpool, where River Plate meat first concentrated,[4] and pre-eminently London, the largest British market and a national distributing centre, handled the greater part of Argentine beef. And the importance of Smithfield, where only 20 per cent of meat was domestic, was that it fixed prices in smaller markets (after allowances for transport), since London firms transferred their price each day to agents and clients in the provinces. Thus, imported Argentine beef seemed to enjoy a disproportionate price-fixing and regulatory function in Britain.[5] In 1908 Weddels *Review* reported:

In effect Smithfield market practically rules the price of imported meat throughout the country; and if any group of operators could secure control of Smithfield they would control the prices of all fresh meat

---

[1] *Diario de Diputados* (Argentina), 27 July 1910, 640; see also ibid., 13 May 1913, 57.

[2] B. R. Duffin, 'The United Kingdom Market for Chilled Beef', *Quarterly Review of Agricultural Economics*, x (1957), 29–33.

[3] *Combinations in the Meat Trade, passim*; *Inter-Departmental Committee on Meat Supplies*, P.P., 1919, xxv, 440; *Second Report of the Imperial Economic Committee on the Marketing and Preparing for Market of Foodstuffs Produced in the Overseas Parts of the Empire*, P.P., 1924–5, xiii, 843 *et seq.*

[4] Weddels, 1899, p. 4, and 1920, p. 7; *R.R.P.*, 17 Feb. 1900, 31, and 1 Sept. 1900, 27. Early operators of refrigerated tonnage (H. & W. Nelson and Houlder Brothers) were based at Liverpool.

[5] *Combinations in the Meat Trade*, 5–7; *Report of the Royal Commission on the Meat Export Trade of Australia*, P.P., 1914–16, xlvi, 18; *The Economist*, 15 May 1909, 1030.

in the United Kingdom and indirectly regulate the value of most of the livestock owned by the British farmer.[1]

Argentine packers also established forward linkages which extended their market powers. Nelsons organized an important retailing network which between 1902 and 1904, when the company also invested in the Colonial Consignment and Distributing Company, was raised from 700 to 1,000 shops, central to the firm's profitability. The River Plate Fresh Meat Company owned forty-six wholesale branches in England, while the Smithfield & Argentine Company employed the commercial services of the respected Smithfield house, Poels & Brewster.[2] The Americans enjoyed an existing marketing organization developed to handle shipments from the United States consisting of representative companies, registered locally but obeying Chicago, which imported for their principals and administered stalls in Smithfield. Their wholesale shops gave the appearance of competition but in fact respected territorial divisions, agreed prices, and maintained a blacklist against recalcitrant clients. Deals were often conducted secretly, and witnesses before investigating committees remained evasive.[3] Vesteys enjoyed the full range of meat-marketing services in Britain: cold stores (Union Cold Storage Company), Smithfield stalls, and retail shops (Dewhursts, Eastmans, and Argenta).[4] A close identity of interest thus existed between packing, importing, and distribution which conferred influence throughout the marketing chain. Such integration, the rarity of which in the competing Australasian trade served to increase officials' and dealers' suspicions, impeded the entry of independent dealers into Argentine beef. As early as 1901, Weddels recognized 'the controlling power wielded by River Plate importers when they work in unison for the regulation of prices'.[5] On the other hand packers' forward linkages probably helped *estancieros*, since

---

[1] Weddels, 1908, p. 4. Such a control on prices could only impose maxima rather than minima and hence would benefit the British consumer, though not the farmer.

[2] *The Times*, 22 Apr. 1903, 3e; 1 May 1903, 13c; 3 May 1904, 13d; 31 May 1904, 13c; 21 June 1906, 14c; and 29 June 1906, 4c. *R.R.P.*, 6 July 1901, 20; 22 Mar. 1902, 675; 28 June 1902, 1307; 26 July 1902, 151; 25 Apr. 1903, 727; and 17 Feb. 1911, 427.

[3] *Combinations in the Meat Trade*, 11 et seq.

[4] *Royal Commission on Food Prices*, QQ. 4334-55; Hanson, op. cit. (1937), p. 207.

[5] Weddels, 1901, p. 8.

profits from retailing, even if manufacturing were unremunerative, maintained prices.

Nevertheless, important restraints existed in the British market. If butchers and consumers depended on Argentina, so *frigoríficos* relied heavily on British sales. Before 1914, tariff barriers, sanitary regulations, popular prejudice, and persistent lobbying by vested agrarian interests largely excluded Argentina from continental European markets. Only Italy, Switzerland, and Portugal imported Argentine beef, albeit on a small scale, before 1914.[1] Abnormal wartime conditions and army contracts raised European consumption, a trend continued erratically into the 1920s. Nevertheless, practically all Argentine chilled beef entered Britain after the war, and in 1923 Britain still imported more than the rest of Europe.[2]

Demand for Argentine beef was also elastic. Consumption depended upon the purchasing power of a large portion of the population, who reacted rapidly to changes in price or income. Unemployment in Lancashire would quickly reduce demand for Argentine beef landed at Liverpool.[3] And while annual *per capita* meat consumption undoubtedly rose in the last quarter of the nineteenth century, some evidence suggests that a peak in consumption was reached in 1908 and that a continuous fall in British demand occurred from 1910 to 1935.[4] This trend, perhaps, reflected the well-established decline in real wages before 1914, wartime strains, and post-war preference for smaller but high-quality joints, which lowered the volume of meat sold over the counter although it raised the number of cattle slaughtered.

At the same time alternative supplies of meat permitted an easy switching of demand. Before 1914 domestic production still satisfied 60 per cent of Britain's meat needs, and after the war 55 per cent. The market for refrigerated beef, an inferior substitute for fresh beef, depends on underselling fresh beef, the market price of which sets a limit above which chilled beef cannot go. British livestock farmers, who also produced lamb and pork, were

[1] Weddels, 1911, pp. 4 and 13; 1912, p. 10; and 1914, p. 11.
[2] Ibid., 1919–25, *passim*.
[3] *R.R.P.*, 28 May 1904, 1041; Weddels, 1906, p. 7.
[4] Gertrude Gronbech, 'Meat Consumption Trends and Patterns', *Agricultural Handbook*, No. 187 (1960), United States Department of Agriculture, cited by Peter H. Smith, *Politics and Beef in Argentina: Patterns of Conflict and Change* (New York, 1969), p. 52; Imperial Economic Committee, op. cit., 842, recorded a fall in British *per capita* meat consumption, between 1911 and 1924, from 138·6 to 135·8 pounds.

not squeezed like British arable farmers who provided 20 per cent or less of domestic grain needs. Although the number of sheep fell from 32 million to 27 million by the mid 1920s, the cattle population rose from 11 to over 12 million. Britain was also the only major importer of lamb, the ready adaption of which to refrigeration ensured plentiful international shipments. The finest imported lamb, enjoying high prices in England, was New Zealand (Table VIII.5). While some Argentine *frigoríficos* sold substantial

TABLE VIII.5

British Imports of Frozen Lamb and Mutton, by Country, 1882–1925

(Quinquennial totals, 000 cwts, rounded to nearest 000)

	Europe	United States	Argentina	Australia	New Zealand	Chile	Uruguay	Total[e]
1882–5	413	135	156[c]	181	623			1,501
1886–90	747	17	1,616	276	2,497			5,305
1891–5	1,066	37	2,724	1,634	4,704	nil		10,240
1896–1900	1,421	8	5,109	3,072	6,659			16,241
1901–5	1,489	93	6,995	1,746	8,308		54[d]	19,041
1906–10	1,101	12	7,256	4,580	9,573	407	282	23,164
1911–15	605	nil	6,311	6,516	11,347	647	358	25,541
1916–20	93	23[b]	3,564	3,353	9,063	951	254	17,194
1921–5	17[a]	nil	8,032	3,631	15,156	1,069	708	28,541

[a] 1921 only.   [b] 1919 and 1920 only.
[c] 1883–5 only.   [d] 1905 only.   [e] From all sources.

SOURCES: *Annual Statements of the Trade of the United Kingdom with Foreign Countries and British Possessions* (Parliamentary Papers); W. Weddel & Co., (Annual) *Review of the Frozen Meat Trade*.

quantities of frozen lamb and mutton—in 1912 Swifts shipped 1·1 million carcasses (30 per cent of the republic's output), Sansinenas exported 720,000 (20 per cent), and works in Patagonia produced mutton—Argentina's share of the British market remained relatively small. Imperial sources provided over 70 per cent of British imports. At the same time, refrigerated mutton (and beef) was increasingly exported from Argentina's neighbours. In 1909 Chile shipped 210,000 carcasses from Rio Seco and San Gregorio in Patagonia;[1] Uruguay developed frozen meat slowly, but had opened several *frigoríficos* by 1911;[2] cattle raising and beef

[1] U.S.M.C.R., May 1910, 356, p. 102, and June 1910, 357, p. 70.
[2] Between 1905 and 1914 output of Uruguayan frozen beef, benefiting from removals of export duties, increased from 2,000 to 69,000 tons: Ruano Fournier, op. cit., p. 369; U.S.M.C.R., Oct. 1909, 349, p. 115.

production became important industries in Brazil,[1] though exports were small (see Tables VIII.2 and VIII.5), and Danish bacon and American pork also provided substitutes. However, large-scale switching of demand did not apparently occur, which suggests that Argentine meat prices in England were acceptable to consumers, and that, therefore, the tactics of the *frigoríficos* were not coercive. In the period 1911–24, annual *per capita* consumption of lamb fell from 30·8 to 22·6 pounds, while beef rose from 68·7 to 70·8 pounds.[2] It must also be admitted that the American packers and Vesteys added participation in the Dominion trades to their Argentine interests, and to some extent reduced competition.[3]

A powerful domestic commercial organization also faced Argentine *frigoríficos*. Seventy per cent of British retailers belonged to united associations which lobbied at local and national levels. Of 762 meat companies in Britain before 1914, the Americans controlled only eight, and owned just thirty-four out of 550 Smithfield stalls. Vestey's 2,000 shops in the 1920s comprised only 6 per cent of total retail outlets. Jobbers, independent wholesalers, and large commission agents, who bought in bulk from importers for domestic butchers, ensured that nearly 20 per cent of Argentine beef reached the consumer without passing through the importers' wholesale machinery.[4] Moreover, the fact that chilled beef was perishable also undermined the price-regulatory function of Argentine exporters. Importers, who had little option or leeway in marketing, had to sell whatever the ruling price, even ex-ship without entering Smithfield if shipments were delayed. Importers would not willingly freeze chilled beef, which could only be sold at a lower price and hence usually at a loss. Indeed, the need for rapid distribution partly accounts for the development of a marketing network by the *frigoríficos*. Normal business considerations, economy and efficiency, not necessarily a desire to coerce and control, governed their decisions.

If the discretion of packers in the *British* meat market was

---

[1] *Diplomatic Despatches of the United States (Brazil)*, David E. Thompson to Hay, 4 June 1903, lxviii, 29; Weddels, 1919, p. 16, and 1920, p. 18.

[2] *Imperial Economic Committee*, 842; Weddels, 1909–12.

[3] Federal Trade Commission, op. cit., i. 184–93; *Meat Export Trade of Australia*, 24–5.

[4] *Interim Report on Meat—Prepared by a Sub Committee Appointed by the Standing Committee on Trusts*, P.P., 1920, xxiii, 548–50.

limited, a prima facie case against their influence in Argentina still existed. The livestock industry in Argentina was of supreme importance to the republic's wealth and standard of living. In 1910 meat and hides accounted for almost 25 per cent of exports. The meat packers were a major employer, each *frigorífico* hiring up to 2,000 men.[1]

In the 1920s one estimate valued Argentine cattle at £280 million of which Buenos Aires province claimed half and neighbouring provinces 40 per cent.[2] Farms were typically large: in 1914, 59 per cent of Buenos Aires farmland lay in holdings of over 1,000 hectares. Yet Consul-General Bennett doubted whether even the most powerful and prestigious *estancieros* 'could successfully hold out against the drastic methods of the Beef Trust'.[3] A quarter of a century later, in 1937, the Committee of Inquiry stressed 'the psychological significance of the mere fact that the producers . . . have been dependent for their outlet on a few powerful concerns financed almost entirely by foreign capital and working in close co-operation'.[4] Inevitably the existence of formal agreements and export quotas lent weight to charges that *frigoríficos* did not compete for purchases.[5] Grading was another area where producers felt cheated, but as buyers normally undervalue purchases so sellers exaggerate their worth. The power of the packers was most strongly felt during a depression: not only did cattle prices fall in keeping with product prices, but packers also passed on to the farmer the higher unit overhead costs which of necessity accompanied reduced throughputs.

Among the *estancieros*, whom Deputy Carlés called 'los dóciles, indefensos, individualistas',[6] divisions prevented the development of a united front against the packer. The deepest division was between fatteners (*invernadores*) and breeders (*criadores*), whose activities were spatially divorced.[7] Since breeding required five to ten times as much land per unit of annual output, it was

---

[1] P.R.O. F.O. 368/785/33417, Tower to Grey, 25 June 1913.

[2] F. Gerrard, ed., *The Book of the Meat Trade* (London, 1955), ii. 181–3.

[3] P.R.O. F.O. 368/266/20436, Bennett to Grey, 24 May 1909. Such an opinion, however, reflected forebodings rather than facts.

[4] *Report of the Joint Committee of Inquiry into the Anglo-Argentine Meat Trade*, P.P., 1937–8, viii, 840.

[5] *Royal Commission on Food Prices*, QQ. 2600–66 and 3175.

[6] *Diario de Diputados* (Argentina), 13 May 1913, 57.

[7] *Anglo-Argentine Meat Trade*, pp. 892 *et seq.*; Smith, op. cit., pp. 43–7; Fuchs, op. cit., pp. 194–5.

restricted to less expensive land.[1] Fatteners and breeders differed greatly in the nature of their vulnerability and their scope for manœuvre. The fattener behaved like the packer in that he effected purchases well in advance of sales and his purchase price reflected production costs, desired profit margins, and anticipated selling price. On a rising market he gained handsomely, whilst on a falling market part of his losses could be passed on in lower future store prices. High costs of fattening chillers on cultivated pastures precluded the withholding of fat cattle from the market for many months, but in compensation the chilled beef packer was faced with a year-round demand and his capital-intensive plant required him to operate at near full capacity. Reliable fatteners, who were usually large *estancieros*, were reasonably treated and benefited from consistent loyalty to one factory. The situation was thus one of mutual dependence. Freezing-grade cattle, fattened on natural pastures in summer, could more cheaply be held over to the next summer in expectation of higher prices; equally, however, the beef-freezing *frigorífico* could stockpile against a period of high cattle prices. But in the face of several years' continued unattractive prices, whether contrived or not, the fattener could usually turn to crop farming either on his own account or through the introduction of tenant farmers.

The cattle breeder, in contrast, could not conduct his operations with the same flexibility. Store-cattle breeding programmes took at least two-and-a-half years to effect; falling store-cattle prices could not be compensated by commensurate cuts in production costs. Breeding herds could not be sold in times of adversity except at a loss, and breeding lands were frequently suitable only for sheep raising as an alternative land use. The only latitude permitted to the breeder was that afforded by fattening his own cattle for the domestic market. Forward estimation of breeding's profitability was, therefore, impossible to make with any precision. Additionally, in *estanciero* society the breeding of high-grade cattle and the winning of prizes at annual livestock shows yielded social prestige which became an end in itself and perhaps prolonged uneconomic production to the benefit of cattle purchasers.

The cattle fattener, furthermore, enjoyed the real benefits of

[1] In Mesopotamia, where cattle transfer costs were high, this meant land remote from the factories; in the Pampas, where rapid haulage was available, it meant lands physically less suitable for fattening (and arable farming).

a more flexible pattern of purchasing than obtained in many commodity trades. He preferred selling at the farm gate under direct negotiations with factory buyers, thus avoiding middlemen, to consigning to agents for grading and sale in the central market at Buenos Aires. While the system permitted buyers to underrate stock—up-country cattlemen might not know current market values—it protected *estancieros* from exploitation by stockyards (an important feature of control in the United States)[1] and from any abnormal loss through flood or disease when delivering cattle on their own account. The system also permitted *frigoríficos* to effect forward purchasing, which earned *estancieros* better prices since delivery could be fitted into a schedule and a smoother throughput achieved than by reliance on daily purchases at auction or the factory gate.

Cattle were also purchased by local speculators, wholesalers, and butchers in an unusually strong domestic business where demand exceeded exports.[2] To the extent that top quality cattle were destined solely for export such competition was more apparent than real. Additionally some *frigoríficos*, notably Sansinena, had a substantial domestic interest, though in 1914–30 they never accounted for more than 20 per cent of slaughterings for home consumption.[3] Thus the local price for beef cattle set a base below which export prices could not go.[4] Local butchers and slaughtermen, nevertheless, were not averse to taking advantage of and even aggravating low cattle prices dictated by world market conditions.[5]

The fact that transportation from farm to factory and thence overseas, though foreign-owned, was not controlled by the

---

[1] *Transportation and Sale of Meat Products*, p. 2.

[2] P.R.O. F.O. 368/785/33418, Tower to Grey, 25 June 1913; *Diario de Diputados* (Argentina), 27 June and 2 July 1913, 350 and 406–14; *Anglo-Argentine Meat Trade*, 807. Already in 1914 2·3 million cattle were consumed in Argentina and only 1·3 million exported: Junta Nacional de Carnes, *Reseña 1957*.

[3] *R.R.P.*, 11 Feb. 1899, 9; 28 Apr. 1900, 9; 20 Oct. 1900, 10; and 2 Mar. 1901, 12; Junta Nacional de Carnes, *Reseña 1957*.

[4] To the extent that the local (Argentine) market sought an inferior grade of fresh beef to the central (British) market, the situation differed from our model; nevertheless the implications were similar.

[5] Hanson, op. cit. (1937), pp. 222–3. This is clearly indicated by the behaviour of Argentine retail prices compared with cattle prices in 1920–3. Expressed as indices (1913–14 = 100), retail prices fell from 134 to 74 but cattle prices declined from 144 to 53: Junta Nacional de Carnes, *Reseña 1957*.

frigoríficos, gave *estancieros* further freedom. Ownership of rail-roads and refrigerated cars was a crucial source of control in the United States where 'exorbitant and rapacious' charges were levied on independent shippers.[1] If *estancieros* had little choice of railway—shrinkage costs prevented haulage to more distant stations—shipments were not impeded. And although river trans-port, important during the period immediately before the re-frigerated beef boom,[2] was not an alternative since few riverside areas were suitable for fattening high-grade cattle, ocean-going steamers by the 1920s were loading direct at up-river factories before calling down river. Riverine beef, thus a day or so older than estuarine beef, commanded a lower price.

Indeed, the shipping companies on whom the packers depended for shipment abroad were also a balancing factor. The nature of British demand, the ban on live exports, and the perishability of chilled beef, compelled packers to use fast steamers. Some links existed between packer and shipowner. The pioneer factories at first loaded their own boats.[3] Thomas Dence, a director of the River Plate Fresh Meat Company and chairman of the Royal Mail Steam Packet Company, negotiated a freight contract between the two firms in 1901; two directors of H. & W. Nelson sat on the board of James Nelson & Sons;[4] and Vesteys introduced their Blue Star Line of insulated ships in the 1920s.[5] Nevertheless, *frigoríficos* preferred to employ independent shipowners. Since such tonnage was expensive and could not be filled on outward journeys, so that outsiders had no possibility of practising so specialized a trade, shipowners contracted with the packers before building suitable steamers and compelled them to pay for empty space.[6] Thus, factories were obliged to ship full cargoes or suffer losses, which limited their discretion to withhold meat until prices improved, and ensured a steady flow from producer to consumer. The merging of ownership among the participating lines after

[1] *Transportation and Sale of Meat Products*, pp. 2 and 17–21; *Combinations in the Meat Trade*, QQ. 2647–52.

[2] *Consular Reports (Rosario)*, P.P., 1898, xciv, 48; *The Times*, 24 June 1901, 4e; *R.R.P.*, 20 July 1901, 99.

[3] *R.R.P.*, 8 Dec. 1894, 18, and 3 Feb. 1911, 331.

[4] Ibid., 11 Aug. 1900, 32, 9 Mar. 1901, 29, and 26 July 1902, 151; Weddels, 1900, p. 14, and 1901, p. 13; *The Times*, 3 May 1904, 13d, and 31 May 1904, 13c.

[5] *Royal Commission on Food Prices*, QQ. 6258–63; *R.R.P.*, 18 Oct. 1912, 983.

[6] *Combinations in the Meat Trade*, QQ. 1411–13; *Royal Commission on Food Prices*, QQ. 6222–6.

1900 into two groups, Royal Mail and Furness-Withy, consoli=
dated the shipowners' position. While the Donaldson Company
was financially independent, it tacitly accepted conditions imposed
by its larger rivals.[1] The Standing Committee on Trusts recognized that shipowners 'should not be overlooked in the consideration of any defence measures against the American meat
companies', and recommended close links with H.M. Government to prevent foreign control of British meat markets.[2]

Although British ownership of *estancias* was important in
Argentina,[3] and although George Drabble, the promoter of the
River Plate Fresh Meat Company, owned local grazing land,[4] the
frigoríficos were not normally breeders or fatteners on their own
account before 1945. Nor did the *frigoríficos* control credit, through
which they might have refused loans to recalcitrant farmers, or
periodicals which published *ex parte* statements, an important
feature of control in the United States. Their ability to influence
Argentina's meat export trade from farm to ship was thus limited.
They could not patronize favoured suppliers against outside
estancieros.

The restraints imposed on *frigoríficos* by flexible purchasing and
independent transportation may have proved illusory under a
falling market, accelerated by combination. The First World War
expanded both the demand for, and the production of, Argentine
cattle to a level above that needed during the 1920s. The *estanciero*
now suffered both from falling beef prices and from higher unit
factory costs, passed on in the form of still lower cattle prices.
Under such conditions, *estancieros*, particularly the small men
whose business relied on marginal production under liberal
credit, sought official assistance (unsuccessfully) rather than pas-
sively awaiting a renewed upturn. The claim that cattlemen were
disorganized and fragmented can be exaggerated, since neighbours
were related and directorships among estate companies inter-
locked.[5] Moreover, from its origins in the 1850s, the Sociedad
Rural, composed of a minority of wealthy, influential ranchers,

[1] *Royal Commission on Food Prices*, QQ. 6228–57; R.R.P., 31 Oct. 1913,
1117.   [2] *Interim Report on Meat*, 552.
[3] J. Fred Rippy, 'Argentina: Late Major Field of British Overseas Investment', *Inter-American Economic Affairs*, vi (1952), 3–13; R.R.P., 5 Jan. 1895,
17, 2 Mar. 1895, 18, and 17 Jan. 1903, 107.
[4] R.R.P., 26 Dec. 1896, 5–6, and 1 June 1901, 25.
[5] *Royal Commission on Food Prices*, QQ. 3108–9, and Appendix xxxii.

was an important, if exclusive, lobbyist in the promotion of good practices and the collection of data. A close link between the Sociedad and Argentine politics was not confined to agricultural legislation.[1] Its members supplied over half the presidents before 1914, 39 out of 93 cabinet appointments, and 15 per cent of all seats in Congress. Before the First World War the aristocratic generation of the 1880s, whom the *estanciero* typified, governed Argentina.

Official participation in the market process was long established. From the 1880s Argentina abolished meat export duties, relaxed tariffs on imported refrigerated machinery, and offered premiums and guarantees on capital to encourage production and competition.[2] Before 1914, when competitive wars between packers raised local livestock prices, officials, who had anyway preferred a *laissez-faire* approach, were dissuaded from action.[3] The arrival of the Americans, who posed as the ranchers' friends, far from being viewed with immediate alarm, was regarded as a means of releasing *estancieros* from the clutches of British firms. Prior, Swifts' representative and a critic of the Anglo-Argentine companies, claimed that limited prices injured *estancieros* and he readily opened his books to confirm that efficient management, better agents in Britain, and the use of by-products ensured a profitable result.[4] 'The ranching interest', explained Tower, 'is strong in Congress, and cattle breeders are reaping a rich harvest.'[5] Similarly, the Board of Trade recognized that 'the operation of a powerful trust may for a long time be advantageous to certain producers'.[6] Carlos Carlés admitted in Congress that both breeder and fattener were 'favourable to the work of the trust which has raised the value of cattle . . .'.[7]

[1] Frank W. Bicknell, 'The Animal Industry of Argentina', *Bureau of Animal Husbandry*, Bulletin xlviii (1903), 10; Smith, op. cit., pp. 21–2 and 47–50.

[2] U.S.M.C.R., Apr. 1889, xxix, 104, pp. 675–80; Liceaga, op. cit., p. 21; *Diario de Diputados* (Argentina), 28 Sept. 1906, 1135, 6 Dec. 1907, 31, 16 June 1910, 176.

[3] Dr. Suarez, director of the livestock department in the Ministry of Agriculture, told Sir Reginald Tower that 'the general opinion in [Argentine] Government circles was to let things take their course': P.R.O. F.O. 368/785/31009, Tower to Grey, 9 June 1913; see also the remarks of Adolfo Mujica (Minister of Agriculture) and of Señor Frers: *Diario de Diputados* (Argentina), 25 and 27 June 1913, 313–19 and 363 *et seq.*; Smith, op. cit., p. 65.

[4] *R.R.P.*, 4 and 18 Apr. 1913, 857 and 979.

[5] P.R.O. F.O. 368/785/31009, Tower to Grey, 9 June 1913.

[6] P.R.O. F.O. 368/785/31848, Board of Trade to Foreign Office, 10 July 1913.

[7] *Diario de Diputados* (Argentina), 13 June 1913, 1089.

Indeed, demands for intervention came rather from the hard-pressed British companies. They claimed that their American competitors' enormous resources enabled them to bear losses which their own more slender reserves could not sustain. The Americans' economies of scale gave them lower unit costs at maximum output, enabling them to pay more for cattle than the smaller British firms. Tower informed Grey that the manager of Nelsons was collaborating with other non-American firms to arouse feeling against a trust in meat, and for this purpose Argentine deputies were 'being sedulously provided with material for future speeches . . . in Congress'.[1] But Mujica, Minister for Agriculture, and Meixa, a former minister, both sympathetic to the British, would not act, and bills authorizing a livestock census and anti-trust legislation were rejected.[2] The Argentines, who preferred to play off one group of *frigoríficos* against the other (since domestic interests appeared unthreatened), placed the responsibility for legislative action with Britain, whose ban against Argentine livestock was still bitterly resented.[3]

Oversupply and agreements between packers changed conditions after the First World War. Grievances over monopoly, grading, and low prices produced talk of an *estancieros'* strike, the expropriation of *frigoríficos*, or government-sponsored factories.[4] Suspension of buying by the *frigoríficos* forced Congress to shelve legislation passed during the cattle crisis of 1922–3, which included minimum cattle prices, action against trusts, regulated weighing, and national factories. But more far-reaching state intervention during the 1930s established a National Meat Board (Junta Nacional de Carnes), the inspection of company accounts, a

[1] P.R.O. F.O. 368/785/33418, Tower to Grey, 25 June 1913; see also P.R.O. F.O. 368/785/31009, 31012 and 32254, letters 11 and 18 June and 9 July 1913. *The Times*, 9 June 1913, 18b and 21d; 13 June 1913, 16d; 17 June 1913, 17c–d; and 20 June 1913, 18d. *The Economist*, 12 July 1913, 70, and 19 July 1913, 119.

[2] *Diario de Diputados* (Argentina), May–June 1913, *passim*; P.R.O. F.O. 368/785/34639, 38642 and 40154, Tower to Grey, 3 and 18 July and 2 Aug. 1913; *The Times*, 18 July 1913, 17d; Smith, op. cit., p. 66; Bicknell, loc. cit., 12.

[3] U.S.M.C.R., June 1909, 345, 109–10; *The Economist*, 28 July 1906, 1253; R.R.P., 9 Oct. 1908, 917 and 931; *Diario de Diputados* (Argentina), 20 July 1910, 516–22, and 8 Aug. 1910, 886–8.

[4] Roger Gravil, 'State Intervention in Argentina's Export Trade between the Wars', *Journal of Latin American Studies*, ii (1970), 147–73. Much of the following is taken from Dr. Gravil's article. See also D. C. Sycks, 'Cattle Raising in Argentina' (*Trade Information Bulletin*, 647, Washington, 1929); Hanson, op. cit. (1937), pp. 260–8; Gerrard, op. cit., ii. 191–6; Weddels, 1923–4.

producers' co-operative (financed by a 1 per cent export duty), government marketing, and official interest in meat packing at Gualeguaychú.[1] Argentina also sought co-operation with rival producers, Brazil and Uruguay, negotiated the Roca–Runciman agreement to safeguard her major market (Britain) now threatened by agricultural protection and imperial preference, and began a campaign to increase consumption, all of which helped to diminish the impact of the world depression on the meat trade. Nor was such state intervention untypical, as successful legislation in Australia and New Zealand after the First World War indicated.[2]

Argentina's meat packing industry, epitomizing foreign capitalist exploitation of the republic's national resources and linked to the notorious Chicago companies, could hardly have expected popularity. Excluding the very good year, 1902, but including the losses of 1911, under conditions of intense competition,[3] the dividends paid by British firms between 1900 and 1913 averaged over 7 per cent according to their published accounts. It is difficult to separate the Argentine business from the larger enterprise of the Chicago packers, but their over-all profits, if not excessive, were still excellent.[4] In Britain, where cheap food was a cornerstone of official policy, and in Argentina, where the livestock and meat export industries were critical elements in the national economy, wider questions were asked.

Yet suspicion and unpopularity are not proof of conspiracy to defraud consumers. In Britain fears that Argentine *frigoríficos*, one of many market influences, would control Britain's trade were exaggerated. Lord Vestey rejected control as 'absurd and wholly untrue'.[5] Rather, under a flexible supply and demand relationship, competition between rival importers and British farmers remained keen, prices changing daily, even hourly.[6] Unduly high prices soon attracted domestic meat traders or switched demand. Indeed, the fact that Australasian meat was entirely frozen gave that sector

[1] *Anglo-Argentine Meat Trade*, 825–7.

[2] Weddels, 1916, p. 12; 1919, p. 12; 1921, p. 15; and 1922, p. 15. *Inter-Departmental Committee on Meat Supplies*, 449–51.

[3] *The Times*, 10 May 1913, 15c, 15f, and 17a, and 20 May 1913, 19d. The River Plate Fresh Meat Company lost £41,000 in 1911.

[4] Federal Trade Commission, op. cit., v; P. Fitzgerald, *Industrial Combination in England* (London, 1927), p. 128. The profits of the Big Five Packers averaged 7·8 per cent 1912–14, and 5·6 to 6·8 per cent in the 1920s.

[5] *Royal Commission on Food Prices*, Q. 4276.

[6] *Interim Report on Meat*, 549.

greater discretion to withhold supplies and raise prices, though no evidence exists that this tactic was employed. Putnam, who claimed that Argentine packers 'are in no position, and . . . never can be in a position, to control prices at Smithfield',[1] goes too far. No doubt abuses occurred, if irregularly and unorganized—though stable prices and output were normally advantageous to butchers. But the final impression is that constraints in Britain's meat trade balanced the options open to the Argentine packer. An official in the Board of Agriculture minuted that 'the meat trade or monopoly seems to me rather a bogey . . .'.[2] Despite questions in the House of Commons and official investigations, no definite legislation emerged, since the arrival of the Americans at Buenos Aires had unquestionably cheapened chilled beef, 1909–11 (see Table VIII.6). Similarly, the Royal Commission on Food Prices in 1925 made no recommendations for intervention. In any case, it was difficult to see what Whitehall, committed to Free Trade and *laissez-faire*, could do. Officials had the unenviable task of reconciling the conflicting interests of British farmers, consumers, and packers, and could hardly interfere directly in what was really an Argentine matter.

In Argentina, the problem was more serious. Undoubtedly foreign capitalists, among them the British, exercised control over the meat trade for limited periods and to a limited extent. Although *estancieros* benefited from buoyant prices until 1920, the disadvantages of laying themselves open to coercion in a falling market, which occurred in the early twenties, were serious. Carlos Carlés recognized that producers believed that favourable pre-war conditions would be permanent, 'when in reality they could only be transitory'.[3] Nevertheless, restraints on the *frigoríficos* such as internal disputes, outside competition, the size of Argentina's domestic market, and the independence of the republic's stockyards, ranchers, and transport—conditions quite different from those which assisted control in the United States[4]—did exist. *Estancieros* also enjoyed important market resources in addition to official intervention. It is, therefore, sensible to consider not only

[1] G. E. Putnam, *Supplying Britain's Meat* (London, 1923), p. 129.
[2] P.R.O. F.O. 368/785/32254.
[3] *Diario de Diputados* (Argentina), 13 June 1913, 1089.
[4] Federal Trade Commission, op. cit., i. 24–5; R. J. Arnould, 'Changes of Concentration in American Meat Packing, 1880–1913', *Business History Review*, xlv (1971), 21–3.

the areas of friction which inevitably existed between producer, packer, and consumer, but also—and this has received less attention—the interdependence between these three market forces and the constraints within which each was compelled to operate.

TABLE VIII.6

Index of Annual Average Prices at Smithfield, 1898–1926

(1913 = 100)

	1898	1899	1900	1901	1902	1903	1904	1905	1906	1907
New Zealand lamb	82	80	84	88	86	90	92	86	82	90
Australian lamb	77	77	77	87	80	87	89	85	78	85
New Zealand mutton	68	82	84	86	88	91	97	94	88	91
Argentine mutton	64	70	85	76	88	88	94	85	85	82
Argentine chilled beef						85	85	83	80	87
Argentine frozen beef						100	82	79	82	88
New Zealand frozen beef	88	94	103	97	121	103	94	85	88	91
Australian frozen beef	68	79	94	88	100	88	75	72	72	88

	1908	1909	1910	1911	1912	1913	1914	1915	1916	1917
New Zealand lamb	94	76	88	86	96	100	106	128	146	162
Australian lamb	87	63	80	77	91	100	104	128	157	174
New Zealand mutton	88	72	88	85	91	100	109	142	173	198
Argentine mutton	85	73	85	85	94	100	112	151	217	259
Argentine chilled beef	95	92	90	85	97	100	115	154	185	240
Argentine frozen beef	91	85	91	91	97	100	133	178	?	?
New Zealand frozen beef	94	88	91	91	100	100	133	178	187	?
Australian frozen beef	91	85	88	88	97	100	135	178	?	?

	1918	1919	1920	1921	1922	1923	1924	1925	1926
New Zealand lamb	214	194	202	194	186	186	186	186	162
Australian lamb	230	208	216	200	178	178	183	191	153
New Zealand mutton	?	250	194	174	168	190	168	187	148
Argentine mutton	316	286	223	180	174	165	174	180	139
Argentine chilled beef	?	?	240	200	135	125	125	140	130
Argentine frozen beef	350	338	300	225	130	130	130	142	136
New Zealand frozen beef	?	?	294	162	112	118	125	136	125
Australian frozen beef	?	?	294	162	112	112	118	130	125

? = Author was unable to obtain accurate figures.
SOURCE: Weddell & Co., (Annual) *Review of the Frozen Meat Trade.*

IV

The Corned Beef and Extract Industries in the Plate, with particular reference to Liebigs

Compared with the refrigerated beef industries, corned beef and extract suffered two major disadvantages: except for Paraguay in the 1920s, these beef products either singly or together never constituted the principal outlet for the cattle of the countries in which they were prepared; secondly, they occupied inferior positions in the hierarchy of beef products in terms of the market value of the products yielded per head of cattle. Hence firms engaged in their manufacture were rarely in a position actively to control cattle prices or successfully to elevate product prices. A tendency serving further to circumscribe the power of firms producing extract and corned beef as primary products was the development of the manufacture of the same items as by-products of refrigerated beef production. Using inferior parts of cattle destined primarily for chilled or frozen beef, the *frigoríficos* were able to produce corned beef, albeit of inferior quality, at lower cost. Actions designed to increase primary producers' profits were, therefore, confined on the one hand to locating their plants in cattle areas at points sufficiently far from rival establishments to afford a transfer-cost barrier to competition; and on the other hand to investing in a range of backward and forward linkages and technological improvements which cumulatively also served to reduce uncertainty. Combination was very rarely possible.

The competition encountered by the various extract and corned beef factories roughly followed the course hypothesized in the introduction to this chapter as the predictable fate of factories at fixed locations: the production of extract within easy reach of cattle; an increase in competition from *saladeros*; consequent conversion to corned beef which could afford heightened ability to compete with *tasajo*; new competition from *frigoríficos* for freezing-grade cattle; conversion to frozen beef . . . In detail, however, the relative duration and timing of specific phases and the precise mechanisms varied; nor were beef-product manufacturers operating under purely *laissez-faire* economic systems.

A common feature of most extract plants was their establishment at or near existing factories where a superior product (usually *tasajo*) was produced, and at a time of falling demand for the superior product.[1] Whilst Colón was exceptional in the latter

---

[1] The circumstances of Liebigs' commencement in Uruguay and Paraguay have already been cited. The circumstances affecting the foundation of other known extract factories are as follows:

(*a*) Argentine *tasajo* exports fell from 38,700 tons in 1877 to 22,400 tons in 1881; Kemmerich founded Santa Elena in 1880, and Delacre's Extract of Beef Co. at La Plata was founded in 1881.

respect, it was also exceptional in that over a third of the slaughter capacity was allocated to corned beef.

Subsequent recovery in the trade of the superior product inevitably brought the threat of excessive competition for cattle, higher prices, and unprofitability. Distance and the opportunity for combination provided the main protection. Fray Bentos felt no need to accept an invitation by the *saladeros* of western Uruguay to join their combination in 1882,[1] yet it undoubtedly benefited since the price it paid fell from $16 in 1882 to under $10 in 1892 despite increased slaughters.[2] Santa Elena must have benefited from its great isolation for three or four decades: mapping of the detailed distribution of *criollo* and *mestizo* cattle in 1895, 1908, and 1914 reveals that improved cattle steadily advanced up the eastern side of Mesopotamia—where *saladeros* were many and rail haulage was available—whilst a wedge of *criollo* cattle persistently stretched along the Paraná as far south as Santa Elena (which enjoyed not only physical isolation from rivals but also a lack of rail facilities).[3] The inference is reasonable that just as competing *saladeros* in the east encouraged improvement with high prices, so isolated Santa Elena discouraged improvement by paying low prices.

Zeballos Cue, Liebigs' factory near Asunción, enjoyed several years' isolation in the 1920s. It paid lower prices than *saladeros* could afford and the General Manager feared the establishment of an *estanciero*-owned *saladero*. Yet Zeballos Cue's extract production

(*b*) Paraguayan *tasajo* exports fell from 2,657 tons in 1903 to 605 tons in 1909; Kemmerich began his San Salvador plant in 1910 not far from Rio Apa and Concepción *saladeros*.

(*c*) The Entre Rios Extract of Meat Co.'s plant at Gualeguaychú (a *saladero* centre) was begun in 1889 and closed in 1895. In those years, however, Argentine *tasajo* exports constantly exceeded 40,000 tons, and 1895 was the peak export year in the country's history.

(*d*) Paraguayan *estancieros* founded Piquete Cue factory near Liebigs' plant in 1929 at a time when Liebigs had combined with I.P.C. (see below) to keep prices down.

Sources: Argentina: *Censo Agropecuario 1908*, iii. 575; British Consular Reports for Paraguay, Annual Series Nos. 3241 (for 1903), 4815 (for 1910), and 5403 (for 1913); 'Argentine Estates of Bovril Ltd.', *La Res* (Buenos Aires), 20 July 1940; J. C. Crossley, 'La contribution britannique à la colonisation et au développement agricole en Argentine' in Centre National de la Recherche Scientifique, *Les Problèmes Agraires des Amériques Latines* (Paris, 1967), pp. 465–6.

[1] Liebigs, Board Minutes, 24 Oct. 1882 and 23 Jan. 1883.
[2] Ibid., various dates 1882–90.
[3] Crossley, op. cit. (1974): Figs. IV. 2, 5; V. 1, 3, 12, 14; VI. 7, 9.

costs equalled the price at which extract could be purchased from third parties; hence higher cattle prices could not be justified.[1] A greater threat came with the reopening of the corned beef factory of Farquhar's International Products Corporation at nearby San Antonio in June 1926. The International Products Corporation, however, had difficulty in producing an acceptable corned beef, and proposed a combination with Liebigs to limit cattle prices. This ran from the start of 1927 to mid-1929 and allowed Zeballos Cue to continue the profitable production of extract. This brief cattle-purchasing combination—the only one known to have existed within or between the extract and corned beef industries, and certainly the only one in which Liebigs ever participated—was brought to an end with the construction of the *estanciero* co-operative extract factory at Piquete Cue. Knowing that extract could not competitively be produced at the higher cattle prices, Liebigs were obliged to convert Zeballos Cue to corned beef production.[2]

In the early days of Liebigs' corned beef boom, from 1909 to 1913, competition continued to come principally from the *saladeros*, and Fray Bentos suffered more than Colón. Although Uruguay achieved its highest *tasajo* exports in history in 1904, with 59,400 tons, the pressure came increasingly from the *saladeros* of Rio Grande do Sul. Following the revolution in Rio Grande in the 1890s, Brazil began increasingly to favour the state's *tasajo* industry by the imposition of import duties on the Uruguayan and Argentine product. According to Acevedo, these rose from the equivalent of $1.25 per animal in 1895 to $9.00 by 1911.[3] The result was the construction of a series of nine new *saladeros* in the interior of Rio Grande and close by the Uruguayan frontier, expressly to process Uruguayan cattle. Enjoying not only tariff protection—and hence an ability to pay high cattle prices—but also access to the Uruguayan rail system, the 'frontier' *saladeros* discomfited not only the Uruguayan *saladeros* but also Fray Bentos. In the period 1901–14, no correspondence may be discerned between the prices paid by Fray Bentos and the volume of cattle

[1] Liebigs, C. D. Noble to K. M. Carlisle, 28 July and 9 Sept. 1925.
[2] Ibid., K. M. Carlisle to C. D. Noble, 5 Feb. 1925; Noble to Carlisle, 24 Apr. 1925, 18 Jan. 1927; Carlisle to Noble, 15 Aug. 1929.
[3] Acevedo, op. cit. (1934), v. 316, 594. Cf. the prices paid by Fray Bentos for steers in 1901–11 which varied between $14 and $23: Liebigs' Slaughter Statistics.

slaughtered there, except for the years 1907–10. In contrast, Colón, less accessible from Rio Grande do Sul, enjoyed a greater command of local cattle resources: in 1905–12 prices paid by Colón closely reflected the volume of its own needs; similarly the Entre Rios *saladero* slaughter varied inversely with Colón's. The weakness of the local *saladeros* was additionally due to duties on imported salt and sacks.[1] Yet in 1912 even Colón had to lament that fatteners serving the Rio Grande *saladeros* were paying more for store cattle than Colón was offering for fat cattle.[2] Following their wartime eclipse, Argentine *saladeros*, now preparing a tenderer type of *tasajo*, enjoyed a resurgence. All six lay in areas whence Colón drew its cattle, paid similar prices and, at least until 1926, constituted for Liebigs 'a thorn in our side'.[3]

But it was from the *frigoríficos* that Liebigs' corned beef factories came increasingly to suffer. Following the opening of the Ibicuy–Zárate rail ferry in 1908, some 52,000 cattle were railed from Entre Rios in January–October 1909. In Uruguay the second *frigorífico* was opened in 1911, following the government's permanent exemption of refrigerated beef from export duties. Immediately Fray Bentos suffered a cattle shortage and prices paid in 1912 and 1913 rocketed. Liebigs observed: 'the basis of our cattle purchases was formerly the value of *tasajo*; now it is, in Uruguay anyhow, already to a very large extent the price the Montevideo freezing works pay for their cattle'.[4] By August 1913 Liebigs were seriously considering closing Fray Bentos.[5]

Saved by the war, Liebigs postponed a decision on Fray Bentos until late 1919, when conversion to a *frigorífico* appeared to present the sensible solution. From January 1923 to April 1924 Fray Bentos operated to produce chilled beef for the British market, but a multiplicity of factors contributed to the failure of the venture: over 150 kilometers from the nearest *frigorífico*, it enjoyed only weekly visits by refrigerated steamers, hence between visits the chilled beef had to suffer deterioration in storage or incur the

---

[1] Liebigs' Slaughter Statistics; Argentina, *Censo Agropecuario 1908*, iii. 91, 366; *S.A.J.*, 1909, ii. 201; Acevedo, op. cit. (1934), v. 594.

[2] Liebigs, Colón, Estancia and Cattle Dept., *Annual Report 1912*.

[3] Liebigs, P. Newkirk to Carlisle, 19 Aug. 1925; Carlisle to Noble, 5 Apr. 1926.

[4] Ibid., Colón, Factory Dept., *Annual Report 1909*; Fray Bentos, Factory Dept., *Annual Report 1911*; Cattle and Estancia Dept., *Annual Report 1913*.

[5] Liebigs, Fray Bentos to London, 6 Aug. 1913, and London to Fray Bentos, 4 Sept. 1913.

additional cost of lighterage to Buenos Aires. Liebigs' plan to slaughter the best animals from both sides of the river was thwarted by the Uruguayan Government's ban on imported cattle, imposed on 1 April 1924. Though ostensibly designed to protect local farmers, the ban was retained despite the support Liebigs received in their petition for its lifting from the Rural Federation of Montevideo, 'in view of the manner in which [Liebigs' activities] have been conducted in the past which have always redounded to the livestock interests and to the national economy'.[1]

For Liebigs' remaining corned beef factory, at Colón, the mid-1920s brought intense pressure on cattle supplies from those *frigoríficos* which catered for the continental frozen trade, as described previously. In contrast, rival manufacturers of corned beef as a primary product were limited to Bovril's plant at Santa Elena. Despite the view of Corrientes *estancieros* to the contrary, the two companies never combined to restrict prices. For purely spatial reasons their areas of supply overlapped only to a limited extent, and any similarity in prices offered was purely a function of their locational, technological, and organizational similarities.[2]

Given the nature of cattle competition, it was through forward and backward linkages that the extract and corned beef industries sought principally to assure their positions and increase their profitability. To a large measure the rapid success of the Liebig Company may be attributed to its establishment of forward linkages. A depot to receive the extract in bulk was immediately opened at Antwerp. That city was also the headquarters of several hide-merchant families who provided much of the Company's capital and received its hides on consignment. By 1868 agencies for

---

[1] *R.R.P.*, 1924, i. 765, quoting *La Nación*, 20 Mar. 1924. For a fuller explanation, see Crossley, op. cit. (1974), pp. 329–59. In the light of the discussion in section III of this chapter, it is pertinent to note that K. R. M. Carlisle (chairman of Liebigs 1958–68) attributes Fray Bentos' failure especially to the fact that hitherto the Company's marketing experience had lain in the more stable grocery sector of the beef product trades and that success in the fickle butchery sector required experience of a very different kind: personal communication, K. R. M. Carlisle to J. C. Crossley, 29 Nov. 1973.

[2] In 1931 Liebigs' Headquarters assured General Manager Noble that cattlemen's assertions of a Liebig–Bovril combination 'were completely unfounded', but, as it would not be believed, it was pointless to publish the assurance: Liebigs, London to Colón, 22 July 1931. Since Liebigs' (private and confidential) correspondence does refer to the Paraguayan combination of 1927–9, this assurance, together with the absence of any other reference to combinations, can be taken at its face value.

the sale of extract had been established in the United States, Mexico, Venezuela, Brazil, Chile, and Batavia, as well as in nearly every European country.[1] Another of the Company's shareholders acted as recipient and distributing agent for the corned beef in the early years. Later, in 1914, a subsidiary company, Oxo Ltd., was founded to handle the whole commercial side; subsequently subsidiaries have been established in many leading European and Commonwealth countries to handle distribution. From the start, therefore, much of the Company's strength lay in its marketing and its virtually exclusive right to the use of the prestigious name of beef extract's inventor. As a result no rival company was ever purchased to reduce competition, but dozens of lawsuits were fought over the right to use the Liebig name.

One such was with Dr. Kemmerich, briefly manager of Fray Bentos in 1874, and founder of Santa Elena. By 1894 he had become in the extract market Liebigs' main, if less successful, competitor. The leasing by Liebigs of the Santa Elena extract factory from 1895 to 1904 (mentioned above) was hailed in the press as a double combination: Kemmerich agreed not to make and sell extract; in return Liebigs agreed to buy beef from Kemmerich and not to compete along the Paraná by building their planned factory or by purchasing cattle. Kemmerich was thus free to extend his *tasajo* side and to monopolize the cattle of the district.[2] The relationship was not a happy one. On its expiry, Kemmerich had difficulty in marketing his extract and twice offered, in 1901 and 1907, to sell out to Liebigs; their derisory offers were a mark either of their marketing strength or of their dislike for Kemmerich.[3] In 1908 Kemmerich and Bovril merged their interests, providing forward and backward linkages for each other.[4] An extract manufacturing and marketing organization was thus created that was soon rivalling Liebigs in both the Plate and Britain.

Much of Bovril's corned beef, however, has been marketed

[1] Liebigs, Board Minutes, 6 Mar. 1868.
[2] Ibid., 31 Oct. and 15 Nov. 1894; *S.A.J.*, 1895, i. 309, quoting *C.D.*
[3] Liebigs, Fray Bentos Local Board Minutes, 23 Apr. 1901; (London) Board Minutes, 30 May 1907, and Board Minutes (Private Meetings), 10 June 1907. The Liebig offer was £70,000.
[4] Kemmerich received almost £500,000: Argentine Estates of Bovril Ltd., Prospectus 1908, Companies Registration Office, File 101243 (Companies House, 55–71 City Road, London, E.C.I.).

under the brand names of other companies, whilst the 'Fray Bentos' brand, exclusive to Liebigs even after the factory's sale, has long been the leader in the corned beef trade, enabling the Company to command a premium over other brands.

The strength of Liebigs' marketing side has had consequences on the production side of particular importance in the context of this book. A purely marketing firm is able to obtain its supplies from the cheapest source whilst a purely manufacturing firm is in serious difficulty once it ceases to produce at competitive prices. In an integrated firm in times of manufacturing adversity, the marketing side is able to support the production side even if it is making a loss. Such action constitutes a transfer of capital to the country of production which is also benefited by the greater regularity of production thereby achieved. Possession of a premium-commanding brand image further enhances such a company's ability to transfer capital back. Equally, however, a highly profitable marketing side allows inefficiency in manufacturing operations to go unheeded. In the absence of a study of internal accounts and of the comparative c.i.f. prices of corned beef and extract produced by independent manufacturers, it is impossible to calculate the extent of such transfers of capital to the producing side of Liebigs' enterprises. K. R. M. Carlisle, however, comments that the Board of Directors viewed the marketing side as the main source of profit in the 1920s, and was content with a marginal profit from the River Plate activities.[1] Ironically, it was the inefficiency of operations that provides the clearest evidence of a transfer of capital. Thus, in the 1928 season, Colón killed 202,000 cattle averaging 388 kilogrammes each to provide the volume of corned beef required, when 175,000 properly finished cattle averaging 420 kilogrammes would have sufficed (the cattle had been killed too soon after they had been bought as store cattle for fattening on Liebigs' *estancias*).[2] Thus Liebigs incurred the unnecessary expenses of buying 27,000 too many store cattle and of slaughtering them. *Estancieros* and factory workers were clearly the beneficiaries.

Liebigs in Uruguay, Argentina, and Paraguay, Kemmerich/Bovril in Argentina, and the International Products Corporation

---

[1] Personal communication K. R. M. Carlisle to J. C. Crossley, 29 Nov. 1973.
[2] Liebigs, H. Gibson (then Local Director of Liebigs) to London, Memo on Colón Factory Supplies, 31 July 1928.

in Paraguay also became involved on a massive scale with backward linkages into cattle fattening and breeding on both rented and owned properties. Acquisitions by Liebigs were begun by Croker, the manager at Fray Bentos, in 1875 for the purposes of smoothing the flow of cattle to the factory (at a time when all animals were delivered on foot) and of participating in the profits of fattening. It reflected the preference of Croker, by training a cattleman, for enhancing the Company's profits from farming rather than through technological improvements at the factory. The policy was fully accepted by the Board only in 1883 when other advantages emerged: 'by having a stock of cattle at our disposal we are rendered more independent of farmers and dealers very much to our advantage'.[1] Yet by 1891 Liebig *estancias* could furnish at most one-eighth of Fray Bentos' fat cattle requirements.

With the election of C. E. Gunther as Liebigs' chairman in 1898, the role of Liebigs' *estancias* became a regular source of conflict between the Board and the River Plate Management. For the latter, the purpose of *estancias* was to facilitate the flow of cattle to the factory, to reduce its need to compete for cattle, and to participate in the profits of fattening. Gunther in contrast took a longer-term view, preferring to expand cattle breeding and improvement and envisaging that, with the extension of rail systems and the increased outreach of *frigoríficos*, such investments would appreciate and provide greater and surer profits than catering for the factory's immediate needs.[2] The corollaries of the first policy were that lands and cattle should continue to serve the factory even when cattle could be sold more profitably elsewhere, and lands could more profitably be turned over to crop farming. The corollaries of the second policy were that great sums had to be invested before the venture became profitable and that the gamble on the lands' physical and locational suitability would ultimately pay off. The second policy can be considered as backward linkage only in so far as it supplied stores for Colón.

The compromise which evolved was, in Argentina, to buy cheap remote lands in Corrientes for breeding and to rent lands in Entre Rios to supply Colón with fat cattle. By 1911 Liebigs owned 307,000 hectares and leased 173,000 hectares in Argentina. Yet

---

[1] Liebigs, Directors' *Annual Report* to Shareholders, 7 June 1883.

[2] Ibid., Fray Bentos Local Board Minutes 6/7 Mar. 1905 (meeting attended by chairman).

the breeding lands contributed relatively little to Colón's needs, nor were many sales made outside: in 1915–21, 33 per cent of Colón's supply came from bought fat cattle, 47 per cent from bought store cattle fattened on Liebig lands, and only 20 per cent from cattle bred and fattened by the Company. In Uruguay Fray Bentos' needs were met from the same sources in the proportions 73:23:4. Additionally, by 1912 Liebigs had invested in Paraguay, Rhodesia, and South West Africa and brought the lands under the Company's control to 1·75 million hectares, most of them undeveloped, yielding little, and absorbing the profits of manufacturing and marketing as well as increases in authorized capital.[1] Following the acquisition of Zeballos Cue, Liebigs proceeded almost to double their Paraguayan territories to 581,000 hectares by mid-1925, with the intention of increasing their fattening capacity.

The consequences for the River Plate countries were varied: the expansion in Argentina of fattening, to supply Colón with up to 140,000 fat cattle a year, served to transfer demand massively to the store cattle sector, raising prices there to the advantage of breeders but to the disadvantage of fatteners and Liebigs alike. The fatteners suffered, too, from the fact that year-to-year fluctuations in Colón's needs were passed on as far as possible to the independent fatteners: thus during the years 1919–24, Liebig-fattened cattle slaughtered at Colón varied between 22,000 and 81,000, whereas purchased fat cattle fluctuated between nil and 149,000. In Uruguay the lesser role of Liebig *estancias* was more beneficial and Liebigs' reputation among cattle farmers was, as already mentioned, high.

Liebigs' breeding activities in contrast were largely beneficial to local cattle breeders in Uruguay and Argentina. By breeding

[1] By such devices as issuing new Ordinary shares at a premium as well as 5 per cent Preference shares, it was possible to raise Ordinary dividends from 20 per cent in 1899 to 22½ per cent in 1912, whilst at the same time distributed profits as a percentage of capital actually raised in fact fell from 26⅔ per cent to 10½ per cent. Although wartime profits were high, ordinary dividends increased only marginally to 25 per cent; the rest was reinvested in lands and cattle in the Plate, as were the proceeds of Fray Bentos' sale in 1924. After further ordinary capital was raised in 1921 and 1924, ordinary dividends fell to 16 per cent and distributed profits as a percentage of actually raised capital remained virtually constant, at 11 per cent, in 1925–30. Since much of this must have come from marketing profits and profits on manufacturing (Oxo cubes) in Britain, it is clear that whilst nineteenth-century activities involved a massive transfer of wealth to Britain (and Europe), twentieth-century transfers have been minimal.

high-grade Hereford and Angus cattle in regions that were tick-infested and hence exposed to Texas Fever, Liebigs created a reservoir of fine stock which was relatively immune to the disease —unlike animals imported from tick-free areas—and hence, through sales of surplus bulls, materially contributed to the improvement of the herds of Mesopotamia and western Uruguay; by the same token they accelerated the rate at which cattle became attractive to the *frigoríficos*, benefiting breeder and fattener alike through the higher prices offered. Through such activities the Company also gained great social prestige among *estancieros*. Economically, however, the gains expected by Gunther had still to materialize: in 1925 a detailed study by Gibson of the Company's Corrientes *estancias* revealed that 73 per cent of the profits came from sheep, *yerba mate*, and subletting, and most of the cattle profits came from fattening; virtually all the breeding *estancias* were losing money on cattle account. The reason, over-breeding, and the solution, introduction of high-grade Zebu stock, were still to be discovered. Only then, fifty years after Gunther's policy began, did good profits justify its implementation.

Besides forward and backward linkages, technological changes played a part in aiding the position of the companies concerned. In the case of Liebigs, improvements in extract technology in 1895 and 1900 reduced the amount of beef needed to make a pound of extract from forty pounds in 1894 to twenty-five pounds in 1900. By 1900 a cheaper but inferior type of extract, liquid Oxo, requiring only twelve pounds of beef per pound of extract, had been invented. From a marketing point of view the major disadvantage of all liquid extracts was the fact that the smallest practicable size of jar was beyond the means of many people. The invention and introduction of the Oxo cube in 1910 solved the problem and opened up the market for extract to a new class of people. As a result Colón's slaughter for Oxo rose from 12,100 cattle in 1909 to 34,800 in 1912.[1] Wartime changes increased the amount of corned beef obtained from each pound of fresh beef by about 10 per cent. At the same period, standard extract and liquid Oxo began to be produced as by-products of corned beef manufacture rather than as primary products.

[1] Liebigs, Fray Bentos Manager's *Annual Reports*, 1895 and 1900; C. Scarborough, *About Oxo* (London, 1965), p. 8; Liebigs, Board Minutes, 17 Feb. 1910; Colón, Factory Department *Annual Reports 1909, 1912.*

The fact remained that such changes, which increased the market value of extract products per head of cattle, only marginally affected the location or date at which extracts had to yield to a superior beef product. As already described, conversion to a superior beef product was the only alternative to closure for specific factories when competition and cattle prices reached crucial levels. For specific companies, in contrast, the alternative of relocation was also available. Liebigs' choice was on several occasions both to convert existing factories to new products and to relocate manufacture of the original product. Bovril in contrast chose only to convert Santa Elena, though in 1926–7 they gave serious consideration to manufacturing extract in northern Paraguay.[1]

The extract and corned beef industries, like refrigerated beef, were also subject to the direct intervention of governments. Liebigs' move to Argentina has been cited by Hanson as the consequence of President Batlle's anti-foreign capitalist attitude in Uruguay.[2] More specifically, Acevedo has written that Liebigs decided to establish Colón in 1906 after Batlle refused to reduce duties on extract to the level of those on *tasajo*, that is, from the equivalent of $1.26 per animal to $0.91.[1] In fact Fray Bentos' manager in his Annual Report dated 1 November 1903, whilst lamenting the lack of progress with the petition to Batlle, still hoped for a favourable outcome. Batlle's rejection must, therefore, have followed the actual legal transfer of Colón,[3] whilst Liebigs' decision to purchase was made in November 1902—before Batlle became President![4] Nevertheless the fact that Argentina had abolished export duties *was* one of many factors, though the main one was probably the shortage of cattle in western Uruguay.[5] The fact also remains that Batlle's attitude did affect Liebigs in their production policies for Fray Bentos and Colón. Following Batlle's rejection, Liebigs successfully petitioned Congress for a reduction in duties in 1905; Batlle, however, vetoed the Bill which was finally enacted when his successor came to power in

---

[1] Following detailed inspection Bovril were offered the 2·5 million hectare Chaco properties of the Carlos Casado Company: J. Campbell to G. A. Ellison, 4 June 1927 (Bovril Ltd., Bovril House, Southbury Rd., Enfield, Middlesex).

[2] Hanson, op. cit. (1938), pp. 19, 199–200.

[3] Acevedo, op. cit. (1934), v. 315.

[4] Liebigs, Board Minutes, 19 Nov. 1903.   [5] Ibid., 6 Nov. 1902.

[6] Ibid., Fray Bentos Local Board Minutes, 15 Nov. 1902.

1907.[1] Available data demonstrate that production costs of corned beef and extract were lower at Colón than Fray Bentos. Thus in 1905–7 extract cost 9·25*d.* per pound more at Fray Bentos, duties accounting for 2·28*d.*; after their reduction in July 1907 they accounted for 1·14*d.* of the 8·10*d.* per pound difference in 1908–12. In 1907 duties on corned beef accounted for 4*s.* 2*d.* of the nine-shilling difference per 100 kilos. The British consul commented: 'As long as Argentina offers such a marked advantage over Uruguay in the matter of import and export duties the development of this important business must inevitably take place in the former country.'[2] Yet even after all duties were removed in 1910, differences remained and Fray Bentos' slaughter, expressed as a percentage of Colón's, actually fell from 81 per cent in 1909 to 57 per cent in 1911.

Of wider general significance than the foregoing have been the frequent restrictions imposed by governments on the movement of cattle across their frontiers. Import prohibitions have been frequently introduced at the time of foot-and-mouth disease outbreaks in neighbouring countries. Export restrictions have been imposed to encourage or protect domestic beef product industries. Such barriers often serve to impede the 'natural' flows of cattle that are inherent in the theory outlined in Section II of this chapter. Two examples may suffice: the Salto Falls on the River Uruguay provide a limit to navigation and made the banks of the lower reaches the logical best locations for *saladeros* as well as Colón and Fray Bentos. The natural flow of cattle was, therefore, southwards from breeding areas in the north to fattening areas in the south near the factories. In Argentina no obstacle to such movement occurred, as only an inter-provincial movement between Corrientes and Entre Rios was involved. On the east bank, however, the areas corresponding to Corrientes and Entre Rios lie respectively in Brazil and Uruguay. Not only did negative restrictions impede the corresponding flow, but Brazil's protection of her native *tasajo* industry actually reversed the flow. Similarly, in the 1920s the natural flow of the cattle of southern Mato Grosso was southwards to lands in northern

[1] *S.A.J.*, 1905, i. 434; 1907, ii. 147.
[2] Liebigs Slaughter Statistics; Fray Bentos Factory Department, *Annual Reports 1906, 1908*; British Consular Reports (Uruguay), Annual Series No. 4052, 1907.

Paraguay which fattened supplies for the *saladeros* and Zeballos Cue. Prohibition by Paraguay on imports in 1927 (for fear of introducing rinderpest) was coupled with other difficulties such as exchange rates which made Brazilian cattle too expensive. As a result Liebigs found that *estancias* acquired just south of the frontier for receiving imported cattle had to be converted to breeding establishments.[1]

Finally, in any discussion of the extent to which business firms exerted control over the environment in which they operated, it should be stressed that decision-taking was exercised not by omniscient, profit-maximizing rational 'economic men' but by normal human beings, whose motives were mixed and not necessarily even economic, whose knowledge was far from perfect—this was especially true of the period under consideration when quite simple geographic facts were not available and companies did not have well-staffed intelligence departments—and whose perceptions and skills were not necessarily adequate to the tasks they were called upon to perform. Let three examples from Liebigs' wide-ranging activities, that had steadily evolved from making extract at Fray Bentos, suffice.

In promoting a long-term policy of large-scale cattle improvement, C. E. Gunther was undoubtedly influenced by his own experience as a successful and independent producer of high grade Hereford/Shorthorn cattle in western Buenos Aires;[2] he could hardly know that the steady refining with Hereford stock of the herds that roamed Liebigs' *estancias* in the humid subtropical north-east corner of Corrientes would thirty years later produce animals incapable of resisting the diseases to which *criollo* cattle were immune.

Secondly, on the evidence of agents (the Rural Belga Company in which Liebigs held shares), 132,000 hectares of land in southern Paraguay were purchased in 1906–7 for the purpose of raising cattle for a factory to be built on the banks of the River Paraguay. But in 1908 the only possible site proved liable to river erosion against which no preventive measures could be taken. Most of the lands proved to be 'swamps [that] are simply frightful to pass

---

[1] Liebigs, Carlisle to Noble, 10 Mar. 1927; Noble to Carlisle, 29 June 1927; Liebigs, Livestock Department, *Annual Report 1930*.

[2] *S.A.J.*, 1904, ii. 376–9; W. H. Koebel, *Modern Argentina* (London, 1907), pp. 207–12.

through and most dangerous for the animals'.[1] Such misfortunes were hardly surprising for, in reporting on his visit to southern Paraguay in October 1905, G. P. J. Lynch prefaced his observations to the Directors with the words: 'The difficulty of obtaining any information of reliable character is only equalled by the great disorganization that prevails in every quarter both in public and private affairs and [has been] quite the natural state of things outside Asunción . . . for the last forty years.' Finally, having failed to extend their backward linkage into successful cattle-breeding in north-eastern Corrientes, Liebigs sought to derive some profit from plantation agriculture. Tree crops were also speculative ventures requiring several years' investment before even the possibility of profit could be accurately assessed. In 1926 Albert Cavanagh, an expert in subtropical horticulture, was placed in charge of the plantations: 'whilst Mr. Cavanagh's main duties must of course be to aid in making the (existing) *yerba* plantations a success . . . he should be allowed, and if necessary encouraged, to make experimental plantations with other shrubs and trees . . . and to divulge advice and knowledge to all'. Agricultural diversification, experimentation, and diffusion thus became the Company's declared policy, objectives that proved congenial to Cavanagh. His own scientific dedication and humanitarianism, coupled with Liebigs' ability to finance loss-making activities for many years in the hope of ultimate gain, were to lead to the introduction of tung trees, the proof of their commercial viability, and the diffusion of the crop to 6,000 small farmers in Misiones.[2] Tea cultivation was also pioneered by Cavanagh and subsequently widely adopted.[3] The crop was not, however, developed on a commercial scale by Liebigs—ironically, because in 1968 the company merged its enterprises with the tea specialists, Brooke Bond!

[1] Liebigs, C. M. Rotter's Report 1906; Board Minutes, 29 Nov. 1906; Fray Bentos, Estancia and Cattle Department, *Annual Reports 1908, 1909*; Factory Department, *Annual Report 1909*.

[2] Liebigs, London to Colón, 3 Nov. 1926, 28 Oct. 1927; Argentina, *Censo Agropecuario 1960*, i. 12. The crop has become second only to *yerba* among the Misiones colonists and the main crop in contiguous areas of Paraguay.

[3] Liebigs, Board Minutes, 15 Mar. 1928; ibid., *Report on Visits to Plantations*, Dec. 1932.

PART IV

BUSINESS AND GOVERNMENT:
THREE CASE STUDIES

CHAPTER IX

Antony Gibbs & Sons, the Guano Trade and the Peruvian Government, 1842–1861

W. M. MATHEW

I

THERE are at least three different ways in which one can define the term 'control' in the context of relations between a foreign merchant house and a national government. There is, first, the deliberate control that the foreigner may exercise over officials, using what power he possesses to bring about decisions favourable to his own operations. Second, there is the more subtle and less obvious form of control in which policies are not wilfully forced upon the government, but which results simply from the circumstances confronting the government as a result of the presence and dispositions of the foreigner. Third, there is the control that manifests itself in mercantile authority and initiative in fields of activity vital to the government's well-being, the government itself lacking the will or the power to restrain the merchant and exercise a jurisdiction of its own.

II

Gibbs's first contract with the Peruvian Government for the export and sale of guano was arranged at the beginning of 1842. Their last contract expired at the end of 1861. Over the intervening twenty years the English firm became the single most important mercantile party in one of South America's largest and most unusual trades. Guano for the British market and for much of Europe and the British Empire as well was consigned exclusively to Antony Gibbs & Sons of London and W. J. Myers & Co. of

M

Liverpool between 1842 and 1849, and to Gibbs alone from 1849 to 1861. Gibbs's dominance of what rapidly became Peru's principal export sector derived from the fact that Britain, their main preserve, purchased more guano than all other foreign markets combined. The period of their participation extends more or less from the start of the trade through and past its phase of most vigorous expansion. In 1858 302,207 tons of Peruvian guano were imported into Britain. This was to be the all-time peak (Table IX.1). 'The real heyday of the guano period had been

TABLE IX.1

British imports (gross) of Guano from Peru, 1841–69

(tons)

1841	2,062	1851	199,732	1861	161,566
1842	14,123	1852	86,293	1862	69,390
1843	1,589	1853	106,312	1863	196,704
1844	16,475	1854	221,747	1864	113,086
1845	14,101	1855	255,535	1865	210,784
1846	22,410	1856	177,016	1866	109,142
1847	57,762	1857	264,230	1867	164,112
1848	61,055	1858	302,207	1868	155,766
1849	73,567	1859	49,064	1869	199,122
1850	95,083	1860	122,459		

SOURCES: Parliamentary Papers, 1852, lii, 215; 1860, lxvi, 10–11; 1865, lii, 314; 1870, lxiii, 305.

passed', writes C. A. McQueen of the early 1860s, 'although the ultimate collapse did not take place until 15 years later.'[1]

There were two houses of Gibbs in the guano trade: Antony Gibbs & Sons of London and Gibbs Crawley & Co. (renamed William Gibbs & Co. in 1847) of Lima. The London firm had been established in 1808, and the Lima branch fourteen years later. Both concentrated on commission work, and the connections between them were intimate. The London house took a share of the Lima concern's profits, and the branch found a good deal of the cash it required for its operations through the sale of bills on the parent. Policies on matters of mutual concern were usually harmonized to the extent that time and distance would permit. The way in which this relatively small and initially rather unambitious family enterprise dominated one of the great trades

[1] C. A. McQueen, *Peruvian Public Finance* (Washington, 1926), p. 38.

of the international economy in the mid-nineteenth century is probably without precedent. Their participation, moreover, brought them into direct contact with the Peruvian Government, for guano was declared state property almost as soon as exporting began. Any merchant house which entered the trade did so only through prior contractual agreement with the government, and the terms of these arrangements were such that traders and officials were in continual communication with each other. The government had the closest interest in the success of the trade, for by the 1850s the fertilizer had become its main source of income and the country's principal earner of foreign exchange. The relationship between Gibbs and the government, therefore, was highly important in both budgetary and commercial terms, and brings into the sharpest focus issues of very central concern to this book.

The literature on the relationship, both contemporary and modern, leaves little doubt that it represents an almost classic case of control in each of the senses alluded to above. Could it have been otherwise? Gibbs were one of the most powerful representatives of European capitalism in Peru, and were backed by the enormous financial resources of the City of London. Peruvian governments, led by economically unsophisticated soldiers, ruled an impoverished and disunited country. The English merchants were visibly enriched by their guano business, and by the latter decades of the nineteenth century were disporting themselves with much poise and confidence in the elevated world of merchant banking. Administrations in Lima, however, staggered from one financial crisis to another. At the end of the guano period, in the 1880s, they governed a debilitated and demoralized country, defeated in war and defaulting on its external bonded debt.

Between 1856 and 1861 a rash of books and pamphlets appeared in Peru and Europe denouncing Gibbs for misconduct in the trade and wilful ruination of Peruvian wealth. Authors like Carlos Barroilhet, Luis Mesones, and José Casimiro Ulloa used their pens as swords to cut into the gross flesh of the English capitalists and force their withdrawal from the trade in 1861. Gibbs's participation in guano exporting, commented Barroilhet, had been 'a complete disaster for Peru, a public calamity'.[1] The consignment

---

[1] Carlos Barroilhet, *Opúsculo sobre el huano dedicado a la nación peruano* (Paris, 1857), p. 6.

system of which they were part was described as 'vicious' by Mesones, involving as it did exorbitant charges and grave damage to the national treasury.[1] According to Ulloa, they wielded 'the greatest despotism that a person or family could exercise over a nation'.[2] They withheld funds from the government at their pleasure, imposed the harshest possible terms when loans were arranged, and perpetrated the excessive depreciation of guano prices in overseas markets in order to energize sales and increase their own commission earnings.[3] Accusations of unnecessary price reductions had also been a principal feature of Barroilhet's critique: in his view these had been a deliberate ploy to impoverish the government and coerce it into heavy financial dependence on the merchants. 'A poor Peru is the one that suits us best' was, he imagined, Gibbs's privately expressed sentiment.[4] In 1857-8, following a resolution of the Convención Nacional, commissioners were sent to Britain, France, and the United States to see whether or not guano *had* been sold at unduly low prices by Gibbs and other consignees and to check if these parties had been working in precise accordance with the terms of their contracts.[5] Gibbs were cleared of malpractice,[6] but this did little to abate the criticism directed against them. In 1861 the newspaper *El Comercio* insisted that considerations of justice, morality, and financial expediency demanded the speedy termination of the Gibbs contract.[7]

Recent writings have served to confirm the notion that Gibbs's influence was insidious and malevolent. Heraclio Bonilla observes that, enjoying 'absolute control . . . over the sale of guano in Europe', they came to hold in their power 'the vital mainsprings of the Peruvian economy'.[8] By the late 1840s, according to Fredrick Pike, 'Peru's economy was largely at the mercy of Antony Gibbs & Sons of London'.[9] Jonathan Levin, noting that under the terms of

[1] Luis Mesones, *El Ministro de Hacienda del Perú en sus relaciones con los administradores del huano en europa* (Besançon, 1859), p. 120.

[2] José Casimiro Ulloa, *Huano (Apuntes Económicos y Administrativos)* (Lima, 1859), p. 116.

[3] Ibid., pp. 5-7, 114-16, 130.

[4] Barroilhet, op. cit., pp. 32-3.

[5] Neptali Benvenutto, *Crónica parlamentaria del Perú*, v (Lima, 1926), 203-4.

[6] *Informe circunstanciado sobre el sistema y la economía de la venta del huano. Volumen especial* (London, 1872), p. xix.

[7] 'El Congreso, El Gobierno y La Casa de Gibbs', *El Comercio*, 17 Jan. 1861.

[8] Heraclio Bonilla, 'Aspects de l'histoire économique et sociale du Pérou au xixᵉ siècle' (unpublished doctoral thesis, Paris, 1970), p. 216.

[9] Fredrick B. Pike, *The Modern History of Peru* (London, 1967), p. 98.

his contracts the guano trader earned commissions on costs met on behalf of the government, suggests that he had a clear interest 'in raising the costs and thereby increasing his commission on them'. He also observes (echoing Ulloa) that the contractor, acting on incentives provided by sales commissions on gross proceeds, wished to sell guano at prices lower than the Peruvian Government, 'the owner of a wasting resource', deemed appropriate. He concludes that on both counts—the holding down of intermediate costs and the maintenance of high monopoly prices—the government suffered losses. Because the contractors' interests were allowed to diverge from the government's while the government lacked any effective means of enforcement, the government's interests suffered.[1] These arguments have been restated in recent accounts of the trade by Peruvian scholars.[2] 'Levin's scissors', if we may call them that, have become an important tool for the dissection of Peru's economic woes in the guano period.

All the indications, then—from superficial observation, from *a priori* assumption, from contemporary comment, and from modern scholarship—point to a clear instance of 'control'. There are, however, four good reasons why such judgements cannot be regarded as definitive. In the first place, the conclusions have not been backed up by reference to the records of traders such as Gibbs. Second, there has been a dearth of information on vital matters such as intermediate costs and market prices: arguments asserting that the former tended to rise and the latter to fall remain totally unsubstantiated. Third, there are contradictions in the Levin model: the scissors do not necessarily snip. By pushing up costs, for example, the contractors may have placed upward pressures on prices, thereby compromising the alleged policy of price depreciation. Fourth, we cannot be certain that contemporary observers who were so critical of Gibbs were objective and disinterested parties: guano was a very live political issue, and the possibility of contract transference from Gibbs was a matter of the greatest economic moment for powerful elements of the Peruvian bourgeoisie.

[1] Jonathan V. Levin, *The Export Economies* (Cambridge, Mass., 1960), pp. 68–71.
[2] Jorge Basadre, *História de la República del Perú 1822–1933* (Lima, 6th edn., 1969), iii. 162; Bonilla, op. cit., pp. 226–7; Luis Pásara, *El Rol del Derecho en la época del guano* (Lima, 1970), p. 15; Ernesto Yepes del Castillo, *Perú 1820–1920; un siglo de desarrollo capitalista* (Lima, 1972), pp. 62–3.

It is our purpose here not merely to cast doubt on some of the judgements that have been offered, but positively to contradict them. It is no part of the argument to suggest that Gibbs were specially virtuous, or that they exercised altruistic self-restraint in their pursuit of profit. Nor is there any wish to convey the impression that foreign traders in backward economies generally knew their place and never seriously compromised the political integrity of the states in which they operated. The Peruvian case may have been a rather unusual one. We shall consider it by examining first of all the contracts governing the export and sale of guano by Gibbs; second, the financial dealings between them and the Peruvian Government; third, their position on guano pricing; fourth, their record on intermediate costs; and fifth, the other abuses that they may have committed. Then we shall return to our categories of 'control' and see which, if any, are applicable.

III

We can begin with some bald and basic details on contracts.[1] Gibbs entered into five successive arrangements with the Peruvian Government: in February 1842, July 1847, December 1847, January 1849, and May 1850. In 1843 they also secured a three-year extension on their 1842 contract (altered in 1846 to one year); and in 1853 they won a six-year *prórroga* on their 1850 contract, thereby gaining security of tenure until the end of 1861. The first three contracts were shared with other parties; the last two were theirs alone. The territorial aspects of these arrangements varied quite a bit. February 1842 and December 1847 gave world-wide trading rights. July 1847 gave all but the United

[1] There is an abundance of information on the contracts in the Gibbs correspondence and in the British Foreign Office General Correspondence and Embassy and Consular Archives relating to Peru (P.R.O. F.O. 61 and F.O. 177 respectively). Reproductions of the 1842, 1846, 1847, 1849, and 1858 arrangements appear in *Anales*, iii. 155–9; iv. 22, 28–9, 30–3, 37–40, 113; v. 22, 35–9, 42. For the 1843, 1850, 1853, and 1854 contracts one has to rely on the Gibbs archive, MS. 11,047: extracts of correspondence between the London Head Office and others concerning the firm's guano business, 1840–56 (hereinafter G.G.C.), letters of 13 Sept. 1843, 16 and 23 May, 12 and 27 July, 17 Sept. 1850. MS. 11,038: copy-book of in-letters addressed to William Gibbs, 1854–5 (hereinafter W.G.C.), Henry Hucks Gibbs to William Gibbs, 24 Mar. and 31 Aug. 1854. MS. 11,036: out-letter books (private) of Henry Hucks Gibbs, 1845–82 (hereinafter H.H.G.C.), vol. ii, Henry Hucks Gibbs to William Gibbs, 3 Feb. 1860.

States. January 1849 was for Britain and the whole of Europe excluding France. May 1850 brought further restriction with the loss of the Spanish market. A special four-year contract for supplying France and her colonies, however, was obtained in January 1858, and around this time Gibbs were also put in temporary charge of Spanish sales.[1] In 1854, they won the right to trade with the West Indies and Australia for seven years.

Under the terms of their first contract, which ran from the beginning of 1842 until the end of 1847, they and their associates had the right to a 25 per cent share in any profits in excess of £6 per register ton.[2] Thereafter all the proceeds went to the government, the contractors operating exclusively on a commission basis. Remuneration of this sort reached its most generous levels in the two-year contract of January 1849 when Gibbs were allowed to take 4 per cent for sales and delcredere guarantee, 1 per cent for brokerage, and 2½ per cent for the arrangement of charters. Rates in earlier and later contracts were lower: commissions on charters, for example, were normally disallowed, and the contract of May 1850 (and its extension in March 1853) gave only 3½ per cent for all the operations connected with selling. Sales commissions throughout applied to *gross* proceeds. In the three contracts up to December 1847 the merchants were also given the right to supply substantial portions of the funds due to the government in the form of debt paper. This was accepted at face value, and as the government was defaulting on both its internal and external debt obligations in the 1840s, the paper could be picked up on the market for very low prices.[3] From the differential, the contractors gained quite large sums. In the process, of course, they were helping the government retire its debt and reduce its obligations to creditors in the event of a funding settlement.

Every single contract required Gibbs to make a loan to the government in advance of sales. Reimbursement came from the

---

[1] No contract, apparently, was drawn up for this arrangement. The fact that Gibbs were serving Spain for a time, however, is clear from their correspondence in 1858–61. See also 'The Trade in Guano', *F.M.* 3rd ser. xv, 4 (Apr. 1859), p. 313, and Charles Stubbs's evidence to the *Royal Commission on Unseaworthy Ships*, P.P. 1873, xxxvi, 48.

[2] A register ton of shipping represented about 1⅓ effective tons of guano. £6 on a register ton, therefore, equals £4. 10s. on an effective ton.

[3] See Levin, op. cit., pp. 44–7, 56–7; W. M. Mathew, 'The First Anglo-Peruvian Debt and its Settlement, 1822–49', *Journal of Latin American Studies*, 2, 1 (May 1970), 81–98, *passim*.

proceeds which they themselves collected abroad. This financial dimension to the contractor–government relationship will be explored more fully in the next section. For the moment we shall simply try to determine what the successive arrangements for the export of guano signify as to the relative power of the government and the traders and the distribution of guano spoils between them.

Gibbs's entry into the trade in 1842 was preceded by the scrapping of two earlier contracts which the government had drawn up with Francisco de Quiros, a prominent Peruvian capitalist, and a number of foreign commercial adventurers who had succeeded in winning the financial backing of W. J. Myers & Co. of Liverpool.[1] The first contract, of November 1840, gave the merchants exclusive rights to sell as much guano as they chose in any part of the world for a period of six years in return for quite paltry payments of cash and debt certificates to the government.[2] Shortly after, the duration was extended by an extra three years.[3] The government was in a state of almost total ignorance as to guano's potential profitability as an export commodity, and no effort was made during the contract negotiations to inform ministers that successful experiments had already been made through Myers in England, and that prices of £24 and more per ton were anticipated.[4] Once exporting began and reports started drifting back to Lima of high returns in the British market, secrecy and deceit could no longer be sustained, and in November/December 1841 the merchants were forced to relinquish their nine-year contract and accept a new, shorter-term arrangement whereby the government secured roughly two-thirds of the profits and a loan of 287,000 pesos (about £57,000).[5] Still not satisfied, and prepared to make the fullest use of the power deriving from its ownership of the guano, the government quickly abandoned the 1841 agreement and coerced the merchants into joining up with a number of other commercial houses in Lima, including Gibbs Crawley & Co., and sign yet

---

[1] Aquiles Allier, Carlos Barroilhet, and Dutez & Co.

[2] *Anales*, iii. 103–5; P.R.O. F.O. 61/82, Wilson to Palmerston, 15 Apr. 1841.

[3] *Anales*, iii. 126.

[4] See Barroilhet, op. cit., p. 18; Aquiles Allier, *Alcance Al Comercio Número 742 Sobre La Cuestión Del Huano* (Lima, 1841), p. 15.

[5] See W. M. Mathew, 'Foreign Contractors and the Peruvian Government at the Outset of the Guano Trade', *Hispanic American Historical Review*, 52, 4 (Nov. 1972), 603–5; *Anales*, iii. 153–5.

another contract in February 1842.[1] An extra 200,000 pesos were grafted on to the December loan, and the government claimed all the profits up to £6 per register ton and 75 per cent of the returns in excess of that figure. The merchants were allowed a free cargo of guano as interest on their advances, and permitted to pay half of the profits due to the government in depreciated debt paper. They were also obliged to undertake all the managerial functions in the trade, and the contract stipulated that 120,000 tons would be exported over the five years of the contract period. 487,000 pesos, moreover, had been lent in advance of sales of a commodity which, despite early market successes, was still largely unknown and untested in Europe and North America. Prices were already falling in Britain.[2] This, combined with high freight costs,[3] bit hard into profits. Antony Gibbs & Sons, who had had no hand in arranging the contract but who were required to act as joint consignees with Myers and meet drafts from Lima, described their branch's entry into the trade on such unbalanced terms as an 'act of insanity'.[4] Gibbs Crawley soon came to agree.[5] Myers tried to pass on his share of the business to half a dozen different merchants, but without success.[6] 'The Peruvian consul in London', an official in Lima recorded, 'could not find a single house prepared to accept the consignment or advance a single peso against its [guano's] value.'[7]

It seems peculiar that the merchants had willingly become party to such an awkward contract .The reason would seem to be that in 1841 and 1842 they had very exaggerated notions of guano's potential profitability.[8] Various houses, eager to get into the trade,

[1] Mathew, 'Foreign Contractors', 609–10; *Exposición que Don Francisco Quiros y Don Aquiles Allier Elevan al Soberano Congreso* (Lima, 1845), pp. 6–10; Barroilhet, op. cit., p. 20; Hac. Arch., Año 1845, *Memoria Sobre La Negociación Del Guano (Por El Encargado De La Cuenta De Ella, Contador Dn. Pedro José Carillo)*.

[2] Gibbs, G.G.C., 1 Mar. and 1 and 15 Apr. 1842. For some figures, see pp. 357–9 below.

[3] The British chargé d'affaires suggested an average of £4. 17s. per ton for 1841 exports. P.R.O. F.O. 61/81, Wilson to Palmerston, 22 Dec. 1841.

[4] Gibbs, G.G.C., 1 Aug. 1842.   [5] Ibid., 8 and 21 Aug. 1842, 8 Apr. 1843.

[6] Ibid., 16 May, 2 June, 8 Aug. 1842. Diaries of Henry Witt, vol. i. (19 July to 17 Nov. 1842). (I am indebted to Sra. Eloyda Garland Melián de Montero for making this extremely valuable and hitherto largely unseen manuscript available for my inspection.)

[7] *Memoria Sobre La Negociación Del Guano.*

[8] See, for example, retrospective remarks in Gibbs, G.G.C., 21 Aug. 1842, and Hac. Arch., *Memorandum Para El Ministro De Hacienda Sobre El Negocio De Huano*, 12 Dec. 1842.

were jostling for position, and the government, as owner of the guano, was able to play one group off against another:[1] in the words of a British consul in Peru at the time, it simply 'took advantage of the avidity of the Monopolists and Speculators'.[2]

Towards the end of 1842 the contractors submitted a memorandum to the Ministry of Finance, describing the condition of the business as 'hazardous' in view of the recent fall in prices and accumulation of unsold stocks, and requesting that their contract period be extended. Short of a drastic reduction in prices, there seemed no hope whatever of selling 120,000 tons by the end of 1846.[3] And if prices were brought down much lower there was a danger that the government might gain receipts insufficient to repay the contract loans.[4] The proposal was rejected,[5] but the merchants persisted.[6] 'I am straining every nerve for an extension of our contract,' wrote John Hayne, the head of Gibbs Crawley & Co., in July 1843, 'without which we would never get back our advances.'[7] Success finally came in September when the government of Manuel Ignacio de Vivanco agreed to a three-year extension,[8] thus giving the contractors the right to sell guano until the end of 1849.

There was, however, no real security in arrangements with governments, as the experiences of 1840–1 had shown. Governments always possessed the crude power to tear up paper agreements when they so chose. And since there was a high rate of executive replacement, one government could simply choose to ignore the commitments of its predecessors. Realizing such dangers, Gibbs and Myers had already made an unsuccessful bid to secure protection for their associates' loans from the British Government, citing 'the fluctuating character of the Governments of the young South American States' as a prime factor in their concern.[9] In 1844 their worst fears were confirmed when the Vivanco

---

[1] Mathew, 'Foreign Contractors', pp. 605–10.

[2] P.R.O. F.O. 61/94, Crompton to Aberdeen, 14 Dec. 1842.

[3] *Memorandum Para El Ministro De Hacienda.*

[4] Only half the proceeds due to the government (i.e. the half in cash) was designated for the repayment of contractor loans. The rest was earmarked for the retirement of the bonded debt. See *Anales*, iii. 157.

[5] *Memoria Sobre La Negociación Del Guano.*

[6] A further memorandum was submitted on 7 Mar. 1843 and led to a series of conversations between merchants and ministers: see ibid.

[7] Gibbs, G.G.C., 15 July 1843; see also 14 Aug. 1843.

[8] Ibid., 13 and 16 Sept. 1843.

[9] P.R.O. F.O. 61/101, Gibbs and Myers to Sandon, 24 Mar. 1843; Canning to Sandon, 20 May 1843.

regime was displaced and the government of Manuel Menéndez declared its acts illegal, 'our proroga among them'.[1] By the spring of 1845 power had passed to Ramón Castilla, who refused to give any clear assurances about the extension.[2] Later in the same year the Castilla administration decided to turn the affair to its own advantage. 'The Government want a loan of $200,000,' wrote Hayne in September, 'and hope to get it as a new advance on Huano—something we must give to ensure our proroga. I should not mind $50,000.'[3] The dispute continued, and in January 1846 Castilla threatened to break entirely with the contractors and transfer the business to local capitalists. 'No chance of getting our proroga now!' declared Hayne.[4] But matters were patched up over the ensuing week and on 7 February Gibbs Crawley & Co. reported that an agreement had at last been reached, giving a one-year extension instead of the previous three, and requiring a loan of 300,000 pesos at an interest rate of $\frac{1}{2}$ per cent per month.[5] A provision of extra time, if required, was granted, but Myers in Liverpool held that this would be quickly forgotten if other parties offered a fresh loan in exchange for exporting rights after the end of the guaranteed year: 'Up to December 17 1847 we have a *right* to the export, after that we have the President's *word*. Weigh that at £60,000!'[6] The contractors had been forced into the uncomfortable situation of having to make new loans in order to protect old ones. It was an instance of fairly blatant opportunism on the part of a government which badly needed some ready cash,[7] and it reveals the relative impotence of the contractors on matters of vital concern to their own well-being. Gibbs tried to recruit the support of the British chargé d'affaires in Lima and the commander-in-chief of the British naval squadron in the Pacific, but without success.[8]

In 1847, as noted, the contractors lost their right to a share in profits, and in the contract of May 1850 Gibbs's commission earnings were substantially reduced from the unusually high

---

[1] Gibbs, G.G.C., 16 Oct. 1844.   [2] Ibid. 28 Apr. 1845.
[3] Ibid. 3 Sept. 1845.   [4] Ibid. 3 Dec. 1845, 31 Jan. 1846.
[5] Ibid. 7 Feb. 1856; *Anales*, iv. 22; P.R.O. F.O. 61/112, Barton to Aberdeen, 2 Mar. 1846.
[6] Gibbs, G.G.C., 26 Aug. 1846; see also 13 Mar. 1847.
[7] See the Finance Minister's report to Congress in October 1845, reproduced in *Anales*, iii. 25–6; also P.R.O. F.O. 61/112, Barton to Aberdeen, 2 Mar. 1846.
[8] Gibbs, G.G.C., 16 Oct. 1845 and 16 Jan. 1846.

levels granted only a year before. In both 1849 and 1850, it was made clear to Gibbs that they were not regarded as indispensable in the trade, and that if they failed to satisfy official requirements the business might well be placed in other hands.[1] A congressional law of 1849, moreover, had insisted that in any future negotiations for exporting rights preference should be given to Peruvian merchants.[2] In consequence of this, and of the six-year contract extension which Gibbs won in 1853, apparently without any competitive bidding from other traders,[3] a congressional commission of 1856 argued that their involvement in the trade no longer had legal justification and that the terms of their arrangement ought to be further revised in the government's favour.[4] The government, as it happened, chose to disregard these proposals,[5] but with the mounting criticism of Gibbs's conduct in the late 1850s and the growing capacity and desire of the local merchants to displace them,[6] it was decided (albeit in very confused circumstances) that they should not be granted a new contract when their current one expired at the end of 1861.[7] Thomas Jerningham, the British chargé d'affaires, noted in August 1860 that Congress was bound to make 'strenuous attempts . . . to change the present system and take it out of Foreign Hands . . .'.[8] He had heard, he wrote in October of the same year, 'that the President was inclined to continue the Huano contract with this Firm [Gibbs], but was overruled by others, who scared him by saying that if he did not give it to a Native Firm, there would be a Revolution'.[9] Gibbs relinquished their monopoly without any great fuss. There was, in fact, an air of guano-weariness about their correspondence in the late 1850s

[1] Gibbs, G.G.C., 12 Feb. 1849, 11 Feb. and 13 Mar. 1850.

[2] Reproduced in *El Peruano*, 28 Mar. 1861.

[3] *Dictamen De La Comisión Especial Sobre Nulidad De Las Prórrogas De Consignación Del Huano* (Lima, 1856), pp. 4, 7.

[4] Ibid., pp. 10, 26–7. There was also a more strongly worded minority report: *Dictamen De La Minoría De La Comisión Especial . . .* (Lima, 1856). See too Gibbs, H.H.G.C., 2, Henry Hucks Gibbs to William Gibbs, 11 Oct. 1856.

[5] See P.R.O. F.O. 61/173, Zevallos to Sulivan, 22 May 1857; Sulivan to Clarendon, 26 May 1857.

[6] Bonilla, op. cit., pp. 261, 269; Levin, op. cit., p. 83; Yepes, op. cit., p. 68.

[7] See, *inter alia*, P.R.O. F.O. 61/193, Jerningham to Russell, 13 Oct. 1860; *Anales*, vi. 52; *El Peruano*, 28 Mar. 1861; *Informe Circunstanciado . . .* op. cit., p. xx; P.R.O. F.O. 61/198, Jerningham to Russell, 13 May 1861; Gibbs, H.H.G.C., 2, Henry Hucks Gibbs to William Gibbs, 14 Aug. and 14, 15, 18 Oct. 1861; Witt Diaries, iv, entries for 1, 8, 14, and 30 Jan. 1862.

[8] P.R.O. F.O. 61/193, Jerningham to Russell, 14 Aug. 1860.

[9] Ibid. 13 Oct. 1860.

and early 1860s. 'If the business does go from us', commented Henry Hucks Gibbs, the head of the London house at the time, 'I shall be quite satisfied that it would have brought more *duras* than *maduras*, more kicks than halfpence, and certainly I should think the new people will find it so to their cost ...'.[1] These were hardly the words of a man on the point of losing profitable control over the affairs of a foreign state.

Gibbs's position depended in the last resort on the patronage of the government. The latter had the power to employ and to dismiss, and to state the terms upon which a merchant could continue in the trade. And even when its own predispositions were towards Gibbs, it had always to act within the context of Peruvian polity. Congress was periodically very lively and critical; liberal elements were suspicious both of Castilla and of the foreign contractors; and Gibbs were apparently powerless to influence the opinions and decisions of the humbler Peruvian politicians.

The government, moreover, claimed the vast bulk of the returns from guano. Gibbs's own earnings are difficult to determine, since guano entries cannot usually be isolated in the London house's accounts. In the 1840s, London's best year for profits was 1840: well ahead of their entry into the trade.[2] The books of the Lima branch in the same decade show a succession of unprofitable guano accounts up to 1847, and a heavy reliance on bond speculation for their contract income.[3] By the 1850s, however, when the trade was assuming very large proportions, the London house's total net earnings from commissions and brokerage averaged £61,393 per annum, compared with only £5,247 in the pre-guano decade of the 1830s.[4] Over-all profits rose from an annual average of £11,480 in the 1830s to £26,828 in the 1840s and to £91,984 in the 1850s. In the 1860s they fell back to £60,984.[5] Gibbs got off to a troubled and uncertain start in the trade, but once guano acquired wide popularity as a fertilizer in Europe their position became both secure and highly profitable. But if Gibbs did well, the Peruvian Government did very much better, and with an absolute minimum of effort. It has been estimated that in the

---

[1] Gibbs, H.H.G.C., 2, Henry Hucks Gibbs to George Gibbs, 1 Nov. 1860.
[2] Gibbs 11,053, London Head Office general ledgers, 1st series, vols. viii–xiii.
[3] Gibbs 11,032, South American branches: Lima, Peru, accounts, 1819–83, file 2, 1837–47. See also G.G.C., 28 Oct. 1843.
[4] Gibbs, 11,053, London ledgers, vols. v–viii and xiiia–xx.
[5] Ibid., vols. v–xxii.

period 1849–61 successive administrations took on average 65 per cent of *gross* sales proceeds from the Gibbs contracts, most of the remainder being claimed by shippers.[1] Official figures for 1840–56 show an average net return to the government of around £4. 16s. on the 1,650,290 tons of guano sold over these years.[2] In 1862 it was calculated that the government's receipts on each ton sold in Britain and the colonies in the period 1854–61 averaged £6. 8s.[3] Whatever charges one can sustain against the contractors, the fact is indisputable that in the distribution of guano proceeds between government and merchants, the former took the lion's share. From the late 1840s on, every last peso of profit went to the government; and in the preceding years, although contractors had a right to profits, in practice net proceeds were rarely high enough to permit significant returns to any parties other than the government. Merchant income always came principally from commissions, interest, and bond and exchange speculation. It was an extraordinarily advantageous arrangement for the government, but this, of course, was perfectly proper. The government, after all, represented a nation; the merchants represented only themselves and their financial backers.

IV

Governments held the whip hand in matters pertaining to contracts, and claimed the great bulk of the profits of the trade. At the same time, however, the continuance of the monopoly-contract system of exporting was associated with mounting governmental indebtedness to the guano merchants, and in particular to Gibbs. The government was always impatient to get guano funds as far in advance of sales as possible. This financial dimension requires close attention, for debt is usually taken as a sign of weakness. Its effects, of course, are not necessarily debilitating: much depends on considerations of cost, frequency, utilization, and capacity to repay. In the Peruvian case, however, the consequences do appear to have been largely adverse. The habit of borrowing became entrenched,

[1] Shane J. Hunt, 'Growth and Guano in Nineteenth Century Peru' (unpublished discussion paper, Princeton University, Feb. 1973), p. 62. (I am grateful to the author for giving me permission to cite this paper.)

[2] P. Dávalos y Lisson, *La Primera Centuria* (Lima, 1919), iv. 118.

[3] Gibbs to S. A. Rodulfo, 19 Mar. 1862, quoted in *Fenn's Compendium of the English and Foreign Funds* (London, 9th edn., 1867), pp. 377–8.

since the premature claiming of funds from one contract meant that relatively little guano money was being received when the next one came to be drawn up, thereby aggravating the need for a fresh cash injection. The whole process, according to some contemporary observers, was tending to limit the government's freedom of action, since the momentum of borrowing could not easily be checked.[1] Interest had to be paid: usually five per cent or more. There was the danger of an undesirable degree of power accruing in the hands of the creditors. The money, so easily obtained, was almost invariably used for unproductive purposes. It reduced the onus on the government to develop alternative and more regular sources of income and economize on wasteful expenditures.[2]

487,000 pesos, or just under £100,000, were borrowed when the 1842 contract was arranged.[3] 300,000 pesos were required in exchange for the 1846 *prórroga*. 700,000 pesos[4] were taken in July 1847, in return for the right to export only 40,000 register tons, and 850,000 pesos in December of the same year. These were all loans from the Lima branch, undertaken in association with fellow contractors and financed to a considerable degree from the sale of bills on the London house.[5] In 1849 Antony Gibbs & Sons agreed to supply £72,000 or 360,000 pesos for the dividends on the recently settled Anglo-Peruvian debt,[6] and as this was to be paid over in advance of sales from the contract of that year, it was treated as a loan. Also in 1849, William Gibbs & Co. contributed more than half of a 472,000 peso advance.[7] The contract of 1850 required an 800,000 peso loan from the London house, and the Lima branch was party to a 384,000 peso loan earlier in the year.[8] The Lima

---

[1] Francisco de Rivero, *Ojeada Sobre El Huano* (Paris, 1860), p. 220. See also remarks of a Peruvian Foreign Minister, Gómez Sánchez, in 1854, cited in Mathew, 'Foreign Contractors', pp. 619–20.

[2] Indeed it permitted the run-down of the internal tax structure in the 1850s. See Levin, op. cit., p. 94; Emilio Romero, *História Económica del Perú* (Buenos Aires, 1949), pp. 365–7.

[3] Unless otherwise indicated, the references for the loans are the same as those given in the previous section for contract terms.

[4] 100,000 in debt certificates taken at face value. See *Anales*, iv. 113. The margin for profit which this allowed the contractors was to serve as interest.

[5] See, for example, evidence cited in Mathew, 'Foreign Contractors', p. 614.

[6] See Mathew, 'Debt', pp. 94–6.

[7] 72,000 in debt certificates, again in lieu of interest. See Gibbs, Lima Branch Accounts, File 3, 1847–62.

[8] Ibid., Peruvian Government Huano Loan Account, 30 Apr. 1851; see also *Anales*, v. 21–2; P.R.O. F.O. 61/126, Adams to Palmerston, 25 May 1850; Gibbs, G.G.C., 13 July 1850.

account books also cite the following 'sundry loans' in 1850–1:
95,000 pesos on 31 August 1850; 86,000 on 31 October; 34,000
on 30 November; 93,000 on 31 December; 30,000 on 31 January
1851; 60,000 on 28 February; 30,000 on 31 March; and 80,000 on
30 April:[1] 508,000 pesos in all. In the nine months following the
prórroga of March 1853, 1,460,000 pesos were handed over:
960,000 in eight monthly instalments of 120,000 pesos each, the
remaining 500,000 in eighteen different payments ranging from
5,000 to 200,000 pesos.[2] In 1854 500,000 pesos were lent in
connection with an Australian and West Indian guano supply
contract, and an agreement was reached to provide the government with additional monthly loans of 200,000 pesos for an un-
specified period.[3] In 1855 500,000 pesos were lent to the new
Castilla regime.[4] The French contract of 1858 required an advance
of 300,000 pesos, and in 1862 and 1864 loans of 600,000[5] and
200,000[6] pesos respectively were given. There is also a reference
in the Gibbs correspondence to a 4,000,000 peso advance
around 1860.[7]

Why were these loans undertaken? Partly through habit, partly
through the momentum of indebtedness, partly through frequent
upswings in expenditure. What is beyond question is that the
principal initiatives came not from Gibbs but from the government. There was little need for the contractors to press their
funds on officials: the demand was there more or less all the time.
In 1841–2 money was needed to prosecute a war against Bolivia.[8]
Of the 487,000 pesos lent to the government under the contract of
February 1842, 410,877 (84 per cent) were used for expenditures
unambiguously connected with military activity: army salaries
and wages, provisions, cannon, shrapnel, sabres, rifles, saddlery,
horseshoes, uniforms, ponchos, water bottles, straw mattresses,

[1] Peruvian Government Huano Loan Account, loc. cit.
[2] Hac. Arch., *Correspond.ᵃ con los Consignat.ˢ del Huano y Gobor. de las Islas
de Chincha*, Año de 1853, letters from Piérola, Saco, Paz Soldan, and others to
William Gibbs & Co. and Antony Gibbs & Sons: 26 Mar.; 19, 25, and 29 Apr.;
2, 9, 11, 12, 28, and 30 May; 25 and 27 June; 15, 20, and 26 July; 3, 4, 6, 10,
and 18 Aug.; 1, 3, 16, and 29 Sept.; 4 and 25 Oct.; 3 Nov.; 21 Dec.
[3] Gibbs, W.G.C., Henry Hucks Gibbs to William Gibbs, 31 Aug. 1854.
[4] Ibid. 20 Feb. 1855.
[5] Witt Diaries, VI, 14 Jan. 1862.
[6] Hac. Arch., Año 1864, Tesorería Principal, loan of 1 Oct. 1864.
[7] Gibbs, H.H.G.C., 3, Henry Hucks Gibbs to William Gibbs, 14 Dec. 1863.
[8] See Mathew, 'Foreign Contractors', pp. 604, 610.

and various other 'articles for the army'.[1] 1847 saw renewed tension with Bolivia, and the government was concerned too by José Flores's preparations in Ireland for an expedition against Ecuador which, if successful, might help re-establish Spanish power in the sub-continent. Funds were required, therefore, to help defend 'the national honour'.[2] In 1849 the Minister of Finance, Manuel Del Río, presented a memorial to Congress lamenting the lack of public funds and answering accusations of malversation. The document, as the British chargé d'affaires, William Pitt Adams, observed, made no suggestion as to how revenue might be increased or expenditure decreased, but confined itself 'to pointing out the necessity of raising an immediate loan on guano to the amount of 6 or 800,000 dollars . . .'.[3] In 1854, the Foreign Minister, Gómez Sánchez, in a defence of the prevailing guano export system, noted how important it was for a country such as Peru, which 'lacks the great resources that old, rich Nations have at their disposal for use in times of conflict', to be able to come by 'substantial loans' in order to meet their most urgent requirements. These could be secured quickly, and avoided the placing of burdensome impositions on the Peruvians themselves.[4] 'Under the present system of contracting with mercantile houses for the sale of guano', commented a North American journal in the same year, 'the government can obtain an advance of money at any time it may be required, without the trouble of negotiating a loan in the manner adopted by other nations. This is found to be very convenient . . .'[5] The Finance Minister in 1860, Juan José Salcedo, noting the scale of indebtedness to the contractors and the perilous state of the country's finances, declared that he had decided to enlarge that debt to help alleviate the situation.[6] The process, of course, was self-defeating. 'The Government's treasury was always without a dollar', observed a guano merchant of the 1860s, Henry Witt; 'they owed much and every sum which entered vanished like smoke, to satisfy the urgent claims of hundreds of creditors'.[7]

---

[1] Hac. Arch., Año 1842, *Razón que manifiesta las cantidades que han ingresado en la Tesorería gral. por adelantos sobre la extracción del Huano, y su inversión desde diciembre de 1841 hasta junio de 1842.*

[2] Basadre, op. cit., (3rd edn., 1946), i. 220–2; *Anales*, v. 111–13.

[3] P.R.O. F.O. 61/121, Adams to Palmerston, 12 July 1849.

[4] P.R.O. F.O. 61/148, Gómez Sánchez to Sulivan, 10 Oct. 1854.

[5] *De Bow's Commercial Review*, xvi (1854), 461.

[6] Dávalos y Lisson, op. cit., iv. 121–2.

[7] Witt Diaries, 1 Jan. 1862. These, of course, included holders of external and

One finds no reference whatever in the Gibbs correspondence to any effort on their part to create lending opportunities prior to some move from the government itself. This *may* have happened, but there is no evidence of it. And quite often the scale of the government's requirements was in excess of what Gibbs considered desirable. The size of the 1842 loan greatly troubled the London house, and soon the Lima branch as well. The *prórroga* loan of 1846 was six times larger than the sum John Hayne was initially willing to supply. He also expressed some concern over the size of the loan he had given for the December 1847 contract.[1] Complaints were made quite frequently in the 1850s about excessive government borrowing,[2] and in 1861 Henry Hucks Gibbs said he wanted to limit the firm's lending activities in the event of their securing a fresh contract.[3] Government loans did not necessarily provide the most remunerative outlets for surplus cash, and there was occasionally the danger that heavy lending could strain the liquidity of the Lima and London houses.[4]

In stressing that the initiative behind the debts lay mainly with the government, however, we should not at the same time assume that Gibbs put themselves at great risk in thus obliging their employers, or that there was any *general* reluctance to lend. Liquidity problems were rare, and repayment came from the sales proceeds that Gibbs themselves collected. There were genuine risks and worries in the early and mid-1840s, given the size of the 1842 and 1846 advances and the uncertain state of the market, but from the end of that decade on, loans were about as risk-free as was possible for such large-scale financial operations. There was normally enough fertilizer afloat or in British and European warehouses to guarantee reimbursement in the event of a contract being torn up in Lima.

The power accruing to Gibbs as a creditor appears to have been

internal debt paper, which had lately much expanded, as well as guano contractors.	[1] Gibbs, G.G.C., 10 Jan. 1848.

[2] Gibbs, W.G.C., Henry Hucks Gibbs to William Gibbs, 18 May 1854 and to John Hayne, 20 Sept. 1855; H.H.G.C., 2, Henry Hucks Gibbs to William Gibbs, 22 Dec. 1858 and 6 Jan. 1859.

[3] Gibbs, H.H.G.C., 2, Henry Hucks Gibbs to William Gibbs, 1 Nov. 1861.

[4] The London firm experienced a crisis of liquidity in late 1855 and early 1856. See Gibbs, W.G.C., Henry Hucks Gibbs to William Gibbs, 11 and 12 Sept., 18 and 22 Oct., 20 and 28 Dec. 1855; H.H.G.C., 2, Henry Hucks Gibbs to William Gibbs, 2 Jan. 1856, and to Tyndall Bright, 8 and 11 Jan., 24 and 30 Apr. 1856.

used mainly for the purpose of continuing in the guano business. The command of loanable funds was a vital factor in their entry into the trade in 1842[1] and in their success in all future contracts up to 1853. The government's reliance on these large advances almost certainly delayed the transfer of the British market from foreign to Peruvian hands. Creditor power, however, did not guarantee permanent occupation, as the events of the early 1860s clearly showed, nor did it result in the imposition of unnaturally onerous conditions on the borrower. The normal interest rate (when paid as a straight percentage rather than through free guano or opportunities for bond speculation) was 5 or 6 per cent. The fact that other parties usually competed with Gibbs for the privileges of contracting and lending was a restraining influence. Referring to their advances of May 1850, the Lima house reported: 'Both Souter and Alsop had offered the loan at 6% so we were obliged to be content with that Interest. . . .'[2] Such rates may appear high given that the risks were so slight, but they were not excessive by international standards, and had they been significantly lower, mercantile incentives to divert funds to other speculations would have been correspondingly greater.

It is difficult to discover clear instances of Gibbs using, or even contemplating the use of, their loan weapon to influence government behaviour on matters other than contract allocation. Towards the end of 1854 they appear to have withheld funds from the tottering Echenique administration. 'Went does not deliver money to the Government faster than he can avoid though he knows that we lose interest in consequence, because he wishes discreetly to keep back for fear of a change in the Government, which now appears to be inevitable when Castilla chooses to attack Lima.'[3] This, however, was probably not part of any concerted plan to weaken Echenique and advance Castilla's cause, for only a few months before, generous lending arrangements had been agreed with the government.[4] It derived from a recognition of realities, and from a wish to leave margins to permit financial assistance to Castilla when he came to power. Castilla, back in the presidency, 'was gratified to find that the income from the Huano had not been

---

[1] See, for example, Quiros y Allier, op. cit., p. 10.

[2] Gibbs, G.G.C., 12 May 1850.

[3] Gibbs, W.G.C., Henry Hucks Gibbs to William Gibbs, 18 May 1854. Samuel Went was manager of Gibbs's Lima house.

[4] See above, p. 352.

more forestalled', thereby proving to Gibbs the prudence of their 'plan of keeping our entregas at the lowest possible point'. The fact that there was money to spare 'delighted Don Ramón's heart exceedingly'.[1] More important, perhaps, was Gibbs's declaration in October 1855 that if official plans for an immediate 18 per cent rise in the price of guano[2] were carried into effect, their capacity to make loans in the future might be seriously impaired.[3] Government policy was in the event implemented, but only fully so fourteen months later. Gibbs's pressure derived from a well-justified fear that a price rise might adversely affect sales, and since their own financial situation at the time was rather tight, any reduction in guano income was bound to limit the resources available for government loans. So they may simply have been stating facts. But it was, without question, a form of pressure, and it was effective in at least delaying the price increase.[4]

It does seem an exaggeration, however, to talk, in the manner of Ulloa, of Gibbs's financial despotism. The worst effect of borrowing—apart from the indebtedness itself—was the way it encouraged the amassing of markets in Gibbs's hands, giving them a range of territories greater than they seem to have been able to supply.[5] It also restricted the number of merchants capable of bidding for contracts and added to the difficulties of indigenous capitalists trying to move into the lucrative British trade.

V

Nothing that has been said so far, however, touches on the Levin thesis of price depreciation and cost elevation: of a damaging conflict of interests in the running of the business between contractors and governments. Accusations of price depreciation, as we have noted earlier, were also levelled against Gibbs in the late 1850s and early 1860s by Carlos Barroilhet and José Casimiro Ulloa.

[1] Gibbs, W.G.C., Henry Hucks Gibbs to William Gibbs, 20 Feb. 1855.

[2] See Rivero, op. cit., p. 340.

[3] Gibbs, W.G.C., Henry Hucks Gibbs to John Hayne, 8(?) Oct. 1855, and to William Gibbs, 10 Oct. 1855.

[4] The delay may, however, have been to the government's advantage, for after the rise (from £11 to £13) was implemented, the trade suffered a quite massive setback. See W. M. Mathew, 'Peru and the British Guano Market, 1840–1870', *Economic History Review*, 2nd ser., xxiii, 1 (Apr. 1970), pp. 112–28, *passim*.   [5] See below, section VII.

The first point that must be established is that there was no secular downward trend in prices: rather the opposite. The lowest levels were reached in 1846–9 and the highest in 1857–8. There was a clear downward movement in the first half of the 1840s; thereafter, almost all the adjustments were in an upward direction. In 1841, the first year of British imports, guano fetched a variety of prices ranging from £14 to £28 per ton.[1] In the first half of 1842, however, the range was considerably lower: £10 to £20.[2] It had been possible to sell very small amounts for experimental purposes at high prices in 1841; it was proving very difficult to sustain such prices for purposes of general agricultural application.[3] In January 1842 Gibbs noted that although £26 had been fetched in the past for samples, returns of this magnitude could not be anticipated 'for real consumption'.[4] Agricultural produce prices, moreover, were falling,[5] thereby impairing the purchasing power of farmers. In August 1842 Gibbs and Myers settled on a fixed scale—£12 minimum and £15 maximum[6]—but the downward drift persisted in the latter months of the year and in January 1843 a new scale of £10 to £12 was formally adopted.[7] The objective, wrote Gibbs, was the promotion of 'steady, large and increasing annual sales. To spread the want throughout the country, we must spread the manure even at a slight sacrifice; and to do this we must in a manner *force* dealers and consumers to buy.'[8] The £10 minimum persisted until April 1846, by which time the Peruvian business was facing massive competition from cheap African guano.[9] African imports had in fact begun as early as the autumn of 1843: in September of that year Gibbs judged the threat as 'formidable'.[10] The decision to persist at £10 for almost three years after the appearance of African guano unquestionably cost them heavily in sales. 'Tho' our sales are almost nil, we keep at £10 . . . We will not yield . . . till the last moment.'[11] The belief was

---

[1] Gibbs, G.G.C., 1 July, 1 and 15 Oct., 23 Nov. 1841.

[2] Ibid., 1 Mar., 1 and 15 Apr., 13 May 1842.

[3] *Memoria Sobre La Negociación Del Huano*.

[4] Gibbs, G.G.C., 1 Jan. 1842.

[5] See Susan Fairlie, 'The Corn Laws and British Wheat Production, 1829–76', *Economic History Review*, 2nd ser., xxii, 1 (1969), p. 97, Fig. 1.

[6] Gibbs, G.G.C., 10 Sept. 1842.

[7] Ibid., 2 Jan. 1843.   [8] Ibid., 28 Feb. 1843.

[9] For an account of the African importations, see Robert Craig, 'The African Guano Trade', *The Mariner's Mirror*, l (1964), pp. 25–55.

[10] Gibbs, G.G.C., 22 Sept. 1843.   [11] Ibid., 16 Nov. 1844.

that the African trade was a temporary affair and that if they were
to reduce their prices substantially they might find it difficult to
pull them back up again after the African challenge had passed.
'No compromise to continue Peruvian sale!' declared Gibbs in
December 1844.[1] As it happened, however, the market was very
heavily glutted and although African imports tailed off after 1845
(when 254,527 tons came in),[2] the disposal of so-called 'second-
hand' stocks went slowly and competition persisted. In April 1846
the consignees felt the time had at last come for a reduction, and
lowered to £8. 10s. (Liverpool) and £9 (London).[3] By January
1847, however, the minimum had been restored to £10.[4] In
October 1847 it returned to £9 at Myers's instigation.[5] A year and
a half later, in the spring of 1849, Gibbs—now alone as British
consignees—settled on a minimum rate of £9. 5s.[6] and there it
remained for the next five years. In January 1854 it was raised to
£10,[7] and in July of the same year to £11;[8] both moves were in
accordance with Peruvian Government instructions and were
caused principally by rising freight costs at the time of the Crimean
War.[9] Government directives were also responsible for two further
increases in 1856: to £12 in July[10] and £13 in December.[11] After
a period of disastrous sales the price was reduced again, to £12,
again on instructions from Lima.[12] In 1862, still with guano to sell,

[1] Gibbs, G.G.C., 20 Dec. 1844.

[2] P.P., 1851, liii, 309. (Only 14,101 tons came in from Peru and Bolivia in the same year.)

[3] Gibbs, G.G.C., 29 Apr., 11 and 16 May 1846.

[4] Ibid. 29 Jan. 1847.

[5] Ibid. 22 and 30 Sept., 14, 15, 18, and 23 Oct., 16 Nov. 1847.

[6] Ibid. 16 May 1849; see also 16 and 17 Aug. 1849.

[7] Antony Gibbs & Sons, *Contestación de la Casa Gibbs a los cargos sobre el guano* (London, 1858), p. 12.

[8] Gibbs, G.G.C., 1 Aug. 1854.

[9] Paz Soldan to William Gibbs & Co., 24 Nov. 1853 (reproduced in Rivero, op. cit., pp. 137–8); Gibbs, G.G.C., 12 Dec. 1853; ibid., Peruvian Govern-
ment to Antony Gibbs & Sons, 18 Mar. 1854; W.G.C., Henry Hucks Gibbs to
William Gibbs, 5 May 1854; Mendiburu to Antony Gibbs & Sons, 10 July 1854
(Rivero, op. cit., p. 140); Antony Gibbs & Sons, op. cit., p. 13.

[10] Gibbs, W.G.C., Henry Hucks Gibbs to William Gibbs, 4 Oct. 1855;
G.G.C., Rivero to Antony Gibbs & Sons, 5 Oct. 1855; Antony Gibbs & Sons,
op. cit., pp. 13–14; Melgar to Peruvian Foreign Minister, 27 Apr. and 2 June
1856 (Rivero, op. cit., pp. 258, 266–7); G.G.C., 5 May, 2 and 30 June 1856.

[11] Melgar to Peruvian Foreign Minister, 2 June 1856, loc. cit.; Antony Gibbs
& Sons, op. cit., p. 14; Gibbs's circular of 24 Dec. 1856 in Rivero, op. cit., p. 81.

[12] P.R.O. F.O. 61/184, Gibbs to Fitzgerald, 1 July 1858; P.R.O. F.O. 61/190,
Osma to Malmesbury, 24 Mar. 1859; Rivero, op. cit., p. 169.

TABLE IX.2

Prices and Sales of Peruvian Guano in Britain, 1843–62

	Price average (£ s. per ton)	Sales (tons)
	£ s.	
1843	10 6	Not available
1844	10 10	,,
1845	10 10	,,
1846	10 10	,,
1847	10 10	,,
1848	9 9	,,
1849	Not available	,,
1849–50 (1 July–30 June)	9 5	77,098
1850–1 ,,	9 5	96,145
1851–2 ,,	9 5	112,638
1852–3 ,,	9 14	118,286
1853–4 ,,	10 5	135,524
1854	11 1	154,271
1855	11 5	161,852
1856	12 2	211,647
1857	13 5	110,490
1858	12 18	122,819
1859	12 1	132,082
1860	12 5	146,145
1861	12 5	161,707
1862	12 18	Not available

SOURCES: Price averages, calculated to the nearest shilling, based on London dealers' quotations, irregularly supplied in monthly editions of the *Farmer's Magazine*. Sales figures for 1849–50 to 1853–4 taken from appendix ('Estado Comparativo de las Ventas de Huano') to Rivero, op. cit.; those for 1854–61, from letter to S. A. Rodulfo from Antony Gibbs & Sons, 19 Mar. 1862, reproduced in *Fenn's Compendium of the English and Foreign Funds* (London, 9th edn., 1867), pp. 377–8.

Gibbs advised and secured a return to £13,[1] but this was brought back to £12 by the new contractors early in 1863,[2] and remained at that level for most of the remainder of the 1860s (Table IX.2). So clearly there was no persistent fall in prices. Two other

[1] Gibbs, H.H.G.C., 3, Henry Hucks Gibbs to William Gibbs, 4 and 27 Mar. 1862; P.R.O. F.O. 61/206, Kernaghan to Russell, 14 June 1862, and Russell to Kernaghan, 23 Sept. 1862.

[2] Pardo to Thomson Bonar & Co., 12 Feb. 1863: in *Correspondencia de los Signatarios del Contrato de Consignación para la Venta del Guano en la Gran Bretaña y sus Colonias, Dirigida á los SS. J. Thomson, T. Bonar y Compañía* (no date), pp. 30–1.

important things should be noted. Price changes in the 1840s were determined principally by the consignees, and not by the government. The policies adopted, however, had always to be explained to the authorities in Lima and appear to have consistently won their approval. This was sometimes given grudgingly and belatedly, but there was never any sustained disagreement or conflict between ministers and merchants. Second, price alterations in the 1850s were largely Lima-inspired. The government took clear charge of policy. And the prices demanded, despite occasional delays in implementation, were not thrust on unwilling merchants. Gibbs indeed wanted a price rise in the spring of 1853 which the government refused to sanction,[1] and argued again for increases in the spring of 1854[2] and in the winter of 1856.[3] Price rises, when effected, always carried the approval of the English house. Gibbs, it may be noted, also advised the government against reductions in January 1850,[4] and again in 1852.[5]

Contrary to what is usually asserted, the contractors had a number of reasons for at times pursuing higher prices or resisting falls. They had an interest, for one thing, in pleasing the government. They also knew that price falls did not necessarily bring about prompt increases in demand. Buyers witnessing one reduction might anticipate another and delay their purchases accordingly. Hostility, too, might be generated among people who had bought the fertilizer before the price falls were carried into effect.[6] In the difficult early years of the trade, moreover, the merchants wished to achieve a level of returns for the government sufficiently high to ensure repayment of the large loans of 1842 and 1846. There was in addition a chance of a small share in profits during most of the 1840s if net proceeds could be raised above £6 per register ton (equivalent to about £4. 10s. per effective ton). Higher prices too could yield higher commission returns without any extra effort,[7] so long as consumption was not too badly impaired.

---

[1] Antony Gibbs & Sons, op. cit., p. 11.

[2] Antony Gibbs & Sons to William Gibbs & Co., 29 Apr. 1854 in Rivero, op. cit., p. 139.

[3] Rivero to Peruvian Foreign Minister, 30 Dec. 1856 in ibid., pp. 64–5; see also Antony Gibbs & Sons, op. cit., p. 14.

[4] Gibbs, G.G.C., 16 Jan. 1850.

[5] Ibid., 16 Feb., 16 June, 16 July, and 16 Sept. 1852.

[6] Ibid., 23 Mar. 1846.

[7] Even Carlos Barroilhet acknowledged that, somewhat inconsistently: Barroilhet, op. cit., p. 71.

Arguments relating contractor interest to price depreciation rest partly on the assumption that the supply situation was elastic: that increased demand supposedly resulting from price falls could be met without much difficulty. In fact, however, supply was frequently limited, meaning that income maximization for Gibbs lay in selling the available quantities at the highest possible price. All the contracts of the 1840s, for example, specified the amount of guano to be exported. There were also very frequent shortages[1] caused by slow loading at the guano islands,[2] ill-timed chartering, and unpredictable climatic and tidal influences. And in the early and mid 1860s Gibbs were unable to replenish stocks for the simple reason that their contract had expired.

Arguments relating Peruvian interest to slow-tempo, high-price sales and the objective of preserving a wasting asset ignore the distinction that has to be drawn between the somewhat abstract entity which was Peru and the hard reality which was a governmental system sunk in debt and chronically beset by a host of urgent political and financial pressures. There is no evidence to suggest that fears of exhaustion were a primary preoccupation of ministers and officials in Lima. They certainly were never cited in the directives sent to England ordering price increases. The government's main concern, it seems, was the maximization of income in the short term. This was sought cautiously up to the early 1850s, and somewhat more recklessly in 1855 and 1856. When prices did begin to move towards the sort of levels that critics like Barroilhet thought appropriate, competition was vigorously stimulated and sales slumped badly.[3]

[1] See, for example, Gibbs, G.G.C., 16 Nov. 1850, 1 Feb. 1853, 16 Feb. 1854; Monthly 'Agricultural Reports', for Jan. Feb., Apr., May, and June 1853; Feb., Apr., and May 1854; Feb., Apr., and May 1855, in appropriate issues of *F.M.*; 'The Guano Crisis', *F.M.*, 3rd ser. xi, 3 (Mar. 1857), p. 266; 'The Manure Difficulty and its Solution', ibid., p. 261; 'The Supply of Guano', ibid. 4 (Apr. 1857), p. 356; Hansard, *Parliamentary Debates*, 3rd ser., cxliv, 6 Mar. 1857, col. 1951.

[2] See, *inter alia*, Gibbs, G.G.C., 16 Nov. 1850; H.H.G.C., 2, Henry Hucks Gibbs to William Gibbs, 8 Nov. 1860; P.R.O. F.O. 61/144, Clarendon to Sulivan, 13 Apr. 1854; P.R.O. F.O. 61/172, Sulivan to Clarendon, 12 Mar. 1857; Hac. Arch., *Correspond.ᵃ Con los Consignat.ˢ del Huano . . .*, Mendiburu to William Gibbs & Co., 10 July 1854; *The Times*, 8 July 1844, p. 6, 26 Nov. 1853, p. 18, 7 Dec. 1853, p. 12, 16 Feb. 1854, p. 7, and 10 Dec. 1866, p. 7; 'The Origin of Guano', *F.M.*, 3rd ser. xiv, 1 (July 1858), pp. 37–8; Nicolás de Piérola, *Informe sobre el estado del carguío de huano en las Islas de Chincha, y sobre el cumplimiento del contrato celebrado con D. Domingo Elias* (Lima, 1853), pp. 9, 11, 18–19.

[3] For analysis, see Mathew, 'Guano Market', pp. 115–16, 119–24.

VI

On the question of intermediate costs, Gibbs did have an incentive to raise these inasmuch as interest was earned in the 1850s on payments made in advance of sales. And on freights specifically, commissions were taken from shipowners. *Commissions* on costs from the *government* are of little consequence here, for these were only paid out over the two years of the 1849 contract, and then only for charters. The evidence to hand does not indicate that Gibbs responded to these incentives. They were afraid, no doubt, of giving offence to the government (as well as to their own branch and its associates in the profit-sharing years up to the late 1840s), and probably obeyed the normal mercantile instinct to move their commodities cheaply rather than expensively. The incentives, moreover, did not exist through most of the 1840s. Nowhere in their private correspondence is there even a hint of a wish for higher costs. When they did write of the desirability of freight increases, for example, this they always related to the need to acquire adequate shipping tonnages and never to any likelihood of increased earnings. High rates, for one thing, could be viewed as a possible source of loss inasmuch as costly shipping might induce the government to raise prices to a level at which consumption would be seriously damaged. In 1853 *El Comercio* complained that the rates Gibbs were offering were unnecessarily *low* and that this was making it difficult to obtain a sufficient capacity of shipping to keep the European market stocked. The English firm, they alleged, was behaving in a 'niggardly' manner; they were failing to show 'a proper liberality in regard to freights' and their policy had 'shaken all confidence in future supplies'.[1] There was justice in this observation: in 1853–4, during the Crimean inflation, Gibbs persisted with unrealistically low rates of £4 and £4. 10s.[2] It was also argued that the monopoly-export system had a generally depressing effect on freights. In 1857 the British chargé d'affaires observed how the organization of the trade, with only one bidder for shipping for any single market, kept rates lower than they would have been under a more competitive system.[3] 'By the

[1] Quoted in *The Times*, 25 Aug. 1853, 7a.
[2] Ibid., 26 Nov. 1853, p. 8; Gibbs, W.G.C., Henry Hucks Gibbs to William Gibbs, 24 Mar., 13 Apr., and 5 May 1854.
[3] P.R.O. F.O. 61/173, Sulivan to Clarendon, 12 May 1857.

centralizing which has existed', commented the *Farmer's Magazine* in 1861, 'tonnage has been obtained upon the most favourable terms, all competition being destroyed. . . .'[1]

A lot of information has been gathered on periodic alterations in freight rates in the 1840s. There are also figures to hand for rates on 2,574 vessels over the years 1849–60. Space does not permit any detailed discussion of these. All that need be said, really, is that there was no long-term upward trend. Rates rose and fell a good deal, within years and between years, in accordance with shifts in demand and supply in world shipping markets. In 1841, as already noted, freights averaged £4. 17s. per ton. In early 1844 they were down to about £2. 10s.[2] In January 1847 they were at £5 for the best vessels.[3] In the early months of 1851 many ships were being hired for less than £3.[4] In July 1852 Gibbs quoted a figure of £2. 15s.[5] During the Crimean War costs rose steadily to reach £5 in April 1854.[6] By the beginning of 1855 they were back down to £4.[7] Three years later they were at £3.[8] In 1859 rates were occasionally as low as £2. 5s.[9] By the start of 1862 the average was at just under £4.[10] Over the years of Gibbs's participation the highest rate appears to have been £5 in 1847 and 1854 and the lowest, £2. 5s. in 1859.

As for other intermediate costs—in relation to docking, unloading, and warehousing—all the evidence shows Gibbs pressing for reductions, never advances—in 1844, 1845, 1849, and 1861.[11] 'We think the extent of the Business may warrant a reduction in the Charges, and we are occupied in the endeavour to attain this.'[12]

---

[1] 'The Manure Trade of the Past Year', *F.M.*, 3rd ser. xix, 2 (Feb. 1861), p. 159.
[2] Gibbs, G.G.C., 11 Jan. and 8 June 1844.
[3] Ibid., 11 Jan. 1847.
[4] Gibbs, 'Statement of Freights on Vessels Chartered on the Coast belonging to 1st Consignment Account to 30 April 1851', Lima Branch Accounts, File 3, 1847–62.
[5] Gibbs, G.G.C., 16 July 1852.
[6] Gibbs, W.G.C., Henry Hucks Gibbs to William Gibbs, 5 May 1854.
[7] Ibid., 3 Feb. 1855, Gibbs.
[8] 'The Trade in Guano,' *F.M.*, 3rd ser. xv, 4 (Apr. 1859), 60.
[9] 'The Manure Trade of the Past Year', ibid., xiv, 2 (Feb. 1861), p. 159.
[10] Gibbs, H.H.G.C., 3, Henry Hucks Gibbs to William Gibbs, 4 Mar. 1862.
[11] Gibbs, G.G.C., 25 Sept. 1844, 8 Mar. 1845, 17 Aug. and 16 Oct. 1849, 16 Jan. 1850; *The Times*, 2 Feb. 1861, p. 5.
[12] Gibbs, G.G.C., 17 Aug. 1849.

VII

Every Peruvian minister who had recently served in London, wrote one of their number, Francisco de Rivero, in 1860, arrived there 'naturally prejudiced against the house of Antony Gibbs & Sons, cherishing, if not the most vulgar notions bred among us, at least some doubts as to their management of the business as honest men.' After observing the consignees at close quarters, however, they had been 'delighted to do full justice to the energy, integrity and probity with which the trade is run'. Only ill-informed and mean-spirited men had taken a different view. Gibbs had been 'vilely, unjustly and crudely attacked by certain individuals full of rancour and envy', by 'communists of a new sort, enemies of their wealth'. Gibbs, in short, were blameless of all sin. Their affairs were conducted with an uncompromised 'purity'.[1] The consignees themselves, not unnaturally, took the same view, although they were sometimes uncertain as to how best to respond to the attacks of Barroilhet and others. 'To enter the lists against such a scoundrel as Barroilhet', wrote Henry Hucks Gibbs, 'is to fight with a Chimney Sweep—you may conquer but you come out grievously soiled from the encounter. We have got to tell the truth—which though it will always prevail with those who understand the subject matter, and I may say with honest men, yet it is not better than a lie with the majority of those whom our opponent addresses, and who are probably neither the one nor the other.' The government knew of their innocence, 'and I would rather have them see that we treat such charges with the contempt they deserve than that we suffered them to give us any uneasiness'.[2] Barroilhet he described variously as a 'convicted scoundrel', a 'rogue and a liar', and 'the Brute'.[3] Luis Mesones, another critic, was viewed as 'personally hostile', a source of 'lying attacks', and a man exhibiting a 'ridiculous ignorance of commercial matters'.[4] The self-righteousness of Gibbs and the encomiums of Rivero are impressive in their way. They are also probably exaggerated.

There are at least four quite serious charges that can be sustained

---

[1] Rivero, op. cit., pp. 33–4.
[2] Gibbs, H.H.G.C., 2, Henry Hucks Gibbs to William Gibbs, 9 Oct. 1857.
[3] Ibid., 22 Aug. 1856, 13 and 24 Oct. 1857.
[4] Ibid., Henry Hucks Gibbs to Francisco de Rivero, 10 Mar. 1860; H.H.G.C., 3, Henry Hucks Gibbs to William Gibbs, 4 Mar. 1862.

against the contractors.[1] In the first place, they claimed a 1 per cent delcredere commission long after they merited it. Gibbs generally appear to have received cash down for their guano sales.[2] The whole point of a delcredere commission, however, arose in relation to purchase by bills. Since there was always a danger that these could not be cashed at maturity, the owner of the commodity was protected by the selling agent guaranteeing to refund him in such an eventuality—and taking a commission for his trouble. 200,000 tons sold in a hypothetical year at £10 a ton, therefore, gave Gibbs £20,000 that they were not entitled to: a direct loss to the government.[3]

Second, throughout the 1850s, if not before, Gibbs took a 2½ per cent commission from either brokers or shipowners on the arrangement of a charter party.[4] Such an unusual charge, it was believed, caused the shipowners to compensate themselves through correspondingly adjusted rates.[5] In 1856, and presumably in earlier years as well, 7½ per cent was charged on charters arranged in Lima, and a third of this was credited to the London house.[6] The 2½ per cent rate may not have been of much consequence by itself as an elevating factor when shippers were competing for guano cargoes in normal times of underemployment.[7] But, in combination with a number of other aggravations in the trade,[8]

---

[1] There are a variety of others, which are either of little importance or cannot be substantiated from the evidence to hand: overcharging on bags in 1845, selling some guano beyond their contract area in the mid-1850s, and demanding unnecessarily high fees from ships' captains in Callao to meet various expenses there and at the Chinchas. Gibbs, needless to say, denied such allegations, although the accusations over bags did cause them some private unease (see Gibbs, H.H.G.C., 2, Henry Hucks Gibbs to William Gibbs, 20 Aug. and 9, 24, 28, and 30 Oct. 1857). Gibbs and Myers also took higher (1 per cent) sales commissions for a time in the early 1840s than those agreed on with their mercantile associates in Lima. This caused quite a lot of dissension between the merchants (see Gibbs, G.G.C., 3 Apr. and 13 Dec. 1843, 22 and 28 Mar. 1844).
[2] See, for example, comments in Gibbs, G.G.C., 17 Dec. 1847.
[3] For critical comment, see Mesones, op. cit., p. 110.
[4] Gibbs, G.G.C., 1 May 1852; Ulloa, op. cit., pp. 51–9; *Anales*, vi. 36–7.
[5] Barroilhet, op. cit., pp. 65–6; Ulloa, op. cit., pp. 54, 57; *Dictamen De La Comisión Especial* . . ., pp. 14–15.
[6] Gibbs, H.H.G.C., 2, Henry Hucks Gibbs to William Gibbs, 21 Aug. 1865.
[7] For comment on the shipping market, see J. R. McCulloch, *A Dictionary of Commerce and Commercial Navigation* (London, 1856 edn.), p. 1169; ibid. (1859 edn.), p. 1168; 'The Trade in Guano', loc. cit., p. 60.
[8] Slow loading; troublesome cargo; rigorous post-1854 vessel inspection system at Callao; requirement in most years that ships had to check in at Callao and Pisco both before and after loading at the Chincha islands. See,

it may well have helped push up costs when the shipping market was tight and shipowners could opt for less onerous charters in other trades.[1] Gibbs, it seems, were taking advantage of their very considerable strength in the shipping market. Their command of patronage, indeed, must have been among the greatest in Western Europe. Over the years 1850–60 as many as 3,051 vessels, of 1,873,630 register tons, were dispatched from Peru under their consignment.[2] It would be difficult to find another merchant house in that decade employing a fleet of equivalent dimensions. They were certainly not claiming payment for any great labour. 'One cannot see any good reason for charging this commission' it was observed in 1856, 'since a business as great as that of guano must attract all the shipowners to the Gibbs office, relieving the consignees of all work in this respect.'[3] In our hypothetical 200,000 ton year, therefore, with an imaginary £4 freight average, Gibbs would take £20,000 at the 2½ per cent rate.

Third, there were notable defects in the geography of British and continental importations. In 1858, for example—the peak importing year—243,957 of the 353,541 tons of guano brought into Britain came through London: almost 70 per cent. The south-east of England, however, did not purchase a great deal of guano. Scotland, which did, received only 24,837 tons.[4] This, of course, necessitated much internal redistribution, obviously costly and price-enhancing for a bulky commodity like guano. There are a number of possible factors here—ship size, harbour facilities, desire to distribute as late as possible so that regional demand could be accurately gauged, efforts to control adulteration, and so on—but a major consideration almost certainly was Gibbs's wish to maximize their income. On guano sold in London they earned their full commission. On guano sold in the so-called 'outports' they had to use agents, and share their commissions. The two outports which were most amply used—taking 71,644 tons[5] (two-thirds

inter alia, Royal Commission on Unseaworthy Ships, loc. cit., pp. 32, 36, 49–50; 'The Guano Diggings', *Household Words*, vi, 131 (25 Sept. 1852), pp. 42–3; *Informe Circunstanciado . . .*, p. 250.

[1] Ibid., pp. 249–51; *The Times*, 22 Feb. 1854, 10.

[2] Royal Commission on Unseaworthy Ships, op. cit., Appendix X, pp. 502–3.

[3] *Dictamen De La Comisión Especial . . .*, p. 14; see also Ulloa, op. cit., p. 58.

[4] *Annual Statement of the Trade and Navigation of the United Kingdom with Foreign Countries and British Possessions in the Year 1858*, P.P. 1859, xxviii, pp. 124–5, 128, 130. The figures are for *all* guano imports (of which roughly 85 per cent were Peruvian).   [5] Ibid., pp. 124–5.

of the non-London imports)—were Liverpool and Bristol, where the associate firms of Gibbs, Bright & Co. were the agents. Antony Gibbs & Sons, then, were reluctant to share their earnings;[1] when they did share, they did so mainly with sister houses. The volume of sales was almost certainly reduced in consequence: Gibbs themselves acknowledged that.[2] As for the European business, the scale of guano re-exporting in the 1840s and 1850s suggests again a high degree of redistribution from London,[3] and a reluctance to encourage direct importing. It was also claimed at the time that Gibbs, with enormous territorial responsibilities, were ineffectual in pushing sales throughout the full extent of their markets[4] (and unnecessarily high prices resulting from indirect imports must have aggravated the problem). Rivero gives sales figures for the different countries, and although these probably exclude guano sold in London for shipment to the Continent, they do convey the impression that the European market was badly served. In 1856, the peak sales year in Britain and Europe, the British figure of 214,707 tons was more than twice that for Gibbs's European territories (then excluding France and Spain). More than half of the continental sales, moreover, were concentrated in Belgium. Sales in Britain and Belgium together amounted to 269,694 tons. In the enormous expanse of Europe east of the Rhine they came to only 50,032 tons.[5]

Fourth, Gibbs deliberately engaged in excessive exporting in 1860–1. There were probably two objectives here: to stockpile and thereby make it awkward for the business to be taken from them; and to ensure that, if they *were* removed from the trade, they would have guano to sell for a year or two after the contract expired. They made no bones about the fact that they were pursuing their own interest at the expense of most other considerations. If, wrote Henry Hucks Gibbs in 1860, 'we can carry away the islands bodily before the 18 December '61 we have *strictly* a right to do so'. In dealing with the government, he claimed, Gibbs had

---

[1] For some contemporary comment, see Ulloa, op. cit., pp. 17–18.

[2] Gibbs, H.H.G.C., 2, Henry Hucks Gibbs to William Gibbs, 30 Dec. 1858; 3, Henry Hucks Gibbs to William Gibbs, 19 Feb. 1862.

[3] See P.P. 1854–5, l, 312–13; 1860, lxiv, 32; 1865, lii, 33; Antony Gibbs & Sons, op. cit., p. 26.

[4] Rivero, op. cit., p. 28; Ulloa, op. cit., pp. 13–19.

[5] Rivero, op. cit., Appendix: Estado Comparativo de Las Ventas de Huano desde 1° de Julio de 1849 hasta 1860 inclusivo.

'never looked to the strict letter of the law, when our doing so would prejudice them, but as against our competitors, and possible successors—every man for himself! We must take whatever hard earned advantage our contract gives us . . .'[1] Attitudes such as these, sustained throughout 1860, activated a policy of energetic chartering. By December their unsold stocks in all markets amounted to 267,944 tons, and a further 254,000 tons were on their way.[2] Gibbs foresaw the possibility of a ban on any more chartering, but were not much troubled: 'we shall have stock for the whole of the season of '62 and some to spare for the Autumn— their diligence comes too late'.[3] In November 1861, just a few weeks before their contract was due to expire, stocks were calculated at 230,000 tons, with a lot more still to come.[4] By then, however, the policy of heavy exporting had been substantially curtailed. William Gibbs, the former head of the house, now in semi-retirement, and John Hayne, the former manager of the Lima branch, both disapproved of Henry Hucks Gibbs's activities and forced him to agree towards the end of 1860 that he had been in error. He confessed that after closely examining the contract he saw that he really had the right only to export sufficient to satisfy *consumption* up to the end of 1861.[5] But it was a conveniently late conversion to propriety, and his firm's behaviour had created a furore in Lima.[6]

VIII

We can now return to our categories of 'control' and see which, if any, are applicable to the relationship between Gibbs and the Peruvian Government.[7]

[1] Gibbs, H.H.G.C., 2, Henry Hucks Gibbs to William Gibbs, 3 Feb. 1860.
[2] Ibid., Henry Hucks Gibbs to John Hayne, 12 Dec. 1860.
[3] Ibid., Henry Hucks Gibbs to Francisco de Rivero, 18 Dec. 1860.
[4] Ibid., Henry Hucks Gibbs to William Gibbs, 1 Nov. 1861; 3, Henry Hucks Gibbs to William Gibbs, 4 Mar. 1862.
[5] Ibid., 2, Henry Hucks Gibbs to William Gibbs, 12 Dec. 1860.
[6] The matter was heatedly discussed in Congress and provoked some scathing comment from *El Comercio*. See Gibbs, H.H.G.C., 2, Henry Hucks Gibbs to William Gibbs, 17 Jan. 1861.
[7] It should be stressed that we have examined only the *British* contractors in this chapter, in conformity with this book's frame of reference. As it happened, of course, Gibbs were easily the most important of the guano merchants. But no firm pronouncements about the monopoly-consignment as a whole can be made until the behaviour of the other contractors has been examined in close detail.

On the issue of direct control over official policy, and the forcing of decisions favourable to mercantile interests, there is not a great deal to be said. Gibbs had considerable power through the provision of loans to the government, and the government was usually ready to defend them against their attackers in a manner that suggests a somewhat conniving and collaborative association.[1] But the power appears to have been used principally in relation to contract allocation. The government wanted loans; Gibbs provided them, and thereby maintained their lien on guano. This, however, was merely the system feeding off itself: and when the Peruvian environment in which they operated turned chilly, Gibbs had little choice but to withdraw.

On the matter of exercising authority and undertaking initiatives in areas of activity vital to the economic strength of Peru, unchecked by the government and contrary to its best interests, one can certainly fault the contractors on the claiming of unearned commissions, the excessive centralization of British and European imports, and the heavy exporting of 1860–1. But on the charges of sustained price depreciation and cost elevation the evidence to hand suggests they must be acquitted. Gibbs certainly made very ample profits, earning interest and commissions on a wide range of activities, but the scale of their income owed much to the vast dimensions of their commerce. And although they undertook virtually all the practical managerial responsibilities of the trade, their remuneration was still only a fraction of that claimed by the government. The latter, in its peculiar position as owner of the export commodity, exercised a considerable authority over contract terms and pricing.

The category of 'control' which seems of most relevance is the second one cited at the start of this chapter: 'in which policies are not wilfully forced upon the government, but which results simply from the circumstances confronting the government as a result of the presence and dispositions of the foreigner'. Gibbs were resident

---

[1] When Barroilhet went to see Castilla in 1856 with allegations of Gibbs's misconduct he was dismissed with angry remarks from the President about charlatans wasting his time and trying his patience. See Barroilhet, op. cit., pp. 14–15. In Sept. 1857 the Finance Minister, Zevallos, gave a vigorous defence of Gibbs's integrity before the Convención Nacional, asserting that they had always behaved with a 'most exact scrupulousness', that their interests did not conflict with those of the government, and that the Convención would do well to ignore assertions made by a man such as Barroilhet whose motives invited only suspicion: *El Comercio*, 6, 7, and 9 Sept. 1857.

in Lima: they were active in the guano sector; and they were backed by the resources of the City of London. They represented metropolitan finance, and held out to a weak, insecure, and inadequately financed governmental system in Lima irresistible temptations to sink ever more deeply into a costly and debilitating indebtedness. They did not thrust money on the Peruvians, but of course they rarely denied them it either. Their interests, like those of all their kind, were in material gain and advancement. They did not care a whit about the Peruvian economy, beyond those fields of activity of consequence for their own well-being.[1] Their position as ready accomplices in the injudicious extravagances of the Peruvian Government is encapsulated in their brief comment in 1854 when they were awarded the Australian and West Indian contract. This required a large loan, and as market returns were likely to be trifling, profits were to be directed from European sales for purposes of reimbursement. Commercially it was an inconsequential arrangement, 'only as the Government would have it, it was better in our hands than another's: It is very bad policy for Peru!'[2]

---

[1] Nor did they display much concern over the wretched circumstances of the contract labourers on the guano islands, who performed the first crucial tasks necessary before contractors could earn any commissions or governments any profits.

[2] Gibbs, W.G.C., Henry Hucks Gibbs to William Gibbs, 8 Sept. 1854.

CHAPTER X

British Firms and the Peruvian Government, 1885–1930

RORY MILLER

I

THE interaction of British business and the Peruvian Government in the middle of the nineteenth century has long been the subject of debate, and Dr. Mathew, who has contributed most substantially to the debate in recent years, has already summarized its elements in Chapter IX above. Far less attention, however, has been given to the relationship between British firms, the government, and the economy of Peru for the years which followed Peru's defeat in the War of the Pacific and the loss of her guano and nitrate to Chile.[1]

In contrast to the earlier period Peru's export trade had become based on a wider range of products. Exports totalling over £p8 million in 1913 were composed, by value, of 22 per cent copper, 18 per cent cotton, 18 per cent sugar, 14 per cent silver, 11 per cent oil, and 10 per cent rubber.[2] Broadly speaking, Britons participated in the Peruvian economy in two distinct directions. The trading houses confined themselves to the marketing and financing of sugar and cotton crops. Unlike the American house of Grace and Company, few British houses took a direct interest in production; their business was the shipment of produce to Britain, Chile, or the United States. Only a few *haciendas* in the north of Lima department and the Cañete valley were directly controlled by British interests, accounting for less than 10 per cent of Peruvian

---

[1] Some of the material for the intervening period has been covered in Robert G. Greenhill and Rory M. Miller, 'The Peruvian Government and the Nitrate Trade, 1873–1879', *Journal of Latin American Studies*, v (1973), pp. 107–31.

[2] Peru, Department of Treasury and Commerce, *Statistical Abstract of Peru, 1923* (Lima, 1924), p. 46. The *libra peruana* was approximately equivalent to and exchangeable for the pound sterling at this period.

sugar production. British firms like Duncan Fox, Graham Rowe, Henry Kendall, or Milne and Co. were, therefore, unlikely to come into conflict with the Peruvian Government; it was the Peruvian plantation owners, through the Sociedad Nacional de Agricultura and other pressure groups, who took charge of negotiations over matters like the imposition of export duties on sugar and cotton in 1915.

In non-agricultural sectors, however, foreign firms participated more directly in the Peruvian economy. Mining became an important American interest after 1902 when the Cerro de Pasco Copper Corporation moved into the central sierra. The bulk of the oil industry remained in British hands until 1913. Even after that date, when Standard Oil of New Jersey bought a controlling share in the major producer (the London and Pacific Petroleum Company), the British were still heavily involved; Standard Oil subsidiaries were registered in London and Toronto, and it was the Foreign Office, not the State Department, that handled the delicate negotiations over the oil concessions. Furthermore, British firms, whether the heavily capitalized Peruvian Corporation or the smaller Chimbote and North Western Companies, owned and operated the greater part of the country's railways. Both the oil and the railway companies worked under government concessions and contracts, and it was from these that the majority of disputes between the Peruvian Government and British firms arose.

II

The British trading houses, therefore, could depend on some identity of interest between themselves and local producers. This avoided the political problems that might arise from too direct a share in the Peruvian economy. Even where a British firm took an interest in production, like Antony Gibbs and Sons in nitrate before the Pacific war, it aimed at 'a quiet and economical style of management'.[1] The house refused to accept government proposals for the reorganization of the nitrate trade in 1878 because it would become too directly involved with the Administration; subsequent to the guano contracts of 1842–9 and 1850–61, Gibbs had preferred in the nitrate trade to deal with the government only through the intermediary of four Lima banks. Peruvian producers

[1] Greenhill and Miller, op. cit., pp. 120, 125–6.

formed a buffer between British trading houses and the government, and it was this class that underpinned most administrations in the early twentieth century. José Pardo, president from 1904 to 1908 and 1915 to 1919, came from a key family in the sugar industry, while Augusto Leguía, president from 1908 to 1912 and 1919 to 1930, had once managed one of the few British-owned sugar estates.

A number of writers on imperialism have underlined the importance to British economic interests abroad of the political collaboration of the local élite. Gallagher and Robinson have argued that once the economies of the South American states had become sufficiently dependent on foreign trade, the classes whose prosperity was derived from it would normally work to preserve the local political conditions for that trade.[1] In a more recent paper Ronald Robinson has emphasized the two types of linkage implicit in the collaborative mechanism: the arrangement between the agents of the metropolis and the indigenous élites, and the compromise that the latter had to be prepared to make with local interests and institutions. The local political élite, in balancing both sets of forces, might ignore foreign interests to maintain domestic credibility.[2]

Peruvian writers have used similar arguments to analyse the nature of the Peruvian ruling class at the end of the nineteenth century. Ernesto Yepes del Castillo saw the rise of *civilismo* as the political reaction of Peru's ruling classes to growing foreign control over Peruvian trade:

They turned their principal efforts towards increasing their participation in the profits generated by the economic system of dependence. . . . They sought to do so by becoming the politically dominant class. . . . In this way that fraction of the dominant class capable of assuring internal order to allow the labour force to be put at the disposal of economic exploitation (principally foreign) could negotiate dividends in exchange.[3]

Nobody, however, has made an empirical study of the practical

[1] J. Gallagher and R. Robinson, 'The Imperialism of Free Trade', *Economic History Review*, 2nd ser. vi (1953), 10.

[2] Ronald Robinson, 'Non-European foundations of European imperialism: sketch for a theory of collaboration' in Roger Owen and Bob Sutcliffe, eds., *Studies in the Theory of Imperialism* (London, 1972), pp. 121–2.

[3] Ernesto Yepes del Castillo, *Perú 1820–1920; un siglo de desarrollo capitalista* (Lima, 1972), p. 158.

applications for Peru of the theory that British interests rested on the collaboration of a sympathetic élite of Peruvian politicians. The relations of British firms with the Peruvian Government provide a well-documented opportunity to test this theory; and such a study may illustrate the points of stress in the normally friendly relations between the administration and foreign firms, the ways in which the government had to compromise between foreign capitalists and local interests, and the role it played when these came into conflict.

The basic assumption behind the theory of the collaborating élite is that the ruling class in the host country accepted the role of foreign capital either from motives of ideological belief or from personal economic interest. This was certainly the case in Peru at the turn of the century. In the philosophy of *civilismo*, foreign investment and immigration were regarded as the most important elements in Peru's future development. Manuel Pardo, Peru's first civilian president (1872–6), epitomized this view:

> We must bring in foreign capital. In order to do so we must create the necessary political and economic conditions, such that it is not only guaranteed an adequate return on the sum invested, but an internal climate to make this investment possible . . . We must provide huge inducements for European investors to overcome the obstacles in their way.[1]

Another *civilista* colleague wrote in 1882 that in the post-war regeneration of Peru 'we trust in an influx of foreign capital and labour more than in the enterprise of our governments and our capitalists'.[2] In 1910 the vice-president tried to attract Lord Cowdray's attention to Peru:

> If a powerful firm like Messrs. Pearson identified themselves prominently in the development of Peru's undoubted resources (in the same manner that they have identified themselves with the progress of Mexico) they would not have cause to regret it and it would be a matter that would be welcomed, not only by the governing classes of the country, but also by the whole of the Peruvian people at large.[3]

It was only in the 1920s that these basic assumptions really came into question, and then from writers like Víctor Raúl Haya

[1] Quoted in Yepes, op. cit., p. 100.
[2] Luís Esteves, *Apuntes para la História Económica del Perú* (Lima, 1882), p. 6.
[3] Balfour Williamson: Guillermo Billinghurst to Sir Archibald Williamson, 1 Sept. 1910.

de la Torre and José Carlos Mariátegui who were outside the spectrum of the ruling oligarchy. Only one government between 1885 and 1930 systematically attacked foreign interests: that of José Pardo (1915–19) in the exceptional situation created by the First World War.

Yet there was no complete identification of interests between foreign firms and the Peruvian oligarchy. Disputes did take place. At times the harmony of interests clearly disappeared. Moreover, these disagreements occupied a place of exceptional importance and bitterness within Peruvian politics. One deputy claimed in 1919 that the major crises of the past fifty years had been those over the Dreyfus concessions, the Grace contract, and the International Petroleum Company.[1] Too ready an acceptance of the theory of a collaborating élite leaves many questions unexplained. Why could Pardo ignore foreign claims during the First World War? Why could the Peruvian Corporation and the Peruvian Government not settle a dispute that had started in 1890 until 1907? Why was the Grace contract, first signed in 1887, not passed by Congress until 1890? Why could the International Petroleum Company (I.P.C.) not obtain its demands in 1915, while achieving a settlement on similar lines in 1922? Did Peru consistently aim to control the entry of foreign capital, or were its motives more opportunistic? The theory of a collaborating élite may help to explain the economic relationship between the metropolis and a dependent economy. It cannot make proper allowance for those tensions and breakdowns in the local political system which occurred even when the host government continued to express a harmony of interests with foreign capital. To explain such situations we must refine the theory by studying the élite's role in mediating between foreign and local interests. Can we put the Peruvian Government in the role of arbitrator between the foreign firms and a critical, antagonistic Congress?

III

Congress played a leading part in all the disputes, a feature that most writers on this subject have ignored. Between 1885 and 1930 no government could afford to forget the interests of Congress which continued in existence throughout the period. Some

---

[1] Peru, Legislatura Ordinaria de 1918, *Diario de Diputados* (Peru), p. 1046 (speech of Sr. Salazar Oyarzaban).

governments, of course, were stronger than others, or had pressing reasons for pushing a proposal through a sceptical Congress. Some presidents gained in authority during their term of office. In 1928 Leguía obtained Congressional approval for a settlement with the Peruvian Corporation which he had not even dared to submit earlier in the decade. But where a president had lost the confidence of the legislature, where his cabinets survived only during the annual recess, he had to take account of the legislature's wishes before he could achieve anything. The life of cabinets indicates the intensity of the conflict between the executive and legislature. In the first three years of his administration (1890–3), General Morales Bermúdez had to reorganize his cabinet seven times.[1] In October 1887 President Cáceres failed to find any politician willing to face his former colleagues in the legislature over the question of the Grace contract, and was reduced to forming a government of the senior officials in each ministry.[2] The one attempt by a president in this period to suppress Congress—Billinghurst's in 1914— ended in his overthrow.[3] In this distribution of power, Congress could exercise three functions in disputes between the government and foreign interests: it could initiate a dispute, delay a settlement by failing to approve government plans, or deter negotiations completely.

Initiation of a dispute generally arose from some damage that a foreign-owned concession was doing, or was expected to do, to the personal interests of the legislators. A senator or deputy had to consider the interests of the region he represented, and, of course, he had to safeguard and advance his own political or financial position. In 1910 the two senators for Ancash attacked the concession granted to a British firm, the Chimbote Coal and Harbour Syndicate, for the construction of a railway from Chimbote (on the Pacific coast) to Recuay (at the head of the Santa valley). The company faced financial problems, and the senators suspected that it would complete the railway only to the coal-mines a few miles from the coast. In this way the company would avoid the costly construction necessary higher up the valley, but scarcely benefit the region's agriculture. Despite President Leguía's support for the company, pressure from the legislature forced the government to annul the concession in 1911. The executive had

[1] *Anales*, xxiii. 7. [2] *El Comercio*, 5 Oct. 1897.
[3] Fredrick B. Pike, *The Modern History of Peru* (London, 1967), pp. 200–1.

been prepared to revise the contract in the company's favour, but it could not risk Congressional opposition. For its part, the company could offer the Government no financial inducement to change its policy, nor even obtain the aid of the British Foreign Office.[1]

One of the strongest groups within Peruvian politics represented the interests of coastal agriculture. As we have said, both President Pardo and President Leguía had strong links with the sugar industry. It was the pressure group representing coastal agriculture which provoked the conflict between the government and the Peruvian Corporation over the latter's rights to export guano under the Grace contract. When the contract was signed in 1890, domestic consumption of guano was insignificant. The negotiations reserved only the depleted stocks of the Chincha islands for internal consumption. However, the increased use of fertilizers formed an important element in the sugar industry's attempts to rebuild after the crisis of the early 1900s. In the first decade of the century demand for guano increased substantially, and in 1909 the government had to establish the Compañía Administradora del Guano to control the trade. But by then the Peruvian Corporation's claim that its exports had priority prevented domestic demands from being met. Under pressure from the Sociedad Nacional de Agricultura, the government divided the deposits into two zones, one for internal consumption and one for export. Four years later, President Billinghurst rescinded the Corporation's licence to load at certain high-grade deposits. Even this did not satisfy the legislature which pressed the government to cancel the 1909 compromise and restrict the Corporation to one, low-grade island. For some time the government delayed action. It did not wish to injure its credit in Europe by an attack on the Peruvian Corporation at a time when it still had to place £300,000 of a loan authorized by the legislature. Circumstances changed during 1914. The outbreak of war made it impossible to think of raising money in Europe while intensifying the fiscal problems of the government. Trade slumped, cutting the government's revenue from import and export duties. Congress proposed to sanction an increase in the price of guano in Peru and thus aid government revenue, while the

---

[1] P.R.O. F.O. 371/970, Huxley (syndicate secretary) to Norman, 19 Sept. 1910; P.R.O. F.O. 371/1205, Des Graz to Grey, 10 Dec. 1910, and Jerome to Grey (telegraphic), 25 Aug. 1911.

Compañía Administradora del Guano offered a loan of £p50,000 secured against future receipts. In January 1915 the executive accepted a law confiscating the Peruvian Corporation's guano rights and annulling the existing division into zones.[1] Agricultural interests, working through both the Sociedad Nacional de Agricultura and sympathetic deputies and senators, had thus forced the executive into a confrontation with a foreign firm. For a time the possibility of gaining easy credit in Europe had postponed government acquiescence in Congressional demands, but once war removed this restraint legislative pressure on the executive was impossible to resist.

Of the three major sets of negotiations between the government and foreign business interests outlined by Sr. Salazar in 1918, two, the Grace contract and the I.P.C. dispute, occurred in this period. In both cases Congress delayed a settlement—to the chagrin of the government. Cáceres's administration first signed an agreement with the Peruvian Bondholders' Committee in May 1887, but the revised contract came into operation only in January 1890. In the other case, I.P.C. proposed a settlement of their dispute with the government late in 1915. Congress discussed it for three years, modifying the government's proposals and incorporating its own amendments, before agreeing to the executive's project for arbitration at the end of 1918. Yet the arbitration award was not given until 1922, and almost exactly resembled the first set of plans for agreement of seven years earlier. There was only one important difference: Congress had added an amendment calling for I.P.C. to pay $1 million in compensation for unpaid taxes, and this was retained in the final award. In the Grace contract Congress rejected one concession agreed between the government and the Bondholders' Committee—the establishment of a bank of issue in Lima. To some extent, therefore, by delaying and revising agreements Congress operated as a check on any tendency of the government to make liberal concessions to foreign interests.[2]

[1] Ministerio de Hacienda, *Memoria del Ministro de Hacienda por el año 1910*, XL and Anexo 86; *West Coast Leader* (Lima), 19 and 26 June 1913; PC/Lim, Peruvian Corporation, Representative's Annual Report, 1915, pp. 17–18; P.R.O. F.O. 371/2082, Rennie to Grey, 29 Apr. 1914.

[2] One of the best accounts of the I.P.C. dispute is still Luís Laurie Solís, *La Diplomacia del Petroleo y el Caso de La Brea y Pariñas* (Lima, 1967); see also Jorge Basadre, *História de la República del Perú* (5th edn., Lima, 1964), viii. 3774, 3885–92; and, for the most recent view, I. G. Bertram, 'Development problems in an export economy: a study of domestic capitalists, foreign firms,

The executive continually had to take into account the attitude of the legislature. To gain Congressional approval for the Grace contract, the Cáceres government had to call four extraordinary sessions. It had to remove the opposition in the Chamber of Deputies, which had first adopted filibustering tactics and then simply refused to make up a quorum in the Chamber. In the confused political situation following the War of the Pacific, attacks on the Grace contract united diverse elements in opposition to Cáceres, though they acted from a variety of motives. Some attacked the assumption that Peru had a debt at all, since Chile had agreed to pay the bondholders a proportion of the proceeds from the guano deposits captured during the war. Others disagreed with the terms of the contract. Manuel Candamo, a future *civilista* president, impugned the settlement on the grounds that it did not settle outstanding diplomatic questions with Chile, nor could Peru afford to pay the bondholders the £80,000 annual subsidy that they demanded. Another prominent *civilista*, Felipe Barreda y Osma, questioned the assumption that foreign control of the railways under the contract would in fact stimulate the expected economic recovery. Cáceres's opponents disputed the right of the executive to sign a contract without first obtaining the approval of the legislature. Local interests also played a part. Representatives from southern Peru were angered by the stipulation in the original proposal that the bondholders should take over the administration of the Mollendo customs. Moreover, other opponents of the scheme used members of Congress to delay its implementation. José María Químper, believed to have taken bribes from Henry Meiggs in the first phase of railway construction, was suspected of being in close contact with rival French interests whose claims conflicted with the bondholders'; at one stage he tried to interpellate the Minister of Foreign Affairs about a French note of protest even before the legation had delivered it.[1] Despite the diverse motives of the contract's opponents, Congress

and government in Peru, 1919–1930' (unpublished D.Phil. thesis, University of Oxford, 1974). For the Grace contract see Basadre, op. cit., vi. 2748–74, W. H. Wynne, *State Insolvency and Foreign Bondholders* (New Haven, Conn., 1951), pp. 109–95, and Rory Miller, 'The Making of the Grace Contract', *Journal of Latin American Studies*, viii (1976), pp. 73–100.

[1] *El Comercio*, 3 and 14 Sept. 1889; F. Barreda y Osma, *Los Ferrocarriles y el Proyecto de los Tenedores de Bonos* (Lima, 1888), pp. 5–9; anon., *La Deuda Externa y la Cámara de Diputados* (Lima, 1888), p. 19; *Panama Star and Herald*, 19 Nov. 1887; P.R.O. F.O. 61/383, Mansfield to Salisbury, 24 Jan. 1889.

succeeded in questioning, delaying, and modifying the government's plans. The executive overcame the opposition only by using methods of doubtful constitutional legality, leaving behind a legacy of bitterness and distrust. Although the government was desperate to conclude the contract and recover its credit in Europe, it could not do so without finding a method of controlling Congress.

In fact, the legislature often tended to echo xenophobic feeling in Peru against an unpopular foreign concessionaire. The bitterness left by the Grace contract meant that, in its early years, the company which had been formed to work the concessions (the Peruvian Corporation) faced hostility everywhere. 'The Corporation does not enjoy popularity amongst the general public in Peru', wrote the British minister, 'and notably possesses few partisans in either chamber.'[1] Legislative opposition deterred the Corporation from exerting its full rights under the contract at a time when the executive was especially weak and fragile. Michael Grace, in Peru to advise the management of the new company, suggested care in the prosecution of the company's tariff policy:

It is not at all prudent that we should force the cabinet into such a position that would involve its fall on a popular question or policy such as that of the reduction of tariffs, in addition to which we must remember the cabinet is composed of friends who stood behind this contract during the whole of the recent Congressional fight.[2]

Even prominent *civilistas* like Alejandro Garland, who usually welcomed foreign capital, opposed the corporation.[3] In an attempt to reconcile their differences, the company's representative reached a settlement with the government in 1905 that was rejected by the London board. The proposals aroused intense opposition in Lima. 'The press has expressed its strong disapproval of the action of the government in accepting them even as a basis of settlement', reported the British chargé d'affaires.[4] Once a company like the Peruvian Corporation became unpopular, Congress echoed the xenophobia. Unless a government was exceptionally strong, or had pressing reasons to conclude a settlement, Congress

[1] P.R.O. F.O. 61/393, Mansfield to Salisbury, 22 July 1892.
[2] PC/UCL, file Z. 99, Michael Grace to Thomas Webb (company secretary), 11 Mar. 1891.
[3] Letter in *S.A.J.*, 28 June 1902.
[4] P.R.O. F.O. 61/446, Alfred St. John to Lansdowne, 25 May 1905.

would prolong the dispute or oppose altogether any attempt at agreement.

The legislature was more independent of foreign pressure than the executive largely because of the differing roles of the two branches of government. The administration had to negotiate directly with the foreign concessionaire and to consider all aspects of a settlement. Congress could simply block, delay, or amend, reflecting 'popular' dislike of a project. Ambitious or troublesome representatives enjoyed establishing themselves in a position of opposition to a foreign company. They jealously guarded legislative privileges. The dispute with I.P.C. during the First World War is one illustration. Early in 1916 a Lima newspaper leaked the terms of the settlement which the government had negotiated with I.P.C. in return for help in issuing a loan on the New York market. This forced the administration to withdraw the bill which it had placed before Congress.[1] According to the British minister:

The recent proposal that the President should be allowed a free hand to contract a loan in the United States through the Standard Oil Company, was met with summary treatment at the hands of the House of Representatives, who insisted that any arrangement for a loan could only be made 'ad referendum' to Congress. The fate of Mexico appears to be looked on as a lesson to Peruvian politicians, that the Standard Oil Corporation must not be allowed to obtain any hold on their country.[2]

When the president did present the legislature with a plan for settlement, the Senate refused to accept it and substituted its own solution. The deputies then rejected the Senate's bill after it had passed the Upper House.[3] The legislature did not settle the question of I.P.C.'s concession, first raised in 1912, until 1918— to the embarrassment of the government and the exasperation of the company.

Congress, free from the responsibilities of government, could and did obstruct the executive's plans for settlement with foreign firms. It could initiate disputes with foreign firms by launching an attack on a concession or contract. More difficult to find, in the absence of full government records, are those instances where fear of legislative opposition deterred a president from even

[1] P.R.O. F.O. 371/2738, Rennie to Grey, 18 Jan. 1916.
[2] P.R.O. F.O. 371/2739, Rennie to Grey, 28 Feb. 1916.
[3] Laurie Solís, op. cit., p. 127; *Diario de Diputados* (*Peru*), 1918, pp. 1154–5.

submitting a settlement to Congress. In 1910, the Peruvian Corporation asked Leguía to consider a plan that would give them perpetual ownership of the railways, in place of the sixty-six-year lease which the Corporation held under the Grace contract. Leguía told the company that he personally regarded the proposal favourably, yet the opposition to him was such that he dared not even submit it to the legislature, let alone hope for approval.[1] In 1921 Congress embarrassed Leguía by rejecting a plan for the commutation of the Peruvian Corporation's guano rights.[2] This rebuff may have influenced Leguía's reaction when the Corporation again suggested negotiating perpetuity in 1925. The Corporation's representative in Lima, a close friend of the president, reported the latter's reaction:

I think the proposal would be mutually advantageous [said Leguía]. But here in Peru there are not a dozen people far-sighted enough to see it in that light. The large majority, especially in view of the length of time still to run, would at once say that I was giving away valuable assets of the State without return and for purely hypothetical reasons. The proposal would have not the slightest chance of acceptance.[3]

The Corporation obtained the concession of perpetual ownership of their lines in 1928, but only after offering their guano rights to the government, together with a substantial cash payment, at a time when it faced financial stringency. By then Leguía's position *vis-à-vis* Congress was such that he gained approval of the settlement within only a few weeks.[4]

Congress was certainly an element in all calculations between 1885 and 1930. Settlement of every dispute had to go before Congress, whose leaders often proved ready to pose as the defenders of national interests against the excessive demands of foreign firms. The legislature, of course, did not have executive responsibilities; it did not have to look to the future; it did not have to worry about diplomatic protests or fiscal crises. Clashes with foreign firms could provide a convenient pretext to attack the president and overthrow his cabinet. Presidents often faced a

[1] PC/UCL, file A. 8, Morkill to Yates, 14 July 1910.
[2] *Memoria del Ministro de Hacienda* (1921), pp. cv–cviii; PC/UCL, *Report of Board of Directors, 1920,* p. 11.
[3] PC/Lim, Informe 1, memo of A. S. Cooper's interview with President Leguía, 20 June 1925.
[4] For Cooper's diary of the negotiations see PC/Lim, Informe 1.

hostile Congress; under the 1860 constitution (which lasted until 1920) presidents were elected every four years, but a third of Congress was renewed every two. At no time in this period could a president ignore the attitude of Congress in his dealings with a foreign firm.

IV

What countervailing pressures were available to the firms themselves? D. C. M. Platt, in his preliminary study of business control in Latin America, argued that 'in finance, given that British government assistance was not available, the strongest weapon of control was the denial of credit'. Platt felt, however, that this sanction was seldom effective in the long term once money had become easier; to be fully effective even in the short term a government had to be anxious to raise new loans, and there had to be a general shortage of credit so that European financiers and investors were not competing amongst themselves to obtain the business.[1] What role did this weapon play in the disputes between British firms and Peru?

The desire to restore Peruvian government credit in Europe, to raise funds for the reconstruction of the country following the War of the Pacific, and more immediately, to finance government expenditure after the loss of the two major pre-war sources of revenue, guano and nitrate, undoubtedly formed part of the reason for the government's acceptance of the Grace contract. The presidential commission which examined the first project in 1886 put the point clearly: 'The bondholders' proposals have for us the capital advantage that we pay off our external debt and recover our credit abroad.'[2] Without settling the outstanding foreign debt, Peru could not participate in the increased spate of Latin American borrowing on European exchanges in the late 1880s. The Bondholders' Committee had already prevented two entrepreneurs, Michael Grace and John Thorndike, from raising capital in London for the reconstruction of the Central and Southern Railways.[3]

Peru had no choice of alternative markets at the time, even in the cheap credit conditions of the late 1880s. Grace tried, and

[1] D. C. M. Platt, 'Economic Imperialism and the businessman: Britain and Latin America before 1914', in Owen and Sutcliffe, op. cit., pp. 297–8.
[2] *El Comercio*, 29 Nov. 1886.   [3] Ibid. 16 Sept. 1889.

failed, to interest New York in his schemes for the reconstruction of the railways.[1] European investors were equally reluctant. As Charles Watson commented: 'No Banking House or Financial Concern would agree to finance such a business unless they could get a Stock Exchange quotation, and the Stock Exchanges of Europe are quite agreed to forbid and refuse any such quotation until the Peruvian bondholders are arranged and settled with.'[2]

Berlin might have been an alternative market. Chile raised a loan there in 1889, although the bondholders in Holland objected that they were in dispute with Chile as well as Peru.[3] However, Chilean credit, after the conquest of the nitrate *pampas* from Peru, was extremely good, and there is no evidence that Peru ever considered this course.

When the Peruvian Corporation came into dispute with the Peruvian Government, it continued to influence investors in other countries. Without any positive action on the part of the Corporation, its misfortunes could clearly deter investors from lending to the Peruvian Government. Conclusive evidence may be difficult to find, but it would be natural enough for a banker or investor to have doubts about lending to a government which maltreated its major creditor. Moreover, after Peru lost the guano and nitrate, its credit rating in the advanced countries slipped dramatically. The poor showing of the Peruvian Corporation, which had had to reduce the interest paid on its debentures between 1896 and 1903, might well have persuaded investors to seek more profitable outlets in other South American countries. In the minds of the investing public, Peru and the Peruvian Corporation were synonymous. Of sixteen articles on Peru in *The Economist* between 1890 and 1902, only three were not specifically about the Corporation.

Furthermore, the directors and management of the Peruvian Corporation actively intervened in the market against Peru. In 1896 the Corporation successfully prevented a French consortium from lending to the Peruvian Government.[4] Peru succeeded in raising a loan on the Paris market in 1909 after a settlement with the Corporation, but found herself facing more problems. The French house of Dreyfus complained that Peru had not settled

[1] PC/Lim, Meiggs papers, Joseph Spinney to Charles Watson, 15 June 1885.
[2] PC/Lim, Meiggs papers, Charles Watson to Charles Watson, jun., 13 June 1888.
[3] *S.A.J.*, 25 May 1889; *Statist*, 25 May 1889.
[4] *S.A.J.*, 8 Oct. 1904.

Dreyfus's outstanding claims, and in consequence the loan did not obtain a listing on the Paris Bourse until 1921.[1] In 1915–16, at the time of the conflict over guano, the Peruvian Corporation successfully applied pressure through W. R. Grace and Co. in New York to prevent the National City Bank from negotiating a loan for Peru.[2] The British minister in Lima reported in 1919 that a group of American bankers, on an exploratory visit to Peru, had rejected the idea of business with the Peruvian Government after hearing of the unsettled dispute with the Corporation over guano.[3]

Foreign creditors, if adequately organized themselves and supported by the more powerful financial houses and brokers, could successfully prevent the government from borrowing in some or all of the principal money markets, although a collusive attempt to restore Peruvian credit, by financiers and the Peruvian Government working in harness, *could* reopen those markets without offering genuine advantages to the ordinary investor. This was the case with the formation of the Peruvian Corporation in 1890, and it has been common enough in the successive 'reorganizations' and 'settlements' of overseas debts for Latin America since Independence.

Foreign creditors might also hope to bring pressure to bear by halting private investment, but this was more difficult to manage successfully, and naturally less influential in dealing with governments. Its effectiveness depended on whether a company needed to turn to public capital markets. If it could raise all the finance it needed by private subscription, its only criteria for investment were business possibilities. The government bondholders, at a time when they were attempting to block Peruvian credit, could not prevent the London and Pacific Petroleum Company from investing in Peruvian oil in 1889, since the company obtained its finance privately. Antony Gibbs and Sons considered financing the export of ores from Cerro de Pasco at the beginning of the twentieth century. The house rejected the business because of uncertainties in profits and staffing; the difficulties of the Peruvian Corporation and the Corporation's claims on Cerro de Pasco had no influence on its decision.[4] A dispute with the Peruvian Government may

[1] Wynne, op. cit., pp. 168–9.
[2] P.R.O. F.O. 371/2738, Yates (company secretary) to Foreign Office, 31 Dec. 1915 and 19 Jan. 1916.
[3] P.R.O. F.O. 371/3893, Rennie to Seymour, 30 May 1919.
[4] Gibbs 11470/19, Valparaíso to London, 22 Feb. 1901.

certainly have delayed further investment by the company concerned. When the Peruvian Corporation at last began to make reasonable profits in the early 1900s and was able to finance new development from its receipts, it invested not in Peru but in Bolivia. The International Petroleum Company refused to sink further capital in the Negritos oilfield until the Peruvian Government had settled its titles. The production of La Brea y Pariñas languished at about 240,000 tons annually during the most serious phase of the dispute from 1915 to 1919; by 1926 it had risen to over a million tons.[1] This could affect the government's interests, since further investment would provide additional employment opportunities, a general expansion of economic activity and, in the case of oil, increased government revenues through payment of the export duty.

How much, then, did the denial of credit influence the government in settling with a foreign firm? In the short term, the timing of an agreement depended more on other forces. Though the Peruvian Government hastened to sign the Grace contract to restore its credit on European markets, the timing of the final settlement was determined by the legislature's willingness to approve the agreement. The pressure applied by the Peruvian Corporation on Peruvian credit in 1896, 1916, and 1919 did nothing to resolve the disputes in question. Similarly, in the long run and at a price, credit was obtainable, and others could be found to undertake the business. It was in the intermediate period, when the government was anxious to take advantage of what might turn out to be only a temporary easing of capital markets, that the foreign firm had its best chance of success. The Peruvian Corporation was in an unusually strong position in this respect. Formed as part of a compromise with Peru's external creditors, the value of its stock tended to be taken as a measure of Peruvian credit. For years prices of Peruvian Corporation stock were listed on the London Stock Exchange not under 'railways' or 'investment trusts' but under 'foreign governments'. The Corporation could depend on this as a powerful element of control over Peru's access to further sources of credit, and its connections outside Peru could make the settlement of outstanding disputes between government and corporation a precondition of further financial aid from abroad.

[1] Jorge Hohagen, 'La Industria Minera en el Perú, 1932 y 1933', *Boletín del Cuerpo de Ingenieros de Minas*, 111 (Lima, 1935), 169–70.

This was clearly an important element in the terms of the 1905 agreement signed by the corporation's representative in Lima, but rejected by his Board. Alfred St. John, the British consul-general, pointed out the motives that had led the government to sign an unpopular agreement: 'Although they considered the terms onerous in the extreme, at that juncture they still feared a rupture with Ecuador and were anxious to raise a loan of six hundred thousand pounds . . . They apprehended that the Corporation would oppose the loan and it would seem that this anticipation was well founded.'[1] Naturally, as this suggests, the key is often to be found in the need of the government for an immediate cash advance. For most of the century after independence the Peruvian Government was continually short of funds. Its ordinary revenues were based substantially on the income from customs duties on imports and exports, while, as Mathew describes in Chapter IX, the government during the guano boom continually followed a policy of demanding advances from prospective consignees against future proceeds. When the government expropriated the expanding nitrate industry in 1875, it followed the same system.[2] The Pacific War then removed these extraordinary sources of finance and left Peru once more almost entirely dependent on the income from duties on foreign trade. This, of course, fluctuated widely as commerce slumped or boomed, and was always insufficient at a time of emergency.

In 1894, when the Cáceres government was gravely threatened by rebellion, the Peruvian Corporation obtained the government's assent to a settlement that incorporated a loan of £23,000. The government took advantage of the expected restoration of its credit to ask Congress for permission to conclude an additional external loan of £150,000. The legislature turned down the plan for settlement with the Corporation on the grounds that the Corporation's loan of £23,000 was insufficient.[3] In 1915, the government was prepared to accept a plan for settlement extremely favourable to the International Petroleum Company in return for the company's help in obtaining a loan in New York.[4] In 1922, the

---

[1] P.R.O. F.O. 61/446, St. John to Lansdowne, 13 July 1905.
[2] Greenhill and Miller, op. cit., *passim.*
[3] P.R.O. F.O. 61/408, Alfred St. John to Kimberley, 6 Nov. 1894.
[4] I.P.C. would have had to pay annual taxes of only £4,600, though their Peruvian opponents claimed that they should pay £124,000 (*West Coast Leader*, 30 Dec. 1915). Their production for 1915 exceeded a million pounds in value:

Leguía government finally accepted a settlement of the dispute with I.P.C. that would bring little in the long term to Peru, but which included a cash payment of $1 million.[1] In 1928 the Peruvian Corporation found its way to a settlement eased by its willingness to include a cash payment of £246,000.[2]

A foreign firm's chances of obtaining a settlement could well depend, therefore, on the state of the government's finances and on the immediate cash benefit to be expected by the government from an agreement. The attitude of President Pardo's government towards foreign interests during the First World War, after the failure of its attempts to raise a loan in New York, shows the reverse side of the coin. Pardo had no further hope of obtaining a foreign loan, while at the same time government finances were improving as new export duties, imposed in 1915, took their effect, and wartime demand in Europe and the United States pushed up prices. Pardo now had nothing to fear from a policy of ignoring foreign claims. The two major, running disputes—over I.P.C.'s titles, and the Peruvian Corporation's guano rights—remained unsettled for the duration of the war. Furthermore, such a policy offered political dividends at home. The British minister explained why there was no hope of a settlement of the guano dispute:

> The present administration seem determined to maintain their stand over this question. Sr. Pardo and his government are apparently resolved to take advantage of the situation created by the war, not only in this, but also in other questions relating to foreign interests. From private conversations I gather that their line in the present case is that Peru, in her times of stress, has been exploited by foreign capitalists, and that now is the time to reassert her rights.
>
> The opportunity offered by the present case seems to be a good one for the President to pose as the defender of the Country's interests . . . The President is likely to fight especially hard in the case of the Corporation's contract which was made, or as Sr. Pardo would say, was forced on Peru at a time when she was compelled to accept any conditions offered.[3]

Carlos Jímenez, 'Estadística Minera en 1915', *Boletín del Cuerpo de Ingenieros de Minas*, 83 (Lima, 1916), 13.

[1] G. S. Gibb and W. R. Knowlton, *The History of Standard Oil* (New York, 1956), p. 368; P.R.O. F.O. 371/7241, Piesse to Eyre Crowe, 28 Apr. 1922.

[2] P.R.O. F.O. 371/12787, Trant to D.O.T., 20 Aug. 1928, and Hervey to Cushenden, 13 Nov. 1928; PC/UCL, *Report of Proceedings, 1928*, pp. 2–3.

[3] P.R.O. F.O. 371/2990, Rennie to Grey (confidential), 27 Nov. 1916.

The British minister summarized the position clearly: 'Threats of loss of credit are no longer likely to have much effect as it is realized here that Peru is unlikely to obtain any financial assistance in Europe so long as the war lasts and probably for some time afterwards.'[1]

V

Settlement of a dispute with a foreign firm could thus depend on the firm's power to damage Peruvian credit on European and American capital markets—but only if the government needed money, and if settlement of the dispute were the only obstacle to obtaining it. Settlement could also be reached at the price of an offer to help the government over short-term financial difficulties, but Congressional approval was necessary and it was not always granted. However, foreign firms possessed other possible weapons of control besides the denial of credit or the capacity to help the government out of financial difficulties, although the use of these alternative methods was less common.

Foreign business occasionally considered a direct threat to the country's economy, though it was seldom put into effect. It was a course which might prove particularly effective in compelling Congress to agree to an unpopular settlement, but it needed nerve. There is no evidence that the Peruvian Corporation ever considered taking such a line. It had too much to lose; it depended almost completely on its Peruvian operations, and these required that relations should be neutral, if not amicable. But the oil companies, the true precursors of the multinational firm, did consider it. Only one company actually carried such a policy through—with impressive results. I.P.C. used the threat of closure and boycott of the Peruvian market to force Congress into action in 1918. Sir Archibald Williamson, chairman of Lobitos Oilfields, had considered a similar policy in 1916 over oil export duties, but he refused to pursue it when I.P.C., the dominant oil company in Peru, failed to agree on a similar line. Moreover, he lacked the courage to close down operations at the most critical moment, when Congress was debating the matter. He would do so only after Congress had closed its sessions so as not to arouse resentment.[2]

[1] Ibid., 26 Nov. 1916.
[2] Balfour Williamson, Forres/4, Williamson to Teagle (president of I.P.C.), 11 July 1916.

Two years later I.P.C. proved more courageous. Early in 1918, exasperated at continual delays in settling its titles, it told the president that unless Congress settled on some acceptable solution it would close down its operations in Peru. In June the company suspended drilling on thirty rigs and threatened to stop all development work within a week, throwing 600 men out of work. The government promised to submit the matter to the deputies as soon as Congress opened its sessions.[1] In October, Congress began to discuss the bill and I.P.C. applied further pressure. Enemy action had left only one tanker on the West Coast to supply domestic Peruvian demand. I.P.C. persuaded the Canadian Government to requisition it, and then immobilized it under repair in Talara. The government had to cut the Lima urban tram service, ration fuel supplies to manufacturing industry, and watch the Central Railway come almost to a standstill. What made the situation more serious was the increasing substitution of oil for coal since 1914.[2] The outcome of the debate was legislative approval for a government project to arrange the dispute by international arbitration.

All foreign firms in dispute with the Peruvian Government tried at one time or another to enlist diplomatic support. The British Foreign Office seldom took official action in such cases, though it often instructed its minister in Lima to make unofficial representations. A firm whose disagreement with the government arose out of an existing contract could not obtain official support until it had shown that it had exhausted its legal remedy of appeal to the local courts. British official policy was clearly outlined by Sir Charles Mansfield in 1893 over the Peruvian Corporation's taxation liability, its failure to fulfil the stipulations on railway construction, and the government's inability to pay the annuity: the company in each case, Mansfield said, had to go before the Peruvian courts. A case of arbitrary confiscation, however, entitled a British firm to official diplomatic support, and it was on these grounds that assistance was given in the Cerro de Pasco dispute.[3]

In practice, Foreign Office intervention was rarely effective. The Peruvian Government knew that the British Government was

[1] P.R.O. F.O. 371/3276, Rennie to Balfour (telegraphic), 24 Apr. 1918; *West Coast Leader*, 29 June 1918 and 6 July 1918.
[2] *Diario de Diputados* (Peru), 1918, pp. 1170 and 1052.
[3] P.R.O. F.O. 61/404, Mansfield to Rosebery (confidential), 20 Feb. 1893.

unlikely to take any action beyond a note of protest. Other pressures on the Peruvian administration determined the amount of notice it was prepared to take of such diplomatic representations. Despite continued official protests over the annulment of the Peruvian Corporation's rights in Cerro de Pasco, the company never gained any redress, and in the end let the matter drop.[1] The rights claimed by the Peruvian Corporation did not deter large-scale American investment in the mines after the turn of the century. Where British firms could bring no financial or direct pressure on the Peruvian Government, the latter could ignore Foreign Office protests completely. Between 1916 and 1918 the Pardo government took no action in any of the disputes about which the British Government protested. The guano dispute with the Peruvian Corporation and a disagreement with the North Western Railway were not settled until after the war, while the conclusion of the dispute with I.P.C. arose from the more direct pressure exerted by the company itself. Wartime intransigence, in fact, provoked the British Government into going beyond the traditional note of protest, the only occasion between 1885 and 1930 that it did so. In the summer of 1917 it embargoed jute supplies to Peru for a month, in an effort to influence the Pardo Government's treatment of British interests. From the first, Britain applied this control half-heartedly. It continued to export jute bags to Chile, for trans-shipment to Peru when the embargo was lifted.[2] What the British Government had not realized was the harm that this measure would do to other firms not in dispute with Peru. It provoked letters of protest from Grace Brothers, Duncan Fox, and Graham Rowe, the three most important houses on the coast. As one of them explained:

The matter is one of vital importance to our Agricultural, Mining and Commercial interests in Peru. We cannot transport the produce of our Sugar Estates, Cotton, Rice, Agricultural Produce, nor Metals without the necessary constant supply of Jute Bags or Hessians. Large quantities of these products such as Sugar, Beans, and Wolfram Ore are sold for delivery to the various Departments of His Majesty's Government.[3]

[1] PC/Lim, Caja 4.ii.2, Morkill to Yates, 30 Oct. 1911.
[2] P.R.O. F.O. 382/1247, Minute (J. C. Leetham) on MacLean to Balfour (telegraphic), 31 May 1917.
[3] Ibid., Grace Bros. to Hardinge, 18 May 1917, Graham Rowe to Hardinge, 21 May 1917, and Duncan Fox to Hardinge, 21 May 1917.

The British Government lifted the controls because of the danger to sugar supplies, further emphasizing the impossibility of using direct methods at such a time.[1]

One other important method existed by which representatives of foreign firms could influence the Peruvian executive and legislature—personal relations and friendships. Its nature makes it almost impossible to detect or document, but in the restricted circles of the Peruvian oligarchy, contacts between foreign businessmen and Peruvians might be close. President Leguía's brother-in-law left a political career to take up the lucrative post of legal adviser to the Peruvian Corporation.[2] The evidence for Peru in this period suggests that the personal relations between a businessman and an influential Peruvian might prove crucial to the settlement of a dispute. The prime minister who decided to eject the minority from its seats in Congress in 1889 to allow the passage of the Grace contract happened to be the lawyer of Michael Grace.[3] In 1915 the Peruvian Government fixed oil export duties at an extremely low level. Probably it did not wish to antagonize I.P.C. while there was still hope of obtaining a loan in New York. But Sir Archibald Williamson commented on the vast amount of work that George Guthrie, Lobitos' representative in Lima, had put in, entertaining Peruvian senators and deputies and financing them in a small way for some months.[4]

It is equally difficult to assess the amount of control that a company could exercise on the local level. This could be vital to the day-to-day operations of a foreign firm which had to rely on local politicians and officials. British Sugar Estates, which monopolized the production of the Cañete valley, found it necessary to intervene in the appointment of the *alcalde* and sub-prefect.[5] The Peruvian Corporation found it vital to have a friendly prefect in Arequipa where they were the largest employer. They had to be able to rely on his support in the case of labour troubles.[6] Without

[1] P.R.O. F.O. 382/1247, Minute (J. C. Leetham) on India Office to Foreign Office, 22 May 1917.
[2] P.R.O. F.O. 371/720, Des Graz to Grey, 8 June 1909.
[3] *El Comercio*, 8 Apr. 1889.
[4] Balfour Williamson, Forres/4, Williamson to Teagle, 29 Nov. 1915.
[5] In 1919 British Sugar Estates paid £220 to the local *alcalde*, concealing it in their accounts: Ronald Gordon to Ward Houghton, 17 Apr. 1919 (letter book shown to the author by Mr. R. M. J. Gordon of Lima, for which the author is glad to record his thanks).
[6] In 1935 the Ferrocarríl del Sur paid out $15,000 in 'gratifications' to the

access to the archives of the oil companies, it is impossible to say whether they followed a similar policy in the north, but it would certainly seem likely that they did.

VI

The small number of disputes between foreign firms and the Peruvian Government from 1885 to 1930, and in particular the complete absence of confrontation between the Peruvian Government and any one of the major trading houses, does suggest that, in the normal course of business as conducted by the rules of the day, they were complementary to each other. Basically the interests of a trading house were the same as those of their Peruvian associates. British houses rarely became involved in direct exploitation of a particular crop or mineral. If they did, there was no reason for them to come into conflict with the Lima government. It was more important for them to retain a close working relationship with the local authorities. The important clashes between the Peruvian Government and foreign interests all occurred over concessions or contracts, outside the normal scope of a trading house. This type of dispute was fairly common and often prolonged. The concessionaire was in a peculiarly vulnerable position, at the whim of the Peruvian administration and Congress. He was seen to be operating under special conditions which aroused resentment. Peruvians might not criticize Peru's reliance on the export of mineral and agricultural products through foreign trading houses, but it was easy to pick on one particular concessionaire. The Peruvian Corporation and the International Petroleum Company, above all, became the targets of popular indignation.

In these disputes the Peruvian Government had a difficult role to play. It had to appease the two houses of Congress, which might use the dispute to focus discontent on an unpopular administration. The legislature easily, and often, obstructed the passage of agreements between the foreign firm and the government. It might gain concessions at the cost of prolonging the dispute. And if we take Congress as being representative of the Peruvian élite, it becomes clear that in some instances it was especially unfavourable towards foreign interests. Too little account, perhaps, has

prefect, police-chiefs, and strike-breakers, and for aeroplanes to move these personnel: PC/Lim Caja 19.8, L. S. Blaisdell to F. H. Hixson, 29 Aug. 1935.

been taken of local politics in the theory of a united collaborative élite. As Robinson points out, the administration had to compromise between its relations with foreign capital and its connections with local interests.[1] The government had also to take into account the pressures that a foreign firm could use to force a settlement. The government's role in these confrontations was to balance the needs of domestic politics with the advantages (especially the financial ones) of concluding a dispute. In a situation where the government had no hope of credit, as in the First World War, the foreign firm could not expect agreement. When the government knew that credit was available and needed money, chances of settlement improved. When credit remained available and the immediate needs of the government were satisfied, relations might again deteriorate with individual firms, although the government's liberty of action depended on its anxiety for even further resources and on the availability at competitive rates of alternative credit. The problem, for both government and foreign firm alike, was to hit the right point in the cycle, and even then all calculations might be upset by an independent and often intransigent Congress.

[1] Robinson, 'Non-European Foundations', op. cit., pp. 121–2.

CHAPTER XI

British Railway Companies and the Argentine Government*

COLIN LEWIS

I

J. FRED RIPPY's calculations for the magnitude and direction of public investment in Latin America indicate the preference of British capitalists for infrastructural projects, particularly railway development. On the eve of the First World War this category accounted for approximately 46 per cent of British capital invested in the region, almost half of which was situated in a single country, Argentina. Investment in the extensive Argentine railway network represented some 21 per cent of all funds placed in public companies and government stock by British investors in Latin America.[1] A little over two decades later, in 1935 before the process of nationalization had begun, an assessment of the British stake in Argentina established that nominal investment in railway scrip stood at £272 million, representing 61 per cent of British funds placed publicly in that country.[2] Even on the basis of market valuation, railway investment accounted for a substantial proportion of British funds. British embassy and Bank of England estimates variously placed the figure at between 36 per cent and 39 per cent of the total.[3] In 1940, an Argentine calculation found

---

* Other aspects of the operation of British railway companies in Argentina are discussed in detail in Dr. Lewis's unpublished Ph.D. thesis, 'The British-owned Argentine Railway Companies, 1857–1947', University of Exeter, 1974.

[1] J. Fred Rippy, *British Investments in Latin America, 1822–1949* (Minneapolis, 1959), p. 68.

[2] Sir Stephen H. M. Killick, *Manual of Argentine Railways for 1935* (London, 1935); *The Times*, 15 Mar. 1935, 16b.

[3] P.R.O. F.O. 371/18628, S. Waley to J. M. K. Vyvyan, 5 June 1935, enclosed Memorandum 31 May 1935.

that British investment in railways accounted for some 36 per cent of all foreign capital invested in the country.[1]

Although the validity of this data may be challenged in several respects, in relative terms it provides a rough indication of the significance of British investment in Latin America, and of the special attention which British investors devoted to the field of railways and to Argentina. Between the 1860s and 1930, the British-owned railways represented by far the greater part of infrastructural investment in Argentina, and also a substantial part of all foreign funds placed in the republic. In addition, the nominal value of this investment represented a large percentage of total Argentine capital stock. Thus the British companies provide an interesting case study for an examination of the relationship between foreign capitalists and the government in Argentina, both in general and within the particular field of railway affairs. Given the British preference for investment in railway companies, and the pattern of railway expansion at home and abroad, there is little reason to suppose that the experience of the Anglo-Argentine companies differed greatly from that of English railway undertakings operating in other regions of Latin America. Moreover, the diversity of the Argentine railway system, covering such a range of types and experience, makes it a particularly appropriate exemplar.

II

The British-owned railway companies in Argentina were not monolithic; the network consisted of a number of individual joint-stock corporations, enjoying varying degrees of profitability and mounting operations of all sizes and shapes. Established at different periods, the companies developed haphazardly. Located in different regions of the country, they were constructed to several gauges. The lines, which had been sponsored by the provincial and national governments, did not share a common financial heritage nor a single pattern of development. It is usual to categorize the companies in accordance with the three main gauges employed—broad, standard, or metre—or in terms of the predominant geographical features of the zones within which they operated—pampean, mesopotamian, etc.; but there remain substantial

[1] United Nations Organization, Economic Commission for Latin America, *Foreign Capital in Latin America* (New York, 1954), p. 36 (U.N. II G. 1954.4).

differences within each sub-division. By the end of the nineteenth century, most of the British-owned companies had established their London offices at River Plate House in Finsbury Circus, and this has given an impression of unity which is not confirmed by the facts. Dealings between the railway managements and the government were conducted upon an individual basis. *El pulpo inglés* (the English octopus) was largely mythical, the dream of cartoonists and authors who read into the radial concentration of railway lines around the city of Buenos Aires a relationship that barely existed. Given the superficial similarity of their situation, it may seem surprising that the various railways did not, in fact, seek to operate in concert, or to institutionalize their common interests. The explanation of this phenomenon lies in the historical development of individual lines, as well as in the effect of government policy.

The political situation in mid-nineteenth-century Argentina ensured that early railway development was centred on Buenos Aires and Rosario. Some two hundred miles apart, these two cities gave expression to the economic and political differences which divided the country. The rejection by the Province of Buenos Aires of the 1853 constitutional settlement, and its autonomous, or near autonomous, existence during the mid-1850s, had important repercussions upon the subsequent course of railway expansion.[1] Within the province, the growth of new economic activities such as wool production, the continued dynamic of cattle raising, and above all the potential of local markets in the city of Buenos Aires itself, stimulated proposals for a number of lines. Although some of these schemes were not successful or immediately profitable, the basic form of railway development was firmly established. Whether financed by domestic interests, such as the Sociedad de Camino de Hierro de Buenos Aires al Oeste, or dependent upon external investors, like the Buenos Ayres and San Fernando Railway Company and the Buenos Ayres Great Southern Railway Company, the lines radiated from the provincial capital, linking existing centres of population.[2] In most

[1] Haydée Garastegui de Torres, *História argentina, la organización nacional* (Buenos Aires, 1971).
[2] London Stock Exchange, Quotations Department Records, 21A 775, 21A 796; Thomas J. Hutchinson, *Buenos Ayres and Argentine Gleanings* (London, 1865), pp. 34–45; and William Hadfield, *Brazil and the River Plate in 1868* (London, 1869), pp. 125–30, 146–53.

cases the promoters associated with these early companies were closely connected with the landed interests, and saw railway development as a means of stimulating the local economy and increasing the value of their estates.[1]

Rosario, on the other hand, witnessed the development of a different type of railway system. Denied the resources of its wealthiest province (Buenos Aires), President Urquiza's Argentine Confederation saw railway construction as a means of imparting a sense of unity to the assorted provinces of which the Confederation was composed. Like many such projects, the initial concept was grandiose, envisaging a network that would first link the Paraná with north-western Argentina and then cross the Andes. The underlying intention was to open adequate communications between the more important provinces of the Confederation; and even in 1870, when the original concession had been completed and some of the political differences between Buenos Aires and her sister provinces were settled, the Argentine Government remained anxious that railway development should continue to open up and unify the provinces of the north-west.[2]

Thus the first companies established in Argentina owed their formation to very different considerations, and it was a disparity in underlying motive that was perpetuated by subsequent developments. Situated in separate regions of the country, the early growth of these companies tended rather to emphasize the differences which divided them than the common features they shared. The companies did not deal with a single government agency. Their relations with Argentine authorities were determined by the accident of formation and by their different experiences with the local officials of the area in which they operated. Companies working out of Buenos Aires, for instance, were especially favoured. Their usually harmonious relationship with the government was founded not only upon economic viability or the close links which existed between their original promoters and the 'governing classes', but also on the fact that they operated from the provincial capital. Since both were established in the city, contacts between the government—

---

[1] John Fair, *Some Notes on my Early Connection with the Buenos Aires Great Southern Railway* (Bournemouth, 1899), p. 5; Winthrop R. Wright, *British-Owned Railways in Argentina: Their Effect on the Growth of Economic Nationalism, 1854–1948* (Austin, 1974), pp. 21 ff.

[2] *R.T.*, 12 Mar. 1864, xxvii. 382–3; Central Argentine Railway Company Ltd., *Annual Report* (London, 1870).

which had issued the concessions—and the companies were physically easy and usually congenial. The Central Argentine Railway Company, on the other hand, despite the fact that it linked the main cities of the Confederation, was not so well placed. It lacked adequate contacts with either the provincial or the national governments, and its interests suffered in any conflict between them. Nor did the Central enjoy the same degree of local landowner support as some of the other lines, and it faced the basic problem of coordinating company policy between head office in London, local office in Rosario, and the perambulating national authorities.

The growth of each company was further moulded by local demographic and geographic factors. In the province of Buenos Aires, a buoyant domestic economy and the receding menace of Indian attack confirmed and encouraged the radial tendency which had existed from the first. To the north, the Central Railway, struggling from Rosario to Córdoba through sparsely settled country, was essentially a trunk route. While the Buenos Aires lines, especially the Great Southern and the Oeste, quickly demonstrated their economic potential, the Central continued to languish, dependent upon government assistance.

Economic differences and jealousies were exacerbated by personal antagonism between the railway managements. When, during the 1860s, both the Great Southern and the Central were canvassing for funds and seeking financial support in London, relations were soured by a conflict of interest between the respective promoters. William Wheelwright, a North American who held the Central concession, attempted to launch his company in London. The success of this venture was largely dependent upon the attitude adopted by the great merchant bankers, Baring Brothers & Co., who were already closely associated with the Great Southern. It seems that Barings saw no difficulty in supporting both railways, but Wheelwright, unfortunately, allowed his name to become linked with a move by the Buenos Aires provincial government to reduce the Great Southern's construction costs. There was at this stage a marked difference in the costing of the Central and the Great Southern, and the guarantee which the provincial authorities had granted the Southern was based upon the cost of construction. While disclaiming any hostile intention towards the other company, and informing the authorities of his dependence upon the good offices of Baring Brothers, Wheelwright foolishly maintained that in the event of the abandonment of the original Southern concession, he would have no difficulty in completing the project upon terms more advantageous to the province.[1] To make it worse, Wheelwright then obtained a concession in the province of Buenos Aires which the Great Southern considered to fall within its sphere of influence, and upon terms less onerous to the province than those accorded to the Great Southern.[2] The Southern interpreted these actions as distinctly unfriendly, and, using its influence with Baring Brothers, caused Wheelwright to abandon his schemes in the province and ultimately to withdraw from the Central project altogether.

The episode serves to underline the frailty of the co-operation which is commonly supposed to exist between the major railway groups in nineteenth-century Argentina. It soured relations between the Central and the Great Southern, and fostered a mood of rivalry which continued almost until nationalization. Noncompetitive in the sense that they were situated in different parts of the country, each railway considered itself the 'premier' Argentine line, jealously guarding its position. Even during the 1920s and 1930s, when events tended to encourage a degree of co-operation amongst the British-owned railways, there remained a marked coolness between the two largest lines.[3]

The dissimilarities occasioned by physical isolation were not reduced when a national network was forged during the 1880s. As the companies converged upon the city of Buenos Aires, the incidence of rivalry between the lines increased in direct proportion to the proximity of their various trunk routes. The emergence of regional railway networks during the early years of the twentieth century emphasized the differences which separated railways, rather than their common interests. As the various groupings evolved, they embarked upon a series of construction programmes designed to create 'spheres of influence'. Given the radial system which developed in Argentina, companies considered the construction of trunk routes as a means of carving out zones which could be preserved from hostile competition. Inevitably, however, competition arose on the fringes of zones where the lines of two groups

---

[1] Baring H.C. 4.1.29 Pt. III, John Fair to David Robertson, 27 June 1863; Frank Parish to Robertson, 30 July 1863.
[2] Ibid., Robertson to Baring Young, 23 Sept. 1863.
[3] P.R.O. F.O. 371/21408, Foreign Office Minute, J. Balfour, 13 Jan. 1938.

marched in parallel formation from the interior provinces to the coast. In such cases, rate-cutting and other inducements to persuade shippers to re-route traffic were common, especially during difficult times when the acquisition of additional traffic became an important consideration.

Lack of co-operation amongst the British companies was notorious. It was not until the 1930s, when expropriation appeared inevitable, that the British-owned railways combined in an attempt to co-ordinate relations with the government. In 1936, the British–Argentine Railway Committee was formed in Buenos Aires. It was composed of the managers and local directors of all the British-owned companies, with the object of 'safeguard[ing] British railway interests in Argentina'.[1] Even so, formal co-operation in London did not occur until the 1940s, when the broad-gauge groupings co-opted the chairmen of sister companies on to their respective boards.[2] Hitherto, despite a number of minor exceptions, the device of interlocking directorships had been employed only amongst companies represented within the regional groupings which had emerged during and after the 1890s.

Company rivalries, while not necessarily encouraged by the state, nevertheless served a useful purpose, and both national and provincial governments often attempted to stimulate a degree of further competition by a judiciously liberal policy in the allocation of concessions. In the 1880s, and subsequently during the period of expansion which preceded the First World War, the ease with which lines were able to obtain concessions encouraged, if it did not initiate, a measure of rivalry. Intervention to prevent collaboration between the railway groups could take a more active form. The national government in particular refused to recognize the institutionalization of co-operation between companies, insisting that in their relations with the state, companies were to be regarded as individual entities whose affairs were governed by their respective concessions.

One of the early exercises in concerted action on the part of the British lines occurred during the years after the Baring crisis, when in 1893 the eight British-owned guaranteed railways formed the Railway Committee, 'composed of men of the highest

---

[1] *The Times*, 8 June 1939, 22b.
[2] *The Universal Directory of Railway Officials and Railway Year Book*, *1944–5* (London, 1945), pp. 164–5, 167–8; *The Times*, 20 Aug. 1943, 9f.

standing in this City [of London] whose opinions should carry considerable weight [in Argentina]'.[1] In the face of common difficulties, occasioned by the non-payment of their guarantees, these lines decided to make joint representations to the Argentine authorities and to the Rothschild Committee (which was currently considering the question of Argentina's external obligations). The government in Buenos Aires, however, refused to take cognizance of the Railway Committee, and insisted upon settling each company's claim separately. Subsequently, while the national government attempted to co-ordinate railway administration and to increase the role of central government at the expense of provincial, the central authorities nevertheless invariably insisted upon dealing with the British-owned lines individually. Joint representations by companies acting in concert, except when extremely informal, were rarely countenanced or successful. When in the late 1920s the Argentine Government appeared poised to intervene for the enforcement of tariff reductions on the major British lines, the companies made separate approaches to the national authorities without any apparent prior consultation amongst themselves.[2]

Consequently, despite the preponderance of British capital in the Argentine railway system, and the formulation of railway policy at head office in London, it would be incorrect to infer that the Anglo-Argentine railway companies acted in concert as an established lobby. While various groups of companies certainly co-ordinated their operations and combined to form zonal systems, there is little evidence to suggest that the groupings undertook inter-regional co-operation for the purpose of applying joint pressure in Argentina. Incongruous though it may seem, the Anglo-Argentine railway companies did not act in concert till the 1930s. Until then the vision of a monolithic infrastructural lobby, capable of mobilizing and exerting massive pressure upon government, was largely a myth. From the 1850s to the 1930s provincial and national governments in Argentina rarely experienced, and certainly never countenanced, concerted pressure from the railway companies.

[1] F. O. Smithers to the Local Board, Villa María and Rufino Railway Company Limited, 2 Feb. 1893: Villa María and Rufino correspondence, Letter Bundle A (nos. 1–23), A4, consignment no. 71, Archivo del Ferrocarril Nacional General San Martín, Buenos Aires; *R.T.*, 4 Feb. 1893, lxiii. 159.

[2] P.R.O. F.O. 371/12738, A. S. Mallett to Sir Austen Chamberlain, 31 July 1928.

III

Although the Argentine Government was anxious not to encourage the development of concerted action among the private companies, individually the lines often enjoyed cordial and sometimes close relations with the state. Representatives of the lines obtained ready access to government. Indeed, many of the individuals connected with the establishment of the early lines were drawn from the government itself, or featured among the classes from which the government was derived. Moreover, in later years most of the companies created local boards and directorships in Buenos Aires, or employed local legal representatives recruited from the same social, or even family, background as the politicians, officials, and interest groups which composed the 'oligarchy'.

The Buenos Ayres Great Southern was a case in point. The rapid development of the railway, and its stable and profitable record, have often been attributed to the close links which existed between the line's directorate and Argentina, and their intimate knowledge of local affairs. From its establishment, the Great Southern enjoyed an enviable relationship with important sectors of *bonaerense* opinion. The company forged firm connections with the provincial government. David Robertson, its director and chairman, was a close personal friend of Norberto de la Riestra, sometime Minister of Finance, who took a marked interest in the fortunes of 'our Southern railway'.[1] It was acknowledged that Robertson's contacts and connections in Buenos Aires assisted the company through several of its early difficulties.[2] The company also numbered amongst its directors the Buenos Aires vice-consul in London.[3] While the Southern might have been fortunate in the variety and extent of its contacts, the company was not exceptional in this respect. From the first the Central's board included a director resident at the Argentine capital, not necessarily a native Argentine but usually a prominent landowner of impeccable local credentials.[4] And most of the other lines formed during the 1850s and 1860s established similar connections. Subsequently the railways retained eminent native lawyers in a

[1] Baring H.C. 4.1.29 Pt. III, Norberto de la Riestra to Robertson, 27 July 1863.

[2] Ibid., Parish to Robertson, 30 July 1863.

[3] *Bradshaw's Railway Guide, Shareholders' Manual and Directory*, xv (1863), 379.   [4] *Bradshaw*, xvii (1865), 407.

number of capacities. Drawn from illustrious Argentine families, these served as local legal representatives or as directors. It was a policy that was not confined to the foreign-owned railway companies, nor to Argentina, but it was developed to great effect by the Anglo-Argentine railways, a number of whose legal officers achieved high political office.[1]

The transition from personal friendship to a more professional relationship between the companies and their local representatives reflected a change that occurred in the financial structure of the railways themselves. The deep personal affinity which had characterized contacts between Robertson and Riestra was less likely in later years. After the 1870s, and particularly during the boom of the 1880s, the railway companies acquired a broader financial base. Previously, most of the capital employed in railway construction had been supplied by individuals already closely interested in Argentina. Railways were seen as a vital means of developing those interests. By the last quarter of the nineteenth century, however, railway operations had achieved a degree of profitability sufficient to attract the general investor. Also, the scale of infrastructural projects had moved beyond the stage where private funding could provide an adequate capital flow. Consequently, both established companies and new railway promotions increasingly looked for support from the London Stock Exchange, thereby marking a change in character from the earlier lines.

Nevertheless, while the railways developed as corporate institutions and their directors came to fulfil a managerial rather than a classically entrepreneurial function, there was no decline in the amicability of company–government relations. Indeed, the establishment of formally constituted local boards, pioneered by the Buenos Ayres and Pacific Railway in 1904, was merely the institutionalization of an existing relationship. Local representatives and visiting railway directors continued to enjoy relatively easy access to Argentine government circles. Even President Hipólito Yrigoyen, whose Radical party replaced the traditional oligarchy in 1916 and whose reputation among other sectors of foreign business in Buenos Aires was not of the highest, was considered by the British-owned railway companies to be extemely approachable. Although during his presidency the companies made considerable concessions to the Argentine authorities, they were not usually

[1] Wright, op. cit., *passim.*

denied access to the Casa Rosada, and there is little to suggest that Yrigoyen did not mean what he said when he told them of his thorough appreciation of 'the immense advantage which the construction of railways by private capital has conferred on my country'.[1]

IV

Access to authority did not imply that the government was necessarily pliable or amenable in the face of representations. The Argentine Government was rarely compliant, and the friendly relationship which it enjoyed with foreign capitalists or their representatives must not be construed as deriving from any subservient or client relationship. Indeed, railway–government relations were not always amicable. There were several areas of friction. The logistics of railway operations, the existence of provincial and central government railway systems within a largely privately owned network, and the relations between foreign railway companies and their customers and employees, were bound to occasion difficulties. The disputes which resulted between companies and government illustrate the limitations of any pressure which could be brought to bear by individual companies, and underline the ultimate sovereignty of the state. Despite an appearance of strength, and the vital position occupied by the foreign companies in the Argentine economy, there was little that the railways could do when Argentine opinion favoured a specific course, no matter how inimical to the interests of the foreign-owned railways. Consultation and persuasion might modify government policy, but when the 'national interest' was involved the lines were invariably unable to hold their own.

The earliest disagreements between the state and the railway companies sprang from the practical difficulties of establishing the first lines upon a profitable and remunerative basis. Often the companies lobbied for the alteration of their concessions, seeking more advantageous terms. All but two of the original companies possessed a government guarantee, the payment of which, as well as the settlement of government debts, provided another area of conflict. Downswings in the economic cycle invariably aggravated

---

[1] P.R.O. F.O. 371/13460, Sir Malcolm Robertson to R. L. Craigie, 14 Mar. 1929, enclosing a memo by H. O. Chalkley.

these problems as the companies sought either to extract further financial support from the state, or to obtain a modification of their terms of operation. Unfortunately, proposals such as these, presented in times of economic crisis, were received by the Argentine authorities when they themselves were ill placed to undertake further commitments. The Central's concession was altered several times in order to make the project more attractive to investors. The original terms provided that the line was to be constructed at a cost of not more than £6,000 per mile. Later the figure was raised, and the land grant which accompanied the concession was also increased.[1] Yet these minor improvements were scarcely generous, and the national government was forced to provide further support, subscribing a substantial portion of the capital required to complete the trunk route from Rosario to Córdoba. Despite the modifications, the Central's concession was not over-generous, and the initial costing turned out to be largely unrealistic.[2] More generous in their estimate of railway construction costs were the Buenos Aires provincial authorities, who allowed £10,000 per mile.

At this juncture, the Argentine national and provincial governments were anxious to create an environment favourable to the construction and operation of railways. Consequently, there was little fundamental opposition to the revision of concessions, nor indeed to the provision of direct financial assistance in the form of a guarantee of interest on invested capital or the purchase of equity. The Great Southern concession was amended several times at the company's request.[3] The Oeste, like the Central, obtained official financing.[4] But by the end of the 1860s, once the companies were established, the Argentine authorities became less tractable. When the Great Southern abandoned its guarantee in 1869, the terms were extremely favourable. The province of Buenos Aires not only waived its claim to the repayment of previous advances, but also agreed to pay the balance due upon unfulfilled guarantees.[5] Some twelve years later, when the Central

[1] *R.T.*, 15 Nov. 1863, xxv. 1618; 21 May 1864, xxvii. 721.

[2] Baring H.C. 4.1.29 Pt. III, Robertson to Baring Young, 29 Oct. 1863; *R.T.*, 23 May 1874, xxxvii. 533.

[3] Fair, op. cit., *passim.*

[4] Wright, op. cit., pp. 21–4; *The Times*, 16 Nov. 1867, 7a; Baring H.C. 4.1.52, George Woolcott to Baring Brothers, 27 Aug. 1875.

[5] Buenos Ayres Great Southern Railway Company Limited, *Report of the*

tried to end its own guarantee upon equally advantageous conditions, the company was rebuffed and forced before agreement to make substantial repayments to the government.[1] Equally, the companies found it more difficult to extract further concessions from the state, and had to offer compensating advantages. The Southern, after completing its main line, attempted to increase earnings by constructing a number of branch lines into established, commercially developed areas which offered the best prospects of a speedy return upon investment. For political and strategic reasons, however, the local authorities wished the company to push its trunk route through less-populated zones. The company refused, deterred by adverse prospects in a frontier area and fearful of the costs involved. In reply the provincial government blocked the railway's other plans. The *impasse* was resolved only when the provincial government granted the desired branch line concession on condition that the trunk line was extended concurrently.[2]

The most divisive problems of the period were financial, arising largely from the guarantees accorded by provincial and national governments. As the attitude to the revision of concessions hardened, so the government's willingness to assist in the financing of railway development was reduced. The government's guarantee of interest on capital subscribed—a standard practice for international railway development in the third quarter of the nineteenth century—was not an outright grant to the railway companies but an interest-free loan, the repayment of which was dependent upon the financial position of the railway concerned. It was a pledge to the private investor that his capital would never earn less than a specific return, usually 7 per cent. So long as the profits on railway operation were insufficient to provide the guaranteed return, the Argentine authorities, national or provincial, supplied the balance. Although the operation of the guarantee was limited to a specific period, normally between twenty and forty years, it was anticipated that the companies would become self-sufficient within a relatively short term, when the government could expect to recoup its early disbursements.

Abuse of the guarantee system was not common, but by the

Directors for the half year January to June, 1869 (London, 1869); *The Times*, 6 Dec. 1868, 6e; 20 Nov. 1869, 6f.

[1] Baring H.C. 4.1.65 Pt. VIII, Nicolas Bouwer to Baring Brothers, 22 Oct. 1881; *S.A.J.*, 21 Feb. 1885, xxii. 94.

[2] *B. & R.P.M.*, 8 Oct. 1870, vii. 1 and 13.

1870s the action of a number of guaranteed companies was beginning to cause the government some financial embarrassment. Guarantees had sometimes been given without proper investigation, and in a number of cases there was little prospect that companies would ever earn the full 7 per cent. A line such as the Buenos Ayres Northern Railway Company Limited, which was badly constructed and inadequately managed and whose capital had been substantially 'watered', was a constant source of annoyance.[1] Others, like the East Argentine Railway Company Limited, unscrupulously obtained an inflated guarantee.[2] Until the guarantee system was finally abolished in the early 1890s, the government's unwillingness to honour some of these claims inevitably created a degree of discord, especially during periods of financial stringency. Moreover, it was normally on these occasions that government insolvency was most likely to affect all companies, for guarantee claims and for more mundane debts.

While the difficulties associated with concessions and guarantees were solved with the passage of time, other sources of conflict were more permanent. Although the greater part of the Argentine railway network was foreign-owned, the central and provincial governments were themselves responsible for the construction and operation of substantial systems. Private and government lines sometimes integrated their services and operations, but more often their relations were less than friendly, and the charge that the foreign-owned private companies were subject to 'unfair competition' was not uncommon. On several occasions it was reported that projected extensions by private companies were delayed or abandoned as the result of opposition from state lines, especially those operated by the province of Buenos Aires.[3] At other times the foreign companies complained that the state was either allowing nationally owned railways to construct in their zones, or offering competitive concessions to other private lines for the same purpose.[4]

An equally perennial problem was that of tariffs. Most, although

[1] *B. & R.P.M.*, 22 Aug. 1865, ii. 469.

[2] Baring H.C. 4.1.65 Pt. I, Bouwer to Baring Brothers, 31 Jan. 1877.

[3] Ibid., Pt. IV, Bouwer to Baring Brothers, 21 Apr. 1879; *Buenos Ayres Standard*, 30 Aug. 1870.

[4] Buenos Ayres Western Railway Company Limited, *Proceedings at the Thirty-eighth Ordinary General Meeting* (London, 1927); *The Times*, 8 Oct. 1913, 19f.

not all, concessions allowed the state to fix railway tariffs, either for the duration of the original concession, or while the guarantee applied. Usually government intervention was determined by the level of profits, the state being entitled to demand a reduction when earnings reached a certain point. The difficulty lay in determining when the point of intervention had been reached, for it was dependent not only upon earnings but also on recognized capitalization, deductible expenses, and so on, all of which were open to argument. Moreover, in order to maintain sterling earnings, the British-owned companies tied railway tariffs to the gold premium, adding yet another controversial element to the calculations. Even the Great Southern, which in the pioneer days of 1862 had persuaded the provincial authorities to forgo the right to fix tariffs, was subject to pressure on this account.[1] Like other lines the Southern established a gold tariff and collected paper currency according to the prevailing premium. Normally the paper tariffs were surcharged 75 per cent of the gold premium, or 50 per cent when the premium was particularly high.[2] Daily movements in the gold premium produced chaos, since 'nobody knows for more than a few days at a time how many dollars it is going to cost to make a journey by rail. Today it may be $50, next week $80, or, with less probability, $40.'[3] Subsequently, the company was persuaded to apply a sliding scale by which a much reduced, variable percentage of the gold premium was added to the paper tariff, thereby introducing a degree of equity, if not stability, to the tariff schedule.[4]

Nevertheless, the tariff question continued to preoccupy the companies, complicated by the appearance of exchange control which placed further pressure upon profits. Essentially the problem was one of remittance. Operating in Argentina, the foreign-owned companies earned a profit which had to be translated into a sterling dividend for their shareholders. In the nineteenth century the return yielded from operations was eroded by the depreciation of the paper peso; during the early twentieth century, when the exchange was stable, profits were squeezed by the increasing cost of labour, and later by the application of exchange

[1] D.G.F., *Estadísticas 1893* (Buenos Aires, 1895), p. 66.
[2] *R.T.*, 1 June 1899, lv. 722.
[3] Thomas A. Turner, *Argentina and the Argentines* (London, 1892), p. 174.
[4] *S.A.J.*, 18 May 1889, xxvi. 622–3.

control. The gradual democratization of Argentine society meant that the demands of railway employees for higher wages and salaries, or for more substantial fringe benefits, commanded the attention of the government, although the companies invariably saw the problem in terms of tariffs.

V

To deal with these difficulties railway managements employed an array of devices of varying effectiveness. In the early days the companies could depend on Argentina's desire to enter the railway age, and on her reliance upon foreign funds to do so. While this continued to be the case it was possible for the railways to threaten non-participation in projects, and to attempt to prevent Argentina from obtaining further foreign capital should they disagree with, or feel aggrieved by, official action. But when the shallowness of these sanctions was revealed, the railways had to find some alternative. In part there was a reversion to earlier, well-tried methods of coercing or influencing the state. Experience during the 1850s and 1860s indicated the benefits of powerful local representation. Local connections had often been allowed to lapse as the companies became fully operational, only to be re-forged at a later date. During the hectic 1880s, when a railway mania seized the country, the scramble for concessions left little time for the cultivation of local opinion or for a careful scrutiny of the terms of new agreements. The price of this neglect, and the consequently reduced influence of the railway lobby, was obvious by the end of the nineteenth century. Thus when a new era of expansion occurred during the 1900s, most of the major British-owned companies increased their local representation in Buenos Aires. The relationship between local representatives and the British companies in the twentieth century was cliental, rather than participatory, as it had been with prominent Anglo-Argentines or Argentines—the Armstrongs, Fairs, and Riestras—of the earlier period. But drawn as they were from the 'governing classes', the Ramos Mexias or the Guerricos fulfilled a similar function. Articulate and familiar with the local situation, they served the railways well. Co-option, however, was not confined to the 'oligarchy'. After the First World War the private lines attempted a general mobilization of sectoral interests in support of their position in Argentina.

Paradoxically, the most effective method open to the railway companies to put pressure on Argentine governments in the earlier period was to hold back. Because of the state's desire to obtain railway construction, an apparent lack of interest in a project was a relatively easy means of coercing national or provincial authorities. The early history of the Oeste indicated that native Argentines were not prepared or able to sink large sums of money in the creation of a basic infrastructure. Further investment funds had to be procured abroad, and foreign investors were determined to 'wait until the terms were right'. During the difficult period when attempts were being made to modify the Great Southern's original concession, its promoters desired that 'English capitalists should *not* interfere, but go hand in hand and aid each other in those distant Countries of South America'.[1] Only competition among railway promoters could break the common front, and there was little prospect of this as yet. Neither could such competition be easily fostered, as Wheelwright and the province of Buenos Aires discovered to their cost.

Britain was the main source of funds at this time, and the structure of the London money market, in which only a small number of firms was concerned with or possessed any knowledge of Latin America, tended to reduce the possibility of genuine competition. Concessions had to be modified and amended until they found favour with foreign capitalists. Various inducements, such as land grants, guaranteed profits, and even subsidies were offered to attract investors, until the correct balance was achieved. The Central Argentine concession, the first draft of which was published in 1854, was subject to several amendments before the definitive version appeared in 1863.[2] Less spectacularly, the Buenos Ayres Great Southern concession was also altered a number of times before it satisfied the promoters.[3]

But this position was not one which could be held indefinitely. Once the companies had actually begun operations in Argentina, their latitude for negotiation was much reduced. Failure to construct an extension, for example, would probably harm the company more immediately than the government. Moroever, by the

[1] Baring H.C. 4.1.29 Pt. III, Robertson to Baring Young, 23 Sept. 1863.

[2] D.G.F. *Estadísticas 1893* (1895), pp. 69–70.

[3] Provincia de Buenos Aires, *Registro Oficial de la Provincia* (1862), pp. 140, 148; (1863), p. 256; Provincia de Buenos Aires, *Recopilación de Prado y Rojas*, vi (1863), 244.

1870s, partly because of its exasperation with some of the private lines, the government began to construct railways on its own account—an alternative now available to it with the improvement of Argentine credit, the profit record of the pioneer companies, and a proved ability to attract foreign investment.

TABLE XI.1

Railway Capitalization in Argentina, British and National, 1873, 1877, and 1880

	British companies	National lines	Total
	£	£	£
1873	3,760,000 (72·3%)	1,440,000 (27·7%)	5,200,000
1877	7,006,659 (64·4%)	3,867,974 (35·6%)	10,874,633
1880	7,623,632 (56·8%)	5,790,000 (43·2%)	13,413,632

SOURCES: Compiled and calculated from *Brazil and River Plate Mail*, 21 Oct. 1873, x. 8; Parliamentary Papers, 1878, lxxii, 2; and *South American Journal*, 5 July 1890, xxix. 19.

The credit rating of a borrowing government is always its most sensitive point. Imputations against credit-worthiness increase the cost of borrowing, or greatly reduce the prospect of obtaining access to foreign capital, so that the desire of a foreign state to place its obligations in the money markets of western Europe provided aggrieved creditors with useful leverage. While the Argentine authorities were more amenable, wishing to maintain their access to the London money market and subscribing to the belief that default or slurs upon their financial rectitude would impair or prevent that access, the railway companies were in a strong position. The Great Southern was the first railway company to avail itself of this weapon. Quoting its experience of unpaid government debts, the Southern called Baring Brothers' attention to the situation, 'knowing how great an interest you take in the credit and well-being of the Argentine Republic'.[1]

But it was the Northern which used the device to greatest effect. After repeatedly complaining to the province of Buenos Aires about its unpaid guarantee, the company approached Baring

[1] Baring H.C. 4.1.67, C.O. Barker to Baring Brothers, 18 Jan. 1877.

Brothers in 1881 and threatened to place its case before the Committee of the Stock Exchange should Barings attempt to obtain the quotation of a projected Buenos Aires loan.[1] The Buenos Aires government agreed to settle, and the Northern repeated the threat on subsequent occasions actually approaching the Committee of the Stock Exchange at one point when it considered Barings' action insufficiently expeditious.

Where the Southern and Northern led, others were soon to follow. The East Argentine, although its claims were against the national authorities, proceeded with equal vigour against both central and provincial governments. Complaining of its unfulfilled guarantees, the company warned Baring Brothers that if it failed to obtain satisfaction in Buenos Aires, it would seek to prevent the quotation of Argentine loans in London, even when issued by the *province* of Buenos Aires, because 'that province is in wealth, population and from its position on the coast practically the whole life and body of the Confederation [and] it cannot be allowed to ignore its responsibilities to the Company'.[2]

Inevitably the success of these approaches depended upon the extent to which all parties subscribed to the conventions relating to credit standing. Baring Brothers, as London bankers of the Argentine Government, were particularly conscious of the dangers arising from imputations against their clients. Indeed, Barings, with Rothschilds the greatest of London merchant banks with a high reputation of their own to safeguard, often showed rather more concern for Argentina's reputation than Argentina herself or than the host of less than respectable company promoters anxiously pressing other people's money on the Argentine authorities.[3] Nevertheless, both the Argentine Government and the general investor attached some importance to credit standing until overtaken by the speculative boom of the 1880s, and while this attitude lasted, the threat to impugn Argentine credit was frequently and successfully employed (though virtually abandoned after the Baring crisis).

Optimistic expectations for Argentine expansion during the 1880s enabled Argentina to encourage competition among the

[1] Ibid., H.C. 4.1.78, C. Seale Hayne to Baring Brothers, 22 Nov. 1881.
[2] Ibid., H.C. 4.1.68, Lawrence Barker to Baring Brothers, 21 Mar. 1882.
[3] Ibid., L.B. 64 (1882), p. 79, Baring Brothers to Bouwer, 3 May 1882; Baring H.C. 4.1.78, Baring Brothers to Seale Hayne, 11 May 1882.

private companies. Concessions were readily taken up by foreign capitalists. Most of the established lines felt threatened at various times during the decade.[1] Under boom conditions the 'concessions game' was a means of persuading recalcitrant companies to modify an unfriendly attitude, or of encouraging the construction of branches by an otherwise cautious railway, driven to build lest its zone should be invaded by a rival. In general, however, the established companies had less to fear from such paper rivals than from the government-owned lines. When the bubble burst in the financial crisis of 1890–1, many concessions lapsed or were revoked.[2] National and provincial government railways proved more formidable rivals, especially in the pampean zone. The state-owned railways provided the government with a useful check upon private operations. Although some of these lines were notoriously inefficient, others were fully competitive. The provincially operated Oeste provided a reliable service, yet contrived to levy substantially lower tariffs than its British-owned competitors.[3] Consequently, the private companies were more sensitive to prospective government rivalry than they were to the intrusion into their zones of newly established foreign railways. And the denationalization of a number of lines after the crisis, in an effort to sustain national and provincial finances, reduced the possible area of friction. At the beginning of 1890, before the process of liquidation began, provincial and national government lines accounted for approximately 26 per cent of the country's operational mileage.[4] In 1900 state lines represented only 12 per cent of the total railway system.[5]

Indeed, the years around the turn of the century witnessed a new mood of co-operation in Argentine railway circles. Both the government and the companies were chastened by financial collapse; denationalization had removed some grievances; and a greater awareness existed among the private lines of the government's position. There was little, in fact, to disrupt a basically amicable relationship, and this was reinforced and maintained by the return of more prosperous times with increasing, though not spectacular, profits. In 1907 the Mitre Law, a remarkably liberal piece of legislation, was enacted by Congress. A recapitulation and

[1] *La Prensa*, 11 Oct. 1887; *R.T.*, 14 July 1888, liv. 52.
[2] *R.T.*, 29 Nov. 1890, lviii. 631; 3 Dec. 1892, lxii. 731.
[3] *S.A.J.*, 9 Feb. 1889, xxvi. 173.
[4] Calculated from *S.A.J.*, 5 July 1890, xxix. 19.
[5] Calculated from P.P. 1901, lxxxi. 37.

recodification of existing statutes, the law was largely successful in its objective of establishing a fair and equitable legal framework for private investment in Argentine railway development. Approved and supported both by the government and the railways, the Mitre Law was a monument to harmony in railway affairs.

VI

Denationalization and a more liberal approach to the private companies should not be represented as a victory for the British-owned railways, or as the policy of a venal government. Greater

TABLE XI.2

Railway Mileage in Argentina, by Nationality of Companies,
1900–29

	Total mileage	British companies		French companies		Argentine companies		National lines	
1900	10,281	8,808	(85·7%)	227	(2·2%)ª	n/aᵇ		1,246	(12·1%)
1909	14,909	11,317	(75·9%)	1,416	(9·5%)	165	(1·1%)	2,011	(13·5%)
1915	20,934	15,032	(71·8%)					2,977	(14·2%)
1920	21,042	15,222	(72·3%)	} n/aᵇ		} n/aᵇ		3,053	(14·5%)
1925	22,419	14,976	(66·8%)					4,271	(19·0%)
1929	22,775	15,665	(68·8%)	2,536	(11·1%)	292	(1·3%)	4,282	(18·8%)

ª French and Argentine companies.   ᵇ Not available due to insufficient data.

SOURCE: Compiled and calculated from República Argentina, Ministerio de Obras Públicas, Dirección General de Ferrocarriles, *Estadística(s) de los Ferrocarriles en Explotación* (various); Parliamentary Papers, Trade and Consular Reports (various); and *Annual Report(s)* of the British-owned companies.

liberality in the awarding of concessions applied not only to the British lines but to other nationalities, thereby establishing an additional element of inter-company rivalry. Whether or not this was the objective, French capital was able marginally to increase its share of Argentine railway development, despite some minor nationalizations and the rapid increase in British investment during the period prior to the inter-war depression.[1] But in general the British-owned companies continued to enjoy reasonably harmonious relations with the state during the early twentieth century. If the Mitre Law illustrated the government's desire to maintain friendly relations with the companies, the railways

[1] A. E. Bunge, *Ferrocarriles argentinos. Contribución al estudio del patrimonio nacional* (Buenos Aires, 1918), pp. 89–90; *S.A.J.*, 5 July 1890, xxix. 19.

responded in good faith and renewed their commitment to Argentine development. Between 1906 and 1914, railways increased their lines from 12,824 miles to 20,857 miles, and capitalization doubled.[1] Conflicts of interest, when they occurred, were usually occasioned by third parties. The first two decades of the new century found the companies subject to conflicting pressure from employees and shippers which inevitably complicated their relations with the government. Effective unionization of railway labour and the general political situation prevailing in the country encouraged railway employees to press for higher wages and more extensive fringe benefits. On the other hand, falling grain prices squeezed arable incomes until farmers clamoured for tariff reductions. The government was sensitive to the claims of both groups, though not necessarily concurrently.

The social and political effervescence which culminated in the *semana trágica* of 1919 did not leave the railways unscathed. Although the main causes for the crisis might have been political, there were substantial underlying economic grievances exacerbated by the First World War. Railway wages had never been high, and some companies had even been charged with discrimination against Argentine nationals.[2] The attraction of a job on the railways lay in the regular nature of the work and the relative security it offered, rather than in high wages. Nevertheless, desertion from construction gangs at harvest time showed that better paid, if seasonal, employment was obtainable. Strikes and stoppages became a regular feature of railway operations after 1904, particularly at harvest time, and relations were further embittered by the companies' hostility to new pension legislation.[3]

Disruption of rail services at the end of the agricultural season was liable to have adverse repercussions for the whole economy, especially when the strikes lasted for several months as was the case in 1907 and 1912. Backlogs of traffic could reduce the whole transport system to chaos, paralysing exports and internal com-

---

[1] D.G.F. *Estadísticas 1913* (Buenos Aires, 1916), pp. 396–8.

[2] *Diario de Diputados* (Argentina), 1891, i. 666.

[3] For a catalogue of strikes and a review of pensions legislation, see Bunge, op. cit., chs. XII and XIV. For the companies' opinion see Buenos Ayres Great Southern Railway Company Limited, *Report of Proceedings at the half-yearly General Meeting, July–December, 1903*, and *Report of Proceedings at the Ordinary General Meeting, 1907* (London, 1904 and 1907); Buenos Ayres Western Railway Company Limited, *Proceedings at the Eighteenth Ordinary General Meeting* (London, 1907); *The Times* (South American Supplement), 25 Sept. 1913, 12a.

munications. Inevitably, this brought government intervention, institutionalized after 1907 with the creation of the Departamento Nacional del Trabajo. Wage increases and the funding of fringe benefits added substantially to costs, and could have spelt financial disaster for many of the less prosperous British-owned companies had they not been offset by compensatory tariff increases. Moreover, the situation was equally critical for the government which, under pressure from an increasingly vociferous and more effectively organized working class, was naturally more inclined to defer to the appeals of its own citizens than to the complaints of foreign capitalists. Consequently, government intervention in labour disputes was viewed with growing apprehension by the British-owned lines. Committed to heavy investment programmes financed normally by the issue of fixed-interest debentures, the railways were in a precarious economic position with little room for manœuvre.

Past experience indicated that the foreign companies would be unable to persuade the Argentine authorities to adopt an unpopular course of action. Therefore, the British railways sought to ally their interests with those of their employees, who had already demonstrated a remarkable ability to gain the ear of the government. By linking the concession of wage demands to increases in tariffs, the railways hoped to get the support of labour in tariff negotiations with the government. They strengthened their arguments for higher tariffs with the threat of retrenchment and the curtailment of services should such support, or a favourable response from the government, not be forthcoming. Although railway profits, freight rates, and wage levels were not formally linked together until the early 1930s, labour showed itself willing from much earlier on to combine with the railway companies against consumers.[1] Where such joint representations failed, unilateral action which threatened jobs and services usually proved effective. In 1922, when the companies felt particularly under pressure, two of the weaker lines informed the authorities that failure to increase tariffs would result in the withdrawal of services and staff redundancies—which proved an equally effective if more

---

[1] For a detailed account of labour disputes during the period 1916–22, and attempts by the railway companies to co-opt labour's support for tariff increases, see P. B. Goodwin, *Los ferrocarriles británicos y la U.C.R., 1916–1930* (Buenos Aires, 1974), chs. I–V.

coercive method of enlisting labour support and successfully 'brought matters to a head'.[1] In this manner railway tariffs steadily increased, keeping pace with rises in the wage bill. Fairly substantial tariff increases were obtained, both of a general and a selective nature. During the period 1914–22, tariffs increased by between 40 per cent and 69 per cent, depending upon the category of traffic and the company.[2]

These successes, however, were deceptive. Rather than indicating the power of the British-owned lines in negotiation with the government, they serve to point to the weakness of the companies' position. Although wage and salary increases were not the sole cause, operating costs rose steadily during the twentieth century. Between 1903 and 1933, for example, the Buenos Ayres Western's working ratio (operating costs expressed as a percentage of gross receipts) mounted from 48 per cent to 82 per cent, the Great Southern's from 47 per cent to 70 per cent.[3] The most effective means of obtaining relief from the inexorable pressure of rising costs was to mobilize local sectoral support. In the late 1910s and early 1920s this tactic was successful because, in co-opting labour, the companies were mobilizing that sector of Argentine society most threatened by the prevailing economic climate. In turn, the alliance of management and labour worked because, despite the opposition which greeted tariff increases, the shippers and producers most affected by increased rail freights could cover their additional costs; they were able, while the short post-war boom lasted, to raise prices in a buoyant external market. Increased rail freights, however, merely disguised the fact that the companies' success was due not to their unaided pressure, but to the activities of their allies. Subsequently, the limitations of such an alliance were demonstrated when other, more powerful interests felt themselves threatened.

Declining prices for primary products during the 1920s indicated the limitations of the railways' new policy. Benefits accruing to the British companies from understandings with domestic interest groups were consequent upon the status of their allies,

[1] *The Economist*, 1 July 1922, 11.

[2] Cámara de Diputados, *Comisión especial de asuntos ferroviarios* (Buenos Aires, 1930), 494–6.

[3] Buenos Ayres Great Southern Railway Company Limited, *Annual Report(s)* (London, 1903, 1933); Buenos Ayres Western Railway Company Limited, *Annual Report(s)* (London, 1903, 1933).

whose own position was often precarious. If organized labour was able to influence government, other groups were equally equipped to lobby the Buenos Aires authorities. In 1928 mounting pressure from grain producers led to government intervention detrimental to railway profits. The accelerating fall in cereal prices after 1926 produced a clamour from the arable sector for government action to ease narrowing profit margins and enable Argentine produce to assume a more competitive position in the world market. Grain producers demanded a reduction in rail tariffs as a solution to both difficulties. Essentially the government was faced with two alternatives: to support existing tariffs, thereby maintaining railway profits and encouraging the continuing process of investment in railway expansion of ultimate benefit to the country at large, or to enforce a reduction in freight rates in order to bring immediate relief to arable interests.[1] The government chose the latter course and instructed two railways—the Great Southern and Central—to reduce rariffs.

At first the government intervened in accordance with the terms of the Mitre Law, maintaining that the companies had infringed prescribed profit limits. The Central was inclined to yield to *force majeure*, but the Southern contested the charge, protesting that its profits had not exceeded the established maximum of 6·8 per cent for three consecutive years. Accordingly, the government modified its approach and applied instead the more amenable Ley General de Ferrocarriles which stated that tariffs should be 'just and reasonable'.[2] Both lines complied with the new instructions and, while reserving their future freedom of action, applied lower tariffs. Having dealt successfully with the two major companies, it was anticipated that the government would pursue a similar course with the other lines. In the event, however, the companies in which the government had not yet intervened were spared, for the return of President Yrigoyen to office in 1928 marked a break with the policies of the previous regime.

Yrigoyen's re-election occurred at a time when North American capitalists were once again expressing a marked interest in Argentina as a field for investment. His undoubtedly cordial relations

[1] H. O. Chalkley, *Commercial, Economic and Financial Conditions in the Argentine Republic* (H.M.S.O., 1928), p. 69.
[2] P.R.O. F.O. 371/12738, Robertson to Chamberlain, 17 July 1928, enclosed memorandum; Mallet to Chamberlain, 31 July 1928; and Lord St. Davids to Chamberlain, 3 Aug. 1928.

with the British-owned railway companies and their representatives were probably occasioned less by animosity towards the retiring administration, or even by any specific regard for the companies themselves (or the influence which the lines were able to command), than by the real fear, often exhibited by Yrigoyen, of North American penetration.[1] The flood of American capital into Argentina during the late 1920s, and the earlier experience of virtual North American domination of the important meat packing industry, alarmed Argentines and not least the Radical administration. Faced with the threat to an even more vital sector of the economy, the newly elected authorities determined to adopt a more conciliatory policy towards British capitalists.

The tariff episode, the last event to disrupt company–government relations prior to the débâcle of the inter-war depression, emphasized the status and position of the British railways in Argentina. It revealed the danger of reliance on sectional support. While the foreign companies sought to justify their policies in terms of general interest, their position was relatively secure. Cultivation of sectional support, on the other hand, meant that the railways as a group were prey to domestic rivalries in Argentina, particularly during periods of economic transition when fundamental structural changes tended to disrupt the *status quo*. During sectional conflicts the government inevitably acceded to the demands of the more powerful group. The weakness of the companies' situation was shown when, despite their protestations, undoubted influence in certain quarters, and attempts to pressurize government, the Great Southern and Central were forced to effect tariff reductions which they considered substantial and likely to have long-term adverse effects upon future earning potential.[2] In addition, the affair suggests further reasons for doubting the existence of co-operation or collusion amongst the British companies. The Central and Southern pursued divergent courses of action when threatened with intervention, while the other lines maintained a discreet silence, anticipating that the government might continue to view 'our modest earnings with respect'.[3]

[1] P.R.O. F.O. 371/13460, Robertson to Craigie, 14 Mar. 1929; telegram, Robertson to Chamberlain, 16 May 1929.
[2] P.R.O. F.O. 371/12738, Mallet to Chamberlain, 31 July 1928; Chalkley, op. cit., p. 68.
[3] Buenos Ayres Western Railway Company Limited, *Proceedings at the Thirty-eighth Ordinary General Meeting* (London, 1928).

When national self-interest was involved (even if sectionally conceived), successive administrations demonstrated a marked reluctance to defer to railway appeals or threats. Indeed, in this instance the companies were able to retrieve their position only when the Argentine Government considered national interest to be threatened. It was the spectre of a North American take-over of the British lines which caused Yrigoyen to pursue a more conciliatory policy, rather than coercion by the companies themselves. Once again, the efficacy of railway representations depended upon an external 'ally' and not on the potency of the British lobby.

VII

The evolving relationship between private companies and the government in Argentina tells us something about the checks and balances on both sides. All governments in the nineteenth century, in Argentina and elsewhere, were cautious in dealing with the new railway systems. The railway companies were on a far larger scale, demanding much greater capital, than anything previously experienced in the private sector. It was only common sense to see railways as monopolies. Though they were not necessarily the only means of linking two termini, they were usually unrivalled in providing transport to and between intermediate points. Governments were well aware of this, and step by step they imposed the necessary legislative safeguards and restrictions. Even in *laissez-faire* Britain, railway companies were subject to a multitude of checks and obligations by the middle of the nineteenth century. The interests of passengers and shippers had to be considered. Minimum standards of service and safety could not be left to the discretion of individual companies. Strategic and economic considerations meant that there had to be at least some degree of uniformity of operation, if not upon a national basis then at least within a regional context.

Argentina was no less aware of these considerations than any other country, and although formal legislation took several decades to emerge, a desire to place constraints upon individual companies was observable from the first. Indeed, this desire partly explains the difficulties experienced with early concessions which, despite repeated modifications, normally retained a basic minimum provision for official intervention. Even the Great Southern concession, after several amendments, still allowed the government to expropriate the line, at cost plus 20 per cent, should the company fail to comply with government requests—especially with respect to the construction of extensions and branch lines under government guarantee.[1] The Central was subject to a similar proviso, and when the guarantee was finally abandoned the national government retained the right to intervene when the company's net profits exceeded 12 per cent.[2]

Even prior to the general codification of railway legislation in 1891, when the *Ley General de Ferrocarriles* was inscribed in the statute book, the Argentine Government had extensive powers to regulate the affairs of private companies. In the case of the lines carrying a government guarantee, their working ratios were fixed at 50 per cent; their operations were open to detailed examination, and if particularly at fault they might find their accounts debited for purchases by the government of rolling stock on their behalf. However, an acceptance of this type of government supervision does not imply that it was agreeable to the railway managements, nor that the foreign companies did not seek to establish greater freedom of action. The British-owned companies certainly attempted to obtain the most advantageous operational environment. It was their duty to their shareholders to do so. But the companies' income in the present and hopes for the future depended on maintaining reasonably harmonious relations with the local authorities. Obviously, they hoped to shape government opinion to their advantage, but advantages could not permanently be secured by obstruction or heavy-handed pressure.

Operating in a foreign land, there was a limit to a company's power of persuasion or coercion. Most companies found their interests best served by reasonably straightforward dealings with the government, based upon simple business considerations. Examples certainly exist of less honest methods of conducting relations with local or national governments. The history of the East Argentine, from the awarding of the concession itself, gives some indication of what might happen. The line was associated with some of the less savoury local politicians, even if it did not

[1] Buenos Ayres Great Southern Railway Company Limited, *Report of Proceedings at the Ordinary General Meeting, 1868* (London, 1869); *B. & R.P.M.* 7 June 1869, vi. 19–21.

[2] *R.T.*, 15 Nov. 1863, xxvi. 1618; *S.A.J.*, 21 Feb. 1885, xxii. 94.

intervene directly in local politics. A price had to be paid, and the company suffered in the shifting pattern of alliances which dominated mesopotamian politics.[1] Nor was the East Argentine alone in this; the Entre Rios Railway was equally in the hands (and pockets) of local officials and *estancieros*.[2] There is little reason to suppose that these mesopotamian companies were unrepresentative of their class. However, such behaviour was usually confined to the weaker, less profitable lines. Unstable, subject to repeated financial reorganizations, and burdened by high operating costs, these companies were easy prey both to their own instinct for self preservation and to officialdom. Cultivation of local connections and association with regional interests appeared to be the only way to make ends meet, since dividends depended on obtaining maximum payments under the government guarantee with the least degree of effective state supervision. Such privileges had their price, like the easy credit terms extended by the Entre Rios Railway to the provincial governor, because he 'is who he is'.[3]

The larger, more viable companies of the pampean region were under no similar pressures. Prosperity was best achieved by a punctilious attention to the details of railway operation. What might be tolerated at Concordia or Paraná was unacceptable in Buenos Aires. It is instructive that three of the more prosperous British-owned broad-gauge lines hardly drew upon state financial assistance: the Great Southern abandoned its guarantee after only three years, while the Rosario and Western Railways never possessed one. Company profits had never depended upon the more questionable methods employed by some of the smaller lines. It is unlikely that they would have been sanctioned by shareholders, or by early managers and promoters of the calibre of Fair, Parish, and Robertson, who were remarkably realistic about what was acceptable, and what was not permissible, in dealings with the local authorities.

In most phases and aspects of railway operation, the relationship between companies and government was based on what was considered at the time to be mutually advantageous. In the early

---

[1] Baring H.C. 4.1.65 Pts. I and XIII, Bouwer to Baring Brothers, 31 Jan. 1877, and 1 Apr. 1886; Raul Scalabrini Ortiz, *Historia de los Ferrocarriles Argentinos* (Buenos Aires, 1958), pp. 347–8.

[2] Mandatos, R.P.T.L.A., Entre Rios Letter Book 184, July 1893–Apr. 1894, Jason Rigby to the River Plate Agency, 28 Aug. 1893, 19 Feb. 1894.

[3] Mandatos, R.P.T.L.A., Entre Rios, 3. Rigby, 19 Feb. 1894.

days the railways demanded the creation of a favourable operational environment, to which governments agreed, provided that it did not compromise sectional, national, strategic, or personal interests. Concessions, the terms of railway operation, and the degree or method of official support, were all negotiable, but only to the extent that a balance of mutual advantage was preserved. Reasonable dividend payments were the means of attracting further funds to Argentina, but spectacular profits were not usual. Indeed, exceptionally high earnings tended to encourage government intervention, for they demonstrated that the balance of advantage had shifted too much in favour of the foreign-owned companies. Even before general limits were laid down under the terms of the Mitre Law, most railway concessions carried profit intervention clauses, while officially determined levels for expenses and public scrutiny of accounts prevented too obvious a manipulation of disguised earnings. High dividends declared upon ordinary stock did not necessarily mean monopoly profits, since much railway investment was in the form of low, fixed-interest bonds, thereby allowing more substantial returns to be paid upon equity capital even when over-all profits remained moderate.

The range within which foreign-owned railways were free to operate depended on the general level of prosperity. During buoyant periods, for example during the 1880s and for the years immediately prior to 1914, the government behaved liberally towards the railway companies in order to encourage further foreign investment. Less prosperous times, such as the 1890s and late 1920s, brought closer scrutiny. Domestic political considerations meant that the government was not, or could not be seen to be, unduly favourable to foreign utilities at a time when various internal interests were threatened. During much of the period of expansion, *estancieros* did encourage railway construction, and the government did defer to railway opinion, but only in so far as it suited their interpretation, sectional though it undoubtedly was, of their own and Argentina's interests.

The growth of mass political awareness and articulation during the twentieth century extended the scope of Argentina's 'national interest'. In order to pressurize or coerce the government, the foreign-owned railways had to convince a larger segment of Argentine society that the interests of foreign capitalists were their own. The task became even more difficult as nationalist sentiment grew. Impinging upon so many aspects of Argentine social and economic life, the railways were both more vulnerable to criticism and less easily supported, even by sympathetic authorities, as governments became more aware of popular demands and resentments. The Argentine national administrations of the 1930s, which supposedly favoured foreign capitalists, can hardly be described as puppets of the foreign railways. The various governments of the Concordancia did allow the railways a more favourable rate of exchange when making essential foreign remittances, but few other favours came their way. The companies were usually refused permission during a period of recession to effect substantial reductions of salaries, staff, or services; they were not allowed to increase tariffs at will; highways and state railway construction were pushed ahead, often in direct competition with the British-owned lines; the profits of the private lines were eroded until they disappeared, and until nationalization offered a welcome release.[1] Even non-democratic governments required a modicum of popular support, and the foreign-owned railways provided a convenient means, when the need arose, of rallying popular opinion. Under these conditions there is little evidence of a coercive rejoinder from foreign capitalists, who tended, for lack of an alternative, to come to accept such attacks as an occupational hazard.

As the client of powerful domestic interests, and subject on occasion to electoral considerations, the willingness of national and provincial governments in Argentina to co-operate with foreign railways was determined by their instinct for survival. Terms of operation which were too advantageous to private companies implied a high cost to the local community; ill-considered railway concessions might stimulate regional or sectional rivalries detrimental to political stability; uncontrolled tariffs were open to constant comment in the press. Seemingly so powerful, the railway lobby had to be seen to be controlled by the government if politicians were to maintain their credibility. In Argentina, despite the apparent strength and power of the British railway community, the state was paramount, its task made easier by an absence of concerted action among railway managements.

---

[1] P.R.O. F.O. 371/15797, for an account of the British railways' situation during the 1930s see J. M. Eddy's memorandum, enclosed in Eddy to D. V. Kelly, 5 Feb. 1932; P.R.O. F.O. 371/19761, Foreign Office Memorandum, 'Means of improving the situation of the United Kingdom Railways in Argentina', 16 July 1936.

These observations apply to direct 'control' and conscious coercion. Equally relevant is the question of the constraints imposed upon Argentina by the shape of railway development in the nineteenth and early twentieth centuries. In recent years much has been written about 'economic dependency' and the restrictions accepted by 'peripheral' countries as they became drawn into the international economy.[1] Concentrating upon explicit pressures, these interpretations tend to ignore the actual, physical limits placed upon economic development at the time, or the influence which these limits naturally had on the pattern of growth. In the Argentine case, it has been stated that the foreign-owned railways actively sponsored the rise to economic hegemony of the littoral. It is true enough that the pattern of railway expansion in Argentina, determined by factors no more sinister than topography, tended to radiate from Buenos Aires, thereby encouraging the continuation of a process observable from late colonial times. Such a development was not the conscious objective of railway policy. On the contrary, it tended to work against railway efficiency, and one of the overriding, but less successful, objectives of railway development after the 1890s was to remedy the operational defects occasioned by the convergence of lines upon the federal capital. Similarly, it is arguable that because of their linkages with the export sector, the railways permitted the rapid growth and easy operation of an 'open' economic system that inhibited a more balanced pattern of development. This does not mean that the British-owned companies 'conspired' to obstruct Argentine industrialization. It was simply that Argentina's exceptionally rapid development as an exporter of grain and meat, of which the railway companies were but one facet, by its very success discouraged any alternative course of development— diversification in agriculture, industrialization, improved north-

---

[1] For a selection of some of the more recent views see: Fernando H. Cardoso and Enzo Faletto, *Dependencia y desarrollo en América Latina* (Mexico, 1969); A. G. Frank, *Capitalism and Underdevelopment in Latin America. Historical Studies of Chile and Brazil* (New York, 1969); Gino Germani, 'Stages of modernization in Latin America', in S. A. Halper and J. R. Sterling, eds., *Latin America. The Dynamics of Social Change* (Bristol, 1972); T. dos Santos, *La Crisis de la teoría de desarrollo y las relaciones de dependencia en América Latina* (Santiago, Chile, 1968), and 'The Structure of Dependence', *American Economic Review*, lx, 2 (1970), 231–6; O. Sunkel, 'National development policy and external dependence in Latin America', *Journal of Development Studies*, vi, 1 (1969), 23–48.

south communications—which, with hindsight, might have been more conducive to long-term, stable growth.

There can be no end to speculation of this kind. It may serve, however, to emphasize what seems to have been the case for Argentina, namely that despite all the literature that now exists on the theme of direct and co-ordinated pressure and coercion by the foreign railway companies, little scope for such pressure and coercion in fact existed; the elemental pressures were to be found in market forces beyond private or governmental control.

Map III. South America

INDEX